Trusts of Lan
Trustee Delegation and the
Trustee Act 2000

Trusts of Land, Trustee Delegation and the Trustee Act 2000
Second Edition

Chris Whitehouse, BA, BCL
Barrister

Nicholas Hassall, BA
formerly a partner at Boodle Hatfield

Butterworths
London, Edinburgh and Dublin
2001

United Kingdom	Butterworths, a Division of Reed Elsevier (UK) Ltd, Halsbury House, 35 Chancery Lane, London WC2A 1EL and 4 Hill Street, Edinburgh EH2 3JZ
Australia	Butterworths, a Division of Reed International Books Australia Pty Ltd, Chatswood, New South Wales
Canada	Butterworths Canada Ltd, Markham, Ontario
Hong Kong	Butterworths Hong Kong, a division of Reed Elsevier (Greater China) Ltd, Hong Kong
India	Butterworths India, New Delhi
Ireland	Butterworth (Ireland) Ltd, Dublin
Malaysia	Malayan Law Journal Sdn Bhd, Kuala Lumpur
New Zealand	Butterworths of New Zealand Ltd, Wellington
Singapore	Butterworths Asia, Singapore
South Africa	Butterworths Publishers (Pty) Ltd, Durban
USA	Lexis Law Publishing, Charlottesville, Virginia

© Reed Elsevier (UK) Ltd 2001

A CIP Catalogue record for this book is available from the British Library.

First published in 1996

ISBN: 0 406 91443 5

Typeset by Letterpart Ltd, Reigate, Surrey
Printed and bound in Great Britain by William Clowes Limited, Beccles and London

Extract from the preface to the first edition

'The reforms in the Bill are, as we have been told, the products of reports from the Law Commission. They are generally welcomed, so far as I can tell, both academically and among practitioners to the north of the Law Courts. Frankly, it is hard to detect the emotional turmoil in Lincoln's Inn on almost any subject. But, as far as I have been able to discover, there is no seething discontent at the changes now proposed.' (Lord Meston in the House of Lords Second Reading: Hansard 1 March 1996, col 1723).

'. . . we are at last going to get a little bit of common sense into the law affecting the matrimonial home, instead of leaving it to people like me to work out what ought to be the simplest thing in the world by reference to Acts designed to deal with the settled estates of the Duke of Omnium. That must be an enormous leap forward.' (Lord Browne-Wilkinson in the House of Lords Second Reading: Hansard 1 March 1996, col 1725).

And the authors devoutly hope that the Act will be a success, whilst (a) fearing that it will not be; (b) believing that the same laws should not regulate the co-ownership of a Hackney bed-sit and the settled estates of the Duke of Omnium; and (c) suspecting that sorting out problems concerning the matrimonial home is never the simplest thing in the world!

Even viewed through sympathetic eyes the Act is a poor thing; appallingly drafted and with an underlying assumption on the part of those responsible that so long as ministerial statements in Parliament are clear and so can be used to supplement the Act, all will be well! An ill-thought out and ultimately unnecessary piece of legislation would seem an apt judgment . . .

In some ways the defects of the Act are encapsulated in a glaring omission from Part II. The legislation there stresses that beneficiaries can 'direct' trustees to retire and/or appoint trustees of their choice but, save in the case of retirement under Section 19, it does not state that trustees must obey and act on these directions. Shakespeare put the matter thus:

> '*Glendower*: I can call spirits from the vastly deep.
>
> *Hotspur*: Why, so can I, or so can any man; but will they come when you do call for them?'

Preface to the second edition

The first edition of this book dealt with the 1996 Act and ventured the view that that particular piece of legislation was 'a poor thing'. Those were, as it now appears, days of innocence and the reform process (using 'reform' in the sense of 'change' rather than 'a making better' or 'removing defects from') can now be judged as a whole.

Undoubtedly the 2000 Act is a valuable measure for trustees giving them wide investment powers and the ability to delegate (comparatively) freely. Certainly there are infelicities of drafting and some uncertainty in the new duties of care but the good outweighs the bad. The same cannot be said of the 1999 Act, a masterpiece of opaque draftsmanship. The tone is set right at the start by s 1(1) which begins 'the donee of a power of attorney is not prevented from doing an act': presumably this might have been rendered, in slightly more comprehensible Queen's English, 'an attorney can act' etc. In the case of this Act the negatives very definitely outweigh the positives.

A word about the arrangement of the book. The first three parts provide a detailed commentary on the legislation; Part IV is a collection of precedents loosely arranged in the order of the legislation although Precedent 1 (a settlement of land on discretionary trusts) contains a full set of administrative provisions taking into account the 2000 Act. The Appendices contain the complete legislation including the Trustee Act 1925 (as mutilated by the 2000 Act). In addition there are extracts from correspondence on the taxation implications of the 1996 Act and a copy of Land Registry Practice Leaflet number 32 which deals with powers of attorney and registered land.

Particular thanks are due to Peter Webber, in-house solicitor at Oxford University, for his acute comments on the legislation, to the team at Butterworth Tolleys and, for battling with manuscripts, to Catherine and Joanna at 8 Gray's Inn Square.

The law is stated as at 5 April 2001.

Chris Whitehouse
Nicholas Hassall
April 2001

Contents

Part IV: Precedents

Table of statutes

References in **bold** type indicate where the section of the Act is set out in part or in full

Table of statutory instruments

Table of cases

Part I:
The Trusts of Land
and Appointment
of Trustees
Act 1996

1

Introduction

The 1925 System

1.1   The value attached to land, not least because of its permanency, ensured that over the centuries a sophisticated legal system developed aimed at dealing, on the one hand with the aspirations of landowners, and, on the other, with the demands of purchasers.

1.2   The law had to accept at any early stage that merely to recognise single ownership of a plot of land was insufficient. Instead, a far more complex pattern emerged with individuals being able jointly to acquire land ('concurrent ownership') whilst landowners were able to fragment the rights inherent in the ownership of their property by, for example, conferring rights to income on one or more persons (typically via the 'life interest' or 'annuity interest') with ultimate entitlement to capital passing to another person (the 'remainder interest') and, at the same time, vesting the management of the land in a third person (commonly the trustees).

1.3   The 1925 property legislation marked the culmination of a period of reform and produced a structure which, in its essentials, survived unchanged for more than 70 years. The system then established was often referred to as 'the dual system' given that whenever successive interests in land were created this had to be done either as settled land under the Settled Land Act 1925 or as an interest taking effect behind a trust for sale[1].

1   The Settled Land Act 1925, s 1(1)(i) defines a settlement (inter alia) as any instrument under which land is 'limited in trust for any persons by way of succession'. Limited interests, other than a term of years, only exist in equity as part of a settlement. As discussed further at para 1.9 below, when successive interests were created then if a trust for sale was not expressly adopted (or imposed by statute) the Settled Land Act 1925 applied: see s 1(7) as inserted by the Law of Property (Amendment) Act 1926, s 7, Schedule.

The Strict Settlement

1.4   The prime objective of the strict settlement was to ensure that land would be retained undivided in the hands of a single family passing through one family member in each generation (essentially via the system of primogeniture). To achieve this objective, given the perpetuity rules, the basic strict settlement involved a conflict or tension between different generations which was resolved by giving father and son comparable bargaining strength as a result of which land was resettled every generation[1]. Land was seen as an engine of wealth to be retained within the dynastic family with key members given being limited interests in that land[2].

1   This process is well described in Lawson & Rudden *The Law of Property* (2nd edn, 1982) ch 12.

2   In 'The Paradox of the Land Law' (1905) 21 LQR at 222 Dicey commented:

> 'The paradox of the modern English Land Law may be thus summed up: the constitution of England has, whilst preserving monarchical forms, become a democracy, but the land law of England remains the land law appropriate to an aristocratic state.'

1.5   In the classic strict settlement, the tenant for life occupied the land and, from the middle of the 19th century, it had become apparent that the division of interests within the structure of the settlement (based in some senses on the political maxim 'divide and rule') meant that in many cases no one person had adequate powers of managing and developing the land whilst a sale was all but impossible. The Settled Land Act 1925 was the culmination of a series of reforming statutes which increased the powers of the tenant for life and ensured that there was someone who could sell the legal estate free from the claims of the family. This implicitly recognised that in the post-First World War conditions, and with changing attitudes to status and gender, the strict settlement had already become moribund[1].

1   'There are no other Acts of Parliament, and few works of literature, which are as redolent as the Settled Land Act of a world which was already dying in 1925 and has long since disappeared – the world of the great landowner, mining his own coal, transporting it over his own tramways to his own docks, building his own gasometer to provide gas and light for his principal mansion house, and providing small dwellings to which his grateful workers return at the end of the working day after their visit to the public baths to decide whether to spend the evening in the literary institute or the working man's club': 'Trust Law for the Twenty-First Century' by Sir William Goodhart QC published in (1996) 10 *Trust Law International* No 2, 40.

The Trust for Sale

1.6   In origin, the trust for sale developed as a mechanism whereby, after death, the testator could ensure that his property was sold and the proceeds divided up in accordance with his wishes. Out of this developed the so-called 'Traders Settlement' established by persons wishing to control property for more than a single generation: typically property that would have come from a successful business venture. Land held in such a settlement was viewed as a commodity with the emphasis being on 'sale value' rather than 'use value'[1]. There was a certain irony in the way in which the trust for sale developed as the primary vehicle for landholding as well as the rather inappropriate device through which the co-ownership of land took effect.

1   See *Transfer of Land, Trusts of Land* (Law Com No 181) para 3.1.

The Alternatives Compared

1.7   The differences between the strict settlement and the trust for sale, enshrined in the 1925 legislation, can simply be stated:

(a)   *Land management.* Land management was vested in a tenant for life in the case of strict settlements and in the trustees in a trust for sale.

(b)   *Power of sale.* A power of sale was given to the tenant for life in a strict settlement and to the trustees in a trust for sale.

(c)   *Overreaching.* A purchaser could, in both cases, acquire the legal estate free from any equitable interests by paying the purchase money to at least two trustees ('overreaching').

(d)   *Concurrent interests.* Concurrent interests normally had to exist behind a trust for sale[1].

1   If land was settled under the Settled Land Act 1925 with joint tenants for life there was no trust for sale: s 19(2). The only permitted concurrent interest in the legal estate was a form of unseverable joint tenancy such as that owned by trustees: legal tenancies in common were abolished by the Law of Property Act 1925, s 34 and every form of beneficial co-ownership could only exist behind a trust for sale. See further para 1.1 above.

Defects in the Settled Land Act Regime

1.8   There were a number of problems, including the following.

The involuntary strict settlement

1.9   Given the paramountcy of the strict settlement, whenever land was to be enjoyed by persons in succession and a trust for sale was not imposed, the provisions of the Settled Land Act 1925 applied, often when this was not the intention of the settlor. As the Law Commission commented, this meant that where trusts of land were created without proper advice it was almost certain that the land would be settled[1]. Most often this would be the case in home-made wills resulting in the need for additional documents and expense. In some cases, giving the life tenant legal title to the land and powers of management corresponded to the testator's wishes[2]; often the existence of a strict settlement passed undetected[3]!

1   See *Trusts of Land* (Law Com Working Paper no 94) para 3.3. For illustrations see *Bannister v Bannister* [1948] 2 All ER 133, CA; *Ungurian v Lesnoff* [1990] Ch 206, [1989] 3 WLR 840; *Costello v Costello* [1996] 1 FLR 805, CA; and cf *Dent v Dent* [1996] 1 All ER 659. Changing the law because the ordinary man in the street does not obtain proper legal advice (for example before making a will) is certainly not a policy that should in all cases be followed.

2   Arguably not in the *Bannister v Bannister* type of case where all that was intended was to confer a right of occupation during Mrs Bannister's lifetime, or so long as she wished to live in the particular house. Vesting Settled Land Act powers in Mrs Bannister (including the right to sell) was certainly not intended!

3   The undetected strict settlement caused problems for a purchaser: see the Settled Land Act 1925, s 13 (the 'paralysing' section) and note the apparent conflict between the Settled Land Act 1925, ss 18 and 110 (now amended by the Trusts of Land and Appointment of Trustees Act 1996, Sch 3, para 2); cf *Weston v Henshaw* [1950] Ch 510 and *Re Morgan's Lease, Jones v Norsesowicz* [1972] Ch 1, [1971] 2 All ER 235. In part these difficulties stemmed from the rather curious view taken of the tenant for life in the Settled Land Act legislation; for most purposes he occupied the position of independent trustee, but for others he still resembled a delegate of the Settled Land Act trustees: see, for example, D W Elliott 'Curing a defective lease granted by a tenant for life' (1971) 87 LQR 338. For difficulties of making title see *Re Duce and Boots Cash Chemists (Southern) Ltd's Contract* [1937] Ch 642.

Conflict of interest

1.10   The legal estate, and all the powers of dealing with the land, was vested in the tenant for life who was made a trustee for other parties interested under the settlement in relation to the exercise of any power under the Settled Land Act 1925[1]. The tenant for life was also the principal beneficiary. Like any other beneficiary/trustee, the tenant for life was therefore in a position of inherent conflict: in this case this was exacerbated by a general lack of control over the powers that he might exercise. The courts, for example, adopted a leisurely view of the tenant for life's position as trustee so that, in effect, he could allow the estate to fall into disrepair and could sell the estate for a relatively low price[2].

1   Settled Land Act 1925, s 107. For an unreasonable refusal to exercise these powers see *Re Thornhill's Settlement* [1941] Ch 24, [1940] 4 All ER 249, CA.
2   In *Wheelwright v Walker* (1883) 23 Ch D 752, Pearson J commented as follows:

> 'So far as I can see, there is no restriction whatever in the Act on the power of a tenant for life to sell. There is nothing that I can see in the Act to enable the Court to restrain him from selling, whether he desires to sell because he is in debt and wishes to increase his income; or whether, without being in debt, he thinks he can increase his income; or whether he desires to sell from mere unwillingness to take the trouble involved in the management of landed property; or whether he acts from worse motives, as from mere caprice or whim, or because he is desirous of doing that which he knows would be very disagreeable to those who expect to succeed him at his death. There is not, so far as I can see, any power either in the Court or in the trustees to interfere with his power of sale.'

> The tenant for life, however, had to act in good faith: in later proceedings in *Wheelwright v Walker* (1883) 31 WR 912 a malicious attempt to sell at a reduced price was prevented.
>   Beneficiaries did not always discover the sale until it had long since been concluded and so were without an effective remedy: see *England v Public Trustee* (1967) 205 Estates Gazette 651, CA. Subject to restrictions, the tenant for life was able to deal with the land for his own purposes: see the Settled Land Act 1925, s 68 as substituted by the Mental Health Act 1959, s 149, Sch 7 Pt I; and *Re Pennant's Will Trusts, Pennant v Ryland* [1970] Ch 75, [1969] 2 All ER 862 when despite the correct procedure not being followed the sale was allowed to stand.

Defects in the Trust for Sale Regime

Definitional problems

1.11   The definition of a trust for sale ('an immediate binding trust for sale')[1] hardly took matters forward[2]. 'Binding', for example, was a somewhat bizarre word to employ given that all trusts are binding.

1   Law of Property Act 1925, s 205(1)(xxix).
2   See generally Maudsley & Burn's *Land Law Cases and Materials* (7th edn, 1998) p 230 et seq.

The duty to sell

1.12   Once widely used as a vehicle for land holding rather than for property investment, the imposition of the overriding duty to sell (coupled with the application of the doctrine of conversion) frequently did not correspond to the settlor's intentions and created problems when it became necessary to decide whether beneficiaries had an interest in the land itself[1].

1   See para 2.122 below.

Termination

1.13   There was no formal procedure for ending a trust for sale so that purchasers had to investigate the trusts to ensure that they had ended[1].

1   Contrast the Settled Land Act 1925, s 17 as amended by the Trusts of Land and
     Appointment of Trustees Act 1996, Sch 3, para 2(6) which provides that where the estate
     owner holds the land free from other equitable interests under a trust instrument, the
     trustees are bound to execute a deed declaring that they are discharged from the trust. A
     purchaser is then entitled to assume that the land has ceased to be settled.

Co-ownership

1.14   A statutory trust for sale was imposed whenever land was conveyed
to co-owners, whether as joint tenants or tenants in common in equity. This,
a mere conveyancing device, was intended to keep the beneficial interests off
the title[1]. Although there are no precise statistics in this area, in 1914 only
7% of the houses in England and Wales were owner-occupied. By 1938 the
figure was still only 43%, whereas by 1984 in Great Britain as a whole it was
61%. Forcing co-ownership into the trust for sale mould raised a number of
problems, including:

(a)   The duty to sell, coupled with expansive views on the ambit of the
       doctrine of conversion, meant that the courts were forced to grapple
       with such basic issues as whether a statutory co-owner had any right of
       occupation, and how to escape from the clutches of the trust for sale
       when one of the co-owners sought a sale and the other party (and
       'equity') suggested that the property should be retained[2].

(b)   To what extent was there a power to compensate a co-owner not in
       possession[3]?

(c)   It had generally been assumed that it was the intention of the 1925
       legislation to impose a trust for sale in all cases of beneficial
       co-ownership. However, the relevant provisions in the Law of Property
       Act 1925, ss 34 and 36, and in the Settled Land Act 1925, s 36[4], whilst
       dealing satisfactorily with beneficial joint tenancies merely provided for
       the imposition of a trust for sale in two instances of *inter vivos* transfers[5]
       on beneficial tenancy in common:

       (i)   first, where land was 'expressed to be conveyed to any persons in
              undivided shares'[6]; and

       (ii)   second, where settled land was held in trust for persons entitled
              in possession in individual shares[7].

       Neither case would appear to cover the situation which arose in *Bull v
       Bull*[8] where mother and son bought a house for their joint occupation,
       contributing unequally to the purchase price. The property was conveyed
       into the son's name alone and he eventually sought to evict his mother.
       The Court of Appeal concluded that a beneficial tenancy in common had
       been created and, given that the Settled Land Act 1925, s 36(4) only
       permitted tenancies in common to arise behind a trust for sale, it held that
       the mother's interest was an interest under a trust for sale.

       The difficulty with this argument is that there was no 'trust instrument'
       as required by the Settled Land Act 1925, s 36(4), and nor was the land
       'expressed to be conveyed . . . in undivided shares' as required in the
       Law of Property 1925, s 34(2). In fact, the property was conveyed to
       the son as absolute owner and the mother's interest arose in a way not

provided for in the legislation. Unsatisfactory though this decision is in terms of doing violence to the wording of the legislation, it was subsequently assumed that in all cases of equitable co-ownership a trust for sale arose. This was accepted without argument throughout the courts in the case of *Williams and Glyn's Bank v Boland*, with Lord Wilberforce in the House of Lords commenting that 'since the [Law of Property] Act, undivided shares in land can only take effect in equity, behind a trust for sale on which the legal owner is to hold the land'[9].

(d) When there were two legal owners, given that they were trustees for sale, one could not appoint the other to be his attorney[10].

1   See the Law of Property Act 1925, ss 34, 36 (now amended by the Trusts of Land and Appointment of Trustees Act 1996, Sch 2, paras 3, 4, Sch 4). The Law Commission in *Trusts of Land* (Law Com Working Paper no 94) para 3.17 commented as follows:

'Wherever a couple buy a house, they become trustees for sale of it although a sale is not what they intend. In 1925, owner-occupation of dwellings was far less usual than nowadays, and where it did exist, it was less likely that a house would be purchased in joint names. The co-ownership envisaged by the Law of Property Act would have arisen in a different context, where, for example, property was left to children in equal shares. In such a case, a sale at some stage was likely. As far as co-ownership is concerned, a system devised for one set of social circumstances is being used for very different circumstances.'

2   For a discussion of these problems see para 2.122 below.
3   See, for example, *Dennis v McDonald* [1981] 2 All ER 632, [1981] 1 WLR 810; affd [1982] Fam 63, [1982] 1 All ER 590, CA and the discussion of this matter by Frank Webb in (1982) 98 LQR 519 *et seq*.
4   Settled Land Act 1925, s 36 (now amended by the Trusts of Land and Appointment of Trustees Act 1996, Sch 3, para 2(11)).
5   For other situations where the legislation did not appear to succeed in imposing a trust for sale see Megarry & Wade *The Law of Real Property* (6th Edn, 2000) para 9-053 and see the comments of Charles Harpum in 'Overreaching, Trustees' Powers and the Reform of the 1925 Legislation' (1990) 49 CLJ 300.
6   Law of Property Act 1925, s 34(2).
7   Settled Land Act 1925, s 36 (1).
8   *Bull v Bull* [1955] 1 QB 234, [1955] 1 All ER 253, CA.
9   *Williams and Glyn's Bank v Boland* [1981] AC 487 at 503, [1980] 2 All 408 at 411, HL.
10   Trustee Act 1925, s 25(2) substituted by the Powers of Attorney Act 1971, s 9(2). (The position has been changed from 1 March 2000 by the Trustee Delegation Act 1999: see paras 8.3 and 8.40 below).

1.15   At first glance there would seem to be little in common between, on the one hand, the traditional strict settlement of a dynastic estate and, on the other, the co-ownership of a flat in Neasden. The Law Commission did consider establishing a new regime for co-ownership distinct from other trusts of land[1]. In the event, the problems that would have arisen were thought to outweigh the advantages.

1   *Trusts of Land* (Law Com Working Paper No 94) Proposal (IV) at para 15.1.

Bare Trusts

1.16   Prior to the Trusts of Land and Appointment of Trustees Act 1996, bare trusts[1] were within neither the Settled Land Act system nor the trust for sale regime. Such a trust arises whenever land originally held in trust for more than one beneficiary has become vested in a single beneficiary (as where land was originally settled on trust for A for life, remainder to B absolutely and A has died) or where land is acquired by a nominee (for example, where C purchases land which is conveyed into B's name)[2].

1   A bare trust is defined in *Snell's Equity* (30th edn, 200) para 6.30 as follows:

'A simple (or bare) trust is one in which property is vested in one person on trust for another, the nature of the trust not being prescribed by the settlor but being left to the construction of the law, as where property is transferred to T "on trust for B absolutely". In such a case, T must permit B to enjoy the trust property, and must obey his instructions as to disposing of it.' See *Transfer of Land, Trusts of Land* (Law Com no 181) para 7.1. Sometimes a bare trust is used in a wider sense: eg to include the situation when more than one person is absolutely entitled: see, for instance, TA 2000, s 34(3) and see also para 14.53 below.

2   For a further example of when a bare trust arises, see *Hodgson v Marks* [1971] Ch 892, [1971] 2 All ER 684, CA.

1.17   The overreaching machinery in the Law of Property Act 1925, s 2 did not apply to a bare trust[1] and so there were situations where a purchaser failed to obtain a good title[2].

1   See further para 1.22 below.
2   Note, however, the protection given by the Law of Property Act 1925, s 23 (repealed by the Trusts of Land and Appointment of Trustees Act 1996, Sch 4) (where a bare trust arose on the ending of a trust for sale a purchaser was entitled to assume that the trust continued).

Overreaching

The principles

1.18   A major problem for any system of landownership is to reconcile, on the one hand, a purchaser (who needs to be sure that he is acquiring the whole of the interest which he contracted to buy) with, on the other, the rights of beneficiaries owning fragmented interests in the land. For a purchaser to ensure that he has identified and dealt with all such interests would be complicated, costly and time consuming. The 1925 legislation solved this dilemma by making land held in trust freely marketable, so that dealings with the legal estate could occur without any need to refer to (or indeed be aware of) equitable interests in the land. This did not mean, however, that those interests were defeated. Instead, the claims of beneficiaries were, on a sale, transferred to the proceeds of sale (by the process of overreaching) provided that the purchase money was paid to at least two trustees or a trust corporation[1]. This was achieved under the Law of Property Act 1925, s 2(1) which provides that 'a conveyance to a purchaser of a legal estate in land shall overreach any equitable interest or power affecting that estate, whether or not he has notice thereof' if various conditions are satisfied.

1   A trust corporation means the Public Trustee or a corporation appointed by the court to act as a trustee in a particular case or a corporation entitled to act as a custodian trustee under rules made pursuant to the Public Trustee Act 1906, s 4(3): Law of Property Act 1925, s 205(1)(xxviii); Settled Land Act 1925, s 117(1)(xxx); Public Trustee Rules 1912/348 r 30 as substituted by SI 1975/1189 and subsequently amended. See further Maudsley & Burn's *Land Law Cases and Materials* (7th edn, 1998) p 226 ff.

1.19   Prior to the Trusts of Land and Appointment of Trustees Act 1996, the Law of Property Act 1925, s 2(1) applied to:

(a)   conveyances under Settled Land Act powers by tenants for life[1];

(b)   conveyances by trustees for sale[2]; and

(c)   conveyances by mortgagees, personal representatives and by order of the court[3].

1   Law of Property Act 1925, s 2(1)(i).
2   Law of Property Act 1925, s 2(1)(ii) (now amended by the Trusts of Land and Appointment of Trustees Act 1996, Sch 3, para 4(2)). See para 1.21 below for the theoretical difficulties with the overreaching mechanism in the case of trusts for sale.
3   Law of Property Act 1925, s 2(1)(iii), (iv).

1.20   The intention was to overreach what may be termed 'family' interests: commercial interests, not susceptible to monetary 'compensation' (such as easements and restricted covenants), remained protected[1].

1   Law of Property Act 1925, s 2(3).

Lacunae

1.21   First, the issue of whether there was a trust for sale in cases such as *Bull v Bull*[1] and *Williams and Glyn's Bank v Boland*[2] which has already been considered above[3]. Whatever the theoretical shortcomings, the courts consistently found a trust for sale to exist in such cases so that the Law of Property Act 1925 Section 2[4] applied to overreach the interests of the beneficiaries (provided that the other conditions were satisfied: eg in *Bull v Bull* the appointment of a second trustee to receive the sale proceeds).

1   *Bull v Bull* [1955] 1 QB 234, [1955] 1 All ER 253, CA.
2   *Williams and Glyn's Bank v Boland* [1981] AC 487 at 503, [1980] 2 All 408 at 411, HL.
3   See para 1.14 above.
4   Law of Property Act 1925, s 2 as amended by the Law of Property (Amendment) Act 1926, s 7, Schedule (now also amended by the Trusts of Land and Appointment of Trustees Act 1996, Sch 3, para 4(2)).

1.22   Second, bare trusts fell outside the scope of the Law of Property Act 1925, s 2[1]. Hence, when land was conveyed to A and B other than as tenants in common or beneficial joint tenants, there was a risk that they held that land as bare trustees with the result that the interests of the beneficiaries may not have been overreached[2]. In the case of unregistered land, a purchaser might have been protected if he did not have notice of the beneficiary's interest (of course, if the beneficiary was in occupation of the property, it is likely that the purchaser would have been aware of this and would have made appropriate enquiries).

1   See generally 'Overreaching, Trustees' Powers and the Reform of the 1925 Legislation' by Charles Harpum (1990) 49 CLJ 277.
2   Charles Harpum, however, took the view that given the Law of Property Act 1925, s 2 was not exhaustive, overreaching applied generally when a power of disposition was exercised *intra vires*.

1.23   In the case of registered land, the purchaser's position was even less secure, given that if the beneficiary was in occupation he would have an overriding interest under the Land Registration Act 1925, s 70(1)(g) binding on a purchaser even if unregistered[1].

1   An overriding interest under the Land Registration Act 1925, s 70(1(g) covers 'the rights of every person in actual occupation of the land . . . save where enquiry is made of such a person and the rights are not disclosed'.

1.24   In *Hodgson v Marks*[1], for example, the owner of a residential property voluntarily transferred legal title to her lodger (after the death of her second husband she regarded the lodger as a man of substance to whom she entrusted the management of all her affairs) on the understanding that she retained full beneficial ownership of the property. He sold the house, but the courts held that her beneficial interest was not overreached[2]. Even if a second trustee had been appointed this would not have protected a purchaser, because it would not have had the effect of converting a bare trust into a trust for sale. Of course, if the beneficiary had not been in occupation a purchaser would have taken free of that person's interest given, in the case of registered land, that purchasers take subject only to entries on the register and overriding interests[3].

1   *Hodgson v Marks* [1971] Ch 892, [1971] 2 All ER 684, CA.
2   She was held to be in actual occupation for the purposes of the Land Registration Act 1925, s 70(1)(g).
3   Land Registration Act 1925, ss 20(1), 23(1).

Overriding interests and overreaching

1.25   Where the legal title was registered in the name of more than one person as trustees for sale, there was a potential conflict between overriding interests and the doctrine of overreaching. In *City of London Building Society v Flegg*[1], although four persons contributed in unequal shares to the purchase price of a property, the conveyance was taken in the names of A and B only (expressly on trusts for sale for themselves as beneficial joint tenants). No mention was made of C and D, although they were entitled to beneficial interests in the property proportionate to their contributions to the purchase price (given unequal contributions, as tenants in common). A and B charged the property by way of legal mortgage to the plaintiffs and defaulted on the payments. The plaintiffs then sought possession against C and D who were in actual occupation of the property throughout. C and D resisted on the basis that their equitable interest, coupled with actual occupation, gave them an overriding interest under the Land Registration Act 1925, s 70(1)(g). The plaintiffs argued that the payment of the purchase money to two trustees for sale overreached those interests which, being transformed into interests in the proceeds of sale, could not take effect as an overriding interest. This argument was accepted by the House of Lords. The position of a beneficiary in occupation as a consequence of this case, and of the lacunae in the overreaching provisions (discussed above), is summarised in the para 1.26 below.

1   *City of London Building Society v Flegg* [1988] AC 54, [1987] 3 All ER 435, HL. Ferris and Battersby in [1998] 62 Conv 168 argue that the 1996 Act has effected a statutory reversal of the decision in *Flegg* as a result of registered land being excluded from the protective provisions of s 16. But see para 2.175 below.

Beneficiaries in occupation

1.26   The position of a beneficiary in occupation prior to commencement of the Trusts of Land and Appointment of Trustees Act 1996 may be summarised as follows:

(a)   If the legal estate was in the hands of a single owner, as in *Hodgson v Marks*[1], such a beneficiary was protected under the Land Registration

Act 1925, s 70(1)(g) unless he failed to respond to questions about his interest. For unregistered land, the doctrine of notice applied[2].

(b) By contrast, if there were at least two trustees for sale and they conveyed and received the purchase price in accordance with the statutory requirements, the beneficial interest was overreached (as in *City of London Building Society v Flegg*[3]). Of course, if the trustees did not hold on trust for sale, but on bare trusts, the position was as in (a) above.

(c) In the case of registered land, a beneficiary in occupation could protect his position (to some extent) by registering a caution[4]. If the interest was protected in some other way, for example, by a restriction as where joint owners were registered and a single survivor was not entitled to give a good discharge for capital money arising on a sale[5], the owner of the relevant interest could then only enter a caution with the Registrar's consent[6]. Protection afforded by a caution was of relatively limited value, since its effect was merely to prevent a dealing with the registered title until the Registrar had served notice on the cautioner giving him time to object. The notice was, of course, served after the transaction had been completed. However, in practice, the caution procedure did provide valuable protection, since no prospective purchaser or mortgagee was likely to proceed having seen such a caution until they were satisfied that they would take free of the interest protected by that caution.

1   *Hodgson v Marks* [1971] Ch 892, [1971] 2 All ER 684, CA.
2   See *Kingsnorth Trust Ltd v Tizard* [1986] 2 All ER 54, [1986] 1 WLR 783.
3   *City of London Building Society v Flegg* [1988] AC 54, [1987] 3 All ER 435, HL.
4   See *Elias v Mitchell* [1972] Ch 652, [1972] 2 All ER 153 in which a partner who was entitled to joint ownership of property registered in the other partner's name lodged a caution against dealings.
5   See the Land Registration Act 1925, s 58(3); Land Registration Rules 1925/1093 r 213.
6   Land Registration Act 1925, s 54(1).

The Reform Impulse

1.27   The Law Commission began a review of trusts for sale and strict settlements in October 1984 and one year later produced a Working Paper on Trusts of Land[1]. A final Report was produced and laid before Parliament in June 1989[2]. The main proposals were as follows[3]:

(a) to produce a system of law applicable to all trusts: similar rules to apply to trusts of land and trusts of personalty;

(b) the concept of a 'trust of land' with trustees of land having power both to sell and retain the land should replace the existing dual structure. There should be no further Settled Land Act settlements and the doctrine of conversion should be abolished;

(c) the new rules should cover both successive and concurrent interests; in the future accidental settlements should become trusts of land and conveyancing difficulties arising from a failure to realise that there was a strict settlement would disappear;

(d) to some extent settlors would be able to replicate the existing machinery under the Settled Land Act 1925 as trustees would be given wide powers of delegation. At least in theory, simplicity would be provided with the abolition of any need for two documents (although in practice it was accepted that it was likely the two document system would continue)[4];

(e) the discretion of the court under the Law of Property Act 1925, s 30 should be put on a wider, statutory, basis;

(f) trustees of land should be given the same wide powers of investment and management as an absolute owner which would include powers to purchase property for occupation by a beneficiary;

(g) beneficiaries with a vested interest in possession should have the right to occupy the land. This coupled with the abolition of the doctrine of conversion, and the proposal to confer wider rights on beneficiaries (eg with regard to consultation) amounted to something of a revolution in the relationship of trustee as against beneficiary;

(h) in the case where all the beneficiaries are ascertained, sui juris and unanimous, they should be able to exercise the right of appointment of new trustees currently vested in the existing trustees.

1 Ie *Trusts of Land* (Law Com Working Paper no 94).
2 See Transfer of Land, Trusts of Land (Law Com no 181).
3 For a pungent criticism of these proposals see 'Trusts of Land Reform' by Roger Smith (1990) Conveyancer 12. Note in particular his strictures on the proposal to extend the ambit of the Law of Property Act 1925, s 30 (powers of the court) to embrace 'the settlement of any dispute which has arisen concerning the trust or the land subject to it'. In the event this proposal was not proceeded with.
4 See para 6.47 below.

1.28   In the course of examining the law relating to trusts of land, the Law Commission identified a need to look separately at the impact of overreaching on beneficiaries in actual occupation of the trust property. As a result, a separate report[1] was produced in December 1989. That Report identified the main question as follows:

'. . . whether beneficiaries are adequately and appropriately protected by having an interest only in the proceeds of sale of the trust land, or whether they should not have a claim *in rem* to continue in occupation notwithstanding the disposal of the property by the trustees.'

1 Transfer of Land Overreaching: Beneficiaries in Occupation (Law Com no 188).

1.29   The Report noted the changing use pattern that had emerged since the legislation of the 1920's and the increased importance of occupation rights, especially in the case of residential property (whether or not that property was a matrimonial home). A right of occupation was often of far greater value than a share in the proceeds of sale, especially in an age of negative equity. Problems with the overreaching mechanism (discussed above)[1] led the Law Commission to consider requiring occupying beneficiaries to register their interest. In the event this was rejected: largely because the ownership of residential property is typified by informal arrangements so that, for example, a contributor to the purchase price of property who enjoyed occupation of that property would probably not realise the need to register his interest until either the property was sold or mortgaged (as happened in *City of London Building Society v Flegg*[2]). The alternative, which commended itself to the Committee, was that if a beneficiary was in occupation this would normally provide sufficient warning to a prospective purchaser so that full enquiries would be necessary. The basic recommendation of the Committee was therefore as follows[3]:

> 'A conveyance of a legal estate in property should not have the effect of overreaching the interest of anyone of full age and capacity who is entitled to a beneficial interest in the property and who has a right to occupy it and is in actual occupation of it at the date of the conveyance, unless that person consents.'

1   See para 1.18 ff above.
2   *City of London Building Society v Flegg* [1988] AC 54, [1987] 3 All ER 435, HL.
3   Transfer of Land Overreaching: Beneficiaries in Occupation (Law Com No 188) para 5.3(i).

The Legislative Process

1.30   Both Reports remained unimplemented for years and their very existence was largely over-looked by practitioners. It was therefore something of a bolt from the blue when the Lord Chancellor introduced a Trusts of Land and Appointment of Trustees Bill in the House of Lords on 23 November 1995. In the explanatory memorandum, the purpose of the Bill was said to be to 'give effect, with minor changes, to the recommendations of the Law Commission concerning successive and concurrent interests in land which were set out in its report on Transfer of Land: Trusts of Land (Law Com. No 181). It also implements the recommendation about bare trustees in the Law Commission's Report on Overreaching (Law Com No 188)'[1].

1   Law reform is never high on the agenda when it comes to allocating Parliamentary time and it is interesting to note that the Act was taken through Parliament during the last full session of the Conservative administration when, in the eyes of at least some commentators, that administration was running short of things to do!

1.31   The progress of the Bill[1] may be charted as follows:

Date	Stage	Principal changes
1995		
23 November	HL First Reading	A number of proposals of the Law Commission not implemented (notably Report No 188 largely ignored).
1996		
1 March	HL Second Reading	
25 March	HL Committee Stage	Delegation provisions first amended; changes in consultation of beneficiaries; and clarification on the appointment of trustees rules.

Date	Stage	Principal changes
22 April	HL Report Stage	Amendments for land held by charities etc; further changes in delegation; rules on appointment of trustees widened to include retirement and reverse the decision in *Re Brockbank*[2].
7 May	HL Third Reading	Further amendments in delegation; and in the retirement of trustees.
7 May	HC First Reading	
12 June	HC Second Reading Committee	
18 June	HC Second Reading	
26 June	HC Commitee Stage	Minor matters
16 July	HC Remaining stages	
22 July	HL approve HC amendments	
24 July	Royal Assent	
1 January 1997	In force	

1   It was a 'dinner bill': ie it was squeezed into the Parliamentary schedule here and there and notably during the lunch or supper interval.

2   *Re Brockbank, Ward v Bates* [1948] Ch 206 at 208, [1948] 1 All ER 287 at 288.

Features of the Legislation

1.32   Taking an overview of the legislation three features stand out:

(a)   Enhanced rights for beneficiaries as against the trustees: see, for example, the consultation process[1], the right to occupy provisions[2], and Part II of the Act[3]. The abolition of the doctrine of conversion[4], coupled with the right to occupy, resolves uncertainties as to the nature of beneficial rights in a trust of land: under the Act the authors consider that there can be no doubt that such rights are rights in land[5].

(b)   The Act applies to all trusts and settlements, both existing and future, with the exception only of existing Settled Land Act settlements[6].

(c)   The Act has not produced a simple pattern of land holding trusts for the immediate future as the diagram below illustrates. Given the existing structure this was probably inevitable[7]: the slow death of the strict settlement (and of some trusts for sale) will, in due course, effect a measure of simplification.

1   Trusts of Land and Appointment of Trustees Act 1996, s 11. See para 2.107 below.
2   Trusts of Land and Appointment of Trustees Act 1996, ss 12, 13. See para 2.120 ff below.
3   See para 3.1 ff below.
4   Trusts of Land and Appointment of Trustees Act 1996, s 3.
5   For a consideration of the former position under trusts for sale, and especially in cases of
     co-ownership of land, see para 1.14 above.
6   Some sections are not retrospective; for example, the doctrine of conversion was not
     abolished in relation to deaths occurring before 1 January 1997: see the Trusts of Land and
     Appointment of Trustees Act 1996, s 18(3). Other provisions may be excluded by existing
     trusts: see s 21(6). Whilst the definition of a trust of land is retrospective, that does not
     affect the accrued rights of beneficiaries, trustees and purchasers so that (to take one
     example) enhanced trustee powers in ibid s 6 cannot be used to validate past transactions
     which were, when carried out, a breach of trust.
7   Although query whether it would have been more satisfactory to have an entirely separate
     system regulating the co-ownership of property: see para 1.15 above.

1.33   The legislation has not cured all the difficulties that had previously
existed: for example, overreaching problems of the type illustrated in
Williams and Glyn's Bank Ltd v Boland[1] remain, whilst some of the deficiencies
in the drafting of the Act ensure that future litigation will be inevitable[2]. It
may also be noted that whilst it was a cardinal principle of the 1925
legislation that land in a strict settlement was to be freely alienable, the new
rules, by allowing the trustees' powers under s 6 to be restricted or excluded,
permit a settlor who is so minded to exclude altogether, or restrict so as to
make inoperable, the power of sale[3].

Trusts of land under the Trusts of Land and Appointment
of Trustees Act 1996

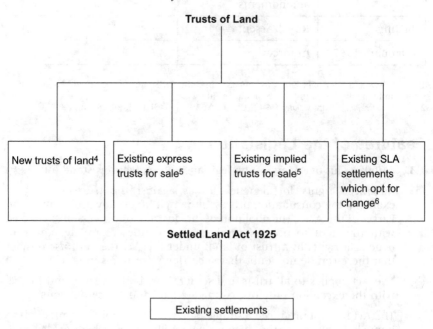

1   *Williams and Glyn's Bank v Boland* [1981] AC 487 at 503, [1980] 2 All 408 at 411, HL. See
     para 1.21 above.
2   See, in particular, the Trusts of Land and Appointment of Trustees Act 1996, s 6(2) and the
     consultation provisions in s 11.

3   And, of course, there is a long history of manic attempts to tie up land or to use land for purposes that might be considered contrary to public policy: see the example of the M'Caigs of Oban discussed in *Maudsley & Burn Trusts & Trustees–Cases & Materials* (5th edn, 1996) at p 325 and *Brown v Burdett* (1882) 21 Ch D 667.
4   Which may be in the form of a trust for sale.
5   Certain provisions (eg as to consultation) do not apply.
6   See the Trusts of Land and Appointment of Trustees Act 1996, s 2(2), (3).

Trust Reform

1.34   The Trusts of Land and Appointment of Trustees Act 1996 marked the beginning of a period of trust reform[1]. The main areas of change and of prospective change are considered below.

1   This was signalled by the appointment of Charles Harpum as a Law Commissioner with the general responsibility for updating the law of trusts. Reform was desperately overdue in many areas: the Law Reform Committee's 'Report on the Powers and Duties of Trustees' (Cmnd 8733) had been almost totally ignored. However, the Goode Committee's 'Report of the Pension Law Review Committee' (Cm 2342) had produced substantial reforms in the area of pension trusts.

Delegation by individual trustees

1.35   The Law Commission published a report on delegation by individual trustees in November 1993[1] and this led to the Trustee Delegation Act 1999 which came into force on 1 March 2000[2].

1   See The Law of Trusts Delegation by Individual Trustees (Law Com No 220).
2   The Act is considered in detail in Part II of this book.

Investment powers of trustees and corporate delegation

1.36   The shortcomings of the Trustee Investments Act 1961 had long been known and much discussed[1]. Some tinkering was carried out: in April 1995, the power of charity trustees to invest in equities was widened by altering the balance between wider and narrower range investments from 50–50 to 75–25[2], and in May 1996 this change was extended to all trusts[3]. The Treasury issued a Consultation Document in May 1996[4] proposing to give trustees powers to invest as if they were the absolute owner of trust property, albeit subject to a statutory duty to have regard to the need for diversification of investments, so far as appropriate in the circumstances of the trust. Existing protection accorded by trust law would have continued in an uncodified form. These changes were to be introduced under the Deregulation and Contracting Out Act 1994 in accordance with which the Report and proposals would be laid before Parliament for 60 days, then a draft order for approval of Parliament examined by the Deregulation Select Committee.

1   The Law Reform Committee in 'Report on the Powers and Duties of Trustees' (Cmnd 8733) commented that the Act had proved to be tiresome, cumbrous and expensive in operation and its provisions widely perceived to be inadequate.
2   Trustee Investment Act 1961, s 13; Charities (Trustee Investment Act 1961) Order 1995/1092.
3   Trustee Investment Act 1961, s 13; Trustee Investments (Division of Trust Fund) Order 1996/845.
4   Ie 'Investment Powers of Trustees'.

1.37 In the event there was considerable uncertainty as to whether the 1994 Act was the appropriate vehicle to remove the restrictions imposed by the 1961 Act[1]. The calling of the 1997 General Election rendered the whole matter academic and the proposal was never revived. Instead, the Law Commission – which had produced a consultation paper entitled 'Trustees' Powers and Duties' in June 1997 – expanded their final report to include trustee investments[2]. This report formed the basis of the Trustee Act 2000 which is considered in detail in Part III of this book.

1   See Law Com No 260, para 2.21.
2   See Law Com No 260 (July 1999).

The reform of perpetuities and accumulations

1.38 The Law Commission[1] has proposed to reform the rule against perpetuities in its application to trusts by introducing a fixed period of 125 years during which equitable interests must vest[2]. It is envisaged that the change will apply to instruments made after the introduction of the reforming statute and so would apply to new trusts and, it appears, to appointments made under existing special powers of appointment. So far as accumulations of income are concerned, the Report envisages that it will be possible to provide for accumulation throughout the new 125-year perpetuity period[3].

1   See Law Com Report on the 'Rules Against Perpetuities and Excessive Accumulations', Law Com No 251 (1998).
2   This will replace the 'life plus 21 years' and 80-year period permitted under the 1964 Act.
3   The principles in the Report have been accepted by the Government and the reform will be introduced when Parliamentary time permits.

The work of the Trust Law Committee

1.39 The privately funded Trust Law Committee has produced a final Report on 'Rights of Creditors Against Trustees and Trust Funds' and Consultation Papers on:

(a)   capital and income of trusts;

(b)   trustee exemption claims;

(c)   equitable problems in the securities market; and

(d)   the proper protection by liens, indemnities or otherwise of those who cease to be trustees.

1.40 The whole question of exemption clauses produced much disquiet in the House of Lords during the passage of the Trustee Act 2000. The Trust Law Committee expressed the provisional view that 'a trustee remunerated for his services as trustee cannot rely on an exemption clause excluding liability for negligence (and worse), at all events where the trustee cannot prove that prior independent advice was given to the settlor'[1]. The matter has now been referred for consideration by the Law Commission.

1   See para 8.1 of the Report (June 1999). This vexed topic has been considered several times by the courts in recent years: see, in particular, *Armitage v Nurse* [1998] Ch 241, CA; *Bogg v Raper* (1998) The Times, 22 April, CLY 4592 and *Walker v Stones* [2000] 4 All ER 412, CA.

2

Part I: Trusts of Land

In this commentary where provisions of the Act have been repealed they are printed in square brackets in italics; where provisions have been inserted they appear in bold.

Section 1 – Meaning of 'Trust of Land'

2.1 Text of section 1

(1) In this Act—

(a) 'trust of land' means (subject to subsection (3)) any trust of property which consists of or includes land, and

(b) 'trustees of land' means trustees of a trust of land.

(2) The reference in subsection (1)(a) to a trust—

(a) is to any description of trust (whether express, implied, resulting or constructive), including a trust for sale and a bare trust, and

(b) includes a trust created, or arising, before the commencement of this Act.

(3) The reference to land in subsection (1)(a) does not include land which (despite section 2) is settled land or which is land to which the Universities and College Estates Act 1925 applies.

'Trust of land'

2.2   A 'trust of land' is the key definition which is widely drawn to include trusts arising expressly as well as implied, resulting and constructive trusts[1]. Charitable trusts are generally included as are trusts for sale and bare trusts. Apart from trusts implied by statute (eg in the case of co-ownership of land[2]) the category of implied trusts is broken down into resulting and constructive trusts (similar terminology to that in the Trusts of Land and Appointment of Trustees Act 1996, s 1(2)(a) is found in the Law of Property Act 1925, s 53(2))[3].

EXAMPLE 1

1.   Terry Testator's will leaves his farmland to T1 and T2 to hold on trust for his wife for life, remainder to his children, if more than one in equal shares. Terry died in March 1997. He has created a trust of land. Had he died in 1996 he would (doubtless inadvertently) have created a Settled Land Act settlement[4].

---

2. Bob and Thelma jointly purchase a house for occupation. Legal title is vested in Bob and Thelma who hold on trust for themselves as either beneficial tenants in common or beneficial joint tenants. Under the Trusts of Land and Appointment of Trustees Act 1996 this is a trust of land whether the purchase occurred before or after 1 January 1997. Prior to the coming into effect of the Act, a transfer to co-owners to hold on the statutory trusts would have resulted in them holding on a trust for sale. By contrast, a transfer after the Act comes into force has the effect of them holding on trust without any trust for sale. The effect of the Act on existing transfers is to convert the statutory trust into a trust of land removing the trust for sale[5].

3. Mrs B owned two cottages which she agreed to sell to her brother-in-law on an oral undertaking that she could continue living in one of the cottages rent free for as long as she wished. On these facts a court decided that the brother-in-law held the cottage on constructive trusts with Mrs B entitled to a life interest determinable on her ceasing to live in the cottage. At the relevant time (1947) this resulted in a strict settlement: from 1 January 1997, any such arrangements when entered into create a trust of land[6].

4. Richard Rich purports to convey land to his infant daughter Miranda. Because minors cannot hold a legal estate in land the attempted conveyance by Richard takes effect as a declaration of trust: Richard will be a trustee of a trust of land[7].

5. X nominee company acquires land for beneficial owner Bertie. The nominee company is a trustee of a trust of land[8].

6. Jason Dodds died in 1994 leaving his residuary estate (which includes land) on trust for sale for a class of beneficiaries including his children and grandchildren. The will trustees became, from 1 January 1997, trustees of a trust of land.

7. Ethelred dies intestate on 1 June 1997. His estate includes real and personal property. His administrators will hold all his real property on a trust of land: the trust for sale that was formerly imposed has been abolished[9].

1   For the distinction between implied, constructive and resulting trusts see eg Gray *Elements of Land Law* (3rd edn, 2001) p 668 *et seq*.
2   'Land' is defined in the Law of Property Act 1925, s 205(1)(ix) (as amended by the Trusts of Land and Appointment of Trustees Act 1996, Sch 4) to include 'land of any tenure, and mines and minerals, whether or not held apart from the surface, buildings or parts of buildings (whether the division is horizontal, vertical or made in any other way) and other corporeal hereditaments; also a manor, an advowson, and a rent and other incorporeal hereditaments, and an easement, right, privilege, or benefit in, over, or derived from land; and "mines and minerals" include any strata or seam of minerals or substances in or under any land, and powers of working and getting the same; and "manor" includes a lordship, and reputed manor or lordship; and "hereditament" means any real property which on an intestacy occuring before the commencement of this Act might have devolved upon an heir.' Contrast land for the purposes of TA 2000 which is defined by reference to the Interpretation Act 1978: see para 11.32 below.
3   Bare trusts are also included: for a definition of a bare trust see para 1.16 above, footnote 1 and see generally para 14.53 below.

4   This settlement would continue to be regulated by the Settled Land Act 1925: see the
     Trusts of Land and Appointment of Trustees Act 1996, s 2.
5   Trusts of Land and Appointment of Trustees Act 1996, Sch 2, paras 3, 4.
6   See *Bannister v Bannister* [1948] 2 All ER 133, CA.
7   See the Trusts of Land and Appointment of Trustees Act 1996, Sch 1, paras 1, 2. Prior to the
     coming into effect of the Act, a conveyance to a minor took effect as an agreement to execute
     a settlement in the form of the appropriate principal vesting deed and trust instrument in
     favour of the minor: Settled Land Act 1925, s 27 (repealed). As from 1 January 1997 that
     agreement ceases to have effect and the conveyance thereafter operates as a declaration that
     the land is held in trust for the minor: see further para 6.33 below.
8   This is a bare trust. These trusts fell outside the dual system of trusts for sale and strict
     settlements and it was one of the objectives of the 1996 legislation to bring them within
     the new unitary arrangement.
9   See the Administration of Estates Act 1925 s 33 as amended by the Trusts of Land and
     Appointment of Trustees Act 1996, Sch 2, para 5.

Co-ownership

2.3   Co-ownership is now governed either by an express trust or by a
statutory (implied) trust:

(a)   *Express trusts.* Express trusts will occur when property is conveyed 'to A
       and B as joint tenants on trust for themselves as beneficial [joint
       tenants *or* tenants in common]'. A trust for sale will no longer need to
       be imposed. As compared to implied or statutory trusts, an express trust
       enables the various powers conferred on trustees in the Trusts of Land
       and Appointment of Trustees Act 1996 to be excluded or modified and
       hence has greater flexibility.

(b)   *Statutory trusts.* The statutory trust for sale formerly imposed by the Law
       of Property Act 1925, ss 34–36[1] has been modified to become a trust of
       land. For example, whenever land is conveyed 'to A and B as beneficial
       [joint tenants *or* tenants in common]' the Trusts of Land and Appoint-
       ment of Trustees Act 1996 will apply. The 'statutory trusts' (ie trusts for
       sale) formerly imposed under the Law of Property Act 1925, s 35 have
       been abolished[2].

(c)   *The statutory lacuna.* The gap in the legislation illustrated by cases such as
       Bull v Bull[3] and *Williams and Glyn's Bank v Boland*[4] has been plugged.
       Because implied trusts are included within the all embracing definition
       of a trust of land, these situations are within the Trusts of Land and
       Appointment of Trustees Act 1996. Whether (theoretically) the trust
       which arises in such cases is statutory or a species of implied (ie
       resulting) trust does not matter.

(d)   *Commencement.* Existing statutory trusts for sale (including *Bull v Bull*
       and *Williams and Glyn's Bank v Boland* situations) became trusts of land
       from 1 January 1997.

1   Law of Property Act 1925, ss 34, 36 (now amended by the Trusts of Land and Appoint-
     ment of Trustees Act 1996, Sch 2, paras 3, 4, Sch 4). As to the former statutory trust for
     sale see para 1.14 above.
2   Trusts of Land and Appointment of Trustees Act 1996, Sch 2, paras 3, 4, Sch 4; for the
     amendment of the Settled Land Act 1925, s 36 see the Trusts of Land and Appointment of
     Trustees Act 1996, Sch 3, para 2.
3   *Bull v Bull* [1955] 1 QB 234, [1955] 1 All ER 253, CA. See paras 1.14 and 1.21 above.
4   *Williams and Glyn's Bank v Boland* [1981] AC 487 at 503, [1980] 2 All 408 at 411, HL. See
     paras 1.14 and 1.21 above.

Formalities for the creation of trusts

2.4   The formalities for the creation of trusts remain unchanged. Accordingly, the creation and disposition of interests in land must be in writing as must any declaration of trust respecting any land or interest in it[1].

1   Law of Property Act 1925, s 53(1): this is subject to s 53(2) which excludes from these requirements resulting, implied and constructive trusts.

Property which consists of, or includes, land

2.5   Trusts comprising realty and personalty fall within the definition of a trust of land. If all land held in the trust fund is sold by the trustees it ceases to be a trust of land: by contrast, if trustees of a trust fund made up entirely of personal property acquire land then they become trustees of a trust of land[1].

1   With the passage of TA 2000 this is of less significance given that all trustees are given powers to acquire land in the UK (see TA 2000, s 8) and all trustees now enjoy wide powers of management and investment (see TA 2000, Pts II–IV). As a result s 17(1), which gave trustees of the proceeds of sale of land power to acquire land in England and Wales, has been repealed (TA 2000, Sch 2, para 47).

Trustees

2.6   For the purposes of the Trusts of Land and Appointment of Trustees Act 1996, trustees generally include personal representatives holding land[1].

1   See the Trusts of Land and Appointment of Trustees Act 1996, s 18, but note the exclusions set out in that section.

Exclusions

2.7   The Trusts of Land and Appointment of Trustees Act 1996 Section 1(3) provides that the Act does not apply to:

(a)   existing Settled Land Act settlements[1]; or

(b)   land to which the Universities and College Estates Act 1925 applies.

1   As defined in the Trusts of Land and Appointment of Trustees Act 1996, s 2.

2.8   Charitable, ecclesiastical and public trusts are, however, included[1].

1   See the House of Lords Report Stage at 571 HL Official Report (5th series) cols 954–955, 22 April 1996:

'The Bill presently draws no distinction between charitable trusts and what may be termed "private" settlements, where land is limited in succession for individuals. As the Bill is presently drafted, all settlements in existence at the time of commencement would remain untouched by the new regime and subject to the Settled Land Act for as long as they remain in existence as settlements. It has been cogently argued, however, that charities would benefit from the more flexible trustee powers conferred on trustees of land, and that while it would not be right to convert existing "private" settlements into trusts of land and change the position of the tenant for life, there is no such problem in the case of charitable trusts.'

See further the Trusts of Land and Appointment of Trustees Act 1996, s 2(5).

2.9   So far as land to which the Universities and College Estates Act applies, the Lord Chancellor (Lord Mackay) commented at Report Stage as follows[1]:

'. . . the trusts of land regime will not apply to such land. This is because land to which that Act applies is in an unusual position, having never been subject to the Settled Land Act scheme but rather having its own detailed, self contained scheme, and representatives of those who deal with such land have indicated that they would prefer to continue to operate in accordance with that separate scheme.'

1   House of Lords Report Stage at 571 HL Official Report (5th series) col 955, 22 April 1996.

Commencement

2.10   Trusts whenever created (including, therefore, those which were created or arose before 1 January 1997) are included, but note that certain parts of the Act either do not apply or may be excluded in relation to existing trusts[1].

1   See, for example, the Trusts of Land and Appointment of Trustees Act 1996, s 3 providing that the abolition of the doctrine of conversion does not apply to will trusts already in existence, and s 11(2) providing that the consultation process does not apply to existing trusts. Despite the retrospective nature of s 1, it will not affect the accrued rights and duties of beneficiaries and trustees.

Section 2 – Trusts in Place of Settlements

2.11   Text of section 2

(1)   No settlement created after the commencement of this Act is a settlement for the purposes of the Settled Land Act 1925; and no settlement shall be deemed to be made under that Act after that commencement.

(2)   Subsection (1) does not apply to a settlement created on the occasion of an alteration in any interest in, or of a person becoming entitled under, a settlement which–

(a)   is in existence at the commencement of this Act, or

(b)   derives from a settlement within paragraph (a) or this paragraph.

(3)   But a settlement created as mentioned in subsection (2) is not a settlement for the purposes of the Settled Land Act 1925 if provision to the effect that it is not is made in the instrument, or any of the instruments, by which it is created.

(4)   Where at any time after the commencement of this Act there is in the case of any settlement which is a settlement for the purposes of the Settled Land Act 1925 no relevant property which is, or is deemed to be, subject to the settlement, the settlement permanently ceases at that time to be a settlement for the purposes of that Act.

In this subsection 'relevant property' means land and personal chattels to which section 67(1) of the Settled Land Act 1925 (heirlooms) applies.

(5)   No land held on charitable, ecclesiastical or public trusts shall be or be deemed to be settled land after the commencement of this Act, even if it was or was deemed to be settled land before that commencement.

(6) Schedule 1 has effect to make provision consequential on this section (including provision to impose a trust in circumstances in which, apart from this section, there would be a settlement for the purposes of the Settled Land Act 1925 (and there would not otherwise be a trust)).

Purpose of the section

2.12 Section 2 prevents the creation (expressly or by implication) of further Settled Land Act settlements on or after 1 January 1997. Successive interests in land must thereafter be dealt with under a trust of land[1].

1   For consideration of how the nearest equivalent of a strict settlement may be created under the new regime see para 2.77 below. The word 'or' in the Trusts of Land and Appointment of Trustees Act 1996, s 2(2)(b) should read 'of'.

Existing settlements

2.13 The Trusts of Land and Appointment of Trustees Act 1996, s 2 preserves the position of existing Settled Land Act settlements as it was not considered acceptable to alter the position of an existing tenant for life[1]. It is not possible for such settlements to 'opt into' the trusts of land regime although note:

(a) further property cannot be added to an existing settlement. In such a case further property, being land, will be held on a trust of land[2];

(b) if 'relevant property' (as defined)[3] ceases to be subject to a settlement then the settlement itself is deemed to cease so that subsequently acquired land will be held on a trust of land[4]. For practical purposes therefore, future management and control will reside in the trustees and the tenant for life will cease to enjoy such powers (unless delegated to him under the Trusts of Land and Appointment of Trustees Act 1996, s 9). The definition of 'relevant property' includes personal chattels (namely furniture, pictures, armour and other family possessions, including a baronetcy) settled so as devolve along with the land[5]. These items are often, although inaccurately, referred to as 'heirlooms';

(c) a new settlement resulting from any alteration of an interest under a Settled Land Act settlement (typically a re-settlement), or occurring as the result of a person becoming entitled under an existing Settled Land Act settlement (for example, as a result of the exercise of a power of appointment), will continue to be governed by the Settled Land Act 1925 unless a relevant instrument provides to the contrary.

EXAMPLE 2

Under the terms of a strict settlement established in 1987, property is held for the benefit of A for life, remainder to his son in tail. The son is 18 years old in June 1997 and joins with A in barring the entail and resettling the property on trust for A for life, remainder to the son for life with further remainders over. The existing Settled Land Act treatment will continue unless the instrument of resettlement provides for it to be treated as a trust of land[6].

---

1   Existing 'accidental' strict settlements are likewise preserved: for situations where such settlements may have arisen see para 1.9 above.

2   The position may of course be different if capital money is used to acquire further land when the Settled Land Act 1925, s 10 will apply assuming that there is never a moment when the settlement does not include 'relevant property'.

3   Trusts of Land and Appointment of Trustees Act 1996, s 2(4).

4   See further the Trusts of Land and Appointment of Trustees Act 1996, Sch 1, para 6 which makes it clear that when a settlement ceases to be a settlement for the purposes of the Settled Land Act 1925 then any property which is (or later becomes) subject to the terms of that settlement is held in trust for the persons interested under the settlement. It is thought that an SLA settlement ends when the only continuing trust is in favour of a person who is absolutely entitled.

     Note that if the tenant for life sells land, simultaneously purchasing replacement land, there is still relevant property and accordingly a Settled Land Act settlement. By contrast, if the sale is concluded before the purchase is completed, there is then a moment when there is no relevant property so that the Settled Land Act regime permanently ceases to apply: see the Trusts of Land and Appointment of Trustees Act 1996, s 2(4). Retaining a small strip of land will ensure that the Settled Land Act rules continue to apply. If, on 1 January 1997, no land is retained within a strict settlement and land is subsequently acquired it is held on a trust of land. (Note that from 1 February 2001 the investment of capital monies is a matter for the SLA trustees: see para 14.48 below).

5   Settled Land Act 1925, s 67; and see Megarry and Wade *The Law of Real Property* (6th Edn, 2000) para 8-041.

6   Trusts of Land and Appointment of Trustees Act 1996, s 2(2), (3). Note that for the purposes of s 2(3) the relevant statement must be in the instrument creating (or one of the instruments creating) the new settlement. A separate document will not therefore suffice.

     On the occasion of a new settlement there will be capital gains tax consequences. Because one or more persons become absolutely entitled as against the settlement trustees there will normally be a deemed disposal of the property in the settlement at its then market value and a reacquisition of that property by the trustees holding as bare trustees for the persons so entitled: Taxation of Chargeable Gains Act 1992, s 71. A line of capital gains tax cases has explored when a 'new' settlement arises; ie when a person (which may be trustees of a new settlement albeit that they are also the same persons as the existing trustees) becomes entitled (not necessarily beneficially) to the settled property as against the trustees: see, for example, *Hoare Trustees v Gardner* [1979] Ch 10, [1978] 1 All ER 791; *Roome v Edwards* [1982] AC 279, [1981] 1 All ER 736, HL; *Bond v Pickford* [1983] STC 517, CA; *Swires v Renton* [1991] STC 490. For the Inland Revenue's interpretation of this case law see the succession of Statements of Practice, namely, SP 7/78, SP 9/81 and (reflecting current views) SP 7/84. The cases are generally concerned with the exercise by trustees of dispositive powers (normally of advancement and appointment) and have drawn a line between a power 'in the wider form' (typically a power of advancement) which when exercised will normally result in the creation of a new settlement, and powers 'in the narrower form' (eg a power of appointment whose function is more akin to filling up a hole left in the settlement by the settlor) whose exercise does not normally create a new settlement. In the case of existing strict settlements, dispositive powers are likely to be in the nature of powers of appointment (the statutory power of advancement not applying) and are unlikely to result in the creation of a new settlement so that the provisions of the Trusts of Land and Appointment of Trustees Act 1996, ss 2(2) and 2(3) will not be in point: see the Trustee Act 1925, s 32(2) as substituted by the Trusts of Land and Appointment of Trustees Act 1996, Sch 3, para 3(8). Of course, if the beneficiaries join together to resettle the property – as in Example 2 – this may involve the termination of the old settlement and creation of a new settlement with consequent CGT implications.

2.14   The tenant for life will inevitably be a party to any decision to switch from the Settled Land Act regime to a trust of land; the typical factors which might influence such a decision are likely to be found in the defects of the Settled Land Act machinery already noted and especially in:

(a)   the cumbersome (and ill-understood, certainly by laymen) conveyancing problems resulting from the double set of deeds; and

(b)   the inherent conflict between the tenant for life *qua* beneficiary and as the person possessing the powers of management.

2.15 In the event of a resettlement excluding the provisions of the Settled Land Act 1925 in the relevant instruments, then, in order to ensure that the trustees hold on a trust of land, the tenant for life must effect a conveyance to the trustees who may then execute a deed of discharge within the Settled Land Act 1925, s 17(1)(a). A purchaser would, in due course, be able to rely on the provisions of Section 17(3)[1].

1   Ie the Settled Land Act 1925, s 17(3) as amended by the Trusts of Land and Appointment of Trustees Act 1996, Sch 3, para 2(6)(c).

Charitable, ecclesiastical and public trusts

2.16 From 1 January 1997, land held on charitable, ecclesiastical and public trusts is not settled land, even if the land was, or was deemed to be, settled before such date[1].

1   For the rationale behind this provision see paras 2.7 and 2.8 above.

Consequential amendments

2.17 The Trusts of Land and Appointment of Trustees Act 1996, Sch 1 makes a number of amendments consequential on Section 2 of the Act. Note in particular that entailed interests cannot be created in the future[1].

1   Trusts of Land and Appointment of Trustees Act 1996, Sch 1, para 5. See further para 6.29 below.

Section 3 – Abolition of Doctrine of Conversion

2.18   Text of section 3

(1)   Where land is held by trustees subject to a trust for sale, the land is not to be regarded as personal property; and where personal property is subject to a trust for sale in order that the trustees may acquire land, the personal property is not to be regarded as land.

(2)   Subsection (1) does not apply to a trust created by a will if the testator died before the commencement of this Act.

(3)   Subject to that, subsection (1) applies to a trust whether it is created, or arises, before or after that commencement.

Conversion and the trust for sale

2.19 Where there was a duty to sell (as in a trust for sale) equity looked on that as done which ought to be done and so 'anticipated' the sale, treating the interests of the beneficiaries as interests in personalty[1]. As a result of this doctrine of conversion, beneficiaries in such cases were generally considered not to have an interest in land, but there were situations where the courts refused to accept this[2].

1   See, for example, *Irani Finance Ltd v Singh* [1971] Ch 59, [1970] 3 All ER 199, CA.
2   See *Williams and Glyn's Bank Ltd v Boland* [1981] AC 487, [1980] 2 All ER 408, HL and especially Lord Wilberforce's comments therein. The matter is considered in the standard

textbooks: see, for example, Gray *Elements of Land Law* (3rd edn, 2001) p 662 *et seq* and Cheshire and Burn *Modern Law of Real Property* (16th edn, 2000) p 218 *et seq*. For a pungent criticism of the modern width of the doctrine see Stuart Anderson 'The Proper, Narrow Scope of the Doctrine of Conversion in Land Law' (1984) 100 LQR 86.

As a result (at least in part) of the doctrine of conversion it has always been treated as axiomatic that trustees for sale will (on selling the land) convert (or overreach) the interests of the beneficiaries into the proceeds of sale.

Abolition by the Act

2.20   With the introduction of the trust of land, enshrining a power to sell and retain, it was felt logical to abolish the doctrine of conversion in this area. However, although certain beneficiaries will now be entitled to interests in land, this will not normally affect a third party purchaser, complying with the relevant formalities, as the overreaching provisions are retained[1].

1   It may be noted that the Law of Property Act 1925, s 25(4) (repealed by the Trusts of Land and Appointment of Trustees Act 1996, Sch 4) provided that where there was a trust to retain or sell land the same was construed as a trust to sell the land and the doctrine of conversion was considered to apply.

Express trusts for sale in the future

2.21   It is still possible to create an express trust for sale (thereby imposing a duty on the trustees to sell land), but in all such cases there will be implied a power to retain, irrespective of any contrary intention[1]. Furthermore, the doctrine of conversion is abolished in such cases so that the interests of the beneficiaries will be in realty[2].

1   Trusts of Land and Appointment of Trustees Act 1996, s 4(2).
2   Trusts of Land and Appointment of Trustees Act 1996, s 3(3). Abolishing the doctrine of conversion ensures that there is no difference between the interest of beneficiaries under a trust for sale and under a trust of land where there is no duty to sell. As to when it will still be desirable to create express trusts for sale, see paras 2.26 and 6.38 below.

Commencement

2.22   In general, s 3 applies to trusts whenever created, but there are two important qualifications to note:

(a)   trusts established in the will of a deceased testator whose death occurred before the commencement of the Act will not be subject to s 3[1];

(b)   when land is held by personal representatives, rather than trustees, s 3 does not apply if the relevant death occurred before the commencement of the Act[2].

1   Trusts of Land and Appointment of Trustees Act 1996, s 3(2).
2   Trusts of Land and Appointment of Trustees Act 1996, s 18(3). Personal representatives who have not assented in writing in their own favour as trustees continue to hold the legal estate in land as personal representatives: *Re King's Will Trusts, Assheton v Boyne* [1964] Ch 542, [1964] 1 All ER 833; *Re Edwards' Will Trusts, Edwards v Edwards* [1982] Ch 30, [1981] 2 All ER 941, CA. For assents by personal representatives in their own favour as trustees see **Precedents 28** and **29** below.

Incorrect side heading

2.23   The doctrine of conversion has only been abolished in certain cases: namely, where land is held by trustees under a duty to sell or personal property under a duty to convert into land. There are, however, other cases where conversion is relevant: for example, under specifically enforceable contracts or under partnership agreements. In these situations the law remains unchanged[1].

1   See generally *Snell's Equity* (30th edn, 2000) p 554 *et seq* and see Pettit (1997) 113 LQR 207.

Conclusions on the abolition of the doctrine

2.24

(a)   The main effect of the abolition of the doctrine of conversion will be in the case of wills leaving personal property to beneficiary A and realty to B. If a deceased had been a beneficial tenant in common in No 4 Railway Cuttings then under the old law his interest in Railway Cuttings was converted and so treated as personalty which passed to beneficiary A. Under the provisions of the Trusts of Land and Appointment of Trustees Act 1996, however, he will own an interest in realty passing to beneficiary B. In practice, it is relatively uncommon for wills to be drafted in this way and the testator would doubtless have intended that his interest in Railway Cuttings would pass to B so that the doctrine more often than not acted as a trap for the unwary.

(b)   The doctrine of conversion had already lost much of its importance with the intestacy rules becoming (from 1925) the same for realty and personalty[1].

(c)   For inheritance tax purposes the Inheritance Tax Act 1984, s 211 provides that any tax for which the personal representatives are liable is a testamentary expense whether that tax arises in respect of realty or personalty[2]. Subject to any contrary provision in the will itself, the tax is paid in accordance with the rules for the application of assets contained in the Administration of Estates Act 1925. There was no equivalent provision in the days of estate duty when it was thought that duty on personal property was a testamentary expense whereas that attributable to realty was not[3]. Formerly, the Inheritance Tax Act 1984, s 237(3) provided that the Inland Revenue charge was not to be applied to personal property which included undivided shares in land held on trust for sale (whether statutory or not). The Trusts of Land and Appointment of Trustees Act 1996, Sch 4 has deleted that provision: such an interest is accordingly to be treated as realty for these purposes.

(d)   As already noted the abolition of the doctrine of conversion makes it clear that there is no difference between the interest of a beneficiary whether land is held on trust for sale or on a trust of land lacking any obligation to sell. It also means that the rationale behind overreaching in the case of trusts of land (including trusts for sale) has to be found in the existence of the trustees' power of sale[4].

1   See the Administration of Estates Act 1925, ss 33, 45 *et seq*. On intestacy before 1926 realty
     devolved on the heir and personalty on the statutory next of kin.
2   See *Re Dougal* [1981] STC 514, Ct of Sess.
3   See *Dymond Capital Taxes* para 27.140.
4   See para 6.64 below.

Section 4 – Express Trusts for Sale as Trusts of Land

2.25   Text of section 4

(1)   In the case of every trust for sale of land created by a disposition there is to
       be implied, despite any provision to the contrary made by the disposition, a
       power for the trustees to postpone sale of the land; and the trustees are not
       liable in any way for postponing sale of the land, in the exercise of their
       discretion, for an indefinite period.

(2)   Subsection (1) applies to a trust whether it is created, or arises, before or
       after the commencement of this Act.

(3)   Subsection (1) does not affect any liability incurred by trustees before that
       commencement.

Express trusts for sale in the future

2.26   It is still possible to create an express trust for sale of land, but there
will be implied into any such disposition a power for the trustees to postpone
sale[1]. In view of this does the creation of such an express trust serve any
useful purpose? It should be borne in mind that, so far as trustees are
concerned, the existence of a trust for sale imposes a mandatory requirement
(a duty to sell) which can only be postponed if there is an unanimous
decision to exercise the power of postponement. If the trustees are not
unanimous the land must therefore be sold[2].

1   And this power to postpone cannot be excluded in the disposition. Note that for these
     purposes a trust for sale means an *immediate* trust for sale: if the sale is not to take effect
     until a future date it is not immediate and there is no need for this provision.
2   One situation where it may continue to be standard practice to use a trust for sale is in the
     residue clause of a will: see para 6.41 below. A mere failure to sell is not a proper exercise
     of the power of postponement.

Definition of a 'disposition'

2.27   'Disposition' is defined in LPA 1925, s 205(1)(ii) and will include an
assurance of property to a trustee and a declaration of trust by the absolute
owner of the property.

Effect of abolition of conversion

2.28   Even though an express trust for sale may still be created, the effect
of the Trusts of Land and Appointment of Trustees Act 1996, s 3 is that the

interests of the beneficiaries will not be subject to the doctrine of conversion: they will therefore be interests in land.

Commencement

2.29   The Trusts of Land and Appointment of Trustees Act 1996, s 4 applies to trusts whenever created, but not so as to affect a liability which arose before 1 January 1997 (see Example 3 at para 2.30).

Old law

2.30   The Law of Property Act 1925, s 25 provided that in a disposition on trust for sale there was implied a power to postpone sale unless there was a contrary intention in the disposition. Under s 25(4) of the Act when there was a trust to retain or sell this was construed as a trust to sell with a power to postpone. Section 25 of the Act was repealed by the Trusts of Land and Appointment of Trustees Act 1996, Sch 4.

EXAMPLE 3

Thad's will imposed a trust for sale (with no power to postpone) over his residuary estate which included land. He died in 1994. The statutory power of postponement under the Law of Property Act 1925, s 25(1) was expressly excluded but, despite this, the land had not been sold on 1 January 1997. Under s 4 of the new Act the trustees have a power to postpone, but this will not affect any pre-existing liabilities. Given that the trustees failed to carry out the trust for sale from 1994 to 1997, it may be that an action would lie against them.

Section 5 – Implied Trusts for Sale as Trusts of Land

2.31   Text of section 5

   (1)   Schedule 2 has effect in relation to statutory provisions which impose a trust for sale of land in certain circumstances so that in those circumstances there is instead a trust of the land (without a duty to sell).

   (2)   Section 1 of the Settled Land Act 1925 does not apply to land held on any trust arising by virtue of that Schedule (so that any such land is subject to a trust of land).

Changes affecting statutory trusts for sale

2.32   All trusts for sale implied by statute have been converted into trusts of land. The Trusts of Land and Appointment of Trustees Act 1996, s 5(1) expressly states that in the cases identified in Sch 2 there is no duty to sell the land. The situations dealt with in that Schedule are as follows[1]:

(a) implied trusts of mortgaged property where the right of redemption is barred;

(b) land purchased by the trustees of a personalty settlement;

(c) joint ownership of land;

(d) intestacy; and

(e) trusts arising on a reverter of sites.

1   These are discussed further at para 5.9 ff below.

A resume of trustees' powers (and duties) regarding sale

2.33   The position under the Trusts of Land and Appointment of Trustees Act 1996 regarding trustees' duties and powers of sale and retention is as follows:

(a) if a disposition made on or after 1 January 1997 imposes an express trust for sale it will take effect subject to s 4(1) of the Act which gives the trustees a power to postpone sale (and protects them if, in exercise of that power, they postpone sale for an indefinite period);

(b) existing express trusts for sale continue, but with the addition of the s 4(1) power of postponement;

(c) existing statutory trusts for sale (as listed in Sch 2 of the Act) have been amended to replace the duty to sell with a power to sell and a power to retain.

2.34   In drafting new trusts of land, it is for the draftsman to decide whether there is any advantage to be obtained from including an express trust for sale, given that it will not be possible to exclude the power to retain set out in s 4(1) and that it will no longer be necessary for land to be held on a trust for sale in order to fall outside the provisions of the Settled Land Act 1925[1].

1   As to involuntary strict settlements see para 1.9 above.

Commencement

2.35   The Trusts of Land and Appointment of Trustees Act 1996, s 5 operates with regard to existing situations in which a trust for sale had been imposed prior to 1 January 1997. Section 5(2) of the Act was therefore included to make it clear that just because a trust for sale no longer arises it does not mean that the Settled Land Act provisions apply.

Nature of a trust of land

2.36   When trustees hold land subject to a power to sell with a power to retain, it may be argued that this is somewhat bizarre and that there should be some sort of underlying obligation[1]. In particular, as trustees must exercise powers unanimously, there should be some guidance as to what is to be done if they are divided. It is no answer to say that the trustees should in such a case simply apply to the court under the Trusts of Land and Appointment of Trustees Act 1996, s 14. In practice, what will occur is that the land will not be sold so that the underlying position is that a trust of land comprises a power to sell backed up by (the equivalent of) a duty to retain[2].

1   See, for example, 'Trusts of Land Reform' by Roger Smith (1990) Conveyancer 12. It may be noted that the Trusts of Land and Appointment of Trustees Act 1996, s 6(1) is the basis for the statement that in a trust of land (assuming that there is no express trust for sale imposed) trustees have a power to sell and to retain. This follows from that subsection conferring on them the powers of an absolute owner.
2   The Lord Chancellor's Department has confirmed in correspondence with the authors that this is their understanding of the position.

Section 6 – General Powers of Trustees

2.37   Text of section 6

(1)   For the purpose of exercising their functions as trustees, the trustees of land have in relation to the land subject to the trust all the powers of an absolute owner.

(2)   Where in the case of any land subject to a trust of land each of the beneficiaries interested in the land is a person of full age and capacity who is absolutely entitled to the land, the powers conferred on the trustees by subsection (1) include the power to convey the land to the beneficiaries even though they have not required the trustees to do so; and where land is conveyed by virtue of this subsection–

(a)   the beneficiaries shall do whatever is necessary to secure that it vests in them, and

(b)   if they fail to do so, the court may make an order requiring them to do so.

(3)   The trustees of land have power to [*purchase a legal estate in any land in England or Wales*] **acquire land under the power conferred by section 8 of the Trustee Act 2000**.

[*(4)   The power conferred by subsection (3) may be exercised by trustees to purchase land–*

(a)   by way of investment,

(b)   for occupation by any beneficiary, or

(c)   for any other reason.]

(5)   In exercising the powers conferred by this section trustees shall have regard to the rights of the beneficiaries.

(6)   The powers conferred by this section shall not be exercised in contravention of, or of any order made in pursuance of, any other enactment or any rule of law or equity.

(7)   The reference in subsection (6) to an order includes an order of any court or of the Charity Commissioners.

(8)   Where any enactment other than this section confers on trustees authority to act subject to any restriction, limitation or condition, trustees of land may

not exercise the powers conferred by this section to do any act which they are prevented from doing under the other enactment by reason of the restriction, limitation or condition.

(9) **The duty of care under section 1 of the Trustee Act 2000 applies to trustees of land when exercising the powers conferred by this section.**

Structure of section 6

2.38   The Trusts of Land and Appointment of Trustees Act 1996, s 6 (which has been amended in important respects by TA 2000) deals with a number of different trustee powers as follows:

(a)   s 6(1) gives a general management power to trustees of land including selling, leasing and mortgaging the land which replaces the Law of Property Act 1925, s 28. Contrast TA 2000, s 8(3) which confers a similar power on trustees who *acquire* land: contrast the position therefore if the land is gifted – see para 11.73 below;

(b)   s 6(2) contains a power for trustees to vest land in beneficiaries who are of full age and capacity and absolutely entitled (replacing the Law of Property Act 1925, s 23);

(c)   s 6(3)-(4) gives trustees of land a specific power to purchase a legal estate in land in England and Wales both for investment and for occupation by a beneficiary (but not to buy an interest in land). Section 6(3) has now been amended by TA 2000 to include land in the UK and s 6(4) has been repealed since the matter is covered by TA 2000, s 8(1);

(d)   s 6(5) is a reminder that the exercise of these powers is subject to general equitable guidelines: in particular, that the trustees must have regard to the rights of the beneficiaries and, in s 6(6), to rules of equity;

(e)   s 6(6)-(8) states that in certain circumstances these powers may not be available or may not be exercisable.

2.39   The Trusts of Land and Appointment of Trustees Act 1996, s 6 may be restricted or extended by the express terms of the relevant trust deed[1], and such provisions may include a requirement that the powers given to trustees under the section can only be exercised with consent[2]. The section applies to all implied trusts and to all pre 1 January 1997 trusts.

1   Trusts of Land and Appointment of Trustees Act 1996, s 8(1).
2   Trusts of Land and Appointment of Trustees Act 1996, s 8(2).

Powers over land

2.40   The Law of Property Act 1925, s 28 gave trustees for sale the same administrative powers as are conferred on the tenant for life and the Settled Land Act trustees of a strict settlement. The Law Commission concluded as follows[1]:

'As regards the nature and extent of the trust powers themselves, we consider that trustees of land should be put in much the same position as an absolute owner. The circumstances of most trusts of land will be such that those persons to whom the legal label of "trustee" is attached are quite likely to regard themselves as the "owners" of the trust land. Even where this is not the case, it is desirable that the trustees should have the powers necessary to make efficient use of the land. Our proposals are designed to reflect this state of affairs whilst maintaining the general equitable duties of trustees. Therefore, although the powers will be approximate to those of an absolute owner, they will not be quite as readily exercisable.

In recommending that trustees of land should have all the powers of an absolute owner, our aim is not simply to tack additional powers on to those which trustees for sale currently possess, so as to arrive at a more "complete" inventory. Rather, it is to make the scheme of powers as broadly based and as flexible as possible. The powers of trustees for sale are expressed as a rather complex and fragmented set, and, in accordance with our policy that trusts of land should be analogous to those of personalty, it is our view that this composite of powers should be dissolved into a simple and widely-framed provision.'

1   Ie *Transfer of Land, Trusts of Land* (Law Com no 181) paras 10.4, 10.5. These powers fell short of those possessed by an absolute owner; eg trustees could not raise the initial purchase price for the property by way of mortgage. For the powers of the tenant for life to deal with the settled land (which equally applied to the trustees for sale) see Megarry and Wade *The Law of Real Property* (5th edn, 1984) p 358 *et seq*. The very restricted powers of leasing and mortgaging should be noted.

The ambit of section 6(1)

2.41

(a)   The power in the Trusts of Land and Appointment of Trustees Act 1996, s 6(1) embraces the management of land (for example, letting, mortgaging etc). If the land is sold the question then becomes one of investing the sale proceeds and that is not dealt with in this section (apart from in s 6(3) which is considered below). Accordingly, in the absence of any express provision to the contrary, the governing authority conferring investment powers on trustees will now be the Trustee Act 2000, Pts II and III.

(b)   The power in s 6(1) is given to the trustees in relation to the land which is subject to a trust. Accordingly, insofar as other property is held in those trusts, this particular power does not apply to that property[1]. Note also that the power may be enjoyed by trustees of a sub-trust which holds an interest in land subject to the trusts of a head trust: an undivided share in land is now 'land' (see para 2.2 above for the definition of land employed in the Act). Given that the definition of a trust of land is wide enough to include bare trusts, it is important to note that bare trustees are now given (for the first time) all the powers of a trustee of land including the power of sale[2].

(c)   Although the power is conferred in the widest terms, its exercise must conform to general equitable requirements: s 6(5) which provides that regard be had to the rights of the beneficiaries is merely an illustration of this[3]. A purchaser of the land is not concerned to see that the requirements in s 6(5) have been complied with[4].

(d) Section 12 confers (in certain circumstances) a right to occupy trust land on beneficiaries. In addition, the powers given under s 6(1) include a power to allow a beneficiary into occupation.

(e) The powers are conferred on the trustees 'for the purpose of exercising their functions as trustees': functions in this context will embrace both the powers and duties of the trustees.

(f) Apart from the s 6(1) powers, trustees retain other detailed powers with regard to sales and mortgages:

– TA 1925, s 12(1): mode of sale;

– TA 1925, s 13: remedies for depreciatory conditions;

– the power to sell includes a power to sell part (however that part is arrived at, eg it may be on the basis of horizontal or vertical division);

– TA 1925, s 24: power to concur with others in the sale of individual shares;

– TA 1925, s 17: protection of mortgagee on mortgage by trustees;

– TA 1925, s 14: power of trustees to give receipts.

1   Note also that the Trusts of Land and Appointment of Trustees Act 1996, s 6(1) does not apply to an existing settlement which remains governed by the administrative provisions of the Settled Land Act 1925.
2   See para 14.53 ff below.
3   And see the Trusts of Land and Appointment of Trustees Act 1996, s 6(6) and para 2.43 below.
4   Trusts of Land and Appointment of Trustees Act 1996, s 16(1).

Trustees to have regard to the rights of the beneficiaries

2.42 The inclusion of this subsection is a total mystery given that trustees' powers should generally be exercised with the interests of the beneficiaries in mind. Why was it ever included? Goodness knows, but TA 2000 does not contain any similar provision in Pt III and the Notes to that Act comment that:

'The express duty to have regard to the interests of the beneficiaries in exercising power under s 6(5) of the 1996 Act is not replicated ... However that provision merely clarifies what is already the law and the omission of an equivalent provision is not intended to diminish the obligations of trustees.'

2.43 Section 6(6) may also be considered an unnecessary inclusion (inserted presumably out of abundant caution!). For instance, the reference to rules of equity is redundant since all trustee powers fall to be exercised with such rules in mind (for example, the trustees must not breach the self dealing rule).

Bringing a trust of land to an end

2.44   Provided that all relevant beneficiaries are of full age and capacity and absolutely entitled to the land, the Trusts of Land and Appointment of Trustees Act 1996, s 6(2) enables the trustees to convey or transfer the land to those beneficiaries without obtaining their consent[1]. In a case where trustees are holding for one such beneficiary who is absolutely entitled, this will have the effect of bringing the trust to an end: if more than one beneficiary is involved, the trust will continue and so the effect of the conveyance or transfer will be to replace the existing trustees with the beneficiaries (or at least with four of those beneficiaries).

EXAMPLE 4

Sad and Sal hold Blackacre on trust for Lucy and Tom contingent on attaining 21 years and if more than one in equal shares absolutely. Tom the younger has just reached 21 years. Under the Trusts of Land and Appointment of Trustees Act 1996, s 6(2), Sad and Sal may transfer the property to Lucy and Tom to hold on trusts for themselves as beneficial tenants in common. For capital gains tax purposes, the trust of Blackacre ended when Tom reached 21 years at which time there was a deemed disposal and reacquisition of the property at its then market value by the trustees[2]. Alternatively, if Lucy was the sole beneficiary, the trustees could convey the land to her 'freed and discharged from the trust'[3].

---

1   Consent is not needed because the object of the provision is to enable a trust to be determined (contrast other powers where consultation is required, see s 11 considered at para 2.107 below). Likewise the beneficiaries are obliged to do whatever is necessary to ensure that the land vests in them: if, for instance, the land is unregistered, the transfer will now trigger compulsory registration (LRA 1925, s 123 substituted by LRA 1997, s 1).
2   See the Taxation of Chargeable Gains Act 1992 ss 60, 71; and see also *Crowe v Appleby* [1975] 3 All ER 529, [1975] 1 WLR 1539.
3   For the deed of discharge that will be appropriate see **Precedent 16** below.

The ambit of section 6(2): a drafting nightmare

2.45   The wording of this subsection is a nightmare! To start with what was intended, the Law Commission in its report *Transfer of Land, Trusts of Land*[1] described the section as a re-enactment of the Law of Property Act 1925, s 23 and, in the draft Bill attached to the report, the section appeared as a separate clause with a side heading 'Duration and termination of trusts of land'[2]. The attached explanatory note suggested that the provision implemented a recommendation of the committee that 'there should be a provision similar to s 17 of the Settled Land Act for all trusts of land'[3]. At this stage the clause envisaged a transfer to a single beneficiary who was *sui juris* and absolutely entitled. When the Bill was finally printed, however, the provision had been subsumed into a general clause on trustees' administrative powers and, in place of a single beneficiary, the reference had become to beneficiaries of full age and capacity being absolutely entitled. This wording was then amended at House of Lords Report Stage into its final form, the Lord Chancellor (Lord Mackay) commenting as follows:

'As to Amendment No 3 itself, the noble Lord, Lord Mishcon, stated in Committee his belief that the trustees' power to convey trust land to beneficiaries under Clause 6(2) is to be exercisable where each of the beneficiaries in question is absolutely entitled; that is, on the basis of concurrent interests, as joint tenants or tenants in common. The amendment to Clause 6(2) is intended simply to make it clear that the noble Lord's belief is entirely correct. The amendment also makes it clear that the power exists where one particular parcel of land is held for the beneficiaries absolutely, regardless of whether absolute interests exist in other land or other assets of the trust[4].'

1   Ie Transfer of Land, Trusts of Land (Law Com No 181).
2   Draft Bill cl 2 as set out in Transfer of Land, Trusts of Land p 36.
3   Transfer of Land, Trusts of Land p 37. This is achieved by the Trusts of Land and Appointment of Trustees Act 1996, s 16(4): see paras 2.51 and 2.170 below.
4   House of Lords Report Stage at 571 HL Official Report (5th series) col 957, 22 April 1996.

2.46   Has the wording achieved that result: ie that the power can only be exercised in cases where there is a single beneficiary absolutely entitled to the land or, in the case of more than one beneficiary, when those beneficiaries are together jointly absolutely entitled (as either tenants in common or joint tenants)?

2.47   It is arguable that the wording does not achieve this result: consider by way of contrast, the wording used in the Trusts of Land and Appointment of Trustees Act 1996, s 7(1) (partition of land amongst co-owners) which refers to beneficiaries of full age being absolutely entitled in undivided shares. There is no similar reference to undivided shares in s 6(2), but merely to beneficiaries interested in the land. Given the definition of beneficiaries in s 22(1) of the Act[1], it then might appear that the provisions of this subsection are wide enough to extend beyond a simple co-ownership situation.

1   Broadly any person having an interest in property subject to the trust: see para 4.2 below.

2.48   It is hard to make sense of the words 'each of the beneficiaries interested in the land is a person of full age and capacity who is absolutely entitled to the land'. If the word 'who' refers back to 'the beneficiaries' then this seems very odd given that the verb which follows is in the singular case. If, however, the reference back is to 'each of the beneficiaries' (which makes sense of the verb) then we seem to pass immediately from the reference to interests in land to a person being absolutely entitled to the land. Perhaps the only way to make sense of this is by interpolating the word 'together', but it is far from satisfactory that the only way of making sense of s 6(2) is to interpolate words that are not there.

2.49   There are two possible constructions of s 6(2): first, that it is limited to a transfer of land to co-owners, and second, that it would apply in a *Saunders v Vautier*[1] situation (ie where all the beneficiaries are *sui juris* and together could end the trust). In the first case s 6(2) performs the role of enabling the trustees to either bring a trust of land to an end or, in the case of more than one co-owner, to transfer the trusteeship to the co-owners (or at least the first four such co-owners)[2]. On the second interpretation, given that the trusts are continuing, it is simply a way of changing the trusteeship and enabling the current trustees to, in effect, retire and be replaced by at least some of the beneficial owners. A further difficulty on the second interpretation would then be thrown up by the limitation on trustees in the Trustee Act 1925, s 34(2) (as amended by the Trusts of Land and Appointment of Trustees Act 1996, Sch 3, para 3(9)). In an appropriate case this would require the trustees to transfer the land to four only of the beneficiaries to hold as trustees for themselves and the other beneficiaries.

1   *Saunders v Vautier* (1841) Cr & Ph 240.
2   See the Trustee Act 1925, ss 34(2), 36(6) as amended by the Trusts of Land and Appointment of Trustees Act 1996, Sch 3, para 3(9), (11); Law of Property Act 1925, s 34 as amended by the Trusts of Land and Appointment of Trustees Act 1996, Sch 2, para 3, Sch 4 (see also para 2.51 note 4 below).

2.50   The authors are inclined to the view that the first interpretation is the one that will be preferred: however, given the manifest defects in the drafting of the provision, a court may well consider that on its face s 6(2) is ambiguous, and therefore have resort to the doctrine of *Pepper v Hart*[1].

1   *Pepper v Hart* [1993] AC 593, [1993] 1 All ER 42, HL. In correspondence with the authors, the Lord Chancellor's Department commented that it did not see much force in the argument that successive interests were included within the subsection, but that in any event the Hansard references are absolutely clear and would be prayed in aid against anyone seeking to persuade the court to the contrary. Given the well publicised difficulties presented by s 6(2) it is surprising to find exactly the same problems presented by the drafting of TA 2000, s 34 (see para 14.4 below).

Specific points on section 6(2)

2.51

(a)   Because the Trusts of Land and Appointment of Trustees Act 1996, s 6(2) does not refer to beneficiaries becoming absolutely beneficially entitled, trustees can use the power when there is a sub-trust (or resettlement) of the land[1].

(b)   Section 6(2) refers to 'any land' so that the trustees may exercise their powers with respect to one parcel of land, albeit that other land remains held on trust[2].

(c)   As a result of s 6(2)(a), it is clear that the beneficiaries can be forced to execute the appropriate transfer or conveyance of the land[3].

(d)   For the protection of purchasers, s 16(4) provides that when the trustees exercise their powers under s 6(2) in favour of persons whom they believe to be absolutely entitled and of full age and capacity, they must execute a declaratory deed stating that they are discharged from the trust in relation to that land.

(e)   When the trustees transfer land to more than four beneficiaries, the limitation on the number of trustees to four will apply (this apparently is put beyond doubt by the Trusts of Land and Appointment of Trustees Act 1996, s 6(8)) so that the first four named beneficiaries (who may therefore be chosen by the trustees) will hold on trust for themselves and the others as either joint tenants or tenants in common[4].

(f)   *Precedents*: for a conveyance pursuant to s 6(2) see **Precedent 5** and for a deed of discharge pursuant to s 16(4) see **Precedent 16**.

1   Compare the Taxation of Chargeable Gains Act 1992, s 71; and see *Hoare Trustees v Gardner* [1979] Ch 10, [1978] 1 All ER 791 and Example 4 above.
2   See para 2.45 above.
3   See the Trusts of Land and Appointment of Trustees Act 1996, s 11(2) excluding the trustees' power under s 6(2) from those functions of the trustees the exercise of which requires prior consultation with the beneficiaries.
4   See the House of Lords Committee Stage debates at 570 HL Official Report (5th series) col 1533, 25 March 1996 per the Lord Chancellor (Lord Mackay):

> 'There is also nothing in Clause 6(2) to suggest that that is not subject to the provisions of Section 34 of the Law of Property Act 1925 as amended by the Bill, which provides, amongst other things, for a conveyance of land to more than four persons in undivided shares to operate as a conveyance to the first four named in the conveyance on trust for all of them. That already enables the trustees to exercise a degree of control, by selecting the first four names and, given that the power in Clause 6(2) is not dependent on the beneficiaries asking for it to be exercised, it is questionable what benefit is to be gained by empowering the beneficiaries to specify which four of them shall be trustees for the others.' It may be noted that this comment was made in response to a proposed amendment which would have specifically referred to a limitation on four trustees being appointed but would have provided for the beneficiaries to select from amongst themselves the four to be trustees.

Power to purchase a legal estate in land

2.52   Because there was no power to purchase land in the Trustee Investments Act 1961, the Trusts of Land and Appointment of Trustees Act 1996, s 6(3) gave trustees of land an extended power of investment. Note in particular the following matters:

(a)   The power extended to the purchase of a legal estate in land in England and Wales: ie a fee simple absolute in possession or term of years absolute[1]. No other restrictions are imposed: in particular, a short leasehold interest may be acquired. Given that a legal estate must be acquired, Section 6(3) of the Act does not extend to the purchase of an interest in land unless the trustees take the legal title. As a result of the extension in this power made by TA 2000, from 1 February 2001 trustees of land have also been able to acquire land in Scotland and Northern Ireland.

(b)   Under TA 2000, s 8(1) land may be purchased for occupation by a beneficiary, albeit that the courts have held that this would not be an investment even under a wide power giving the trustees the investment powers of an absolute owner[2].

(c)   The power in s 6(3) is stated to be exercisable by trustees of land, but s 17(1) of the Act formerly provided that it could also be used by trustees of a trust of proceeds of sale of land. A 'trust of proceeds of sale of land' is defined in s 17(3) to include not only the situation where proceeds are held on trust, but also the situation where property representing such proceeds is held on trust. Provided therefore that land was at any time owned by trustees, and that either the proceeds of that sale or replacement assets were still held in trust, the s 6(3) power was available to the trustees[3]. With the passage of TA 2000, s 17(1) was repealed since trustees of the proceeds of sale of land have power to buy land under TA 2000, Pt III in any event so that it is no longer necessary to treat them as if they were trustees of land and hence authorised under s 6(3).

(d) At Report Stage[4] amendments in the definition of a trust of land to include charitable, ecclesiastical and public trusts were made, thereby enabling those trusts to take advantage of the more flexible trustee powers given by the Trusts of Land and Appointment of Trustees Act 1996[5].

1   See the Law of Property Act 1925, s 1(1) for the definition of a legal estate.
2   See *Transfer of Land, Trusts of Land* (Law Com No 181) paras 10.7, 10.8:

> 'Trustees of land will have a power to apply proceeds of sale of trust land, or any part thereof, to the purchase of land, either for occupation by the beneficiaries or for investment. Although trustees for sale do have a power to apply trust money to the purchase of land, the courts have interpreted the scope of this power rather restrictively. Thus, in *Re Power's Will Trusts* it was held that, where the trustees were expressly given all the powers of investment of an absolute owner, this power could not be exercised to purchase land for occupation by beneficiaries. Similarly, it has been held that where all the trust land has been sold the trustees cease to be trustees for sale and hence cease to be within the statutory provisions.

> Our recommendation is that trustees should have a broad power to apply some or all of any proceeds of sale to the purchase of land, either as an investment or for occupation by the beneficiaries. This power would extend to the purchase of freehold or leasehold legal estates. It would not be restricted to property where the lease has more than sixty years left to run: we felt that such a restriction was neither necessary nor desirable in today's economic climate, in which shorter leases may often be regarded as good and prudent investments, appropriate to the particular circumstances of the trust and beneficiaries. The fixing of a minimum period, of whatever length, could only be the result of an arbitrary decision and, bearing in mind that there are circumstances in which it is quite conceivable that even a freehold might represent an imprudent or inappropriate investment, it seemed sensible to give trustees maximum flexibility, leaving general equitable rules to govern the use of such flexibility. In addition, the powers of trustees of land to mortgage, lease, or sell the land should be analogous to those held by absolute owners. Any money realised by the exercise of these powers will be held upon the same trusts as the land is or was held.'

3   Note the Trusts of Land and Appointment of Trustees Act 1996, s 17(5) which makes it clear that the definition does not apply to land held under a continuing Settled Land Act settlement.
4   House of Lords Report Stage at 571 HL Official Report (5th series) col 955, 22 April 1996.
5   See para 2.8 above and para 6.7 below.

Relationship between s 6(1) and TA 2000, s 8(3)

2.53   Section 6(1) confers on trustees of land in relation to land subject to the trust 'all the powers of an absolute owner' whereas s 8(3) of TA 2000 provides that a trustee who *acquires* land under s 8 has 'all the powers of an absolute owner in relation to that land'. These provisions overlap in cases where trustees acquire land thereby becoming trustees of land: see further para 11.73 below.

The statutory duty of care

2.54   From 1 February 2001 this has been extended to trustees when exercising their powers under s 6[1]. It is in relation to the absolute owner powers, which include selling, leasing, improving the property, mortgaging etc that trustees will need to be especially aware of the new duty. Case law has established a series of obligations to which trustees should have regard when exercising their powers of sale, for instance:

(a) the sale must take place under every possible advantage to the beneficiaries and paying regard to the interests of the different beneficiaries;

(b) trustees must ensure that there is proper competition and avoid anything (eg a misdescription of the property) likely to lead to reduction in the price;

(c) commercial morality should not dictate the refusal of a higher offer;

(d) although a trustee can impose reasonable conditions of sale he is not entitled to impose wholly unreasonable restrictions that would have the effect of depreciating the price;

(e) there is a power to sell part including minerals and the s 6(1) power would enable a sale to occur at a valuation and a sale to be for a consideration other than money. In such cases the trustees must act reasonably in line with their duty of care;

1   For a general consideration of the duty of care, see para 10.1 ff below. Section 6 is curiously omitted from the list in TA 2000, Sch 1.

2.55   The beneficial owner power in s 6(1) is widely enough drawn to include the sale of leaseholds by way of underlease selling property and leaving the purchase money outstanding on mortgage[1] and gives the trustees the power to make improvements[2].

1   This was formerly regulated by TA 1925, s 10(2) which was repealed by TA 2000: see para 14.49 below.
2   Formerly given by LPA 1925, s 28 imported from SLA 1925.

Section 7 – Partition by Trustees

2.56   Text of section 7

(1) The trustees of land may, where beneficiaries of full age are absolutely entitled in undivided shares to land subject to the trust, partition the land, or any part of it, and provide (by way of mortgage or otherwise) for the payment of any equality money.

(2) The trustees shall give effect to any such partition by conveying the partitioned land in severalty (whether or not subject to any legal mortgage created for raising equality money), either absolutely or in trust, in accordance with the rights of those beneficiaries.

(3) Before exercising their powers under subsection (2) the trustees shall obtain the consent of each of those beneficiaries.

(4) Where a share in the land is affected by an incumbrance, the trustees may either give effect to it or provide for its discharge from the property allotted to that share as they think fit.

(5) If a share in the land is absolutely vested in a minor, subsections (1) to (4) apply as if he were of full age, except that the trustees may act on his behalf and retain land or other property representing his share in trust for him.

Origins

2.57   The Trusts of Land and Appointment of Trustees Act 1996, s 7 replaces the Law of Property Act 1925, s 28(3), (4) which, with appropriate amendments, is extended to all trusts of land[1].

1   For partition amongst co-owners see generally Megarry and Wade *The Law of Real Property* (6th edn, 2000) para 9-100. The power may be expressly excluded by a provision in the disposition creating the trust of land or made subject to the trustees obtaining some consent: see s 8(1)(2) considered at para 2.69 below.

Requirements

2.58   Partition of land amongst co-owners requires:

(a)   the consent of all the relevant beneficiaries; and

(b)   the exercise by the trustees of their s 7 powers.

2.59   In the event that a beneficiary refuses his consent, or that the trustees are unwilling to partition the land on request, an application may be made to the court under the Trusts of Land and Appointment of Trustees Act 1996, s 14. The court may, *inter alia*, order a partition or sale of the land[1].

1   See the Trusts of Land and Appointment of Trustees Act 1996, s 14(2)(a): an order relating to the exercise by the trustees of their functions. It would appear from the reference to 'beneficiaries' rather than to 'each of the beneficiaries' that part of the land could be partitioned amongst beneficiaries absolutely entitled to a share in the land held on trust.

Meaning of beneficiary

2.60   Reference to a beneficiary 'absolutely entitled in undivided shares to land' does not require him to be beneficially so entitled: therefore a partition can be made to a trustee or personal representative[1].

1   Compare the Trusts of Land and Appointment of Trustees Act 1996, s 6(2) and see s 22(2).

Formalities of partition

2.61   Any conveyance by the trustees must be by deed[1].

1   See the Law of Property Act 1925, s 52 as amended by the Law of Property (Miscellaneous Provisions) Act 1989, s 1(8), Sch 1, para 2. On a partition it will often be necessary for accounts to be taken between the former co-owners: see *Re Pavlou* [1993] 1 WLR 1046.

Beneficiaries under a disability

2.62   A mental patient is entitled to his share with the consent of his receiver which is sufficient to protect the trustees: in the case of a minor, the trustees may act on his behalf and retain land or other property representing his share.

Purchasers

2.63   A purchaser of land is not concerned to see that the requirement of consent imposed on the trustees under the Trusts of Land and Appointment of Trustees Act 1996, s 7(3) has been complied with[1].

1   Trusts of Land and Appointment of Trustees Act 1996, s 16(1).

EXAMPLE 5

North and South Farm were held on trust for A for life, remainder to such of B and C as attained 21 years and if more than one in equal shares. A and C (who had attained 21 years) were killed in a car accident. The trustees (under s 7) may now decide to partition the two farms between B and C's personal representatives. For example, North Farm to B and South Farm to the personal representatives.

Capital gains tax aspects

2.64   The capital gains tax position when land is partitioned amongst beneficial co-owners is dealt with by Inland Revenue extra-statutory concession D26. Under this concession, where interests in land which is in the joint beneficial ownership of two or more persons are exchanged after 19 December 1984 and either:

(a)   a holding of land is held jointly and, as a result of the exchange, each joint owner becomes sole owner of part of the land formerly owned jointly; or

(b)   a number of separate holdings of land are held jointly and, as a result of the exchange, each joint owner becomes sole owner of one or more holding;

a relief along the lines of the Taxation of Chargeable Gains Act 1992, ss 247, 248 (relief for compulsory acquisition of land) may be claimed to alleviate the charges to capital gains tax which would otherwise arise. The relevant relief is a form of roll-over relief enabling any gain arising to be rolled over into the cost of acquiring the replacement land. Assume, for example, that the base costs of the land to the two joint tenants was £100 and that the land was divided between them: each would have base costs of £50 attributable to the piece of land to which he becomes absolutely entitled.

2.65   Reference should also be made to the 'pooling' cases of *Booth v Ellard*[1] (dealing with shares) and *Jenkins v Brown*[2] (dealing with land).

1   *Booth v Ellard* [1980] 3 All ER 569, [1980] 1 WLR 1443, CA.
2   *Jenkins v Brown* [1989] 1 WLR 1163.

Stamp duty aspects

2.66   For partitions of any estate or land, a fixed duty of £5 is charged unless consideration in excess of £100 is given for equality[1].

1   FA 1999, Sch 13, para 21.

Precedents

2.67 For a consent to partition, see **Precedent 6** and for a conveyance giving effect to a partition, see **Precedent 7**.

Section 8 – Exclusion and Restriction of Powers

2.68 Text of section 8

(1) Sections 6 and 7 do not apply in the case of a trust of land created by a disposition in so far as provision to the effect that they do not apply is made by the disposition.

(2) If the disposition creating such a trust makes provision requiring any consent to be obtained to the exercise of any power conferred by section 6 or 7, the power may not be exercised without that consent.

(3) Subsection (1) does not apply in the case of charitable, ecclesiastical or public trusts.

(4) Subsections (1) and (2) have effect subject to any enactment which prohibits or restricts the effect of provision of the description mentioned in them.

Restricting sections 6, 7

2.69 The powers of trustees of land given in the Trusts of Land and Appointment of Trustees Act 1996, ss 6 and 7 can generally be restricted or excluded by the disposition creating the trust[1]. If restriction or exclusion is the draftsman's objective this should be done by express reference to the relevant section(s): whilst a court might hold that the disposition contained express provisions which were implicitly inconsistent with these statutory powers (and which were accordingly to that extent excluded) it is not safe to rely on mere implication. Alternatively, the disposition creating the trust may require one or more consents to be obtained before the ss 6 and 7 powers can be exercised[2].

---

1   For a consideration of how the exclusion or restriction should be effected and, in particular, the meaning of the 'disposition' in this context see **Precedent 8 note 1** below. In the case of registered land, any limitation on the trustees' powers will need to be entered on the register as a restriction since a proprietor of registered land has all the powers of an absolute owner (subject only to any restrictions on the register). In *Private Trusts of Land* (2nd Edn, April 2000), Practice Advice Leaflet No 13, published by HM Land Registry, the matter is explained as follows:

'In unregistered conveyancing, where the powers of the trustees of a private trust are limited by virtue of section 8 of the 1996 Act, they are under an obligation to take all reasonable steps to bring the limitation to the notice of any purchaser of the land from them (TOLATA 1996, s 16(3)(a)(b)). In registered conveyancing, the rules impose a corresponding obligation in the form of a duty to apply for a restriction in Form 11A ...

These restrictions are entered for the protection of the rights of the persons beneficially interested in the land (LRA 1925, s 94(4)). In the absence of a restriction a purchaser of registered land from trustees is not concerned to see that any necessary consent has been obtained, or any limitation on the trustees' powers of disposition in the disposition creating the trust has been complied with' (see para E2.3).

2   The consent required need not be that of a beneficiary: it can be of any person. Although a purchaser is protected if any two consents are obtained (see the Trusts of Land and Appointment of Trustees Act 1996, s 10(1)), the trustees will be guilty of breach of trust if they do not obtain all requisite consents. Contrast the Law of Property Act 1925, s 26(2) (repealed by the Trusts of Land and Appointment of Trustees Act 1996, Sch 4) and note the Land Registration Act 1925, s 58(1) giving the Registrar power to enter restrictions on the register including consents. For the power of the Court to relieve trustees of their obligation to obtain the consent of any person, see s 14(1)(2) considered at para 2.145 below.

Purchasers

2.70   The position of purchasers of the relevant land is dealt with in the Trusts of Land and Appointment of Trustees Act 1996, s 10 (consents)[1] and s 16(3)[2].

1   See paras 2.100 and 6.65 below.
2   See paras 2.169 and 6.66 below.

Charities etc

2.71   The Trusts of Land and Appointment of Trustees Act 1996, s 8(3) preventing the restriction of charitable trustees' powers was inserted at the House of Lords Report Stage in order to restore the effect of the Settled Land Act 1925, s 106 for charitable, ecclesiastical or public trusts which become trusts of land[1]. The reason is that such trustees must administer the trust as effectively as possible with a view to achieving the charitable objects and this might be made more difficult if their powers could be fettered.

1   See House of Lords Report Stage at 571 HL Official Report (5th series) col 955, 22 April 1996.

Pension trusts

2.72   The particular reason for the inclusion of the Trusts of Land and Appointment of Trustees Act 1996, s 8(4) was explained by the Lord Chancellor in the House of Lords Committee Stage debates as follows[1]:

'Section 35(4) of the Pensions Act 1995 . . . prevents the powers of occupational pension scheme trustees being fettered by reference to requirements to obtain the consent of the employer, and it is right that this specific provision, aimed at a particular need in defined circumstances, should not be overridden by the general provisions of Clause 8. The same principle is applicable to specific provisions in other enactments which prohibit restriction on trustees' powers in certain circumstances, and the provision . . . has been drafted so as to apply to all such provisions, not just the pensions legislation.'

1   House of Lords Commitee Stage at 570 HL Official Report (5th series) col 1534, 25 March 1996.

Power of sale

2.73   It would appear that a settlor or testator is able to exclude the power of sale by imposing a suitable limit on the trustees' power under the Trusts of Land and Appointment of Trustees Act 1996, s 6(1)[1].

1   Contrast the Settled Land Act 1925, s 106. Trustees for sale could always have their powers restricted by a requirement of consent (eg from persons who the settlor knew would never consent to a sale!): see, for example, *Re Inns, Inns v Wallace* [1947] Ch 576 where land was, in effect, inalienable. The relevant provisions were in the Law of Property Act 1925, s 26. As already noted, in the case of registered land, any such limitation will need to appear on the register as a restriction: see para 2.69 note 2 above. Otherwise it will not prevent land being sold by the trustees. When the power of sale is excluded trustees may seek such a power under TA 1925, s 57 but it is not thought likely that the Court will be prepared to grant such a power. (Contrast *Re Cockerell's Settlement Trusts* [1956] Ch 372.) Alternatively, the trustees could apply to the Court for the exclusion to be removed under s 14 (see para 2.157 below).

Consent of persons under a disability

2.74   In the case of a minor the trustees must obtain the consent of a parent or guardian although a purchaser is not concerned with this[1]. If a person is mentally incapable, there is no such protection for a purchaser[2] who must ensure that the trustees have obtained the consent of the receiver. If consent cannot be obtained an application may be made to the court[3].

1   Trusts of Land and Appointment of Trustees Act 1996, s 10(3).
2   Contrast the Law of Property Act 1925, s 26(2) repealed by the Trusts of Land and Appointment of Trustees Act 1996, Sch 4.
3   Trusts of Land and Appointment of Trustees Act 1996, s 14(2)(a).

Commencement

2.75   The powers conferred on trustees under the Trusts of Land and Appointment of Trustees Act 1996, ss 6 and 7 apply to all existing trusts and cannot be excluded. Similarly, they will apply to all implied trusts whenever arising. It is therefore only in post-1996 express trusts of land that advantage can be taken of s 8.

Precedents

2.76   For a clause excluding the Trusts of Land and Appointment of Trustees Act 1996, ss 6(2) and 7 see **Precedent 8** below.

Section 9 – Delegation by Trustees

2.77   Text of section 9

(1)   The trustees of land may, by power of attorney, delegate to any beneficiary or beneficiaries of full age and beneficially entitled to an interest in possession in land subject to the trust any of their functions as trustees which relate to the land.

(2)   Where trustees purport to delegate to a person by a power of attorney under subsection (1) functions relating to any land and another person in good faith deals with him in relation to the land, he shall be presumed in favour of that other person to have been a person to whom the functions could be delegated unless that other person has knowledge at the time of the transaction that he was not such a person.

And it shall be conclusively presumed in favour of any purchaser whose interest depends on the validity of that transaction that that other person dealt in good faith and did not have such knowledge if that other person makes a statutory declaration to that effect before or within three months after the completion of the purchase.

(3) A power of attorney under subsection (1) shall be given by all the trustees jointly and (unless expressed to be irrevocable and to be given by way of security) may be revoked by any one or more of them; and such a power is revoked by the appointment as a trustee of a person other than those by whom it is given (though not by any of those persons dying or otherwise ceasing to be a trustee).

(4) Where a beneficiary to whom functions are delegated by a power of attorney under subsection (1) ceases to be a person beneficially entitled to an interest in possession in land subject to the trust–

(a) if the functions are delegated to him alone, the power is revoked,

(b) if the functions are delegated to him and to other beneficiaries to be exercised by them jointly (but not separately), the power is revoked if each of the other beneficiaries ceases to be so entitled (but otherwise functions exercisable in accordance with the power are so exercisable by the remaining beneficiary or beneficiaries), and

(c) if the functions are delegated to him and to other beneficiaries to be exercised by them separately (or either separately or jointly), the power is revoked in so far as it relates to him.

(5) A delegation under subsection (1) may be for any period or indefinite.

(6) A power of attorney under subsection (1) cannot be an enduring power within the meaning of the Enduring Powers of Attorney Act 1985.

(7) Beneficiaries to whom functions have been delegated under subsection (1) are, in relation to the exercise of the functions, in the same position as trustees (with the same duties and liabilities); but such beneficiaries shall not be regarded as trustees for any other purposes (including, in particular, the purposes of any enactment permitting the delegation of functions by trustees or imposing requirements relating to the payment of capital money).

[(8) *Where any function has been delegated to a beneficiary or beneficiaries under subsection (1), the trustees are jointly and severally liable for any act or default of the beneficiary, or any of the beneficiaries, in the exercise of the function if, and only if, the trustees did not exercise reasonable care in deciding to delegate the function to the beneficiary or beneficiaries.*]

(9) Neither this section nor the repeal by this Act of section 29 of the Law of Property Act 1925 (which is superseded by this section) affects the operation after the commencement of this Act of any delegation effected before that commencement.

2.78 [Section 9A Duties of trustees in connection with delegation etc

(1) **The duty of care under section 1 of the Trustee Act 2000 applies to trustees of land in deciding whether to delegate any of their functions under section 9.**

    (2)   Subsection (3) applies if the trustees of land–

        (a)   delegate any of their functions under section 9, and

        (b)   the delegation is not irrevocable.

    (3)   While the delegation continues, the trustees–

        (a)   must keep the delegation under review,

        (b)   if circumstances make it appropriate to do so, must consider whether there is a need to exercise any power of intervention that they have, and

        (c)   if they consider that there is a need to exercise such a power, must do so.

    (4)   'Power of intervention' includes–

        (a)   a power to give directions to the beneficiary;

        (b)   a power to revoke the delegation.

    (5)   The duty of care under section 1 of the 2000 Act applies to trustees in carrying out any duty under subsection (3).

    (6)   A trustee of land is not liable for any act or default of the beneficiary, or beneficiaries, unless the trustee fails to comply with the duty of care in deciding to delegate any of the trustees' functions under section 9 or in carrying out any duty under subsection (3).

    (7)   Neither this section nor the repeal of section 9(8) by the Trustee Act 2000 affects the operation after the commencement of this section of any delegation effected before that commencement.]

A contentious section!

2.79   The Trusts of Land and Appointment of Trustees Act 1996, s 9, in the form of the original draft Bill produced by the Law Commission, was the subject of intense criticism in the House of Lords as a result of which a substantially amended provision was produced at Committee Stage[1]. Even thereafter further amendments were made on Report[2] and Third Reading[3]. Subsequently (with effect from 1 February 2001) further changes were made to the section by TA 2000 with the deletion of sub-section (8) and the inclusion of a new section 9A.

1   See House of Lords Commitee Stage at 570 HL Official Report (5th series) cols 1535-1540, 25 March 1996.
2   See House of Lords Report Stage at 571 HL Official Report (5th series) cols 958-961, 22 April 1996.
3   See House of Lords Third Reading at 572 HL Official Report (5th series) cols 94-97, 7 May 1996.

Delegation by trustees[1]

2.80   The Law of Property Act 1925, s 29, which was replaced by this section, allowed trustees for sale to delegate revocably their powers of management (including the power to grant and accept surrenders of leases). That section did not, however, enable the power of sale to be delegated and so the powers of an attorney appointed under it could not in any sense be compared with those of the tenant for life under a strict settlement[2].

1   For delegation by an individual trustee of his functions see TDA 1999 considered in Part II of this book. The changes made to collective delegation by trustees in TA 2000, Pt IV are considered at para 12.1 ff below.

2   The tenant for life in a strict settlement is not able to assign his powers (Settled Land Act 1925, s 104) but may delegate his discretions (like any other trustee) under the Trustee Act 1925, s 25(10) inserted by TDA 1999. In practice delegation under the Law of Property Act 1925, s 29 was rare.

2.81   The essential feature of the delegation permitted by the Trusts of Land and Appointment of Trustees Act 1996 Section 9 is its 'corporate' nature: ie it is a delegation by the trustee body.

Delegation as an alternative to the strict settlement

2.82   The Law Commission envisaged that the power of delegation to be conferred on trustees of land may be employed to achieve much the same results as under the traditional strict settlement[1]. The restriction in the Trusts of Land and Appointment of Trustees Act 1996, s 9(7), which apparently prevents an attorney from receiving capital money, means that although the powers of sale may be delegated and the attorney may enter into a contract to sell land, at the stage of completion it will be necessary for the trustees to receive the sale money.

1   Transfer of Land, Trusts of Land (Law Com No 181) para 4.5:

> 'Besides the "family" settlement, there are other examples of situations in which the strict settlement might be preferred to the trust for sale or trust under the new system. In the context of matrimonial arrangements, it may, for example, be desired that the survivor should have the powers of a life tenant but that the capital should ultimately pass to the children of a previous marriage. In many of these instances, it may be simpler to do this by way of the Settled Land Act machinery. More generally, it might be considered appropriate that the current occupier of the land, being uniquely placed to do so, should have responsibility for the overall maintenance of the property, or for the collection of rents. We consider that these facilities should, in substance, continue to be available; settlors should be allowed to place control of the trust in the hands of those beneficiaries who are most directly interested in the trust land. Thus, our recommendations include a proposal that the new system should include such powers of delegation as are necessary to permit this.'

> In the event, although trustees of land are given power to delegate 'any of their functions as trustees which relate to the land' (Trusts of Land and Appointment of Trustees Act 1996, s 9(1)) there remain differences with the tenant for life under a strict settlement: in particular, the legal estate remains in the trustees and the attorney is treated as being in the same position as those trustees, but only in relation to the exercise of these functions: s 9(7). Of course, the attorney must also act in the name and on behalf of the trustees. There is not thought to be any difficulty in an individual trustee granting a trustee power of attorney under the Trustee Act 1925, s 25 as substituted by TDA 1999, s 5 (eg to cover a period of absence from the UK) which would enable the attorney eg to give receipts for capital money on a sale (see Trusts of Land (Law Com Working Paper No 94 para 8.4) or to exercise investment powers alongside a Trusts of Land and Appointment of Trustees Act 1996, s 9 delegation by all the trustees. It should be borne in mind that the s 9 power must be exercised collectively and the trustees can only delegate functions which relate to the land. So far as the wording of s 9(7) is concerned, it has been stated in the text that an attorney cannot give a receipt for capital money and that is believed to be the intention of the concluding part of the subsection. However, it may be argued that the subsection imposes the duties of a trustee on an attorney in relation to the exercise of the trustees' functions, but so that the attorney shall not otherwise be regarded as a trustee and, in particular, shall not be so regarded in relation to a receipt of capital money. On this view, the attorney can receive such money, but will not in that respect act qua trustee.

Who can be an attorney?

2.83 Only a beneficiary of full age who is beneficially entitled to an interest in possession[1] in the land can be appointed an attorney. If there is more than one such beneficiary then a joint appointment is possible[2]. Can the trustees delegate to an interest in possession beneficiary of a sub trust? Assume, for instance, that trustees are holding land for A and B as beneficial tenants in common and that B settles his interest on trust for (*inter alia*) C for life. In this case can the trustees of the land exercise their powers under s 9 in favour of C? It is thought not: C's interest is in the property in the sub trust; it is the trustees of that sub trust who have an interest in possession in the land in the 'head' trust (and they are not beneficially entitled).

1   For the definition of an interest in possession see para 4.2 below and note the Trusts of Land and Appointment of Trustees Act 1996, s 22(3) which excludes an annuitant. A trustee or personal representative cannot be beneficially entitled as such.
2   The Trusts of Land and Appointment of Trustees Act 1996, s 9(1). For a power of attorney granted pursuant to s 9, see **Precedent 9** below. Contrast delegation to an agent under TA 2000, Pt IV where that agent cannot be a beneficiary (TA 2000, s 12(3)).

What can be delegated?

2.84 The trustees may delegate 'any of their functions as trustees which relate to the land'. This enables all the powers conferred on the trustees by the Trusts of Land and Appointment of Trustees Act 1996, s 6 (ie the powers of an absolute owner, including the power of sale) to be delegated either indefinitely, or for a limited period[1], to an attorney acting in the trustees' name. When the trust contains a number of separate parcels of land, the trustees may choose to delegate their functions with regard to one parcel only and not to the rest: if there is also more than one beneficiary with an interest in possession, there may be a delegation to one beneficiary with regard to one parcel of land and to another beneficiary with regard to a separate parcel[2].

1   Trusts of Land and Appointment of Trustees Act 1996, s 9(5).
2   The power is limited to the trustees' functions in relation to land and hence does not extend, for example, to their investment powers in relation to the proceeds of sale of land. It is also considered that it is administrative functions (what TA 2000 refers to in s 11(2) as 'delegable functions') which are capable of delegation and not, for example, the exercise of dispositive discretions.

Mandatory delegation

2.85 The trust instrument may require the trustees to delegate to the life tenant; for example, because of the settlor's wish to set up the 'nearest equivalent' to a strict settlement[1].

1   Although the power to delegate under the Trustee Act 1925 may be excluded by the settlor (s 69(2)) it is not thought that the Trusts of Land and Appointment of Trustees Act 1996, s 9 can be so excluded. It seems to the authors that mandatory delegation sits uneasily with the concept of trusteeship (and with the revocation powers given by the section).

Protection of third parties[1]

2.86 Section 9 (2) affords protection to a third party dealing with the attorney 'in good faith'. In his favour it is presumed that the attorney is a person to whom functions could have been delegated (ie that he is a beneficiary enjoying an interest in possession and of full age). This is qualified in the case where a third party had knowledge[2], at the time of the transaction, that he was not such a person (although very often such knowledge will itself mean that the third party is not acting in good faith).

1   Compare the Law of Property Act 1925, s 29(1) which is replaced by the Trusts of Land and Appointment of Trustees Act 1996, s 9.

2   The section uses the word 'knowledge' rather than 'notice'.

2.87   A subsequent purchaser whose title depends on the original dealing with the attorney is given conclusive protection in the second part of s 9(2), provided that a statutory declaration is made by the person who dealt with the agent before or within three months of completion of the purchase[1].

1   For a statutory declaration pursuant to the Trusts of Land and Appointment of Trustees Act 1996, s 9(2), see **Precedent 10** below.

2.88   Concern was expressed in the House of Lords debates[1] at the opportunities that these provisions presented for fraud: however, the provisions of s 9(7) would in practice impose substantial restraints on any possible fraudulent activities.

1   House of Lords Third Reading at 572 HL Official Report (5th series) col 96, 7 May 1996.

2.89   The Powers of Attorney Act 1971, s 5 protects third parties in the event of a revocation of the power[1].

1   The Powers of Attorney Act 1971, s 5 is in the following terms:

'(1) A donee of a power of attorney who acts in pursuance of the power at a time when it has been revoked shall not, by reason of the revocation, incur any liability (either to the donor or to any other person) if at that time he did not know that the power had been revoked.

(2) Where a power of attorney has been revoked and a person, without knowledge of the revocation, deals with the donee of the power, the transaction between them shall, in favour of that person, be as valid as if the power had then been in existence.

(3) Where the power is expressed in the instrument creating it to be irrevocable and to be given by way of security then, unless the person dealing with the donee knows that it was not in fact given by way of security, he shall be entitled to assume that the power is incapable of revocation except by the donor acting with the consent of the donee and shall accordingly be treated for the purposes of subsection (2) of this section as having knowledge of the revocation only if he knows that it has been revoked in that manner.

(4) Where the interest of a purchaser depends on whether a transaction between the donee of a power of attorney and another person was valid by virtue of subsection (2) of this section, it shall be conclusively presumed in favour of the purchaser that that person did not at the material time know of the revocation of the power if—

(a)   the transaction between that person and the donee was completed within twelve months of the date on which the power came into operation; or

(b)   that person makes a statutory declaration, before or within three months after the completion of the purchase, that he did not at the material time know of the revocation of the power.

(5) Without prejudice to subsection (3) of this section, for the purposes of this section knowledge of the revocation of a power of attorney includes knowledge of the occurrence of any event (such as the death of the donor) which has the effect of revoking the power . . .'

As a power of attorney (albeit rather unique) it is considered that all relevant provisions of the Powers of Attorney Act 1971 and of the common law, save where expressly excluded or varied, apply to the trustees' delegation under s 9. The statutory declaration referred to in the Trusts of Land and Appointment of Trustees Act 1996, s 9(2) may be combined with a declaration to take advantage of the Powers of Attorney Act 1971, s 5(4)(b).

Making and revoking an appointment

2.90 The trustees must be unanimous in appointing an attorney: his authority may then be revoked by any one trustee[1].

> **EXAMPLE 6**
>
> Sad and Sal, trustees of the Blackthorn Trust, appoint Pierse, the life tenant, to exercise their powers under the Trusts of Land and Appointment of Trustees Act 1996, s 9(1):
>
> (a) if Sal died the power would continue unless revoked by Sad;
>
> (b) if a new trustee, Tim, is appointed to replace Sal, the power is revoked and a new power will be needed reappointing Pierse;
>
> (c) if Pierse surrenders his life interest the power ceases[2];
>
> (d) if the power had been granted jointly to Pierse and Rudolph (who enjoyed a concurrent life interest in the property with Pierse), the death of Pierse would not revoke the power so far as Rudolph was concerned[3]; a similar result applies if the power had been granted separately (or jointly and separately)[4].

1   Trusts of Land and Appointment of Trustees Act 1996, s 9(3).
2   Trusts of Land and Appointment of Trustees Act 1996, s 9(4)(a).
3   Trusts of Land and Appointment of Trustees Act 1996, s 9(4)(b).
4   Trusts of Land and Appointment of Trustees Act 1996, s 9(4)(c). Note that the section uses the word 'separately' rather than 'severally'.

2.91 The qualification to the above rules on revocation 'unless [the power is] expressed to be irrevocable and to be given by way of security' was explained by the Lord Chancellor (Lord Mackay) in the House of Lords debates as follows[1]:

> 'Although the power of attorney by which functions are delegated must be made unanimously, so that where the power is revocable it may be revoked by any one of the trustees, this does not override Sections 4 and 5(3) of the Powers of Attorney Act 1971, which covers powers of attorney which are expressed to be irrevocable and given by way of security for a proprietary interest of the attorney or for the performance of an obligation owed to him. It is possible that such a power might be used, for example, in the context of an employee relocation scheme which operates by using a trust mechanism, and since such powers may in general be revoked only with the attorney's consent [this provision] excludes them from the revocation provisions of clause 9(3). Accordingly, where the trustees

delegate functions to a beneficiary by a power which is expressed to be irrevocable and to be by way of security, the power may only be revoked in accordance with Section 4 of the Powers of Attorney Act 1971.'

1   House of Lords Third Reading at 572 HL Official Report (5th series) col 95, 7 May 1996.

The attorney as trustee

2.92   The Trusts of Land and Appointment of Trustees Act 1996, s 9(7) provides for the attorney to be in the position of a trustee insofar as the exercise of his powers is concerned[1]. The attorney is, for example, prohibited from any exercise which may confer on him a personal benefit. Although an agent's behaviour is therefore regulated by trust law, he is not a trustee and cannot sub-delegate or apparently receive capital money[2]. A purchaser will be aware that he is dealing with an attorney[3] and so the position will be similar to a transfer by the tenant for life under a strict settlement with the attorney executing the transfer and the trustees joining in to give a receipt for the proceeds of sale.

1   Compare the Law of Property Act 1925, s 29(3) (repealed by the Trusts of Land and Appointment of Trustees Act 1996, Sch 4).
2   See para 2.82 note 1 above.
3   '. . . delegation to a beneficiary should not affect the statutory machinery for overreaching, so that capital money must still be paid to or by the direction of two trustees or one trustee being a trust corporation . . .:' House of Lords Committee Stage at 570 HL Official Report (5th series) col 1536, 25 March 1996, per the Lord Chancellor.

Liability of the trustees for acts of the attorney

2.93   The Trusts of Land and Appointment of Trustees Act 1996, s 9(8) was much amended during the passage of the legislation and was repealed, by TA 2000, as from 1 February 2001. The Law Commission originally recommended that[1]:

'One effect of delegation under section 29 of the Law of Property Act is that the trustees are no longer liable to the other beneficiaries for the acts or defaults of the person(s) to whom the powers of management have been delegated. It is our view that this makes the trustees' liability too narrow. As it is our recommendation that delegation should take place within the terms of section 25 of the Trustee Act 1925, so it will follow that trustees of land will be liable to the other beneficiaries for the acts or defaults of the donee(s). Therefore, the trustees will have a clear incentive to adopt a supervisory role.'

1   Transfer of Land, Trusts of Land (Law Com no 181) para 11.3.

2.94   This would have reversed the existing rule in the Law of Property Act 1925, s 29(3)[1] and, indeed, the position that Settled Land Act trustees occupied.

1   Law of Property Act 1925, s 29(3) (repealed by the Trusts of Land and Appointment of Trustees Act 1996, Sch 4).

2.95 At the Committee Stage in the House of Lords debates[1], the Government accepted that there was substance in the widespread criticism of this approach. The main items focused on by the critics were as follows:

(a) the stringent liability laid on trustees would have discouraged the use of the Trusts of Land and Appointment of Trustees Act 1996, s 9 which would have become a 'white elephant';

(b) if the settlor made it a mandatory condition that the trustees should delegate to the life tenant then there was a risk that individuals would refuse to accept such a trusteeship, involving as it then would an obligation to hand over their functions to a person whose actions they could not control but for which they would be vicariously liable;

(c) a court could order the trustee to delegate, but then hold such a trustee accountable for the acts of his attorney which would be inequitable.

1   House of Lords Commitee Stage at 570 HL Official Report (5th series) cols 1536-1537, 25 March 1996.

2.96 To counter this criticism, the Government accepted a narrowing in the liability of trustees (it was at this stage proposed that liability would be limited to cases where 'it was not reasonable to delegate the function to the beneficiary') balanced, to some extent, by making the beneficiary/attorney a trustee for certain purposes[1]. This suggested test based on reasonableness (designed to retain vicarious liability if the delegation was, for example, to a beneficiary who was weak or feckless) did not appease the critics who were concerned at the imposition that the test itself involved and a final amendment was made at Report Stage[2]. The Lord Chancellor, Lord Mackay, then commented:

'The amendment is intended to require the trustees to observe the precautions of a reasonably prudent person in deciding whether to delegate those particular functions to that beneficiary or beneficiaries in the particular circumstances of the trust. That is in line with the well-settled test in *Speight v Gaunt*[3].'

1   House of Lords Commitee Stage at 570 HL Official Report (5th series) cols 1536, 25 March 1996. See the Trusts of Land and Appointment of Trustees Act 1996 s 9(7).
2   House of Lords Report Stage at 571 HL Official Report (5th series) col 959, 22 April 1996.
3   *Speight v Gaunt* (1883) 9 App Cas 1, HL.

2.97 Section 9(8) as finally enacted required reasonable care to be exercised:

(i) in deciding to delegate; and

(ii) in deciding to delegate to that beneficiary.

2.98 If this requirement was satisfied, the subsequent acts of the attorney could not be visited on the trustees. Section 9(8) was concerned solely with vicarious liability: trustees could themselves commit breaches of trust, for example by failing to act in cases where an attorney had manifestly acted against the interests of the trust fund/other beneficiaries (in this situation trustees' liability was primary and could not be avoided). This liability could attach to trustees, albeit that they were protected against vicarious liability under the terms of Section 9(8)[1].

1   In correspondence with the authors, the Lord Chancellor's Department confirmed that this was the assumption underlying the drafting of the subsection. Even in cases where trustees delegate all their functions, they retain the ability to revoke their power of attorney and hence can still be considered to have responsibilities as trustees.

The position of trustees from 1 February 2001

2.99   From this date s 9(8) was repealed and a new s 9A introduced into the 1996 Act. The consequences are as follows:

(a)   s 9(8) was capable of imposing vicarious liability on trustees in respect of the acts of an attorney from 1 January 1997 to 1 February 2001. Its repeal is consistent with the policy adopted in TA 2000 in respect of agents appointed under Part IV of that Act whereby a trustee's liabilities are limited to his own breach of duty (see further para 12.90 below);

(b)   the new s 9A (taking effect from 1 February 2001) imposes the statutory duty of care[1] on trustees of land:

　　(i)   in deciding whether to delegate their functions to an interest in possession beneficiary (normally the duty applies once the decision has been taken to appoint an agent: ie it does not apply to the taking of the decision and in this sense s 9A is unique). The trustees should accordingly consider the suitability of the beneficiary and whether it is desirable for them to delegate their functions to that person;

　　(ii)   during the delegation the trustees must keep the position under review (ie ensure that the attorney is acting in a proper fashion) and, where relevant, consider intervening and, if necessary, intervene. In exercising these duties the trustees must act as reasonable men in accordance with the statutory duty of care. The duties do not apply if the delegation was irrevocable,

(c)   s 9A(6) provides that a trustee is not liable for the act or default of a beneficiary unless he has failed to comply with the duty of care. What therefore occurs if the trustee does breach the statutory duty of care? Does it follow that he then becomes vicariously liable for the acts etc of the attorney? Although the wording could be clearer, this is not what the sub-section says and it is considered that the better view is that a trustee's liability is determined on the basis of his own breach of duty. Accordingly, if a failure to review the activities of the attorney results in a loss to the trust fund the trustee will, *because of his breach* of duty which allowed the loss to occur, be liable to make good that loss[2].

1   As laid down in TA 2000, s 1: see for the content of this duty the discussion at para 10.1 ff below.
2   See the same wording in TA 2000, s 23 which is considered at para 12.90 below.

Section 10 – Consents

2.100   Text of section 10

(1)   If a disposition creating a trust of land requires the consent of more than two persons to the exercise by the trustees of any function relating to the land, the consent of any two of them to the exercise of the function is sufficient in favour of a purchaser.

(2)   Subsection (1) does not apply to the exercise of a function by trustees of land held on charitable, ecclesiastical or public trusts.

(3)   Where at any time a person whose consent is expressed by a disposition creating a trust of land to be required to the exercise by the trustees of any function relating to the land is not of full age–

(a)   his consent is not, in favour of a purchaser, required to the exercise of the function, but

(b)   the trustees shall obtain the consent of a parent who has parental responsibility for him (within the meaning of the Children Act 1989) or of a guardian of his.

Position of section 10

2.101   The Trusts of Land and Appointment of Trustees Act 1996, s 10, together with the following five sections, is primarily concerned with the rights of beneficiaries and with the duties owed by trustees to their beneficiaries. Section 8 of the Act[1] envisages that the general powers of the trustees, and the power of partition, may be restricted in the disposition creating the trust. Section 10 is concerned with the effect that any requirement for consents has on purchasers of the land and should be considered alongside s 16[2].

1   See para 2.68 above.
2   See para 2.165 below. For the position where the person in question suffers from a disability (ie infancy or lunacy) see para 2.74 above. In the case of registered land the fundamental principle is that the registered proprietor can exercise all powers of disposition *unless* some entry on the register limits those powers. Hence, the requirement for consent should be entered as a restriction on the register and the trustees' disposition must be in accordance with that restriction: see *Private Trusts of Land* (2nd Edn, 2000) Practice Advice Leaflet No 13 (see section F2 on the position of personal representatives).

Antecedents

2.102   The forerunner of the Trusts of Land and Appointment of Trustees Act 1996, s 10 is the Law of Property Act 1925, s 26[1]. Under the trusts for sale regime there were two different 'procedures': the consent procedure in s 26(1) and the consultation procedure in s 26(3). (In the Settled Land Act regime it is not possible to fetter the powers of the tenant for life[2].) In the case of trusts for sale, it was common to make the sale of the land dependant upon the consent of the interest in possession beneficiary who might thus be enabled to enjoy the property *in specie* if he so wished. Of course, there were cases where the relevant consent would never be forthcoming, and some commentators have queried whether such a *de facto* prohibition on sale was compatible with the existence of a trust for sale[3].

1   Law of Property Act 1925, s 26 (repealed by the Trusts of Land and Appointment of Trustees Act 1996, Sch 4).
2   Settled Land Act 1925, s 106.
3   *Re Inns, Inns v Wallace* [1947] Ch 576; and see Megarry & Wade *The Law of Real Property* (6th edn, 2000) para 8-114. Under the Law of Property Act 1925 and the Trusts of Land and Appointment of Trustees Act 1996, the persons whose consent is required do not have to be beneficiaries.

Effect of failure to obtain consents

2.103   Although in the situation addressed in the Trusts of Land and Appointment of Trustees Act 1996, s 10(1) a purchaser is only concerned with any two consents, the trustees are obliged to obtain all requisite consents and failure to do so would invalidate the exercise of the power thereby rendering them liable to an action for breach of trust.

Ambit

2.104   The Trusts of Land and Appointment of Trustees Act 1996, s 10(1) does not apply in relation to charities, ecclesiastical and public trusts. 'Purchaser' is defined in s 23(1) of the Act by reference to the Law of Property Act 1925[1]: broadly speaking, a purchaser must be in good faith and give valuable consideration. The Trusts of Land and Appointment of Trustees Act 1996, s 10 does not apply to personal representatives[2].

1   See the Law of Property Act 1925, s 205(1)(xxi).
2   Trusts of Land and Appointment of Trustees Act 1996, s 18(1). Under the Administration of Estates Act 1925, s 36(7) a purchaser is not entitled to see the contents of the will: all that will be shown to him is proof of the death of the former estate owner (or registered proprietor in the case of registered land) and the fact of the grant of probate. The purchaser is then protected and is not concerned whether consents have been obtained or even whether there is any requirement in the will to obtain consents.

Law Commission

2.105   The Law Commission[1] in its report on overreaching recommended:

'A conveyance of a legal estate in property should not have the effect of overreaching the interest of anyone of full age and capacity who is entitled to a beneficial interest in the property and who has a right to occupy it and is in actual occupation of it at the date of the conveyance, unless that person consents[1].'

1   Transfer of Land Overreaching: Beneficiaries in Occupation (Law Com No 188) para 4.3.

2.106   This (the basic recommendation of the Report) has not been implemented.

Section 11 – Consultation with Beneficiaries

2.107   Text of section 11

(1)   The trustees of land shall in the exercise of any function relating to land subject to the trust–

(a)   so far as practicable, consult the beneficiaries of full age and beneficially entitled to an interest in possession in the land, and

(b)   so far as consistent with the general interest of the trust, give effect to the wishes of those beneficiaries, or (in case of dispute) of the majority (according to the value of their combined interests).

(2)   Subsection (1) does not apply–

(a)   in relation to a trust created by a disposition in so far as provision that it does not apply is made by the disposition,

(b)   in relation to a trust created or arising under a will made before the commencement of this Act, or

(c)   in relation to the exercise of the power mentioned in section 6(2).

(3)   Subsection (1) does not apply to a trust created before the commencement of this Act by a disposition, or a trust created after that commencement by reference to such a trust, unless provision to the effect that it is to apply is made by a deed executed–

(a)   in a case in which the trust was created by one person and he is of full capacity, by that person, or

(b)   in a case in which the trust was created by more than one person, by such of the persons who created the trust as are alive and of full capacity.

(4)   A deed executed for the purposes of subsection (3) is irrevocable.

Antecedents

2.108   The Trusts of Land and Appointment of Trustees Act 1996, s 11 is largely modelled on the Law of Property Act 1925, s 26(3)[1] which, in summary, provided as follows:

(a)   *Consultation.* The trustees had to consult 'so far as practicable' with interest in possession beneficiaries of full age.

(b)   *Implementation.* So far as consistent with the general interest of the trust the trustees had to give effect to those wishes or (in the case of a dispute) of the majority (in terms of combined value).

(c)   *Third party protection.* A purchaser was not concerned to see that these provisions had been complied with[2].

1   Law of Property Act 1925, s 26(3) as substituted by the Law of Property (Amendment) Act 1926, s 7, Schedule (repealed by the Trusts of Land and Appointment of Trustees Act 1996 Sch 4).

2   These provisions only applied to statutory trusts and, given that it was not always clear whether a trust was statutory or express, problems could arise: compare *Bull v Bull* [1955] 1 QB 234, [1955] 1 All ER 253, CA. In practice the procedure was rarely used. The contrast between the Law of Property Act 1925 s 26(3) and the consultation provisions in the Trusts of Land and Appointment of Trustees Act 1996 is striking and should be carefully noted.

Views of the Law Commission and changes during passage of the Act

2.109   The Law Commission[1] recommended relatively minor tinkering: ie for existing trusts for sale these provisions should apply unless expressly excluded (contrast the Law of Property Act 1925, s 26(3)[2] which provided that consultation with beneficiaries did not apply to express trusts for sale unless expressly included)[3]. The Bill, as originally drafted, provided in the case of existing trusts for a settlor to have the power to exclude the operation of the consultation provisions (only of use if he was still alive!) and, as first amended, for beneficiaries during a transitional period (envisaged to be of one year) to be able to waive consultation. This was manifestly unsatisfactory:

'These provisions have been reconsidered in the light of representations from the legal profession, pointing out that a trust cannot be 'opted out' if there is at commencement no settlor living and of full capacity. A settlor who has died or who has lost capacity might well have set up the trust in the knowledge that beneficiaries would not have the opportunity to control trustees' decisions in this way unless he spelt out the intention that they should have it; and it is therefore argued that the present transitional provisions will have the effect of changing the terms of some trusts but not others on a capricious basis. There has also been criticism of the provision for opting out for beneficiaries on the basis that it adds complication for little benefit. No-one would wish to do that[4].'

1   Transfer of Land, Trusts of Land (Law Com No 181) para 35.
2   Law of Property Act 1925, s 26(3) as substituted by the Law of Property (Amendment) Act 1926, s 7, Schedule (repealed by the Trusts of Land and Appointment of Trustees Act 1996 Sch 4).
3   The views expressed by the Law Commission in Trusts of Land (Law Com Working Paper no 94) para 8.6 were even more lukewarm:

'Like the statutory power to postpone, it is arguable that this duty [to consult] is an implicit recognition of the inappropriateness of the duty to sell in some of the situations where the 1925 legislation imposed one. Once there is no duty to sell, there seems less need for any special provision regarding consultation. The trustees have a general duty to exercise their powers for the benefit of the beneficiaries. That, coupled with an extension of the rights of beneficiaries to apply to the court, might be sufficient protection. However, the existence of the duty to consult may ensure that the beneficiaries are aware of some action by the trustees so that they can take steps to prevent it before it is too far advanced. In this respect the duty to consult is valuable, although, in its present form, probably too weak to be of use. If it is thought necessary to retain some similar provision, then a more definite right to be informed as to the trustees' future actions would be preferable.'

4   House of Lords Committee Stage at 570 HL Official Report (5th series) col 1541, 25 March 1996, per the Lord Chancellor. There is a fascinating contrast with the provisions in the Trusts of Land and Appointment of Trustees Act 1996, Pt II which apply to existing trusts unless expressly excluded, as had been envisaged in this section!

Position of existing wills

2.110   Further changes were made in the House of Lords at Report Stage[1]: in particular, what is now the Trusts of Land and Appointment of Trustees Act 1996, s 11(2)(b) dealing with trusts arising under existing wills was added. Although a will made before the commencement of the Act is of no effect until death (which may occur after the date of commencement) when the testator made his will there was no consultation requirement. Given that the resultant trust would (on the above facts) arise after the commencement date, the trustees would be subject to the consultation requirements. This was considered unreasonable (especially since wills are in many cases never revised!). The Government at this stage also removed any time limit for existing trusts to 'contract in'.

1   House of Lords Report Stage at 571 HL Official Report (5th series) col 961, 22 April 1996. It is thought that for these purposes a will is made when it is executed and that a codicil executed after 1996 will not affect the position: see generally *Towns* in 1998, SJ p 378.

'Created or arising under a will'

2.111   These words are taken from the Family Law Reform Act 1969, Sch 3, para 6. They are intended to cover not only will trusts proper, but also trusts that may be created by an assent from personal representatives to a trustee or beneficiary under the will[1].

1   House of Lords Report Stage at 571 HL Official Report (5th series) col 961, 22 April 1996.

'Or a trust created after that commencement by reference to such a trust'

2.112   These words were added at the House of Lords Third Reading stage[1] to deal with the situation where land is added to an existing trust after the Trusts of Land and Appointment of Trustees Act 1996 has come into force (typically by the settlor adding further land). The wording appears wide enough to cover the following situations:

(a)   Trust A is in existence and the settlor (or indeed any other person) adds further land to that trust.

(b)   A new trust (trust B) is created with a provision that the property comprised in it is to be held on the same trusts as trust A (there are different trustees possessed of different administrative powers).

(c)   By exercise of a power of advancement under the Trustee Act 1925, s 32 the trustees of trust A establish a new settlement[2]. In this case, it is not absolutely clear that the Trusts of Land and Appointment of Trustees Act 1996, s 11(3) would apply given that the new settlement need not in any way be referential to the old (albeit that the trustees derived their power to advance from that trust). In these circumstances, expressly excluding s 11 in the advancement is advised.

1   House of Lords Third Reading at 572 HL Official Report (5th series) col 97, 7 May 1996.
2   On the creation of new settlements by exercise of a power of advancement (or any other power 'in the wide form') see para 2.13 note 6 above.

Third parties

2.113   As to the protection of purchasers see the Trusts of Land and Appointment of Trustees Act 1996, s 16(1)[1].

1   The duty to consult does not apply where the trustees convey the property to adult
     beneficiaries under the Trusts of Land and Appointment of Trustees Act 1996, s 6(2): see
     s 11(2)(c).

How workable is the provision?

2.114   If trustees fail to consult beneficiaries in circumstances when the
Trusts of Land and Appointment of Trustees Act 1996, s 11(1) applies they
are in breach of trust[1]. The main remedy open to such a beneficiary is to seek
a direction that the trustees shall consult and to set aside whatever action
(other than a sale) was entered into without consultation. However, establishing a breach may not be easy given the imprecision of the wording; for
example, what is meant by:

(a)   'so far as practicable'–presumably this involves issues such as the
       availability of the beneficiary and the urgency of exercising the relevant
       trustee function.

(b)   'any function'[2]–can there really be a duty to consult on a relatively
       minor matter?

(c)   'so far as consistent with the general interest of the trust'–if the
       beneficiary's wishes are manifestly absurd or purely self-seeking they
       must, presumably, be ignored. In addition, the trustees should have
       regard to the interests of other beneficiaries (eg remaindermen and
       others without an interest in possession). Maintaining a balance
       between the different beneficial interests, and seeking to act in the best
       interests of all, will in practice be the most common reason for trustees
       to reject the views of the interest in possession beneficiary.

(d)   'the majority'–in the case of a dispute it is not absolutely clear how the
       value rule operates. Taking two concurrent life tenants, presumably
       actuarial values of both interests must be computed and the more
       valuable interest then holds sway (ie the race goes to the youngest and
       fittest!). Given that the overriding requirement remains the general
       interest of the trust, this may not be thought to be entirely satisfactory[3]!

1   The Trusts of Land and Appointment of Trustees Act 1996, s 11 does not apply to personal
     representatives: s 18(1). It is in any event doubtful whether any beneficiary could be said
     to have an interest in possession in an estate in the course of administration: compare the
     Inheritance Tax Act 1984, s 91.
2   For the meaning of 'function' see para 2.41 (e) above.
3   The Law of Property Act 1925, s 26(3) (repealed) only applied to concurrent interests
     where there can be no question of taking actuarial values. It is with the extension of these
     provisions to succession trusts that the problems arise. There may also be an element of
     absurdity with these provisions in, for example, a trust where 10% of the fund is held on
     interest in possession with the remaining 90% being settled on accumulation and
     maintenance trusts. In such a case, the view of beneficiaries entitled to only 10% of the
     fund will need to be canvassed and 'so far as consistent with the general interest of the
     trust' followed.

Waiver

2.115   A beneficiary can waive his rights to be consulted.

Time limit

2.116 Trustees are entitled to impose a time limit on the consultation process.

Trustee delegation under TA 2000, Pt IV

2.117 Trustees may not delegate their function under TA 2001, Pt IV on terms that would prevent them from consulting a relevant beneficiary under s 11 of the 1998 Act[1].

1   See TA 2000, s 13(4)(5) and see para 12.27 below.

Drafting and practical implications

2.118 Consider the impact of the Trusts of Land and Appointment of Trustees Act 1996 on (a) new trusts and (b) old trusts. For a clause pursuant to s 11(2) excluding the consultation provisions, see **Precedent 11** below. As compared to the Law of Property Act 1925, s 26 (repealed) it should be noted that the Trusts of Land and Appointment of Trustees Act 1996, s 11 applies to all trusts of land (not just to statutory trusts for sale as did the Law of Property Act 1925, s 26) and crucially outside the area of co-ownership. Thus if a trust fund is invested partly in realty, and partly in stock exchange investments, the trustees must consult the life tenant as regards the land (albeit acquired as an investment), but not as regards the stock exchange investments. The manifest inconvenience that s 11 is capable of causing has encouraged trust draftsmen to make the exclusion of s 11 a standard term of modern trusts. Of course as a matter of practical good sense trustees will normally consult the principal beneficiary before taking any major decision relating to the trust land[1].

1   Note s 15(3) in the context of applications to the court and see Megarry and Wade, *Law of Real Property* (6th edn, 2000) at para 8.14.

Summary

2.119 When does the Trusts of Land and Appointment of Trustees Act 1996, s 11 apply?

	Operation of Section 11
Existing express trusts	See s 11(3). Section 11 does not apply unless included by a deed made by the settlor or such of the settlors as are alive and of full capacity. Such deeds are irrevocable and presumably consultation is then required from the date of such deed. (see **Precedent 12**.)
Pre-commencement wills	See s 11(2)(b). Section 11 does not apply.

Referential trusts	As for existing express trusts.
'New' trusts (and existing implied trusts)	See s 11(2)(a). Section 11 applies unless expressly excluded by the disposition – subsequent documents or statements will not do.

Section 12 – The Right to Occupy

2.120 Text of section 12

(1) A beneficiary who is beneficially entitled to an interest in possession in land subject to a trust of land is entitled by reason of his interest to occupy the land at any time if at that time—

    (a) the purposes of the trust include making the land available for his occupation (or for the occupation of beneficiaries of a class of which he is a member or of beneficiaries in general), or

    (b) the land is held by the trustees so as to be so available.

(2) Subsection (1) does not confer on a beneficiary a right to occupy land if it is either unavailable or unsuitable for occupation by him.

(3) This section is subject to section 13.

Ambit of sections 12 and 13

2.121 The Trusts of Land and Appointment of Trustees Act 1996, s 12 is concerned with the right of a beneficiary, who is beneficially entitled to an interest in possession, to occupy trust land. Section 13 deals with the ability of the trustees to exclude, restrict or impose conditions on such occupation[1].

1   For the position of pension trusts see para 6.57 below. For an agreement with a beneficiary for occupation of a trust property see **Precedent 15** below.

Position under a trust for sale

2.122 The right of a beneficiary to occupy land that had been held under a trust for sale (especially an implied trust when the beneficiaries were co-owners) prior to 1 January 1997 was much debated[1].

1   See, for example, Cheshire and Burn's *Modern Law of Real Property* (16th edn, 2000) pp 218–9 and Gray *Elements of land law* (3rd edn, 2001) pp 662–3. On one view (the 'traditional' view) occupation in the case of a trust for sale was not a right but a privilege which depended on the exercise by trustees of their fiduciaries powers of management. As such, an occupying beneficiary was a mere tenant at will whose tenancy was determinable at any time on the trustees' demand for possession. The other view (the 'modern' view) considered that a right of occupation was an integral part of the rights enjoyed by a beneficiary especially in cases of co-ownership. In *City of London Building Society v Flegg* [1988] AC 54, [1987] 3 All ER 435, HL, for example, Lord Oliver based such rights either on an agreement between the beneficiaries or on the basis of the purpose for which the trust was originally created. So far as the trust purpose is concerned, the law in this area may be traced back to Lord Denning's judgment in *Bull v Bull* [1955] 1 QB 234, [1955] 1 All ER 253, CA (as interpreted in *Jones v Challenger* [1961] 1 QB 176, [1960] 1 All ER 785,

CA) in which a right of occupation was accorded to a mother who was an equitable tenant in common behind an implied trust for sale of residential property.

The Law Commission, considering the right of residence in *Trusts of Land* (Law Com Working Paper no 94), concluded at para 8.7 as follows:

'The tenant for life of settled land clearly has the right to occupy the land. That is, generally speaking, the purpose of the settlement. Under a trust for sale, the position may depend on whether the land is held on express trusts for sale, when there may be no rights of residence [*Barclay v Barclay* [1970] 2 QB 677], or on the statutory trusts for sale imposed on co-owners, where there are. The rights of residence of co-owners depend on the pre-1926 law, and have been a matter of some dispute. The difference between the two systems seems to arise because the trust for sale in the latter case is a mere conveyancing device, in other words, wholly artificial. Once again, the imposition of an unnecessary duty to sell has made the law more complex than it need be. We would suggest that all beneficiaries who have present (as opposed to future) interests in land should have a right to occupy the land unless specifically excluded by the settlor or unless the trustees have been given discretion to choose which beneficiary can occupy. This would mean that those entitled on intestacy might acquire rights of residence if the administrators retained the property after the "initial stage" . . . While this is probably a change from the present position, there does not seem anything wrong with the result, because such a situation is likely to arise where there are infant beneficiaries or a widow with a life interest. The right of residence should not apply to, for example, rented property which the trustees hold for investment purposes.'

The authors would merely add that in the case of an 'ordinary' trust for sale (ie excluding co-ownership) under a standard investment clause, trustees had no power to purchase property for occupation and so in practice would only be able to do so if there was express provision to that effect in the trust deed (this has, of course, now been reversed by TA 2000, Pt III). They incline to the view therefore that in such trusts an interest in possession beneficiary had no right to occupy.

Parliamentary passage

2.123   Section 12 passed through the Parliamentary process unamended and without any debate. It applies to all trusts of land whenever created.

A qualifying beneficiary

2.124   To enjoy the right to occupy land, the beneficiary must have a beneficial interest in possession in that land[1]. If a trust is in discretionary form, no beneficiary will satisfy this requirement unless an appointment is made by the trustees whereby an interest in possession is created. In such cases, the trustees may of course permit one or more beneficiaries to occupy land either in accordance with the wide power of management etc given in the Trusts of Land and Appointment of Trustees Act 1996, s 6, or under an express power in the trust instrument, but that is not the same as saying that a beneficiary has a right to occupy[2]. In the case of land held on accumulation and maintenance trusts, given that the definition of such trusts prohibits the existence of any interest in possession, there can be no beneficiary with a right to occupy under s 12(1)[3].

1   For a discussion of the meaning of 'interest in possession' see para 4.9 below and note also the Trusts of Land and Appointment of Trustees Act 1996, s 22. For the position of sub trusts, see para 2.83 above.

2   *Transfer of Land, Trusts of Land* (Law Com no 181) para 13.2 stated that there was some uncertainty as to whether allowing a beneficiary to occupy land would be a proper use of the trustees' powers under the Trusts of Land and Appointment of Trustees Act 1996, s 6(1). Hence an express right to occupy was suggested. This argument is far from

persuasive: in the first place it is not thought that ibid s 6(1) would be construed in this restrictive fashion; in the second, if it was thought to be so restrictive then the remedy would surely have been to confer this power expressly on the trustees rather than giving the beneficiary a right to occupy the property.

3   Accumulation and maintenance trusts are the creature of the capital transfer tax/inheritance tax legislation: see further the Inheritance Tax Act 1984, s 71. Where a dwelling house is held on such trusts for minors, an express clause should always be included giving the trustees powers to permit beneficiaries to occupy the property (it is not thought that the existence, or exercise, of such powers takes the trusts outside the s 71 definition). An interest in possession beneficiary of a sub trust will not have a right to occupy land in the head trust, but a purchaser of an interest in possession in the head trust may.

Nature of the land

2.125   The land must not be unavailable (for example, tenanted land) or unsuitable for occupation by the beneficiary (for example, a large rambling property in the case of an invalid beneficiary)[1]. It is thought that the unsuitability may arise either from the nature of the land or from the characteristics of the relevant beneficiary. What was contemplated was occupation of a 'residence', but there is no such limitation in the wording of the legislation[2].

1   See the Trusts of Land and Appointment of Trustees Act 1996, s 12(2).
2   See para 2.129 below. Land may be unsuitable if a beneficiary with no farming experience seeks to occupy a farm.

The right to occupy

2.126   Subject to the restrictions of s 13, and to the land being available and suitable, a beneficiary has the right to occupy if either of two conditions is satisfied:

(a)   First, the purposes of the trust include making the land available for occupation[1]. In general:

    (i)   land jointly purchased for residential occupation will usually satisfy the test[2];

    (ii)   the test will be satisfied if merely one of the purposes of the trust includes beneficial occupation.

    How are the purposes of the trust to be gleaned? There may be an express recital to the effect that the purpose (or one of the purposes) is to make land so available, or there may be other terms in the trust which make that apparent. The existence of a power to allow occupation by a beneficiary (which is commonly included as a standard form additional trustee power) may even suffice. Apart from the instrument itself, evidence may be gleaned from other statements made by the settlor; for example, in a letter of wishes. If the settlor is still alive at the relevant time, he may indicate what his purposes were in establishing the trust. Having said this, the purposes of the trust may (in many cases will) change in accordance with the needs of beneficiaries and the prevailing circumstances[3]. The statutory test is what the purposes were 'at that time'; ie not necessarily when the trust was created, but at any time when a beneficiary is entitled to an interest in possession so that the question of occupying trust land is in issue. Given that the purposes of the trust may evolve in this fashion, although the wishes of the settlor are of importance, it will be for the trustees themselves to decide what the current purposes are.

(b)   Second, the land is held by the trustees to be available for beneficial occupation. The draft bill produced by the Law Commission[4] referred to land 'acquired' by the trustees for these purposes and this is obviously one of the meanings of 'held'. In simple terms, if the trustees decide to allow an interest in possession beneficiary into occupation it may then be said that the land has been held by those trustees to be so available.

1   In considering this requirement some assistance may be gleaned from the case law referred to in para 2.122 note 1 above.
2   But not always, see *Barclay v Barclay* [1970] 2 QB 677, [1970] 2 All ER 676, CA where an express trust for sale in a will provided for the sale of a bungalow with division of the proceeds. The sole trustee was a daughter-in-law of the deceased who wished to sell with vacant possession. One of the beneficiaries (a son) was in possession. The trustee was successful in an action for possession, because the son in occupation only had an interest in the proceeds of sale. Cf the position in *Bull v Bull* [1955] 1 QB 234, [1955] 1 All ER 253, CA in which the occupier was considered to have an interest in the land.
3   See, for example, *Jones v Challenger* [1961] 1 QB 176, [1960] 1 All ER 785, CA.
4   *Transfer of Land, Trusts of Land* (Law Com No 181) Draft Bill cl 7(1)(a) p 50.

Trust drafting

2.127   For the impact of these rules on the drafting of new trusts of land, see further para 2.126 above.

2.128   In cases where the settlor does not wish any beneficiary to enjoy a right of occupation, it is important that the trust instrument so indicates: expressly excluding the Trusts of Land and Appointment of Trustees Act 1996, s 12(1) does not appear to be contemplated by the Act, but a recital that it is not the wish of the settlor that any beneficiary should enjoy such a right and stating that any beneficial occupation should always be a matter exclusively within the discretion of the trustees is possible (see **Precedents 13** and **14**)[1].

1   Kessler in *Drafting Trusts and Will Trusts* (5th Edn, 2000) at para 18.36 suggests that the section can be excluded commenting that 'it is a fundamental principle of trust law that it is up to the settlor to decide what rights to confer under the trust. Restrictions on freedom of disposition should not be lightly inferred'. Faced with s 12 a settlor may avoid an interest in possession trust: does it follow from s 12 that the trustees' rights of disposition are restricted? See para 2.129 (point c) below.

Nature of the 'right' conferred on a beneficiary

2.129   Although hedged about with uncertainties and limitations, s 12 does, in appropriate circumstances, confer a 'right' on a beneficiary. In a simple case, this will involve the occupation of a dwelling house, but s 12 is not so limited and may include, for example, the occupation of a farm or, indeed, of a landed estate. Of course, s 12 only deals with occupation: it does not confer management powers (this would be a matter for the trustees under s 9 of the Act). So far as the nature of the 'right' is concerned, the following points may be noted:

(a) along with the right to be consulted, and with the provisions of Part II of the Act, s 12 is part of the shift in power from trustees to beneficiaries;

(b) with the abolition of conversion, s 12 emphasises that beneficiaries under trusts of land have rights in the land;

(c) how does this square with the trustees' management powers? In a typical case the occupation agreement made with the beneficiary will be in the form of a licence thereby permitting the trustees to terminate it and sell the property[1]. It may, of course, be argued that if there is a 'right' in the beneficiary, is that consistent with a mere licence to occupy which is determinable at the trustees' will? (as to which it may be said that the trustees are entitled to regulate beneficial occupation by means of a licence under their powers in s 13(3)). In practice, of course, a sale will be impossible unless the beneficiary agrees to leave the premises since it will be a rare purchaser who is willing to acquire a lawsuit;

(d) in the case of co-ownership (to which this provision is presumably primarily addressed) it will often be the case that there are competing beneficial 'rights' and therefore (given that the beneficiaries are also the trustees) deadlock[2];

(e) as already noted, beneficiaries now enjoy real rights under the Trusts of Land and Appointment of Trustees Act 1996 and therefore any charging order under the Charging Orders Act 1979 will be against the land rather than against the proceeds of sale[3];

(f) the right will end if the qualifying interest of the beneficiary comes to an end (eg if a determinable life interest is determined).

1   For an occupation agreement, see **Precedent 15** below.
2   See the discussion of the Trusts of Land and Appointment of Trustees Act 1996, s 13 at para 2.131 below.
3   Under the Charging Orders Act 1979, the court can make an order charging a debtor's beneficial interest 'under any trust' which will include a trust for sale. There were, however, difficulties over the registration of a charging order. If the debtor, or debtors, owned the whole beneficial interest together, then the order could be made against the legal estate and would be registrable under the Land Charges Act 1972, s 6 as amended. However, if the order affected only part of the equitable interest, then it was not registrable due to the doctrine of conversion: *Perry v Phoenix Assurance* [1988] 3 All ER 60, [1988] 1 WLR 940. With the abolition of the doctrine of conversion this difficulty has been removed.

Conclusions

2.130

(a) It is interesting that the Law Commission in its Working Paper[1] commented as follows:

'The settlor should be able to exclude the right of residence if he so wishes. The right of residence would be capable of being overreached if the land were sold and the purchase price paid to at least two trustees or a trust corporation. Once a sale took place the beneficiaries would no longer have any interest in the land and would thus have no right of residence in it. It is important to make this point so that it is not thought that the right of residence we propose is a new separate right, capable of subsisting on its own.'

Unfortunately, it is by no means certain that those aspirations have been carried through in the legislation!

(b)   The difficulty with ss 12 and 13 is that they are concerned with two very different situations: co-ownership where the trustees are the beneficial owners when the prime purpose of the acquisition is usually to provide a residence for the owners, and the ordinary succession trust where interest in possession beneficiaries have only a limited interest in the land to be weighed against that enjoyed by remaindermen, discretionary beneficiaries etc. As regards the latter, it would arguably have been more satisfactory to have given trustees a statutory power similar to that usually conferred in settlements, whereby the trustees have a discretionary power to allow a beneficiary to occupy trust property on such terms as the trustees may agree. But that, of course, would fit uneasily into the co-ownership situation.

(c)   It is not made clear whether the right to occupy given by the 1996 Act has replaced any common law right that was available to a beneficiary or whether it has conferred an additional right. *Barnsley*[2] considers that such pre-Act rights of occupation which co-owners had (namely a non-exclusive right to occupy) continue to exist and may be relied upon in cases where they are preferable to the rights conferred by the 1996 Act. And, of course, s 12 cannot affect the rights of a beneficiary under a bare trust (given that the trustees are nominees for him and it is not thought that they can impose conditions on his occupation)[3].

1   *Trusts of Land* (Law Com Working Paper No 94) para 8.9.
2   [1998] CLJ 123.
3   His conclusion that the effect of the Act is that an equitable co-owner no longer enjoys unity of possession is dismissed in Megarry and Wade's *Law of Real Property* (6th Edn, 2000) at para 9-063 as 'more apparent than real'.

Section 13 – Exclusion and Restriction of Right to Occupy

2.131   Text of section 13

(1)   Where two or more beneficiaries are (or apart from this subsection would be) entitled under section 12 to occupy land, the trustees of land may exclude or restrict the entitlement of any one or more (but not all) of them.

(2)   Trustees may not under subsection (1)–

        (a)   unreasonably exclude any beneficiary's entitlement to occupy land, or

        (b)   restrict any such entitlement to an unreasonable extent.

(3)   The trustees of land may from time to time impose reasonable conditions on any beneficiary in relation to his occupation of land by reason of his entitlement under section 12.

(4)   The matters to which trustees are to have regard in exercising the powers conferred by this section include–

> (a) the intentions of the person or persons (if any) who created the trust,
>
> (b) the purposes for which the land is held, and
>
> (c) the circumstances and wishes of each of the beneficiaries who is (or apart from any previous exercise by the trustees of those powers would be) entitled to occupy the land under section 12.

(5) The conditions which may be imposed on a beneficiary under subsection (3) include, in particular, conditions requiring him–

> (a) to pay any outgoings or expenses in respect of the land, or
>
> (b) to assume any other obligation in relation to the land or to any activity which is or is proposed to be conducted there.

(6) Where the entitlement of any beneficiary to occupy land under section 12 has been excluded or restricted, the conditions which may be imposed on any other beneficiary under subsection (3) include, in particular, conditions requiring him to–

> (a) make payments by way of compensation to the beneficiary whose entitlement has been excluded or restricted, or
>
> (b) forgo any payment or other benefit to which he would otherwise be entitled under the trust so as to benefit that beneficiary.

(7) The powers conferred on trustees by this section may not be exercised–

> (a) so as prevent any person who is in occupation of land (whether or not by reason of an entitlement under section 12) from continuing to occupy the land, or
>
> (b) in a manner likely to result in any such person ceasing to occupy the land,

unless he consents or the court has given approval.

(8) The matters to which the court is to have regard in determining whether to give approval under subsection (7) include the matters mentioned in subsection (4)(a) to (c).

Purpose of section 13

2.132   Section 13 deals with two principal matters:

(a) imposing reasonable conditions on a beneficiary who occupies land because of his entitlement under s 12[1];

(b) in a case where two or more beneficiaries would be entitled to occupy under s 12, permitting trustees to exclude or restrict the occupation of some but not all[2].

---

1   Trusts of Land and Appointment of Trustees Act 1996, s 13(3). Under this subsection the trustees may require a beneficiary to contribute to the cost of adapting the property to make it suitable for his occupation: see *Rodway v Landy* below.

2   See Trusts of Land and Appointment of Trustees Act 1996, s 13(1), (2), (6). Note that although the trustees cannot exclude all the beneficiaries, they can restrict the occupation of all of them. See further *Rodway v Landy*, 4 April 2001, CA. Peter Gibson LJ held in that case that 'in relation to a single building which lends itself to physical partition the trustees (can) exclude or restrict one beneficiary's entitlement to occupy one part and at the same time exclude or restrict the other beneficiary's entitlement to occupy the other part'.

2.133 These powers may not be exercised so as to interfere with present occupation: for example, where prior to 1 January 1997 the trustees for sale have already allowed a beneficiary and his family into occupation (unless the beneficiary consents or the court so orders)[1]. Note in this connection that s 13(7) protects 'any person' in occupation: this would cover the spouse, partner or child of a qualifying beneficiary. The real problems in this area are likely to arise in co-ownership situations.

1   Trusts of Land and Appointment of Trustees Act 1996, s 13(7). In a co-ownership situation where, on a falling out of the proprietors, one of them walks out of the residential property leaving the other in occupation, does s 13(7) then apply to protect that person's occupation? Is the leaving party afforded any protection at common law (*viz* as a legal owner he has a non-exclusive right to occupy). See further *Barnsley* [1998] CLJ 123.

Power to impose conditions on section 12 occupations

2.134 The Trusts of Land and Appointment of Trustees Act 1996, s 13(4) outlines the general factors that the trustees must consider in exercising their powers to impose conditions: note that the intentions of the settlor and the purpose for which the land is held are included[1]. Section 13(5) of the Act provides a non-exhaustive list of conditions that may be imposed; for example, the payment of outgoings or the assumption of other obligations in relation to the land.

1   For a discussion of these matters see para 2.126 above. For an agreement with a beneficiary for occupation of trust property see **Precedent 15** below.

Power to exclude one or more beneficiaries

2.135 The trustees must not act unreasonably in exercising the power to exclude one or more beneficiaries[1]. Section 13(6) is specifically concerned with conditions that may be imposed when there are a number of beneficiaries, some of whom have to be excluded from occupation.

EXAMPLE 7

1.   Tim and Tom are beneficial tenants in common of Blackacre, an estate burdened with substantial running costs. Tim occupies the estate as he has always done and the trustees have made him responsible for the payment of all running costs[2]. Tom prefers to live quietly at the seaside in his own cottage. As can be seen, the position is not complicated given that Tom has no wish to live on the trust estate, nor to be paid any compensation[3].

2.   As in (a) above, except that the trustees now agree that Tim shall pay a 'rent' to Tom[4]. Tim claims to deduct this sum (which amounts to £5,000 per annum) as an outgoing of the estate for his income tax purposes, but Tom does not consider that the payment should attract income tax in his hands[5].

3.   A trust comprises a substantial dwelling ('White Gates') and a stock exchange portfolio. There are two concurrent life tenants: Tony occupies White Gates and as a result of the exercise of the

---

trustees' powers under s 13(6)(b), Tandy, the other life tenant, receives 70% of the dividend income from the portfolio[6].

4. Ted is a life tenant in half of the trust fund: the other half-share having been resettled on to discretionary trusts for the children of Ted's brother Sid. Because of the requirement in s 12 that a beneficiary must be 'beneficially entitled' only Ted qualifies: accordingly, the 'compensation' arrangements in s 13(6) are not in point. The same position would apply if one of Sid's children enjoyed an interest in possession under the sub-settlement.

If land accounts for the bulk (in terms of value) of the trust fund, the trustees should consider imposing reasonable conditions on occupation under s 13(3); imposing an obligation merely to discharge outgoings would not appear reasonable so far as the beneficiaries of the sub-settlement are concerned. It is therefore suggested that a compensation payment could be ordered in lieu of income from the estate to be paid to the trustees of the sub-settlement (s 13(5) does not so provide, but it is not exhaustive of the conditions that may be imposed by the trustees).

1   Trusts of Land and Appointment of Trustees Act 1996, s 13(2) and see *Rodway v Landy*, 4 April 2001, CA.
2   See Trusts of Land and Appointment of Trustees Act 1996, s 13(5)(a).
3   See Trusts of Land and Appointment of Trustees Act 1996, s13(6)(a).
4   See Trusts of Land and Appointment of Trustees Act 1996, s13(6)(a). This may be described as 'compensation' for Tom being excluded from occupation: compare *Re Evers' Trust* [1980] 1 WLR 1327, CA, and *Dennis v McDonald* [1982] Fam 63, CA.
5   As to the taxation implications see para 2.138 below.
6   As to the taxation of the trust income in the hands of the beneficiaries see para 2.138 below.

Protection for beneficiaries

2.136   The terms of s 13(7) should be noted. Beneficiaries are given protection by s 13(7) in cases where the trustees purport to stop them occupying land: either where their action directly has that effect[1] or where the trustees act 'in a manner likely to result in any such person ceasing to occupy the land'[2]. The court has the power to approve the trustees' conduct when it will be required to take into account the factors set out in s 13(4)[3]; for example, the purpose of the trust.

1   Trusts of Land and Appointment of Trustees Act 1996, s 13(7)(a).
2   Trusts of Land and Appointment of Trustees Act 1996, s 13(7)(b).
3   Trusts of Land and Appointment of Trustees Act 1996, s 13(8).

Theoretical matters

2.137

(a)   A beneficiary excluded from occupying land under the Trusts of Land and Appointment of Trustees Act 1996, s 13(1) is still thought to retain a vestigial interest in possession in that land. Accordingly, on the death of the other (occupying) beneficiary and assuming that the first beneficiary thereupon becomes sole life tenant of the trust fund, he can no longer be excluded from occupation under s 13(1) of the Act, nor be required to pay compensation under s 13(6).

(b)   A beneficiary is in occupation under s 12(1), but the trustees wish to sell the land. What is the nature of the occupying beneficiary's interest? Can he prevent a sale?[1]

1   See para 2.129 above. For a licence to occupy see **Precedent 15** below.

Taxation aspects

2.138   Correspondence between the Law Society and the Inland Revenue on the likely taxation implications of the 1996 Act is reproduced in Appendix 5 below. The following are some of the issues arising:

(a)   Is there a charge to income tax on the recipient of payments of 'rent' (compensation)? In Example 7 (point 2) above, the payment of a compensation 'rent' to Tom might fall within the definition of a receipt for Schedule A purposes, being 'any payment in respect of any licence to occupy or otherwise to use any land . . .'[1]. The analysis would have to be that the sum was paid for the occupation of Tom's interest in the land. As against that, it might be argued that the payment was made because of the conditions imposed on Tom by the trustees under the Trusts of Land and Appointment of Trustees Act 1996, s 13(6). Accordingly, the payments are to be categorised as 'compensation' which then leads to the question of whether they fall within the income tax net at all: clearly they are (or are capable of being) recurrent and so it might be thought that they fall within Schedule D Case III (annuities and annual payments). However, given that annual payments made by individuals were generally taken outside the income tax net in 1988 this may lead to the conclusion that they are not taxed in Tom's hands[2].

(b)   Is there an income tax deduction for payment of compensation? In cases where the occupying beneficiary carries on a business on the land, the compensation payment may be a deductible expense under the Income and Corporation Taxes Act 1988, s 74(1)(a)[3].

(c)   What is the income tax position on the unequal division of the stock exchange portfolio in Example 7 (point 3)? It is thought that the income tax position will follow the actual payments made so that Tandy will be taxed on 70% of all the portfolio income. Given that the occupation of 'White Gates' does not involve an income tax liability on Tony, the tax suffered by Tandy should be taken into account by the trustees in deciding the level of compensation.

(d)   What is the inheritance tax position when there are several beneficiaries with interests in possession, some of whom are excluded from occupation? The matter is by no means free from doubt, but the following is thought to be the position:

(i)   For inheritance tax purposes, the definition of a 'settlement' in the Inheritance Tax Act 1984, s 43 does not extend to co-ownership. The interest of a tenant in common or beneficial joint tenant must, therefore, be valued on normal principles[4] with, in appropriate cases, a discount.

(ii) In cases where there is a settlement for inheritance tax purposes with, say, two concurrent life tenants, the basic tax treatment is laid down in the Inheritance Tax Act 1984, s 49(1): namely, 'a person beneficially entitled to an interest in possession in settled property shall be treated . . . as beneficially entitled to the property in which the interest subsists'. In relation to concurrent interests in income, the treatment is then expanded in s 50 which states (inter alia) that 'the interest shall be taken to subsist in such part only of the property as bears to the whole the same proportion as the part of the income to which he is entitled bears to the whole of the income'[5]. Joint use and enjoyment of trust property is then dealt with in s 50(5), but there is a significant omission in s 50 which fails to deal with cases where the settled property comprises both land which is enjoyed *in specie* by one of the beneficiaries and other assets which produce income.

(iii) For the Inheritance Tax Act 1984, s 50 to apply, there must be an 'interest in possession' which has been judicially defined as:

> '. . . "in possession" must mean that your interest enables you to claim now whatever may be the subject of the interest. For instance, if it is the current income from a certain fund your claim may yield nothing if there is no income, but your claim is a valid claim, and if there is any income you are entitled to get it. But a right to require trustees to consider whether they will pay you something does not enable you to claim anything[6].'

Take the case (as in Example 7 (point 3)) where one beneficiary is in occupation of land, 'White Gates', the other being compensated by receiving more of the income from the trust investments. Given that the trustees have acted properly, and in accordance with the provisions of the Trusts of Land and Appointment of Trustees Act 1996, ss 12 and 13, it may be argued that for inheritance tax purposes:

(a) Tony has an interest in possession in White Gates and in 30% of the assets comprising the stock exchange portfolio;

(b) Tandy has an interest in possession in 70% of the portfolio;

From this analysis it would follow that:

(c) assume that prior to 1 April 1997 White Gates had been tenanted and so unavailable for beneficial occupation. When the trustees obtain vacant possession they decide to allow Tony to occupy White Gates and to compensate Tandy accordingly. Whilst the land was tenanted, Tony and Tandy both enjoyed interests in possession in all the assets in the trust fund and, under s 50, each was treated as owning one-half of the entirety. As a result of the new arrangements, however, there may be an alteration in the amount of trust property attributed to each beneficiary. For example, if White Gates was worth £1m and the portfolio £750,000, the value of Tandy's share becomes £525,000 (ie 70% of the portfolio value) instead of £875,000 (which was 50% of the total value of the trust fund), whilst Tony's share increases from £875,000 to £1,225,000. The reduction in Tandy's estate under present legislation, would be a potentially exempt transfer[7];

(d)   assuming that Tony dies, inheritance tax is then charged on £1,225,000 of the trust fund: £1,000,000 of that is White Gates on which tax may, at the trustees' election, be paid by instalments. If Tandy is now the sole surviving interest in possession beneficiary, the value of his interest in the trust fund is increased to £1,750,000[8].

Some support for this interpretation of the inheritance tax legislation is found in Inland Revenue Statement of Practice 10/79, which provides as follows:

'When there is no interest in possession in the property in question, the Board do not regard the exercise of power as creating one if the effect is merely to allow non-exclusive occupation or to create a contractual tenancy for full consideration. The Board also take the view that no interest in possession arises on the creation of a lease for a term or a periodic tenancy for less than full consideration, though this will normally give rise to a charge to tax under IHTA 1984, s 65(1)(b) .... On the other hand if the power is drawn in terms wide enough to cover the creation of an exclusive or joint residence, albeit revocable, for a definite or indefinite period, and is exercised with the intention of providing a particular beneficiary with a permanent home, the Revenue will normally regard the exercise of the power as creating an interest in possession. And if the trustees in exercise of their powers grant a lease for life for less than full consideration, this will be regarded as creating an interest in possession in view of IHTA 1984 ss 43(3)-50(6) ....

A similar view will be taken where the power is exercised over property in which another beneficiary had an interest in possession up to the time.'

Most of this Statement is taken up with an analysis of the position regarding discretionary (ie no interest in possession) trusts. However, the final sentence is directly relevant to the matter under consideration.

(iv)   If a beneficiary who enjoys a right to occupy under the Trusts of Land and Appointment of Trustees Act 1996, s 12(1) gives up that right in favour of another beneficiary, on the above analysis he has made a potentially exempt transfer[9].

1   Income and Corporation Taxes Act 1988, s 15(1), Sch A, para 1(3)(a).
2   Income and Corporation Taxes Act 1988, s 347A as inserted by the Finance Act 1988 s 36.
3   Income and Corporation Taxes Act 1988, s 74(1)(a) as amended by the Finance Act 1994, s 144(2), but note that if the payment is untaxed in the recipient's hands (eg on the basis that it is an annual payment) then there may be no deduction for the payer: Income and Corporation Taxes Act 1988, s 74(1)(m).

4   See, in particular, the Inheritance Tax Act 1984, s 160 and note *Wight v IRC* [1984] RVR 163.
5   Inheritance Tax Act 1984, s 50(1).
6   *Gartside v IRC* [1968] AC 553 at 607, [1968] 1 All ER 121 at 128 per Lord Reid, HL and see the discussion at Para 4.4 below.
7   See the Inheritance Tax Act 1984, s 3A as inserted by the Finance Act 1986, Sch 19, para 1 and amended by the Finance (No 2) Act 1987, s 96 and Sch 9, Pt III.
8   See the Inheritance Tax Act 1984, ss 227–228 for the option to pay tax by instalments. For a further consideration of the meaning of 'interest in possession' see para 4.9 below and see generally *McCutcheon on Inheritance Tax* (3rd edn) p 562 *et seq.*
9   From the correspondence in Appendix 5 below it will be seen that the Revenue may draw a distinction between cases where 'compensation' has been paid in return for occupation (when the existing position of attributing a share of the trust fund to the relevant beneficiaries will not be disturbed) and where no payment is made for occupation when the change in the IHT position described above will apply. The authors are not convinced by this analysis but incline to the view that the trustees have no power under s 13 to vary the beneficial trusts merely to impose arrangements of an administrative nature on the beneficiaries. Hence the interests in the fund enjoyed by the beneficiaries are not disturbed. See also *Woodhall (Woodhall's Personal Representative) v IRC* [2000] STC (SCD) 558.

Section 14 – Applications for Order

2.139   Text of section 14

(1)   Any person who is a trustee of land or has an interest in a property subject to a trust of land may make an application to the court for an order under this section.

(2)   On an application for an order under this section the court may make any such order–

(a)   relating to the exercise by the trustees of any of their functions (including an order relieving them of any obligation to obtain the consent of, or to consult, any person in connection with the exercise of any of their functions), or

(b)   declaring the nature or extent of a person's interest in property subject to the trust,

as the court thinks fit.

(3)   The court may not under this section make any order as to the appointment or removal of trustees.

(4)   The powers conferred on the court by this section are exercisable on an application whether it is made before or after the commencement of this Act.

Law Commission recommendations

2.140   The Trusts of Land and Appointment of Trustees Act 1996 is the replacement for the Law of Property Act 1925, s 30[1]. The Law Commission[2] explained the purpose of these new provisions as follows:

'The courts have interpreted section 30 of the Law of Property Act so broadly as to enable them, in settling a dispute relating to a trust for sale, to give effect to what they perceive to be the purpose of the trust or the intention of the parties in acquiring the trust land. It is our view that the courts should have a similarly broad power to settle disputes concerning trusts of land under the new system . . .

As with the question of trust powers generally, our aim is to express the courts' powers by way of a broad provision rather than by drawing up an inventory. This may not give the courts many more powers than they currently exercise in relation to trusts for sale; our recommendations as to the making of applications and orders may be of greater importance in securing added flexibility. Similarly, if the trustees have more powers, then the courts' overall "capacity" will be increased accordingly.

Generally, this broad power will include powers to interfere with the trustees' exercise of any of the trust powers, to dispense with any consents, or to regulate beneficiaries' occupation of land.'

1   Law of Property Act 1925, s 30 as amended by the County Courts Act 1984, s 148(1), Sch 2, para 2 and by the High Court and County Courts Jurisdiction Order 1991/724 (repealed).
2   *Transfer of Land, Trusts of Land* (Law Com No 181) paras 12.1, 12.7 and 12.8.

2.141   The intention is to permit any interested person to intervene in any dispute concerning a trust of land[1].

1   The Trusts of Land and Appointment of Trustees Act 1996, s 14 also applies to a trust of the proceeds of sale of land: see s 17(2).

Relevance of existing case law

2.142   The Law of Property Act 1925, s 30[1] was hampered by its restrictive words and by the overriding duty to sell: restrictions that do not apply to the new section. The Law Commission considered that 'there will be much of value in the existing body of case law, even though these cases assume that there is a duty to sell'[2].

1   Law of Property Act 1925, s 30 as amended by the County Courts Act 1984 s 148(1), Sch 2, para 2 and by the High Court and County Courts Jurisdiction Order 1991/724 (repealed) which applied in circumstances where the trustees for sale refused to sell or otherwise to exercise their powers.
2   For the courts approach to the Law of Property Act 1925, s 30, and for a consideration of the relevant case law, see in particular Gray *Elements of Land Law* (2nd edn, 1993) p 585 *et seq*. Note especially the case of *Re Evers' Trust, Papps v Evers* [1980] 3 All ER 399, [1980] 1 WLR 1327, CA. As to why there should be an express provision enabling an application to be made to the court in the case of trusts of land, the Law Commission in *Trusts of Land* (Law Com Working Paper No 94) para 10.4 commented as follows: 'It might be suggested that it is unnecessary to confer special powers on the court where trusts of land are concerned. Where other trusts are concerned, the courts can and will act to restrain a breach of trust, but the courts do not normally interfere with the exercise of discretion by the trustees unless their discretion is so exercised that the exercise of the discretion is itself a breach of the trust. Why is a special power needed? It is probably true that where express trusts are concerned, the trustees are managing investments for the benefit of a number of beneficiaries, and disagreement among the trustees to the point where they can no longer operate the trust is unlikely. Even if such a disagreement were to exist, the solution would probably be for some of the trustees to retire and, in the meantime, the effect of the disagreement would be unlikely materially to affect the interests of the beneficiaries. However, where trusts of land arising out of co-ownership are concerned, the trustees and the beneficiaries are likely to be one and the same. The case law shows that all too often disputes can arise as to the occupation of the trust property, and failure to agree may lead to one or more of the trustees or beneficiaries being homeless. Therefore in this area, the courts have found it necessary to interfere with the exercise of the trustees' discretion.' For the attitude being shown by the judges to the existing law, see Neuberger J in *Mortgage Corpn Ltd v Shaire*, considered at para 2.163 below.

Who may apply to the court?

2.143 Apart from trustees[1], s 14(1) states that 'any person who . . . has an interest in property subject to a trust of land' may make an application to the court. An interest in personal property held on a trust of land therefore suffices. As originally drafted, the clause referred to 'a beneficiary under a trust of land', but it was considered that these words were unduly restrictive. The following persons can apply under s 14 of the Act:

(a) an interest in possession beneficiary;

(b) a remainderman (whether vested or contingent)[2];

(c) a discretionary beneficiary[3];

(d) the secured creditor of a beneficiary; and

(e) trustees (and beneficiaries) of a sub-trust (because the 'interest' does not have to be owned beneficially)[4].

1   Note that the Trusts of Land and Appointment of Trustees Act 1996, s 14 does not apply to personal representatives: s 18(1). For the definition of 'the court' for these purposes see s 23(3).
2   Contrast the relatively weak position of remaindermen under the Settled Land Act 1925: see para 1.10 above.
3   As to the position of beneficiaries of a discretionary trust see para 4.4 below.
4   Under LPA 1925, s 30 when there was a trust for sale and *either* the trustees refused to sell or to exercise any of their other powers *or* any requisite consent would not be obtained *any person interested* could apply to the court. This phrase was widely interpreted, see Megarry and Wade, *The Law of Real Property* (6th Edn, 2000) at para 8.142.

Typical applications

2.144 The provision may be used:

(a) by trustees seeking directions as to the application of the right to occupy provisions in the Trusts of Land and Appointment of Trustees Act 1996, ss 12 and 13; and

(b) by beneficiaries critical of the actions of a life tenant to whom the trustees have delegated their functions.

2.145 The court may make any order relating to the exercise by the trustees of their functions including:

(a) dispensing with consents or the need to consult;

(b) ordering a sale or refusing to order a sale;

(c) a partition (including the payment of equality money); and

(d) ordering the payment of an occupation rent.

Declaratory relief

2.146 Note that the declaratory relief in the Trusts of Land and Appointment of Trustees Act 1996, s 14(2)(b) is couched in similarly wide terms ('a person's interest') to s 14(1). It is not thought that this provision gives the court the power to vary the rights of any person: the court is given a discretion whether to make the order or not.

Appointing or removing trustees

2.147 Trustees cannot be appointed or removed under the Trusts of Land and Appointment of Trustees Act 1996, s 14[1].

1   Trusts of Land and Appointment of Trustees Act 1996, s 14(3). As to the appointment and removal of trustees see para 3.8 below.

Commencement

2.148 Section 14 applies to applications already commenced before 1 January 1997 under the Law of Property Act 1925, s 30[1]. Rather surprisingly, therefore, standing applications have benefited from the wider jurisdiction given to the court under s 14[2].

1   Law of Property Act 1925, s 30 as amended by the County Courts Act 1984, s 148(1), Sch 2, para 2 and by the High Court and County Courts Jurisdiction Order 1991/724 (repealed).
2   See the Trusts of Land and Appointment of Trustees Act 1996, s 14(4). Orders already made were unaffected.

Section 15 – Matters Relevant in Determining Applications

2.149 Text of section 15

(1) The matters to which the court is to have regard in determining an application for an order under section 14 include—

   (a) the intentions of the person or persons (if any) who created the trust,

   (b) the purposes for which the property subject to the trust is held,

   (c) the welfare of any minor who occupies or might reasonably be expected to occupy any land subject to the trust as his home, and

   (d) the interests of any secured creditor of any beneficiary.

(2) In the case of an application relating to the exercise in relation to any land of the powers conferred on the trustees by section 13, the matters to which the court is to have regard also include the circumstances and wishes of each of the beneficiaries who is (or apart from any previous exercise by the trustees of those powers would be) entitled to occupy the land under section 12.

(3) In the case of any other application, other than one relating to the exercise of the power mentioned in section 6(2), the matters to which the court is to have regard also include the circumstances and wishes of any beneficiaries of full age and entitled to an interest in possession in property subject to the trust or (in case of dispute) of the majority (according to the value of their combined interests).

(4)   This section does not apply to an application if section 335A of the Insolvency Act 1986 (which is inserted by Schedule 3 and relates to applications by a trustee of a bankrupt) applies to it.

Law Commission views

2.150   Section 15 sets out some of the factors that the court is to have in mind when an application for an order is made under s 14 of the Act. The Law Commission commented[1]:

'As regards the exercise of these powers, it is our view that the court's discretion should be developed along the same lines as the current "primary purpose" doctrine. This approach was moulded to practical requirements, and we consider that it gets the balance more or less right. Nevertheless, we recommend that section 30[2] should set out some guidelines for the exercise of the court's discretion, the aim being to consolidate and rationalise the current approach. The criteria which the courts have evolved for settling disputes over trusts for sale are ones which will continue to have validity in the context of the new system. One function of the guidelines will be to put these criteria on a statutory footing.'

1   *Transfer of Land, Trusts of Land* (Law Com No 181) para 12.9.
2   It was originally envisaged that the Law of Property Act 1925, s 30 would be amended: in the event, the new Trusts of Land and Appointment of Trustees Act 1996, ss 14, 15 completely superseded this section.

2.151   The list is not exhaustive and the factors may, in a particular case, conflict with each other.

'The welfare of any minor . . .'

2.152   On this guideline the Law Commission commented[1]:

'. . . although it seems clear that the courts will not be slow to protect the interests of children, much may depend upon whether the trust purpose is deemed to be the provision of a "matrimonial" home or of a "family" home. Our recommendation here is that the welfare of the children should be expressly defined as an independent consideration. The aim is to ensure that the interests of children are not linked to the interests of particular beneficial owners[2].'

1   *Transfer of Land, Trusts of Land* (Law Com No 181) para 12.9.
2   When the purpose is to provide a 'family' home then providing for children is implicit in that purpose. By contrast, if a 'matrimonial' home is envisaged then the interest of children may be linked to those of the beneficial owners. Among the relevant cases are *Dennis v McDonald* [1982] Fam 63, [1982] 1 All ER 590, CA; *Re Holliday (a bankrupt), ex p Trustee of the Property of the Bankrupt v Bankrupt* [1981] Ch 405, [1980] 3 All ER 385, CA; and *Re Evers' Trust, Papps v Evers* [1980] 3 All ER 399, [1980] 1 WLR 1327, CA. There is much to be said for the view of Waite QC sitting as a deputy judge in *Cousins v Dzosens* (1981) Times, 12 December that the authorities were not really in conflict and that 'while there were differences in language and emphasis, they were really attributable to the choice of language influenced by different circumstances'. See further para 2.158 below.

2.153   The Law Commission accepted that the way in which these guide-lines have been drawn up may influence the exercise of the court's discre-tion: for example, if the welfare of children is seen as a factor independent of the beneficiary's interest, the court may be less willing to order a sale than at present despite the interests of creditors. Of course, the interest of minors is only relevant in the context of a home.

Secured creditors

2.154   In respect of the Trusts of Land and Appointment of Trustees Act 1996, s 15(1)(d), the main illustration of a secured creditor in the case of a jointly owned residential property is a mortgagee. Also included is a creditor who has obtained a charging order under the Charging Orders Act 1979 against any person for whose benefit the land, subject to the trust, is or may be held[1].

1   See the discussion at para 2.163 and for the way in which the 1996 Act has changed the rights of creditors see *Mortgage Corpn Ltd v Shaire* [2000] WTLR 357.

Beneficiaries' rights of occupation

2.155   Section 15(2) provides that, in relation to applications in connection with the beneficiary's right to occupy trust property and with the trustees' powers under s 13 of the Act, the circumstances and wishes of each adult interest in possession beneficiary are to be taken into account (contrast s 15(3) which applies in most other cases).

Other applications

2.156   Section 15(3) applies in cases other than rights of occupation under s 15(2) of the Act and other than the trustees' power to transfer land under s 6(2). The Law Commission[1] considered to what extent the wishes of life tenants should be given priority over other beneficiaries and concluded as follows:

'It may, in this context, be appropriate to consider whether the life tenant's wishes should be given priority over the wishes of other benefici-aries, particularly as we are concerned that the new system should, as much as possible, enable settlors to reproduce the conditions of a strict settlement. It is, however, our view that there should be no restrictions upon the exercise of the court's discretion.'

1   *Transfer of Land, Trusts of Land* (Law Com No 181) para 12.13. In the case of disagreement, the court is to have regard to the views of the majority ascertained according to the value of their combined interests (compare para 2.114 (d) above for a discussion of how to value beneficiaries' interests).

Can the court override an express exclusion by the settlor of all or some of the s 6 powers?

2.157   Assume that the trustees are prohibited in the trust deed from selling, letting or mortgaging land by a settlor who wishes to keep the land in the trust throughout its duration[1]. If the trustees request the court, for example, to give a power of sale, does the court have power to accede to their request? It is thought that the court has such power: it can, for instance, override any consent requirement imposed by the settlor[2]. Furthermore, the court may make 'any such order . . . relating to the exercise by the trustees of any of their functions'[3] and, given that 'functions' includes the trustees' duties to act in the best interest of the beneficiaries, faced with the argument that it is in their interest for the trustee to have a power of sale, it is considered that the court must have power to make an appropriate order.

1   See s 8(1) discussed at para 2.69 above.
2   Section 14(2)(a).
3   Section 14(2)(a).

Exercise of the court's powers in cases of co-ownership

2.158   It is common for disputes to arise between co-owners when, as a result of the breakdown in the relationship between them, one wishes the property to be sold while the other does not, often because he or she is continuing to live in it. The matters to which the court is required to have regard under the 1996 Act in exercising its discretion are based upon the principles developed in the case law which had evolved under LPA 1925, s 30. The list is not exhaustive; the factors may overlap and, in a particular case, can conflict, but these factors are to be taken into account in all cases irrespective of the identity of the applicant (except when an order is being applied for by a trustee in bankruptcy[1]).

1   As to which see para 2.164 below. Note s 15(2) which is limited to the court's discretion under s 13 (exclusion or restriction of right to occupy) and contrast s 15(3) which requires the circumstances and wishes of adult interest in possession beneficiaries to be taken into account in all cases other than s 13 applications and applications relating to the s 6(2) power to partition.

(i) The intentions of the person who created the trust

2.159   Obviously this factor is easier to apply when an express trust – rather than the statutory trust – is created. Take the example of a young couple buying a flat where it is not unlikely that the relationship will terminate within a few years. It may be sensible for the purchase to be on an express trust for sale with the intention being stated that the purchase is for joint occupation so that either party should be able to force a sale.

(ii) The purposes for which the property subject to the trust is held

2.160   The overlap with (i) is considerable[1] and again: it may be desirable for the purpose to be spelt out in an express trust for sale (although the purposes may have changed by the time the matter comes before the court). The pre-1997 cases established that where there were no children the purpose of the purchase was to provide a home for both parties to the relationship and so neither should be able to force a sale until the termination of that relationship[2]. Of course, it has to be borne in mind that, under the old law, all that the court could do was order (or refuse) a sale: it now has the widest powers. For instance:

(a)   it could decline to order a sale on the basis that the person in occupation compensates the other party; or

(b)   it could order a sale at a future date (ie postponed on terms);

(c)   in the case of an unmarried couple with children, providing a home for the children may be the factor which prompts the court to postpone any order for sale until the children reach 18 or leave full-time education (see also factor (iii)).

1   But see *Rodway v Landy*, 4 April 2001 (CA) where Peter Gibson LJ commented that '(in s 15(1)(b)) I emphasise the present tense which shows that the relevant purposes are those subsisting at the time the court is determining the application'. In this case the trustees were ordered to exercise their powers under s 13 to restrict the entitlement of the beneficiaries and to impose conditions on their occupation.

2   See, for instance, *Jones v Challenger* [1961] 1 QB 176, CA; *Rawlings v Rawlings* [1964] P 398, CA. For a recent illustration see *TSB Bank plc v Marshall* [1998] 2 FLR 769 where the court ordered a sale on behalf of the Bank which had an equitable charge over the defendant's equitable interest because the collateral purpose of purchasing the property had been satisfied. The court failed to take account of the width of the new provisions and proceeded on the basis that it must order a sale unless there was a subsisting collateral purpose. The judge's conclusions were rejected in *Mortgage Corpn Ltd v Shaire* [2000] WTLR 357, 80 P & CR 280. The issues in this paragraph have also been considered in social security cases involving an assessment of capital available to an applicant. In *Wilkinson v Chief Adjudication Officer* [2000] 2 FCR 82 the Court of Appeal decided in the context of a brother and sister who had jointly inherited a house under the will of their mother:

> 'It was a gift by Mrs Thomas jointly to her two children in equal shares. It was an absolute gift in the sense that there was no restriction or super-added purpose expressed in the will. This was not a case like *Palfrey* where property was acquired by joint owners for a collateral purpose, such as accommodation for both joint owners, and that purpose would be defeated if one of those acquiring the property were to insist on a sale while that purpose was still subsisting. In such a case there is, as Hobhouse LJ said "nothing obscure or abstruse in the conclusion that the amount of capital which the applicant's joint possession of that dwelling house represents may fall, for the time being, to be quantified in a nominal amount." On the contrary this is a case where an order for sale would give effect to the testamentary purpose of Mrs Thomas in leaving the house to both of her children for the benefit of both of them equally. Mr Brian Thomas's share in the house and his rights in the house were no greater than those of Mrs Wilkinson, either before or after he went into occupation. If he wished to remain in occupation of the house he could only justly do so on payment to Mrs Wilkinson of the value of her share or at least payment to her of a market rent' (Mummery LJ).

2.161   When co-owners are married any application of sale should be heard by the court dealing with the ancillary relief claim under the Matrimonial Causes Act 1973[1].

1   In *Tee v Tee and Hillman* [1999] 2 FLR 613, CA, Thorpe LJ commented:

> 'The respective roles of family law and Chancery law in this field are very well established. Plainly, in view of the fact that one of the spouses had invoked the Matrimonial Causes Act, that was the dominant statute for the determination of their respective rights and interests . . . Since 1971, when the Matrimonial Proceedings and Property Act 1970 came into force, real property and trust law has had a much reduced role in determining distribution and division of realty between spouses.'

(iii) The interests of any minor who occupies or who might reasonably be expected to occupy the land as his home

2.162   Prior to 1997 when co-owners had minor children (whether or not the parents were married) the court would sometimes refuse an order for sale on the basis that the property had been purchased to acquire a family home[1]. However, the cases were not always consistent and on other occasions the court considered that the children were not beneficiaries under the trust for sale[2]. Section 15(1)(c) resolves the matter by providing that the court must take into account the welfare of any minor[3].

1   *Williams v Williams* [1976] Ch 278, CA; *Re Evers' Trust* [1980] 1 WLR 1327, CA.
2   *Burke v Burke* [1974] 1 WLR 1063, CA; *Re Densham* [1975] 1 WLR 1519.
3   When the parties are married the matter of a sale of the property will be dealt with under the claim for ancillary relief under the Matrimonial Causes Act 1973. When unmarried, a claim could be made under the Children Act 1989 as an alternative to the 1996 Act.

(iv) The interests of a secured creditor of any beneficiary

2.163   The interests of a creditor are now one factor (but not necessarily the decisive factor) for the court to take into account on any application for an order. The pre-1997 cases which suggested that, save in exceptional circumstances, the creditor would obtain an order for sale of the property, were based on the close analogy with the position when the matter involved an application by a trustee in bankruptcy. Under the 1996 Act that link has been broken and the factors set out in s 15 do not apply to such claims[1]. This would suggest that a more flexible approach might be adopted with, for instance, a sale being refused in cases where the creditor's security was not in jeopardy, provided that arrangements could be agreed to deal with payments of interest. This is the approach to the construction of s 15 which commended itself to Neuberger J in *Mortgage Corpn Ltd v Shaire*[2]:

'His Lordship said that raised question: had the law relating to the way in which the court would exercise its power to order a sale at the suit of a chargee changed? It had.

First, if there had been no intention to change the law it was hard to see why Parliament had set out in subsections (2) and (3) the factors that specifically had to be taken into account when the court was exercising its jurisdiction to order a sale.

Second, it would be surprising if Parliament had intended to confirm the law as laid down in *Byrne*[3] given that the interest of the chargee was just one of the four specified factors to be taken into account in section 15(1) and there was no suggestion that it was to be given any more importance than the interests of children residing in the house.

Third, the very concept of trust for sale and the law as it had been developed by the courts suggested that, in the absence of a clear reason to the contrary, the court should order sale. There was nothing in the language of the new code as found in the 1996 Act which supported that.

Fourth, it was clear from the reasoning in *Byrne* that the law under section 30 of the 1925 Act was that the court should adopt precisely the same approach to a case where one of the co-owners was bankrupt as where one of the co-owners had a charge and the chargee was seeking to enforce it.

It was quite clear that Parliament now considered that a different approach was appropriate in the two cases. The Law Commission report that gave rise to the 1996 Act Transfer of Land, Trusts of Land (Law Comm No 181, 1989) tended to support the view that the law had changed.

The way in which the 1996 Act and in particular section 15 had been drafted suggested that the Law Commission's proposals were very much in the mind of the legislature.

In his Lordship's judgment, Parliament had intended to relax the law so as to enable the courts to have more discretion in favour of families and against banks and other chargees.

Having reached that conclusion, the next question was to decide the extent to which the old authorities were of assistance. In his Lordship's judgment it would be arrogant to throw over the wealth of learning and thought given by so many eminent judges to the problem which was thrown up on application for sale of a house where competing interests existed.

Nevertheless, in light of the change in the law introduced by section 15, they should be regarded with caution.'

1   TOLATA 1996, s 15(4) and see para 6.1 below.
2   [2000] WTLR 357, 80 P & CR 280.
3   *Lloyds Bank plc v Byrne* [1993] 1 FLR 369, CA.

Applications under the Insolvency Act 1986

2.164   When the Insolvency Act 1986, s 335A[1] applies, s 15 is excluded from applying to the application under s 14[2].

1   Insolvency Act 1986, s 335A as inserted by the Trusts of Land and Appointment of Trustees Act 1996, Sch 3, para 23.
2   Trusts of Land and Appointment of Trustees Act 1996, s 15(4). See further para 6.1 below and the comments in *Transfer of Land, Trusts of Land* (Law Com no 181) paras 12.11, 12.12.

Section 16 – Protection of Purchasers

2.165   Text of section 16

(1)   A purchaser of land which is or has been subject to a trust need not be concerned to see that any requirement imposed on the trustees by section 6(5), 7(3) or 11(1) has been complied with.

(2)   Where–

   (a)   trustees of land who convey land which (immediately before it is conveyed) is subject to the trust contravene section 6(6) or (8), but

   (b)   the purchaser of the land from the trustees has no actual notice of the contravention,

   the contravention does not invalidate the conveyance.

(3)   Where the powers of trustees of land are limited by virtue of section 8–

   (a)   the trustees shall take all reasonable steps to bring the limitation to the notice of any purchaser of the land from them, but

(b)   the limitation does not invalidate any conveyance by the trustees to a purchaser who has no actual notice of the limitation.

(4)   Where trustees of land convey land which (immediately before it is conveyed) is subject to the trust to persons believed by them to be beneficiaries absolutely entitled to the land under the trust and of full age and capacity–

    (a)   the trustees shall execute a deed declaring that they are discharged from the trust in relation to that land, and

    (b)   if they fail to do so, the court may make an order requiring them to do so.

(5)   A purchaser of land to which a deed under subsection (4) relates is entitled to assume that, as from the date of the deed, the land is not subject to the trust unless he has actual notice that the trustees were mistaken in their belief that the land was conveyed to beneficiaries absolutely entitled to the land under the trust and of full age and capacity.

(6)   Subsections (2) and (3) do not apply to land held on charitable, ecclesiastical or public trusts.

(7)   This section does not apply to registered land.

Continued protection for purchasers

2.166   The Trusts of Land and Appointment of Trustees Act 1996 is not intended adversely to affect the position of a purchaser[1] in that the overreaching mechanism in the Law of Property Act 1925 (which had applied to trusts for sale) is now extended to all trusts of land[2]. Indeed, the position of a purchaser has been improved in that:

(a)   as no new strict settlements will be created, problems concerning ineffective dispositions of settled property and the unrecognised strict settlement will disappear; and

(b)   the overreaching rules have been extended to bare trusts[3].

1   'Purchaser' means a person who acquires an interest in, or charge on, property for money or money's worth: Law of Property Act 1925, s 205(xxi). For the protection of mortgagees see the Trustee Act 1925, s 17.

2   See the Law of Property Act 1925, ss 2 (as amended by the Law of Property (Amendment) Act 1926, s 7, Schedule and by the Trusts of Land and Appointment of Trustees Act 1996, Sch 3, para 4(2)), 27 (as amended by the Law of Property (Amendment) Act 1926, s 7, Schedule and by the Trusts of Land and Appointment of Trustees Act 1996, Sch 3, para 4(8)). See further para 6.63 below.

3   In this respect, the Trusts of Land and Appointment of Trustees Act 1996 implements the recommendations of the Law Commission in its report *Transfer of Land Overreaching: Beneficiaries in Occupation* (Law Com No 188).

2.167   Section 16 is needed because of the requirements in the Act laid on trustees and the possibility of limitations on their powers being laid down in the relevant instrument. In relation to post-1996 dealings, a purchaser is entitled to assume that trustees have the wide Section 6 powers (contrast the position with regard to earlier transactions in which the trustees' powers were commonly more limited). Of course the limitations considered in s 16(2) and (3) must refer to invalidity in equity given that, as the legal estate is vested in the trustees, they have the power to convey it[1].

1   See further *Ferris and Battersby* in [1998] 62 Conv p 168.

2.168   It has already been noted that, when the consents of more than two people are required to the exercise of any trustee function, a purchaser is protected provided that the consent of any two of them is obtained[1].

1   Section s 10(1) replicating LPA 1925, s 26(1) which had applied to trusts for sale prior to 1997. Note the exception for land held on charitable, ecclesiastical or public trusts in s 10(2).

Unregistered land

2.169   The Trusts of Land and Appointment of Trustees Act 1996, s 16 makes provision for the protection of purchasers of unregistered land. The section divides into two as follows:

(a)   A purchaser is not concerned with whether[1]:

   (i)   the trustees, in exercising their powers, have considered the rights of beneficiaries[2];

   (ii)   the consent of beneficiaries has been obtained to a partition of land[3]; or

   (iii) the requirement to consult and to give effect to the wishes of the beneficiaries with interests in possession have been complied with[4].

(b)   A purchaser is only concerned in cases where he has actual notice[5] that:

   (i)   the trustees are exercising their powers in contravention of s 6(6) or 6(8) of the Act (ie exercise of powers which are in contravention of any other enactment or any rule of law or equity or subject to restrictions etc)[6];

   (ii)   the trustees are exercising powers which are limited under s 8 of the Act[7]; or

   (iii) the trustees conveyed land to beneficiaries under s 6(2) of the Act in a situation where the beneficiaries were not of full age and capacity and absolutely entitled[8]. Provided in this case that the purchaser obtains a declaratory deed from the trustees, he is protected in the absence of an actual notice of the irregularity[9].

1   Trusts of Land and Appointment of Trustees Act 1996, s 16(1) and see para 6.63 below. Note that the wording is 'need not be concerned to see': contrast 'shall not be concerned with the trusts affecting . . .' in the Law of Property Act 1925, s 27(1) as substituted by the Trusts of Land and Appointment of Trustees Act 1996, Sch 3, para 4(8). Despite this difference, it is thought that the effect of the two provisions is the same. Note that these provisions do not apply to land held on charitable, ecclesiastical or public trusts
2   See the Trusts of Land and Appointment of Trustees Act 1996, s 6(5) and paras 2.38 above and 6.66 below. It is odd that the general equitable duty (enshrined in s 6(6)) is not included.
3   See the Trusts of Land and Appointment of Trustees Act 1996, s 7(3) and para 2.58 above.
4   See the Trusts of Land and Appointment of Trustees Act 1996, s 11(1) and paras 2.107 above and 6.65 below. In contrast to the consent requirements it therefore appears that these obligations are personal to the trustees and do not touch the land as such.
5   It would seem that actual notice is limited to something known by the purchaser or his agent: *Ferris and Battersby* [1998] 62 Conv 168 at p 178.
6   Trusts of Land and Appointment of Trustees Act 1996, s 16(2).

7   Trusts of Land and Appointment of Trustees Act 1996, s 16(3). Trustees have a duty to bring these restrictions to the notice of a purchaser, but, if they do not, a purchaser without actual notice takes free of the limitation: s 16(3). In the case of registered land, trustees must apply for a restriction to be entered on the register and beneficiaries may apply for a restriction or caution to protect their interests. There is no such facility for beneficiaries in the case of unregistered land. If a purchaser is aware of a consent requirement, s 10 will apply so that any two consents will generally suffice.

8   See Trusts of Land and Appointment of Trustees Act 1996, s 16(4), (5).

9   For a deed of discharge pursuant to Trusts of Land and Appointment of Trustees Act 1996, s 16(4) see **Precedent 16** below.

Deeds of discharge

2.170   The ending of a Settled Land Act settlement imposed a requirement on the trustees to execute a deed of discharge to indicate that this had happened[1]. There was no equivalent provision for trusts for sale, a defect that was cured by s 16(4). When trustees convey land to beneficiaries of full age and capacity whom they believe to be absolutely entitled to it, they must execute an appropriate deed of discharge and, if they fail to do so, can be ordered to do so by the court. A subsequent purchaser or registrar on an application to register the land, in the absence of actual notice to the contrary, is entitled to assume that the trust has ended. In practice, it is registrars who will be affected by s 16(4) given that any conveyance of unregistered land by trustees on the termination of a trust is now an occasion for first registration[2].

1   SLA 1925, s 17.

2   LRA 1925, s 123 (substituted by LRA 1997, s 1) from April 1998. Such a conveyance is a 'gift': see s 123(6). In the case of registered land, the trustees should apply to the registrar to remove any restrictions: see LRR 1925, r 236B. The application should be on Form 77: see generally *Private Trusts of Land* (PAL No 13) 2nd Edn (April 2000) published by HM Land Registry at H4.

Position of beneficiaries

2.171   The trustees may be subject to an action for breach of trust in cases where they fail to obtain consents, fail to consult or act in excess of a limitation on their powers.

Registered land

2.172   The Trusts of Land and Appointment of Trustees Act 1996, Sch 3, para 5(8) amends the Land Registration Act 1925, s 94. Registered land subject to a trust of land is to be registered in the name of the trustees and 'there shall also be entered on the register such restrictions as may be prescribed, or may be expedient, for the protection of the rights of the persons beneficially interested in the land'[1].

1   Land Registration Act 1925 s 94(4) as inserted by the Trusts of Land and Appointment of Trustees Act 1996, Sch 3, para 5(8)(c). This is because of the basic principle that 'in registered conveyancing it is fundamental that any registered proprietor can exercise all or any powers of disposition unless some entry on the register exists to curtail or remove those powers' (see *State Bank of India v Sood* [1997] Ch 276 at 284, CA, per Peter Gibson LJ).

2.173   The practice of the Land Registry is set out in *Private Trusts of Land* (April 2000), Practice Advice Leaflet No 13 and may be summarised as follows[1]:

(a)   because the 1996 Act gives trustees of land all the powers of an absolute owner the only restriction that will normally be entered on the register is Form 62[2] (except in the case of charity land);

(b)   in the case of limitations with which a purchaser of unregistered land is not concerned[3] 'these obligations cannot be made the subject matter of a restriction, so a purchaser of registered land will be in the same position unless there is a caution on the register';

(c)   in the case of contraventions which do not invalidate a conveyance of unregistered land to a purchaser without notice[4] the practice in registered conveyancing depends upon the state of the register:

> 'If it does not contain a restriction preventing the registration of a disposition in contravention of the provision, a purchaser will be able to complete his purchase even though he is aware of the contravention. If it does contain such a restriction, however, the purchaser must insist on the restriction being complied with' (PAL No 13 at E2.2).

The Form 76 should be used to apply for a restriction: the application may be made by any person interested in the land or having a sufficient interest to prevent the contravention (see rr 236(1) and (3); 236(4) and 236(2));

(d)   in the case of limitations which trusts must bring to the notice of a purchaser of unregistered land[5] there are corresponding obligations in registered conveyancing in the form of a duty to apply for a restriction in Form 11A (see rr 59A and 106A). The Form is in the following terms:

> 'Except under an order of the registrar no disposition (*or transfer, or charge, or lease for more than* (*specify longest permitted term*), *or as the case may be*) by the proprietors of the land is to be registered unless they make a statutory declaration, or their solicitor or licensed conveyancer certifies, that the disposition is in accordance with (*specify the disposition creating the trust*) or some variation thereof referred to in the declaration or certificate[6].'

The Practice Leaflet concludes as follows:

> 'In unregistered conveyancing, where the powers of the trustees of a private trust are limited by virtue of section 8 of the 1996 Act, they are under an obligation to take all reasonable steps to bring the limitation to the notice of any purchaser of the land from them. In registered conveyancing, the rules impose a corresponding obligation in the form of a duty to apply for a restriction in Form 11A.
>
> These restrictions are entered for the protection of the rights of the persons beneficially interested in the land. In the absence of a restriction a purchaser of registered land from trustees is not concerned to see that any necessary consent has been obtained, or any

limitation on the trustees' powers of disposition in the disposition creating the trust has been complied with.'

1   See Part E.
2   The form of this restriction is as follows:

> 'No disposition by a sole proprietor of the land (not being a trust corporation) under which capital money arises is to be registered except under an order of the registrar or of the Court.'

3   See s 16(1): the relevant provisions – essentially personal obligations of the trustees – are those in ss 6(5), 7(3) and 11(1).
4   See s 16(2).
5   See s 16(3)(a) which applies when the powers of the trustees are limited by s 8.
6   See further PAL No 13, section E3.

2.174   When trustees execute a deed under the Trusts of Land and Appointment of Trustees Act 1996, s 16(4) stating that the land is no longer subject to a trust because all the beneficiaries are absolutely entitled to the land and are of full age and capacity, the Registrar is entitled to assume that the land is not subject to the trust unless he has actual notice to the contrary[1].

1   Land Registration Act 1925, s 94(5) as inserted by the Trusts of Land and Appointment of Trustees Act 1996, Sch 3, para 5(8)(c). See para 2.170 above.

The Ferris/Battersby argument

2.175   The article in *The Conveyancer*[1] argued that the 1996 Act had, perhaps unintentionally, overruled *City of London Building Society v Flegg*[2] in respect of certain trustees of registered land. In simple terms, because of the restrictions that can be imposed on a trustee's powers under s 6, dispositions of trustees may be *ultra vires* and, because the additional purchaser protection given by s 16 does not apply to registered land, equitable owners in occupation may find that they have overriding interests against a purchaser or mortgagor[3]. If correct, this result will have very serious consequences. The following points may be noted:

(a)   there is no evidence that the 1996 Act was intended to overturn one of the fundamental tenets of the 1925 legislation and it appears from the Law Commission report that it was intended to leave overreaching impact[4];

(b)   the views are not shared by HM Land Registry[5];

(c)   it is thought likely that the courts will strive to interpret the legislation so that *first* the trustees have all the powers of an *absolute owner* subject only to entries on the register (thereby protecting a purchaser) whilst, *secondly*, accepting that there are an increasing number of situations where trustees may act in breach of trust (and so be liable to a beneficiary);

(d)   in *Birmingham Midshires Mortgage Services Ltd v Sabherwal (Sudesh)*[6] the Court of Appeal followed the *Flegg* case in deciding that the mortgage had overreached the interests of the beneficiaries. This was because: (a) the mortgage (started in 1990) predated the changes made by the 1996 Act; (b) that Act 'contains nothing to exclude the essential overreaching promise contained in s 2(1)(ii) of LPA 1925[7] and that provision had merely been amended in line with the new terminology and (c) the abolition of the doctrine of conversion has had no effect on overreaching. This case illustrates what is thought to be a strong judicial bias in favour of overreaching, albeit that *Flegg* was not directly challenged in the case and the *Ferris/Battersby* argument not fully rehearsed.

1   [1998] 62 Conv 168.
2   [1988] AC 54, HL, see para 1.25 above.
3   Under the so called '*Boland* Principle': see para 1.14 above.
4   See generally Report No 181, 'Transfer of Land: Trusts of Land'.
5   See para 2.172 above.
6   (1999) 80 P & CR 256.
7   Per Robert Walker LJ.

Section 17 – Application of Provisions to Trusts of Proceeds of Sale

2.176   Text of section 17

[*(1)   Section 6(3) applies in relation to trusteees of a trust of proceeds of sale of land as in relation to trustees of land.*]

(2)   Section 14 applies in relation to a trust of proceeds of sale of land and trustees of such a trust as in relation to a trust of land and trustees of land.

(3)   In this section 'trust of proceeds of sale of land' means (subject to subsection (5)) any trust of property (other than a trust of land) which consists of or includes–

  (a)   any proceeds of a disposition of land held in trust (including settled land), or

  (b)   any property representing any such proceeds.

(4)   The references in subsection (3) to a trust–

  (a)   are to any description of trust (whether express, implied, resulting or constructive), including a trust for sale and a bare trust, and

  (b)   include a trust created, or arising, before the commencement of this Act.

(5)   A trust which (despite section 2) is a settlement for the purposes of the Settled Land Act 1925 cannot be a trust of proceeds of sale of land.

(6)   In subsection (3)–

  (a)   'disposition' includes any disposition made, or coming into operation, before the commencement of this Act, and

  (b)   the reference to settled land includes personal chattels to which section 67(1) of the Settled Land Act 1925 (heirlooms) applies.

Purpose of section 17

2.177   The Trusts of Land and Appointment of Trustees Act 1996, s 17 indicates which provisions of the Act apply to trustees of a trust containing the proceeds of sale of land (as defined).

'Trust of proceeds of sale of land'[1]

2.178 The width and uncertainty of this definition may be noted[2]. It should also be noted that in the case of Settled Land Act trusts which become trusts of land on 1 January 1997, earlier dispositions of land (including heirlooms falling within the Settled Land Act 1925)[3] will be covered. The wording of the Trusts of Land and Appointment of Trustees Act 1996, s 17(3) means that in future, strict settlements which become trusts for land will likewise qualify.

1   See the Trusts of Land and Appointment of Trustees Act 1996, s 17(3).
2   Note that it includes property representing such proceeds.
3   Trusts of Land and Appointment of Trustees Act 1996, s 17(6)(b).

Applicability

2.179 The following provisions of the Act apply to trusts of the proceeds of sale:

(a)   ss 14 and 15 (application to the court); and

(b)   prior to 1 February 2001, s 6(3) with the result that such trustees were given the power to buy land (this solved the difficulty that a trust of land ended when the last piece of land was sold). With the implementation on TA 2000 this provision became redundant given that *all* trustees (including trustees of the proceeds of sale of land) have the power to buy land under TA 2000, Pt III.

Section 18 – Application of Part I to Personal Representatives

2.180   Text of section 18

(1)   The provisions of this Part relating to trustees, other than sections 10, 11 and 14, apply to personal representatives, but with appropriate modifications and without prejudice to the functions of personal representatives for the purposes of administration.

(2)   The appropriate modifications include–

(a)   the substitution of references to persons interested in the due administration of the estate for references to beneficiaries, and

(b)   the substitution of references to the will for references to the disposition creating the trust.

(3)   Section 3(1) does not apply to personal representatives if the death occurs before the commencement of this Act.

Law Commission recommendations

2.181 The Law Commission[1] recommended that trusts of land arising on death should be similar in nature to *inter vivos* trusts. Accordingly, personal representatives should be given all the powers conferred on trustees of land. The Trusts of Land and Appointment of Trustees Act 1996 Section 18 largely implements this policy.

1   Transfer of Land, Trusts of Land (Law Com No 181) para 19.3.

Exclusions

2.182   The following provisions in the Trusts of Land and Appointment of Trustees Act 1996 do not apply to personal representatives:

(a)   the relaxation of the requirement for consents in favour of a purchaser in s 10 of the Act;

(b)   the requirement to consult in s 11; and

(c)   the ability to apply to the court under s 14 (contrast the position under the Law of Property Act 1925, s 30)[1].

1   Ie the Law of Property Act 1925, s 30 as amended by the County Courts Act 1984, s 148(1), Sch 2, para 2 and by the High Court and County Courts Jurisdiction Order 1991/724 (repealed).

2.183   In other cases, note that the imposition of the legislation (for example, the beneficiary's right of occupation under the Trusts of Land and Appointment of Trustees Act 1996, s 12) is without prejudice to the functions of the personal representatives in the administration of the estate[1].

1   Trusts of Land and Appointment of Trustees Act 1996, s 18(1).

Doctrine of conversion

2.184   The abolition of the doctrine of conversion[1] does not apply to personal representatives in respect of deaths occurring before 1 January 1997[2].

1   See the Trusts of Land and Appointment of Trustees Act 1996, s 3 and para 2.18 above.
2   The Trusts of Land and Appointment of Trustees Act 1996, s 18(3).

Administrative powers

2.185   The enhanced powers in the Act apply in the case of deaths occurring on or after 1 January 1997. Suitable amendments are made to the Law of Property Act 1925, s 33[1] and to the Administration of Estates Act 1925, s 39[2].

1   Law of Property Act 1925, s 33 as amended by the Trusts of Land and Appointment of Trustees Act 1996, Sch 3, para 4(9).
2   Administration of Estates Act 1925, s 39 as amended by the Trusts of Land and Appointment of Trustees Act 1996, Sch 3, para 6(2).

Delegation

2.186   The powers of delegation in the Trusts of Land and Appointment of Trustees Act 1996, s 9 are given to personal representatives.

Intestacy

2.187   The statutory trusts for sale which arose on intestacy have been abolished[1]:

'Our proposals are not designed to alter the relationship between personal representatives and beneficiaries under either an intestacy or an express trust for sale. We do, however, recommend that trusts for sale should no longer automatically arise on intestacy, since no practical justification for this could be perceived. Accordingly, we propose that section 33 of the Administration of Estates Act 1925 be amended so as to provide that, in cases of intestacy, the deceased's estate should be held by his personal representatives on trust under the new system. The personal representatives would hold the property, after meeting those costs and expenses which are at present set out in subsection 33(2), on the same terms as those of subsections 33(2)-(7). This amendment is designed to affect both real and personal property.'

1   See the Administration of Estates Act 1925, s 33 as amended by the Trusts of Land and Appointment of Trustees Act 1996, Sch 2, para 5 and note *Transfer of Land, Trusts of Land* (Law Com No 181) para 19.2.

Will drafting

2.188   For the effect of the Act on will drafting, see para 6.39 below.

3

Part II: Appointment and Retirement of Trustees

Background

3.1   The Trusts of Land and Appointment of Trustees Act 1996, Pt II, concerning the appointment and retirement of trustees, occupied almost as much debating time as the remainder of the statute even though it comprises only three sections. In part this stems from the fact that the original recommendations of the Law Commission were ill thought out. The end result is radically different from what was envisaged and the impression from reading the Parliamentary Debates is of the Government making wholesale amendments at the behest (largely) of the Law Society without at any stage pausing to reflect on whether the changes were either necessary or desirable. In the event, it is likely that the powers to remove and appoint trustees which have been given to beneficiaries will only affect a relatively small number of trusts. However, a radical principle ('beneficiary power') has been established and, as may have been presaged in the House of Commons Debates (in which a suggestion was considered that for larger trusts there should be a majority rule, akin to the 90% shareholder rule for companies)[1], further in-roads may be made in the future into the traditional division between the powers and duties of the trustees on the one hand and the rights of beneficiaries on the other. Part II of the Act is not limited to trusts of land.

1   HC Official Report, SC A (Trusts of Land and Appointment of Trustees Bill), 26 June 1996, cols 4-7.

3.2   By way of background, the Law Commission made the following recommendations[1]:

'Where a trust arises by way of a conveyance to co-owners, the trustees will, as at present, be the first four named in the conveyance. They will, however, hold the legal estate on trust under the new system rather than on trust for sale. Where new trustees are to be appointed, we recommend that section 36 of the Trustee Act 1925 should apply as at present, subject however to an amendment. We recommend that where the beneficiaries are ascertained, *sui juris*, and unanimous, they should be able to exercise the right of appointment currently exercised by the remaining trustees. The beneficiaries' right would take priority over the trustees' right under section 36(1)(b). However, in order that purchasers might continue to enjoy the protection of section 38 of the Trustee Act, the beneficiaries will exercise their right indirectly. In other words, they will merely direct the appointment of a new trustee, the formal deed of appointment being executed by the remaining trustees. Where the mental disorder of an existing trustee necessitates the new appointment, the beneficiaries would be able to give the direction to the trustee's receiver or (if no receiver was acting) to any person authorised for that purpose by the Court of Protection. In order to avoid confusing distinctions, the amendment will apply to trusts of personalty as well as trusts of land.

Where successive interests are created, the trustees will be either those persons appointed by the settlor or, failing this, whoever has the legal estate currently vested in him. Where necessary, the court will have recourse to the power which it currently possesses under section 41 of the Trustee Act 1925.'

1   *Transfer of Land, Trusts of Land* (Law Com No 181) paras 9.1, 9.2.

3.3   It may be noted that:

(a)   no reasons were given for the proposals;

(b)   the relevant comments were mainly concerned with co-ownership although it was envisaged that the change would also to apply to trusts with successive interests;

(c)   the proposed change was to apply to all trusts (ie not just to trusts of land); and

(d)   the proposal concerned the appointment of a new trustee (either to replace an existing trustee or an addition to existing trustees) and did not envisage beneficiaries having the power to remove trustees[1].

2   In *Trusts of Land* (Law Com Working Paper no 94) para 7.6 the possibility of giving the tenant for life a right to be appointed a trustee was considered. The conclusion arrived at was that this had some merit:

'When there is a tenant for life, one of the disadvantages of the proposed new trust is that the tenant for life would no longer have the powers of disposition and management that he has at present . . . Increased powers of delegation may assist, but one other idea is to give the tenant for life a right to be appointed as a trustee. This would give him a direct voice in the management of the property, while the other trustees (there would have to be at least one other if the land were to be sold) would ensure that the interests of other beneficiaries were protected.'

In the event the matter was not considered in the final Report. In para 7.1, the Working Paper mentioned the possibility of beneficiaries in a trust of land having power to appoint new trustees since 'such a provision recognises the strong position of such beneficiaries'. They concluded, however, that to extend that power beyond trusts of land would raise matters beyond the scope of this report.

3.4   The Law Commission in their Report did not mention the case of *Re Brockbank*[1] in which the testator's residuary estate was held on trust for his widow for life and then for his children absolutely. One of the trustees and all the beneficiaries (all of whom were *sui juris* and of sound mind) wished the trustees to retire and be replaced by Lloyds Bank. The other trustee refused to retire and Vaisey J commented:

'It is said that where all the beneficiaries concur, they may force a trustee to retire, compel his removal and direct the trustees, having the power to nominate their successors, to appoint as such successors such person or persons or corporation as may be indicated by the beneficiaries, and it suggested that the trustees have no option but to comply.

I do not follow this. The power of nominating a new trustee is a discretionary power, and, in my opinion, is no longer exercisable and, indeed, can no longer exist if it has become one of which the exercise can be dictated by others. But then it is said that the beneficiaries could direct the trustees to transfer the trust property either to themselves absolutely, or to any other person or persons or corporation, upon trusts identical with or corresponding to the trusts of the testator's Will. I agree, provided that the trustees are adequately protected against any possible claim for future death duties and are fully indemnified as regards their cost, charges and expenses . . .

It seems to me that the beneficiaries must choose between these two alternatives . . . The claim of the beneficiaries to control the exercise of the defendant's fiduciary power of making or compelling an appointment of the trustees is, in my judgment, untenable. The court itself regards such a power as deserving of the greatest respect and as one with which it will not interfere.'

1   *Re Brockbank, Ward v Bates* [1948] Ch 206 at 208, [1948] 1 All ER 287 at 288.

3.5   Curiously by Report Stage in the passage of the Trusts of Land and Appointment of Trustees Act 1996, the Lord Chancellor was introducing amendments on the following basis[1]:

'The approach of this group of amendments is to give a wider power to the beneficiaries, in essence reversing the 1948 decision in the case of *Re Brockbank.*'

1   House of Lords Report Stage at 571 HL Official Report (5th series) col 963, 22 April 1996.

3.6   Even though the beneficiaries may not force a removal and replacement of trustees under the *Brockbank* judgment they could of course (given their unanimity and legal competence) bring the trust to an end under the so-called *Saunders v Vautier* principle. They could then, if so minded, resettle the property on identical trusts, but with their own choice of trustees; but (and it is a major 'but') the price in fiscal terms is likely to be considerable. Assume a simple case where a father leaves property on trust for his son A for life with remainder to his grandson B. A and B both being of full age and sound mind may demand that the trust property be divided between them: for example, in the ratio of 60:40. For capital gains tax purposes, the consequent ending of the trust will result in a deemed disposal of all trust property at that time on the basis of its then market value and a reacquisition of the property by the trustees as (in effect) bare trustees for A and B[1]. If the assets have increased in value, the resultant chargeable gain may be unacceptably large[2].

1   Taxation of Chargeable Gains Act 1992, ss 60, 71.
2   The circumstances when hold-over relief is available to enable any tax charge to be postponed are now severely limited: see Taxation of Chargeable Gains Act 1992, ss 165, 260.

3.7   For inheritance tax purposes, under the original settlement A will be treated as entitled to the entire capital value of the trust fund and therefore, insofar as 40% of that value is given to B on break-up of the trust, he will make a potentially exempt transfer of that amount[1]. If the property is then resettled by A and B, although no capital gains tax is likely to be charged (given that the assets will not have increased in value from the time of the deemed disposal on the termination of the trust) A and B will now be settlors so that any gain realised by their trustees will be taxed as theirs to the extent of the property that they contributed[2]. For inheritance tax, whilst A's resettlement on himself will not be a transfer of value (since he remains treated for inheritance tax purposes as the owner of the property in which he has a life interest) B's settlement on A for life will amount to a potentially exempt transfer.

1   Inheritance Tax Act 1984, ss 49(1), 52. So far as a potentially exempt transfer is concerned tax will be payable if A fails to survive by seven years.

2   Taxation of Chargeable Gains Act 1992, ss 77-79 as amended by the Finance Act 1995, s 74, Sch 17, paras 27-29, Sch 29 Pt VIII(8).

Section 19 – Appointment and Retirement of Trustee at Instance of Beneficiaries

3.8   Text of section 19

(1)   This section applies in the case of a trust where–

    (a)   there is no person nominated for the purpose of appointing new trustees by the instrument, if any, creating the trust, and

    (b)   the beneficiaries under the trust are of full age and capacity and (taken together) are absolutely entitled to the property subject to the trust.

(2)   The beneficiaries may give a direction or directions of either or both of the following descriptions–

    (a)   a written direction to a trustee or trustees to retire from the trust, and

    (b)   a written direction to the trustees or trustee for the time being (or, if there are none, to the personal representative of the last person who was a trustee) to appoint by writing to be a trustee or trustees the person or persons specified in the direction.

(3)   Where–

    (a)   a trustee has been given a direction under subsection (2)(a),

    (b)   reasonable arrangements have been made for the protection of any rights of his in connection with the trust,

    (c)   after he has retired there will be either a trust corporation or at least two persons to act as trustees to perform the trust, and

    (d)   either another person is to be appointed to be a new trustee on his retirement (whether in compliance with a direction under subsection (2)(b) or otherwise) or the continuing trustees by deed consent to his retirement,

he shall make a deed declaring his retirement and shall be deemed to have retired and be discharged from the trust.

(4)   Where a trustee retires under subsection (3) he and the continuing trustees (together with any new trustee) shall (subject to any arrangements for the

protection of his rights) do anything necessary to vest the trust property in the continuing trustees (or the continuing and new trustees).

(5) This section has effect subject to the restrictions imposed by the Trustee Act 1925 on the number of trustees.

Purpose of section 19

3.9 In certain circumstances, the Trusts of Land and Appointment of Trustees Act 1996, s 19 allows beneficiaries to:

(a) force one or more of the trustees to retire;

(b) nominate their successor(s); and

(c) add further trustees up to the permitted maximum[1].

1 The permitted maximum is four trustees: see the Trustee Act 1925, ss 34, 36(6) as amended by the Trusts of Land and Appointment of Trustees Act 1996, Sch 3, para 3(9), (11). The reason given for beneficiaries acting indirectly (that purchasers will then be protected under the Trustee Act 1925, s 38) appears to be irrelevant given that the replacement will not (necessarily) be for reasons stated in the Trustee Act 1925, s 36(1).

When does Section 19 not apply?

3.10

(a) The Trusts of Land and Appointment of Trustees Act 1996, s 19 does not apply when the instrument creating the settlement states who should appoint new trustees[1]. Often the settlor will retain this power during his lifetime, but thereafter it is common for the express power of appointment to lapse so that under the Trustee Act 1925, s 36[2] it is the existing trustees who then have the power to appoint new or replacement trustees[3]. There is, however, nothing to stop the power of appointing new trustees being conferred on identified individuals in succession. For example:

   (i) on the settlor during his life;

   (ii) on his elder son during his life; and

   (iii) thereafter on the eldest grandson etc.

   The wording of the Trusts of Land and Appointment of Trustees Act 1996, s 19(1)(a) ('there is no person nominated . . .') is thought to require that at the relevant time there is someone with the capacity to make such an appointment. Accordingly, the fact that the trust instrument originally nominated such a person who is now either dead or incapable of making the appointment will not prevent s 19 from applying and nor will a clause in the trust instrument which applies the statutory power to the trust.

(b) In the case of a settlement created before 1 January 1997, s 19 will apply unless excluded by a deed executed by the settlor (or, if more than one, by those of the settlors who are alive and of full capacity)[4].

(c) The beneficiaries have to be unanimous[5] and *sui juris*.

1   Trusts of Land and Appointment of Trustees Act 1996, s 19(1)(a).
2   Trustee Act 1925, s 36 as amended by the Trusts of Land and Appointment of Trustees Act 1996, Sch 3, para 3(11).
3   See generally the Trustee Act 1925, s 36(1) which provides as follows:

> '(1) Where a trustee, either original or substituted, and whether appointed by a court or otherwise, is dead, or remains out of the United Kingdom for more than twelve months, or desires to be discharged from all or any of the trust or powers reposed in or conferred on him, or refuses or is unfit to act therein, or is incapable of acting therein, or is an infant, then, subject to the restrictions imposed by this Act on the number of trustees,–
>
> (a)   the person or persons nominated for the purpose of appointing new trustees by the instrument, if any, creating the trust; or
>
> (b)   if there is no such person, or no such person able and willing to act, then the surviving or continuing trustees or trustee for the time being, or the personal representatives of the last surviving or continuing trustee;
>
> may, by writing, appoint one or more other persons (whether or not being the persons exercising the power) to be a trustee or trustees in the place of the trustee so deceased remaining out of the United Kingdom, desiring to be discharged, refusing, or being unfit or being incapable, or being an infant, as aforesaid.'

There is no statutory power to dismiss a trustee; only to replace in limited circumstances (eg for unfitness to act or for refusing to act). For a clause conferring an express power to appoint trustees given to the settlor during his life see **Precedent 1, clause 13.1** below. There is no reason why the power cannot be conferred, after the settlor's death, on his eldest son for life thereafter on that son's son and so on. The perpetuity rules do not apply. It is rare for a trust deed to confer a power to remove trustees; the main examples are pension trusts and offshore trusts.

4   See the Trusts of Land and Appointment of Trustees Act 1996, s 21(6) which is discussed further at para 3.31 below. For a deed made pursuant to s 21(6) see **Precedent 24** below.
5   See para 3.27 below.

Conditions to be satisfied by the beneficiaries

3.11

(a)   Under the Trusts of Land and Appointment of Trustees Act 1996, s 19(1)(b) '[all] the beneficiaries under the trust' must be of full age and capacity and taken together must be absolutely entitled to the trust property.

EXAMPLE 1

1.   Ron and Eth are the beneficial tenants in common of Roseacre. Given that they are adult and sane they satisfy the test in s 19(1)(b) of the Act.

2.   Colonel Pickering left his residuary estate on trust for his wife for life, remainder to his son. His wife and son (given sanity and the son being an adult) satisfy s 19(1)(b); compare the facts in *Re Brockbank, Ward v Bates*[1].

3.   Professor Higgins' will left property on trust for his housekeeper for life, remainder to Eliza Dolittle if she is living at the death of the housekeeper and remainder to her children if any, if more than one in equal shares. The housekeeper and Eliza are not together absolutely entitled, and given that Eliza at present has no children there is the possibility of a reversion to Professor Higgins' estate. The conditions of s 19(1)(b) are not satisfied[2].

---

4. The property is held on trust for such of the children of the settlor and his sister as the trustees may, in their absolute discretion, select. Both the settlor and sister are now dead and there are ten living children. Provided that they are all of full age and capacity they will together satisfy the s 19(1)(b) test. Of course obtaining the agreement of so many beneficiaries may prove impossible[3]. When a discretionary trust includes an open-ended class of beneficiaries which is incapable of being listed, the requirements of s 19(1)(b) will not be satisfied[4].

5. Tiger Tim's estate is held on trust (a) to pay an annuity of £1,000 per annum to his aunt Miss Moneypenny; and (b) to divide the residue into two equal parts and to hold one such part for his daughter Sally and the other for his sister Bunty. Bunty has just died whilst some years ago Sally settled her moiety on trusts for her infant children. Section 19(1)(b) will be satisfied on the basis that the beneficiaries for this purpose are Moneypenny, Bunty's personal representatives and the trustees of Sally's moiety. The definition of 'beneficiary' in s 22(1) includes any person interested in trust property (hence encompassing the personal representatives and trustees); the added requirement (a 'beneficiary who is beneficially entitled') does not apply to s 19(1)(b)[5]. Similarly, an annuitant is a beneficiary for these purposes.

6. The Lovejoy accumulation and maintenance trust split into three funds after the three beneficiaries became 25. Each fund comprises separate property and has separate trustees. Under the A Fund the trustees are X, Y and Z and the beneficiaries A (for life) and B (in remainder). It is thought that A and B can together force the removal of all or any of X, Y and Z. The existence of other funds with separate assets and trustees is to be ignored.

(b) The phrase 'taken together' is intended to encompass the situation where beneficiaries are entitled in succession, or are objects of a discretionary trust as well as being co-owners. As such, there is a contrast with the wording in s 6(2) which refers to each of the beneficiaries being absolutely entitled, and which is believed to be limited to beneficiaries who are all beneficial tenants in common or joint tenants. For a parallel, consider the wording and interpretation of the Taxation of Chargeable Gains Act 1992, s 60 which applies only to beneficial co-owners (or, as the courts have put it, to persons entitled to the same interest)[6] and not in the wider circumstances envisaged by the Trusts of Land and Appointment of Trustees Act 1996, s 19(1)(b).

(c) The beneficiaries must be unanimous in agreeing the appointment and/or retirement[7].

1   *Re Brockbank, Ward v Bates* [1948] Ch 206, [1948] 1 All ER 287.
2   Of course if Eliza was past the age of child bearing there would then be an ultimate remainder in Professor Higgins' estate. Depending on who would be entitled the conditions of the Trusts of Land and Appointment of Trustees Act 1996, s 19(1)(b) could then be satisfied.

3 The meaning of 'beneficiary' as used in the Trusts of Land and Appointment of Trustees Act 1996 is considered at para 4.1 below. It is there suggested that 'beneficiary' may be given a wide meaning to include the beneficiaries of a discretionary trust. If, however, 'interest in property' was given a restricted meaning and excluded such persons then even if all such persons were of full age and wished to use the s 19 power they would not be able, given that the 'beneficiaries' as (restrictively) defined would not together be absolutely entitled.

4 See *McPhail v Doulton* [1971] AC 424, [1970] 2 All ER 228, HL; *Re Smith, Public Trustee v Aspinall* [1928] Ch 915.

5 Contrast, for example, the Trusts of Land and Appointment of Trustees Act 1996, s 12(1) and see ss 22(2), (3). It is *not* thought that the courts would adopt a broad-brush approach in treating the original disposition into trust and the disposition creating the sub-trust as together constituting a trust of the property held in the trust (thereby requiring the consent of beneficiaries of the sub-trust).

6 See, for example, *Tomlinson v Glyns Executor and Trustee Co* [1970] Ch 112, [1970] 1 All ER 381, CA; *Kidson v MacDonald* [1974] Ch 339, [1974] 1 All ER 849; and *Stephenson v Barclays Bank Trust Co* [1975] 1 All ER 625, [1975] 1 WLR 882.

7 See further the Trusts of Land and Appointment of Trustees Act 1996, s 21(1) which is considered at para 3.27 below.

Directions

3.12   Section 19(2) indicates that the beneficiaries may direct in writing either or both of the following:

(a)   that some or all of the trustees are to retire from the trust. No reasons need be stated: the beneficiaries are simply given the right to remove trustees[1]; and

(b)   that the trustee(s) for the time being appoint as a trustee one or more persons specified in the direction. The reference to a trustee 'for the time being' indicates that the direction must be served on all the trustees (including one who is being directed to retire)[2].

1 The power to remove trustees formed no part of the original proposals for the Trusts of Land and Appointment of Trustees Act 1996. It was only accepted by the Government at the House of Lords Report Stage: see 571 HL Official Report (5th series) col 964, 22 April 1996. There is nothing to prevent the beneficiaries from requiring the appointment of persons who are not resident in the UK to act as trustees (subject to safeguarding the retiring trustees, eg against any capital gains tax liabilities that might then result), nor from directing the appointment of themselves. For a written direction and a deed of retirement see **Precedents 17** and **18** below.

2 For a written direction and a deed of appointment, see **Precedents 19** and **20** below.

3.13   Although s 19(2)(b) contains a direction that new trustee(s) should be appointed in writing, in practice it will be desirable for such appointment to be by deed in order to take advantage of the provisions of the Trustee Act 1925, s 40 (vesting of property in new or continuing trustees)[1].

1 Trustee Act 1925, s 40 as amended by the Trusts of Land and Appointment of Trustees Act 1996, Sch 3, para 3(14). Note that s 19(3) requires a trustee to retire by deed and that after his retirement there shall be at least two persons or a trust corporation to perform the trust.

3.14   Section 19(5) makes it clear that the Trustee Act 1925, s 34 (and perhaps s 36(6)) apply to restrict the number of trustees who may be appointed[1].

1 The permitted maximum is four trustees in the case of non charitable trusts of land and settled land: see the Trustee Act 1925, s 34 as amended by the Trusts of Land and Appointment of Trustees Act 1996, Sch 3, para 3(9). Under s 36(6) as amended by

TOLATA 1996, Sch 3, para 3(11) the number of additional trustees who may be appointed under that sub-section is limited to four but it is arguable that any appointment of additional trustees under s 19 is made under s 19(2)(b) and not under s 36(6) so that the limitation does not apply.

3.15 The statutory requirements concerning the directions to be given by beneficiaries are contained in the Trusts of Land and Appointment of Trustees Act 1996, s 21(1)[1].

1   See para 3.27 below.

Position of the trustees

3.16

(a)   Despite the provisions of the Trusts of Land and Appointment of Trustees Act 1996, s 19, the ordinary powers of appointing replacement or additional trustees which (subject to the existence of 'nominated person') are exercisable under the Trustee Act 1925, s 36(1)(b) by the existing trustees continue to apply.

(b)   A trustee served with a notice under s 19(2)(a) (ie with a direction to retire) is entitled to remain in office until reasonable arrangements have been made for his protection[1]. Note that such arrangements must have been concluded: it is not sufficient for them merely to have been proposed[2]. The arrangements in question would normally include:

(i)   reimbursement of expenses incurred;

(ii)   an indemnity against contractual liabilities incurred by the trustees to third parties;

(iii)   an indemnity against tax liabilities of the trust for the period when the retiring trustee was a trustee (together with some protection against a possible capital gains tax liability under the Taxation of Chargeable Gains Act 1992, s 82)[3];

(iv)   an indemnity for contingent and future liabilities in a case where he would have a right of retention against the trust fund.

Normally when a trustee retires it is the continuing trustees who will give him a suitable indemnity. Will those trustees be willing to co-operate in cases where the trustee is being removed under s 19? It is difficult to see that they can be forced to co-operate but does that mean that the trustee removed under s 19 is forced to rely on his continuing equitable charge over the trust property in respect of future and contingent liablilities[4]?

(c)   If a trustee is served with a direction to retire, the Trusts of Land and Appointment of Trustees Act 1996, s 19(3)(c) and 19(3)(d) are similarly worded to the existing rules on retirement contained in the Trustee Act 1925, s 39 ('retirement of trustee without new appointment')[5]. However, there are differences, and it appears that the retirement takes effect under s 19(3) rather than under the Trustee Act 1925, s 39. Note, in particular, that the consent of the continuing trustees is not necessary if another person is appointed on his retirement[6].

1   Trusts of Land and Appointment of Trustees Act 1996, s 19(3)(b).
2   See the House of Lords Report Stage at 571 HL Official Report (5th series) col 964, 22 April 1996; House of Lords Third Reading at 572 HL Official Report (5th series) col 98, 7 May 1996.
3   See the Taxation of Chargeable Gains Act 1992, s 82(3) and SP 5/92 para 5. For a deed of retirement by a trustee pursuant to the Trusts of Land and Appointment of Trustees Act 1996, s 19(3) see **Precedent 18** below. For an indemnity clause see **Precedent 22** below.
4   See generally '*The Proper Protection by liens etc of those who cease to be trustees*' (Trust Law Commission Consultative Paper, Dec 1999).
5   Retirement is permitted under the Trustee Act 1925, s 39 provided that:

(i)   after the retiring trustee's discharge there will be either a trust corporation or at least two persons to perform the trust: note that s 39(1) formerly referred to two 'individuals'; 'persons' was substituted by the Trusts of Land and Appointment of Trustees Act 1996, Sch 3, para 3(13) and the implications, especially for offshore trusts, are considered at para 6.70 below;

(ii)   the retiring trustee's co-trustees, and the person (if any) entitled to appoint new trustees, consent by deed to his retirement; and

(iii) the power in the Trustee Act 1925, s 39 is not negatived by the trust instrument: s 69(2).

Special rules regulate the retirement of a judicial trustee (Judicial Trustees Act 1896, s 4) and the retirement of a trustee when the continuing trustee is the Public Trustee (Public Trustee Act 1906, s 5(2)).

6   See further para 3.18 below.

Vesting of trust property

3.17   The retiring trustee must (along with the continuing trustees) do all in his power to vest the trust property in the continuing trustees[1]. There are automatic vesting provisions in the Trustee Act 1925, s 40[2], although in view of the exclusions (notably stocks and shares)[3] an express transfer or conveyance of property into the continuing trustees' names is commonly required. There is no provision dealing with the appointment of additional trustees as a result of a section 19 direction, presumably TA 1925, s 37(1)(d) which is in similar terms will apply. If difficulties arise, for example if the continuing trustees are uncooperative, a vesting order may need to be obtained.

1   Trusts of Land and Appointment of Trustees Act 1996, s 19(4).
2   Trustee Act 1925, s 40 as amended by the Trusts of Land and Appointment of Trustees Act 1996, Sch 3, para 3(14).
3   Trustee Act 1925, s 40(4).

Mandatory force of any direction

3.18   The position of trustees served with a valid direction is that they are given no option (subject only to reasonable arrangements being concluded under the Trusts of Land and Appointment of Trustees Act 1996, s 19(3)(b)) but to retire. Similarly, continuing trustees appear to have no option but to comply with a direction. In exercising the powers under these provisions, the beneficiaries are not acting in a fiduciary capacity[1]. Accordingly, it is thought that even if a new trustee chosen by the beneficiaries appears to be wholly unsuitable, the trustees have no choice but to make the appointment in accordance with the direction given[2].

1   An express power to remove trustees is considered to be fiduciary: see *IRC v Schroder* [1983] STC 480; *Von Knieriem v Bermuda Trust Co Ltd ('Star Trusts')* [1994] 1 Offshore Cases and Materials 116.

2   Of course the new trustee must be capable of acting: he cannot, for example, be a minor (if he lacks mental capacity, the s 20 power may be used by the beneficiaries). However, the restriction in the Trustee Act 1925, s 36(6) as amended by the Trusts of Land and Appointment of Trustees Act 1996, Sch 3, para 3(11) that the appointor cannot appoint himself as an additional trustee does not apply to appointments under the Trusts of Land and Appointment of Trustees Act 1996, s 19.

Source of the power

3.19   The Trusts of Land and Appointment of Trustees Act 1996, s 19(2)(b) simply refers to a written direction to the existing trustees to appoint, by writing, a person specified in the direction. Section 19(2)(b) of the Act does not, in terms, confer a power of appointment on those trustees. In many cases, the appointment could be made under the Trustee Act 1925, s 36[1], but what if that provision has been excluded? In such a case, to prevent s 19(2)(b) being wholly without effect, the courts will be forced to conclude that there is an implicit power to appoint in s 19[2].

1   Trustee Act 1925, s 36 as amended by the Trusts of Land and Appointment of Trustees Act 1996, Sch 3, para 3(11).

2   See further the discussion of the Trusts of Land and Appointment of Trustees Act 1996, s 20 where the problem is even more starkly presented. The Lord Chancellor's Department in correspondence with the authors confirmed that Part II of the Act is not (unlike the original provisions in the Bill) linked to the Trustee Act 1925, s 36. Instead, the power to appoint new or additional trustees is conferred by 'necessary implication' by Part II itself. At Report Stage, Lord Mackay observed that 'the new clause [ie the Trusts of Land and Appointment of Trustees Act 1996, s 19] operates independently rather than by reference back to the Trustee Act 1925, and so certain aspects of s 36 of that Act must be spelt out since they are no longer incorporated by reference': House of Lords Report Stage at 571 HL Official Report (5th series) col 964, 22 April 1996. See also the extension of the Trustee Act 1925, s 36(7): para 3.29 below.

Section 20 – Appointment of Substitute for Incapable Trustee

3.20   Text of section 20

(1)   This section applies where—

    (a)   a trustee is incapable by reason of mental disorder of exercising his functions as trustee,

    (b)   there is no person who is both entitled and willing and able to appoint a trustee in place of him under section 36(1) of the Trustee Act 1925, and

    (c)   the beneficiaries under the trust are of full age and capacity and (taken together) are absolutely entitled to the property subject to the trust.

(2)   The beneficiaries may give to—

    (a)   a receiver of the trustee,

    (b)   an attorney acting for him under the authority of a power of attorney created by an instrument which is registered under section 6 of the Enduring Powers of Attorney Act 1985, or

(c)   a person authorised for the purpose by the authority having jurisdiction under Part VII of the Mental Health Act 1983,

a written direction to appoint by writing the person or persons specified in the direction to be a trustee or trustees in place of the incapable trustee.

Replacement of an incapable trustee

3.21   Section 20 is concerned with the appointment of one or more replacement trustees for an incapable trustee[1]. It only applies if there is no person both entitled and willing and able to make such an appointment under the Trustee Act 1925, s 36[2]. If there are other trustees, then it would be surprising (and a cause for criticism) if they did not take steps under the Trustee Act 1925, s 36(1)(b) to make the replacement appointment themselves. This provision is, therefore, aimed at the situation where the incapable trustee is the sole (surviving) trustee.

1   As defined by the Trusts of Land and Appointment of Trustees Act 1996, s 20(1)(a). This section may be excluded: see para 3.31 below.
2   There is authority that if a nominated person cannot be found (*Cradock v Witham* [1895] WN 75) or if such persons disagree (*Re Sheppard's Settlement Trusts* [1888] WN 234) there is then no person able and willing to make an appointment. The section may apply if there is some person who is entitled, able and willing to make an appointment under an *express* power.

Conditions to be satisfied by beneficiaries

3.22   The conditions to be satisfied by beneficiaries before they are able to replace an incapable trustee are the same as in the Trusts of Land and Appointment of Trustees Act 1996, s 19[1].

1   See the Trusts of Land and Appointment of Trustees Act 1996, s 20(1)(c) and para 3.8 above.

Who is directed to make the appointment?

3.23   A written direction[1] is to be given to certain persons acting on behalf of the incapable trustee, requiring them to appoint a particular person, or persons, as trustee or trustees; namely:

(a)   a receiver of the trustee;

(b)   an attorney acting under a registered power under the Enduring Powers of Attorney Act 1985; or

(c)   a person authorised under the Mental Health Act 1983, Pt VII.

1   'Written directions' are considered further in the discussion of the Trusts of Land and Appointment of Trustees Act 1996, s 21: see para 3.26 ff below.

How is the appointment made?

3.24   The question of by what authority an appointment can be made under the Trusts of Land and Appointment of Trustees Act 1996 has been addressed in the context of s 19 of the Act[1]. In the case of s 20, it is assumed that the person receiving a written direction in accordance with s 20(2) will make the appointment; for s 20 to have any force, the relevant authority must implicitly be conferred in s 20 itself, given that that person will have no authority under the Trustee Act 1925, s 36[2].

1   See para 3.19 above.
2   Trustee Act 1925, s 36 as amended by the Trusts of Land and Appointment of Trustees Act 1996, Sch 3, para 3(11).

Omissions?

3.25   The Trusts of Land and Appointment of Trustees Act 1996, s 20 raises a number of difficulties; for example:

(a)   in a case where the automatic vesting of trust property under the Trustee Act 1925, s 40[1] does not apply (for example, stocks and shares), there is no provision in the section enabling the person who receives the direction (or indeed anyone else) to act on behalf of the incapable trustee in vesting the trust property in the names of the replacement(s). It is thought that an attorney under a registered enduring power may make the necessary property transfer on the basis, not that he is acting as a trustee, but that he is carrying out an administrative act for the *former* trustee;

(b)   whilst trustees who are replaced under the Trusts of Land and Appointment of Trustees Act 1996, s 19 are entitled to an indemnity under s 19(3)(b), there is no equivalent provision for the incapable trustee under s 20 of the Act;

(c)   although s 20 permits the giving of a written direction to the persons listed in s 20(2), it does not require those persons to act on that direction[2]!

1   Trustee Act 1925, s 40 as amended by the Trusts of Land and Appointment of Trustees Act 1996, Sch 3, para 3(14).
2   The Trusts of Land and Appointment of Trustees Act 1996, s 19 is likewise silent in relation to directions under s 19(2)(b): it is only the 'retiring' trustee who is expressly required to comply.

Section 21 – Supplementary

3.26   Text of section 21

(1)   For the purposes of section 19 or 20 a direction is given by beneficiaries if—

     (a)   a single direction is jointly given by all of them, or

     (b)   (subject to subsection (2)) a direction is given by each of them (whether solely or jointly with one or more, but not all, of the others),

     and none of them by writing withdraws the direction given by him before it has been complied with.

(2)   Where more than one direction is given each must specify for appointment or retirement the same person or persons.

(3)   Subsection (7) of section 36 of the Trustee Act 1925 (powers of trustees appointed under that section) applies to a trustee appointed under section 19 or 20 as if he were appointed under that section.

(4)   A direction under section 19 or 20 must not specify a person or persons for appointment if the appointment of that person or those persons would be in contravention of section 35(1) of the Trustee Act 1925 or section 24(1) of the Law of Property Act 1925 (requirements as to identity of trustees).

(5)   Sections 19 and 20 do not apply in relation to a trust created by a disposition in so far as provision that they do not apply is made by the disposition.

(6)   Sections 19 and 20 do not apply in relation to a trust created before the commencement of this Act by a disposition in so far as provision to the effect that they do not apply is made by a deed executed—

(a)   in a case in which the trust was created by one person and he is of full capacity, by that person, or

(b)   in a case in which the trust was created by more than one person, by such of the persons who created the trust as are alive and of full capacity.

(7)   A deed executed for the purposes of subsection (6) is irrevocable.

(8)   Where a deed is executed for the purposes of subsection (6)—

(a)   it does not affect anything done before its execution to comply with a direction under section 19 or 20, but

(b)   a direction under section 19 or 20 which has been given but not complied with before its execution shall cease to have effect.

Unanimity

3.27   Given that the beneficiaries must be unanimous, any direction on behalf of individual beneficiaries must specify that the same person, or persons, are to retire and/or the same person, or persons, are to be appointed. Whilst it is obviously convenient for a single written direction to be signed by all beneficiaries, this is not a requirement[1].

1   Trusts of Land and Appointment of Trustees Act 1996, s 21(1). The Act contains no provisions concerning when a direction is treated as having been communicated etc (contrast the Law of Property Act 1925, s 196).

Withdrawal of direction

3.28   Any beneficiary can (in writing) withdraw his direction[1] (whether this direction was given in a joint document signed by all the beneficiaries or in a separate document) at any time before it has been acted upon (ie before a trustee has retired and/or a new trustee appointed). During the passage of the Trusts of Land and Appointment of Trustees Act 1996 through Parliament, it was felt that there could be cases where one beneficiary exercised an excessive influence on the others in persuading them to agree to sign a direction removing trustees. It was considered proper, therefore, to permit a beneficiary to change his mind; for example, after discussing the position with the trustee in question[2].

1   For a notice to trustees of withdrawal of a direction see **Precedent 21** below.
2   House of Lords Committee Stage at 570 HL Official Report (5th series) col 1549, 25 March 1996.

Extension of provisions

3.29   Because ss 19 and 20 are wholly independent of the Trustee Act 1925, s 36, it was necessary to extend expressly the provisions of the Trustee Act 1925, s 36(7) (new trustees have vested in them all trust powers etc) to those appointed under the Trusts of Land and Appointment of Trustees Act 1996[1].

1   Trusts of Land and Appointment of Trustees Act 1996, s 21(3).

Appointing new trustees of settlements and trusts for sale

3.30   The amendments to the Trustee Act 1925, s 35(1) made by the Trusts of Land and Appointment of Trustees Act 1996, Sch 3, para 3(10), and to the Law of Property Act 1925, s 24 made by the Trusts of Land and Appointment of Trustees Act 1996, Sch 3, para 4(7) should be noted[1].

1   For a consideration of the continuing use of two instruments see para 6.47 above.

Excluding sections 19 and 20

3.31

(a)   The Trusts of Land and Appointment of Trustees Act 1996, ss 19 and 20 can be excluded expressly (in whole or in part) in any disposition creating the trust. This enables all trusts coming into effect on or after 1 January 1997 (whether created *inter vivos* or by will) to exclude these provisions[1].

(b)   So far as trusts created before 1 January 1997 are concerned, ss 19 and 20 of the Act will apply unless the settlor, being of full capacity, by deed provides for their exclusion[2]. If there is more than one settlor, the sections can be excluded provided that suitable deeds are executed by those of the settlors who are alive and of full capacity[3]. Crucially, therefore, the position with regard to existing trusts is the exact opposite from that which applies to, for example, consultation under Part I of the Act (the provisions do not apply unless a deed executed by the settlor etc expressly so provides)[4]. In the case of a will trust coming into effect before 1 January 1997, the provisions of this Part must always apply.

(c)   Deeds executed by settlors in these circumstances are irrevocable[5].

1   Trusts of Land and Appointment of Trustees Act 1996, s 21(5). For a clause for insertion in a disposition excluding the provisions of ss 19, 20 see **Precedent 24** below.
2   Trusts of Land and Appointment of Trustees Act 1996, s 21(6). For a deed excluding the provisions of ss 19, 20 see **Precedent 24** below.

3   If property is added to an existing trust does the person making the addition become a
    settlor and hence a person able to exclude these sections in respect of that trust?
4   See para 2.119 above.
5   Trusts of Land and Appointment of Trustees Act 1996, s 21(7).

Review of wills

3.32   Existing wills, where the testator is still alive, should be reviewed to
consider whether the Trusts of Land and Appointment of Trustees Act 1996,
ss 19 and 20 should be excluded.

No time limit

3.33   For existing trusts there is no time limit, or transitional period,
within which the settlor must act if he wishes to exclude the Trusts of Land
and Appointment of Trustees Act 1996, ss 19 and 20. Section 21(8) of the Act
recognises that before a deed of exclusion is executed, beneficiaries may have
exercised their powers under ss 19 and 20. If those directions have already
been acted upon by the trustees before an excluding deed is executed, the
execution of that deed does not undo what has been done. By contrast, if the
direction has not been acted upon it ceases to have effect.

EXAMPLE 2

S established a family trust on 1 January 1990. His son is life tenant,
and grandson the remainderman, and the trust does not give any
person an express power to appoint trustees. Both are of full age and
immediately on commencement of the Trusts of Land and Appointment
of Trustees Act 1996 they directed the existing trustees (Bill and Ben) to
retire in favour of themselves. Bill and Ben were unhappy at this
proposal and wrote to S who immediately executed a deed under the
Trusts of Land and Appointment of Trustees Act 1996, s 21(6) thereby
ensuring that the directions were of no effect. Contrast the position if
Bill and Ben had complied with the directions and only subsequently
had S become aware of what had happened. The beneficiaries having
become trustees could not be removed by the settlor.

4

Part III: Supplementary

Section 22 – Meaning of 'Beneficiary'

4.1   Text of section 22

(1)   In this Act 'beneficiary', in relation to a trust, means any person who under the trust has an interest in property subject to the trust (including a person who has such an interest as a trustee or a personal representative).

(2)   In this Act references to a beneficiary who is beneficially entitled do not include a beneficiary who has an interest in property subject to the trust only by reason of being a trustee or personal representative.

(3)   For the purposes of this Act a person who is a beneficiary only by reason of being an annuitant is not to be regarded as entitled to an interest in possession in land subject to the trust.

Basic definitions

4.2   Beneficiaries enjoy various rights and have various powers under the 1996 Act. In some sections it is sufficient for a person to be a beneficiary simpliciter: in others, he must enjoy an interest in possession in land subject to the trust. Some of the permutations are set out below.

(a)   The basic definition in the s 22(1) is 'any person who under the trust has an interest in property subject to the trust'. It is explicitly stated that trustees and personal representatives may satisfy this requirement: ie trustees of a sub-trust and personal representatives of a dead benefici- ary. It is thought that beneficiaries of a sub-trust do not fall within the definition: it may well be the case that the trustees of the main trust have no details of such persons and therefore it would be inappropriate for them to be included[1].

The interest has to be in 'property' subject to the trust (not necessarily in land); this, of course, is relevant in the context of Part II of the Act which is not limited to trusts of land.

The main question to be considered in relation to this definition is whether it is wide enough to embrace the objects of a discretionary trust or power (see para 4.4 below).

Beneficiaries under the Trusts of Land and Appointment
of Trustees Act 1996

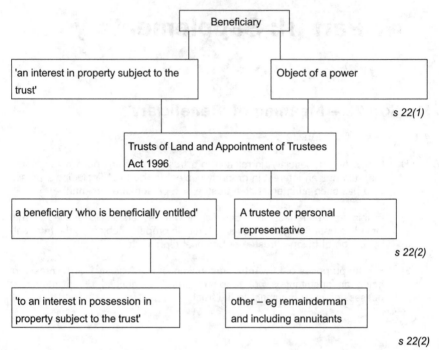

The requirement that the interest must arise 'under the trust' excludes secured creditors, but it is thought that it is wide enough to include the purchaser of a beneficial interest (since that interest arises 'under the trust').

(b)   When the Act refers to a beneficiary who is beneficially entitled, s 22(2) confirms that this will exclude personal representatives and trustees. Assume, for example, that land is held on trust for A and B as beneficial tenants in common. On the death of B his personal representatives, although constituting a 'beneficiary' under s 22(1), are not beneficially entitled.

(c)   When the Act refers to a beneficiary who is entitled to an interest in possession in land subject to the trust, s 22(3) excludes annuitants. The main issue for consideration in this situation is whether an 'interest in possession' otherwise bears the limited meaning given to that phrase by the House of Lords in the capital transfer tax/inheritance tax case of *Pearson v IRC*[2].

1   This view has been adopted in relation to a beneficiary's rights under s 12: see para 2.124 above. Of course, if a broad view was taken then it could be argued that the original disposition into trust and the sub-trust should be considered together as constituting the trusts which effect the property but this is considered unlikely.

2   *Pearson v IRC* [1981] AC 753, [1980] 2 All ER 479, HL.

References to terms in the Act

4.3

Beneficiary	Beneficiary entitled to an interest in possession
Section 6(2)[1]	
Section 6(5)	
Section 7(1)[2]	
	Section 9
	Section 11
	Sections 12,13
Section 14	
Sections 19, 20	

1   In both cases (albeit the position of the Trusts of Land and Appointment of Trustees Act 1996, s 6(2) is not free from all doubt: see para 2.45 above) the beneficiaries must be of full age who are together absolutely entitled in undivided shares to the land.

2   Wider than just beneficiaries; 'any person' includes secured creditors.

The position of beneficiaries or objects of a discretionary trust

4.4   Beneficiaries of a discretionary trust are usually considered to have the following rights:

(a)   to be considered by the trustees before they exercise their (dispositive) discretions;

(b)   to ensure that the trust is properly administered, to see all trust documents and, if necessary, bring an action for breach of trust[1]; and

(c)   to join together (provided that all can be ascertained and are *sui juris*) and bring the trust to an end[2].

1   See *Re Londonderry's Settlement, Peat v Walsh* [1965] Ch 918, [1964] 3 All ER 855, CA.

2   *Re Smith, Public Trustee v Aspinall* [1928] Ch 915. A distinction may, however, be drawn between the distinction of objects of a *mere power* and of a *trust power*. Under the latter the donee of the power (usually the trustees) can do no more than make a selection since the class of beneficiaries is to make in any event. By contrast, in the case of a mere power, the objects may take nothing since there will usually be provisions (in favour of other persons) which take effect in the event that the power is not exercised. Unless and until the power is exercised in their favour it is difficult to see that the objects of a mere power are interested in the property subject to the trust. For the rights of trust beneficiaries to information etc, see 'Rights of beneficiaries to information regarding a trust', (Jersey Law Commission Final Report, October 1998) and *Re Rabaiotti's Settlements* [2000] WTLR 953.

4.5   Unlike beneficiaries under a fixed interest trust, beneficiaries of a discretionary trust do not enjoy an interest in trust assets (in the sense of a right to enjoy). The leading case in which the nature of the rights of a discretionary beneficiary was analysed is *Gartside v IRC*[1] in which the Inland Revenue claimed that such beneficiaries enjoyed either an interest in the trust fund or an interest in possession for estate duty purposes. The House of Lords unanimously rejected that argument. The two fully argued speeches (by Lords Reid and Wilberforce) stressed that the issue for consideration had arisen in the context of fiscal legislation; as Lord Wilberforce commented[2]:

'We are concerned here with a taxing Act, and if one thing is necessary about taxes it is that the amount of them should be ascertained with precision. The subsection must, then, contemplate that some definite portion of the property should be ascertainable when an interest ceases.'

1   *Gartside v IRC* [1968] AC 553, [1968] 1 All ER 121, HL.
2   *Gartside v IRC* above at 616 and 133.

4.6   The setting in which the rights of discretionary beneficiaries were being reviewed by the House was therefore crucial and difficulties in quantifying the interest of a discretionary beneficiary for taxing purposes are obviously considerable[1]. In a key passage, Lord Wilberforce further commented as follows[2]:

'It can be accepted that 'interest' is capable of a very wide and general meaning. But the wide spectrum that it covers makes it all the more necessary, if precise conclusions are to be founded upon its use, to place it in a setting: Viscount Radcliffe, delivering the Board's judgment in *Stamp Duties Comr (Queensland) v Livingston*[3] shows how this word has to do duty in several quite different legal contexts to express rights of very different characters, and that to transfer a meaning from one context to another may breed confusion.

No doubt in a certain sense a beneficiary under a discretionary trust has an 'interest': the nature of it may, sufficiently for the purpose, be spelt out by saying that he has a right to be considered as a potential recipient of benefit by the trustees and a right to have his interest protected by a court of equity. Certainly that is so, and when it is said that he has a right to have the trustees exercise their discretion 'fairly' or 'reasonably' or 'properly' that indicates clearly enough that some objective consideration (not stated explicitly in declaring the discretionary trust, but latent in it) must be applied by the trustees and that the right is more than a mere spes. But that does not mean that he has an interest which is capable of being taxed by reference to its extent in the trust fund's income: it may be a right with some degree of concreteness or solidity, one which attracts the protection of a court of equity, yet it may still lack the necessary quality of definable extent which must exist before it can be taxed.'

1   See, for example, the procedure adopted in the Finance Act 1969, s 36 which inserted s 2(1)(b)(iii) into the Finance Act 1894.
2   *Gartside v IRC* above at 617 and 134.
3   *Stamp Duties Comr (Queensland) v Livingston* [1965] AC 694, [1964] 3 All ER 692, PC.

4.7   In the context of the Trusts of Land and Appointment of Trustees Act 1996, the issue is whether discretionary beneficiaries (meaning specifically the objects of a trust power) have a sufficient interest in the trust property:

(a)   for the trustees to be required to have regard to their rights under s 6(5) in the exercise of their statutory powers under s 6(1);

(b) to be able to apply to the court under s 14; and

(c) to be able collectively to exercise the powers of appointment and retirement of trustees under ss 19 and 20.

4.8 In all three contexts it would be hard to justify excluding such a beneficiary. Arguably, s 6(5) does no more than confirm an already existing equitable duty; the category of applicant under s 14 is intended to embrace all persons concerned in the trust of land (including secured creditors, personal representatives and sub-trustees); whilst it would be rare in any event for the discretionary beneficiaries collectively to be in a position to use the Part II power. The authors are therefore of the opinion that a discretionary beneficiary is, for the purposes of this Act, 'a person who under the trust has an interest in property subject to the trust'.

Meaning of an 'interest in possession'

(1) Background to Pearson v IRC[1]

4.9 As the Table set out in para 4.3 above shows, the crucial rights under the Act are given to beneficiaries who enjoy an 'interest in possession' in the land subject to the trusts: the meaning of this term is therefore fundamental to the operation of the legislation. In recent years, it has been widely used in tax legislation stemming from the capital transfer tax legislation introduced in the Finance Act 1975 which is now consolidated in the Inheritance Tax Act 1984. For the purpose of inheritance tax, the treatment of settlements depends upon the existence or otherwise of an interest in possession. A beneficiary who enjoys an interest in possession in trust property is treated as the owner of the capital in which his interest subsists[2], with the result that on his death that capital is taxed as part of his death estate. By contrast, a settlement which lacks an interest in possession is treated as a separate taxable entity with inheritance tax being levied at ten yearly intervals on the then value of the settled property and with interim charges (commonly referred to as 'exit' charges) when property ceases to be held on such trusts[3].

1 *Pearson v IRC* [1981] AC 753, [1980] 2 All ER 479, HL.
2 Inheritance Tax Act 1984, s 49.
3 Inheritance Tax Act 1984, ss 58–85.

4.10 Given these two radically different regimes, it is crucial to be able to identify circumstances when an interest in possession exists and it is against this background that the House of Lords decision in *Pearson v IRC* must be approached. Broadly speaking, that decision is to the effect that 'grey areas' are to be treated as falling into the 'non-interest in possession' category of trust. If the prime goal in all taxation matters is certainty, then there is little doubt that this has been provided by the decision.

(2) The decision in Pearson v IRC[1]

4.11 The facts of the case were simple. Both capital and income of the fund were held on trust for the settlor's three adult daughters in equal shares, subject to three overriding powers exercisable by the trustees:

(a)   to appoint capital and income amongst the daughters, their spouses and issue;

(b)   to accumulate so much of the income as they should think fit; and

(c)   to apply any income towards the payment or discharge of any taxes, costs or other outgoings which would otherwise be payable out of capital.

1   *Pearson v IRC* [1981] AC 753, [1980] 2 All ER 479, HL.

4.12   The trustees regularly exercised their powers to accumulate the income and what caused the disputed tax assessment was the irrevocable appointment of some £16,000 from the fund to one of the daughters. There was no doubt that, as a result of the appointment, the daughter obtained an interest in possession in the appointed sum; but did she already have such an interest under the original terms of the trust? If so, no inheritance tax would be chargeable on the appointment: if not, there would be a charge because the £16,000 would cease to be held on a 'no interest in possession' trust.

4.13   The Inland Revenue contended that the existence of the overriding power to accumulate, and the provision enabling all expenses to be charged to income, deprived the settlement of any interest in possession. It was common ground that whether such powers had been exercised or not was irrelevant in deciding the case. The overriding power of appointment over capital and income was not seen as endangering the existence of any interest in possession.

4.14   For the bare majority of the House of Lords, the presence of the overriding discretion to accumulate the income was fatal to the existence of any interest in possession. 'A present right to present enjoyment' was how an interest in possession was defined and the beneficiaries in this case did not have such a present right. 'Their enjoyment of any income from the trust fund depended on the trustees' decision as to the accumulation of income' (per Viscount Dilhorne), and the majority refused to draw any distinction between a trust to pay income to a beneficiary (with an overriding power to accumulate) and a trust to accumulate (with power to pay). Therefore, in the following examples there is no interest in possession:

(a)   to A for life but the trustees may accumulate the income; and

(b)   income shall be accumulated but the trustees may make payments to A.

4.15   For there to be an interest in possession, the beneficiary had to be entitled to income as it arose. Were this test to be applied strictly, however, even a trust with a life tenant receiving income might fail to satisfy the requirement, because the trustees may always deduct management expenses from income so that few beneficiaries are entitled to the gross income as it arises. This problem was considered by Viscount Dilhorne as follows:

'Parliament distinguished between the administration of a trust and the dispositive powers of trustees . . . A life tenant has an interest in posses-sion but his interest only extends to the net income of the property, that is to say, after deduction from the gross income of expenses etc properly incurred in the management of the trust by the trustees in the exercise of their powers. A dispositive power is a power to dispose of the net income. Sometimes the line between an administrative and a dispositive power may be difficult to draw but that does not mean that there is not a valid distinction.'

4.16   In *Pearson v IRC* the trustees had an overriding discretion to apply income towards the payment of any taxes, costs, or other outgoings which would otherwise be payable out of capital, and the Inland Revenue took the view that the existence of this overriding power was a further reason for the settlement to lack an interest in possession. Was this power administrative (in which case its presence did not affect the existence of any interest in possession) or dispositive (fatal to the existence of such an interest)? Viscount Dilhorne decided that the power was administrative. It should, however, be stressed that the House of Lords did not have to decide whether the Revenue's contention was correct or not: Viscount Dilhorne's observations were therefore obiter and it is notable that the Inland Revenue still adheres to its original view[1].

1   An Inland Revenue Press Notice dated 12 February 1976 provides as follows:

> '. . . an interest in settled property exists where the person having the interest has the immediate entitlement (subject to any prior claims by the trustees for expenses or other outgoings properly payable out of income) to any income produced by that property as the income arises; but . . . a discretion or power, in whatever form, which can be exercised after income arises so as to withhold it from that person negatives the existence of an interest in possession. For this purpose a power to accumulate income is regarded as a power to withhold it, unless any accumulation must be held solely for the person having the interest or his personal representatives.

> On the other hand the existence of a mere power of revocation or appointment, the exercise of which would determine the interest wholly or in part (but which, so long as it remains unexercised, does not affect the beneficiary's immediate entitlement to income) does not . . . prevent the interest from being an interest in possession.'

> Broadly speaking the decision in *Pearson v IRC* above is on all fours with the statements expressed in this notice.

(3)   What is the meaning of 'interest in possession' in the context of the Trusts of Land and Appointment of Trustees Act 1996?

4.17   According to the Lord Chancellor's Department, the decisions in *Pearson v IRC*[1] and *Gartside v IRC*[2] were in the minds of those responsible for drafting the Trusts of Land and Appointment of Trustees Act 1996. These cases will certainly provide a starting point in looking at the meaning of the words in the context of the Act: as with the discussion of the position of the discretionary beneficiary[3], however, it may be that in the different context of the Act a slightly different meaning will be given to the words. The authors believe that the position is as follows:

(a)   The term 'an interest in possession' is primarily used by way of contrast to 'an interest in remainder'. Both may be vested, but the latter is merely vested in interest whilst the former is in possession[4].

(b)   An annuitant, who would normally be considered to have an interest in possession, is for the purposes of the Trusts of Land and Appointment of Trustees Act 1996 excluded[5].

(c)   *Pearson v IRC* divided the judiciary: the taxpayers had been successful before the High Court and before a majority in the Court of Appeal, but lost by a bare majority decision in the House of Lords (two Law Lords finding in their favour but three against). Lord Keith, for the majority, stressed that 'in the end it comes down to a question of ascertaining the meaning intended by the legislature to be attached to the expression "interest in possession" in the particular context of Finance Act 1975. . . . this seems to me to require that the concept of interest in possession should in this context be a clear and definite one'[6].

1   *Pearson v IRC* [1981] AC 753, [1980] 2 All ER 479, HL.
2   *Gartside v IRC* [1968] AC 553, [1968] 1 All ER 121, HL.
3   As to the position of beneficiaries of a discretionary trust, see para 4.4 above.
4   *Preston's Elementary Treatise on Estates* (2nd edn, 1820) p 89 declares that an interest in possession gives 'a present right of present enjoyment' as contrasted with an estate in remainder conferring merely 'a right of future enjoyment'. In *Fearne's Contingent Remainders* (10th edn, 1844) vol 1 p 2, it is stated that an estate is vested when there is an immediate fixed right of present or future enjoyment; that an estate is vested in possession when there exists a right of present enjoyment; that an estate is vested in interest when there is a present fixed right of future enjoyment; and that an estate is contingent when a right of enjoyment is to accrue on an event which is dubious and uncertain. See further the speech of Viscount Dilhorne in *Pearson v IRC* at p 772 and 484 and SLA 1925, s 20.
5   See the Trusts of Land and Appointment of Trustees Act 1996 ,s 22(3) and the discussion of pension trusts at para 6.57 below.
6   *Pearson v IRC* at p 785 and 494.

4.18   Do the same factors apply in the 1996 Act? The particular benefits conferred on interest in possession beneficiaries are:

(i)   the right to be consulted under s 11;

(ii)   the ability to exercise the delegated powers of the trustees under s 9; and

(iii) the right to occupy trust property under s 12.

4.19   In none of these situations is there is any justification for giving the words an unduly restricted meaning. Unlike the position in the inheritance tax legislation therefore, it is suggested that in this Act grey areas (for example, the situation where trustees have an overriding power to accumulate income) should be considered to fall within the definition of an interest in possession.

Section 23 – Other Interpretation Provisions

4.20   Text of section 23

(1)   In this Act 'purchaser' has the same meaning as in Part I of the Law of Property Act 1925.

(2)   Subject to that, where an expression used in this Act is given a meaning by the Law of Property Act 1925 it has the same meaning as in that Act unless the context otherwise requires.

(3)   In this Act 'the court' means–

(a)   the High Court, or

(b)   a county court.

'Purchaser' defined

4.21   'Purchaser' under the Law of Property Act 1925 is defined as follows[1]:

' "Purchaser" means a purchaser in good faith for valuable consideration and includes a lessee, mortgagee or other person who for valuable consideration acquires an interest in property except that in Part I of this Act and elsewhere where so expressly provided "purchaser" only means a person who acquires an interest in or charge on property for money or money's worth; and in reference to a legal estate includes a chargee by way of legal mortgage; and where the context so requires "purchaser" includes an intending purchaser; "purchase" has a meaning corresponding with that of "purchaser"; and "valuable consideration" includes marriage but does not include a nominal consideration in money.'

1   Law of Property Act 1925, s 205(1)(xxi).

Registered land

4.22   So far as registered land is concerned, it is an essential feature of the system that a transferee is entitled to act in accordance with the information shown on the register and nothing else[1]. A major problem is therefore posed by 'overriding interests' which, although not contained in the register, nonetheless bind a purchaser[2].

1   See the Land Registration Act 1925, s 20 as amended by the Finance Act 1975, s 52(1), Sch 12 paras 2, 5(1), (2) for freeholds and the Land Registration Act 1925, s 23 as amended by the Finance Act 1975, s 52(1), Sch 12 paras 2, 5(1), (3) for leasehold interests: for the position where valuable consideration is not provided see the Land Registration Act 1925, ss 20(4) and 23(5).
2   See Gray *Elements of Land Law* (3rd edn, 2001) at p 971 ff.

Unregistered land

4.23   With the reduction in the number of legal estates, and the concept of overreaching, the legislative simplification, confirmed in 1925, has ensured that fragments of benefit (treated as equitable interests) are protected but are transferred into the purchase money whilst, at the same time, permitting the free alienation of land[1].

1   As to overreaching prior to the Trusts of Land and Appointment of Trustees Act 1996 see para 1.18 ff above. The overreaching mechanism is now extended to all trusts of land: see para 6.64 below.

Section 24 – Application to Crown

4.24   Text of section 24

(1)   Subject to subsection (2), this Act binds the Crown.

(2)   This Act (except so far as it relates to undivided shares and joint ownership) does not affect or alter the descent, devolution or nature of the estates and interests of or in–

   (a)   land for the time being vested in Her Majesty in right of the Crown or of the Duchy of Lancaster, or

   (b)   land for the time being belonging to the Duchy of Cornwall and held in right or respect of the Duchy.

Parliamentary statement

4.25   Introducing the Third Reading Debate in the House of Lords, the Lord Chancellor commented as follows:

'I have it in command from Her Majesty the Queen and His Royal Highness the Prince of Wales to acquaint the House that they, having been informed of the purport of the Trusts of Land and Appointment of Trustees Bill, have consented to place their prerogatives and interests, so far as they are affected by the Bill, at the disposal of Parliament for the purposes of the Bill[1].'

1   House of Lords Third Reading at 572 HL Official Report (5th series) col 94, 7 May 1996.

Section 25 – Amendments, Repeals etc

4.26   Text of section 25

(1)   The enactments mentioned in Schedule 3 have effect subject to the amendments specified in that Schedule (which are minor or consequential on other provisions of this Act).

(2)   The enactments mentioned in Schedule 4 are repealed to the extent specified in the third column of that Schedule.

(3)   Neither section 2(5) nor the repeal by this Act of section 29 of the Settled Land Act 1925 applies in relation to the deed of settlement set out in the Schedule to the Chequers Estate Act 1917 or the trust instrument set out in the Schedule to the Chevening Estate Act 1959.

(4)   The amendments and repeals made by this Act do not affect any entailed interest created before the commencement of this Act.

(5)   The amendments and repeals made by this Act in consequence of section 3–

   (a)   do not affect a trust created by a will if the testator died before the commencement of this Act, and

   (b)   do not affect personal representatives of a person who died before that commencement;

and the repeal of section 22 of the Partnership Act 1890 does not apply in any circumstances involving the personal representatives of a partner who died before that commencement.

Comments in Parliament

4.27   At the House of Lords Report Stage[1], the Lord Chancellor tabled amendments to the Bill which provided that land held on charitable, ecclesiastical or public trusts would cease to be subject to the Settled Land Act[2]. With reference to Chequers, and the Chevening Estate, he then commented as follows[3]:

> 'The changes effected by this group of amendments do not apply in relation to the deeds of settlement for the Chequers Estate and the trust instrument for the Chevening Estate, which are set out by statute. The settlements of those two estates are in a very unusual position in that they are not charitable, ecclesiastical or public trusts within Section 29 of the Settled Land Act so as to be part of the class of trusts which this group of amendments sets out to effect; but they are not "private" settlements in the ordinary sense either. Those responsible for administering these settlements believe it would be better for them to be treated for the purposes of the Bill like private settlements, so that they will remain subject to the Settled Land Act in the same way as at present, since it would be a very complex and delicate task to amend the statutory deeds.'

1   House of Lords Report Stage at 571 HL Official Report (5th series) cols 954-955, 22 April 1996.
2   See para 2.7 above and para 6.7 below.
3   House of Lords Report Stage at 571 HL Official Report (5th series) cols 955-956, 22 April 1996.

Section 26 – Power to Make Consequential Provision

4.28   Text of section 26

(1)   The Lord Chancellor may by order made by statutory instrument make any such supplementary, transitional or incidental provision as appears to him to be appropriate for any of the purposes of this Act or in consequence of any of the provisions of this Act.

(2)   An order under subsection (1) may, in particular, include provision modifying any enactment contained in a public general or local Act which is passed before, or in the same Session as, this Act.

(3)   A statutory instrument made in the exercise of the power conferred by this section is subject to annulment in pursuance of a resolution of either House of Parliament.

Purpose of section 26

4.29   The Trusts of Land and Appointment of Trustees Act 1996, s 26 gives the Lord Chancellor sweeping powers over all areas of English trusts and land law (subject to the rather unsatisfactory negative resolution procedure of Parliament). The justification offered for what at first sight would seem to be unwarrantedly wide powers is that the 1996 Act has an impact (albeit often minor) on many areas of legislation and therefore it is possible that minor tinkering (of the type illustrated by the repeals and amendments listed in Schedule 4) will be necessary (compare TA 2000, s 41.

Section 27 – Short Title, Commencement and Extent

4.30   Text of section 27

   (1)   This Act may be cited as the Trusts of Land and Appointment of Trustees Act 1996.

   (2)   This Act comes into force on such day as the Lord Chancellor appoints by order made by statutory instrument.

   (3)   Subject to subsection (4), the provisions of this Act extend only to England and Wales.

   (4)   The repeal in section 30(2) of the Agriculture Act 1970 extends only to Northern Ireland.

Commencement

4.31   The Trusts of Land and Appointment of Trustees Act 1996 came into force on 1 January 1997 by virtue of SI 1996/2974.

5

Schedules

Schedule 1 – Provisions Consequential on Section 2

5.1   Text of Schedule 1

The text of the Trusts of Land and Appointment of Trustees Act 1996, Sch 1 is set out in Appendix 2.

Purpose of Schedule 1

5.2   Schedule 1, which is consequential on s 2 of the Act, makes provision for situations which, under the Settled Land Act 1925, involve the imposition of a strict settlement. From 1 January 1997, a trust of land is imposed in the circumstances set out below.

Minors

5.3   Provision for minors is made in the Trusts of Land and Appointment of Trustees Act 1996, Sch 1, paras 1, 2. The position of minors is considered at para 6.31 ff below.

Family charges

5.4   Provision for family charges is made in the Trusts of Land and Appointment of Trustees Act 1996, Sch 1, para 3. These are cases where land is charged:

(a)   voluntarily;

(b)   in consideration of marriage; or

(c)   by way of family arrangement

with a rent charge for a person's life or with the payment of capital, annual or periodic sums to any person. Under the Settled Land Act 1925, s 1(1)(v), a strict settlement was imposed in all such cases[1]: as from 1 January 1997, there will instead be a declaration of trust with the land being held on trust to give effect to the charge[2]. A trustee may then either convey the land as encumbered by the charge or, alternatively, ensure that there is a second trustee so as to overreach the charge in accordance with the Law of Property Act 1925, s 2[3]. This change applies to instruments coming into operation after 1996.

1   This was done in order to provide a convenient way for the land to be sold with the purchaser being able to take free of the charge provided that the other formalities were observed.
2   For a discussion of the drafting of this provision see House of Lords Commitee Stage at 570 HL Official Report (5th series) cols 1554-1555, 25 March 1996.
3   Law of Property Act 1925 s 2 as amended by the Law of Property (Amendment) Act 1926, s 7, Schedule and by the Trusts of Land and Appointment of Trustees Act 1996, Sch 3, para 4(2).

Charitable, ecclesiastical and public trusts

5.5   Provision for charitable, ecclesiastical and public trusts is made in the Trusts of Land and Appointment of Trustees Act 1996, Sch 1, para 4. The position of these trusts is considered at para 6.7 ff below.

Entailed interests

5.6   Provision for entailed interests is made in the Trusts of Land and Appointment of Trustees Act 1996, Sch 1, para 5. The position of entailed interests is considered at para 6.24 ff below[1].

1   *Transfer of Land, Trusts of Land* (Law Com No 181) para 16.1 mistakenly states that 'entailed interests can only be constituted behind a strict settlement'. Hence their demise is included in this Schedule!

Position when a Settled Land Act settlement ends

5.7   Provision where property is held on a settlement ceasing to exist is made in the Trusts of Land and Appointment of Trustees Act 1996, Sch 1, para 6. The position is considered further at para 2.13 above.

Schedule 2 – Amendments of Statutory Provisions Imposing Trust for Sale

5.8   Text of schedule 2

The text of Sch 2 is set out in Appendix 2.

General

5.9   Schedule 2 is consequential upon s 5 and modifies certain statutory provisions which had imposed trusts for sale. From 1 January 1997, there has instead been a trust of land without any duty to sell: this change was effective in relation to existing statutory trusts as well as to new trusts arising on or after that date.

Mortgaged property held by trustees after redemption barred/land purchased by trustees of personal property etc – Schedule 2, paras 1, 2

5.10   The 1925 legislation ensured that land purchased by trustees of a personalty settlement, or by trustees of a trust for sale, was treated as held on trust for sale unless the settlement otherwise provided; for example, by directing that a house be used as a residence[1]. Similarly, if trustees had lent money on the security of a mortgage of land and the relevant property subsequently became vested in them freed from the equity of redemption (for example, by limitation, foreclosure or otherwise) then that land was held on trust for sale by those trustees[2]. In both cases, the character of the trust property as personalty was thereby preserved (in the case of a trust for sale via the doctrine of conversion) and the land was not caught in the provisions of the Settled Land Act 1925.

1   Law of Property Act 1925, s 32 (now repealed by the Trusts of Land and Appointment of Trustees Act 1996, Sch 4). Trustees for sale were thought to have power to reinvest the proceeds of sale of land in the purchase of other land; this power being derived from the Settled Land Act 1925, s 73(1)(xi) as impliedly incorporated in the Law of Property Act 1925, s 28(1) (now repealed by the Trusts of Land and Appointment of Trustees Act 1996, Sch 4). There was, however, the possibility of this power being lost if the trustees did not retain at least some land on the trusts for sale: see *Re Wakeman* [1945] Ch 177 at 181, but compare *Re Wellsted's Will Trusts* [1949] Ch 296 at 319, CA. This difficulty was solved as a result of the power in the Trusts of Land and Appointment of Trustees Act 1996, s 6(3) to purchase land being given to the trustees of the proceeds of sale of land: see s 17(1) (now repealed by TA 2000 and the equivalent power being given to all trustees by Part II of the Act).
2   Law of Property Act 1925, s 31 (amended by the Trusts of Land and Appointment of Trustees Act 1996, Sch 2, para 1, Sch 4).

5.11   The implied trust for sale was replaced by a trust of land. In the former case, the Law of Property Act 1925, s 32 was repealed in relation to land purchased after 31 December 1996; in the latter, the new system applied irrespective of when the right of redemption was discharged (although this did not affect dealings or arrangements made before 1 January 1997).

Statutory co-ownership – Schedule 2, paras 3, 4

5.12   The automatic imposition of a trust for sale in the case of co-ownership was one of the most criticised features of the 1925 legislation[1]. Accordingly, the Trusts of Land and Appointment of Trustees Act 1996, Sch 2, paras 3 and 4 replaced the statutory trusts for sale with a trust of land under which the trustees have a power (but no duty) to sell[2]. The following matters are worthy of note:

(a)   The change applies to statutory trusts already in existence as well as those coming into existence on or after 1 January 1997.

(b)   Apart from changes consequent upon the replacement of a trust for sale with a trust of land, no other changes of substance were made to the Law of Property Act 1925, ss 34 and 36[3]. Hence, the lacuna discussed at para 1.21 above still exists. Under the Trusts of Land and Appointment of Trustees Act 1996 it is quite clear, however, that situations such as that illustrated in *Bull v Bull*[4] will now fall under the definition of a trust of land in s 1 of the Act[5]. Whether that is on the basis that they are statutory trusts (as such cases suggested) or implied (or resulting) trusts no longer seems relevant.

(c)   Are there situations where it will still be desirable to create an express trust for sale in a conveyance to co-owners[6]?

1   As to co-ownership see para 1.4 above.
2   Trusts of Land and Appointment of Trustees Act 1996, s 5. The result is that beneficiaries enjoy interests in land (rather than in the proceeds of sale): this being emphasised by the abolition of the doctrine of conversion. As to the abolition of the doctrine of conversion, see para 2.18 above.
3   The Law of Property Act 1925, ss 34, 36 are amended by the Trusts of Land and Appointment of Trustees Act 1996, Sch 2, paras 3, 4, Sch 4. The Law of Property Act 1925, s 35 ('meaning of the statutory trusts') is repealed by the Trusts of Land and Appointment of Trustees Act 1996, Sch 4.
4   *Bull v Bull* [1955] 1 QB 234, [1955] 1 All ER 253, CA. See further paras 1.14 and 1.21 above.
5   See para 2.2 above.
6   See para 6.34 below.

Intestacy – Schedule 2, para 5

5.13   Prior to the Trusts of Land and Appointment of Trustees Act 1996 land (and personal property) forming part of an intestate's estate was subject to a trust for sale[1]. The position was different under testate succession where executors did not hold land (or indeed other property) on trust for sale unless such a trust was imposed in the will[2]. Personal representatives, however, were generally given wide powers (including the power of sale) under the Administration of Estates Act 1925, s 39[3] and it was thought that the administrator would act under that section until such time as he became a trustee and so fell under s 33 of the Act[4].

1   Administration of Estates Act 1925, s 33 (now amended by the Trusts of Land and Appointment of Trustees Act 1996, Sch 2, para 5).
2   As to the desirability of imposing an express trust for sale over a testator's residuary estate see para 6.40 below.
3   Administration of Estates Act 1925, s 39 as amended by the Trusts of Land and Appointment of Trustees Act 1996, Sch 3, para 6(2), Sch 4.
4   There is some uncertainty as to whether an assent is required at that stage.

5.14   In line with the abolition of other statutory trusts for sale, s 33(1) was amended so that the intestate's estate (whether comprised of realty or personalty) became held on trust with a power but no duty to sell. This change was effective from 1 January 1997, whether the death occurred before or after that date.

Reverter of Sites Act 1987 – Schedule 2, para 6

5.15   The Lord Chancellor commented upon the Reverter of Sites Act 1987 and the Trusts of Land and Appointment of Trustees Act 1996 changes made to it as follows[1]:

'Section 1 of the Reverter of Sites Act 1987 concerns any enactment (such as the School Sites Act) which provides for land to revert to the ownership of a particular person where that land was made available for particular purposes and has ceased to be used for those purposes. The land, instead of reverting, vests on trust in the persons in whom it was vested before the particular use ceased; and the trust in question is an express trust to sell the land and hold the net profits until sale and the net proceeds after costs and expenses on trust for the people who would, but for these provisions, be entitled to the land on reverter. The present amendments . . . substitute for this trust for sale a trust of land, with a power to sell and to retain, and a duty to consult certain beneficiaries. Practitioners in this specialised area . . . have, however, alerted my department to possible practical problems with this approach which the present group of amendments sets out to rectify.

The great advantage of the present provisions of Section 1 of the Reverter of Sites Act 1987 is that they make the position of trustees very clear and simple in cases where there are often no beneficiaries, only people claiming to be beneficiaries whose entitlement may be difficult to sort out. Irrespective of the identity of the beneficiaries, the trustees can sell the land, and out of the proceeds of sale, deduct all their costs and expenses and meet the capital gains tax liability which they have as trustees. They can sort out the difficult question of entitlement later, if necessary going to court for directions with the proceeds of sale available to cover their costs of doing so in good faith. . . . as amended by the Bill at present, however, the question of sale is neutral and there is a duty to consult.

The difficulty which has been identified is that the trustees are put at risk if they sell against the wishes of a claimant who asks for the land to be conveyed to him *in specie* but whose entitlement is in doubt. If that claimant's entitlement is subsequently established in court proceedings, he may sue for loss as a result of the land being sold rather than conveyed to him *in specie*. Trustees will also be faced with the difficulty that if claimants do not wish them to sell and there are difficult issues which need the directions of the court, they may have to incur the costs out of their own resources before they have any proceeds of sale out of which they can be paid.

In view of the fact that the trustees in Reverter of Sites cases have the trust thrust upon them and will often be such persons as the incumbent and church wardens (particularly in the case of school sites), there appears to be a strong case for treating this as a special case, rather analogous to the position of personal representatives of a person who dies intestate . . . [the amendments] . . . ensure that the trust imposed permits the trustees to sell the land and hold the proceeds for the putative beneficiaries without being required to consult them or allow them to occupy the land, and with provision for meeting necessary costs, expenses and taxes.'

1   See House of Lords Commitee Stage at 570 HL Official Report (5th series) col 1556, 25 March 1996.

Schedule 3 – Minor and Consequential Amendments

5.16   Text of schedule 3

The text to the Trusts of Land and Appointment of Trustees Act 1996, Sch 3 is set out in Appendix 2 below.

Conditional and determinable fees

5.17   The policy of the 1925 legislation was that an interest being less than a fee simple absolute in possession (which was recognised as a legal estate) must take effect behind a trust of the legal estate. Base and determinable fees fell within the Settled Land Act 1925, s 1(1)(ii)(c)[1]; a provision which appeared wide enough to catch, in addition, a fee simple defeasible by condition subsequent[2]. However, the Law of Property Act 1925, s 7(1)[3] provides for a fee simple which is subject to a legal or equitable right of entry or re-entry to be a fee simple absolute and therefore a legal estate. Although primarily aimed at rent charges ('fee farm rents'), the legislation was so widely drawn as to apparently catch all conditional fees.

1   Settled Land Act 1925 s 1(1)(ii)(c) (now amended by the Trusts of Land and Appointment of Trustees Act 1996, Sch 3, para 2(2)).
2   For the distinction between determinable fees and fees subject to conditions subsequent (a distinction of some subtlety) see Megarry and Wade *The Law of Real Property* (6th edn, 2000) para 3-065.
3   Law of Property Act 1925, s 7(1) as amended by the Reverter of Sites Act 1987, s 8(2), (3), Schedule and by the Law of Property (Amendment) Act 1926, s 7, Schedule.

5.18   It was assumed, although the matter was not free from all doubt, that the Law of Property Act 1925, s 7 took precedence over the provisions in the Settled Land Act 1925. That is now made explicit in Sch 3. So far as base and determinable fees are concerned, if created after 31 December 1996, these take effect behind a trust of land (in line with the general abolition of new strict settlements in the Trusts of Land and Appointment of Trustees Act 1996, s 2) with the trustees being either the grantor or personal representatives (as appropriate).

Settled land where there is more than one life tenant

5.19   If two or more persons are jointly entitled as tenants for life, the land remains settled and they together constitute a 'composite' life tenant[1]. By contrast, if they are entitled as tenants in common, the land cannot be settled and formerly was held on trust for sale. The amendments to the Settled Land Act 1925, s 36[2] ensure that when this situation arises on or after 1 January 1997, the land will be held on a trust of land.

1   Settled Land Act 1925, s 19(2).
2   Settled Land Act 1925, s 36 as amended by the Trusts of Land and Appointment of Trustees Act 1996, Sch 3, para 2(11).

Trustees' power of insurance

5.20   With the enhanced powers given to trustees of land under the Trusts of Land and Appointment of Trustees Act 1996, s 6(1) the trustees were given a power to insure up to the full value of the property (and against any risk). The woefully inadequate provisions in the Trustee Act 1925[1] were therefore limited to personal property and, with the deletion of the reference to fire, such property could, from 1 January 1997, be insured against all risks (albeit that the limit of cover to three-quarters of value remains). The position has now been put on a far more satisfactory footing as a result of the further amendments made to TA 1925, s19 by TA 2000, s 34[2].

1   Trustee Act 1925, s 19 (now amended by the Trusts of Land and Appointment of Trustees Act 1996, Sch 3, para 3(4)). Precisely how the Trusts of Land and Appointment of Trustees Act 1996, s 6(1) operated in the context of insuring the land was not entirely clear given that the powers conferred were in relation to land. Did it mean that premiums could only be paid out of rents from the land (if any)? With TA 2000 – which gives all trustees a power to insure whatever the trust property – this debate has become academic.
2   These changes are considered at para 14.1 below.

Notices under the Trustee Act 1925, s 27

5.21   The ambit of the Trustee Act 1925, s 27 has never been free from doubt since it appears to apply only to trustees of a settlement (ie a Settled Land Act settlement), trustees of a disposition on trusts for sale and personal representatives[1]. There is even an argument that the reference to advertisements in a newspaper where the land is situated implies that the provision is limited to land whether held on strict settlement or on trust for sale, albeit that in the latter case this would include the proceeds of sale[2]. The amendments in the Trusts of Land and Appointment of Trustees Act 1996, Sch 3 now make it clear that the Trustee Act 1925, s 27 can be used by Settled Land Act trustees (as before), by trustees of a trust of land and by trustees for sale of personal property[3].

1   In practice the main use of this provision is by personal representatives.
2   In practice it is not thought that there is much substance in this particular argument. If no land is concerned, current practice is to advertise in a newspaper circulated in the district most likely to be affected; for example, that in which the deceased lived. As Pettit *Equity and the Law of Trusts* (8th edn, 1997) points out at p 367, there is authority to the effect that 'the Sporting Life' is a paper which circulates in Westminster whilst 'The Times' is a local paper circulating in Rickmansworth.
3   Trustee Act 1925, s 27 as amended by Law of Property (Amendment) Act 1926, ss 7, 8(2), Schedule and by the Trusts of Land and Appointment of Trustees Act 1996, Sch 3, para 3(7).

The power of advancement

5.22   The power of advancement in the Trustee Act 1925, s 32 permits capital money (including assets in specie)[1] to be paid or applied for the 'advancement or benefit' of any person entitled to the capital of the trust or any share in it. It is generally available where the property is money or securities, or property held on trust for sale[2], but not capital money arising under the Settled Land Act 1925. As originally drafted, the consequential amendments in the Trusts of Land and Appointment of Trustees Bill would have limited the power to cases where the property consisted of money or securities not applicable as capital money for the purposes of the Settled Land Act 1925. This would have altered the position concerning property subject to a trust for sale by excluding trusts of land. After representations[3], the legislation was amended so that the redrafted s 32(2) now merely excludes capital money arising under the Settled Land Act 1925[4].

1   *Re Collard's Will Trusts, Lloyds Bank v Rees* [1961] Ch 293, [1961] 1 All ER 821.

2   *Re Stimpson's Trusts, Stimpson v Stimpson* [1931] 2 Ch 77 provided that there was no trust for
     reconversion of the proceeds of sale into land (which would be most unusual). The power
     of advancement is given to trustees and has never applied to land held by the tenant for
     life under a strict settlement.
3   House of Lords Committee Stage debates at 570 HL Official Report (5th series) col 1557,
     25 March 1996.
4   Trustee Act 1925, s 32(2) as substituted by the Trusts of Land and Appointment of Trustees
     Act 1996, Sch 3, para 3(8).

'Persons' instead of 'individuals' in the Trustee Act 1925, s 39

5.23   The Trustee Act 1925, s 39 formerly referred to two 'individuals';
'persons' was substituted by the Trusts of Land and Appointment of Trustees
Act 1996, Sch 3, para 3(13)[1].

1   For the consequences of this change for offshore trusts, see para 6.68.

Vesting of trust property – Trustee Act 1925, s 40

5.24   Amending the 'statutory power'[1] to include a reference to the Trusts
of Land and Appointment of Trustees Act 1996, s 19 (although interestingly
s 20 is not included) shows that it was intended that s 19 would be
freestanding; ie would not take effect via the provisions of the Trustee Act
1925[2].

1   Trustee Act 1925, s 40 as amended by the Trusts of Land and Appointment of Trustees Act
     1996, Sch 3, para 3(14).
2   As to the Trusts of Land and Appointment of Trustees Act 1996, s 19 see para 3.8 ff above.

Overreaching – Law of Property Act 1925, ss 2, 27

5.25   The position regarding overreaching in the light of the Trusts of Land
and Appointment of Trustees Act 1996 changes is considered at para 6.64[1]
below.

1   See also para 2.166 above.

'Two instruments' – Law of Property Act 1925, s 24

5.26   For a discussion of the continuing use of two instruments see para
6.47 below. The amendment to the Law of Property Act 1925, s 24(1)[1] is
somewhat odd in its reference to 'any trust of the proceeds of sale of the
land': one might have expected similar wording to that employed in s 27[2], ie
'trusts affecting the land, the net income of the land or the proceeds of sale of
the land . . .'.

1   Law of Property Act 1925, s 24(1) as substituted by the Trusts of Land and Appointment of
     Trustees Act 1996, Sch 3, para 4(7).
2   Law of Property Act 1925, s 27(1) as substituted by the Trusts of Land and Appointment of
     Trustees Act 1996, Sch 3, para 4(8).

Land Registration Act 1925, s 94

5.27 A new Land Registration Act 1925, s 94(4) provides for restrictions to be entered on the register in accordance with prescribed rules or as a matter of expediency for the protection of beneficiaries' rights[1]. Section 94(5) of the Act affords protection to the Registrar acting on a deed of discharge executed under the Trusts of Land and Appointment of Trustees Act 1996, s 16(4): ie in the absence of any actual notice, the Registrar may assume that the trustees were entitled to convey the land to the named beneficiaries[2]. Although the Trusts of Land and Appointment of Trustees Act 1996, s 16 is concerned only with unregistered land[3], in registered conveyancing there is a corresponding obligation in the form of a duty to apply for a restriction on Form 11A[4].

1   Land Registration Act 1925, s 94(4) as inserted by the Trusts of Land and Appointment of Trustees Act 1996, Sch 3, para 5(8)(c).
2   Compare the protection given to purchasers under the Trusts of Land and Appointment of Trustees Act 1996, s 16(5).
3   The Trusts of Land and Appointment of Trustees Act 1996, s 16(7): see para 2.165 ff above for a discussion of the ambit of s 16.
4   See para 2.173 above and *Private Trusts of Land* (PAL No 13), HM Land Registry (2nd edn, April 2000).

Personal representatives' power of management

5.28 Amendments to the Administration of Estates Act 1925, s 39[1] make it clear that whilst the powers of management for personal property are unaltered, so far as land is concerned personal representatives are given wide powers in the Trusts of Land and Appointment of Trustees Act 1996, s 6[2].

1   Administration of Estates Act 1925, s 39 as amended by the Trusts of Land and Appointment of Trustees Act 1996, Sch 3, para 6(2).
2   The wording of the amended Administration of Estates Act 1925, s 39(1)(ii) is a little odd in its reference to the 'functions' conferred on personal representatives by the Trusts of Land and Appointment of Trustees Act 1996, Pt I. 'Functions' is used to cover both powers and duties (see para 2.41 above): apart from the powers given in s 6(1) coupled with the limitation imposed in later subsections of that section, personal representatives are not subject to the consultation rules (s 18(1) excluding ibid s 11(1)) and, given that there cannot be an interest in possession in an unadministered estate, the delegation provisions (s 9) and right of occupation provisions (ss 12–13) are likewise inapplicable. It is somewhat odd that it was considered necessary expressly to exclude the consultation provisions. For the purposes of inheritance tax, the Inheritance Tax Act 1984, s 91 deems there to have been an interest in possession in an estate from the date of the testator's death.

Infants and deemed entails – Administration of Estates Act 1925, s 51(3)

5.29 Because an infant cannot make a will (unless privileged as a solder or mariner) his property passes on death under the intestacy rules, except for the rather odd position provided for in the Administration of Estates Act 1925, s 51(3). Prior to 1 January 1997, when a infant was equitably entitled to a vested estate in fee simple under a settlement, provided that he was unmarried he was deemed to have an entailed interest and the land devolved accordingly. The purpose of this provision appears to have been to remove the need for probate and to ensure that the land would revert to the settlor or his estate. With the abolition of entails[1], the Administration of Estates Act 1925, s 51(3) has been amended[2] to provide for the infant to have a deemed life interest; the same results are achieved so far as the devolution of the property is concerned, as on the death of the infant a resulting trust for the settlor will arise. The opportunity has, however, been taken to include an additional condition for the operation of the section ('and without issue') to reflect the enhanced rights of illegitimate children[3].

1   Trusts of Land and Appointment of Trustees Act 1996, Sch 1, para 5: see para 6.24 below.
2   Administration of Estates Act 1925, s 51(3) as amended by the Trusts of Land and Appointment of Trustees Act 1996, Sch 3, para 6(4).
3   For a discussion of the subsection generally see Megarry and Wade *The Law of Real Property* (6th edn, 2000) at 20.015; Cheshire and Burn's *Modern Law of Real Property* (16th edn, 2000) p 1002.

Charging orders against the interest of a beneficiary

5.30   Section 6(1A) is inserted into the Land Charges Act 1972 with the intention of avoiding problems that would arise if charging orders on beneficial interests in land were registrable as land charges under s 6 of that Act[1].

1   Note that the definition of land in the Land Charges Act 1972, s 17(1) still excludes undivided shares in land. With the abolition of conversion, beneficiaries under a trust of land will commonly have an interest in that land. As Lord Browne-Wilkinson explained in *Perry v Phoenix Assurance* [1988] 3 All ER 60, [1988] 1 WLR 940 'that step [ie registering charging orders] would cut right across the whole system of conveyancing whereby the equitable estate is treated as being separate from the beneficial interests in equity.' See generally Megarrry and Wade, *The Law of Real Property* (6th edn, 2000) at 9-074 *et seq.*

Applications by a trustee in bankruptcy – Insolvency Act 1986, s 335A

5.31   The Insolvency Act 1986, s 335A is inserted by the Trusts of Land and Appointment of Trustees Act 1996, Sch 3, para 23. This new provision is considered at para 6.1 ff below.

Schedule 4 – Repeals

5.32   Text of Schedule 4

The text of the Trusts of Land and Appointment of Trustees Act 1996, Sch 4 is set out in Appendix 2.

Repeals

5.33   Amongst the repeals the following may be noted:

(a)   The Settled Land Act 1925, s 27 (conveying land to a minor: see para 6.31 below); s 29 (charitable and public trusts: see para 6.7 below).

(b)   The Trustee Act 1925, s 10 (powers of investment amended); s 19 (power of insurance amended); s 68(19) (trusts for sale definition amended, *inter alia*, to exclude 'immediate': see para 1.11 above).

(c)   The Law of Property Act 1925:

    (i)   s 19 (conveyances of legal estates to minors);

    (ii)   s 23 (duration of trusts for sale: see now the Trusts of Land and Appointment of Trustees Act 1996, s 16(4));

    (iii)   s 25 (power to postpone sale: see now the Trusts of Land and Appointment of Trustees Act 1996, s 4);

    (iv)   s 26 (consents: see now the Trusts of Land and Appointment of Trustees Act 1996, s 8);

    (v)   s 28 (powers of management: see now the Trusts of Land and Appointment of Trustees Act 1996, s 6);

    (vi)   s 29 (delegation: see now the Trusts of Land and Appointment of Trustees Act 1996, s 9);

    (vii) s 30 (powers of court when trustees refuse to sell: see now the Trusts of Land and Appointment of Trustees Act 1996, ss 14-15);

    (viii) s 31 (mortgaged property: see now the Trusts of Land and Appointment of Trustees Act 1996, Sch 2, para 1);

    (ix)   s 32 (implied trusts for sale and personalty settlements);

    (x)   s 35 (the statutory trusts in co-ownership);

    (xi)   s 42(6) (contracts to convey undivided shares);

    (xii) s 130 (repealed in part: creation of entailed interests).

(d)   With the wide powers given to trustees of the land under the Trusts of Land and Appointment of Trustees Act 1996, s 6, provisions in various Acts which applied the Settled Land Act rules on the payment of expenditure either out of capital or income and which were applicable to trusts for sale are repealed (eg Landlord and Tenant Act 1927, s 13; Hill Farming Act 1946, s 11(2); Coast Protection Act 1949, s 11(2); Landlord and Tenant Act 1954, Sch 2, para 6; Agricultural Tenancies Act 1995, s 33).

(e)   The Inheritance Tax Act 1984, s 237(3)(extension of the Inland Revenue charge under the Inheritance Tax Act 1984, s 37(3): see para 2.24 (c) above)[1].

1   House of Lords Committee Stage debates at 570 HL Official Report (5th series) col 1558, 25 March 1996.

6

Specialist Topics

Bankrupts

Introduction

6.1   The original provisions in the Insolvency Act 1986, s 336 (and the two following sections) were produced as amendments during the passage of the legislation through Parliament in 1985 and were described by the ministerial spokesman (Lord Lucas of Chilworth) as follows[1]:

'The amendments represent a compromise between two conflicting interests and in our view achieve a reasonable balance between the rights of the creditor, who could only look to the bankrupt's assets for payment of his debt, and those of the family, who will normally be able to remain in the property concerned for a reasonable period so as to give them an opportunity to adjust to their changed circumstances and make arrangements either for alternative accommodation or for the buying out of the bankrupt's interest in the property.'

1   See the House of Lords Debates at 467 HL Official Report (5th series) col 1268, 23 October 1985. As to creditors see generally *Muir Hunter on Personal Insolvency* at para 3-283 *et seq.*

Application to the court

6.2   In the case of a bankrupt who is beneficially interested in land held in trust, any application (eg for sale) by the trustee in bankruptcy under the Trusts of Land and Appointment of Trustees Act 1996, s 14 must be made to the bankruptcy court and those provisions in s 15 specifying matters which the court is to take into account on such applications are excluded (see s 15(4))[1].

1   See the Insolvency Act 1986, s 335A as inserted by the Trusts of Land and Appointment of Trustees Act 1996, Sch 3, para 23. The Trusts of Land and Appointment of Trustees Act 1996, Sch 4 makes consequential amendments to the Insolvency Act 1986, s 336.

Court order

6.3   The court is required to make such order as it considers just and reasonable having regard to[1]:

(a)   the interests of the bankrupt's creditors;

(b)   in the case of a dwelling house that is or was the matrimonial home:

    (i)   the conduct of the (former) spouse in contributing to the bankruptcy[2];

(ii)   the needs and financial resources of the (former) spouse; and

(iii)   the needs of any children.

(c)   all the circumstances of the case other than the needs of the bankrupt.

1   Insolvency Act 1986, s 335A(2) as inserted by the Trusts of Land and Appointment of Trustees Act 1996, Sch 3, para 23. A trustee in bankruptcy is required to act in the best interests of the bankrupt's estate (see, for instance, *Re Ng* [1998] 2 FLR 386) which, in the absence of evidence to the contrary, will be presumed: see *Judd v Brown* [1999] 1 FLR 1191, CA.
2   The provision does not apply to an unmarried couple: see *Re Citro* [1991] Ch 142 at 159, CA.

6.4   Once the bankrupt's estate has been vested in the trustee in bankruptcy for at least 12 months[1], save in exceptional circumstances, the court must assume that the interest of the creditors is paramount[2].

1   Insolvency Act 1986, s 335A(3) as inserted. The first vesting of the bankrupt's estate in the trustee takes place under ibid s 306 when the trustee's appointment takes effect, or when the official receiver becomes the trustee.
2   See, for example, *Re Lowrie, ex p Trustee of the Bankrupt v Bankrupt* [1981] 3 All ER 353; compare *Re Citro (a bankrupt)* [1991] Ch 142, [1990] 3 All ER 952, CA; and see (1991) 107 LQR 177. *Re Lowrie, ex p Trustee of the Bankrupt v Bankrupt* is a case noted for the robust judgment of Walton J which included at 355 and 356 the following gem:

   'in exceptional circumstances there is no doubt that the trustee's voice will not be allowed to prevail in equity and the sale will not be ordered. A brilliant example of just such a situation is to be found in *Re Holliday (a bankrupt)* [1980] 3 All ER 385, [1981] 2 WLR 996, where the petition in bankruptcy had been presented by the husband himself as a tactical move, and quite clearly as a tactical move, to avoid a transfer of property order in favour of his wife, or ex-wife, at a time when no creditors whatsoever were pressing and he was in a position in the course of a year or so out of very good income to discharge whatever debts he had. He had gone off leaving the wife in the matrimonial home, which was the subject matter of the application, with responsibility for all the children on her own. One can scarcely, I think, imagine a more exceptional set of facts, and the court gave effect to those exceptional facts. . . .

   One can very well see the case that is from time to time put up where the children are going to be interrupted at a sensitive stage in their schooling, for example taking O levels, or more particularly, because O levels or CSE are not in general all that important, when taking their A levels.'

   See also *Re Mott, ex p Trustee of the Property of the Bankrupt v Mott and McQuitty* [1987] CLY 212.

Exercise of discretion

6.5   The guiding principle is that 'a person must discharge his liabilities before there is any room for being generous'[1]. In an insolvency an immediate sale of the land will therefore be ordered by the court even when the co-owners are spouses in the absence of exceptional circumstances, such as when:

(a)   the bankrupt's spouse was seriously ill[2]; and

(b)   the house had been specially adapted for a handicapped child or spouse[3].

1   *Re Bailey* [1977] 1 WLR 278 at 283 per Walton J and see generally *Re Citro* [1991] Ch 142, CA.
2   *Judd v Brown* [1998] 2 FLR 360.
3   *Re Bailey* [1977] 1 WLR 278 at 284. These statutory provisions largely codified the common law under which the underlying purpose for which the property was acquired was largely considered to be irrelevant.

Secured creditors

6.6   The position of secured creditors has been considered at para 2.154 above. The effect of the 1996 Act on charging orders is considered at para 5.30 above.

Charitable Trusts

Charitable land to be held on a trust of land

6.7   Notwithstanding the fact that Settled Land Act settlements already in existence will continue, the Trusts of Land and Appointment of Trustees Act 1996, s 2(5) provides that no land held on 'charitable, ecclesiastical or public trusts' is deemed to be settled land after the commencement of the Act even if it was, or was deemed to be so, before the commencement. Under the terms of the Settled Land Act 1925, s 29(1)[1], land vested in trustees for charitable, ecclesiastical or public trusts or purposes was deemed to be settled land and the trustees had, as regards such land, all the powers conferred by that Act on the tenant for life and on trustees of the settlement[2].

1   The Settled Land Act 1925, s 29 is repealed by the Trusts of Land and Appointment of Trustees Act 1996, Sch 4.
2   As an exception to the general principle of the 1925 legislation, the purchaser had to ensure that all necessary consents were obtained.

6.8   As from 1 January 1997, therefore, any such land instead of being held as settled land has been held by the trustees as a trust of land and, instead of the powers conferred by the Settled Land Act 1925, trustees have the powers conferred by the Trusts of Land and Appointment of Trustees Act 1996. This was a relatively easy transition given that such land is already vested in the trustees. Land held on trust for sale for charitable etc purposes is not affected[1].

1   The authors' experience is that in the majority of recently established charitable trusts, land has been held on trust for sale.

Conveyances of charitable etc land

6.9   The Trusts of Land and Appointment of Trustees Act 1996, Sch 1, para 4 contains consequential provisions arising from Section 2 of the Act and applies in the case of land held on charitable, ecclesiastical or public trusts (other than land to which the Universities and College Estates Act 1925 applies). It states that where there is a conveyance of such land, then if neither the Charities Act 1993, ss 37(1) or 39(1) apply to the conveyance, that conveyance shall state that the land is held on such trusts.

6.10   The Charities Act 1993, s 37(1) provides that in any contract for the sale, lease or other disposition of land held in trust for a charity, and in any conveyance, transfer, lease or other instrument effecting such a disposition it must be stated:

(a)   that the land is held by or in trust for the charity;

(b) whether the charity is an exempt charity (ie one of certain categories of charity which do not have to register pursuant to the Charities Act 1993, s 3); and

(c) whether the disposition comes within certain paragraphs of the Charities Act 1993, s 36.

6.11 If the relevant charity is not exempt, and the disposition does not come within those paragraphs, then it is land to which the restrictions on disposition imposed by s 36 apply. This section (broadly) requires the order of the court, or the order of the Charity Commissioners, to a sale, lease or disposal of charitable land except if certain conditions are complied with.

6.12 The Charities Act 1993, s 39(1) applies to mortgages and provides that if there is any mortgage of land held by or in trust for a charity, it must be stated:

(a) that the land is held by or in trust for the charity;

(b) whether the charity is an exempt charity; and

(c) whether the mortgage comes within certain paragraphs of s 38 of the Act.

6.13 If the relevant charity is not an exempt charity, and the mortgage does not come within those paragraphs, then the mortgage is one to which the restrictions imposed by s 38 apply. The Charities Act 1993, s 38 therefore does for mortgages what s 36 does for sales and leases: ie it makes an order of the court, or Charity Commissioners, necessary in the case of any mortgage of land held by or in trust for a charity unless certain conditions are complied with.

6.14 Accordingly, the effect of Sch 1, para 4(2)(a) is that if the fact that the land is held on charitable trusts does not have to be stated by reason of either the Charities Act 1993, s 37(1) or s 39(1), there is nonetheless a requirement to state it under this paragraph.

6.15 Schedule 1, para 4(2)(b) goes on to provide that if neither the Charities Act 1993, ss 37(2) or 39(2) have been complied with (ie that an order has not been obtained), and assuming that the conditions under which an order is not necessary do not apply, then a purchaser who has notice that the land is held on such trusts must see that any consents or orders necessary to authorise the transaction have been obtained.

Powers of trustees

6.16 Section 6(6) provides that the powers conferred by s 6(1) of the Act are not to be exercised in contravention of (or of any order made in pursuance of) any other enactment or any rule of law or equity, and s 6(7) provides that the reference in s 6(6) to an order includes any order of any court or of the Charity Commissioners.

Excluding (or restricting) Sections 6, 7

6.17   Section 8(3) provides that s 8(1) does not apply in the case of charitable, ecclesiastical or public trusts. It is not therefore possible to cut down or restrict the provisions of ss 6 and 7 of the Act[1].

1   This repeats the effect of the Settled Land Act 1925 s 106: see House of Lords Report Stage at 571 HL Official Report (5th series) col 955, 22 April 1996.

Trustees' delegation

6.18   The delegation provisions in s 9 have no application to charities whose 'beneficiaries' are their charitable objects. Hence there cannot be a beneficiary of full age entitled to an interest in possession.

Consents

6.19   Section 10(1), does not apply in the case of the exercise of a 'function' by trustees of land held on charitable, ecclesiastical or public trusts[1]. This means that in the case of such land, if the consent of more than two persons is required, then so far as a purchaser is concerned he will have to make sure that all the necessary consents are obtained and it is not sufficient that only two of the consents have been obtained.

1   Trusts of Land and Appointment of Trustees Act 1996, s 10(2).

Sections 11–13

6.20   The provisions of s 11 (regarding consultation) and of ss 12 and 13 (regarding rights of beneficiaries to occupy) have no application to charitable trusts in view of the fact that there are no beneficiaries entitled to an interest in possession.

Purchaser protection

6.21   The purchaser protection offered by s 16 is cut down in the case of charitable trusts. Section 16(6) of the Act provides that the provisions of s 16(2), (3) do not apply in the case of land held on charitable, ecclesiastical or public trusts.

Part II of the Act

6.22   The Trusts of Land and Appointment of Trustees Act 1996, Pt II has no application to charities since the power to give directions bestowed on beneficiaries is only given when beneficiaries are of full age and capacity and, taken together, absolutely entitled to the property subject to the trust.

Miscellaneous

6.23 There are some very minor amendments to the Charities Act 1993, s 23 contained in Sch 3, para 26 which consist of the substitution, in certain cases, of the word 'trust' for the words 'trust for sale', of 'trustee' for 'trustee for sale' and of 'trustees' for 'trustees for sale'. This section relates to reverter under the Reverter of Sites Act 1987.

Entailed Interests

Introduction

6.24 The entailed interest was widely used as an essential component of the traditional strict settlement. In such a settlement land would be settled (frequently on marriage) to the eldest son for life and with the remainder to his son in tail. That entailed interest would be limited so that in the event of the death without issue of the son an entailed interest was given to the second son and so on. Given the nature of an entailed interest there would be an ultimate reversion to the settlor.

6.25 The key to understanding the concept of a resettlement is to realise that for the estate to be preserved in the direct line it was essential that it did not fall into the possession of an entailed beneficiary since he could then disentail and so, if he pleased, dispose of the property. Less dangerous, although there was still a risk, was the position when the son reached 21 years (ie an adult remainderman) since he could then turn the entailed interest into a base fee which was marketable, albeit at a substantial discount.

6.26 The classic resettlement strategy aimed at avoiding these pitfalls and involved resettling every generation. In this example, on the son becoming 21 years he would agree with the life tenant (his father) to disentail the property and they would then create a new settlement. Typically, the opportunity would be taken to provide for junior members of the family and to enter into various administrative arrangements concerning the management of the estate. Having done this, however, the estate as an entity would then be resettled on the father for life, then the son for life with an entailed interest to that son's children born or unborn.

6.27 Both parties in a resettlement had bargaining counters. The son could take the view that he only had to wait for his father's death for the property to fall into possession and for him to disentail and obtain a fee simple. However, the father would be able to point out that that might be many years into the future and meanwhile the son would be kept on very short rations. Under the resettlement, an income would be provided for the son outside the father's control.

Law Commission

6.28 In Working Paper No 94, the Law Commission noted that since 1925 entails could only exist in equity and (largely because of the imposition of taxation) had become something of an 'anachronism'[1]. The recommendation was for existing entails to be converted into fee simple estates and for new entailed interests to be forbidden[2]. In the final report, the Law Commission mistakenly commented that entailed interests could only exist behind a strict settlement and on the basis of that advocated the ending of such interests whether in realty or personalty[3].

1   *Trusts of Land* (Law Com Working Paper No 94) para 6.8.
2   *Trusts of Land* (Law Com Working Paper No 94) para 6.8.
3   Transfer of Land, Trusts of Land (Law Com No 181) para 16.1.

Creation of new entails prevented

6.29   The Trusts of Land and Appointment of Trustees Act 1996, Sch 1, para 5 does not affect existing entails, but as from 1 January 1997 any attempt to create a new entailed interest in another (for example 'to X in tail male') is treated as a declaration that the property is held in trust for that person absolutely (ie it becomes held on trust for X absolutely so that X can call for a transfer of the property assuming that he is adult and sui juris). Any attempt to declare oneself a tenant in tail is ineffective[1].

1   This latter provision was the result of an amendment introduced in the Committee Stage at the House of Lords when the Lord Chancellor commented as follows:

'Amendment No 30 closes a possible loophole; namely where a person attempts to create an entailed interest not by granting it direct to another but by declaring himself a trustee in tail. In that case, the declaration of trust in tail is simply ineffective, and the effect may be illustrated by an example. If A purports to declare himself trustee in tail for B, he will simply remain the owner; and if he purports to declare himself trustee for B for life and C in tail thereafter, B's life interest will not be affected, but the property will simply revert to A, or his estate, when that life interest ceases.'

Conclusions

6.30   The authors (contrary to the findings of the Law Commission) have encountered entailed interests (of chattels) behind a trust for sale. For a titled family desirous of ensuring that the 'family treasures' are kept in the male line (together with the title), an entailed interest offers the most appropriate vehicle. The passing of such interests is to be lamented.

Minors

Capacity

6.31   A minor[1] cannot hold a legal estate in land[2].

1   Traditionally a person attained full age at the first moment of the day preceding the 21st anniversary of his birth: however, from 1 January 1970 the age of majority was reduced to 18 years which was attained at the first moment of the 18th anniversary of that person's birth: Family Law Reform Act 1969, ss 1, 9.
2   A minor can, however, own an equitable interest in land and, of course, other property. Although a minor cannot be appointed an express trustee (Law of Property Act 1925 s 20), he may become an implied, resulting or constructive trustee: *Re Vinogradoff, Allen v Jackson* [1935] WN 68.

Old law

6.32   Under the 1925 system, the Settled Land Act 1925 applied whenever there was an attempted conveyance of land to a minor[1]. Under the Settled Land Act 1925, s 27(1)[2] a conveyance to a minor took effect as a contract for valuable consideration to execute a full settlement, but in the meanwhile the grantor held the land in trust for the minor. Because a minor could not be a tenant for life, the Settled Land Act 1925, s 26 provided for the trustees of the settlement to have the powers of the tenant for life. In cases where land was conveyed to a minor together with an adult as either joint tenants or tenants in common, a trust for sale was imposed with the adult holding the land for himself and the minor[3]. The Law Commission in their Working Paper[4] proposed that under the new system there would be simplification without substantive changes being made.

1   Law of Property Act 1925, s 1(6); Settled Land Act 1925, s 1(1)(ii)(d).
2   Law of Property Act 1925, s 27(1) repealed by the Trusts of Land and Appointment of Trustees Act 1996, Sch 4.
3   Law of Property Act 1925, s 19 repealed by the Trusts of Land and Appointment of Trustees Act 1996, Sch 4.
4   *Trusts of Land* (Law Com Working Paper No 94) para 6.6.

The new system

6.33   In place of the existing trust based upon the Settled Land Act 1925, the new system[1] operates as illustrated in the following example:

EXAMPLE 1

1.   A purports to convey land to M (a minor). A will hold the property on a trust of land for M (similarly, if the conveyance is to more than one minor, either as joint tenants or tenants in common).

2.   By will, A leaves land to M. His personal representatives will hold the land on a trust of land for M (a similar position obtains on intestacy).

3.   A gives land to M and T (an adult) as beneficial joint tenants or tenants in common. T will hold the land on a trust of land for himself and M as either joint tenants or tenants in common[2].

---

1   Ie the Trusts of Land and Appointment of Trustees Act 1996, Sch 1, paras 1, 2.
2   With this simplification the Law of Property Act 1925, s 19 was repealed. In the case of registered land there are equivalent provisions identifying the person who is the registered proprietor and to ensure that no minor is registered (see LRA 1925, s111(1)-(3)).

Co-ownership

Position under the Act

6.34   As from 1 January 1997, the Trusts of Land and Appointment of Trustees Act 1996 converted statutory trusts for sale into trusts of land. As a result, in the case of all existing statutory trusts, instead of a trust for sale the land is held on trust with a power to sell (and a power to retain)[1]. Of course, if land was held on an express trust for sale, that trust continues but the trustees are given a statutory power to postpone sale.

1   Trusts of Land and Appointment of Trustees Act 1996, s 5, Sch 2.

Bull, Boland and the lacuna

6.35   The so-called lacuna cases[1] were treated by the courts as statutory trusts for sale, albeit at considerable violence to the actual wording of the statute. Accordingly, it is assumed that the position from 1 January 1997 is as set out in para 6.34 above. If, however, the correct analysis of these cases is that they are a species of resulting trust, then although they would come within the wide definition of a trust of land in the Trusts of Land and Appointment of Trustees Act 1996, s 1 (and, incidentally, within the over-reaching machinery), it is an interesting point whether or not under the terms of such resulting trust there was implied a trust for sale. If there had been, then there is nothing in the legislation to convert that trust for sale into a mere power to sell as from 1 January 1997.

1   Ie *Bull v Bull* [1955] 1 QB 234, [1955] 1 All ER 253, CA; *Williams and Glyn's Bank v Boland* [1981] AC 487 at 503, [1980] 2 All 408 at 411, HL.

New implied trusts

6.36   As from 1 January 1997, a simple conveyance to A and B as (joint tenants or tenants in common) has taken effect as a conveyance to A and B to hold the land on trust for themselves as beneficial joint tenants or tenants in common. There is no duty to sell. All the powers of the Trusts of Land and Appointment of Trustees Act 1996 are given to the trustees and, as the trust is implied by statute[1], the consultation provisions in s 11 apply as do the occupation rights in ss 12 and 13.

1   Under the Law of Property Act 1925, ss 34, 36 as amended by the Trusts of Land and Appointment of Trustees Act 1996, Sch 2, paras 3, 4, Sch 4.

New express trusts

6.37   A conveyance of land may recite that it is to be held by 'A and B on trust for themselves as beneficial joint tenants/tenants in common'. This creates an express trust of land under which modifications may be made; for example, in the powers of trustees under the Trusts of Land and Appointment of Trustees Act 1996, s 6 and in the consultation provisions.

6.38   As an alternative (which will certainly appeal to some practitioners), the conveyance may impose a trust for sale so that it will read 'to A and B on trust for sale to hold the proceeds of sale for themselves as beneficial joint tenants/tenants in common'[1]. Whilst co-ownership of residential property is on the increase, so also are disputes concerning that property on the break-up of the relevant relationship. In the event of such a dispute, given that the beneficial owners will normally be the trustees, both the consultation and right to possession provisions may well be inoperable and, if the property is held on a trust of land simpliciter, the resultant deadlock may make court proceedings inevitable. On the other hand, if the property is held subject to an overriding trust for sale, then any disagreement between the trustees as to the exercise of the power of postponement means that the overriding duty to sell will become paramount. This, in the eyes of some practitioners, is more satisfactory than the deadlock position that could so easily be arrived at under the statutory trusts.

1   There will of course be implied a power to postpone (irrespective of any provision to the contrary): Trusts of Land and Appointment of Trustees Act 1996, s 4.

Will Drafting

Involuntary strict settlements

6.39   With the demise of Settled Land Act settlements, the problem of involuntary strict settlements[1] no longer arises: accordingly, a provision enabling the testator's mother to live in his country cottage 'for as long as she wishes' now takes effect as a trust of land with the mother enjoying a beneficial interest in possession for her life (or until such time as she no longer wishes to live in the cottage)[2].

1   As to involuntary strict settlements see para 1.9 above.
2   Problems that could arise *inter vivos* in cases such as *Bannister v Bannister* [1948] 2 All ER 133, CA have also been avoided. Curiously, the recent case of *Dent v Dent* [1996] 1 All ER 659 shows that the courts may adopt a very different approach to this kind of problem. In that case, a son gave undertakings under seal to his father and step-mother granting exclusive occupation of a farmhouse to his father during his lifetime and thereafter to the step-mother. After the father's death the step-mother contended that the exclusive right of occupation gave her a life interest in the property which constituted a settlement under the Settled Land Act 1925, s 1. The court held, however, that the exclusive right to occupy in the context of the facts of this case was merely a personal obligation which was not intended to confer any proprietary interest. Accordingly, no Settled Land Act settlement had been created. The court further held that even if such an interest had arisen that was clearly not the intention of the son and so the arrangement would have been set aside for mistake. This commonsense approach meant that no trust had been created: the decision is not therefore affected by the Trusts of Land and Appointment of Trustees Act 1996.

Residue clauses

6.40   Traditionally a residue clause has been drafted along the following lines:

'I GIVE AND BEQUEATH all my property both movable and immovable of whatever nature and whosoever situated except property otherwise disposed of by this Will or by any Codicil hereto to my Trustees UPON TRUST to sell call in and convert the same into money (so far as not already consisting of money) with power to postpone the sale calling in and conversion thereof (even as regards property of a terminable hazardous or wasting nature) in the absolute and uncontrolled discretion of my Trustees without being liable for loss and to hold the net proceeds and my ready money upon the following trusts: . . .'

6.41   In part this provision was designed to ensure that any land not otherwise dealt with by way of specific devise, and which therefore fell into residue, was not caught by the Settled Land Act 1925. However, in cases where residue is to be divided amongst a number of beneficiaries, it will normally be necessary for the assets to be sold and the proceeds of sale then to be distributed. In such cases, a trust for sale is obviously appropriate. It is therefore thought that although trusts for sale are no longer necessary to deal with the problem of land which forms part of the residue, it will often remain the case that such a trust will remain part of any residue clause[1].

1   Contrast the view of Richard Wallington in 'The Trusts of Land and Appointment of Trustees Bill' (1996) 146 NLJ 960. The author's suggestion that the 'incidental effect' of omitting a trust for sale from residue will be the exclusion of the equitable apportionment rules (ie *Howe v Earl of Dartmouth* (1802) 7 Ves 137 and *Re Chesterfield's (Earl) Trusts* (1883) 24 Ch D 643) without the need for further express provision is not thought to be correct.

Statutory will forms

6.42   The use of statutory will forms is nowadays comparatively rare[1]. These have not been updated by the Trusts of Land and Appointment of Trustees Act 1996 and accordingly Form 8 ('Administration Trusts') continues to provide for real property to be held on trust for sale.

1   See the Law of Property Act 1925, s 179 which enables the Lord Chancellor to prescribe forms to which a testator may refer in his will: the Statutory Will Forms 1925, SR & O 1925/780 was made under these provisions in 1925 and has not been updated since.

Inheritance tax planning

6.43   Ideal inheritance tax planning for a husband and wife is for full use to be made of both inheritance tax nil-rate bands. In a case where the house is jointly owned, this is frequently only possible when the matrimonial home is divided between the surviving spouse and children as follows:

(a)   the beneficial joint tenancy is severed so that couple become beneficial tenants in common;

(b)   on the first death the share of the deceased spouse is left on discretionary trusts[1] for the benefit of the children (and possibly grandchildren), but excluding the surviving spouse; and

(c)   the surviving spouse continues to occupy by virtue of her interest as a beneficial tenant in common.

1   It is not generally considered satisfactory to leave the interest in the property to the children outright, nor to leave it on fixed interest trusts, as quite apart from the possibility of disagreements within the family, there may then be problems in the event of children divorcing or becoming bankrupt. The paramount objective in this situation is to ensure that the surviving spouse's occupation of the property remains undistributed.

6.44   Some concern has been expressed as to the efficacy of this arrangement: in particular, it has been suggested that because the surviving spouse occupies the entire property, he would be considered to have an interest in possession in the entirety so that on his death inheritance tax would be charged on the full value of the property (instead, as was intended, on his half share alone)[1].

1   See 'Splitting up the Home' by James Kessler in *Taxation*, 2 May 1996, p 113.

6.45   Under the Trusts of Land and Appointment of Trustees Act 1996, the position on the death of the first spouse is as follows:

(a)   there is an implied trust of land[1];

(b)   the survivor will be beneficially entitled to an interest in possession in the property: the half share passing on the death of the first spouse is held on discretionary trusts (so that there is no interest in possession as regards that portion);

(c)   accordingly, under s 12 of the Act the survivor has a right of occupation and under s 13 the trustees may impose 'reasonable conditions' on that occupation[2], such as discharging outgoings on the property[3].

1   Assuming that an express trust for sale was not created when the house was purchased by the couple.
2   Trusts of Land and Appointment of Trustees Act 1996, s 13(3); but note s 13(7) which will presumably apply in a case like this where the spouse is already in occupation.
3   Trusts of Land and Appointment of Trustees Act 1996, s 13(5).

6.46   When the position of the surviving spouse (say, Mrs A) and of the discretionary trustees is examined it is not thought that the argument that *simply because* the surviving spouse occupies the property she *must* have obtained an interest in possession in the discretionary trust will hold water. Consider the following:

(a)   Mrs A has a right to live in the property by virtue of her interest as an equitable tenant in common;

(b)   her rights are backed up by statutory provisions in the Trusts of Land and Appointment of Trustees Act 1996, s 12;

(c)   from the trustees' perspective the property that they own is a beneficial interest in the house. This interest does not carry any right of occupation. What are the trustees to do? They could of course ask Mrs A (who is the sole surviving trustee holding the legal estate) to sell the property but if she refuses and the trustees apply to the court for a sale (under the 1996 Act) it seems unlikely that the court will make the appropriate order. Of course, the trustees could seek to sell their share in the property, but finding a buyer will be problematic and any payment that they receive would represent a substantial discount on the value of a full half share in the property. What sensible trustees will therefore do is to accept that the asset that they have (whilst not generating any income) is likely to show capital appreciation which will be realised when the property is sold or, at the latest, on the death of Mrs A. Retaining the asset seems therefore to be the prudent course for the trustees to undertake.

The 'Two Instruments'

Position under the 1925 legislation

6.47   Two documents were required to create a strict settlement: the vesting instrument containing the information that a purchaser needed and which vested legal title to the land in the tenant for life, and the trust instrument which contained details of the settlement and which was of no concern to the purchaser (and therefore was 'behind the curtain')[1]. These requirements, introduced for settled land in 1925, were adaptations of the practice of conveyancers which had long been used for *inter vivos* trusts for sale.

1   Settled Land Act 1925, ss 4(1), 6, 8(1).

6.48   In fact a trust for sale could be created by only one instrument, albeit that this practice was undesirable. Given that under trusts for sale beneficial interests were considered to be in money, there was an added reason why the trusts should be kept off the title. Hence, the instrument setting out the trusts was a document for retention by the trustees, whilst the conveyance to the trustees was an essential link in the purchaser's title. Accordingly, the conveyance would require the trustees to hold the net proceeds of sale, and net rents and profits until sale, on the trusts of a separate trust instrument.

6.49   In the case of wills, before 1926 the will was invariably the only document. After 1925 a written assent became necessary to vest the legal estate in the trustees for sale[1]. Hence there were two documents, with the assent performing the function of the conveyance, so that the purchaser was not concerned with the terms of the will. Even if the trustees for sale were the same persons as the personal representatives, it was necessary for them as personal representatives to make a written assent to themselves as trustees for sale[2].

1   Administration of Estates Act 1925, s 36(4).
2   *Re King's Will Trusts, Assheton v Boyne* [1964] Ch 542, [1964] 1 All ER 833; and see Precedents 27 and 28.

Appointing new trustees when there was a trust for sale

6.50   In the exceptional cases where only one instrument was used to create a trust for sale, the appointment was by a single document (which should have been a deed)[1] with a memorandum being endorsed on the instrument creating the trust for sale stating who were the trustees after the appointment was made[2].

6.51   In the normal case of two instruments the procedure involved:

(a)   the appointment of new trustees of the conveyance;

(b)   the appointment of new trustees of the trust of the proceeds of sale; and

(c)   an endorsement on the conveyance on trust for sale stating the names of those who were the trustees for sale after the appointment.

1   So as to allow automatic vesting of the legal estate under the Trustee Act 1925, s 40.
2   The Trustee Act 1925, s 35(3) (now amended by the Trusts of Land and Appointment of Trustees Act 1996, Sch 3, para 3(10)).

6.52   The Trustee Act 1925, s 35(1)[1] provided that new trustees of:

(i)   a conveyance on trust for sale; and

147

(ii)   a settlement of the proceeds of sale

were to be appointed by separate instruments, but so that the same persons became trustees of both.

1   Trustee Act 1925, s 35(1) (now amended by the Trusts of Land and Appointment of Trustees Act 1996, Sch 3, para 3(10)) and see LPA 1925, s 24(1) as amended by Sch 3, para 4(10) of the 1996 Act .

Position under the Act

6.53   From 1 January 1997, strict settlements have been abolished: however, existing settlements continue so that the appointment of new trustees will continue to be necessary in such cases.

6.54   It remains possible to create trusts for sale (albeit with, in all cases, an implied power to postpone) and, of course, a trust for land in which there is no overriding duty to sell. In both cases, there is no prescribed procedure, so that a single document will suffice. There is no doubt, however, that as trusts for sale were in practice always set up by two instruments as discussed above, the same position is likely to apply to trusts of land[1].

1   The Trustee Act 1925, s 35 was amended by the Trusts of Land and Appointment of Trustees Act 1996, Sch 3, para 3(10) to replace 'trusts for sale' with 'trusts of land'. It has been suggested that because under the two instrument system the only trust of land was the one created by the conveyance, whilst the trustees of the settlement are merely trustees of the proceeds of sale, that the latter is not, for general purposes, a trust of land (see, for instance, s 17 of the 1996 Act dealing with the proceeds of sale of land). It is not thought that this approach will commend itself to the courts given that it would, in such cases, stultify ss 9 and 12 of the Act. In essence, the two trust device was for conveyancing purposes only and with the spread of registered land is likely to disappear.

Precedents

6.55   The following Precedents are included[1]:

(a)   conveyance and transfer of land to trustees to be held on trust of land or trust for sale;

(b)   express discretionary trust of land;

(c)   appointment by supplemental deed of a new trustee of a conveyance; and

(d)   appointment by supplemental deed of a new trustee of the trust instrument.

1   See Precedents 1–4.

Termination of trusts and settlements

6.56   Under the Settled Land Act 1925, s 17[1], where the estate owner (ie the person with the legal title) holds the land free from other equitable interests under a trust instrument, the trustees are bound to execute a deed declaring that they are discharged. No such provision had existed for trusts for sale, but under the Trusts of Land and Appointment of Trustees Act 1996 trustees of land who convey land to beneficiaries absolutely entitled (whether under s 6(2) of the Act or otherwise[2]) must execute a deed declaring that they are discharged from the trust in relation to that land[3].

1   Settled Land Act 1925, s 17 as amended by the Trusts of Land and Appointment of Trustees Act 1996, Sch 3, para 2(6).
2   See para 2.45 above.
3   Trusts of Land and Appointment of Trustees Act 1996, s 16(4) which applies to unregistered land: in the case of registered land see Sch 3, para 5(8) and para 2.172 above.

Pension Trusts

Pensions funds as 'trusts of land'

6.57   Pension funds frequently own land and, given the width of a definition of a trust of land in the Trusts of Land and Appointment of Trustees Act 1996[1], such funds will fall within the legislation.

1   For the definition of a 'trust of land' see para 2.2 above.

Concerns about the legislation

6.58   In the Second Reading Debate in the House of Lords, Lord Browne-Wilkinson raised the spectre of 'people, pensioners or pending pensioners, being entitled to occupy number 22 Smithfield. That is an admirable provision when applied to the matrimonial home, but not entirely apposite when brought to bear on pension schemes and any other large trust fund which is invested in land[1].' Concern was also expressed that the consultation provisions in s 11 would apply to pension trusts.

1   House of Lords Second Reading at 569 HL Official Report (5th series) cols 1725, 1 March 1996.

Applicability

6.59   The fears, expressed on behalf of pension trusts, are felt to be groundless in the light of the definition of 'beneficiary' in the Trusts of Land and Appointment of Trustees Act 1996, s 22[1] and of the express wording of the relevant sections of the Act since:

(a)   the sections of the Act only confer rights on beneficiaries who are entitled to interests in possession. Pension scheme members either do not have an interest in possession or, in those cases where they do, are annuitants (and annuitants are by s 22(3) not regarded as enjoying an interest in possession for this purpose);

(b)   in the case of the right of occupation conferred by s 12, beneficial occupation must either have been one of the purposes of the trust (which, in the case of a pension fund, is not the position) or the land must be held by the trustees so as to be so available (which, again, is not the case). Furthermore, the right does not apply to land which is either unavailable or unsuitable; for example, a commercially let office development (the classic investment of pension funds!).

1   For a discussion of the meaning of 'beneficiary', see para 4.1 ff above.

Consents

6.60   The Pensions Act 1995, s 35(4) provides that:

'Neither the trust scheme nor the statement may impose restrictions (however expressed) on any power to make investments by reference to the consent of the employer.'

6.61   Section 8 of the 1996 Act which generally permits the powers of trustees of land to be restricted (for example, by a requirement that consents be obtained) is accordingly limited in s 8(4) so as not to cut across this provision[1].

1   See para 2.72 above.

Part II of the Act

6.62   As originally drafted, it was feared that the provisions for appointing trustees would apply to pension trusts. However, with the amendments during the passage of the legislation through Parliament which resulted in only beneficiaries who are together absolutely entitled and able to bring the trust to an end being permitted to exercise these powers, it follows that they have no application to pension trusts[1]. Even in small self-administered schemes, there will normally be the possibility of the company admitting new members or of unascertained widows and children being entitled to a benefit on the death of a member.

1   It is interesting to note that unlike most private trusts, pension trusts commonly enable the principal employer to appoint and remove trustees at will (which will, of course, exclude the operation of the Trusts of Land and Appointment of Trustees Act 1996, s 19). Under the Pensions Act 1995, s 3, trust deeds and rules of pension schemes are overruled to allow the Occupational Pensions Regulatory Authority ('OPRA') to prohibit a person from being a trustee.

Purchasers

General position

6.63   The position of a purchaser of land from trustees is not in general terms affected by the Trusts of Land and Appointment of Trustees Act 1996. The overreaching machinery, for example, still enables a purchaser (provided that the requisite formalities are complied with) to take free of equitable interests under the trust instrument. Indeed, the position of a purchaser has been strengthened in that:

(a)   bare trusts are included in the definition of a trust of land (whereas in the 1925 legislation they fell through a gap in the legislation)[1]; and

(b)   on the ending of a trust of land the trustees must now execute a deed of discharge which affords protection to a purchaser[2].

1   See para 1.16 above.
2   Trusts of Land and Appointment of Trustees Act 1996, s 16(4): see **Precedent 16** below.

Overreaching after the Act

6.64   The theoretical basis for overreaching is more confused than ever. The Law of Property Act 1925, s 2(1)(ii) provides for overreaching in the case of trusts of land either under the provisions of s 2(2) (which is limited to *ad hoc* trusts of land[1]) or 'independently of that sub-section' provided, in both cases, that capital money is paid in accordance with the Law of Property Act 1925, s 27 (ie to two trustees or a trust corporation)[2]. Prior to 1 January 1997, overreaching outside s 2(2) was sometimes explained in the case of trusts for sale on the basis of the doctrine of conversion[3]. With the abolition of that doctrine in the Trusts of Land and Appointment of Trustees Act 1996, s 3, a new basis has to be found for overreaching in the case of trusts for land which must lie in the powers of sale enjoyed by the trustees[4].

1   On *ad hoc* trusts, see Megarry and Wade *The Law of Real Property* (6th edn, 2000) at para 8.168.
2   See the Law of Property Act 1925, s 2(1)(ii) as amended by the Trusts of Land and Appointment of Trustees Act 1996, Sch 3, para 4(2); Law of Property Act 1925, s 27 as amended by the Trusts of Land and Appointment of Trustees Act 1996, Sch 3, para 4(8). The Law of Property Act 1925, s 27 does not make it clear that the protection in s 27(1) is dependent on the s 27(2) procedure being followed, although that is how the section has been interpreted.
3   *City of London Building Society v Flegg* [1988] AC 54, [1987] 3 All ER 435, HL; and see Megarry & Wade *The Law of Real Property* (5th Edn, 1984) pp 398, 137 'the overreaching effect of trusts for sale was automatic, and needed no assistance by statute . . . when land is held upon trust for sale, any purchaser will have notice of the trusts from the title deeds. But since sale by the trustees is the very thing the trust commands, the purchaser will not be concerned with the equitable interests. From the moment of sale these attach, by the terms of the trust itself, not to the land but to the purchase-money.'
4   Trusts of Land and Appointment of Trustees Act 1996, s 6(1) and see the comments of Charles Harpum in 'Overreaching, Trustees' Powers and the Reform of the 1925 Legislation' (1990) 49 CLJ 300.

Consultation and consents

6.65   Purchasers are not concerned to see that the consultation process[1] is carried through. Where trustee powers can only be exercised with consents, any two of those consents suffice so far as a purchaser is concerned[2].

1   See the Trusts of Land and Appointment of Trustees Act 1996, s 11(1) and para 2.107 ff above.
2   The Trusts of Land and Appointment of Trustees Act 1996, s 10(1). Note that the requirement for consents must be contained in the disposition creating the trust.

Limitations on trustee powers

6.66   Purchasers of unregistered land are not concerned to ensure that the requirements in the Trusts of Land and Appointment of Trustees Act 1996, s 6(5) (trustees to have regard to the interests of beneficiaries) or s 7(3) (consent to partition) have been met[1]. A breach of s 6(6) and 6(8) of the Act only affects a purchaser with actual notice[2]. When trustee' powers are limited under s 8 then although trustees have a duty to bring those limits to the attention of a purchaser, the purchaser is not affected unless he has actual notice of the limitation[3].

1   Trusts of Land and Appointment of Trustees Act 1996, s 16(1). For the position of registered land, see para 2.172.

2   Trusts of Land and Appointment of Trustees Act 1996, s 16(2).

3   Trusts of Land and Appointment of Trustees Act 1996, s 16(3). For these purposes knowledge of a solicitor is attributed to his client and note the protection in s 9(2) for a purchaser dealing with an attorney.

Sale by a single trustee

6.67   On the sale by a single trustee the interest of a beneficiary is not overreached. Accordingly, a purchaser will only take free from that interest if:

(a)   in the case of unregistered land the purchaser does not have notice[1];

(b)   in the case of registered land, if there is no entry on the register and the beneficiary is not in occupation so as to enjoy an overriding interest[2].

1   Equitable interests cannot be registered under the Land Charges Act 1972.

2   *Williams and Glyn's Bank v Boland* [1981] AC 487, [1980] 2 All 408, HL.

Offshore Trusts

Trustee Act 1925, s 37(1)(c)

6.68   The considerable capital gains tax attractions of establishing offshore trusts in the years after 1981 led to something of a boom in that field[1]. Either a new trust was established in a tax haven or an existing UK trust was exported[2]. This was achieved by the replacement of UK resident trustees by foreign residents and by ensuring that the general administration of the trust was carried on outside the UK[3].

1   The system of taxing offshore gains introduced in 1981 meant that a deferral of tax could be achieved (by ensuring that no 'capital payments' were made to UK domiciled and resident beneficiaries) or, in some cases, an exemption from tax (by ensuring that capital payments were made, but to non-UK beneficiaries). The new system introduced in 1991 put a halt on the flow of exports: see now the Taxation of Chargeable Gains Act 1992, ss 80-98A.

2   Some doubt was expressed about the validity of exporting UK trustees by Pennycuick VC in *Re Whitehead's Will Trusts, Burke v Burke* [1971] 2 All ER 1334, [1971] 1 WLR 833 on the basis that such appointment although acceptable might be 'improper'. However, since that case it would appear that judicial attitudes have changed, so that provided the export can be shown to be for the beneficiaries advantage (for example in saving tax) the courts are unlikely to interfere: see the later case of *Richard v McKay* (14 March 1987, unreported).

3   Taxation of Chargeable Gains Act 1992, s 69(1); but note the exclusion contained in s 69(2) for UK professional trustees when the settlor is non-domiciled.

6.69   The former wording of the Trustee Act 1925, s 37(1)(c) (supplemental provisions as to the appointment of trustees) provided something of a trap for the unwary in its requirement that in most cases 'a trustee shall not be discharged from his trust unless there will either be a trust corporation or at least two individuals to act as trustees to perform the trust'. Given that foreign companies and banks cannot be trust corporations, it was necessary to find at least two individuals in the overseas jurisdiction who were willing to act as trustees. Frequently, this was not done (for example, a sole foreign trust company being appointed as a new trustee) and the existing UK trustees were not discharged. As a result the trust would remain resident in the UK for capital gains tax purposes[1].

1   See *Adam & Co International Trustees Ltd v Theodore Goddard* [2000] 13 LS Gaz R 44.

6.70   The Trusts of Land and Appointment of Trustees Act 1996 has solved this particular problem by replacing 'individuals' with 'persons' in the Trustee Act 1925, s 37(1)(c)[1] and now enables two foreign corporations to replace UK trustees. It will remain common practice, however, to include in a trust deed a clause ensuring that non-resident trustees can be validly appointed and a further clause enabling a single foreign corporation to be appointed thereby ousting the continuing requirement in s 37(1)(c) for at least two persons[2].

1   Trustee Act 1925, s 39(1)(c) as amended by the Trusts of Land and Appointment of Trustees Act 1996, Sch 3, para 3(12).
2   When a 'defined person' is one of the beneficiaries, offshore gains are since 1991 taxed on UK settlors as they arise and further there is an 'export charge' when a UK trust appoints foreign resident trustees (accordingly, retiring UK trustees who may be subject to the payment of this charge will normally seek some form of protection: see, for example, **Precedent 18, clause 2** below).

Part II:
Trustee Delegation
Act 1999

7

Introduction

7.1   The Act received Royal Assent on 15 July 1999 and came into effect on 1 March 2000 (TDA 1999, s 13(1): SI 2000/216). The genesis of the Act was a Law Commission Consultation Paper (issued in 1991: CP No 118) which was followed by a Law Commission Report in 1994 (*'The Law of Trusts: Delegation by Individual Trustees'*: Law Com No 220). With only relatively minor changes it is the draft Act attached to that Report which was enacted as TDA 1999.

Scope and Purposes of the Act

7.2   The Act is concerned with the delegation of his powers and duties by an *individual* trustee (for instance, by a trustee going abroad for a six-month holiday). It is not concerned with delegation by the trustee body *collectively* (this matter is considered at para 12.5 below).

7.3   Trustees are only allowed to delegate in restricted circumstances: Courts of Equity have adapted the maxim *'delegatus non potest delegare'* from the law of agency by way of justification[1]. Only if the case falls within a recognised exception is delegation permitted and (prior to 1 March 2000) for an individual trustee these were:

(a)   if the instrument creating the trust specifically authorised delegation;

(b)   if the delegation was agreed by all the beneficiaries who were adult and sane; or

(c)   if delegation was permitted by statute (notably under TA 1925, s 25).

1   The maxim has also been invoked in the continuing debate over the extent to which discretionary trusts can be created by exercise of the statutory power of advancement: see, for instance, Upjohn J in *Re Wills' Will Trusts* [1959] Ch 1.

7.4   It was the purpose of the TDA 1999 to overhaul the statutory rules and specifically to deal with problems that had been created by s 3(3) of the Enduring Powers of Attorney Act 1985. In performing this 'tidying up' exercise the Act has introduced a special rule for co-owners of real property and a safeguard to ensure that, when appropriate, the 'two trustee' rule will be met[1].

1   As such the Act set itself relatively limited objectives but it has not escaped censure. The editor of the *Conveyancer and Property Lawyer* has commented as follows:

'The Act has more quaint detail than can be dealt with in a note such as this. In the main it reflects a convoluted academic approach to law reform which has become the hallmark of Law Commission attempts in this area. Things that work (exchange of contracts, making deeds, covenants for title, trusts of land, powers of attorney) are made more obscure. The amount of law sloshing about the world increases. It represents a genuine effort of intellectual skill but is in large measure no more use than scrimshaw or topiary and they at least are ornamental.'

By contrast, in the Third Reading debate on the Act in the House of Lords, Lord Goodhart welcomed 'this minor but useful Act' (Hansard Vol 598, No 49 at 128).

The Use of Powers of Attorney by Trustees: Some Background Factors

7.5 A power of attorney is a document (under the 1971 Act it must be in the form of a deed[1]) by which a person gives another power to act on his behalf and in his name. The person giving the power is commonly referred to as the donor[2] although in some precedents, 'principal' is employed[3]. The recipient of the power is accordingly the donee (or, if the person creating the power is referred to as the principal, the agent). The following further matters may be noted:

(a) there is no statutory definition of a power of attorney: the 1971 Act merely states that 'an instrument creating a power of attorney shall be executed as a deed'[4];

(b) the power may be general and so entitle the donee to do (virtually) everything that the donor could do[5], or may be limited to certain defined acts and objectives. An individual who is a trustee may, for instance, wish to appoint an attorney to exercise all his powers (including those which he possesses as a trustee), or only to exercise powers which he possesses in his individual capacity or in his trustee capacity[6];

(c) the practical use of a power of attorney is to provide the donee with a document which he can use as evidence to third parties with whom he is dealing and which will show that he has authority to act in the relevant transaction;

(d) a power of attorney confers on the attorney a power to act but it does not impose on him any duty to act[7]. Of course, this position may be altered by contractual agreement between the parties and, once the attorney has carried out an act under the power, obligations may then attach to him (for instance, in relation to the disposal of monies received on a sale of the donor's property). Because the power is, however, essentially 'one sided' it is normally executed only by the donor[8];

(e) A donee cannot, unless expressly allowed, further delegate his authority by himself granting a power of attorney[9];

(f) reflecting the 'one-sided' nature of a power of attorney it can normally be revoked unilaterally by the donor[10]. Exceptions to this rule exist: for instance in the case of a registered enduring power[11] and in the case of power given by way of security[12]. A third party who deals with a donee not knowing of the revocation of his power to act is protected[13];

(g)   powers of attorney are automatically revoked if the donor becomes mentally incapable unless the power was granted under the EPA 1985. In this case, at the onset of mental incapacity, the donee has a duty to register the power[14].

1   PAA 1971, s 1(1).
2   This term is, for instance, used in the 1971 Act.
3   This reflects the fact that a power of attorney is merely a species of agency.
4   Formerly, a power of attorney, as a matter of legal necessity, only had to be created by deed if the agent was himself to be given power to execute a deed.
5   For an exception, see Inland Revenue Statement of Practice A 13 (completion of return forms by attorneys).
6   In the former case (ie where he wishes to delegate everything) he will usually need to execute a 'section 25 trustee power' to deal with the trusts and a section 10 power for his personal affairs.
7   A trustee power under s 25 does not, for instance, make the donee a trustee in place of the donor trustee.
8   Enduring powers of attorney are subject to different rules and impose obligations on the donee: hence the standard form instrument must be executed by both donor and donee: for the standard form see **Precedent 31** below.
9   See further para 7.3 above where it is noted that trustees are seen as delegates and so can only delegate their powers in certain restricted circumstances. See also TA 2000, s 14(3) and para 12.32 below.
10   Of course if he has contracted not to revoke the power this may render the donor liable to the donee in damages. On revocation of enduring powers of attorney, see *Re E, X v Y* [2000] 3 All ER 1004.
11   See EPA 1985, s 7(1)(a) which requires the court to confirm any revocation of a registered enduring power under s 8(3).
12   PAA 1971, s 4.
13   PAA 1971, s 5(2).
14   EPA 1985, s 1.

Delegation Permitted by Statute

7.6   Before 1 March 2000 a trustee could delegate his powers and duties:

(a)   by power of attorney under the Trustee Act 1925, s 25[1] which was subject to various safeguards:

–   the period of delegation must not exceed 12 months,

–   a trustee could not delegate to his sole co-trustee unless that person was a trust corporation,

–   notice of the delegation had to be given to co-trustees,

–   the donor trustee remained liable for the acts of the attorney[2].

(b)   under the Enduring Powers of Attorney Act 1985 s 3(3)[3]. This permitted an attorney under an enduring power (whether or not that power had been registered) to execute any trust power or discretion vested in the donor without the requirement of obtaining any consent and to give a good receipt for capital or other money paid. It contrasted strikingly with s 25:

–   it permitted delegation for an unlimited period of time,

–   it permitted delegation to continue after the donor became incapable[4],

–   delegation of the trustee function could occur inadvertently under the standard form enduring power of attorney which allowed the delegation of any powers possessed by the donor as trustee,

–   it appeared to override other safeguards: for instance, in permitting the attorney to act without obtaining a consent which was required before the donor could act, whilst the ability to give a good receipt appeared to override the statutory requirement that capital money must be paid to two trustees[5].

1   As amended by the Powers of Attorney Act 1971. Formerly the section permitted a trustee who intended to remain out of the UK for more than a month to delegate his powers. The 1971 Act extended the scope of the section to all trustees, not just those going abroad. However, it did not amend the side note which continued to read 'power to delegate trusts during absence abroad'. A power of attorney in general form under PAA 1971, s 10 did not permit the delegation of trustee functions.

2   The section was frequently used – as had never been intended – by the trustees as a body to delegate their powers of investment: para 8.52 below.

3   Section 3(3) was in the following terms:

'subject to any conditions or restrictions contained in the instrument, an attorney under an enduring power, whether general or limited, may (without obtaining any consent) execute or exercise all or any of the trusts, powers or discretions vested in the donor as trustee and may (without the concurrence of any other person) give a valid receipt for capital or other money paid.' ('Instrument' refers to the document creating the enduring power.)

4   Which is, of course, a ground for removing a trustee: see TA 1925, s 36(1).

5   See para 8.60 below. The use of s 3(3) by professionals was defended in *The Conveyancer and Property Lawyer* (2000) at pp 187-8 as follows:

'In a solicitor's firm with a substantial private client practice the senior practitioner may be trustee of several hundred funds and estates. Section 3(3) of the 1985 Act allowed a single enduring power to be used to delegate these trustee functions. The use of such a power allowed the large and sensible use of wide discretion to be used by one of the professional trustees' partners during the periods of absence or capacity (*sic*). This was an extremely desirable state of affairs and posed no risk to the client funds additional to that involved in entrusting money to such unimpeachable law firms – that is no risk whatsoever.'

The Cause of the Chaos: Co-ownership and the *Walia* Case

7.7   To understand why s 3(3) was enacted it is necessary to bear in mind two matters:

(a)   that the normal statutory power of attorney under the Powers of Attorney Act 1971, s 10 which can be used by individuals, did not apply to trustees who, if they wished to delegate their functions, had to use 'the s 25 (ie the trustee) power of attorney'; and

(b)   that jointly owned land is held by the beneficial co-owners on a statutory trust[1].

1   LPA 1925, ss 34-6 as amended by TLATA 1996: see para 5.12 above.

7.8   In *Walia v Michael Naughton Ltd*[1] freehold property was jointly owned by A, B and C. A made C his attorney under a section 10 (ie non trustee) power of attorney. The defendant agreed to purchase the property and the transfer was executed by B and C personally and by C as attorney for A. The defendant agreed to sell on the property to the plaintiff before that transfer had been registered at the Land Registry and the purchaser refused to accept that the defendant had a valid title on the basis that the power of attorney should have been granted by A under s 25. It was argued for the defendant that in executing the transfer A, B and C were not exercising a trustee function but were making the transfer *in their capacity of beneficial* owners so that the s 10 power was appropriate. This argument was rejected by Judge John Finlay QC (sitting as a High Court Judge) who declared:

> '. . . the power of attorney in the section 10 form is not appropriate to entitle the donee to execute on behalf of the donor a transfer in which the transferor, whether or not he is purporting to transfer as beneficial owner, is inevitably exercising the function of a trustee. He is exercising the function of a trustee because it is as trustee that he is registered as one of the three joint proprietors. The trusts of course do not come on the title, but the very fact that there is more than one proprietor must . . . mean that the proprietors (and each of them) are trustees of the land. That they may also be beneficial owners appears to me to be neither here not there. . . . It should have been a power of attorney under section [25 of the 1925 Act].'

1   [1985] 1 WLR 1115.

7.9   As a result of the decision a co-owner wishing to delegate his rights over the property (eg to sell or lease it) could only do so by a trustee power under s 25 and, in the common case of a house owned by a married couple, could not give the power to his spouse. Further, the power would terminate if the donor became mentally incapable.

7.10   At the time when the *Walia* case was decided the Enduring Powers of Attorney Act was passing through Parliament. As then drafted, it provided that trustee powers could not be enduring powers[1]. As a result of the *Walia* case the Bill was amended in some haste and what became section 3(3) was added. The then Lord Chancellor (Lord Hailsham of St Marylebone) explained the need for this provision in the following words:

> 'necessitated by a decision of the High Court [*Walia*] . . . The result of this decision, together with clause 2(8) of the Act, is that an attorney under an enduring power cannot dispose of any of the donor's property held on trust. Most married couples nowadays hold the matrimonial home upon a trust for sale, so that the inability of an attorney under an enduring power to dispose of trust property would have widespread effect and reduce the efficacy of the scheme contained in the Bill. This amendment seeks to remedy this defect.[2]'

1   See clause 2(8) of the draft Bill which stated:

>   'A power of attorney under s 25 of the Trustee Act 1925 (power to delegate trusts by power of attorney) cannot be an enduring power.'

    The Law Commission (which had produced the Act) had taken the view that the 12-month limitation in s 25 was inconsistent with the idea of an enduring power whilst the incapacity of a trustee was a ground for his removal under the Trustees Act 1925, s 36(1).

2   Hansard (HL) Vol 465, 24 June 1985 cols 548-9. It is interesting to note that a measure aimed at dealing with problems arising from the statutory trust in co-ownership cases was

so drafted as to have wider ramifications. This process has subsequently been repeated! Many couples unaware of the existence of the statutory trust would assume that the EPA would be effective in this case and there was no real justification for preventing one co-owner from delegating to the other or granting an enduring power as a precaution against the onset of mental incapacity.

7.11   The anomalies arising from the introduction of s 3(3) between, on the one hand, the use of an enduring power and, on the other, a trust power, are highlighted in the table below.

Scope	Section 25	Section 3(3)
Attorney	No delegation to the sole co-trustee, unless trust corporation	No restriction
Notice	To be given to co-trustees and person with power to appoint	No notice required
Form	No prescribed form	Prescribed form compulsory
Mental incapacity	Grant of power does not survive	Grant of power does survive
Duration	12-month limit	Indefinite
Personal representatives	Can delegate powers	Not expressly mentioned

The 1999 Act – a Summary

7.12   The main provisions of the 1999 Act are summarised in the list below. As will be seen in the detailed analysis of legislation it has also succeeded in producing its own problems!

- **repeal** s 3(3) (see ss 4 and 12) subject to transitional rules;

- special regime for **co-owners** (ss 1-3);

- **modernising** s 25 (ss 5 and 6):
    - duration clarified;
    - use of enduring power;
    - retained safeguards;

- protecting the **two-trustee** rule (s 7);

- donee of **incapable donor** can appoint new trustees (ss 8 and 9).

8

Analysis of the Legislation

8.1   The first four sections of the Act deal with two matters:

(a)   a new provision allowing the delegation of his functions by a trustee who has a beneficial interest in land subject to the trusts; and

(b)   the consequent repeal, save for transitional cases, of s 3(3) of the EPA 1985.

Section 1 – Exercise of Trustee Functions by Attorney

8.2   Text of section 1

(1)   The donee of a power of attorney is not prevented from doing an act in relation to–

    (a)   land,

    (b)   capital proceeds of a conveyance of land, or

    (c)   income from land,

by reason only that the act involves the exercise of a trustee function of the donor if, at the time when the act is done, the donor has a beneficial interest in the land, proceeds or income.

Purpose of the section

8.3   Section 1 introduces an exception to the general rule that a trustee can only delegate his functions by a power of attorney falling under TA 1925, s 25. The section applies when the trustee's functions relate to land, capital proceeds of a conveyance of land or income from land *provided that* the trustee has a beneficial interest in that land; capital proceeds or income. In these cases the delegation may be effected by:

(a)   a trustee power of attorney under s 25: *or*

(b)   an enduring power of attorney; *or*[1]

(c)   a section 10 (ie non-trustee) power of attorney.

[1]   At Third Reading in the House of Commons (*Hansard* 2000, vol 335 No 123 col 534) Mr Nick Hawkins raised a query about the type of power which would fall within s 1 (the query was apparently prompted by concerns expressed by Macfarlanes, a firm of solicitors). In essence, he feared that the section would not permit delegation under an

enduring power at a time when the donor had lost mental capacity because 'the power of attorney provided for in clause 1 is not an enduring one'. It is not thought that there is any substance in this concern for the following reasons:

(a)   the section applies to a donee acting under a power of attorney which covers the case of a donee of a registered enduring power (which is merely one type of power of attorney). The type of power falling within the section is not in any way limited;

(b)   other sections of the Act indicate that the section applies to registered enduring powers: see, for instance, s 4(6) and; s 8(1)(6B)(a).

The Land Registry accept that any type of power may fall within s 1: see *Powers of Attorney and Registered Land* (PL 32) reproduced in Appendix 6 below.

EXAMPLE 1

Bill and Betty jointly own their house, 2 Railway Cottages. On 1 March 2001 Bill executes an enduring power of attorney in favour of Betty. Unless the power is limited (see s 1(3)) this will enable Betty to exercise all Bill's powers in relation to the property.

Notes

(a)   An enduring power is effective from the moment of its execution to confer powers on Betty unless the contrary is expressed in the instrument (the current form for an enduring power *which must be used* is printed as **Precedent 31** below).

(b)   If Bill becomes mentally incapable Betty must register the power: she continues to be able to exercise Bill's trustee functions under s 1.

(c)   If Betty wishes to sell the house, s 1 enables her to do so (in her capacity as trustee and attorney for her co-trustee Bill) but capital monies must be received by two trustees (see further para 8.58 below).

8.4   The s 25 restrictions are absent so that delegation can be for an unlimited period and (as with the amended s 25) delegation can be to a sole co-trustee. The prime target of the section is the co-owner of land but, as will be considered below, it has wider implications.

The donor (trustee) must have a beneficial interest in the land, proceeds or income

8.5   There is no definition of a 'beneficial interest' for these purposes but the following matters may be noted:

(a)   that s 1 is not limited to co-owners under the statutory trust;

> **EXAMPLE 2**
>
> 1. Whiteacre is held on a trust of land for A for life remainder to B. The trustees are B and X. B can delegate his trustee powers to Z under s 1 (hence he may delegate by enduring power and without any of the s 25 safeguards). By contrast, if X wishes to delegate his trustee functions to B he must use a s 25 (trustee) power of attorney. This is a somewhat bizarre position!
>
> 2. Bill and Ben jointly owned Nursery Cottage as beneficial tenants in common. Bill gave his equitable half share to his cousin Bettina. Bill and Ben remain as trustees and Ben can delegate his functions under s 1 whereas Bill cannot since he no longer has a beneficial interest in the land[1].

(b) the beneficial interest can be of any size and, when the doctrine of conversion applies, includes an interest in the proceeds of sale[2];

(c) the interest of co-owner and any interest under fixed interest trusts (for instance a life interest and remainder interest) are beneficial interests for these purposes but what of the interest of a beneficiary under a discretionary trust? It is thought that such a person does not fall within the ambit of s 1[3];

(d) it is necessary for the donor to have a beneficial interest 'at the time when the act is done'. Beneficial interests can, of course, terminate (for instance, an interest limited to A until his remarriage with a gift over to B will terminate on A's remarriage) and may be assigned, voluntarily or for consideration. It is not sufficient for the donor to have an interest at the time when the power was created: however, if the donor of a section 10 power subsequently acquires an interest in land subject to trusts of which he is a trustee, his attorney under that power may then fall within the provisions of s 1. The delegation rules in s 1 may pose problems for third parties dealing with attorneys. Section 2(2) provides that 'an appropriate statement' by the attorney is to be a complete protection for purchasers etc[4], whilst s 5 of the Powers of Attorney Act 1971 deals with the position if the power has been revoked[5]. What, however, if s 1 had – unbeknown to the third party – been excluded by the trust instrument?

1   See Law Com No 220, paras 4.21-4.25. It is clear that the purpose of s 1 is to deal with the case where the trustees of the land are also the beneficial owners but the Law Commission accepted that the section could be used in cases where some beneficiaries were not trustees. It may be asked why such beneficiaries are entitled to less protection than in the normal situation where a beneficiary is protected by the s 25 rules.

2   See Law Com No 220, para 4.29; TDA 1999, s 1(7) and TLATA 1996, s 3(1) which is considered at para 2.18 above.

3   Consider the use of 'beneficiary' in TLATA 1996, s 22 which is discussed in detail at para 4.1 above.

4   See further para 8.19 below and consider TLATA 1996, s 9(2) and **Precedent 33** below in Part IV. Law Com No 260, para 4.34 cites other analogous situations: for instance the Administration of Estates Act 1925, s 36(6) which provides for a statement by personal representatives that they have not made or given a conveyance or assent and Law of Property (Joint Tenants) Act 1964, s 1(1) providing for a survivor of joint tenants to state that he is solely and beneficially interested in the property.

5   See para 8.20 below.

The function must relate to land; the proceeds of sale or the income thereof

8.6   'Land' is defined in s 11(1) as having the same meaning as in the Trustee Act 1925[1] whilst the capital proceeds of a 'conveyance' incorporate the wide definition of conveyance which is taken from the Law of Property Act 1925, s 205(1)(ii)[2]. The attorney can join in disposing of the proceeds of sale and of the income from the land but note that:

(a)   the 'two trustee' rule is preserved: see TDA 1999, s 7 and, generally para 8.58 below; and

(b)   once capital monies have been disposed of (for instance by investment in an equity portfolio) the s 1 power of attorney will cease to be effective in relation to that invested property.

1   TA 1925, s 68 contains the following definition:

> '(6) "Land" includes land of any tenure, and mines and minerals whether or not severed from the surface, buildings or parts of buildings, whether the division is horizontal, vertical or made in any way, and other corporeal hereditaments; also a manor, an advowson, and a rent and other incorporeal hereditaments, and an easement, right, privilege, or benefit in, over, or derived from land; and in this definition "mines and minerals" include any strata or seam of minerals or substances in or under any land, and powers of working and getting the same, and "hereditaments" mean real property which under an intestacy occurring before the commencement of this Act might have devolved on an heir.'

2   'Conveyance' is defined in that Act as follows:

> '(ii) "Conveyance" includes a mortgage, charge, lease, assent, vesting declaration, vesting instrument, disclaimer, release and every other assurance of property or of an interest therein by any instrument, except a will; "convey" has a corresponding meaning; and "disposition" includes a conveyance and also a devise, bequest, or an appointment of property contained in a will; and "dispose of" has a corresponding meaning.'

8.7   A power of attorney over the donor's land is deemed to include any estate or interest that he has in that land[1].

1   See TDA 1999, s 10(2): see para 8.75 below.

'A trustee function'

8.8   This somewhat inelegant phrase comprises the trusts powers and discretions vested in the donor as trustee[1]. Section 1(8), which did not form part of the Law Commission's Draft Bill, makes it clear that an attorney is not to be regarded as exercising the s 1(1) power in cases where his authority derives from the trust instrument. It is, for instance, common for a well drafted trust deed to permit trustees as a body to delegate their functions[2].

1   See also TLATA 1996, s 9(1) permitting the delegation of 'any of their functions as trustees'; TDA 1999, s 6 'for the purpose of exercising their functions as trustees' and TA 2000, Pt IV.
2   See, for instance, **Precedent 1, Sch 1, para 21**. It is rare today for an express power to be given to individual trustees: for a precedent, see Form 40. When s 25 was restricted to cases where trustees were about to go abroad for more than one month (prior to the 1971 changes) express clauses were quite often found in trust deeds. Curiously the Standard Provisions of the Society of the Trust and Estate Practitioners (1st Edn, para 3(11)) appear to permit individual delegation but do not confer a power of collective delegation on the trustees. It may be thought that s 1(8), apart from being obscurely worded, is unnecessary.

Liability of donor for acts of donee

8.9   A trustee is not liable for the mere act of empowering an attorney under s 1 but is liable for what that attorney does or fails to do in the same way as if the acts or omissions of the attorney had been his acts or omissions.

EXAMPLE 3

Z, in Point 1 of *Example 2*, acting both in his capacity as trustee and as attorney for A invests capital money from a sale of land in a speculative and unauthorised investment. A may be liable if a loss arises (as will Z in his trustee capacity). Of course, if the trustee deed contained only a restrictive investment power and Z was acting in the interests of the beneficiaries when he made the investment then, if a wide exclusion clause had been included in the trust deed, this might protect both Z and A (see, for instance, **Precedent 1, clause 11** below and Trustee Act 2000, s 1 (see para 10.20 below) and *Armitage v Nurse* [1997] 2 All ER 705, CA.

8.10   A similar liability rests with the donor in the case of a trustee power of attorney[1] but the position when a 'collective' delegation occurs under TLATA 1996, s 9 and TA 2000, Pt IV is somewhat different[2].

1   Section 25(7), considered at para 8.46 below.
2   See s 9A of the 1996 Act and TA 2000, s 23.

A contrary intention

8.11   Section 1(1) does not apply if (or to the extent that) there is a contrary intention in the instrument creating the power of attorney[1]. A trustee may, for instance, give a general power of attorney over his personal affairs and a separate power over his trusteeships. Section 1(5) further provides that subsections (1) and (4) will only apply if and so far as a contrary intention is not expressed in the trust instrument. The vicarious liability of the donor under s 1(4) for the acts of his attorney may accordingly be limited by the trust deed and the power to appoint an attorney under s 1 may likewise be restricted. A settlor may, for example, provide that his trustees can delegate their functions but only by a trustee power of attorney, hence preventing the possible anomalies considered above from arising[2].

1   TDA 1999, s 1(3).
2   See para 8.5, and **Precedent 34** below. See also Law Com No 220 para 4.31.

Stocks and shares

8.12   At first sight, s 1(6) is perplexing given that an attorney under s 1 can only deal with land, capital money or income from land. The apparent explanation is that the subsection is needed to deal with the situation where an attorney invests capital money from land in the acquisition of stocks and shares[1]. The company in such cases can ignore the notice of the trust which it would otherwise receive when dealing with the attorney[2].

1   See also TA 1925, s 25(9), considered at para 8.48 below.
2   Under the Companies Act 1985, s 360 a company registered in England and Wales is
    prohibited from entering a notice of any trust on its register of members.

Which powers of attorney fall within the section?

8.13   As a general rule, s 1 only applies to powers of attorney created after
the end of February 2000[1]. The one exception is for enduring powers of
attorney already in existence on 1 March 2000[2]. If such powers are registered
before 1 March 2001, s 3(3) continues so that the attorney can exercise all
the trustee functions of the donor (including those in relation to land falling
within s 1). If, however, the power remains unregistered then s 3(3) ceases to
apply but the attorney can exercise the power in the circumstances set out in
TDA 1999 s 1. Hence, in most cases it will not be necessary for existing
enduring powers to be renewed after February 2001.

1   TDA 1999, s 1(9).
2   TDA 1999, s 4(6) and see para 8.32 below.

Practical problems caused by the 'two-trustee' rule

8.14   The 'two-trustee' rule is considered in detail at para 8.88 ff below. It
should be noted, however, that it will give rise to difficulties in the example
considered below and this may influence the choice of attorney.

EXAMPLE 4

Dan and Doris are joint owners of *Dunromin* and Dan grants Doris a
power of attorney over all his property. Dan then goes to work in Outer
Mongolia where he cannot be contacted and, having received an
excellent offer for the property, Doris wishes to sell. She cannot give a
good receipt to a purchaser and short of going to court to remove Dan
as a trustee cannot proceed with the sale.

8.15   To avoid this problem consider whether the power should have been
granted, for example to the couple's solicitor. (Note that TDA 1999, s 8 will
only be of assistance in limited circumstances.)

Precedents

8.16   See the following in Part IV below:

- **Precedent 32**: General power of attorney permitting the attorney to
  join with the co-owner to sell land.

- **Precedent 33**: An appropriate statement under s 2(2).

- **Precedent 34**: Clause excluding the operation of s 1.

- See also *Powers of Attorney and Registered Land* (PL 32) reproduced in
  Appendix 6.

Section 2 – Evidence of Beneficial Interest

8.17   Text of section 2

(1)   This section applies where the interest of a purchaser depends on the donee of a power of attorney having power to do an act in relation to any property by virtue of section 1(1) above.

In this subsection 'purchaser' has the same meaning as in Part I of the Law of Property Act 1925.

(2)   Where this section applies an appropriate statement is, in favour of the purchaser, conclusive evidence of the donor of the power having a beneficial interest in the property at the time of the doing of the act.

(3)   In this section 'an appropriate statement' means a signed statement made by the donee—

(a)   when doing the act in question, or

(b)   at any other time within the period of three months beginning with the day on which the act is done,

that the donor has a beneficial interest in the property at the time of the donee doing the act.

(4)   If an appropriate statement is false, the donee is liable in the same way as he would be if the statement were contained in a statutory declaration.

Purpose of the section

8.18   Section 1 only permits an attorney to act on behalf of a trustee who has a beneficial interest in land, etc and s 2 affords protection to a purchaser[1] who receives an appropriate written statement signed by that attorney[2]. Accordingly, a purchaser does not have to investigate equitable interests in the property and the so called 'curtain principle' is preserved[3].

1   'Purchaser' is defined in LPA 1925, s 205(1)(xxi) for the purposes of Part I of the Act as follows:

'(xxi) "Purchaser" means a purchaser in good faith for valuable consideration and includes a lessee, mortgagee or other person who for valuable consideration acquires an interest in property except that in Part I of this Act and elsewhere where so expressly provided "Purchaser" only means a person who acquires an interest in or charge on property for money or money's worth; and in reference to a legal estate includes a chargee by way of legal mortgage; and where the context so requires "purchaser" includes an intending purchaser; "purchase" has a meaning corresponding with that of "purchaser"; and "valuable consideration" includes marriage but does not include a nominal consideration in money.'

2   See **Precedent 33** below.
3   See Law Com No 220, para 4.33 and para 8.20 below and see generally *Powers of Attorney and Registered Land* (PL 32) reproduced in Appendix 6.

Requirements of an 'appropriate statement'

8.19   It must be in writing, signed by the donee and made by him either at the time when he did the relevant act (for instance entered into a contract to sell trust land to the purchaser) or made within three months after doing that act[1]. A statement used in connection with a prior transaction will accordingly not suffice. The statement must indicate that the donor has (at the time when the donee did the act) a beneficial interest in the property.

1   The statement may be included in any transfer of land sold or may be in a separate document. For a similar three-month period, see the Powers of Attorney Act 1971, s 5(4)(b).

Extent of protection for purchaser

8.20   The statement affords 'conclusive evidence' that the donor had the necessary beneficial interest in the land: as such, it affords good protection to a purchaser whose title depends upon the attorney being duly authorised under s 1. He is not, however, protected in the event that the statement contains an inaccuracy on its face[1] (for instance, if it stated that the donor had a beneficial interest at the time when the power was granted rather than when it was exercised) or if it is tainted by fraud. Nor is he protected against the possibility of a specific provision in the trust instrument which prohibits delegation to an attorney.

1   See *Re Caratal (New) Mines Ltd* [1902] 2 Ch 498.

8.21   Fraud could arise on the part of the purchaser who deals with an attorney in full knowledge that the power purportedly exercised does not meet the conditions of s 1. In this situation, because the definition of 'purchaser' requires him to act in good faith, he will be unable to rely on the statement. If the fraud is on the part of the attorney then it is likely that he is acting for his own ends and so the trust beneficiaries and the purchaser are likely to be innocent parties. In this situation the purchaser remains protected and any resultant loss will fall upon the beneficiaries[1], although the beneficiary will have a right of action against the trustee donor under TDA 1999, s 1(4). In cases where no statement is made, the purchaser may still be protected provided that he is able to show that, on the facts, the conditions of s 1 are met.

1   See Law Com No 220, paras 4.36-4.37.

Liability of donee for false statement

8.22   Any inaccuracy in the statement is subject to the penalties which apply to the making of false statutory declarations under the Perjury Act 1911, s 5 (viz a penalty on summary conviction of imprisonment for up to six months and/or a fine not exceeding £5,000: on indictment the penalty is imprisonment for up to two years and/or an unlimited fine).

Section 3 – General Powers in Specified Form

8.23   Text of section 3

In section 10(2) of the Powers of Attorney Act 1971 (which provides that a general power of attorney in the form set out in Schedule 1 to that Act, or a similar form, does not confer on the donee of the power any authority to exercise functions of the donor as trustee etc), for the words 'This section' substitute 'Subject to section 1 of the Trustee Delegation Act 1999, this section'.

8.24 Normally, a general power of attorney under the Powers of Attorney Act 1971, s 10 does not permit the donee to exercise trustee functions. This section introduces an exception for powers falling within s 1 of the TDA 1999. Hence:

(a)   to this extent it reverses *Walia v Michael Naughton Ltd* (See para 7.8 above);

(b)   as a result, any power of attorney (whether a trustee power under s 25, a general power under s 10 or enduring power) will confer on the donee the power to exercise trustee functions provided that the conditions of s 1 are satisfied.

Section 4 – Enduring Powers

8.25   Text of section 4

(1)   Section 3(3) of the Enduring Powers of Attorney Act 1985 (which entitles the donee of an enduring power to exercise any of the donor's functions as trustee and to give receipt for capital money etc) does not apply to enduring powers created after the commencement of this Act.

(2)   Section 3(3) of the Enduring Powers of Attorney Act 1985 ceases to apply to enduring powers created before the commencement of this Act—

    (a)   where subsection (3) below applies, in accordance with that subsection, and

    (b)   otherwise, at the end of the period of one year from that commencement.

(3)   Where an application for the registration of the instrument creating such an enduring power is made before the commencement of this Act, or during the period of one year from that commencement, section 3(3) of the Enduring Powers of Attorney Act 1985 ceases to apply to the power—

    (a)   if the instrument is registered pursuant to the application (whether before commencement or during or after that period), when the registration of the instrument is cancelled, and

    (b)   if the application is finally refused during or after that period, when the application is finally refused.

(4)   In subsection (3) above—

    (a)   'registration' and 'registered' mean registration and registered under section 6 of the Enduring Powers of Attorney Act 1985, and

    (b)   'cancelled' means cancelled under section 8(4) of that Act.

(5)   For the purposes of subsection (3)(b) above an application is finally refused—

    (a)   if the application is withdrawn or any appeal is abandoned, when the application is withdrawn or the appeal is abandoned, and

    (b)   otherwise, when proceedings on the application (including any proceedings on, or in consequence of, an appeal) have been determined and any time for appealing or further appealing has expired.

(6)   Section 1 above applies to an enduring power created before the commencement of this Act from the time when (in accordance with subsections (2) to (5) above) section 3(3) of the Enduring Powers of Attorney Act 1985 ceases to apply to it.

Purpose of the section

8.26   The difficulties caused by s 3(3) of the Enduring Powers of Attorney Act 1985 have already been considered[1]. Section 4 repeals s 3(3) in respect of enduring powers created after February 2000 with transitional provisions applying to existing enduring powers.

1   See para 7.6 above.

The basic principle: new enduring powers

8.27   Section 3(3) does not apply but the donee of the power may be able to act under s 1 provided that the relevant conditions for the operation of that section are met[1].

1   TDA 1999, s 4(1); 4(6).

Existing but unregistered enduring powers

8.28   Section 3(3) ceases to apply to such powers on 1 March 2001. Until then a donee could continue to exercise all the trustee functions of his donor[1]. From 1 March 2001 s 1 may apply to such powers.

1   TDA 1999, s 4(2)(b); 1(9); 4(6). An enduring power must be registered when the attorney has reason to believe that the donor is, or is becoming, mentally incapable (EPA 1985, s 4(1)). For the registration procedure, see s 6. Until registration an enduring power operates as an ordinary power.

Existing powers where an application to register is refused

8.29   If the application to register is made before 1 March 2001, s 3(3) continues to apply until that application is finally refused. From that time it ceases to apply and s 1 will apply provided that the requisite conditions are satisfied[1].

1   TDA 1999, s 4(2)(a); 4(3)(b); 1(9); 4(6). Section 4(5) sets out when such a power is finally refused. Note that this may be at the end of the appeal process. Refusal to register may therefore have the effect of curtailing the period for which an existing EPA may be used: hence, confirmation should be sought whenever reliance is placed on s 3(3) in the case of a pre March 2001 unregistered power that an application to register has been made and not been refused.

Existing powers which are, or which become, registered

8.30   Section 3(3) continues to apply to:

(a)   powers which were registered on 1 March 2000; and

(b)   powers where an application to register is made before 1 March 2001 and which become registered.

8.31   It will only cease to apply when the registration of the instrument is cancelled[1].

1   TDA 1999, s 4(2)(a); 4(3)(a). For the cancellation procedure in respect of a registered enduring power, see EPA 1985, s 8(4).

Rationale for the transitional rules and s 4(6)

8.32   The transitional rules in the case of enduring powers in existence on 1 March 2000 were introduced to enable donors (who are mentally capable) to make new arrangements whilst the exception for registered powers will preserve the effect of delegations where the donor is no longer capable of delegating his functions. However, s 4(6), which did not appear in the Law Commission Draft Bill[1], has the result that, even if a donor is capable of making a new delegation, the existing enduring power may still be effective to deal with property falling within s 1.

1   See Law Com No 220, paras 4.1-4.4 and see generally *Powers of Attorney and Registered Land* (PL 32) reproduced in Appendix 6 below.

Trustee Delegation under s 25 of the Trustee Act 1925

8.33   This part of the Act makes various detailed changes to the operation of s 25 as a result of the Law Commission recommendations. It should be remembered that s 25 is a statutory fall back which will apply if the trust instrument itself makes no provision for a trustee to delegate his functions. In modern trust deeds such provision is commonly made and trustees are allowed to delegate with greater freedom than is permitted under s 25[1].

1   See TA 1925, s 69(2) which permits s 25 to be overridden by the trust instrument. Exceptionally, the instrument may prevent delegation altogether and, of course, if all the beneficiaries are of full age and capacity they can authorise delegation by a trustee in any circumstances. It is unheard of for a purchaser to refuse to accept a section 25 power without sight of the trust instrument despite the fact that delegation might have been forbidden (or restricted) by the settlor!

8.34   By way of background to the changes that have been made by TDA 1999, it should be remembered that s 25 contained a number of built-in safeguards:

(a)   a 12-month time limit on delegation[1];

(b)   because of the time limit an enduring power could not be used to effect a delegation under s 25[2];

(c)   delegation to a sole co-trustee, other than a trust corporation, was prohibited;

(d)   the trustee must give notice to his co-trustee(s) and the person (if any) with the power to appoint new trustees;

(e)   the trustee may be liable for the acts and omissions of the attorney that he appoints; and

(f)   sub-delegation by the attorney is prohibited.

1   However, the power may be renewed year on year: the Law Commission commented:

'the need for repeated powers of attorney, every year, was seen as a small but useful means of discouraging permanent delegation'

See Law Com No 229, para 4.6 footnote. The time limit was fixed by an analogy with the period in TA 1925, s 36(1) (removal of a trustee remaining out of the UK for 12 months).

2   EPA 1985, s 2(8).

8.35   The Law Commission reviewed the operation of the section and whether the safeguards continued to be necessary and, as a result, changes were made by TDA 1999, ss 5-6.

Section 5 – Delegation under Section 25 of the Trustee Act 1925[1]

8.36   Text of section 5

(1)   For section 25 of the Trustee Act 1925 substitute–

'25   Delegation of trustee's functions by power of attorney

(1)   Notwithstanding any rule of law or equity to the contrary, a trustee may, by power of attorney, delegate the execution or exercise of all or any of the trusts, powers and discretions vested in him as trustee either alone or jointly with any other person or persons.

(2)   A delegation under this section–

(a)   commences as provided by the instrument creating the power or, if the instrument makes no provision as to the commencement of the delegation, with the date of the execution of the instrument by the donor; and

(b)   continues for a period of twelve months or any shorter period provided by the instrument creating the power.

(3)   The persons who may be donees of a power of attorney under this section include a trust corporation.

(4)   Before or within seven days after giving a power of attorney under this section the donor shall give written notice of it (specifying the date on which the power comes into operation and its duration, the donee of the power, the reason why the power is given and, where some only are delegated, the trusts, powers and discretions delegated) to–

(a)   each person (other than himself), if any, who under any instrument creating the trust has power (whether alone or jointly) to appoint a new trustee; and

(b)   each of the other trustees, if any;

but failure to comply with this subsection shall not, in favour of a person dealing with the donee of the power, invalidate any act done or instrument executed by the donee.

(5)   A power of attorney given under this section by a single donor–

(a)   in the form set out in subsection (6) of this section; or

(b)   in a form to the like effect but expressed to be made under this subsection,

shall operate to delegate to the person identified in the form as the single donee of the power the execution and exercise of all the trusts, powers and discretions vested in the donor as trustee (either alone or jointly with any other person or persons) under the single trust so identified.

(6)   The form referred to in subsection (5) of this section is as follows–

"THIS GENERAL TRUSTEE POWER OF ATTORNEY is made on [*date*] by [*name of one donor*] of [*address of donor*] as trustee of [*name or details of one trust*].

I appoint [*name of one donee*] of [*address of donee*] to be my attorney [*if desired, the date on which the delegation commences or the period for which it continues (or both)*] in accordance with section 25(5) of the Trustee Act 1925.

[*To be executed as a deed*]."

(7)   The donor of a power of attorney given under this section shall be liable for the acts or defaults of the donee in the same manner as if they were the acts or defaults of the donor.

(8)   For the purpose of executing or exercising the trusts or powers delegated to him, the donee may exercise any of the powers conferred on the donor as trustee by statute or by the instrument creating the trust, including power, for the purpose of the transfer of any inscribed stock, himself to delegate to an attorney power to transfer, but not including the power of delegation conferred by this section.

(9)   The fact that it appears from any power of attorney given under this section, or from any evidence required for the purposes of any such power of attorney or otherwise, that in dealing with any stock the donee of the power is acting in the execution of a trust shall not be deemed for any purpose to affect any person in whose books the stock is inscribed or registered with any notice of the trust.

(10) This section applies to a personal representative, tenant for life and statutory owner as it applies to a trustee except that subsection (4) shall apply as if it required the notice there mentioned to be given–

(a)   in the case of a personal representative, to each of the other personal representatives, if any, except any executor who has renounced probate;

(b)   in the case of a tenant for life, to the trustees of the settlement and to each person, if any, who together with the person giving the notice constitutes the tenant for life; and

(c)   in the case of a statutory owner, to each of the persons, if any, who together with the person giving the notice constitute the statutory owner and, in the case of a statutory owner by virtue of section 23(1)(a) of the Settled Land Act 1925, to the trustees of the settlement."

(2)   Subsection (1) above has effect in relation to powers of attorney created after the commencement of this Act.

> (3) In section 34(2)(b) of the Pensions Act 1995 (delegation by trustees of trustee scheme under section 25 of the Trustee Act 1925), for 'during absence abroad' substitute 'for period not exceeding twelve months'.

1   In the Draft Bill prepared by the Law Commission, s 5 was drafted as a series of amendments to TA 1925 (which it should be remembered had already been amended by PAA 1971). In the Committee Debates during the passage of the Act in the House of Lords, Lord Brightman proposed the insertion of a new clause which would introduce a schedule setting out the terms of the revised s 25. The Government resisted this amendment with Lord Falconer of Thoroton commenting that:

> 'The amendment tabled by Lord Brightman would result in the inclusion of what is called "a Keeling Schedule" in the Act. Introduced in 1937 these Schedules – named after a member of another place whose enquiries of the then Prime Minister gave rise to their use – are now little used. They tend to give rise to handling difficulties during the passage of bills and set the amended provision in aspic. Further amendments to the provision would not show up on a Keeling Schedule and it might become a trap for the unwary at a later date.'

Instead the Government introduced at Third Reading an amendment setting out the whole of the new s 25.

Purpose of the section

8.37   The section 'tidies up' s 25 in respect of powers of attorney granted after the end of February 2000. The most significant practical change is the removal of the general prohibition on delegating to a sole co-trustee.

Subsection (1)

8.38   This repeats the old s 25(1) with the exception of the 12-month limitation which is clarified in new sub-s (2). The old, and out-of-date, side heading, is replaced by 'delegation of trustee's functions by power of attorney'. The subsection itself eschews 'trustee functions' in favour of the 'trusts, powers and discretions' vested in a trustee[1].

1   The wording suggests that an attorney can appoint an additional trustee under TA 1925, s 36(6): compare TDA 1999, s 8 considered at para 8.63 below.

Subsection (2)

8.39   This sets out in detail the 12-month limitation on powers of attorney granted under s 25[1]. The period will begin on the date of execution of the instrument by the trustee unless the instrument which creates the power makes express provision for when the delegation is to commence (for instance, the power of attorney might provide that it will begin in six weeks time (on such and such a date) being the time when the donor leaves for an extended foreign holiday or, in the case of an enduring power, the date on which it is registered)[2]. What is the effect of a delegation without an express time limit? It is now provided[3] that the power will continue for a period of 12 months but will then cease. Of course, the instrument creating the power may expressly provide for its continuance for a shorter period than 12 months. As a result of the provision which limits an apparently unlimited power to 12 months, there is now no objection to using an enduring power of attorney to effect a section 25 delegation and this is considered further in the discussion of s 6 of the Act[4].

1   See Law Com No 220, paras 4.6-4.10.
2   The donor must, of course, still be a trustee at the chosen date of commencement.
3   Amended TA 1925, s 25(2)(b).
4   The section 1 power can also be delegated to a sole co-trustee: see para 8.3 above.

Subsection (3)

8.40   This replaces the old s 25(2) but with the important removal of the prohibition on delegation to a sole co-trustee (other than a trust corporation). The old prohibition had not always been effective. It could, for instance, have been circumvented:

(a)   by the delegation by several trustees to a single attorney; or

(b)   if two or more trustees delegated to one co-trustee.

8.41   The Law Commission further concluded that it was not supported in principle and that the precise purpose of the restriction was unclear. It is also worth remembering that there is no rule against a trust being established with a single trustee[1]. However, there are statutory provisions which require a minimum of two trustees (or a trust corporation) namely:

(a)   the proceeds of sale of land held on a trust of land must be paid to, or at the direction of, at least two trustees[2].

(b)   capital money arising under the Settled Land Act must be paid to, or at the direction of, at least two trustees[3];

(c)   a receipt for such payments must be given by at least two trustees[4]; and

(d)   equitable interests and powers in land subject to a trust of land are overreached when the land is sold provided that the proceeds are paid to at least two trustees[5].

1   It is not unusual for trusts to be declared by a settlor who becomes the first trustee and, of course, a single trustee may come into existence on the death of his co-trustee. As a matter of policy, however, leaving a single trustee to run the trust may not be recommended.
2   LPA 1925, s 27(2) as amended.
3   SLA 1925, s 18(1)(c); 94(1). Capital monies are then defined in s 117(1)(ii).
4   TA 1925, s 14(2) as amended.
5   LPA 1925, s 2(1)(ii) as amended.

8.42   To bolster these rules (which it considered should be preserved) the Law Commission advocated that the provisions governing delegation by trustees should be restricted so that one person could not, in however many capacities he may be acting, satisfy the statutory provisions requiring two trustees to act. This proposal has been implemented in TDA 1999, s 7 which is considered below[1].

1   See para 8.58 ff below.

Subsection (4)

8.43   This repeats the existing sub-s (4) without any substantive change. The notice should, *inter alia*, indicate when the power is to come into effect and state the reason why it was granted. For a specimen notice, see **Precedent 37** below. Failure to give notice does not affect a third party.

Subsections (5) and (6)

8.44   These provisions are new and provide a standard form power of attorney. It is intended for use by a trustee who wishes to delegate all his trustee functions in relation to a single trust to a single donee. If the statutory form is not used it is provided that the delegation may be effected (still apparently by a single donor to a single donee) in a form 'to the like effect but expressed to be made under this subsection'. The notes issued to accompany the legislation state that 'a power of attorney *differing in immaterial respects only* (italics supplied) has the same effect as the power in the prescribed form'. It is not, however, clear that the statutory words are intended to limit the powers that may expressly be created: for instance, it was accepted by the Law Commission that there can be delegation to joint attorneys and, likewise, it is considered that a single form can be used to delegate the functions of more than one trusteeship. In such cases delegation will be authorised under s 25(1) and it is not considered that s 25(5) was intended to restrict the operation of that sub-section[1].

1   See Law Com No 220, paras 4.18-4.20 explaining the background to the standard form which is based on that provided in Sch 1 of the 1971 Powers of Attorney Act. It is curious to note that this standard form caters for the appointment of joint attorneys but the Law Commission rejected this approach in the case of a standard form for trustee delegation on the somewhat curious grounds that because only four trustees can act in relation to land held in trust (see TA 1925, s 34(1); LPA 1925, s 34(2)) if 'one trustee appoints more than one attorney to act in his place this limit may in practical terms be exceeded'. As an attorney under s 25 does not become a trustee, the objection is presumably to the unwieldy number of persons who would have to be consulted before a trustee decision can be reached. See **Precedent 36** below and see also *Powers of Attorney and Registered Land* (PL 32) reproduced in Appendix 6 below.

8.45   In the following situations the prescribed form will be inappropriate and an express power of attorney, made pursuant to s 25, will be required if:

(a)   the donor is not delegating all his trustee functions but, for instance, merely powers in relation to one trust property;

(b)   more than one attorney is to be appointed;

(c)   the trustee's functions in relation to several trusts are to be delegated;

(d)   more than one trustee is to delegate using a single form. In practice this commonly occurred when s 25 had been used to delegate the trustee powers of investment (essentially a collective delegation)[1]. With the passage of the Trustee Act 2000 this will no longer be necessary and the use of a single instrument by several trustees is capable of giving rise to difficult questions: for instance, if one of the donors ceases to be a trustee or becomes mentally incapable, what is the status of the instrument so far as the other donors and their attorneys are concerned[2]?

1   See para 12.2 below.
2   Law Commission No 220, para 4.20(a).

Subsection (7)

8.46   This relates to the liability of the donor for the acts or defaults of the donee (re-enacting the old s 25(5))[1]. A trustee owes a duty of care in:

(a)   selecting an appropriate attorney to act on his behalf; and

(b)   supervising that attorney once appointed[2].

1   See the identical wording in s 1(4)(a) considered at para 8.9 above.
2   The vicarious liability imposed on a donor under s 25 (and under TDA 1999, s 1) may reflect the fact that such delegation is for a temporary period and is not intended to permit the donor to escape from his duties. Hence, there is no provision permitting the attorney to be paid: contrast collective delegation under TA 2000, Pt IV.

Subsection (8)

8.47   This repeats the old s 25(6) without any substantive change. Note that it prevents further sub-delegation by the attorney: in practice this was rarely expressly authorised in the trust instrument although trustees will frequently delegate their powers of investment to a broker and permit him to hold the investments through a nominee.

Subsection (9)

8.48   This replaces the old s 25(7) and has been considered above in relation to the similarly worded s 1(6)[1].

1   See para 8.12 above.

Subsection (10)

8.49   This repeats the old s 25(8) without substantive changes. A personal representative can delegate under s 25 but not under s 1[1].

1   The powers of the tenant for life under a strict settlement are discussed at para 1.10 above.

Other matters

8.50   Section 5(2) tidies up the wording of s 34 of the Pensions Act 1995 so that it corresponds to the new s 25. The re-worded s 25 applies to powers of attorney granted after February 2000.

8.51   The other significant change in the ambit of s 25, that the relevant power of attorney can be an enduring power, is dealt with in the commentary on s 6 which follows.

8.52   Subsection (3) of s 25 had required a power of attorney to be attested by at least one witness. This provision became obsolete as a result of the general requirements for all deeds laid down in the Law of Property (Miscellaneous Provisions) Act 1989, s 1(3) and has accordingly been repealed. It does not appear that there is any power for the attorney to be remunerated out of the trust funds: TDA 1999, s 5 has make no change in this respect and it is not considered that TA 2000, s 32 applies to individual delegation[1].

1   The authors are aware that when s 25 was used to collectively delegate the trustee's investment powers (no longer necessary after the passage of TA 2000, Pt IV) such attorney was regularly paid out of the trust funds.

Precedents

8.53

- **Precedent 35**: delegation by EPA falling within TA 1925, s 25.

- **Precedent 37**: notice to co-trustees).

- **Precedent 36**: delegation to a single attorney of several trusteeships.

- See generally *Power of Attorney and Registered Land* (PL 32) reproduced in Appendix 6.

Section 6 – Section 25 Powers as Enduring Powers

8.54   Text of section 6

Section 2(8) of the Enduring Powers of Attorney Act 1985 (which prevents a power of attorney under section 25 of the Trustee Act 1925 from being an enduring power) does not apply to powers of attorney created after the commencement of this Act.

Purpose of the section

8.55   Formerly, the fact that s 25 powers had to be limited to a maximum period of 12 months was considered to be incompatible with the use of an enduring power (which is, of course, not limited in duration). However, the insertion of s 25(2)(b), which operates to impose a 12-month limit on a power which is not on its face restricted in duration to 12 months or less, means that the objection falls away and hence the prohibition on using an enduring power of attorney to effect a delegation under s 25 has been repealed.

How significant is the change?

8.56   It is hard to get over-excited by this change. The trustee may delegate his functions by an enduring power; become mentally incapable so that the power is registered and the attorney may continue to exercise that power but only for a maximum period of 12 months[1].

1   See Law Com No 220, para 4.10: 'this (change) is not likely to be of great practical value, because the delegation limited to one year is incompatible with the fundamental purpose of an enduring power, the effect of which is indefinite; nevertheless, it will prevent the power of attorney granted by a trustee being completely invalid simply because the wrong form is used'. The maximum use of a registered power will be 12 months in a case where the section 25 delegation is to commence on registration.

Completing and registering the EPA

8.57   Assume that T uses an EPA to delegate his trustee functions: it would appear possible to amend the prescribed form to make it clear that the delegation is for a maximum period of 12 months (see the space on page 3 of the form for the insertion of restrictions and conditions whch would permit the inclusion of a statement that the delegation was only to be for one year). The legislation contemplates a power expiring otherwise than by the death of the donor: see EPA 1985, ss 8(4)(d) and 9(2)(c). Of course, if the form is unlimited in time the 12-month cut off will be imposed by s 25(2)(6). What if an application to register were made during the 12-month period? It would seem that T's co-trustees are not entitled to notice of the application: if the power were registered what would happen at the end of 12 months? The power lapses and so it should therefore be cancelled.

Section 7 – Two-trustee Rules

8.58   Text of section 7

(1)   A requirement imposed by an enactment–

(a)   that capital money be paid to, or dealt with as directed by, at least two trustees or that a valid receipt for capital money be given otherwise than by a sole trustee, or

(b)   that, in order for an interest or power to be overreached, a conveyance or deed be executed by at least two trustees,

is not satisfied by money being paid to or dealt with as directed by, or a receipt for money being given by, a relevant attorney or by a conveyance or deed being executed by such an attorney.

(2)   In this section 'relevant attorney' means a person (other than a trust corporation within the meaning of the Trustee Act 1925) who is acting either–

(a)   both as a trustee and as attorney for one or more other trustees, or

(b)   as attorney for two or more trustees,

and who is not acting together with any other person or persons.

(3)   This section applies whether a relevant attorney is acting under a power created before or after the commencement of this Act (but in the case of such an attorney acting under an enduring power created before that commencement is without prejudice to any continuing application of section 3(3) of the Enduring Powers of Attorney Act 1985 to the enduring power after that commencement in accordance with section 4 above).

The purpose of the section

8.59   It is possible, under both s 1 and the revamped TA 1925, s 25, for a trustee to delegate his trustee functions to a single co-trustee. That person, albeit in two capacities, will then act as the sole trustee of the trust. It is the purpose of this section to ensure that this does not detract from legislation which, in certain circumstances, requires there to be two trustees.

When are two trustees required?

8.60   The circumstances are as follows:

(a)   capital monies arising from land must be paid to, or at the direction of, at least two trustees (SLA 1925, ss 18(1)(c) and 94(1); LPA 1925, s 27(2));

(b)   a valid receipt for such capital monies must be given otherwise than by a sole trustee (TA 1925, s 14(2)); and

(c)   a conveyance or deed must be made by at least two trustees to overreach any powers or interests affecting a legal estate in land (LPA 1925, s 2(1)(ii)).

A 'relevant attorney'

8.61   Section 7(1) provides that a 'relevant attorney' does not satisfy the two-trustees requirement. This term is defined in s 7(2) as a person acting in more than one capacity (for instance, as trustee and attorney for his sole co-trustee) and who is acting alone. There is the usual saving for a trust corporation.

EXAMPLE 5

A and B are the trustees of the Crypton settlement:

(a)   A appoints B his attorney under s 25. B acting alone will not satisfy the two-trustee rule;

(b)   A and B appoint C as their attorney. C acting alone does not satisfy the two-trustee rule;

(c)   A appoints D his attorney and D acts with B so that the rule is satisfied;

(d)   A appoints D his attorney and B appoints C. C and D can act together and will satisfy the rule;

(e)   A appoints C and D his joint attorney as does B. C and D can act together to satisfy the two-trustee rule.

Commencement

8.62   Section 7 applies to powers of attorney whenever created with the exception of enduring powers of attorney to which s 3(3) of the 1985 Act continues to apply by the virtue of the transitional rules in s 4[1].

1   See para 8.25 ff above. It is, of course, not possible to exclude s 7 in the trust instrument.

EXAMPLE 6

Bill and Ben are trustees of the Bloggs family trust. In 1998 Bill appoints Ben his attorney under an enduring power which is registered on 1 February 2001. By virtue of TDA 1999, s 4(2)(a) and 4(3) Ben is able to exercise all the trustee powers in relation to the family trust (including giving a good receipt for capital monies).

Section 8 – Appointment of Additional Trustee by Attorney

8.63   Text of section 8

(1)   In section 36 of the Trustee Act 1925 (appointment of trustees), after subsection (6) (additional trustees) insert–

'(6A) A person who is either–

    (a)   both a trustee and attorney for the other trustee (if one other), or for both of the other trustees (if two others), under a registered power; or

    (b)   attorney under a registered power for the trustee (if one) or for both or each of the trustees (if two or three),

may, if subsection (6B) of this section is satisfied in relation to him, make an appointment under subsection (6)(b) of this section on behalf of the trustee or trustees.

(6B) This subsection is satisfied in relation to an attorney under a registered power for one or more trustees if (as attorney under the power)–

    (a)   he intends to exercise any function of the trustee or trustees by virtue of section 1(1) of the Trustee Delegation Act 1999; or

    (b)   he intends to exercise any function of the trustee or trustees in relation to any land, capital proceeds of a conveyance of land or income from land by virtue of its delegation to him under section 25 of this Act or the instrument (if any) creating the trust.

(6C) In subsections (6A) and (6B) of this section "registered power" means a power of attorney created by an instrument which is for the time being registered under section 6 of the Enduring Powers of Attorney Act 1985.

(6D) Subsection (6A) of this section–

    (a)   applies only if and so far as a contrary intention is not expressed in the instrument creating the power of attorney (or, where more than one, any of them) or the instrument (if any) creating the trust; and

    (b)   has effect subject to the terms of those instruments.'

(2)   The amendment made by subsection (1) above has effect only where the power, or (where more than one) each of them, is created after the commencement of this Act.

Purpose of the section

8.64   The two-trustee rule, as strengthened by TDA 1999, s 7, could have had the effect of frustrating a section 1 legislation. Assume, for instance, that John and Jane jointly own 'Westwinds' and that John grants Jane an enduring power of attorney, subsequently becoming mentally incapable so that Jane registers the power. She wishes to sell Westwinds but the convey-ance can only by executed and a receipt given for capital monies by two trustees[1]. It is to deal with this problem that s 8 permits Jane to appoint an additional trustee thereby ensuring that the two-trustee rule is met. The section achieves this result by inserting new sub-s 36(6A)-(6D) into TA 1925, s 36.

1   On such facts Jane would have to apply to the Court of Protection for an order to procure the appointment of a new trustee (see the Trustee Act 1925, s 36(9)).

Who can appoint an additional trustee?

8.65   It is only an attorney under a registered power who can make the appointment: 'registered power' is defined in s 36(6C) as one created by an instrument under the 1985 Act and registered on the mental incapacity of the donor.

The circumstances when the attorney can make an appointment

8.66   The somewhat confusing requirements are as follows.

8.67   First, either of the following preconditions has to be met:-

(a)   the attorney must be both trustee and attorney for one or more trustees under registered power(s); or

(b)   he must be attorney under a registered power for the trustee or, if more than one, trustees.

8.68   Then one of the following conditions laid down in s 36(6B) has to be met:

(a)   that the attorney intends to exercise any trustee function by virtue of TDA 1999, s 1(1). Note that the function may not be one which will trigger the 'two-trustee' rule; or

(b)   that he intends to exercise any trustee function in relation to the matters dealt with in s 1 (ie land; capital proceeds of a conveyance of land or income from land) by virtue of a delegation to him under s 25 or in the trust instrument.

EXAMPLE 7

Bill and Ben are trustees of the Bloggs family trust. On 1 June 2000 Bill delegated his trustee powers to Ben under an enduring power of attorney falling within s 25. On 1 September 2000 the power is registered and on 1 December 2000 Ben decides to let part of the trust land and appoints Cecil as an additional trustee under s 36(6)(b).

Notes:

(a)   the requirement in s 36(6A)(a) is satisfied;

(b)   the condition in s 36(6B)(b) is met given that Ben intends to let the land;

(c)   delegation under s 25 is, of course, only effective for a maximum period of 12 months (ie until 1 June 2001) but this does not prevent the appointment of Cecil as an additional trustee. When the s 25 enduring power expires Cecil will therefore remain a trustee with Bill and Ben;

(d)   the letting of the land may produce a capital sum in the form of a premium so triggering the two-trustee rule (which will of course be met) or it may be in consideration of the payment of a rent.

The power that is exercised

8.69   If the various conditions and requirements are met the attorney may exercise the s 36(6)(b) power to appoint an additional trustee or trustees. Although unlikely to be a problem in this situation, it should be remembered that the number of trustees may not be increased beyond four as the result of this appointment[1].

EXAMPLE 8

As in **Example 7** but Ben decides to appoint Cecil and Dougal as additional trustees under s 36(6)(b).

---

1   It is thought that if the appointment purports to create more than four trustees then its exercise is wholly void. It should also be noted that it is because of the four-trustee limit that s 36(6A)(a) refers to two other trustees (apart from the attorney trustee) and s 36(6A)(b) to a maximum of three donee trustees.

The nature of the appointment

8.70   In making the appointment the attorney is acting on behalf of the trustee or trustees and the appointee will become a 'full' trustee of the settlement: ie the appointment is not in any sense an appointment limited to the exercise of the relevant trustee function. Accordingly, although a specific function in relation to trust land is required for the new trustee to be appointed, the appointment is not confined to acting in relation to that specific matter[1] (indeed it may be that the particular function is never so exercised).

1   Law Com No 220, para 4.41.

Other matters

8.71   The changes effected by s 8 only apply to powers created after February 2000[1] and are subject to a contrary intention in the instrument creating the power of attorney or the instrument creating the trust and they have effect subject to the terms of those instruments (see s 36(6D)). It should also be remembered that s 36(6)(b) – the power for existing trustees to appoint additional trustees – can only be exercised if there is no person named in the trust instrument as having that power or if such person is unable and unwilling to act.

1   TDA 1999, s 8(2).

Section 9 – Attorney Acting for Incapable Trustee

8.72   Text of section 9

(1)   In section 22 of the Law of Property Act 1925 (requirement, before dealing with legal estate vested in trustee who is incapable by reason of mental disorder, to appoint new trustee or discharge incapable trustee), after subsection (2) insert–

'(3)   Subsection (2) of this section does not prevent a legal estate being dealt with without the appointment of a new trustee, or the discharge of the incapable trustee, at a time when the donee of an enduring power (within the meaning of the Enduring Powers of Attorney Act 1985) is entitled to act for the incapable trustee in the dealing.'

(2)   The amendment made by subsection (1) above has effect whether the enduring power was created before or after the commencement of this Act.

Purpose of the section

8.73   Section 22(2) of the LPA 1925 provides that if land is held on a trust of land and is vested either solely or jointly in a trustee who is incapable, because of mental disorder, of acting as a trustee then he must be discharged before there is any dealing with the legal estate[1]. In cases where an attorney acting under a registered enduring power (falling under either TDA 1999, s 1 or TA 1925, s 25) wishes to deal with the legal estate this provision would presumably prevent that from happening. Accordingly, s 9 introduces a new sub-s (3) into LPA 1925, s 22 which provides that the incapable trustee does not need to be discharged (ie it disapplies s 22(2)) if there is an attorney under an enduring power who is capable of acting.

1   Note s 22(1) which deals with the position when a receiver acts for the person suffering from mental disorder.

Commencement

8.74   The new sub-s (3) applies whenever the enduring power was created.

Section 10 – Extent of Attorney's Authority to Act in Relation to Land

8.75   Text of section 10

(1)   Where the donee of a power of attorney is authorised by the power to do an act of any description in relation to any land, his authority to do an act of that description at any time includes authority to do it with respect to any estate or interest in the land which is held at that time by the donor (whether alone or jointly with any other person or persons).

(2)   Subsection (1) above–

    (a)   applies only if and so far as a contrary intention is not expressed in the instrument creating the power of attorney, and

    (b)   has effect subject to the terms of that instrument.

(3)   This section applies only to powers of attorney created after the commencement of this Act.

Purpose of the section

8.76   Assume that A and B are joint owners of 'Westwinds'. Each is a trustee of the legal estate which is held for the two of them as beneficial tenants in common. The effect of a power of attorney granted by A which permits the attorney to act in relation to 'my interest in Westwinds' might be construed as limited to A's beneficial interest in the property and accordingly not permit the attorney to deal with A's legal or fiduciary interest[1]. The purpose of this section is to introduce a presumption that any reference to the interest of a donor in land subject to a power of attorney is a reference to all his interest in that land.

1   See Law Com No 220, paras 4.43-4.45.

A contrary intention

8.77   Subsection (1) – which introduces the presumption – takes effect subject to a contrary intention in the instrument creating the power of attorney. It will, for instance, commonly be the case that what is delegated are the trustee powers of the donor so that the attorney's powers do not extend to any dealing in the trustee's beneficial interest in the property.

Commencement

8.78   This rule of interpretation applies only to powers created after February 2000.

Section 11 – Interpretation

8.79   Text of section 11

(1)   In this Act–

'land' has the same meaning as in the Trustee Act 1925, and

'enduring power' has the same meaning as in the Enduring Powers of Attorney Act 1985.

(2)   References in this Act to the creation of a power of attorney are to the execution by the donor of the instrument creating it.

Section 12 – Repeals

8.80   Text of section 12

The enactments specified in the Schedule to this Act are repealed to the extent specified in the third column, but subject to the note at the end.

Section 13 – Commencement, Extent and Short Title

8.81   Text of section 12

(1)   The preceding provisions of this Act shall come into force on such day as the Lord Chancellor may by order made by statutory instrument appoint.

(2)   This Act extends to England and Wales only.

(3)   This Act may be cited as the Trustee Delegation Act 1999.

Purpose of these provisions

8.82   They are essentially administrative in nature. The following matters are worthy of mention:

(a)   for the purposes of TDA 1999 a power of attorney is created when executed by the donor even if it is subsequently executed – as in the case of an enduring power – by the attorney;

(b)   two sections of the EPA 1985 have been repealed: s 3(3), subject to the transitional provisions set out in TDA 1999, s 4[1] and s 2(8)[2]. PAA 1971, s 9 – also repealed – had effected changes to TA 1925, s 25 which has, of course, been wholly recast by TDA 1999, s 5;

(c)   the Act came into effect on 1 March 2000 as a result of SI 2000/216;

(d)   the Hansard reference for the TDA are as follows:

Stage	Date	Hansard reference
House of Lords		
Introduction	3 December 1998	Vol 595 Col 605
Second Reading	11 January 1999	Vol 596 Cols 11-20
Committee	2 February 1999	Vol 596 Cols 1421-3
Report	2 February 1999	Vol 596 Cols 1421-3
Third Reading	9 March 1999	Vol 598 Cols 125-9
House of Commons		
Introduction	9 March 1999	–
Second Reading Committee	17 March 1999	Second Reading Committee Hansard
Second Reading	14 June 1999	Vol 327 Col 115 (formal)
Committee (SCF)	22 June 1999	Standing Committee F Hansard
Third Reading	14 July 1999	Vol 335 Cols 534-6
Royal Assent –	15 July 1999	House of Lords Hansard Vol 604 Col 601(3) House of Commons Hansard Vol 335, Col 648

1   See para 8.26 above.
2   See para 8.54 above.

PART III:
Trustee Act
2000

9

Introduction

Background

9.1   The Trustee Act 2000 (TA 2000) derived from a Law Commission Report Trustees Duties and Powers[1]. The origin of that Report, however, lay in two separate reform impulses.

1   Law Com 260; Scot Law Com 172 (July 1999). The subject had earlier (in 1982) been considered by the Law Reform Committee in their 23rd Report, The Powers and Duties of Trustees, Cmnd 8733. For trust reform generally, see para 1.34 ff above.

Trustee investment

9.2   The restrictive nature of the Trustee Investments Act 1961 prompted the Treasury to issue a Consultation Document on its possible repeal[1]. As a result the then Conservative Government proposed to do away with the 1961 Act and to give trustees all the powers of an absolute owner in relation to the investment of trust assets (this reflected the general response to the consultation exercise). This change was to be achieved by means of an Order under the Deregulation and Contracting Out Act 1994[2]. It then become apparent, however, that this process was fundamentally flawed[3]. In the event, and probably fortunately, the Draft Order was lost with the calling of the General Election in 1997.

1   Investment Powers of Trustees; A Consultation Document by HM Treasury, May 1996. There had been an earlier consultation exercise carried out by the Treasury the previous year when it was proposed to adjust the proportion of wider range investments that could be held under the 1961 Act.
2   This Act does not confer a general power to alter the law, merely to remove burdens, including restrictions imposed by an enactment, when this can be done without taking away any 'necessary protection' and the eventual draft Deregulation Order brought forward in February 1997 did not propose the repeal of the 1961 Act in its entirety.
3   It proposed to amend the Act to remove the requirement for fund splitting and the restrictions on the making of certain investments. A separate order was to be made under TIA 1961 s 12 extending the list of possible investments. The changes were prompted by representations on behalf of the Chancery Bar Association that the 1961 Act was not a burden on Trustees since it had extended the power of investment which trustees had formerly enjoyed!

Trustees' powers and duties

9.3   These were the subject of a Consultation Paper produced by the Law Commission in June 1997 in consultation with the Trust Law Committee. This addressed trustees' powers to delegate their discretions; to employ nominees and custodians; to purchase land for investment occupation or otherwise; to insure the trust property and, in the case of professional trustees, to charge for their services.

9.4   The Law Commission Report in 1999 then brought these matters together and addressed both the issue of what investments could be made by trustees and how trustees could achieve and effect the efficient administration of the trust by, for instance, delegating and using nominees. The draft Bill attached to that Report became, with only minor changes, the Trustee Act 2000.

The Importance of the Trustee Act 2000

9.5   The Act effects a major reform in the area of trustees' *default* powers. Well drafted modern settlements already dealt expressly with all the matters included in the Act. In **Precedent 1** below, for instance:

(a)   trustees' investment powers are dealt with in para 1 of the Schedule;

(b)   the powers of trustees collectively to delegate their discretions is in para 21;

(c)   the power of trustees to leave trust property in the name of a nominee is dealt with in para 18;

(d)   the remuneration of trustees is dealt with in clause 9;

(e)   a wide power for the trustees to insure trust property is given by para 19; and

(f)   so far as the duties of the trustees are concerned, note the wide exculpation clause (clause 11).

9.6   It is likely (for reasons that will be considered later) that trust draftsmen will continue to incorporate the above express powers. Hence, the powers conferred by the Act are likely to be 'default' powers, not usually relevant to the professionally drafted settlement but of great value:

(a)   when the trusts arise under an intestacy;

(b)   to new settlements which (for whatever reason) do not incorporate a full range of express powers; and

(c)   to old settlements which do not incorporate a satisfactory range of express powers.

9.7   Does the Act do more? In particular does it place extra burdens on all trustees, notably in the form of the statutory duty of care? These issues will be considered in subsequent pages but it may be noted at this stage that:

(a)   although the statutory duty of care can be excluded (see, for instance, **Precedent 41** below) it is thought unlikely that this is the course that will be followed by trust draftsmen. It is unclear whether the statutory duty merely codifies existing common law rules (would these have to be excluded as well?) and it is relatively rare to see these excluded under existing trust deeds save in specific instances. At least for the time being it is therefore likely that, insofar as trustees are to be protected, it will be by means of exculpation clauses[1].

(b) much of the Act is driven by the need to enable trustees to invest the trust fund in equities and a number of the provisions will be difficult to apply in situations like the following:

EXAMPLE 1

The Wonker Trust was established to hold shares in Wonker Chocolates Ltd, a private company. Trustees and beneficiaries are family members and many have employment with the company. It is not envisaged that the shares (or indeed any of them) will be sold and the opportunities for diversification of the trust fund are therefore nil.

EXAMPLE 2

The Jermyn-Mervyn estates are held on trust and the relevant management and business activities are carried on by the trustees. The estates have been in the family for generations and there is no wish amongst either trustees or adult beneficiaries to undertake substantial property sales so as to switch the investment strategy of the trust.

EXAMPLE 3

Jason Dodds established a discretionary trust to hold a terraced house for occupation by his son, Jasper, whilst he is studying at Liverpool University. Once Jasper's studies are complete it is envisaged that the house will be sold and the trust wound up (this is a common example of trusts being used as 'single purpose' vehicles).

In such cases how will the trustees deal with their duties under the Trustee Act 2000, s 4 to have regard to the 'standard investment criteria' and, in s 5, to obtain advice?

(c) the Act generally applies to existing and new trusts and to all types of trust (including therefore charities, pension funds and commercially geared trusts[2]);

(d) only relatively minor changes were made to the Bill during its passage through Parliament and certain infelicities remain. The precise ambit of s 24, for instance, is not readily apparent!;

(e) the Law Commission saw themselves as being involved in a balancing act: giving trustees wider powers (notably of investment) whilst ensuring that they exercise those powers prudently to safeguard trust capital[3]. Have they got the balance right? Already there are critics who consider that trustees remain over regulated: Kessler, for instance, comments that 'this approach is well intentioned but misguided'[4];

(f) the Hansard references are:

Stage	Date	Hansard reference
House of Lords		
First Reading	20 January 2000	Vol 608, col 1245
Second Reading	14 April 2000	Vol 612, col 373
Committee	7 June 2000	Vol 613, col CWH 1
Report	23 June 2000	Vol 614, col 561
Third Reading:	29 June 2000	Vol 614, col 1070
House of Commons		
First Reading	29 June 2000	
Second Reading	26 July 2000	Vol 354, col 1132
Standing Committee A	26 and 30 October 2000	
Report/Third Reading	8 November 2000	Vol 356, col 350
Royal Assent	25 November 2000	

(g) the Act came into force on 1 February 2001 as a result of the Trustee Act 2000 (Commencement) Order 2001/49 (C2).

1   See **Precedent 42** below and the notes thereto. The Trust Law Committee produced a consultation paper, 'Trustee Exculpation Clauses', which came down in favour of outlawing clauses excusing professional trustees from negligence (and worse). During the House of Lords debates, the Lord Chancellor (Lord Irvine of Lairg) agreed to refer the matter to the Law Commission for their consideration. He commented that:

> 'I believe that there should be extensive consultation, taking into account, amongst other matters, other statutory provisions on the exclusion of liability, the regulatory impact of such provisions and what seems to be a risk – it is certainly claimed to be – that first-class people might be discouraged from acting as trustees and that some of those persons might be driven offshore. One must give consideration to the economic impact of that' (House of Lords, Hansard, 14 April 2000, Col 394).

2   But see ss 36-38 which provide for certain exclusions in the cases of pensions, charities and authorised unit trusts.
3   Law Com No 260, para 2.19.
4   *'Trusts and Will Trusts*, (5th Ed) 2000 at para 18.1

10

Part I: The Duty of Care

Background

Introduction

10.1 Trustees have always been required to exercise their powers in accordance with a standard of care developed by the Courts of Chancery and a failure to do so has involved a breach of trust. The purpose of the duty of care laid down in TA 2000 is 'to bring certainty and consistency to the standard of competence and behaviour expected of trustees'[1]. The Law Commission viewed the introduction of the statutory duty as something of a *quid pro quo* for the generally enhanced default powers that were given to the trustees by the Act[2].

1   See Explanatory Notes to the Act para 10 and Law Com No 260, para 3.1.
2   Law Com No 260, para 3.8.

The existing common law

10.2 The overriding duty of trustees is to exercise their powers in the best interests of the present and future beneficiaries of the trust. There are, however, specific duties such as:

(a)   a duty not to profit from the trust – this is the essence of the fiduciary nature of trusteeship and is sometimes expressed as the 'self dealing rule'; and

(b)   a duty to comply with the terms of the trust and to have regard to the interests of the beneficiaries entitled on the one hand to income and on the other to capital[1].

1   See generally para 11.16 below for Hoffmann J's analysis of the trustees' duty as being to act fairly in making investment decisions rather than as a duty to hold the scales evenly between the beneficiaries.

10.3 In considering the exercise of his powers (including dispositive powers such as the payment of income or capital to a beneficiary) a trustee must act within the scope of the relevant power and, having considered the correct questions, must not then arrive at a wholly perverse decision. When it comes to actually exercising his discretions, *Snell* summarises the duty laid upon trustees as follows:

'In exercising his discretions, a trustee must act honestly and must use as much diligence as a prudent man of business would in dealing with his own private affairs; in selecting an investment he must take as much care as a prudent man would take in making an investment for the benefit of persons for whom he felt morally bound to provide. If he is a majority shareholder, he will not, as a prudent business man, be content with only such information on the company's activities as a minority shareholder would expect to receive. If he takes the same care of the trust property as a man of ordinary prudence would take of his own, he will not be liable for accidental loss, such as theft of the property whilst in his possession or in the possession of others to whom it has been entrusted in the ordinary course of business, or a depreciation in the value of securities upon which the trust funds have been rightfully invested[1].'

1   *Snell's Equity* (30th Edn) at para 11.02.

10.4   The overriding obligation is sometimes expressed as the prudent man of business standard which requires more than mere honesty, good faith and sincerity[1]. In the case of a professional trustee and a trustee who holds himself out as having special expertise beyond the norm a higher standard will be expected[2].

1   See, for instance, *Speight v Gaunt* (1883) 9 App Cas 1, HL, and see Megarry VC in *Cowan v Scargill* [1985] Ch 270.
2   *National Trustees Co of Australasia Ltd v General Finance Co of Australasia Ltd* [1905] AC 373 PC; *Barlett v Barclays Bank Trust Co Ltd* [1980] Ch 515.

Analysis of TA 2000, Part 1 and Schedule 1

Section 1 – The Duty of Care

10.5   Text of section 1

(1)   Whenever the duty under this subsection applies to a trustee, he must exercise such care and skill as is reasonable in the circumstances, having regard in particular–

   (a)   to any special knowledge or experience that he has or holds himself out as having, and

   (b)   if he acts as trustee in the course of a business or profession, to any special knowledge or experience that it is reasonable to expect of a person acting in the course of that kind of business or profession.

(2)   In this Act the duty under subsection (1) is called 'the duty of care'.

Section 2 – Application of Duty of Care

10.6   Text of section 2

Schedule 1 makes provision about when the duty of care applies to a trustee.

Schedule 1 – Application of Duty of Care

10.7   Text of schedule 1

Investment

1

The duty of care applies to a trustee–

(a)   when exercising the general power of investment or any other power of investment, however conferred;

(b)   when carrying out a duty to which he is subject under section 4 or 5 (duties relating to the exercise of a power of investment or to the review of investments).

Acquisition of land

2

The duty of care applies to a trustee–

(a)   when exercising the power under section 8 to acquire land;

(b)   when exercising any other power to acquire land, however conferred;

(c)   when exercising any power in relation to land acquired under a power mentioned in sub-paragraph (a) or (b).

Agents, nominees and custodians

3

(1)   The duty of care applies to a trustee–

(a)   when entering into arrangements under which a person is authorised under section 11 to exercise functions as an agent;

(b)   when entering into arrangements under which a person is appointed under section 16 to act as a nominee;

(c)   when entering into arrangements under which a person is appointed under section 17 or 18 to act as a custodian;

(d)   when entering into arrangements under which, under any other power, however conferred, a person is authorised to exercise functions as an agent or is appointed to act as a nominee or custodian;

(e)   when carrying out his duties under section 22 (review of agent, nominee or custodian, etc).

(2)   For the purposes of sub-paragraph (1), entering into arrangements under which a person is authorised to exercise functions or is appointed to act as a nominee or custodian includes, in particular–

(a)   selecting the person who is to act,

(b)   determining any terms on which he is to act, and

(c)   if the person is being authorised to exercise asset management functions, the preparation of a policy statement under section 15.

Compounding of liabilities

4

The duty of care applies to a trustee—

    (a)   when exercising the power under section 15 of the Trustee Act 1925 to do any of the things referred to in that section;

    (b)   when exercising any corresponding power, however conferred.

Insurance

5

The duty of care applies to a trustee—

    (a)   when exercising the power under section 19 of the Trustee Act 1925 to insure property;

    (b)   when exercising any corresponding power, however conferred.

Reversionary interests, valuations and audit

6

The duty of care applies to a trustee—

    (a)   when exercising the power under section 22(1) or (3) of the Trustee Act 1925 to do any of the things referred to there;

    (b)   when exercising any corresponding power, however conferred.

Exclusion of duty of care

7

The duty of care does not apply if or in so far as it appears from the trust instrument that the duty is not meant to apply.

Structure

10.8   Section 1 prescribes what is termed 'the duty of care' and section 2 introduces Schedule 1 which identifies the situations when the duty will apply.

A duty of care

10.9   The term itself is something of an oddity in the trust field with connotations derived from the tort of negligence. As such it is perhaps inappropriate given that the duties owed by trustees derive neither from tort nor from contract. What they owe is a duty *to take care* which has hitherto been tested by the prudent man of business standard.

Deciding whether to exercise a trustee power

10.10 The decision whether or not to exercise a power is not subject to the statutory duty of care[1]. As already discussed, in deciding whether to exercise a power a trustee must act in good faith, consider the right questions etc and the court will generally be reluctant to intervene in the decision that he then takes. By way of illustration consider the investment of the trust fund. Trustees have a duty to make the fund productive but should they appoint a discretionary fund manager to take control of the assets? If the trustees decide that they will exercise their power to appoint such a person (it may be an express power or be that given in Part IV of the Act) then the manner in which they exercise the power is subject to the statutory duty of care.

1   With the exception of the decision whether or not to delegate under TLATA 1996, s 9: see para 10.14 below.

The reasons for the introduction of the statutory duty

10.11 The are two main reasons:

(a)   it was considered desirable to define the duty of care applicable to the new enhanced powers given in TA 2000 to trustees[1]; and

(b)   with the new powers of delegation in Pt IV it was considered appropriate to sweep away the old provisions in TA 1925 and to prescribe the relevant duty of care[2].

1   The element of 'balancing' involved has already been noted at para 10.1 below.
2   The difficulties presented by the 1925 provisions and, in particular, the duty laid upon trustees in their exercise are considered at para 12.2 below.

When does the statutory duty apply?

10.12 The situations when the duty applies are set out in the First Schedule to the Act as follows:

(a)   when investing, whether under the power given by Pt II of the Act or under a power in the trust instrument[1], and when reviewing the investments under ss 4 and 5 (these duties are not, it seems, capable of exclusion in the trust instrument);

(b)   when buying land – whether under Pt III or under an express power – and when exercising a power in relation to such land (typically any power of management). Notice, however, that the duty does not apply in the case of the exercise of an *express* power over land which has either been *conveyed* by the settlor or *bequeathed* by the testator;

(c)   when employing an agent custodian or nominee, whether under Pt IV or under an express power, and in reviewing such an arrangement;

(d)   when insuring, whether under the new statutory power in TA 1925, s 19 (as inserted by s 34 of the Act) or under an express power in the trust instrument (and see the extension of this power to settled land by amendments to SLA 1925 s 102(2)(e) and s 107 by Sch 2 paras 15 and 17 of the Trustee Act).

1   Note that the duty applies whatever the origin of the power so that although the text above refers to an express power given in the trust instrument (which will in practice be the most likely source of the power apart from the Trustee Act) the duty is not limited to such express powers. This point was made expressly by the Lord Chancellor when introducing an amendment at Committee Stage in the House of Lords on 7 June 2000:

'(The amendment) ensures that the duty of care provided for in clauses 1 and 2 of the Bill applies to the exercise of the trustees' powers regardless of the origin of the powers. As published, the Schedule referred only to powers derived from the trust instrument. However, that overlooked the fact that trustees may derive relevant powers from other sources such as orders of the Court, orders and schemes made by the Charity Commission and from legislation. That being so and the policy that the duty of care should apply to the exercise of all relevant powers, unless expressly excluded by a trust instrument, the amended wording so applies' (Lords Hansard Col CWH 12).

10.13   The Trustee Bill was subsequently amended to include the following additional cases:

(a)   when exercising the power in the Trustee Act 1925, s 15 to compromise or any similar power in the trust instrument. In making this addition the Lord Chancellor (Lord Irvine) commented:

'This amendment is made for the sake of consistency. As the Bill repeals section 23 of the Trustee Act 1925, with its concept of good faith and replaces it with the powers in the Bill to appoint agents nominees and custodians, to which, of course, the duty of care applies, we have thought it sensible, for the sake of consistency, to apply the duty to section 15 of the Act which also gives a power to trustees but, at present, relies on a test of good faith[1].'

There is some illogicality in this statement: the test of good faith was considered inappropriate in the context of the new delegation powers conferred on trustees by Pt IV of the Act. Hence s 23(1) of TA 1925 was repealed and the duty of care introduced. But does it follow that the concept of good faith is equally unsuitable when the trustees exercise a power to compromise liabilities etc? The draftsman of the amendments appears simply to have replaced any reference which he spotted in the Trustee Act 1925 to good faith with the new statutory duty of care (see also the change to ss 22-23 of that Act which is considered below). The Law Commission certainly did not consider any alleged deficiencies in TA 1925, s 15 and one wonders whether the introduction of the new duty will make it that much harder for trustees to enter into compromises and agreements[2].

(b)   when exercising the power in s 22(1) and (3) of TA 1925 to value property or any express power. This provision was also introduced at the same time as (a) above with the Lord Chancellor offering a similar justification:

'This amendment is also made for the sake of consistency. As I said in speaking of the previous amendment, as the Bill repeals section 23 of the Trustee Act, with its concept of good faith, this amendment applies the duty of care in an analogous way to s 22(1) and (3) of the Act, which also gives powers to trustees but, at present, relies on a test of good faith[3].'

1   Lords Hansard 7 June 2000 Col CWH 12.
2   The operation of the section is discussed in detail in *Snell's Equity* 30th Edn at 12.27.
3   House of Lords, Hansard 7 June 2000 Col CWH 13.

10.14   Also amended (although this time in the original Bill) was section 9 of the Trusts of Land and Appointment of Trustees Act 1996. Under this amendment:

(a)   the duty of care applies to trustees *in deciding* whether to delegate their functions to an interest in possession beneficiary (note it is the *making* of the decision as well as its implementation that is caught); and

(b)   the duty then applies to the review etc of that delegation[1].

1   For a detailed consideration of s 9, see para 2.77 above.

To whom does the duty apply?

10.15   The statutory duty applies to trustees of both existing and new trusts (and, of course, to PRs[1]). Given that it applies to express powers as well as to those conferred by statute it is important that trustees of existing trusts are aware that, as from 1 February 2001, they became subject to this statutory duty of care. In particular, in appointing agents and exercising powers of compromise such trustees are now subject to enhanced duties of care[2].

1   TA 2000, s 35.
2   Of course, the existing trust may contain a wide exculpation clause which would protect trustees against any breach of duty. The question of excluding the duty is considered at para 10.20 below. Trustees may have appointed an agent before 1 February 2001, under their power in TA 1925, s23(1) and on the understanding that, provided the appointment was in good faith, they owed no further duties to supervise the agent. As from 1 February 2001 that appointment falls within TA 2000 and so trustees must review the appointment and are subject to the statutory duty of care. There is no transitional saving for such existing appointments.

10.16   The duty does not apply to trustees of pension schemes when exercising their express powers which are the equivalent of the statutory powers of investment and investment management given by Pts II-IV of the Act (buying and managing investments and land and appointing agents to manage the investment etc)[1].

1   TA 2000 s 36.

What is the duty of care?

10.17   The duty is laid down in s 1. It is akin to the standard used in the tort of negligence: it depends on what is 'reasonable in all the circumstances'. The higher standard expected of the professional (set out in sub clauses (a) and (b)) applies whether or not the professional charges for his services[1]. A number of further matters are worthy of note:

(a)   The Law Commission rejected the more familiar (at least to trust lawyers) test based on the prudent man of business. This preference for the reasonable man test was, at the end of the day arrived at because:

—   to retain the prudent man test would be no more than a restatement of the traditional common law rule[2];

—   the standard adopted permits express regard to be had to the particular skill and position of the trustee (see TA 2000, s 1(a) and (b))[3];

— 'the standard of care must be a robust and, within reason, a demanding one'; and

— 'there may, in fact, be little difference between the two alternatives'.

The case in favour of replacing the prudent man of business with the reasonable man test is therefore hardly persuasive[4].

(b) How far is the test subjective? It is intended to be a standard which increases when a professional trustee is involved *but* 'this does not mean that an incompetent trustee should be absolved from responsibility just because he or she was plainly unsuited to the task. Every trustee should be required to exercise such care and skill as is reasonable in the circumstances. However, the level of care and skill which is reasonable may increase if the trustee has special knowledge of skills . . .'[5].

Taking the ignorant missionary trustee as an example[6] what standard does he owe under s 1? He is not a professional so that the special features in s 1(a) and (b) can be ignored which leaves the question of what is a reasonable standard to apply to him in the circumstances? The phrase 'in the circumstances' with its heavily subjective connotations may suggest that regard must be had to his ignorance so that, provided he has acted honestly, he will have satisfied the test[7]. The prudent man of business test offered an idealised figure against which to measure the performance of particular trustees.

(c) Is the statutory test different from the standard adopted by the common law? From the foregoing discussion it will be appreciated that the answer would appear to be yes which raises interesting questions about the relationship between the two tests and the extent to which the common law test is now redundant.

1   The wording is similar to that in the Insolvency Act 1986 s 214(4) which deals with the duty of care owned by a director in the context of wrongful trading and is as follows:

'the facts which a director of a company ought to know or ascertain, the conclusions which he ought to reach and the steps which he ought to take are those which would be known or ascertained, or reached or taken, by a reasonably diligent person having both:

(a)   the general knowledge, skill and experience that may reasonably be expected of a person carrying out the same functions as are carried out by that director in relation to the company, and

(b)   the general knowledge, skill and experience that that director has.'

The relationship between limbs (a) and (b) is far from clear. Take the example of a solicitor in a small high street practice with limited experience of trusts and compare him with a private client partner in a leading practice. Both are professional and both will charge (doubtless at very different rates!) but are they both subject to the same standard of care? It is thought that there must be a minimum standard required of all solicitor trustees but that the private client partner will presumably be subject to a higher standard by reference to his special skills. Remuneration is not expressly mentioned in the legislation and it is curious that a professional appears to attract a higher standard even though he may not be remunerated (as, for instance, might be the case with a retired solicitor acting as trustee or with a professional but who acts on the basis of being a family friend).

2   See LC No 260 at para 3.24. The prudent man of business standard is, of course, adopted in the Pensions Act 1995, s 34(4) in relation to the delegation of investment decisions to a fund manager (it is also employed by the Uniform Prudent Investor Act in the USA).

3   The existing common law, of course, did permit such an allowance to be made: see para 10.4 above and *National Trustee & Co of Australasia v General Finance Co of Australasia* [1905] AC 373, PC. In *Bartlett v Barclays Bank Trust Co Ltd* [1980] 1 All ER at p 139 Brightman J commented:

> 'So far, I have applied the test of the ordinary prudent man of business. Although I am not aware that the point has previously been considered, except briefly in *Re Waterman's Will Trust* [1952] 2 All ER 1054, I am of the opinion that a higher duty of care is plainly due from someone like a trust corporation which carried on a specialised business of trust management. A trust corporation holds itself out in its advertising literature as being above ordinary mortals. With a specialist staff of trained trust officers and managers, with ready access to financial information and professional advice, dealing with and solving trust problems day after day, the trust corporation holds itself out, and rightly, as capable of providing an expertise which it would be unrealistic to expect and unjust to demand from the ordinary prudent man or woman who accepts, probably unpaid and sometimes reluctantly from a sense of family duty, the burdens of a trusteeship. Just as, under the law of contract, a professional person possessed of a particular skill is liable for breach of contract if he neglects to use the skill and experience which he professes, so I think that a professional corporate trustee is liable for breach of trust if loss is caused to the trust fund because it neglects to exercise the special care and skill which it professes to have. The advertising literature of the bank was not in evidence (other than the scale of fees) but counsel for the bank did not dispute that trust corporations, including the bank, hold themselves out as possessing a superior ability for the conduct of trust business, and in any event I would take judicial notice of that fact.'

4   The authors were tempted to add a fifth reason as follows:

> '(5) Er . . . that's it.'

5   Law Com No 260 at para 3.24. Contrast the original wording produced by the Law Commission for option (5) in CP No 146 at para 111 which was subsequently rejected on the basis of excessive subjectivity:

> '(5)act with the care and diligence that may reasonably be expected having regard to the nature, composition and purposes of the particular trust, the skills which the trustees actually have, or if they are employed as professional trustees, those which they either ought to have or hold themselves out as having'.

6   See Maugham J commenting on the trustee in *Re Vickery* [1931] 1 Ch 572 at 573 that he 'had spent his life as a missionary in the city of London and . . . was completely ignorant of business affairs'.

7   In the context of the similar wrongful trading test in *Re DKG Contractors Ltd* [1990] BCC 903 it was noted that 'Patently, (the Directors') own knowledge, skill and expertise were hopelessly inadequate for the task they undertook. That is not sufficient to protect them.' It should, however, be noted that IA 1986, s 214 is couched in more objective terms than the TA 2000 duty: in particular:

    (i)   in s 214(3) the Director is required to take 'every step' with a view to 'minimising' the potential loss to the company's creditors;

    (ii)   s 214(4)(a) refers to the knowledge, skill and experience to be expected of a person carrying out the same functions as are carried out by the director in relation to the same company.

Nature of the statutory duty of care

10.18   It is not thought that what has occurred is a statutory codification of the common law: rather a new test has been introduced. So what is the position of the common law test[1]? The Explanatory Notes published with the Act state that:

> 'The duty will take effect in addition to the existing fundamental duties of trustees (for example to act in the best interests of the beneficiaries and to comply with the terms of the trust) but will exclude any common law duty of care which might otherwise have applied.[2]'

1   The prudent businessman test will continue to apply to certain situations not falling within the section 1 test: eg to trustees in exercising a power to carry on business.

2   See paragraph 10. Speaking at the STEP London Central Conference in October 2000 Charles Harpum (the Law Commissioner) commented on the duty of care as follows:

> 'when it applies, it requires a trustee to exercise such skill and care as is reasonable in the circumstances, having regard to two factors. The first is any special knowledge or experience that he has or holds himself out to have. The second, which only applies where he acts as a trustee in the course of a business or profession, is any special knowledge or experience that it is reasonable to expect of a person acting in the course of that kind of business or profession. This duty is, therefore, in part objective and in part subjective. It was an attempt to codify the common law duty of care that has been applied to trustees in relation (for example) to investment or trust management.'

10.19   Nowhere, however, has the common law been abolished which suggests that the two duties must coexist: if the statutory duty is excluded, for instance, the common law may still apply[1]. There is also some uncertainty about the position of a trustee who breaches the new statutory duty: is that a straightforward breach of trust or a breach of statutory duty? If the latter will there be important differences in terms of causation, remoteness and applicable limitation periods? Pending resolution of these problems it may be attractive to frame any claims for breach of duty under alternative heads. Of course a court is likely to be heavily influenced by what the Law Commission intended to do (and believes that it has succeeded in doing) and it would therefore be no great surprise for the robust view to be taken that in the circumstances listed in Sch 1 the common law duty has been wholly superseded!

1   See para 10.20 below and **Precedent 41** below. Of course the exclusion clause may also exclude the common law duty of care as well. It is thought that the statutory duty will be treated as a further equitable duty laid on trustees and hence giving rise to a claim in equity (rather than to a tortious claim for breach of statutory duty).

Excluding the duty of care

10.20   This is permitted by Sch 1 para 7: the duty can be excluded both in relation to the exercise of the statutory powers and powers expressed in the trust instrument[1]. Alternatively, it may be replaced by the lesser duty to act in good faith. In practice, for new trusts, it is likely that, if the settlor considers that the trustees require protection, this will be by means of an exculpation clause. In the case of existing trusts it will not, of course, be possible to exclude the statutory duty which may now apply to them (although many such trusts will also include a trustee exculpation clause).

1   See **Precedent 41** below and consider whether any exclusion should also cover any (still extant) common law duty. Paragraph 7 was amended at Committee Stage in the House of Lords by the deletion of the words 'to power conferred by the trust instrument' after 'the duty of care does not apply': See House of Lords Hansard 7 June 2000 Col CWH 13.

The repeal of TA 1925 s 30

10.21   Section 30 has been repealed in its entirety[1] and hence the provision that a trustee 'is answerable and accountable only for his own acts receipts, neglects or defaults and not for those of any other trustee' has disappeared from the legislation. It has always been the law, however, that a trustee is not vicariously liable for the acts of his co-trustees but only for his own defaults[2]. Arguably, therefore, this repeal has not changed the law although there will be some draftsmen who will wish to include an express provision in a trust instrument which incorporates the substance of the now repealed statutory indemnity[3].

1   By TA 2000, Sch 2, para 24. Section 30(1) replaced part of TA 1893, s 24 which in turn had replaced LP (Am) A 1859, s 31.
2   See *Townley v Sherborne* (1633) J Bridg 35 at 37-38 and, see generally, *Snell's Equity* (30th Edn) para 13.07.
3   See **Precedent 42(c)** below.

11

Parts II and III:

Trustee Investment and

Acquiring Land

Background

Introduction

11.1   Trustees must exercise their investment powers in accordance with the purpose of the trust: normally this has required them to make the maximum return consistent with the prudent man of business standard[1]. Trust deeds drafted in recent years have invariably provided expressly for trustees to have a free choice in deciding what investments are appropriate for the particular trust. By contrast, prior to TA 2000, statutory default powers of investment proceeded on the basis of an authorised list.

1   On commercial return consider, for instance, *Buttle v Saunders* [1950] 2 All ER 193 (duty to obtain the best price, even 'gazumping'!) and *Cowan v Scargill* [1985] Ch 270. The prudent man of business yardstick is considered at para 10.3 above. Trustees have a *duty* to invest the trust fund and a *power* to make any particular investment that is authorised under the terms of the trust deed or by statute.

Statutory regulation of trust investments

11.2   For over 250 years trustees have (in the absence of express powers) only been allowed to put trust monies into specific authorised investments. Originally only mortgages or Bank of England 3% Consolidated Annuities ('Consols') were permitted and it was not until the Law of Property Amendment Act 1859 that certain fixed interest stocks were included. A further expansion of the list allowing investment in a range of securities issued by the Government and various public bodies was effected by the Law of Property Amendment Act 1860; the Trustee Investment Act 1889; the Trustee Act 1893 and s 1 of the Trustee Act 1925 (which recast the list). During this period the attitude of the courts to trustee investment was that it should be targeted to preserving capital and avoiding, or at the least minimising, risk. Hence the attraction of fixed interest securities – by contrast, ordinary shares were considered to be unacceptably speculative. For most of this period economic circumstances favoured this approach: the economy was stable with little or no inflation. Many trusts and especially those established by will (which amounted to the vast majority) were intended to preserve wealth for future generations of the family. This was a world, and these were the attitudes, that disappeared as the Twentieth

Century progressed with its World Wars, high levels of taxation and inflation. As a result trustees who were limited in their investments by the provisions of the 1925 Trustee Act saw the real value of their trust fund fall whilst, at the same time, real growth was being achieved by equity stocks and shares which were, of course, not permitted by that legislation.

Trustee Investment Act 1961

11.3   This Act replaced the Trustee Act 1925, s 1 but persisted with the approach of an authorised list of investments[1]. The Act adopted a novel approach in permitting investments to be divided 50/50 into two groups known as 'narrow range' and 'wider range investment'[2]. The former comprised, in the main, gilt edged and other fixed interest securities (eg National Savings) whilst the latter comprised securities in UK companies which satisfied various criteria; Building Society shares and units in authorised unit trusts[3].

1   Critics of the Act are of the opinion that its approach was already out of date whereas others, and notably *Snell's Equity* 30th Edn take the view that 'it did much to meet (the) criticisms (of the existing law)': see paragraph 11.66.
2   The permitted proportion of the fund that could be invested in wider range investments was increased to 75% by the Trustee Investments (Division of Trust Fund) Order 1996 (SI 1996/845).
3   Securities had to satisfy five conditions:

   (i)   to be issued in the UK by a company incorporated in the UK;

   (ii)   which company had a total issued and paid up share capital of not less than £1 million; and

   (iii) in each of the five years preceding the current year in which the investment was made had paid a dividend on its shares which ranked for dividend in that year;

   (iv)   the price of the securities had to be quoted on a recognised investment exchange; and

   (v)   the securities had to be fully paid up or by terms of issue fully paid up within nine months of the date of issue.

11.4   Reviewing the 1961 Act some 38 years later the Law Commission commented:

'Before 1961, trustees without a wide express power of investment were limited to the narrow categories of investment set out in the Trustee Act 1925 or the Trusts (Scotland) Act 1921 (principally fixed interest securities and loans secured over land and buildings). The purpose of the Trustee Investments Act 1961 was to allow trustees to invest in assets with a greater potential for return, in particular in shares, without taking an undue risk with the trust capital. Although investment in shares has historically proved a good measure of protection against inflation, it carries a degree of risk of capital loss, because of the failure of a company, which is not present with assets such as fixed interest UK Government securities. It was therefore considered appropriate in the absence of express powers to ensure that trusts contained a core of investments of the latter type. Trusts funds which could only be invested in this way came to suffer serious losses in real terms because the value of the investments was severely reduced by inflation[1].'

1   Law Comm, No 260, paragraph 2.5. The Trust Law Committee provided the following
     figures for alternative investments for charities:

Capital value in 1963 – £1.5 billion	Capital value in 1994	Income in 1994
50% gilts/50% equities	£12.3 billion	£515 million
25% gilts/75% equities	£18.0 billion	£735 million
100% equities	£23.7 billion	£950 million

The use of express investment powers

11.5   Express investment clauses were used before the 1961 Act to correct the deficiencies of the 1925 list and have, of course, been widely used in recent times. A standard express clause permits trustees to make investments of whatever kind on the basis that they are to be treated as if they were absolute owners of the trust property. In simple terms this type of clause therefore replaces the limited list with a broad power which is, however, circumscribed by the requirements of the trust and the overriding duty of care of the trustees[1]. The effect of express investment clauses depends on a proper construction of the words used and, initially, the courts took the view that such clauses should be strictly construed. Farwell LJ commented:

'Investment clauses purporting to add to the wide range of investments now authorised by law should be construed strictly for the protection of trustees and remaindermen[2].'

1   As to which, see para 10.3 above: from 1 February 2001 the statutory duty applies.
2   *Re Maryon-Wilson's Estate* [1912] 1 Ch 55 at pp 66–77, CA.

11.6   The modern view does not adopt such a restrictive approach and instead gives the words of the clause a natural – rather than a restrictive – interpretation. This approach may be illustrated by *Re Harari's Settlement Trusts*[1] in which the trustees were given power to invest 'in or upon such investments as to them may seem fit'. Jenkins J declared that:

'I think the trustees have power, under the plain meaning of those words, to invest in any investments which . . . they "honestly think" are desirable investments for the investment of monies subject to the trusts of the settlement.'

1   [1949] 1 All ER 430.

Obtaining wider investment powers

11.7   After initial doubts[1] the courts have been willing to widen trustee investment powers beyond what was permitted by the 1961 Act, on an application being made either under the Variation of Trusts Act 1958 or, more usually, under the Trustee Act 1925, s 57[2]. This extension has been justified on the basis that the provisions of the 1961 Act were inadequate judged by current investment practice. At the same time the judiciary commented adversely on that Act[3].

1   See *Re Kolb's Will Trusts* [1962] Ch 531.

2   See, for instance, *Mason v Farbrother* [1983] 2 All ER 1078; *Anker-Petersen v Anker-Petersen* [2000] WTLR 581.
3   *Trustees of the British Museum v AG* [1984] 1 WLR 418; *Steel v Wellcome Custodian Trustees Ltd* [1988] 1 WLR 167 at 172; *University of Glasgow, Petrs* 1991 SLT 604.

Powers of trustees of occupational pension funds

11.8   The Goode Report on Pensions Law of 1993 rejected the 1961 Act provisions as being 'widely regarded as excessively rigid and quite unsuited to modern investment needs and practices'[1]. It recommended the adoption of flexible guidelines for trustees of occupational pension schemes and these were conferred by the Pensions Act 1995, s 34:

> 'The trustees of the trust scheme have, subject to any restrictions imposed by the scheme, the same power to make an investment of any kind as if they were absolutely entitled to the assets of the scheme[2].'

1   Report of the Pension Law Review Committee (1993 CM 2342-1).
2   It should be noted that no attempt was made to define an investment: a similar policy has been followed in the Trustee Act 2000: see further para 11.22 below.

11.9   Section 35 then provides for a statement of investment principles[1] in the following terms:

> '(1)   The trustees of a trust scheme must secure that there is prepared maintained and from time to time revised a written statement of the principles governing decisions about investments for the purposes of the scheme.
>
> (2)   The statement must cover, amongst other things:
>
>   (a)   the trustees' policy for securing compliance with section 36 and 56; and
>
>   (b)   their policy about the following matters.
>
> (3)   Those matters are:
>
>   (a)   the kinds of investments to be held;
>
>   (b)   the balance between different kinds of investments;
>
>   (c)   risk;
>
>   (d)   the expected return on investments;
>
>   (e)   the realisation of investments; and
>
>   (f)   such other matters as may be prescribed.'

1   See also para 11.20 below.

Experience elsewhere

11.10   Many foreign jurisdictions abandoned an authorised list of trustee investments in favour of a prudent person rule: ie a power to invest as if the trustees were the absolute owners of the fund but subject to the needs, requirements and objects of the trust and to a duty of care[1]. In the USA many states have adopted the provisions of the Uniform Prudent Investment Act which allows a trustee to invest in any kind of property (or type of investment) that is consistent with the requirements of the trust: ie which satisfies the risk and return objectives and otherwise amounts to prudent investing. The USA Re-statement 3rd of the Law of Trusts (Prudent Investor Rule) is as follows:

'General standard of prudent investment

The trustee is under a duty to the beneficiaries to invest and manage the funds of the trust as a prudent investor would, in the light of the purposes, terms, distribution requirements, and other circumstances of the trust.

(a)   This standard requires the exercise of reasonable care, skill and caution and is to be applied to investments not in isolation but in the context of the trust portfolio and as a part of an overall investment strategy which would incorporate risk and return objectives reasonably suitable to the trust.

(b)   In making and implementing investment decisions, the trustee has a duty to diversify the investments of the trust unless, under the circumstances, it is prudent not to do so.

(c)   In addition, the trustee must:

(1)   conform to fundamental fiduciary duties of loyalty and impartiality;

(2)   act with prudence in deciding whether and how to delegate authority to others; and

(3)   incur only costs that are reasonable in amount and appropriate to the investment responsibilities of the trusteeship.'

1   New Zealand (since 1988) and most of the states of Australia are examples.

Trustees and modern portfolio theory

11.11   The theory, developed by economists and financial analysts, may be expressed in the following propositions:

(a)   investment decisions must be based upon the two extremes of risk and return;

(b)   from this it follows that the greater the risk the greater the return;

(c)   this balance between risk and return has to be taken into account in the overall management of a portfolio and because diversification is fundamental to managing risk is a basic consideration in all prudent investment management.

11.12   From these factors it can be seen that the making of a particular investment cannot be characterised as *in itself* prudent or imprudent: rather it must be considered as part of the overall composition of the portfolio. It may therefore be concluded that:

(a)   there is no such thing as a speculative investment per se; and

(b)   low risk investment may be judged imprudent.

11.13 It may be said under the tenets of modern portfolio theory that trustees should invest the trust fund, in the light of the particular circumstances of the trust (which determines the investment strategy to be pursued), with a view to the proper management of risk: a wholly different approach from the Nineteenth Century view that the paramount duty of a trustee was to maintain the value of the trust fund[1].

1 'Preservation of real values can be no more than an aspiration which some trustees may have the good fortune to achieve:' Hoffmann J in *Nestlé v National Westminster Bank plc* [2000] WTLR 795 at 803.

11.14 To what extent should trustees embrace modern portfolio theory and, specifically, how will it affect actions for breach of trust brought against trustees? Hoffmann J, at first instance, in the *Nestlé* case, commented:

'Modern trustees acting within their investment powers are entitled to be judged by the standards of current portfolio theory, which emphasises the risk level of the entire portfolio rather than the risk attaching to each investment taken in isolation.[1]'

1 Although given in 1988, the Judgment has only recently been reported in 10 TLI 113 and at [2000] WTLR 795. On appeal reported in [1993] 1WLR 1260 at 1268, CA, Dillon LJ commented that trustees are entitled to be judged according to modern economic and financial conditions. However, the specific comments of Hoffmann J were not commented upon by the Court of Appeal.

11.15 Extra judicially Lord Nicholls of Birkenhead has commented as follows:

'(Investment) policy is aimed at producing a portfolio of investments which is balanced overall and suited to the needs of the particular trust . . . Such a strategy falls to be judged likewise, that is overall. Different investments are accompanied by different degrees of risk, which are reflected in the expected rate of return. A large fund with a widely diversified portfolio of securities might justifiably include modest holdings of high risk securities which will be altogether imprudent and out of place in a smaller fund.

In such a case it would be inappropriate to isolate one particular investment out of a vast portfolio and enquire whether that can be justified as a trust investment. Such a "line by line" approach is misplaced. The enquiry, rather, should be to look at a particular investment and enquire whether that is justified in a holding in the context of the overall portfolio. Traditional warnings against the need for trustees to avoid speculative or hazardous investments are not to be read as inhibiting trustees from maintaining portfolios of investments which contain a prudent and sensible mixture of low risk and higher risk securities. They are not to be so read, because they were not directed at a portfolio which is a balanced exercise in risk management.[1]'

1 In 9 TLI p71 see also Underhill and Hayton *'Law of Trusts and Trustees'*, (15th Edn p 599).

11.16 Much will obviously depend on the strategy that is appropriate for a particular trust fund and, as made clear in Lord Nicholls' article, the size of the fund is a crucial factor. So too will be evidence that the settlor wished the life tenant to be viewed as the principal beneficiary so that trustees may be justified in investing with a view to the production of greater income, albeit at the expense of capital growth, than would otherwise have been the case[1].

1   Commenting on the observations of Megarry VC in *Cowan v Scargill* [1985] Ch 270 that trustees have a duty 'to exercise their powers in the best interests in the present and future beneficiaries of the trust, holding the scales impartially between the different classes of beneficiaries', Hoffmann J in the *Nestlé* case noted that 'a trustee must act fairly in making investment decisions which may have different consequences for different classes of beneficiaries . . . the trustees have a wide discretion. They are, for example, entitled to take into account the income needs of the tenant for life or the fact that the tenant for life was a person known to the settlor and a primary object of the trust whereas the remainderman is a remoter relative or stranger. Of course, these cannot be allowed to become overriding considerations but the concept of fairness between classes of beneficiaries does not require them to be excluded. It would be an inhuman rule which required trustees to adhere to some mechanical rule for preserving the real value of capital when a tenant for life was the testator's widow who had fallen upon hard times and the remainderman was young and well off.'

11.17   The portfolio theory also predicates that investment should not be dictated by the need to produce a certain income return. Ideally on this theory income may be viewed as a maximum amount that an individual can consume in a week and still expect to be as well off at the end of the week as he was at the beginning, treating capital gains as if they were income available for distribution[1]. Normally, however, the legal distinction between income and capital is crucial and will affect the investment strategy of the trustees: for instance, in the case of the standard life interest trust. However, even in this situation trustees may find that they have a power to pay capital to the life tenant thereby enabling the income return to be supplemented if appropriate[2].

1   See JR Hicks, *Value and Capital* (1938) at p 177.
2   With care capital used for this purpose will not be taxed as income: contrast *Brodie's Will Trustees v IRC* (1933) 17 TC 432 and *Cunard, Trustees v IRC* [1946] 1 All ER 159, 27 TC 122, CA (illustrating that trustees should not be required to make the income of the life tenant up to a prescribed level out of the capital if it would otherwise suffer a deficiency) with regular payments made in the trustees discretion in *Stevenson v Wishart* [1987] 2 All ER 428, CA. The rules taxing dividends introduced in by F(No2)A 1997, effective from 6 April 1999 in the case of individuals and trusts, have produced new problems for trustees of certain discretionary and accumulation trusts. The classification of receipts as income or capital is the subject of a Trust Law Committee Consultation Paper (see para 1.39 above). A growing number of FTSE companies now adopt a nil dividend policy leaving investors to realise any profits by disposals.

Ethical Investment[1]

11.18   It is important to be clear what is meant by an ethical (or social) investment policy. In simple terms trustees may pursue three different investment strategies:

(a)   Strategy 1: a neutral strategy based purely on financial return (ie which balances risk and reward);

(b)   Strategy 2: an investment strategy which is sensitive to social or ethical considerations without being dictated by such considerations. As between two competing investments, therefore, each offering an equal return a decision may be made on ethical or social grounds;

(c)   Strategy 3: an investment policy which is dictated by ethical considerations. This may involve a sacrifice of the 'prudence' standard of investment.

1   For cases on the subject see *Evans v London Co-operative Society* (1976) Times, 6 July, Brightman J; *Cowan v Scargill* [1985] Ch 270; *Martin v Edinburgh City Council* 1988 SLT 329 and *Harries v Church Comrs for England and Wales* [1993] 2 All ER 300.

11.19   Of course, the settlor may expressly lay down the investment policy to be pursued by the trustees: he may, for instance, indicate that trustees are to pursue a Strategy 3 investment policy and, in such cases, trustees cannot be criticised for acting in accordance with the express terms in their trust instrument. In other cases the position is as follows:

(a)   Trustees are obliged to put the interests of their beneficiaries first and in pursuing an investment strategy should ignore their own personal views. Megarry VC in *Cowan v Scargill* commented:

> 'Trustees may have strongly held social or political views. They may be firmly opposed to any investment in South Africa or other countries, or they may object to any form of investment in companies concerned with alcohol, tobacco, armaments or many other things. In the conduct of their own affairs . . . they are free to abstain from making any such investments. Yet under a trust, if investments of this type would be more beneficial to the beneficiaries than other investments, the trustees must not refrain from making the investments by reason of the views that they hold.[1]'

(b)   In acting for the 'benefit' of the trust beneficiaries, it will normally be sufficient for the trustees to be concerned with financial benefit but there will be (exceptional) trusts where non-financial benefit also falls to be considered. In *Harries v Church Comrs for England and Wales* the Bishop of Oxford argued that the Church Commissioners (whose object was to promote the Christian faith) should not invest in a manner that was at odds with that purpose even if the result was significant financial detriment. Nicholls VC rejected this argument holding that the purpose of any trust will normally be best served by the trustees seeking to obtain the maximum financial return. He accepted that, in rare cases, certain investments might conflict with the objects of a charitable trust and so should be avoided even at the risk of a significant financial detriment[2]. Interestingly the commissioners already pursued an ethical investment policy, which precluded the making of investments in armaments, gambling, alcohol, newspapers etc, on the basis that members of the Church of England objected to such concerns on religious or moral grounds[3]. It was accepted that the commissioners could exclude such investments since they were still left with an adequate spread of alternative options.

(c)   Apart from particular considerations that will affect charitable trustees, acting in the best interests of beneficiaries will mean that if *all* the beneficiaries are fiercely opposed to a particular range of investments (for instance in armaments) then if the trustees ignored such feelings and duly made investments in that area it is likely that their conduct would be vulnerable to attack in the courts. Similarly, where the principal beneficiary holds entrenched views, the trustees should seek to accommodate those views within their investment strategy. In practice it is likely that only when Strategy 3 is pursued will the trustees be open to a claim for compensation based on a breach of trust:

'The assertion that trustees could not be criticised for failing to make a particular investment for social or political reasons is one that I would not accept in its full width. If the investment in fact made is equally beneficial to the beneficiaries, then criticism would be difficult to sustain in practice, whatever the position in theory. But if the investment in fact made is less beneficial, then both in theory and in practice the trustees would normally be open to criticism.[4']

1   [1984] 2 All ER 750 at 761.
2   Two examples given were (a) a cancer research charity and investments in the tobacco industry and (b) a temperance society with shares in brewing and distilling. If the plaintiffs had been successful in this case 30% of all UK listed companies would have been excluded from investments open to the Church Commissioners.
3   The Commissioners investment policy had been set out in their annual report for 1989 which contained the following.

'The primary aim in the management of our assets is to produce the best total return, that is capital and income growth combined . . .

Whilst financial responsibilities must remain of primary importance (given our position as trustees) as responsible investors we also continue to take account of social, ethical and environmental issues . . . as regards our stock exchange holdings this means that we do not invest in companies whose main business is armaments, gambling, alcohol, tobacco and newspapers. It also means that we must continue to be vigilant in our monitoring of the activities of those companies where we do have a shareholding.'

4   Megarry VC in *Cowan v Scargill* [1984] 2 All ER 750 at 761.

11.20   The Pensions Act 1995 requires trustees to produce a statement of investment principles (ie indicating the kind of investments to be held; the balance of investments; level of risk and expected return) and from July 2000 this statement has to include their approach to ethical investments[1].

1   The Occupational Pension Schemes (Investment, and Assignment, Forfeiture, Bankruptcy etc) Amendment Regulations 1999 (SI 1999/1849) which provides:

'(a) the extent (if at all) to which social environmental or ethical considerations are taken into account in the selection retention and realisation of investments; and (b) their policy if any in relation to the exercise of the rights (including voting rights) attaching to investments.' See para 11.9 above.

Analysis of the Trustee Act 2000, Part II

Section 3 – General Power of Investment

11.21   Text of section 3

(1)   Subject to the provisions of this Part, a trustee may make any kind of investment that he could make if he were absolutely entitled to the assets of the trust.

(2)   In this Act the power under subsection (1) is called 'the general power of investment'.

(3)   The general power of investment does not permit a trustee to make investments in land other than in loans secured on land (but see also section 8).

(4)   A person invests in a loan secured on land if he has rights under any contract under which—

(a)   one person provides another with credit, and

(b)   the obligation of the borrower to repay is secured on land.

(5)   'Credit' includes any cash loan or other financial accommodation.

(6)   'Cash' includes money in any form.

Purpose of the section

11.22   This section gives trustees 'the general power of investment' (see s 3(2)). Important points to appreciate are that:

(a)   the section replicates the common express investment clause in allowing a trustee to make 'any kind of investment that he could make if he were absolutely entitled to the assets of a trust'. This represents the abandonment of the previous statutory approach of proceeding by an authorised list[1].

(b)   the power does not extend to investments in land[2] with the exception of a 'loan secured on land'. The meaning of this phrase is set out in s 3(4)-(6)[3].

(c)   an 'investment' is not defined. The Law Commission considered that this was not appropriate for the following reasons:

'Although the concept (of an investment) has, until now, been defined by reference to lists of "authorised" investments in the context of trustees *statutory* powers, this is certainly not the case when it comes to express powers of investment in trust instruments – wide and unqualified investment powers are common.

The notion of what constitutes an investment is an evolving concept, to be interpreted by the courts. Originally an investment was regarded as something which must not only safeguard capital, but which must produce income (see *Re Somerset* [1894] 1 Ch 231 at 247, CA, per Kekewich J). In *Re Wragg* [1919] 2 Ch 58 the key characteristic of an investment was said to be an expectation that it would yield some interest or profit. Today, there can be little doubt that "profit" can be in the form of capital appreciation rather than income yield. Trustees might, for example, legitimately invest (depending on the circumstances of the trust) in antiques, silver or paintings in the expectation that they will increase in value. In *Harries v Church Comrs* [1992] 1 WLR 1241, Sir Donald Nicholls VC said (at 1246) that one reason why trustees hold property is "for the purpose of generating money, whether from income or capital growth, with which to further the work of the trust. In other words, property held by trustees as an investment. Where property is so held, *prima facie* the purposes of the trust will be best served by the trustees seeking to obtain therefrom the maximum return, whether by way of income or capital growth, which is consistent with commercial prudence"[4].'

1   For the previous approach, see para 11.2 above. For a similar power to that contained in s 3, see the Pensions Act 1995 s 34.

2   But see TA 2000, s 8 which gives trustees power to acquire land whether as an investment or otherwise.

3   The definition is taken from the Financial Services and Markets Act 2000, Sch 2, para 23.

4   Law Comm 260 para 2.28 footnote 56.

11.23   The curious case of *Khoo Tek Keong v Ch'ng Joo Tuan Neoh* [1934] AC 529, PC decided that an unsecured loan was not an investment (whereas a secured loan was!). It is not thought likely in view of current attitudes to the meaning of an 'investment' that the case would be followed today: of course, trustees should have regard to their overriding duty of care before making any such investment.

11.24   A power of investment does not permit trustees to purchase chattels for use by a beneficiary: eg works of art to adorn the walls of the life tenant's house or a Stradivarius to be played by the life tenant. Express clauses need to be inserted into the trust deed to cover those situations[1].

1   See **Precedent 1, clause 1** and **Precedent 47** below for a power to run a business.

Purchasing property jointly

11.25   It was formerly considered that, because trust property has to be controlled by the trustees, the trustees did not have power to acquire property jointly (for instance with the principal beneficiaries)[1].

1   *Webb v Jonas* (1888) 39 Ch D 660.

11.26   In practice, wide express investment clauses were considered to permit this and it was not uncommon to find trustees putting up part of the purchase monies to acquire a house for occupation by the life tenant or to acquire business assets for his use. The Law Commission consider that the s 3(1) power now permits trustees so to invest[1]. There is no doubt, however, that, before making such an investment, trustees should consider most carefully the difficulties which it presents in terms of management, control and future use and sale. Should trustees reserve an overriding right to sell if they consider it in the best interests of the trust so to do? Would failure to do so be regarded as involving a fettering of their discretion[2]?

1   Law Comm No 260, para 2.28. The power to purchase a house jointly with a beneficiary for his occupation is not covered by the general power of investment: see para 11.71 below for a consideration of s 8 and the trustees' powers in relation to the purchase of the land. Kessler in *Drafting Trusts and Will Trusts* (5th Ed) 2000 at 18.25 considers an express power to purchase property jointly to be desirable 'for the avoidance of doubt'.

2   Law Comm No 260 at para 2.28, footnote 54 equates the issues that arise from joint ownership with the use of agents and nominees. The situations are, however, quite different: in the latter control is retained by the trustees whereas in the case of jointly owned property it is shared.

'Programme-related' investments and 'total return'

11.27   In the House of Lords Debates on the Bill, Lord Dahrendorf raised the issues of 'programme-related' investment and 'total return':

'I wonder, however, whether the arrangement as foreseen takes sufficient account of complexity and new opportunities of financial markets. Is there not a case for opening up even further the possibilities of investment for charitable trusts? Does the Bill allow programme-related investments? That term is not yet common in this country but is quite frequently used in the United States. Those investments have a direct relationship with the policy intentions of trusts. Above all, will it be possible for trustees to adopt what are called 'total return policies' in which the rigid and often quite inadvisable distinction between capital and income is abandoned and to look at the total return of investments and thereby have even more freedom to benefit the purposes for which trusts are set up[1]?'

1   See Lords Hansard, 14 April 2000, Col 385.

11.28   In the same debate Lord Wilberforce confessed that '. . . two trusts with which I have some association already operate on the basis of total return. Perhaps we have been acting illegally[1].' As has been discussed above, recent cases have, in the light of modern portfolio theory, accepted that income production is not a requisite for each and every investment made by a trustee[2].

1   See Lords Hansard, 14 April 2000, at Col 392
2   See especially the discussion at para 11.11 above and contrast the approach of the court in *Re Power* [1947] Ch 572.

How should trustees exercise the general power of investment?

11.29   Inevitably the power is not unfettered, for instance:

(a)   trustees remain subject to their overriding fiduciary duties (eg to act in the best interests of their beneficiaries and to avoid conflicts of interest);

(b)   to have regard to the statutory duty of care laid down in Pt I of the Act[1];

(c)   to follow the standard investment criteria as laid down in TA 2000 s 4 and to obtain advice (TA 2000, s 5).

1   See para 10.12 above.

Meaning of an 'asset'

11.30   The term is defined[1] as 'including any right or interest.' It is thought that the term is wide enough to embrace any *form of property* which is capable of being held on trust[2].

1   In TA 2000, s 39(1).
2   For a recent illustration of what 'property' is capable of being held on trust, see *Swift v Dairywise Farms Ltd* [2000] 1 All ER 320.

Mortgages

11.31   The 1961 Act included in the list of Pt II investments (narrow range with advice) mortgages of freehold property in England, Wales and Northern

Ireland and of leasehold property provided that the unexpired term of the lease was at least 60 years. It was commonly thought that if trustees wished to invest in mortgages then they were further restricted by case law which prescribed that the mortgage must be a first legal mortgage (not therefore a second or equitable mortgage) and that contributory mortgages were unauthorised[1]. Under TA 1925 provided that if a trustee lent no more than two thirds of the value of the property and complied with a number of other requirements, he was protected from any allegation that he had committed a breach of trust by lending too much in the event that the property fell in value so that part of the loan was irrecoverable[2]. Under s 3(3) these restrictions have been swept away and the power is simply to lend on the security of land. Questions of the appropriate amount to lend and the nature of the security are matters which now affect the exercise of the power: ie whether it is appropriate for trustees to make the particular loan on the terms proposed (and, of course, in exercising their powers, the statutory duty of care applies).

1   See generally *Snell's Equity*, 30th Ed, paras 11-17.
2   TA 1925, s 8 (which repeated TA 1893 s 8). The whole of TA 1925, Pt I – which dealt with investments – has now been repealed by TA 2000, Sch 2, Pt II, para 18.

Meaning of 'land'

11.32   The definition adopted is that the Interpretation Act 1978, whereby 'land' includes:

'Buildings and other structures, land covered with water, and any estate, interest, easement, servitude or right in or over land[1].'

1   Contrast TOLATA 1996 which adopted (and amended) the definition in LPA 1925, s 205(i) (ix): see para 2.2 above.

11.33   Accordingly, under s 3 of the Act, there is no power for trustees to invest in:

(a)   buildings and other structures;

(b)   an estate or interest in land (presumably including estates capable of subsisting in land outside the UK under the relevant foreign law); and

(c)   any interest in land which will include an undivided share in equitable interests arising under land and a trust of land (the existence of a trust for sale is irrelevant given the abolition of the doctrine of conversion by TOLATA 1996, s 3[1]). Easements and profits á prendre are included and it would seem that there is no power to invest in rent charges[2].

1   See para 2.18 above.
2   TIA 1961, Sch 1, Pt II (narrow range with advice) para 14 permitted investment in some rent charges.

Section 4 – Standard Investment Criteria

11.34   Text of section 4

(1)   In exercising any power of investment, whether arising under this Part or otherwise, a trustee must have regard to the standard investment criteria.

(2)   A trustee must from time to time review the investments of the trust and consider whether, having regard to the standard investment criteria, they should be varied.

(3)   The standard investment criteria, in relation to a trust, are—

    (a)   the suitability to the trust of investments of the same kind as any particular investment proposed to be made or retained and of that particular investment as an investment of that kind, and

    (b)   the need for diversification of investments of the trust, in so far as is appropriate to the circumstances of the trust.

Purpose of the section

11.35   In exercising any power of investment[1] a trustee *must* have regard to the 'standard investment criteria' laid down in sub-s (3). Note especially the following matters:

(a)   the section imposes a duty on all trustees who exercise a power of investment whether or not the power is granted by TA 2000 s 3. Hence it applies to a trustee exercising an express power granted in the trust investment;

(b)   the section cannot be excluded or limited by the trust instrument;

(c)   the trustees must review the trust investments from time to time (a further mandatory duty laid on all trustees) and must at that time have regard to the standard investment criteria;

(d)   the general duty of care applies in relation to the application of the standard investment criteria (see TA 2000, Sch 1, Para 1(b)).

1   It is considered that ss 4–5 are relevant when land is bought as an investment under s 8(1)(a).

The standard investment criteria

11.36   These are defined in s 4(3) *in relation to any particular trust* as

(a)   suitability; and

(b)   the need for diversification.

The suitability of an investment

11.37   Assume that the trustees are minded to invest £100,000 in shares in a publicly quoted oil company. The criteria that they must consider are:

(a)   is that kind of investment appropriate for the trust? In the example under consideration this presumably involves the trustees in deciding further, *first*, whether it is appropriate for £100,000 to be invested in equities (this will involve a consideration of the overall balance of the investments in the trust fund) and, second, whether in an oil company is the appropriate segment of the equity market in which to invest;

(b)   whether the particular investment proposed (the 'X Oil Co plc') is a suitable investment within that segment of the market[1].

1   The questions to be considered relate to 'size and risk'.

11.38   The same factors have to be applied in a case where the trustees are considering whether to retain an existing investment in the X Oil Co plc[1].

1   A further factor in this case may be the tax costs involved in selling an existing investment and acquiring a replacement asset: CGT may be payable on the sale and stamp duty on the purchase.

The need for diversification

11.39   Apart from the need to achieve a balanced portfolio in terms of risk management the trustees should also consider the balance between income and capital growth which is required to meet the needs of the trust[1]. The general duty of the trustee in this area was explained by Hoffmann J in *Nestlé v National Westminister Bank plc* in the following terms:

'The trustee must act fairly in making investment decisions which may have different consequences for different classes of beneficiaries. There are two reasons why I prefer this formulation to the traditional image of holding the scales equally between tenant for life and remainderman. The first is that the image of the scales suggests a weighing of known quantities whereas investment decisions are concerned with predictions of the future. Investments will carry expectations of their future income yield and capital appreciation and these expectations will be reflected in their current market price, but there is always a greater or lesser risk that the outcome will deviate from those expectations. A judgment on the fairness of the choices made by the trustees must have regard to these imponderables. The second reason is that the image of the scales suggests a more mechanistic process than I believe the law requires. The trustees have in my judgment a wide discretion. They are, for example, entitled to take into account the income needs of the tenant for life or the fact that the tenant for life was a person known to the settlor and a primary object of the trust whereas the remainderman is a remoter relative or a stranger. Of course, these cannot be allowed to become the overriding considerations but the concept of fairness between classes of beneficiaries does not require them to be excluded. It would be an inhuman law which required trustees to adhere to some mechanical rule for preserving the real value of the capital when the tenant for life was the testator's widow who had fallen upon hard times and the remainderman was young and well off.'

1   For the duty to 'hold the scales evenly' between the beneficiaries, see *Snell's Equity* (30th Ed) 2000, paragraph 11.35: this equitable principle underpins the rule in *Howe v Earl of Dartmouth*. See further para 11.11 above.

11.40   Trust draftsmen occasionally exclude the duty to diversify: the STEP Standard Provisions, for instance, provide that:

'3(1)(b)The trustees may decide not to diversify the trust find.

3(4)The trustees may decide not to hold a balance between conflicting interests of persons interested in Trust Property[1].'

1   Provisions of this nature should only be included in a trust deed after the matter has been
     discussed with the settlor. In the standard life interest trust, for instance, it is likely that a
     balance is precisely what the settlor will wish the trustees to preserve (albeit that it may be
     difficult to achieve in practice!). It is not therefore thought that these clauses are suitable
     for a standard precedent.

11.41   In such circumstances, although the trustees are bound to have
regard to the standard investment criteria, they may conclude that in the
particular circumstances of the trust it will be appropriate to invest (say) for
capital growth given that the settlor has authorised them not to hold a
balance between the demands of a life tenant and remainderman[1].

1   It may be that the life tenant does not need further income and is content for the trustees
     to invest for capital appreciation. In exercising this power, however, the trustees should
     ensure that they are acting reasonably in relation to the beneficiaries.

A comparison with the Trustee Investments Act 1961

11.42   The wording of TA 2000, s 4(3)(b) is identical to that in TIA 1961,
s 6(1)(a) whilst TA 2000, s 4(3)(a) is a slightly expanded version of TIA 1961,
s 6(1)(b) and uses the word 'kind' instead of 'description[1]'.

1   It was widely assumed (although not, for instance, by the Charity Commissioners) that the
     1961 Act requirements only applied to investments made under that Act.

The duty to review the investments

11.43   This is considered to codify the existing law which was stated as
follows by Leggatt LJ in *Nestlé v National Westminster Bank plc*:

'a trustee with a power of investment must undertake periodic reviews of
the investments held by the trust[1].'

1   [1993]1 WLR 1260 per Leggatt LJ at 1282. For a salutary case where trustees failed to
     diversify their investments, see *Re Mulligan* [1998] 1 NZLR 481. In the situation where
     trustees have acquired land as an investment under TA 2000, s 8 it is thought that the duty
     to review will apply to that land.

11.44   How often should the trustees review their investments? Clearly
much will depend upon the size and composition of the particular trust fund
but it may be suggested that it should be at least annually and for many
funds (and especially larger funds) quarterly reviews will be appropriate.

11.45   The combination of the investment powers given to trustees by TA
2000, s 3 and the obligation to review existing investments make it clear that,
in relation to the assets of the trust, all trustees must possess an implied
power of sale[1].

1   An express power is given to trustees of land: see Trusts of Land Act 1996, s 6(1)
     considered at para 2.41 above.

11.46   There will be trusts where the settlor has requested the trustees to
retain a particular asset (commonly shares in his family company) and in
such cases this will be a further factor for trustees to consider in reviewing
their investments.

Ethical investments

11.47 In considering the suitability of an investment, ethical (or social) considerations may be relevant[1].

1   See para 11.18 above.

Australian legislation

11.48 Section 4 does not particularise specific factors to which trustees are to have regard and may be contrasted with legislation in other countries. The legislation in the State of Victoria, for instance, provides as follows:

'Without limiting the matters that a trustee may take into account when exercising a power of investment, a trustee must, so far as they are appropriate to the circumstances of the trust, have regard to:

(a)   the purpose of the trust and the needs and circumstances of the beneficiaries;

(b)   the desirability of diversifying trustee investments;

(c)   the nature of and risk associated with existing trust investments and other trust property;

(d)   the need to maintain the real value of the capital or income of the trust;

(e)   the risk of capital or income loss or depreciation;

(f)   the potential for capital appreciation;

(g)   the likely income return and the timing of income return;

(h)   the length of the term of the proposed investment;

(i)   the probable duration of the trust;

(j)   the liquidity and marketability of the proposed investment during, and on the determination of, the term of the proposed investment;

(k)   the aggregate value of the trust estate;

(l)   the effect of the proposed investment in relation to the tax liability of the trust;

(m)   the likelihood of inflation affecting the value of the proposed investment or other trust property;

(n)   the costs (including commission, fees, charges and duties payable) of making the proposed investment;

(o)   the results of a review of existing trust investments.'

Section 5 – Advice

11.49 Text of section 5

(1)   Before exercising any power of investment, whether arising under this Part or otherwise, a trustee must (unless the exception applies) obtain and

consider proper advice about the way in which, having regard to the standard investment criteria, the power should be exercised.

(2)   When reviewing the investments of the trust, a trustee must (unless the exception applies) obtain and consider proper advice about whether, having regard to the standard investment criteria, the investments should be varied.

(3)   The exception is that a trustee need not obtain such advice if he reasonably concludes that in all the circumstances it is unnecessary or inappropriate to do so.

(4)   Proper advice is the advice of a person who is reasonably believed by the trustee to be qualified to give it by his ability in and practical experience of financial and other matters relating to the proposed investment.

Purpose of the section

11.50   It links in with s 4 (standard investment criteria) in requiring a trustee to obtain and consider advice (a) before making a proposed investment and (b) when reviewing the trust investments.

A duty on all trustees

11.51   As with the standard investment criteria, obtaining advice is a duty laid on all trustees whether exercising the statutory power of investment under s 3 or acting under an express power in the trust instrument. It is not a duty which can be excluded. The general duty of care applies when trustees carry out this duty (see TA 2000, Sch 1, para 1(b)).

The exception

11.52   The trustees need not obtain advice if they reasonably conclude that in all the circumstances it is unnecessary or inappropriate to do so (s 5(3)).

EXAMPLE 1

1.   Tom, an investment analyst is one of the trustees of the Ffrancom Trust. In investing the trust fund the trustees take his advice. The exception in s 5(3) applies.

2.   Jason set up a bare trust for his infant son, Jasper, by purchasing a capital appreciation (ie non income producing bond). There are taxation attractions in making this investment since any income produced in the trust would be taxed on Jason. Although bare trustees are subject to the duties of ss 4 and 5 in these circumstances it will be appropriate to retain the bond and unnecessary for the trustees to take advice under s 5[1]. It is suggested that as a matter of good practice the trustees should minute this decision to show that they have addressed their minds to the requirements of ss 4 and 5.

---

1   A further situation where trustees would be justified in not taking advice is if the proposed investment is so small that the cost of taking advice would be disproportionate to any benefit gained from so doing.

The person who gives the advice

11.53   This must be a person:

(a)   who the trustees believe to be qualified to give it by his ability and practical experience. Hence the trustees are expected to confirm the professional qualifications and track record of the advisor and merely entrusting the matter to someone met at a cocktail party and who claims in-depth knowledge and experience of the area would not satisfy this requirement; and

(b)   the relevant practical experience must be of financial and other matters relating to the proposed investment. Hence, if the trustees are proposing to invest in X Oil Co plc the advisor must have experience in the equities market, specifically, including oil shares (accordingly an expert in government issues would not suffice).

11.54   It may be thought that the test laid down in s 5(4) is too restrictive. What is required is advice on how the investment power should be exercised having regard to the standard investment criteria which involves a consideration of far more than the suitability of the proposed investment. An expert in oil equities might be well placed to advise the trustees to invest in Y Oil Co plc rather than X Oil Co plc but is unlikely to be qualified to give the 'overview' required by s 4[1].

1   The Law Commission included 'and other matters' in s 5(4) to cater for the situation where an investment in works of art is envisaged so that the advice should be from an expert in the relevant field. They also gave the example of a proposed investment in land and obtaining advice including a valuation of land (land is not, of course, a permitted investment under s 3).

A comparison with the old law

11.55   When acting under powers given to him by the TIA 1961 a trustee was obliged to take advice before investing in wider range and most narrow range investments[1]. When acting under express powers of investment there was no duty to take advice and the matter therefore depended on whether reasonable prudence dictated that advice should be taken.

1   TIA 1961 s 6(2).

Best practice

11.56   Although there is no requirement that advice must be in writing (contrast TIA 1961, s 6(5)[1]) commonly it will be furnished in writing (and often this will be desirable) but, if not, it will be important for the trustees to record the advice that they were given (eg if it was given orally at a trustee meeting). The trustees are also obliged to consider the advice and meetings at which advice is looked at by the trustees should be carefully minuted to show that appropriate consideration was given to it. Of course trustees do not have to accept advice: the position of a trustee in receipt of advice was pungently summarised by Megarry VC in *Cowan v Scargill*[2]:

> 'although a trustee who takes advice on investments is not bound to accept and act on that advice, he is not entitled to reject it merely because he sincerely disagrees with it, unless in addition to being sincere he is acting as an ordinary prudent man would act.'

1   'A trustee shall not be treated as having complied with [the obligation to take and consider advice] unless the advice was given or has been subsequently confirmed in writing.' Contrast the wording of TIA 1961, s 6 (4): '. . . proper advice is the advice of a person who is reasonably believed by the trustee to be qualified by his ability in and practical experience of financial matters; and such advice may be given by a person notwithstanding that he gives it in the course of his employment as an officer or servant.'

2   [1985] Ch 270 at 289.

11.57   In general the provisions of ss 4-5 are likely to pose few problems for the professionally run trust where investment powers are delegated to brokers or trustees act on advice and by and large the fund is invested in equities. Their application in other cases eg when the fund comprises private company shares or chattels, is more problematic (see, for instance, the Examples given at para 9.7 above). In considering a trust which was set up purely to hold shares in the family trading company it is unlikely that the trustees will wish – or indeed be in a position – to diversify. In establishing such trusts today it is suggested that a recital is included indicating that the purpose of the trust is to hold such shares and in the operative part of the deed state that the trustees have power to retain the shares and shall not be liable for the consequences of so acting[1]. Further, although s 4 cannot be excluded, a statement that trustees shall not be obliged to diversify[2] will be relevant in determining whether diversification is appropriate for circumstances of the trust[3]. What of existing trusts? Again it is suggested that in considering their duties under the Act the trustees must take into account the circumstances of the trust (why it was set up etc) and the needs of the beneficiaries but, in addition, they will have to bear in mind the problems that would be involved in diversifying out of a private company shareholding. For instance, what would the potential capital gains tax costs be and, often more significant, the difficulties involved (or it may be the sheer impossibility) in finding a buyer. With this range of considerations in mind it will commonly be the case that the trustee who retains the shares is acting reasonably and is not open to criticism. Of course, trustees should be alert to the opportunity to diversify especially if the holding is a minority one and should not retain the shareholding out of mere sentiment or inertia. When the shareholding is substantial they should ensure that they are represented on the Board of Directors. Similar considerations will doubtless be relevant when the trust fund comprises a landed estate or artefacts long connected with the family of the settlor and beneficiaries. In all such cases it is important to note the wide and flexible ambit of the words 'appropriate to the circumstances of the trust'.

1   See **Precedent 45**.
2   See para 11.40 above.
3   TA 2000, s 4(3)(b).

Section 6 – Restriction or Exclusion of this Part etc

11.58   Text of section 6

(1)   The general power of investment is–

(a)   in addition to powers conferred on trustees otherwise than by this Act, but

(b)   subject to any restriction or exclusion imposed by the trust instrument or by any enactment or any provision of subordinate legislation.

(2)   For the purposes of this Act, an enactment or a provision of subordinate legislation is not to be regarded as being, or as being part of, a trust instrument.

(3)   In this Act 'subordinate legislation' has the same meaning as in the Interpretation Act 1978.

Purpose of the section

11.59   The investment powers given by TA 2000, s 3 are default provisions and so apply in addition to express powers given in the trust instrument but are subject to any restriction or exclusion in that instrument. The following matters may be noted:

(a)   the section is dealing only with the power of investment: duties to have regard to the standard investment criteria and to take advice apply to all trusts and cannot be excluded in the trust instrument;

(b)   the wording used in this section is similar to that used by the draftsman in TA 1925, s 69(2)[1];

(c)   the position of existing trusts is dealt with in TA 2000 s 7[2];

(d)   ss 36-38 exclude the provisions of Pt II from occupational pension schemes, authorised unit trusts and certain schemes under the Charities Act 1993.

1   'The powers conferred by this Act on trustees are in addition to the powers conferred by the instrument, if any, creating the trust, but those powers, unless otherwise stated, apply if and so far only as a contrary intention is not expressed in the instrument, if any, creating the trust, and have effect subject to the terms of that instrument.'

2   See para 11.61 below.

Practical implications

11.60

(a)   A trust instrument enabling the trustees to make 'such investment as the law allows' permits trustees to invest under the s 3 power;

(b)   Will draftsmen still draft express investment clauses? In many cases the answer is likely to be yes for the following reasons:

(i)   *inertia*: an express clause detailing powers of investment etc will be on the draftsman's word processor and, given that it has been evolved through usage, will doubtless be adopted on the basis of familiarity and because it 'cannot be wrong';

(ii) the section does not deal with investment in land (see, however, s 8) and the draftsman may prefer to have a simple clause which:

    – deals with all types of asset;

    – permits the acquisition of an asset as an investment or for use by a beneficiary or otherwise;

    – enables land outside the UK to be purchased[1].

(c) There will be cases where the settlor wishes to restrict the trustee powers of investment. Consider the following:

EXAMPLE 2

1. Sid settles 75% of the shares in his trading company which he wishes the trustees to retain for at least seven[2] years provided that the company is trading satisfactorily and affording employment for the family (many of whom are beneficiaries of the trust).

2. Laura wishes her trustees to pursue an ethical investment policy.

3. Jacob wishes his trustees to invest for capital appreciation and only to make income payments (or indeed capital advances) to beneficiaries who are in 'need'.

4. William does not wish his trustees to invest in any business having any connection with France (he suffered severe homesickness in that country when a young man).

---

1   This matter is considered at para 11.74 below.
2   Sid is mindful of the possibility of a claw back of IHT business property relief: see IHTA 1984, s 113 A and, perhaps, of the desirability of full business assets taper for CGT purposes: see TCGA 1992, Sch 1A.

Section 7 – Existing Trusts

11.61   Text of section 7

(1) This Part applies in relation to trusts whether created before or after its commencement.

(2) No provision relating to the powers of a trustee contained in a trust instrument made before 3rd August 1961 is to be treated (for the purposes of section 6(1)(b)) as restricting or excluding the general power of investment.

(3) A provision contained in a trust instrument made before the commencement of this Part which—

(a) has effect under section 3(2) of the Trustee Investments Act 1961 as a power to invest under that Act, or

(b) confers power to invest under that Act,

is to be treated as conferring the general power of investment on a trustee.

Purpose of the section

11.62   It is primarily concerned with trusts in existence on 1 February 2000. As a general rule the statutory power of investment applies to trusts irrespective of when they were but created subject to restrictions or exclusions in the trust instrument. Section 7(2) and (3) deal specifically with the implications of this rule in the case of existing trusts.

Trust instruments made before 3rd August 1961

11.63   The general power of investment will apply to all such trusts so that no provision in the instrument is to be treated as restricting or excluding that power. The reason for this is that the Trustee Investment Act 1961 applied to all trusts subject only to legislative restrictions[1]. The 1961 Act came into force on 3 August 1961 and hence the purpose of TA 2000, s 7(2) is 'to ensure that old restrictions overcome by the 1961 Act do not revive to restrict the benefits of the new general power of investment'.

1   See TIA 1961 s 1(3) which provided that 'no provision relating to the powers of a trustee contained in any instrument . . . made before the passing of this Act shall limit the powers [*viz* the new powers of investment] conferred by this section'.

Trust instruments made after 2 August 1961

11.64   If the trust instrument gives the trustees power to invest under the 1961 Act or permits trustees 'to invest property in any investment for the time being authorised by law for the investment of trust property' (this power was treated as allowing the trustee to invest under the 1961 Act: see TIA 1961, s 3(2)) then TA 2000, s 7(3) provides that the general power of investment shall apply to those trusts.

Restrictions in post 2 August 1961 trust instruments

11.65   The general principle of s 6(1)(b) is that the general power of investment is subject to restriction or exclusion in the trust instrument. As has been discussed above this principle does not apply to trusts already in existence on 3 August 1961 but it does apply to all trusts subsequently created. What will amount to a restriction or exclusion of the general power of investment? In the notes to the Act the Lord Chancellor's Department provided the following illustration:

'Take for example, an express power of investment in a post 2 August 1961 trust instrument authorising trustees to invest 'only in Government bonds'. This power would be taken to exclude the general power of investment (s 6(1)(b)). On the other hand, an express power in another instrument at the same date to invest 'in shares quoted on the London Stock Exchange, but not in shares of X plc' would take effect as the general power investment subject to the restriction on investing in X plc (s 6(1)). Had the trust instruments predated 3 August 1961, the general power of investment would have applied free of either limitation (s 7(5)) as would the new statutory powers conferred under the 1961 Act when it came into force (TIA 1961, s 1(3)).'

Modifications at Committee stage in the House of Lords[1]

11.66   The Trustee Bill as originally drafted provided that 'this Part does not confer the general power of investment on trustees who immediately before its commencement have special statutory powers of investment'[2]. In moving the deletion of these provisions at Committee Stage the Lord Chancellor (Lord Irvine of Lairg) commented that:

'The purpose of this amendment is to give the new powers of investment to all existing trustees, subject to clause 6(1)(b) which makes the new general power of investment subject to any restriction or exclusion imposed by the trust instrument or by legislation. Without this amendment there are some in the charity sector, in particular, who would be excluded from the new regime. These include those whose current powers are granted by what the published Bill called 'special statutory powers of investment'. That might be particular charities or non-charitable trusts governed by an enactment or by subordinate legislation, or those who belong to a class whose powers derive from legislation or who have been granted additional statutory powers. Certain classes of religious and educational charities may have such powers; and charities which are subject to schemes or orders made by the Charity Commission or the Home Secretary under the Charities Act 1993. We believe that, if the restriction in the published Bill is to be dropped for charitable trusts, it should be dropped for non-charitable trusts as well.

In providing charities and other trusts with wider powers it will not be possible to predict whether or not they will be used appropriately in every case in which they will apply. But there are four factors which, we believe, make the risk acceptable; first, that trustees should have the wider powers that are proposed in the Bill; secondly, the exercise of these powers will be subject to safeguards, including the duty of care; thirdly, the application of the new powers will be subject to any restriction or exclusion in the trust instrument or any enactment; and fourthly, even where the new regime applies, it is for the trustees to determine in the particular circumstances the extent to which it is appropriate to exercise the powers conferred.'

1   Lords Hansard, 7 June 2000, CWH 1-2.
2   See clauses 7(1)-(3) in the Bill which was ordered to be printed on 20 January 2000.

Exclusions

11.67   Part II does not apply to the following:

(a)   occupational pension schemes (TA 2000, s 36);

(b)   authorised unit trusts (TA 2000, s37); and

(c)   certain schemes made under the Charities Act 1993 (TA 2000, s 38).

Analysis of the Trustee Act 2000, Part III

Power to acquire freehold and leasehold land

11.68   Text of section 8

(1)   A trustee may acquire freehold or leasehold land in the United Kingdom—

    (a)   as an investment,

    (b)   for occupation by a beneficiary, or

    (c)   for any other reason.

(2)   'Freehold or leasehold land' means—

    (a)   in relation to England and Wales, a legal estate in land,

    (b)   in relation to Scotland—

        (i)   the estate or interest of the proprietor of the dominium utile or, in the case of land not held on feudal tenure, the estate or interest of the owner, or

        (ii)   a tenancy, and

    (c)   in relation to Northern Ireland, a legal estate in land, including land held under a fee farm grant.

(3)   For the purpose of exercising his functions as a trustee, a trustee who acquires land under this section has all the powers of an absolute owner in relation to the land.

Purpose of the section

11.69   The section is modelled on s 6(3) and (4) of the Trusts of Land and Appointment of Trustees Act 1996. Those provisions gave *trustees of land* power to purchase a legal estate in any land in *England or Wales* whether as an investment; for occupation by a beneficiary or for any other purpose[1]. Section 8 now extends this power to *all trustees* and permits the acquisition of freehold or leasehold land *in the UK*. Consequential amendments are made to the 1996 Act.

1   See further para 2.38(c) above. Trustees of a settlement under the SLA 1925 likewise enjoyed a power to employ capital monies in the purchase of 'freehold land or leasehold land held for sixty years or more unexpired at the time of purchase '(see SLA s73(1(xi)). The purchase would usually be directed by the tenant for life. Trustees of a personalty settlement did not have default powers to purchase land. For the meaning of 'land' for the purposes of TA 2000, see para 11.32 above.

'Freehold or leasehold land'

11.70   The phrase is defined in s 8(2) in relation to England and Wales (see s 8(2)(a)); Scotland (s 8(2)(b)) and Northern Ireland (s8(2)(c)). The power thus extends to the purchase in England and Wales of a fee simple absolute in possession or a term of years absolute[1]. No other restrictions are imposed and hence a short leasehold interest may be acquired by trustees (although they would need to be mindful of their overriding duty to preserve the trust fund before making any such purchase).

2   See LPA 1925, s 1(1) for the definition of a legal estate. The Law Commission concluded that s 8(1) allows trustees to acquire land with the aid of a mortgage but it is not clear that this is the case (see LC No 260 para 2.44).

11.71   Because the power is to acquire a legal estate in land it is not possible to purchase a beneficial interest in land. Land may, however, be acquired jointly with other persons provided that legal title to the property is taken in the names of the trustees.

EXAMPLE 3

1.   Jakob is the principal beneficiary of his family trust of which the trustees are Sid and Sad. A substantial leasehold property is purchased by Jakob and the trustees for occupation by Jakob:

–   the trustees have power to purchase a legal estate in property jointly with Jakob under TA 2000 s 8(1) provided that legal title to the property is taken in the names of the trustees only;

–   further they may purchase the property (in this case their interest in the property) for occupation by a beneficiary (s 8(1)(b)).

Alternatively the Trustees may lend money to Jakob to enable him to purchase the property either under TA 2000 s 3(3), if the loan is secured on the land, or under an express power in the trust instrument.

2.   Assume that Suzanna wishes to raise money on her substantial residence in Purley. If the trustees agree to buy a stake in the property they must ensure that they acquire the legal estate (ie it is not sufficient to purchase (say) a 50% beneficial interest in the property from Suzanna).

Purposes for which trustees may acquire land

11.72   The familiar trio (as an investment, for beneficial occupation or for any other reason) were first set out in the Trusts of Land and Appointment of Trustees Act 1996, s 6(4) (now repealed). The first two situations are straightforward whilst the Lord Chancellor confirmed that the phrase 'for any other reason' would include the purchase of functional land by charitable trustees for carrying out the purposes of the charity (for instance, a school buying land to serve as a playing field)[1]. It is thought that the powers given to the trustees are administrative in nature and so cannot be exercised so as to alter the beneficial trusts: for instance, purchasing a house to be occupied rent free by the life tenant (or by a beneficiary of a discretionary trust) is permitted but there is no power to purchase a house for occupation by the remainderman.

1   See Lords Hansard 7 June 2000 Col CWH3. Another illustration would be if the trustees already carried on a trade and acquired further land for use in connection with that business or acquired a 'ransom strip' with a view to maximising the consideration on a future sale of trust land.

Power in relation to land acquired under s 8

11.73   By s 8(3) trustees have all the powers of an absolute owner in relation to such land. The width of this wording has been discussed in connection with the similar provision in s 6(1) of the Trusts of Land and Appointment of Trustees Act 1996[1]. The relationship between s 6 of the 1996 Act and s 8 is slightly unusual:

(a)   s 6(1) is concerned only with the powers of trustees of land. A trust of land is a trust of property which consists of or includes land and hence a trustee of land is a trustee of such a trust[2]. For these purposes it is irrelevant how the land came into the trust: it could, for instance, have been acquired by trustees under TA 2000, s 8 or it could have been gifted by the settlor;

(b)   by contrast s 8(3) gives all the powers of an absolute owner in relation to the land to a trustee who *acquires* land under s 8. Note, therefore, that this section does not apply in cases where the land is gifted to the trust but this does not matter given that the trust in such a case will be a trust of land and hence the trustees will have the s 6(1) powers. Indeed it would appear that when land is acquired under s 8 the trustees become trustees of land and hence have the s 6(1) powers of an absolute owner. It would, therefore, seem that the powers given in s 8(3) are wholly redundant!

1   See para 2.41.
2   Trusts of Land and Appointment of Trustees Act 1996, s 1(1).

Limitations on the s 8 power

11.74   Although wider than the power conferred originally in the 1996 Act (which had permitted only the acquisition of land in England and Wales) s 8 is still restricted to land in the United Kingdom[1]. Accordingly, there is no statutory power to invest in land elsewhere although trustees may, of course, invest in shares in a company (including a foreign company) which owns such land under their general powers of investment in TA 2000, s 3. Express powers of investment will also commonly permit trustees to acquire 'property (moveable or immoveable) of whatever nature and wherever situated'[2]. The Law Commission decided, however, that a default power should be restricted to the UK given that the concept of a trust is not universally recognised and that even in countries which have adopted the Hague Convention on the Law Applicable to Trusts and on their Recognition, foreign laws do not necessarily afford full protection for the interests of beneficiaries against claims of third parties[3]. The problems identified by the Law Commission are obviously matters which should be taken into account by trustees before exercising an express power to acquire land outside the UK.

1 The 'United Kingdom' comprises England, Scotland, Wales and Northern Ireland.
2 See **Precedent 1** below.
3 The views of the Law Commission are fully set out in No 260 at para 2.42 and footnote 88.

Why does the Act confer a separate power to acquire land?

11.75 The general power of investment might have been widened to include the acquisition of land and might further have provided that land could also be acquired for occupation or indeed for any other purpose. The Law Commission felt, however, that dealing with land in a separate part of the Trustee Act would facilitate consequential amendments to the investment powers of some bodies which, though not trustees, were subject to the provisions of the Trustee Investments Act 1961[1].

1 Law Com No 260, para 2.41, footnote 86 and see also para 2.23.

Section 9 – Restriction or Exclusion of this Part etc

11.76 Text of section 9

The powers conferred by this Part are–

    (a)   in addition to powers conferred on trustees otherwise than by this Part, but

    (b)   subject to any restriction or exclusion imposed by the trust instrument or by any enactment or any provision of subordinate legislation.

Purpose of the section

11.77 It serves the same function as s 6 in relation to Pt II: investment powers[1]. The power to acquire land is in addition to the trustees' other powers but is subject to any restrictions laid down in the trust instrument or to any provision of subordinate legislation (subordinate legislation has already been defined in TA 2000, s 6(2)(3)).

1 See the discussion of s 6 at para 11.58 above.

Section 10 – Existing Trusts

11.78 Text of section 10

    (1)   This Part does not apply in relation to–

        (a)   a trust of property which consists of or includes land which (despite section 2 of the Trusts of Land and Appointment of Trustees Act 1996) is settled land, or

        (b)   a trust to which the Universities and College Estates Act 1925 applies.

    (2)   Subject to subsection (1), this Part applies in relation to trusts whether created before or after its commencement.

Purpose of the section

11.79   It fulfils the same function as s 7 in relation to the Pt II powers. The Pt III powers apply to all trustees irrespective of when the trust was created. Note, however, that in this case there are no special rules for pre-3 August 1961 trusts. Accordingly, a trust already in existence at that time and which permitted only the investment of the trust fund in 'government stock' would be overridden for the purpose of the s 3 general investment power but not for s 8 purposes. The trustees therefore (unless the trust was already a trust of land) will not have power to acquire land.

Amendments at committee stage

11.80   The changes made to s 7 have been noted at para 11.66 above and similar amendments were made to s 10. The Lord Chancellor (Lord Irvine of Lairg) explained that:

> 'The purpose of this amendment . . . is to expand the numbers of trusts that can benefit from the new regime being set up by the Bill, in this case by giving new powers of land acquisition to all existing trustees, subject to clause 9(b). I shall not weary the Committee by repeating the argument in detail but will repeat that the Charity Commission would welcome the introduction of the amendment.

> Settled land and bodies subject to the Universities and College Estates Act 1925 are subject to their own specific regimes in relation to the matters covered by Pt III of the Bill – the purchase of land. The remainder of the amendment allows those well understood regimes to continue to operate as they now do.'

Duty of care

11.81   The general duty of care laid down in TA 2000 s1 applies to:-

(a)   the exercise of the statutory power to acquire land under s 8;

(b)   the acquisition of land under an express power in the trust instrument; and

(c)   in both cases to the exercise of any power in relation to the land acquired[1].

1   TA 2000, Sch 1, para 2: see para 10.12 above.

Exclusions

11.82   There are exclusions, similar to those in Pt II for occupational pension schemes; authorised unit trusts and certain schemes made under the Charities Act 1993[1].

1   See para 11.67 above.

12

Part IV: Delegation by Trustees: Agents, Nominees and Custodians

Background

12.1   The 17 sections that make up Pt IV of the Act may be divided as follows:

(i)   Sections 11-15 give trustees, acting collectively, the power to appoint agents and, in particular, make provision for the appointment of asset management.

(ii)   Sections 16-20 are concerned with the appointment of nominees and custodians to hold trust property.

(iii)   Sections 21-23 deal with the trustees' obligations in connection with the supervision of agents, nominees and custodians and their liability for the acts of those persons.

(iv)   Sections 24-27 contain supplemental provisions which deal, *inter alia,* with the exclusion of this Part of the Act and which trusts are affected by it.

12.2   Courts of Equity took the view that trustees could not, in the absence of express authorisation, delegate their discretions. By contrast, the carrying out of an administrative act was delegable after 1925 even if it was a matter that the trustees could have done themselves so that delegation was not necessary[1]. Trustees could therefore engage a fund manager to advise them on the appropriate trust investments and then direct him to sell/purchase as appropriate but the decision to sell or buy (which constituted the exercise of a fiduciary discretion) was a matter for the trustees.

1   See TA 1925, s 23(1) which apparently changed the law in permitting trustees to employ an agent (a) even if there was no legal or moral necessity to do so and (b) indicated the trustees were not liable for the acts of that agent provided that he was employed 'in good faith'. Liability had formerly been based on the obligation of the trustees to act as reasonable men in both the selection and supervision of the agent: see generally *Re Vickery* [1931] 1 Ch 572; for a forceful criticism see (1959) 22 MLR 381 and generally *Snell's Equity* (30th Ed) at 12.17.

12.3   The Law Commission took the view that the deficiencies in the existing law were not as to *when* trustees could delegate but as to *what* they could delegate. The Commission concluded:

'While certain limitations on trustees' powers of delegation are wholly appropriate, others now constitute a serious impediment to the administration of trusts. Trusteeship is an increasingly specialised task that often requires professional skills that the trustees may not have. Far from promoting the more conscientious discharge of the obligations of trusteeship the prohibition on the delegation of fiduciary discretions may force trustees to commit breaches of trust in order to achieve the most effective administration of the trust.[1]'

1   Law Com No 260, para 4.6.

12.4   In two areas the law had developed differently:

(a)   pension trusts: under the Pensions Act 1995, s 34 trustees may delegate any discretion involving the making of a decision about investments to a fund manager who satisfies certain requirements. The trustees have to prepare a written statement of principles governing investment decisions. The legislation requires trustees to exercise care and skill in that delegation[1].

(b)   Charities: They are generally subject to the normal equitable principles against delegation but the Charity Commissioners have power under the Charities Act 1993, s 26 to permit an extension of the trustees' powers of delegation. Specific conditions will be imposed on such trustees who will be expected to exercise reasonable care[2].

1   See generally the commentary in Law Commission No 260, appendix C para 14. See also paras 11.9 and 11.20 above.
2   See generally 1994 2 Decisions of the Charity Commissioners p29. The Charity Commissioners will normally exercise their discretions when the fund is worth in excess of £100,000 and the frequency of transactions is such as to warrant the appointment of a fund manager. The Commissioners have devised a model order which is in the following terms:-

   1.   The Trustees may appoint as the investment manager for the Charity a person who they are satisfied after inquiry is a proper and competent person to act in that capacity and who is either:

      (i)   an individual of repute with at least 15 years' experience of investment management who is an authorised person within the meaning of the Financial Services Act 1986; or

      (ii)   a company or firm of repute which is an authorised or exempted person within the meaning of that Act otherwise than by virtue of s 45(1)(j) of that Act.

   2.   The Trustees may delegate to an investment manager so appointed power at his discretion to buy and sell investments for the Charity on behalf of the Trustees in accordance with the investment policy laid down by the Trustees. The Trustees may do so only on terms consistent with this Order.

   3.   Where the Trustees make any delegation under this Order they shall:

      (a)   inform the investment manager in writing of the extent of the Charity's investment powers;

      (b)   lay down a detailed investment policy for the Charity and immediately inform the investment manager in writing of it and of any changes to it;

      (c)   ensure that the terms of the delegated authority are clearly set out in writing and notified to the investment manager;

      (d)   ensure that they are kept informed and review on a regular basis the performance of their investment portfolio managed by the investment manager and on the exercise by him of his delegated authority;

    (e)   take all reasonable care to ensure that the investment manager complies with the terms of the delegated authority; and

    (f)   review the appointment at such intervals not exceeding 24 months as they think fit.

4.   Where the Trustees make any delegation under this Order they shall do so on the terms that:

    (a)   the investment manager shall comply with the terms of his delegated authority;

    (b)   the investment manager shall not do anything which the Trustees do not have the power to do;

    (c)   the Trustees may with reasonable notice revoke the delegation or vary any of its terms in a way which is consistent with the terms of this Order; and

    (d)   the Trustees shall give directions to the investment manager as to the manner in which he is to report to them all sales and purchases of investments made on their behalf.

5.   The Trustees may:

    (a)   make such arrangements as they think fit for any investments of the Charity or income from those investments to be held by a corporate body as the Trustees' nominee; and

    (b)   pay reasonable and proper remuneration to any corporate body acting as the Trustees' nominee in pursuance of this clause.

Analysis of TA 2000, Part IV

Section 11 – Power to Employ Agents

12.5   Text of section 11

(1)   Subject to the provisions of this Part, the trustees of a trust may authorise any person to exercise any or all of their delegable functions as their agent.

(2)   In the case of a trust other than a charitable trust, the trustees' delegable functions consist of any function other than–

    (a)   any function relating to whether or in what way any assets of the trust should be distributed,

    (b)   any power to decide whether any fees or other payment due to be made out of the trust funds should be made out of income or capital,

    (c)   any power to appoint a person to be a trustee of the trust, or

    (d)   any power conferred by any other enactment or the trust instrument which permits the trustees to delegate any of their functions or to appoint a person to act as a nominee or custodian.

(3)   In the case of a charitable trust, the trustees' delegable functions are–

    (a)   any function consisting of carrying out a decision that the trustees have taken;

    (b)   any function relating to the investment of assets subject to the trust (including, in the case of land held as an investment, managing the land and creating or disposing of an interest in the land);

    (c)   any function relating to the raising of funds for the trust otherwise than by means of profits of a trade which is an integral part of carrying out the trust's charitable purpose;

(d)   any other function prescribed by an order made by the Secretary of State.

(4)   For the purposes of subsection (3)(c) a trade is an integral part of carrying out a trust's charitable purpose if, whether carried on in the United Kingdom or elsewhere, the profits are applied solely to the purposes of the trust and either–

(a)   the trade is exercised in the course of the actual carrying out of a primary purpose of the trust, or

(b)   the work in connection with the trade is mainly carried out by beneficiaries of the trust.

(5)   The power to make an order under subsection (3)(d) is exercisable by statutory instrument which shall be subject to annulment in pursuance of a resolution of either House of Parliament.

Purpose of the section

12.6   It introduces the general power for trustees *as a body* to delegate certain of their functions: it does not affect delegation by individual trustees which continues to be dealt with by TA 1925, s 25 (as recast by TDA 1999, s 5)[1]. A number of general matters should be borne in mind when considering the ambit of this section:

(a)   it is a default provision which may be excluded or modified in the trust instrument (see TA 2000, s 26);

(b)   there are special rules for pension trusts, authorised unit trusts and funds established under schemes made under the Charities Act 1993, ss 24-25 (see TA 2000, ss 36-38);

(c)   the statutory duty of care applies to a trustee 'when entering into arrangements under which a person is authorised under s11 to exercise functions as an agent' (see TA 2000, Sch1, para 3(1)(a) and see para 3(2))[2];

(d)   the section distinguishes between charitable trusts and others; compare the power to delegate under s 11(3) with that available to non-charitable trustees under s 11(2);

(e)   there is no requirement that the delegation should be by power of attorney nor indeed that it should be in writing (but contrast the special restrictions that apply to asset management: see TA 2000, s 15(1));

(f)   delegation may be to an outside agent (for instance a fund manager) or to an employee of the trust. When a landed estate is held in trust many of the functions of the trustees in relation to the running of that estate will be delegated to a land agent who will frequently be a full-time employee of the trust;

(g)   it may be that an agent has the statutory power to appoint a nominee or custodian (note that the restriction in s 11(2)(d) refers to 'any other enactment or the trust instrument' but not to 'this Act'). Accordingly, a fund manager appointed as the trustees' agent may (it appears) appoint a nominee to hold the assets under the statutory power; and

(h) for delegation of the power to insure in the case of bare trusts, see TA 1925, s 19(2)–(4) inserted by TA 2000, s 34.

1   See further para 8.36 above.
2   These provisions are considered in detail at para 10.12 above.

What are delegable functions in the case of non-charitable trustees?

12.7   Such trustees have a general power to delegate all or any of their delegable functions. It had been suggested that the line should be drawn between 'dispositive' and 'administrative' powers with only the latter being capable of delegation[1]. At para 4.8 of their Final Report the Law Commission concluded that:

'The distinction between administrative powers (which would be delegable) and distributive powers (which would not) would, if left unqualified, enable trustees to delegate in one case where this would be inappropriate, namely in relation to powers to appoint and replace trustees. Although such powers are evidently not 'distributive' in nature, it is equally clear that trustees should not be able to delegate their discretions in such matters without express authority in the instrument creating the trust.'

1   This distinction was considered by the House of Lords in *Pearson (or Pilkington) v IRC* [1981] AC 753: see further para 4.11 ff above. In its Consultation Paper ('Trustees Powers and Duties': Law Com CP No 146) the Law Commission rejected the distinction that had been enshrined in s 23(1) of TA 1925 between ministerial acts and fiduciary powers in favour of a distinction drawn between powers to administer the trust and dispositive powers. This was, however, rejected in the Law Com Final Report.

12.8   As a result the concept of a delegable function allows trustees to delegate matters of administration, including powers of investment and management, but excluding dispositive powers (ie any decision as to whether or in what way assets of the trust should be distributed: See TA 2000, s 11(2)(a)) and also excluding any power to appoint a person to be a trustee of the trust (see TA 2000, s 11(2)(c))[1].

1   See generally the comments of the Law Commission in their Final Report, No 260 at para 4.7 *et seq.*

The interpretation of s 11(2)(a)

12.9   This is intended to prevent the delegation of the trustees' powers to distribute income or capital amongst beneficiaries: typically, therefore, discretionary trustees cannot delegate their powers to pay and apply capital or to effect a resettlement of the trust fund. Curiously the function which is non-delegable relates to the distribution of 'assets' of the trust and assets are defined as 'including any right or interest' (see TA 2000, s 39(1)). The implication is that the restriction is limited to the assets comprising the capital of the trust fund which might therefore suggest that trustees are free to delegate decisions relating to the distribution of the income produced by those assets. It is surprising that the draftsman did not employ the phrase 'trust funds' in dealing with this non-delegable function given that that phrase is defined as comprising both income and capital. In any event it is the undoubted intention that decisions regarding both income and capital are non-delegable and doubtless the courts will construe 'asset' as including trust income. The decision to accumulate income (involving a withholding of assets from the beneficiary) is not delegable and nor is the exercise of powers of appointment, advancement and revocation. Powers of appropriation (for instance splitting the trust into separate funds) are also, it is thought, covered by s 11(2)(a)[1].

1   Although the wording is limited to 'in what way any assets of the trust should be distributed' it is thought that 'to a beneficiary or beneficiaries' is necessarily implied. A sale of trust assets and the retention of assets to meet the trustees' lien would be delegable whilst the exercise of a power to make donations to a charity (when charity is not otherwise a beneficiary of the trust) would appear to be non delegable. Essentially the line is drawn at gratuitous dispositions of trust property.

The interpretation of s 11(2)(b)

12.10   Trust instruments may give trustees a discretion to charge certain payments against either the capital or the income of the trust fund. The Trustee Act 2000 itself provides examples: in s 31 a trustee is entitled to be reimbursed out of the trust funds whilst in s 34, the recast power of insurance, the trustees can pay premiums on an insurance policy out of trust funds which as the amended TA 1925, s 19(5) indicates, means any income or capital. None of these powers is capable of delegation, presumably on the basis that they affect what is capable of being distributed to or for the benefit of beneficiaries.

Delegation by charitable trustees

12.11

Although the old restrictions on collective delegation could be overcome by an application to the Charity Commissioners for an order under the Charities Act 1993, s 26[1], the Law Commission concluded that:

'The fact that a mechanism exists to address the problem caused by the worst failings of the law in this regard does not mean that charity should be excluded from the proposed reforms of trustees' powers of delegation. Sections 23 and 30 of the Trustee Act 1925 are so unsatisfactory that it would not be appropriate to leave them on the statute book solely to regulate the delegation powers of charity trustees.[2]'

1   As to which see para 12.2 above.
2   Law Com No 260 at para 4.38.

12.12   The Commission identified particular problems in framing new rules for charities since it is more difficult in such cases to differentiate between the 'core functions' (which must be performed by the trustees) and functions which should be capable of delegation. To the suggestion that the 'charitable purposes' of the trust should not be delegable it was objected that 'the legal concept of "charitable purposes" is much wider than the particular charitable objects for which the trust exists'.

12.13   Accordingly:

'Although it may initially appear attractive to replace the differentiation by reference to "distributive" functions which is proposed for other trusts with one focusing on the charitable purposes of the trust, it is clear that the legal concept of "charitable purposes" is much wider than the particular charitable objects for which the trust exists. To prohibit charity trustees from delegating all functions falling under the umbrella of "charitable purposes" would therefore substantially *narrow* their powers, and would impede rather than assist the performance of their functions.[1]'

1   Law Com No 260 para 4.38. See also the comments made in the Consultation Paper (CP No 146) at para 6.63:

'The courts have interpreted very widely what constitutes an application of money for charitable purposes. It has been held to include, in the context of revenue legislation, the donation of funds to another charity, the reinvestment of surplus income, and (probably) payments made for administrative purposes, such as the payment of the salaries of a charity's staff. To prohibit charity trustees from delegating all matters that fall within the umbrella of "charitable purposes" would therefore substantially *narrow* their powers, and would impede rather than assist their functions.'

12.14   To resolve these issues the legislation makes a distinction between:

(a)   the management of the fund with a view to generating income to finance the charitable purposes of the trust; and

(b)   the execution of the trust's charitable purposes.

12.15   In principle, the functions in category (a) can be delegated: those in category (b) only in so far as ministerial matters are involved (thereby preserving the existing law for this category). Section 11(3) hence lists what may be delegated: for instance s 11(3)(a) permits the delegation of administrative tasks (ministerial matters); s 11(3)(b) of investment functions and s 11(3)(c) fundraising projects. Two points should be noted:

(a)   s 11(3)(c) excludes trading activities where the trade is an integral part of carrying out the charitable purpose of the trust (see s 11(4) for the meaning of an integral part). The example which is set out in the Law Commission's Final Report is of the Incorporated Council of Law Reporting in England and Wales which operates as a business providing a public service. Funds are raised by publishing Law Reports at a moderate price which is also the charitable purpose[1];

(b)   charitable trustees can delegate their powers of managing land and of creating or disposing of an interest in it[2]. The Charities Act 1993 imposes restrictions on dealing with land held by charities in that the trustees can only sell, lease or mortgage the land (unless they get an order of the Charity Commissioners or the court), if they comply with certain conditions (for instance, to consider proper advice) before entering into the transaction. There is however nothing in that Act which requires these powers to be exercised by the trustees personally.

1   See *Incorporated Council of Law Reporting for England and Wales v AG* [1972] Ch 73, CA.
2   At Committee Stage in the House of Lords the wording of s.11(3)(b) was amended to replace 'acquired' with 'held' thereby making it clear that the subsection covers land which is bequeathed to a charity and then held as an investment. (Compare the wording of TA 2000 s.8(3).)

12.16 It was recognised that the 'list approach' adopted in this subsection might be too narrow, too wide or insufficiently certain. Section 11(3)(d) goes some way to meeting such problems by enabling the Secretary of State to add to the list of delegable functions.

12.17 The Charity Commissioners can still sanction additional powers under the Charities Act 1993, s 26 if they consider that to be necessary.

Foreign property

12.18 A curiosity of the old law was that trustees could delegate their functions (both administrative and discretionary) in relation to foreign property which was held in the trust fund[1]. Initially the Law Commission favoured retaining this provision by enabling trustees in such cases to delegate their distributive functions[2] but by the time of the Final Report it accepted that there was no justification for this. Rather the provision was a relic of an age of slow communications and 'now that global communication is instantaneous, and foreign property is much more commonly held by English trustees than it used to be, it would be anomalous to give trustees different powers merely because of the geographical location of the property concerned'[3].

1   TA 1925, s 23(2) now repealed by TA 2000, Sch 2, Pt II, para 23 but with savings for existing delegations: see Sch 3, para 6. Section 23(2) codified the existing common law power: with the repeal of this provision has the common law power survived? The Law Commission do not think so!
2   Law Com CP 146 para 6.26.
3   Law Com No 260 para 4.13.

Section 12 – Persons who may Act as Agents

12.19   Text of section 12

(1)   Subject to subsection (2), the persons whom the trustees may under section 11 authorise to exercise functions as their agent include one or more of their number.

(2)   The trustees may not authorise two (or more) persons to exercise the same function unless they are to exercise the function jointly.

(3)   The trustees may not under section 11 authorise a beneficiary to exercise any function as their agent (even if the beneficiary is also a trustee).

(4)   The trustees may under section 11 authorise a person to exercise functions as their agent even though he is also appointed to act as their nominee or custodian (whether under section 16, 17 or 18 or any other power).

Purpose of the section

12.20   The section deals with the person (or persons) who can be appointed to act as the trustees' agent. In general no restriction is placed on the person who may be appointed. Note, however, that if more than one agent is appointed to exercise the same trustee function, those persons must act jointly (there is no power to act jointly and severally[1]).

1   This may cause problems when the operation of a trustee bank account, typically in the case of a landed estate, is delegated to the chief land agent and his deputy. In such cases it is common to require only one signature on cheques up to a prescribed limit. It is suggested that the restrictions imposed in s 12(2) are unnecessary and should be amended in the trust deed: see **precedent 56**.

Excluding the appointment of a beneficiary (s 12(3))

12.21   The one person, however, who cannot be appointed to act as agent is a beneficiary whether or not he is also a trustee (note that under s 11(1) a trustee can delegate their functions to one or more of their number)[1]. At first sight this limitation is surprising: there is, for instance, a striking contrast between the position adopted by this section and s 9 of the Trusts of Land and Appointment of Trustees Act which allows trustees of land to delegate to a beneficiary with an interest in possession 'any of their functions as trustees which relate to the land'[2]. The Law Commission indicated that delegation under s 9 'is subject to restrictions which do not apply to (s 11 of the Act). Subsection (3) prevents the avoidance of those restrictions'. This reasoning is far from satisfactory and it will be desirable to extend the power to include beneficiaries[3].

1   See also, in the context of individual delegation, s 25(3) inserted by TDA 1999 s 5 and considered at para 8.40 above.
2   Section 9 is considered at para 2.77 ff above. Such delegation must be by power of attorney.
3   See **Precedent 56** below.

12.22   A further problem with s 12(3) is that it does not define a 'beneficiary'. This is in contrast to the Trusts of Land and Appointment of Trustees Act 1996 which, in s 22, defines a beneficiary as any person with an interest in property subject to the trust. The difficulties posed by this definition have been considered earlier[1] but for the purposes of s 12(3) there is no reason to think that the court will apply the s 22 definition (whatever that means). They may prefer to treat the term as including all persons for whose benefit the trustees must deal with the property[2] which will include the beneficiaries of a discretionary trust.

1   See para 4.1 above.
2   See *Underhill & Hayton* 'Law of Trusts and Trustees' (15th Ed) p 3.

Delegation to one of the trustees

12.23   This is permitted by s 12(1). It had already been allowed in the case of individual delegation under TA 1925, s 25 (as amended by TDA 1999) and probably under the now repealed TA 1925, s 23(1) in the case of purely ministerial functions. Two points are worthy of note:

(a)   originally it had been proposed that trustees should be vicariously liable for the acts and defaults of the trustee agent but this was rejected and the normal standard of care applies[1]. This duty of care under s 1 is, of course, limited to trustees and does not apply to an agent in the performance of his agency. Such persons will, however, owe duties of care under the general rules of agency;

(b) a trustee who acts as an agent may be remunerated for so acting (see TA 2000, s 29(6)(a)) and may recover out of pocket expenses (see TA 2000, s 31(2)(a))[2].

1   As to which, see para 10.5 above. See also Law Com No 260, para 4.31. Vicarious liability is imposed under TA 1925, s 25; and under the Pensions Act 1995, s 34 when investment delegation is to one or more of the trustees.

2   See Law Com CP No 146, para 6.10 and for the requirement that a trustee's right to be reimbursed out of the trust fund is qualified by the requirement that the expenses be properly incurred, see *Holding and Management Ltd v Property Holding and Investment Trust* [1989] 1 WLR 1313, CA.

Section 13 – Linked Functions etc

12.24   Text of section 13

(1)   Subject to subsections (2) and (5), a person who is authorised under section 11 to exercise a function is (whatever the terms of the agency) subject to any specific duties or restrictions attached to the function.

For example, a person who is authorised under section 11 to exercise the general power of investment is subject to the duties under section 4 in relation to that power.

(2)   A person who is authorised under section 11 to exercise a power which is subject to a requirement to obtain advice is not subject to the requirement if he is the kind of person from whom it would have been proper for the trustees, in compliance with the requirement, to obtain advice.

(3)   Subsections (4) and (5) apply to a trust to which section 11(1) of the Trusts of Land and Appointment of Trustees Act 1996 (duties to consult beneficiaries and give effect to their wishes) applies.

(4)   The trustees may not under section 11 authorise a person to exercise any of their functions on terms that prevent them from complying with section 11(1) of the 1996 Act.

(5)   A person who is authorised under section 11 to exercise any function relating to land subject to the trust is not subject to section 11(1) of the 1996 Act.

Purpose of the section

12.25   An agent may be appointed to exercise a trustee power which is subject to restrictions. It is the purpose of this section to ensure that such restrictions bind the agent: ie so that it is not possible, by the simple act of delegating, to remove the restrictions that affect the function delegated. The section only applies to delegation under the statutory power and cannot be excluded or modified by the trust instrument.

Delegation of the power of investment

12.26 As an illustration, s 13(1) provides that such an agent is subject to the duties laid down in TA 2000, s 4 (to have regard to the standard investment criteria). Section 13(2), however, provides that the duty to obtain and consider advice (under s 5) shall not apply if the agent himself would be a proper person to give that advice[1]. Note that s 13(1) appears to impose a statutory obligation directly on the agents which is not capable of modification by the trust instrument. (It may be doubted whether it will always be possible for the agent to apply the standard investment criteria to a proposed investment: will he be in full possession of all the relevant facts?) In appropriate cases the agent's liability may be restricted: see s 14(2); (3)(b).

1   See also s 5(3) which exempts trustees from this duty if in all the circumstances it is unnecessary or inappropriate (eg if a trustee is appropriately qualified).

Section 11 of the Trusts of Land and Appointment of Trustees Act 1996[1]

12.27 This section requires trustees of land to consult, before exercising any function relating to the land, any beneficiary who is entitled to an interest in possession in the land. TA 2000, s13(4) provides that an agent may not be appointed on terms that would prevent the trustees from carrying out their obligation to consult: for instance, a blanket delegation of management functions would not be appropriate given that before each and every exercise of any power of management the life tenant would need to be consulted. By contrast, delegating the collection of rents would not infringe s 13(4). Section 13(5) provides that the obligation to consult remains with the trustees and must be exercised by them personally. These restrictions on the ability of trustees to delegate their functions in relation to land provide a further reason for excluding s 11.

1   This section is considered at para 2.107 above. It is commonly excluded in trust deeds.

Delegation of non-investment functions

12.28 Although fund management is likely to be the most commonly delegated trustee function, s 11 is not so limited. Charity trustees may, for instance, delegate functions in relation to land under s 11(3)(b) and the Charities Act 1993, ss 36-39 imposes restrictions on dispositions and mortgages of land owned by charities[1]. Accordingly any agent appointed in such cases will be required to comply with these restrictions.

1   For a consideration of these restrictions, see Picarda, 'The Law and Practice relating to Charities', 3rd Ed (1999) at p 503 *et seq.*

Section 14 – Terms of Agency

12.29 Text of section 14

(1)   Subject to subsection (2) and sections 15(2) and 29 to 32, the trustees may authorise a person to exercise functions as their agent on such terms as to remuneration and other matters as they may determine.

(2)   The trustees may not authorise a person to exercise functions as their agent on any of the terms mentioned in subsection (3) unless it is reasonably necessary for them to do so.

(3)   The terms are—

(a)   a term permitting the agent to appoint a substitute;

(b)   a term restricting the liability of the agent or his substitute to the trustees or any beneficiary;

(c)   a term permitting the agent to act in circumstances capable of giving rise to a conflict of interest.

Purpose of the section

12.30   The section deals with the terms on which trustees may appoint an agent: subject to certain restrictions it shall be 'on such terms as to remuneration and other matters as they may determine'. Commonly agents will be appointed in writing: if exceptionally this is not the case then trustees should record (in writing) the terms on which that agent has been appointed. Notice in connection with this section that:

(a)   the delegation of asset management is separately regulated under the provisions of TA 2000, s 15[1];

(b)   TA 2000, s 29(6) provides for the remuneration of a professional trustee who has been appointed to act as an agent either under the Pt IV power or in the trust instrument;

(c)   unlike TA 2000, s 13 this section is not expressly limited to an agent appointed under the statutory power.

1   Considered at para 12.35 below.

Sub-delegation; limitations on liability and conflicts of interest

12.31   Section 14(3) lists three situations where terms may only be included in an agency agreement if they are 'reasonably necessary'. These relate to the ability of an agent to appoint a substitute, to any term limiting the liability of an agent (or duly appointed substitute) to the trustees or beneficiaries, and any term permitting the agent to act in circumstances where there may be a conflict of interest. These are all situations which the Law Commission identified as involving 'a degree of risk to the trust (which is) significantly higher than it is in the ordinary case where trustees employ an agent'[1].

1   Law Com No 260 para 4.24 *et seq.*

12.32   So far as sub-delegation is concerned the law had been that an agent could not be engaged on terms which permitted him to sub-delegate except (a) in the case of foreign property held in the trust (as to which see TA 1925, s 23(2) now repealed) and (b) when this was expressly authorised in the trust instrument. However, there will be circumstances when delegation on such terms will be necessary: for instance, if a fund manager is to be appointed then it will usually be on his firm's standard terms and conditions which may well include provisions for sub-delegation and which are likely to limit the liability of the fund manager. As was noted by the Law Commission the provisions in the Trustee Act involve 'a pragmatic approach: the law should recognise that, in practice, trustees often have little option but to delegate on such terms'[1].

1   Law Com No 260 para 4.26.

12.33 Similar issues arise in the context of conflicts of interest: trustees cannot of course, enter into transactions which conflict (or which may conflict) with their fiduciary duties[1] and so it would be somewhat anomalous were trustees to be able to appoint agents who were placed in positions of conflict. Nonetheless there may be situations where this is inevitable: fund managers will commonly be allowed to enter into transactions in which they have a material interest and so involve a potential conflict with that fund manager's duty to the trustees (its customer).

1   This is sometimes called the 'self dealing' rule: see further *Snell's Equity*, 30th Ed, at para 11.68 *et seq*. In practice the self dealing rule is commonly modified in the trust instrument.

What is meant by 'reasonably necessary'

12.34 In practical terms it is important for trustees who are proposing to appoint an agent on terms falling with any of s 14(3)(a)-(c) to show, recorded in a trustee minute:

(a) that the trustees were aware of the general restriction involved in including such terms in the appointment of an agent;

(b) but that in the circumstances they considered that it was reasonably necessary to agree such terms for the reasons which are then set out. Key factors will be that the trustees considered (reasonably!) that the appointment was in the best interests of the trust and that there was no practical alternative (for instance, because any such appointment would be on similar standard form terms).

Section 15 – Asset Management: Special Restrictions

12.35 Text of section 15

(1) The trustees may not authorise a person to exercise any of their asset management functions as their agent except by an agreement which is in or evidenced in writing.

(2) The trustees may not authorise a person to exercise any of their asset management functions as their agent unless–

(a) they have prepared a statement that gives guidance as to how the functions should be exercised ('a policy statement'), and

> > (b) the agreement under which the agent is to act includes a term to the effect that he will secure compliance with–
> >
> > (i) the policy statement, or
> >
> > (ii) if the policy statement is revised or replaced under section 22, the revised or replacement policy statement.
>
> (3) The trustees must formulate any guidance given in the policy statement with a view to ensuring that the functions will be exercised in the best interests of the trust.
>
> (4) The policy statement must be in or evidenced in writing.
>
> (5) The asset management functions of trustees are their functions relating to–
>
> > (a) the investment of assets subject to the trust,
> >
> > (b) the acquisition of property which is to be subject to the trust, and
> >
> > (c) managing property which is subject to the trust and disposing of, or creating or disposing of an interest in, such property.

Purpose of the section

12.36 It imposes special requirements on trustees who delegate their asset management functions. TA 2000, s 15(5) defines 'asset management functions' as the trustees' functions in relation to the investment of the trust fund and to its acquisition, disposal and management. The definition is widely framed and the following matters should be noted:

(a) it applies to the delegation of any trustee function falling within the definition of what is delegable: it is not limited to the delegation of a discretion;

(b) if the trustees engage brokers to offer investment advice it is not thought that they are delegating a function in relation to the management of the property so that a policy statement is not required. In practice, however, something very like a policy statement will be required if the broker is to be able to give appropriate advice;

(c) if the trustees decide to sell a cottage forming part of the trust property and employ an estate agent for that purpose then they would appear to be delegating a function relating to the disposal of property and hence a policy statement is required. In this case the statement is likely to say no more than that the trustees wish to obtain the best price for the property!

The width of the section is somewhat uncertain: is it limited to the situation when an agent is appointed under s 11 of the Act or does it also apply to appointments under express powers? The section is certainly not expressly limited to s 11 appointments (contrast, for instance, s 13 which is so restricted). Prudent trustees – who would probably produce the equivalent of a policy statement in any event! – should therefore assume that it will apply to all agents who exercise asset management functions however they are appointed. A further point on the section is that it appears to impose mandatory requirements which are not capable of modification or exclusion in the trust instrument.

The requirement for a written agreement

12.37 There is no general requirement for agency contracts to be in writing[1] but an agreement delegating asset management functions must:

(a)   be in writing or evidenced in writing; and

(b)   require the agent to comply with 'the policy statement' (or any revision of it).

1   See para 12.30 above.

The policy statement

12.38 This need not be in any particular form but it must be in writing or evidenced in writing and the guidance given in it must ensure that the investment function will be exercised 'in the best interests of the trust' (see s 15(3))[1]. Obviously, the policy statement must be prepared before the agent is able to act although it can be revised or replaced (see TA 2000, s 22(2)) and, for the obligations that must be laid on the agent, s 15(2)(b)). The duty of care applies to the preparation of the policy statement (see Sch 1, para 3(2)(c)).

1   See **Precedent 55** below. The statement must be prepared by the trustees: it is not sufficient for them simply to complete the blanks in a standard asset management agreement.

12.39 It has always been best practice for trustees when delegating investment powers under an express provision in the trust instrument to prepare a guidance note on what will be appropriate investments (specifically, of course, the attention of the agent has to be drawn to any restrictions in the trust instrument on the trustees' investment powers). It may also be noted that provisions in the Pensions Act 1995 require trustees to produce a statement of investment principles indicating the kind of investments to be held, the level of risk which is acceptable, the expected return and the approach to be adopted to ethical investment[1].

1   See paras 11.9 and 11.20 above.

How should trustees formulate the policy statement?

12.40   *First*, the trust instrument has to be considered: in particular, it may impose restrictions on permitted investments. Even if the trustees have wide investment powers (such as the default powers in TA 2000, s 3) the exercise of those powers has to be considered in relation to provisions of the trust instrument. For instance, if there is a life tenant with a need for a significant income returned from the trust. Typically the statement will deal with the balance between income and capital growth.

12.41   *Second*, in the case of an *inter vivos* trust, it is likely that the settlor will have views as to the policy to be pursued and the trustees will normally consult him.

12.42 *Third,* the tax position of the trust and its beneficiaries should be considered. It may be, to take a not untypical example, that the assets of the trust are pregnant with unrealised capital gains so that any disposals will involve a substantial liability to tax. Hence any radical switch in investment policy will need to be considered against this background.

EXAMPLE 1

Mr Bash sets up a trust for his infant son Bruiser absolutely. Income produced in the trust will be taxed on Mr Bash and, accordingly, the trustees may pursue a policy which invests for capital growth provided that it is consistent with the needs of the infant Bruiser.

12.43 *Fourth,* the wishes, as well as the needs, of the beneficiaries should be considered. They may wish the trustees to pursue an ethical investment policy or the principal beneficiary may need a house to live in and may accordingly wish the trustees to exercise their powers under TA 2000, s 8.

12.44 *Finally,* trustees will need to have regard to any prospective liabilities of the trust and to its likely duration.

EXAMPLE 2

Trustees hold the trust fund for Bilbo Baggins contingent on his becoming 25. He is aged 20 and became entitled to the income of the fund at 18. The trustees should have in mind that the trust will come to an end in five years time and that there will at that stage be a capital gains tax liability[1].

---

1   TCGA 1992, s 71. Hold-over relief will only be available at that time if the property in the fund comprises business assets: see s 165.

Landed estates[1]

12.45 Section 15 is not limited to securities: it is concerned with any delegation of the trustees functions relating to, *inter alia,* the management of property subject to the trust. Accordingly, in a case where the trust fund comprises a landed estate and the trustees wish to delegate their estate management functions, the requirements of the section have to be observed. It will be common in such cases for the land agent to be given day-to-day management of the rental properties, to be entrusted with the selection of new tenants when properties fall vacant and to deal with rent review clauses. The decision to sell, mortgage or let on long lease is, however, likely to be reserved to the trustees.

1   See Law Com CP No 146, para 235 *et seq.*

Section 16 – Power to Appoint Nominees

12.46 Text of section 16

(1) Subject to the provisions of this Part, the trustees of a trust may–

  (a) appoint a person to act as their nominee in relation to such of the assets of the trust as they determine (other than settled land), and

  (b) take such steps as are necessary to secure that those assets are vested in a person so appointed.

(2) An appointment under this section must be in or evidenced in writing.

(3) This section does not apply to any trust having a custodian trustee or in relation to any assets vested in the official custodian for charities.

Purpose of the section

12.47 The section gives trustees power to appoint a person to act as their nominee and to vest relevant assets in him. The section does *not* apply to:

(a) pensions trusts (see TA 2000, s 36(8));

(b) authorised unit trusts (TA 2000, s 37);

(c) funds established under schemes made under the Charities Act 1993, s 24 or s 25 (TA 2000, s 38);

(d) trusts which have a custodian trustee in whom the trust property must be vested (TA 2000, s 16(3)); or

(e) trusts where the trust instrument provides to the contrary.

12.48 The duty of care applies to the appointment of a nominee (TA 2000, Sch 1, para 3(1)(b)).

What is a nominee?

12.49 A nominee is a person appointed by the trustees to hold trust property in his own name. For instance, company shares may be registered in the name of a person who acts as nominee for the trustees of a trust fund (contrast the definition of 'a custodian': see para 12.55 below). A person appointed as nominee becomes a bare trustee so that he holds the assets which are in his name for the trustees and must normally act in accordance with their directions. As a result, the trustees do not drop out of the picture and remain subject to their fiduciary duties and responsibilities with regard to the beneficiaries as well as being under a duty to keep under review the appointment and performance of the nominee[1].

1 See generally Law Com No 260 at para 5.4 and especially footnote 3. See also Law Com CP No 146 at para 7.18. It is not considered that a nominee is obliged to act in accordance with all directions given to him by the trustees: he could, for instance, refuse to act if to do so would involve him in personal liability: see Millett LJ in *Ingram v IRC* [1997] 4 All ER 395 at 424.

When are nominees likely to be appointed?

12.50   The illustrations given by the Law Commission are as follows:

(a)   to provide an administration service in relation to investments. In such cases the nominee will collect the dividend; provide statements for the benefit of the trustees and complete paperwork in relation to the relevant tax returns;

(b)   to facilitate dealings with a discretionary fund manager[1]. Using a nominee ensures that securities can be transferred without the need to obtain all the trustees' signatures on the transfer documents;

(c)   as one way of using CREST; in many ways this affords the simplest way since the nominee will be a 'user' (ie a CREST member who may send and receive properly authenticated computer instructions not just on his own account but also on behalf of other persons);

(d)   for overseas investments which are traded using computerised clearing systems; and

(e)   when registered land is held in trust to avoid the need for changes in the register every time there is a change of trustees[2].

1   See Law Com CP No 146, para 2.24 *et seq*. Often the user will not be the fund manager but a connected nominee company.
2   In the case of unregistered land, the deed of appointment of a new trustee automatically vests title to the land in the new trustee without the need for any conveyance: see TA 1925, s 40.

The dangers of appointing a nominee

12.51   Prior to TA 2000 and in the absence of any express authority in the trust instrument, trustees were generally prohibited from using a nominee, primarily because of the requirement that they had to retain control of the trust assets. The appointment of a nominee also carries with it two potential risks:

(a)   *First,* the risk to the trust fund which would arise if the nominee was fraudulent; made an unauthorised delivery of property to a third person etc[1]. The Law Commission concluded that these risks had largely been dealt with by the Financial Services Act 1986 and the Financial Services and Markets Act 2000; and

(b)   *Second,* problems which arise because the nominee is the registered owner of the trust securities so that the trustees suffer a loss of shareholder rights; notably to vote at meetings, receive shareholder benefits etc[2].

1   For a complete catalogue of potential disasters, see Law Com CP No 146, para 2.14.
2   This was the subject of a joint consultation document produced by the DTI and Treasury entitled 'Private Shareholders: Corporate Governance Rights' (June 1996) which considered whether investors under nominee schemes should receive company information and any benefits flowing from share ownership as well as participating in corporate governance. No proposals for reform have so far resulted from this document. Similar problems may arise in the case of land registered in the name of a nominee in respect of notices to the Land Registry.

12.52   In their Report the Law Commission concluded that:

'The Law Commission does not consider that either of these disadvantages is a sufficient reason for denying trustees the benefit and convenience that can result from the employment of nominees. Nevertheless, as a safeguard for beneficiaries it has concluded that trustees should only be able to employ persons or bodies to act as nominees or custodians in the course of their business. Subject to the special position of charities, however, the Commission does not think that there should be other restrictions on the bodies that trustees might employ for these purposes[1].'

1   Law Com No 260 para 5.5.

A custodian trustee

12.53   When there is a custodian trustee the trust property must be transferred into its name as if it were a sole trustee and it will have custody and possession of all securities and documents of title relating to the trust property. The other trustees ('the managing trustees') retain all the trust powers and discretions[1].

1   See generally Public Trustee Act 1906, s 4.

12.54   Apart from the public trustee, certain other corporations may be appointed as custodian trustees[1].

1   See *Snell's Equity (30th Edn)* para 10.20 and *Underhill and Hayton* Law of Trusts and Trustees (15th Edn) p 775 where it is noted that 'custodian trusteeship has not generally commended itself to the Public' . . .

12.55   There is an important distinction between a custodian trustee and a bare trustee: the latter must act in accordance with the directions of the trustees whereas a custodian trustee should not so act if it would involve him in a breach of trust.

Settled land

12.56   At Report Stage in the House of Lords, the Lord Chancellor commented on the position of settled land as follows:

'By section 4(2) of the Settled Land Act 1925, the legal estate in settled land is to be held by the tenant for life or the statutory owner. Thus the legal estate can never properly be held by the trustees of the settlement *qua* trustees and although it seems that there are good reasons why it should be possible for land, held on a trust of land, to be vested in a nominee, there are no obvious reasons why a nominee would be needed in relation to settled land.'

12.57   The proceeds of sale of settled land may, however, be vested in a nominee.

The official custodian for charities[1]

12.58   Under the Charities Act 1993 s 2 the Official Custodian for Charities acts as custodian trustee although his functions have been reduced and the only property that he is now able to hold comprises:

(a)   land; and

(b)   other property vested in him by order of the Charity Commissioners made for the protection of the relevant charity.

1   See generally Law Commission CP 146 paragraph 7.12 *et seq.*

12.59   At Report Stage in the House of Lords the Lord Chancellor commented[1]:

> 'The power to appoint nominees (does not apply) in the case of any trust having a custodian trustee, because the power conferred by the clause is incompatible with the statutory duties of a custodian trustee under the Public Trustee Act 1906. The Charity Commission has made the point that trustees should also be deprived of the powers . . . in relation to property which is for the time being vested in the official custodian for charities. This is because section 22 of the Charities Act 1993 provides that where property is vested in the official custodian in trust for a charity he shall have the same powers, duties and liabilities as a corporation-appointed custodian trustee under section 4 of the Public Trustee Act 1906. It would, therefore, be inappropriate for a nominee or custodian to be appointed under the bill in respect of the relevant property. In addition, where bearer securities are held by the official custodian there should be no duty to appoint a custodian under clause 18 . . .'

1   House of Lords Hansard, 7 June 2000 CWH 4.

Section 17 – Power to Appoint Custodians

12.60   Text of section 17

    (1)   Subject to the provisions of this Part, the trustees of a trust may appoint a person to act as a custodian in relation to such of the assets of the trust as they may determine.

    (2)   For the purposes of this Act a person is a custodian in relation to assets if he undertakes the safe custody of the assets or of any documents or records concerning the assets.

    (3)   An appointment under this section must be in or evidenced in writing.

    (4)   This section does not apply to any trust having a custodian trustee or in relation to any assets vested in the official custodian for charities.

Purpose of the section

12.61   It enables trustees to appoint a custodian, as defined in s 17(2). The provision is similar to that for the appointment of a nominee and, accordingly, the section does not apply, therefore, in the situations discussed at para 12.59 above (see s 17(4)).

What is a custodian?

12.62   A person who undertakes the safe custody of the assets or of any documents or records concerning the assets. Unlike a *nominee,* the ownership of assets is not vested in a custodian. The power to appoint a custodian trustee has been considered above[1] where it was noted that this power has been rarely used: in particular a custodian trustee is not able to perform the functions of a nominee in the conduct of investment business[2] whilst the restriction on persons who can act, to corporations of a particular kind, means that firms of solicitors and accountants are prevented from acting. By contrast, a custodian appointed under s 17 is not a trustee but a particular kind of agent with whom trust property has been deposited.

1   See para 12.53 above.
2   He could not act as custodian trustee on standard investment management terms which confer much wider powers than are available to him in his capacity as such trustee.

Provisions in the Trustee Act 1925

12.63   Under s 21 of that Act a trustee could deposit any documents relating to the trust or to the trust property with any banker or banking company or other company whose business included providing safe custody for documents. Any fees charged had to be paid out of trust income. Under s 7 trustees had a duty to deposit bearer securities with a banker or banking company for safe custody and for the collection of income. The trustees were not responsible for a loss arising from such deposit. Both these sections have now been repealed by TA 2000[1].

1   See TA 2000, Sch II, Part II, paras 18 and 21. The position of bearer securities is now regulated by TA 2000, s 18.

Section 18 – Investment in Bearer Securities

12.64   Text of section 18

(1)   If trustees retain or invest in securities payable to bearer, they must appoint a person to act as a custodian of the securities.

(2)   Subsection (1) does not apply if the trust instrument or any enactment or provision of subordinate legislation contains provision which (however expressed) permits the trustees to retain or invest in securities payable to bearer without appointing a person to act as a custodian.

(3)   An appointment under this section must be in or evidenced in writing.

(4)   This section does not apply to any trust having a custodian trustee or in relation to any securities vested in the official custodian for charities.

Purpose of the section

12.65   It replaces the Trustee Act 1925 s 7 and requires trustees who hold (or acquire) bearer securities to appoint a person to hold them as custodian. Note:

(a)   the restrictions of TA 1925, s 7 – that the custodian must be a banker or banking company and must be charged with the collection of income – are not repeated (for who can be appointed a custodian for these purposes, see TA 2000, s 19);

(b)   the decision whether to retain or acquire bearer securities is an investment decision for the trustees: tax considerations may be relevant (for instance, if such securities are held outside the UK then they will become non UK situs for inheritance tax purposes);

(c)   s 18 does not apply if the trust instrument permits trustees to hold bearer securities without appointing a custodian, if the trust has a custodian trustee, or to securities vested in the official custodian for charities;

(d)   nor does the section apply to a sole trustee who is a trust corporation (see TA 2000, s 25(2)).

Transitional

12.66   Any banker or banking company holding bearer securities deposited with him under the Trustee Act 1925, s 7(1) is deemed to be a custodian appointed under TA 2000, s 18 (see TA 2000, Sch 3, para 1(2)). The fact that the appointment may not have been in writing or evidenced in writing (as required by s 18(3)) is irrelevant for these transitional purposes.

Section 19 – Persons who may be Appointed as Nominees or Custodians

12.67   Text of section 19

(1)   A person may not be appointed under section 16, 17 or 18 as a nominee or custodian unless one of the relevant conditions is satisfied.

(2)   The relevant conditions are that–

  (a)   the person carries on a business which consists of or includes acting as a nominee or custodian;

  (b)   the person is a body corporate which is controlled by the trustees;

  (c)   the person is a body corporate recognised under section 9 of the Administration of Justice Act 1985.

(3)   The question whether a body corporate is controlled by trustees is to be determined in accordance with section 840 of the Income and Corporation Taxes Act 1988.

(4)   The trustees of a charitable trust which is not an exempt charity must act in accordance with any guidance given by the Charity Commissioners concerning the selection of a person for appointment as a nominee or custodian under section 16, 17 or 18.

(5)   Subject to subsections (1) and (4), the persons whom the trustees may under section 16, 17 or 18 appoint as a nominee or custodian include–

  (a)   one of their number, if that one is a trust corporation, or

  (b)   two (or more) of their number, if they are to act as joint nominees or joint custodians.

(6) The trustees may under section 16 appoint a person to act as their nominee even though he is also–

    (a) appointed to act as their custodian (whether under section 17 or 18 or any other power), or

    (b) authorised to exercise functions as their agent (whether under section 11 or any other power).

(7) Likewise, the trustees may under section 17 or 18 appoint a person to act as their custodian even though he is also–

    (a) appointed to act as their nominee (whether under section 16 or any other power), or

    (b) authorised to exercise functions as their agent (whether under section 11 or any other power).

Purpose of the section

12.68 The risks that arise from vesting trust property in a nominee or from using a custodian[1] resulted in the introduction of this section which, by restricting the persons who may be appointed, is intended to afford protection to the beneficiaries.

1   See para 12.51 above and see Law Commission CP No 146, para 7.48 which rejected a proposal to give trustees powers to insure against loss or damage to property or to trust documents when such were vested in a nominee or custodian and whether that loss or damage resulted from accident, negligence or fraud on the part of that person.

Who can be appointed?

12.69 Only a person who satisfies one of the 'relevant conditions' set out in s 19(2). The conditions are:

(a) *either* that the person carries on a business which comprises or includes acting as a nominee or trustee[1]. Provided that this condition is satisfied the trustees may appoint one of their number (being a trust corporation) or two or more of their number (not being trust corporations)[2]. There is no bar on a relevantly qualified beneficiary being appointed[3]; *or*

(b) if the person is a body corporate which is controlled by the trustees[4]. This provision is intended to encourage trustees to use special purpose vehicles for nominee and custodian purposes. The relevant company would not trade or carry on any business within the ordinary meaning of that expression; *or*

(c) if the person is a body corporate recognised under the Administration of Justice Act 1985, s 9. This provision was inserted at Report Stage in the House of Lords when the Lord Chancellor commented as follows:

    'This is another amendment for the avoidance of doubt. It should be possible to be appointed as a nominee or custodian under the Bill only if the proposed appointee is in the business of providing nominee or custodianship services. Subsection (2)(b) is included in the draft in order to cater for the possibility that trustees might wish to set up special purpose vehicles in order to act as their nominees.

However concern was expressed as to whether the clause as drafted was sufficiently wide to enable trustees to utilise the services of solicitors' nominee companies, which are recognised under rules prepared by the Law Society under section 9 of the Administration of Justice Act 1985. Where such companies in England and Wales are owned by solicitors, they can only function as recognised bodies within the Solicitors' Incorporated Practice Rule. Therefore we believe that solicitors' nominee companies should be suitable for appointment as nominees or custodians under the Bill and that the clause should be wide enough to allow for this[5].'

1   Contrast the definition of when a trustee 'acts in a professional capacity': see TA 2000, s 28(5).
2   TA 2000, s 19(5)(a); s 19(5)(b).
3   Contrast s 12(3) which prohibits a beneficiary from acting as agent.
4   Control for these purposes is defined in TA 1988, s 840.
5   House of Lords Hansard, 7 June 2000, Column CWH 6.

Charitable trusts

12.70   Charitable trustees (other than those for an exempt charity) must comply with any guidance about the selection of a nominee or custodian issued by the Charity Commissioners[1]. (An exempt charity is one which is exempt from the supervisory jurisdiction of the Charity Commission.) The rationale for this limitation is a desire to ensure a higher degree of protection for the trust fund and to recognise that in the past when allowing charity trustees to use nominees the Charity Commission has imposed restrictions on the persons or bodies who may be appointed (especially that they should be corporations with a place of business in England and Wales so as to be within the jurisdiction of the High Court or if the nominee is overseas, that there should be procedures to ensure regulation and review of the nominee and the manner in which the property is held)[2].

1   'Charitable trust' and 'exempt charity' are defined in TA 2000, s 39(1).
2   See Law Commission CP No 146, para 7.13.

Nominees, custodians and agents

12.71   A person appointed as custodian or agent may also be appointed a nominee and likewise an agent or nominee may be appointed a custodian (see TA 2000, s 19(6); 19(7)).

Section 20 – Terms of Appointment of Nominees and Custodians

12.72   Text of section 20

(1)   Subject to subsection (2) and sections 29 to 32, the trustees may under section 16, 17 or 18 appoint a person to act as a nominee or custodian on such terms as to remuneration and other matters as they may determine.

(2)   The trustees may not under section 16, 17 or 18 appoint a person to act as a nominee or custodian on any of the terms mentioned in subsection (3) unless it is reasonably necessary for them to do so.

(3)   The terms are—

(a)   a term permitting the nominee or custodian to appoint a substitute;

(b)   a term restricting the liability of the nominee or custodian or his substitute to the trustees or to any beneficiary;

(c)   a term permitting the nominee or custodian to act in circumstances capable of giving rise to a conflict of interest.

Purpose of the section

12.73   It provides for the terms on which nominees and custodians can be appointed and mirrors the provisions of s 14 dealing with the terms of appointment of agents. Accordingly reference should be made to the commentary on that section[1].

1   See para 12.29 above.

Section 21 - Applications of Sections 22 and 23

12.74   Text of section 21

(1)   Sections 22 and 23 apply in a case where trustees have, under section 11, 16, 17 or 18—

(a)   authorised a person to exercise functions as their agent, or

(b)   appointed a person to act as a nominee or custodian.

(2)   Subject to subsection (3), sections 22 and 23 also apply in a case where trustees have, under any power conferred on them by the trust instrument or by any enactment or any provision of subordinate legislation—

(a)   authorised a person to exercise functions as their agent, or

(b)   appointed a person to act as a nominee or custodian.

(3)   If the application of section 22 or 23 is inconsistent with the terms of the trust instrument or the enactment or provision of subordinate legislation, the section in question does not apply.

Purpose of the section

12.75   Sections 21-23 deal with the obligations of trustees to review the appointment of agents, custodians and nominees and set out the liabilities of the trustees for the acts and defaults of such persons.

To what trusts do the sections apply?

12.76   The sections apply to any appointment under:

(a)   TA 2000, s 11 (agents); TA 2000, s 16 (nominees); and TA 2000, ss 17-18 (custodians); or

(b)   a power conferred in the trust instrument or under any provision of subordinate legislation provided that if the application of these sections would be inconsistent with the terms of that instrument or legislation then the section or sections shall not apply.

Section 22 – Review of Agents, Nominees and Custodians etc

12.77   Text of section 22

(1)   While the agent, nominee or custodian continues to act for the trust, the trustees–

(a)   must keep under review the arrangements under which the agent, nominee or custodian acts and how those arrangements are being put into effect,

(b)   if circumstances make it appropriate to do so, must consider whether there is a need to exercise any power of intervention that they have, and

(c)   if they consider that there is a need to exercise such a power, must do so.

(2)   If the agent has been authorised to exercise asset management functions, the duty under subsection (1) includes, in particular–

(a)   a duty to consider whether there is any need to revise or replace the policy statement made for the purposes of section 15,

(b)   if they consider that there is a need to revise or replace the policy statement, a duty to do so, and

(c)   a duty to assess whether the policy statement (as it has effect for the time being) is being complied with.

(3)   Subsections (3) and (4) of section 15 apply to the revision or replacement of a policy statement under this section as they apply to the making of a policy statement under that section.

(4)   'Power of intervention' includes–

(a)   a power to give directions to the agent, nominee or custodian;

(b)   a power to revoke the authorisation or appointment.

Purpose of the section

12.78   It imposes a duty on trustees in relation to the review of any agent, nominee or custodian who has been appointed.

A duty to keep under review (s 22(1)(a))

12.79   This duty comprises a number of elements;

(a)   is it still appropriate for the function to be delegated?

(b)   is the person appointed still the appropriate person to exercise the function?

(c)   should the terms of appointment be varied? and

(d)   how satisfactorily has the delegate been performing his functions?

12.80   No guidelines are laid down as to how trustees are to discharge this duty: it will depend on what is reasonable in all the circumstances. As a matter of best practice, however, it will be important for the trustees to review the position at least once every 12 months and, in many cases, a more frequent review will be called for. In cases where one of the trustees is appointed as an agent of the trust there is an element of 'self-review'!

A duty to consider whether they should exercise any power of intervention that they have (s 22(1)(b))

12.81   This duty to consider the exercise of the power to intervene (defined in s 22(4)) arises 'if circumstances make it appropriate to do so'. For instance, if doubts have been expressed as to the financial integrity of an agent to whom monies have been entrusted then the trustees should consider intervening to revoke that agency (other examples would be where the functions are not being discharged effectively or where the general suitability of the agent is in question).

A duty to exercise the power of intervention (s 22(1)(c))

12.82   Not only must the trustees consider exercising the power but, 'if they consider there is a need' to exercise it, then they must do so.

The overriding duty of care

12.83   When carrying out the s 22 duties, trustees are subject to the duty of care (TA 2000, Sch 1, para 3(e)).

The delegation of asset management functions

12.84   The duty under s 22(1) is extended when the agent is exercising asset management functions[1]. The policy statement[2] must be reviewed and revised or replaced as appropriate. Note that there is also a duty to assess whether the statement is being complied with. It has already been indicated that the investment performance of any fund manager should be monitored on a regular basis and, at the same time, the duties imposed on the trustees by s 22(2) should be discharged. Of course, events may occur which necessitate a radical reconsideration of the policy statement: the death of a life tenant who had a pressing need for income may mean that the emphasis can now switch to capital growth; the collapse of the retail sector of the stock market would indicate a switch into other (hopefully safer) sectors, whilst changes in the burden of taxation might dictate a revised investment strategy[3].

1   For the delegation (and meaning of) asset management functions, see para 12.36 above.
2   See TA 2000, s 15(2).
3   As has happened in the case of certain trusts following the change in the income tax treatment of company distributions made by F (No 2) A 1997.

Section 23 – Liability for Agents, Nominees and Custodians etc

12.85   Text of section 23

(1)   A trustee is not liable for any act or default of the agent, nominee or custodian unless he has failed to comply with the duty of care applicable to him, under paragraph 3 of Schedule 1–

    (a)   when entering into the arrangements under which the person acts as agent, nominee or custodian, or

    (b)   when carrying out his duties under section 22.

(2)   If a trustee has agreed a term under which the agent, nominee or custodian is permitted to appoint a substitute, the trustee is not liable for any act or default of the substitute unless he has failed to comply with the duty of care applicable to him, under paragraph 3 of Schedule 1–

    (a)   when agreeing that term, or

    (b)   when carrying out his duties under section 22 in so far as they relate to the use of the substitute.

Purpose of the section

12.86   The section deals with the circumstances when a trustee can be made liable for the acts or defaults of any agent, nominee or custodian.

Defects in the previous law resulting from the provisions in the Trustee Act 1925

12.87   The liability of trustees for their agents, in the absence of any express provision in the trust deed, had primarily been governed by various provisions in the 1925 Trustee Act[1].

(a)   s 23(1) exonerated trustees who had acted in good faith from loss resulting from the appointment of an agent to carry out ministerial functions (it was unclear whether in appointing that agent a trustee had to act with reasonable prudence);

(b)   s 23(2) dealt with agents for trust property sited aboard and provided that the trustees were not to be liable for any loss arising 'by reason only of their having made such appointment' (but did that leave the trustees with a duty to supervise?);

(c)   s 23(3) dealt with the appointment of certain types of agent and preserved the liability of the trustee if property was left with the agent 'longer than reasonably necessary' although this was something of a dead letter given that the agent could have been appointed under s 23(1) with its seemingly lesser duty of care;

(d)   s 30(1) provided that a trustee should not be liable for any loss caused by the act or default of anyone else unless it resulted from the trustee's own wilful default (ie conscious breach or reckless performance of duty). Simple negligence on the part of a trustee did not give rise to any liability under s 30(1). The ambit of s 30 was far from clear[2] but when it did not apply (for instance, when an agent was required merely to transfer trust property from one person to another) trustees could be made liable for any resultant loss unless they had acted with reasonable prudence.

1   Prior to 1926 (when TA 1925 came into force) the common law had required trustees to exercise reasonable prudence in choosing an agent, in negotiating the terms on which he was to act and in supervising him: see Law Commission CP No 146, para 4.2.

2   The history of the section is traced in the Law Commission CP No 146 at para 4.6 *et seq*. In the much criticised case of *Re Vickery* [1931] 1 Ch 572, Maugham J set out what he regarded as the relationship between the various sections of the 1925 Act.

12.88   It may be noted that different criteria were employed by the Charity Commission when making orders under the Charities Act 1993, s 26 which gave trustees power to appoint a fund manager and imposed a duty to take reasonable care[1] whilst under the Pensions Act 1995, s 34 there is a general obligation on pension trustees to exercise care and skill when delegating to a fund manager.

1   The Model Order drawn up by the Charity Commission is set out at para 12.4 above.

12.89   As recommended by the Law Commission, ss 23(1) (2) (3) and 30(1) of the 1925 Act have all been repealed by TA 2000[1].

1   See Sch 1, paras 23-24.

The basic rule under s 23(1)

12.90   A trustee who satisfies the duty of care laid down in TA 2000, s 1 and Sch 1, para 3 (appointment and review of agents etc) is not liable for the acts and defaults of the agent. Note that if the trustee falls short of the duty of care liability is then imposed upon him for the acts of the agent but, because this only occurs as a result of the personal defaults of the trustee, this is not a case of vicarious liability[1].

1   Vicarious liability may be defined as 'liabilty falling on one person for the fault of another irrespective of any fault of the first person' (see CT Emery 'Delegation by Trustees – Reforming the Law' (1983) 133 NLJ 1095). For an illustration of vicarious liabilty being visited on trustees see TA 1925, s 25 (inserted by TDA 1999, s 5). Contrast the Trusts of Land and Appointment of Trustees Act 1996 s 9(8) which had imposed such liability but

which has now been repealed by TA 2000, Sch 2, para 46 and a new subsection (9A) inserted which imposes the statutory duty of care on trustees of land in such circumstances. Making trustees vicariously liable (in effect strict liability) for the acts of their agents was rejected by the Law Commission in CP No 146, para 6.48.

Substitute agents etc

12.91 The same test for trustee liability applies in a case where the agent has appointed a substitute, in relation to the acts or defaults of that substitute. Bear in mind, however, the restrictions on permitting agents to appoint such substitutes (see TA 2000, s 14(2)(a) and 20(2)(a)).

Section 24 – Effect of Trustees Exceeding their Powers

12.92   Text of section 24

A failure by the trustees to act within the limits of the powers conferred by this Part–

(a)   in authorising a person to exercise a function of theirs as an agent, or

(b)   in appointing a person to act as a nominee or custodian,

does not invalidate the authorisation or appointment.

Purpose of the section

12.93   This section is intended to facilitate dealings by agents, nominees and custodians with third parties. In favour of such persons they will be entitled to assume that the delegate has been properly authorised or appointed. It is curious to note that the section is not expressly drafted in favour of third parties but refers generally to the authorisation or appointment not being invalid or ineffective. In this respect there is a contrast with the various provisions in the Trusts of Land and Appointment of Trustees Act 1996 which precisely spell out the position of a purchaser[1].

1   See, for instance, the Trusts of Land and Appointment of Trustees Act 1996, s 16 and generally para 2.165 above.

Typical cases where an appointment is made by a trustee in excess of his powers

12.94   The Law Commission identified a number of situations which would fall within the section:

(a)   the appointment of a beneficiary as an agent contrary to the prohibition in TA 2000, s 12(3)[1];

(b)   trustees of land appoint an agent on terms which mean that they cannot consult a relevant beneficiary as they are required to do by s 11 of the 1996 Act[2];

(c) the terms of an appointment allow the agent to appoint a substitute although this was not 'reasonably necessary'. In this case it is thought that merely by including this term in the agency agreement the entire appointment is outside the powers of the trustees: it is irrelevant whether or not a substitute is actually appointed[3];

(d) An agent is appointed to exercise a function which is not delegable[4]. If, for instance, an asset manager were to be permitted to exercise the trustees' discretions over income produced by the investments and he duly distributed income amongst the beneficial class his authority to act is not apparently invalid. Is a beneficiary who receives income therefore protected against any claim that it has been wrongly paid out to him?

1   For this restriction, see para 12.21 above and **Precedent 56** below.
2   See para 12.27 above.
3   TA 2000, s 14(2) and see para 12.30 above.
4   TA 2000, s 11(2) and see para 12.7 above.

Position of a trustee who exceeds his powers

12.95 The section does not affect the position or authority of the agent to act but, as far as the trustees are concerned, they have acted in excess of their powers and have therefore committed a breach of trust.

Position of the agent

12.96 He is not invalidly appointed or authorised accordingly to the terms of the section but it is suggested in the explanatory notes to the Act that 'if a person is authorised to exercise a function as an agent, that person may also be liable, as trustee *de son tort*, if the function in question is not properly delegable under s 11. Both parties to the appointment have therefore an interest in ensuring that the appointment can properly be made'.

Section 25 – Sole Trustees

12.97 Text of section 25

(1) Subject to subsection (2), this Part applies in relation to a trust having a sole trustee as it applies in relation to other trusts (and references in this Part to trustees – except in sections 12(1) and (3) and 19(5) – are to be read accordingly).

(2) Section 18 does not impose a duty on a sole trustee if that trustee is a trust corporation.

Purpose of the section

12.98 The delegation power given to trustees in Pt IV of the Act must be exercised collectively and the section refers throughout to 'trustees'. This section makes it clear, however, that the provisions apply equally to a trust with a sole trustee.

A trust corporation as sole trustee

12.99   The trust corporation need not appoint a custodian for any bearer securities[1].

1   TA 2000, s 18 and see para 12.65 above.

Agents, nominees and custodians

12.100   A sole trustee cannot be his own agent nominee or custodian: hence the exclusion in s 25(1) of s 12(1) and (3) and s 19(5).

Section 26 – Restriction or Exclusion of this Part etc

12.101   Text of section 26

The powers conferred by this Part are–

(a)   in addition to powers conferred on trustees otherwise than by this Act, but

(b)   subject to any restriction or exclusion imposed by the trust instrument or by any enactment or any provision of subordinate legislation.

Purpose of the section

12.102   This section provides that the powers given to trustees in Pt IV are default powers: ie they apply to all trusts (but see s 27) in addition to any express powers which the trustees have but subject to any limitations in the trust instrument or in subordinate legislation. Similar words are employed in s 6(1) (in relation to the Pt II powers) and in s 9 (the Pt III powers).

Section 27 – Existing Trusts

12.103   Text of section 27

This Part applies in relation to trusts whether created before or after its commencement.

12.104   Part IV applies to trusts whenever created. As with Pts II and III it does not apply to:

(a)   authorised unit trusts (TA 2000, s 37); or

(b)   schemes under the Charities Act 1993, ss 34-35 (TA 2000, s 38).

But it does apply, with modifications, to pension trusts (TA 2000, s 36(4)-(8)).

13

Part V: Remuneration and Trustee Expenses

Background

Basic principles

13.1   As a general rule trustees cannot charge for their services. The reasons for this stem from the linked principles that a trustee should not benefit from the trust property and that to allow him to charge would be to produce a conflict between his duties to the trust and his own self interest[1]. Accordingly, a solicitor-trustee is allowed to charge only for his out of pocket expenses for business that he carries out for the trust whether of a contentious or non-contentious nature[2]. Is it not, however, the case that remuneration is considered to be incompatible with acting as a trustee: Lord Normand put the matter as follows:

> 'It is not that reward for services is repugnant to the fiduciary duty, but that he who has the duty shall not take any secret remuneration or any financial benefit not authorised by the law, or by his contract, or by the trust deed under which he acts, as the case may be. In England, moreover, the Court has power to order payments to be made to trustees for whom the truster has made no such provision, a power which it is difficult to reconcile with a general principle that remuneration is repugnant to trusteeship[3].'

1   The rule is of great antiquity: in *Robinson v Pett* (1734) 3 P Wms 249 at 251, 24 ER 1049 Lord Talbot LC commented 'a trustee, executor or administrator shall have no allowance for his care and trouble'. The rationale for the rule was analysed in depth in (1983) 46 MLR 289. A trustee, of course, can always refuse to act!
2   *Re Barber* (1886) 34 Ch D 77: *Re Pooley* (1888) 40 Ch D 1, CA.
3   *Dale v IRC* [1954] AC 11 at 27, HL.

Trustee indemnification

13.2   Although there is no general principle permitting a trustee to charge, he is entitled to be paid his out of pocket expenses. He has a lien against the trust property (being a first charge on all the property, both income and capital, although it will usually be satisfied out of the corpus of the fund) for all costs, expenses and liabilities incurred in administering the trust. These rules of equity were enshrined in TA 1925, s 30(2) (which provided that 'a trustee may reimburse himself or pay or discharge out of the trust premises all expenses incurred in or about the execution of the trusts or powers)'. That section has now been repealed by TA 2000, Sch 2, Pt II, para 24 and replaced by section 31 which is considered in detail in para 13.34 below.

Exceptions to the basic rule that a trustee cannot be remunerated

13.3   The most important situations where remuneration has been allowed are:

(a)   Where remuneration is authorised by the trust instrument[1]

13.4   'Charging clauses' which allow a trustee or personal representative to charge have always been strictly construed against the trustee or personal representative so that, unless the trust deed or will provides otherwise, a charging clause allowing a trustee who carries on a profession to charge for his services will only permit payment out of the trust fund to be made for services which were within the scope of the profession in question[2]. It has therefore been common practice for charging clauses allowing a trustee or personal representative who carries on a profession or business to provide that a charge may be made for services *whether or not the services rendered are within the scope of such trustee's profession or business*[3]. As will be discussed in para 13.17 below, it is no longer necessary to include this wording in a charging clause to allow a trustee who is 'acting in a professional capacity' – as defined in TA 2000 s 28(4) – to charge because s 28(1) provides that, unless its provisions are inconsistent with the terms of the trust deed or will in question, a provision in a trust deed or will entitling a trust corporation or a trustee who acts in a professional capacity to receive payment in respect of his or its services out of the trust funds is to be treated as authorising payment in respect of services which could be provided by a 'lay' trustee.

1   See, for instance, **Precedent 1, clause 9**. The validity of such clauses was established by the mid Eighteenth Century: see *Ellison v Airey* (1748) 1 Ves Sen 111 at 115, 27 ER 924 at 927.

2   Hence a trustee could not charge for services which could have been undertaken by a lay trustee and which did not require professional expertise: see *Re Chapple* (1884) 27 Ch D 584; *Clarkson v Robinson* [1900] 2 Ch 722.

3   However, there is some authority that this extended clause requires the express instructions of the client otherwise it will not be valid. In *Re Chapple*, Kay J commented that '[U]nless the testator has expressly instructing him insert those very words' (at 587). As the Law Commission indicated this injunction is widely ignored in practice!

(b)   Where remuneration is sanctioned by statute

13.5   There are a number of specific measures: for instance, when the Public Trustee acts as trustee[1].

1   Public Trustee Act 1906, s 9.

(c)   When remuneration is authorised by the court

13.6   The court has an inherent jurisdiction to permit existing (and prospective) trustees to be remunerated when the trust instrument makes no provision for this. It also has power to vary (and increase) the remuneration provided for in the trust instrument[1]. Instances where remuneration has been ordered include:

(a) where the services of a particular trustee are of special value and he refuses to act without payment; and

(b) where the duties have proved to be unexpectedly onerous.

1   See generally *Re Duke of Norfolk's Settlement Trusts* [1982] Ch 61, CA: the basis for the jurisdiction is that the court is 'exercising its ancient jurisdiction to secure the competent administration of the trust property' (per Fox LJ at p 78). It is not based on any supposed contract between the settlor and the trustee.

(d) Agreement with the beneficiaries

13.7   Beneficiaries who are of full age and sound mind can contract with the trustee to provide for his remuneration on such terms as may be agreed. Such contracts are, however, jealously scrutinised by the court and no pressure must have been brought to bear on the beneficiary if the contract is to be valid.

(e) The rule in Cradock v Piper[1]

13.8   A solicitor trustee is entitled to profit costs when he acts as solicitor in legal proceedings – whether or not hostile – on behalf of himself and his co-trustee jointly[2].

1   (1850) 1 Mac & G 664. The rule is wholly anomalous (cp (1983) 46 MLR 289 at 306).
2   For the ramifications of this so called rule, see *Snell's Equity* (30th Ed) at paras 11-91.

Reform – the views of the Law Commission

13.9   The rationale for introducing a statutory charging clause is found in para 10.18 of the Consultation Paper[1] and paras 7.6-7.7 of the Report[2]. In 1982 the Law Reform Committee[3] had come down against such a measure on the basis that it was unsuitable as a default provision[4]; that any such clause would be open to abuse and that it would encroach unduly on the principle that a trustee should not profit from his trust. The Law Commission however was unpersuaded by this reasoning, taking the view that proper administration of the trust was of paramount importance and that it frequently required professional skills. Further the underlying assumption that trusts were essentially honorary – 'a burden upon the honour and conscience of the person intrusted' – was an outmoded view to be consigned to the dustbin of history.

1   Law Com No 146.
2   Law Com No 260.
3   23rd Report, (1982) Cmnd 8733, paras 3.42-3.55.
4   Ie remuneration of a professional trustee was on this view always a matter on which instructions should be taken.

Remuneration as bounty

13.10   For most purposes charging clauses have been viewed by the courts as involving the payment of a gift or legacy rather than as a payment for services rendered[1]. The origins of the rule can be traced back to the mid-eighteenth century and it was apparently adopted to overcome objections to the validity of express charging clauses[2]. Viewing remuneration as bounty is not, however, a principle which has been universally applied: for instance, for the purposes of income tax, trustee remuneration is treated as earned income[3] whilst remuneration ordered by the court is not considered to involve any change in the beneficial interests of the trust but rather is a payment to secure their proper administration[4].

1   'The clause . . . is really a gift on condition, It is a gift of the privilege of charging, which the solicitor and trustee . . . would not otherwise have' (Re White [1898] 1 Ch 297 at 299 per Kekewich J)

2   See Lord Hardwicke LC in Ellison v Airey (1748) 1 Ven Sen 111 at 115, 27 ER 924 at 927 where he commented 'this was a legacy to the trustees; to whom the testator may give this satisfaction, if he pleases'.

3   Dale v IRC [1954] AC 11, HL, where Lord Normand commented that even if the payment was in the nature of a conditional gift it had to be earned by serving as trustee. Such payments will commonly be taxed under Schedule D Case III ('interest annuities and other annual payments'). Given that Schedule E applies to 'offices and employments' this may be thought somewhat surprising given that a trusteeship would appear to be an office (arguably there is no employer). In the case of professional firms (taxed under Schedule D Case II) for whom holding trusteeships is an integral part of the business, the Revenue will normally permit the payments to be taxed as part of the firm's profits.

4   See Re Duke of Norfolk's Settlement Trusts [1982] Ch 61, CA.

13.11   The Law Commission recommended the sweeping away of this rule which smacked of 'gentleman amateurs' and a recognition that payments were to be treated as remuneration for services rendered[1].

1   Law Com No 260, para 7.19.

Analysis of TA 2000, Part V

Section 28 – Trustee's Entitlement to Payment Under Trust Instrument

13.12   Text of section 28

(1)   Except to the extent (if any) to which the trust instrument makes inconsistent provision, subsections (2) to (4) apply to a trustee if–

(a)   there is a provision in the trust instrument entitling him to receive payment out of trust funds in respect of services provided by him to or on behalf of the trust, and

(b)   the trustee is a trust corporation or is acting in a professional capacity.

(2)   The trustee is to be treated as entitled under the trust instrument to receive payment in respect of services even if they are services which are capable of being provided by a lay trustee.

(3)   Subsection (2) applies to a trustee of a charitable trust who is not a trust corporation only–

(a)   if he is not a sole trustee, and

(b)   to the extent that a majority of the other trustees have agreed that it should apply to him.

(4)   Any payments to which the trustee is entitled in respect of services are to be treated as remuneration for services (and not as a gift) for the purposes of–

   (a)   section 15 of the Wills Act 1837 (gifts to an attesting witness to be void), and

   (b)   section 34(3) of the Administration of Estates Act 1925 (order in which estate to be paid out).

(5)   For the purposes of this Part, a trustee acts in a professional capacity if he acts in the course of a profession or business which consists of or includes the provision of services in connection with–

   (a)   the management or administration of trusts generally or a particular kind of trust, or

   (b)   any particular aspect of the management or administration of trusts generally or a particular kind of trust,

and the services he provides to or on behalf of the trust fall within that description.

(6)   For the purposes of this Part, a person acts as a lay trustee if he–

   (a)   is not a trust corporation, and

   (b)   does not act in a professional capacity.

Purpose of the section

13.13   The section applies when the trust instrument contains a charging clause and lays down new rules of construction for such clauses. Note that these new rules only apply in favour of trustees who are trust corporations or are trustees acting in a professional capacity.

When does a trustee act in a professional capacity?

13.14   Sub-section (4) provides that for the purposes of this Part of the Act a trustee 'acts in a professional capacity' if acting in the course of a profession or business which consists of or includes the management or administration of trusts generally or a particular kind of trust. A corporation, not being a trust corporation, but which is a trustee would benefit under the provisions of sub-s (1) if it qualified as 'acting in a professional capacity'. Sub-section (5) provides that a person acts as a 'lay' trustee if he is not a trust corporation and does not 'act in a professional capacity'.

13.15   The charging clauses used in professionally drawn settlements and wills are often widely worded. Commonly they provide that a trustee or personal representative engaged in 'any profession or business' may charge for his services[1]. Such a clause would authorise the payment for services rendered by a trustee or personal representative who was engaged in some profession or business even if he does not 'act in a professional capacity' within the meaning of sub-s (4). Such a trustee or personal representative does not enjoy the benefit of the new rules of construction.

1   See **Precedent 53** below.

Reversal of the rule that remuneration is a pecuniary legacy

13.16 The power of a personal representative or trustee to charge formerly ranked as a pecuniary legacy[1]. Accordingly, the charging provision was void if the personal representative in question or his spouse witnessed the will, unless being a partner he arranged that he, as distinct from the other partners, did not benefit from any charges made[2]. Also, for the purposes of the application of assets in the case of an insolvent estate under the Administration of Estates Act 1925, s 34(3), such entitlement to charge ranked as a pecuniary legacy. This has now been reversed by s 28(4) in the case of deaths occurring on or after 1 February 2001. Entitlement to charge ceased to be treated as a pecuniary legacy and instead is treated as remuneration for services and hence as an administrative expense. The fact that a personal representative or his spouse has witnessed the testator's signature on the will, does not affect the entitlement to charge, and the remuneration to which such a personal representative is entitled now ranks as an administrative expense for the purposes of the Administration of Estates Act 1925, s 34(3) and for any provision giving reasonable administration expenses priority over the preferential debts listed in the Insolvency Act 1986, Sch 6 in the case of an insolvent estate.

1   See para 13.10 above and note that the provisions of the Act apply to personal representatives, see TA 2000, s 35.
2   Wills Act 1837, s 15.

Which services are covered by a professional charging clause?

13.17 Section 28(2) reverses the rule that charging clauses are strictly construed so that a professional trustee could only be rewarded for services which could not have been provided by a lay trustee[1]. When this sub-section applies a trust corporation or a trustee acting in a professional capacity is entitled to payment even for services which could have been rendered by a lay trustee.

1   See para 13.4 above and **Precedent 55** below in Part IV which includes within a professional charging clause payments for services which could have been rendered by a lay trustee.

The operation of s 28

13.18 The section applies:

(a)   to trusts whenever created (TA 2000, s 33) provided that the section is not inconsistent with the terms of the trust instrument (s 28(1)(c));

(b)   but the section only applies to services provided on or after 1 February 2001; and

(c)   the reversal of the rule that a charging clause is a pecuniary legacy only takes effect for deaths occurring on or after 1 February 2001.

Section 29 – Remuneration of Certain Trustees

13.19 Text of section 29

(1) Subject to subsection (5), a trustee who–

(a) is a trust corporation, but

(b) is not a trustee of a charitable trust,

is entitled to receive reasonable remuneration out of the trust funds for any services that the trust corporation provides to or on behalf of the trust.

(2) Subject to subsection (5), a trustee who–

(a) acts in a professional capacity, but

(b) is not a trust corporation, a trustee of a charitable trust or a sole trustee,

is entitled to receive reasonable remuneration out of the trust funds for any services that he provides to or on behalf of the trust if each other trustee has agreed in writing that he may be remunerated for the services.

(3) 'Reasonable remuneration' means, in relation to the provision of services by a trustee, such remuneration as is reasonable in the circumstances for the provision of those services to or on behalf of that trust by that trustee and for the purposes of subsection (1) includes, in relation to the provision of services by a trustee who is an authorised institution under the Banking Act 1987 and provides the services in that capacity, the institution's reasonable charges for the provision of such services.

(4) A trustee is entitled to remuneration under this section even if the services in question are capable of being provided by a lay trustee.

(5) A trustee is not entitled to remuneration under this section if any provision about his entitlement to remuneration has been made–

(a) by the trust instrument, or

(b) by any enactment or any provision of subordinate legislation.

(6) This section applies to a trustee who has been authorised under a power conferred by Part IV or the trust instrument–

(a) to exercise functions as an agent of the trustees, or

(b) to act as a nominee or custodian,

as it applies to any other trustee.

Purpose of the section

13.20 It has reversed the usual rule that a trustee can only be paid for his or its services if and to the extent that the trust instrument so provides. Now, in cases where there is no provision in the trust instrument (or in any applicable enactment or subordinate legislation) entitling a trustee to remuneration (a) a trust corporation and (b) a trustee, not being a trust corporation or a sole trustee who 'acts in a professional capacity' (but only if the other trustee or trustees have all agreed in writing) is entitled to receive reasonable remuneration out of the trust funds. Trust funds here as elsewhere in the Act means the income or capital of the trust (TA 2000, s 39(1)). Section 29 does not apply to the trustees of a charitable trust.

Remuneration of trustees who act in a professional capacity

13.21   A trustee 'acting in a professional capacity' has the same meaning as for s 28[1] and includes a trustee which is a corporation, but not a trust corporation, and which so acted. A trustee who qualifies under s 29 is entitled to be remunerated for services which could be rendered by a 'lay trustee', which term has the same definition as in s 28[2]. The section also applies

(a)   to a trustee who has been authorised under the provisions of Pt IV of the Act or of the trust instrument to act as an agent of the trustees or as a nominee or custodian as to any other trustee[3]; and

(b)   the provisions of the section apply to personal representatives[4].

1   See para 13.14 above.
2   Section 29(4). The definition of a person 'acting as a lay trustee' is contained in s 28(5).
3   Section 29(6).
4   Section 35.

Trust corporations

13.22   The provisions apply to a trust corporation whether it is the sole trustee or personal representative or acts with other trustees or personal representatives, and if it does act with another or others it does not need his or their agreement (ie there is an automatic right to reasonable remuneration). A trust corporation does not need to qualify as a trustee who acts in a professional capacity.

Sole trustees

13.23   A sole trustee or personal representative (not being a trust corporation), although acting in a professional capacity, does not come within s 29. Accordingly, if A dies leaving B as the sole trustee, B is not entitled to remuneration until a further trustee is appointed and who consents to that remuneration.

Consent of the other trustees

13.24   In giving his or their agreement to the remuneration of a trustee who acts in a professional capacity the other trustee or trustees must have regard to the interests of the beneficiaries (both present and future). The consent requirements are not free from all uncertainty: because 'each other trustee' has to agree, the appointment of a new trustee will mean that his consent will be required. Further, there is no reason why the other trustees should not consent for a limited period (eg during the next 12 months) leaving the remuneration to be reviewed at the end of that period. On the death of the other trustee the consent ends and the sole remaining trustee will not be able to charge under the statutory provision.

Meaning of 'reasonable remuneration'

13.25 'Reasonable remuneration' is defined in s 29(3) as being such remuneration as is reasonable in the circumstances for the provision of the services in question by that trustee. Regard should therefore be had to the nature of the trusts, the size of the trust fund, the sort of assets held and the services and the extent of the services being provided by the trustee.

Exclusions from s 29

13.26 A trustee does not come within the provisions of s 29 if there is any provision concerning his remuneration in the trust instrument or in any enactment or subordinate legislation. This includes a provision *prohibiting* his remuneration.

13.27 The explanatory notes to the Act express the view that an unconditional legacy in favour of a personal representative or trustee does not amount to provision for the remuneration of the legatee but that a legacy *conditional* on the personal representative proving the will would be a provision for remuneration. If this is correct then the commonly found bequest of a pecuniary legacy to an executor conditional on his proving the will means that such executor, even though acting in a professional capacity, will not come within the provisions of s 29. Since what matters is whether the trust instrument (in such a case the will) makes provision for the trustee's remuneration, the disclaimer by the trustee of the pecuniary legacy would not bring him within s 29.

The operation of s 29

13.28 The rules are the same as for s 28 and reference should therefore be made to the discussion in that section[1].

1   See para 13.18 and TA 2000, s 33.

Drafting express remuneration clauses in trusts and wills[1]

13.29 Section 29 should be viewed as a default provision and as no substitute for a properly drafted remuneration clause. Note in particular:

(a)   for a trustee (other than a trust corporation) s 29 only affords assistance if he is acting 'in a professional capacity'. If the settlor or testator wishes to remunerate other trustees (for instance any trustee engaged in any business) then an express clause is essential;

(b)   a sole trustee (not being a trust corporation) is outside the section and in other cases the other trustees have to agree to the payment of reasonable remuneration. Of course the sole trustee without the benefit of an express remuneration clause may appoint an additional trustee so he may then fall within the provisions of s 29. Bear in mind, however, that the power to appoint new trustees is a fiduciary power and must be exercised in the best interests of all the beneficiaries and not as a means to obtain reasonable remuneration;

(c) if co-trustees refuse to agree remuneration for the professional it will be difficult to challenge their decision (and, of course, all co-trustees – not just a majority – must agree); and

(d) a testator may well wish a professional executor to be remunerated for his services and at the same time desire him to receive a legacy for agreeing to act as executor. Again express provisions are necessary to achieve this result.

1   See **Precedent 53** below.

Section 30 – Remuneration of Trustees of Charitable Trusts

13.30   Text of section 30

(1)   The Secretary of State may by regulations make provision for the remuneration of trustees of charitable trusts who are trust corporations or act in a professional capacity.

(2)   The power under subsection (1) includes power to make provision for the remuneration of a trustee who has been authorised under a power conferred by Part IV or any other enactment or any provision of subordinate legislation, or by the trust instrument–

(a)   to exercise functions as an agent of the trustees, or

(b)   to act as a nominee or custodian.

(3)   Regulations under this section may–

(a)   make different provision for different cases;

(b)   contain such supplemental, incidental, consequential and transitional provision as the Secretary of State considers appropriate.

(4)   The power to make regulations under this section is exercisable by statutory instrument, but no such instrument shall be made unless a draft of it has been laid before Parliament and approved by a resolution of each House of Parliament.

Purpose of the section

13.31   Section 30 relates to charitable trusts and gives the Secretary of State for Education power to make regulations providing for the remuneration of trustees of charities who are trust corporations or who act in a professional capacity. This power extends to provisions for the remuneration of a trustee who under the powers contained in Part IV of the Act or the trust instrument has been authorised to act as an agent for the trustees of the charity or to act as a nominee or custodian.

The current position

13.32   On 15 September 1999 the Charity Commission launched a debate on whether charity trustees should be paid. The results were announced in a Press Release of 31 October 2000:

'THUMBS DOWN TO PAYING TRUSTEES

The majority of those responding to the Charity Commission's consultation on whether trustees should be paid have given the idea a firm thumbs down. Most who responded to the consultation, launched in September 1999, felt that trustees should not be paid unless there was strong justification for doing so.

These responses are consistent with the present law, which is reflected in the new guidance CC11 "Payment of Charity Trustees" published by the Commission in September 2000. The guidance looks at a range of factors which charities need to take into account when considering whether their trustees should be paid. For the first time, this includes acknowledgement that charities may wish to recruit trustees from social and economic backgrounds who cannot afford to act as trustees unless paid. The guidance also provides a helpful explanation of the difference between payment and expenses, an area that can cause confusion.'

13.33   Strong views were expressed during the passage of the Act through the House of Lords on the propriety of charity trustees being remunerated. It seems unlikely that any order will be made under s 30.

Section 31 – Trustee's Expenses

13.34   Text of section 31

(1)   A trustee–

(a)   is entitled to be reimbursed from the trust funds, or

(b)   may pay out of the trust funds,

expenses properly incurred by him when acting on behalf of the trust.

(2)   This section applies to a trustee who has been authorised under a power conferred by Part IV or any other enactment or any provision of subordinate legislation, or by the trust instrument–

(a)   to exercise functions as an agent of the trustees, or

(b)   to act as a nominee or custodian,

as it applies to any other trustee.

Purpose of the section

13.35   It has replaced:

(a)   the Settled Land Act 1925, s 100 which had provided that the trustees of a Settled Land Act settlement could reimburse themselves or pay out of 'the trustee property' all expenses properly incurred by them; and

(b) the Trustee Act 1925, s 30(2) which had provided that a trustee could reimburse himself or pay out of the 'trust premises' all expenses incurred in or about 'the trusts or powers'. Both sections have been repealed.

13.36 There is now, therefore, a common provision in respect of reimbursement of expenses applying to all trusts with payment out of the 'trust funds' being the expression generally used in the Act and meaning both the capital and income of the trust. As to which should meet the expense, see Underhill and Hayton *'Law of Trusts and Trustees'* (15th Ed) Article 86 to the effect their 'income' expenses should come out of income and 'capital' out of capital. Has TA 2000 changed the law in this regard by giving trustees a discretion (to be exercised having regard to the duty to act fairly between life tenant and remainderman) to charge any expenses to income or capital. Such a change would be startling: a CGT bill could, for instance, be satisfied out of income and an income tax liability out of capital. The Law Commission Report gives no hint that such a change is intended but Kessler in *'Drafting Trusts and Will Trusts'* has concluded:

> 'It is surprising that this important change was made without express discussion . . . it appears to have been unintentional. However, it is the only natural construction . . . it is also a highly satisfactory result as the former law was complex, uncertain, unworkable and ignored in practice[1].'

Such a conclusion does not seem warranted by the terms of the section: indeed it is thought that the wording is little different from that in TA 1925, s 30(2) which it has replaced. It is therefore suggested that all the section does is to give trustees the power to discharge expenses or to reimburse themselves out of either the income or capital of the trust fund but does not address the question of whether the burden of that expense should then rest with the income or the capital. The trustees may, as an illustration, resort to income to discharge a CGT liability but should then make an appropriate adjustment so that the income deficiency is made good out of capital as soon as circumstances permit[2].

1   5th Ed, 2000, at para 18.29 footnote 53.
2   Law Com No 260 at paras 5.13 and 8.33 accept that the costs of employing a nominee or custodian (not apparently an agent) and insurance premiums should be apportioned between income or capital in the trustees' discretion but (a) they did not make any wider recommendation and (b) it may be doubted whether the Bill as drafted gave effect to these proposals.

An entitlement to payment or reimbursement

13.37 Section 31 confers an entitlement to reimbursement or payment of expenses properly incurred rather than, as in the provisions it replaced, a power to reimburse or pay. As originally drafted the Bill provided only for a reimbursement – this was amended at Committee Stage in the House of Lords – see the comments of Lord Goodhart in the debate on 14 April 2000: 'most liabilities incurred by a trustee on behalf of a trust are not paid by the trustee himself and then reimbursed to him, but are paid directly out of the trust fund. As in the provisions it replaced the expenses concerned may be either reimbursed to a trustee who has met them or be paid direct. The provisions of s 31 apply to a trustee who, under the powers contained in Part

IV of the Act or the trust instrument, has been appointed as an agent of the trustees or to act as a nominee or custodian.'

Commencement

13.38 Section 31 applies to trusts wherever created. It will apply to expenses incurred on or after 1 February 2001 (s 33(1)).

Section 32 – Remuneration and Expenses of Agents, Nominees and Custodians

13.39 Text of section 32

(1) This section applies if, under a power conferred by Part IV or any other enactment or any provision of subordinate legislation, or by the trust instrument, a person other than a trustee has been–

(a) authorised to exercise functions as an agent of the trustees, or

(b) appointed to act as a nominee or custodian.

(2) The trustees may remunerate the agent, nominee or custodian out of the trust funds for services if–

(a) he is engaged on terms entitling him to be remunerated for those services, and

(b) the amount does not exceed such remuneration as is reasonable in the circumstances for the provision of those services by him to or on behalf of that trust.

(3) The trustees may reimburse the agent, nominee or custodian out of the trust funds for any expenses properly incurred by him in exercising functions as an agent, nominee or custodian.

Purpose of the section

13.40 Section 32 gives to the trustees power where, under the powers contained in Part IV of the Act or the trust instrument, a person, (other than a trustee), has been appointed as agent for the trustees or appointed as a nominee or custodian, to remunerate the agent, nominee or custodian out of the trust funds if the appointment has been on terms that the appointee is entitled to remuneration and the amount is reasonable in the circumstances. The trustees are also given power to reimburse the expenses 'properly incurred' by such an agent, nominee or custodian.

Commencement

13.41 Section 32 applies to trusts whenever created and to personal representatives. It applies to services rendered or expenses incurred on or after 1 February 2001[1].

1   Section 33(1).

Section 33 – Application

13.42   Text of section 33

(1)   Subject to subsection (2), sections 28, 29, 31 and 32 apply in relation to services provided to or on behalf of, or (as the case may be) expenses incurred on or after their commencement on behalf of, trusts whenever created.

(2)   Nothing in section 28 or 29 is to be treated as affecting the operation of—

(a)   section 15 of the Wills Act 1837, or

(b)   section 34(3) of the Administration of Estates Act 1925,

in relation to any death occurring before the commencement of section 28 or (as the case may be) section 29.

Purpose of the section

13.43   The section deals with the application of the preceding ss 28-32. In particular, provisions for remuneration or reimbursement of expenses only apply to services rendered and expenses incurred on or after the commencement date (1 February 2001). The treatment of remuneration as an administration expense operates in relation to deaths on or after the commencement date.

14

Part VI: Miscellaneous and Supplementary

Section 34 – Power to Insure

14.1   Text of section 34

(1)   For section 19 of the Trustee Act 1925 (power to insure) substitute–

[19   Power to insure

(1)   A trustee may–

    (a)   insure any property which is subject to the trust against risks of loss or damage due to any event, and

    (b)   pay the premiums out of the trust funds.

(2)   In the case of property held on a bare trust, the power to insure is subject to any direction given by the beneficiary or each of the beneficiaries–

    (a)   that any property specified in the direction is not to be insured;

    (b)   that any property specified in the direction is not to be insured except on such conditions as may be so specified.

(3)   Property is held on a bare trust if it is held on trust for–

    (a)   a beneficiary who is of full age and capacity and absolutely entitled to the property subject to the trust, or

    (b)   beneficiaries each of whom is of full age and capacity and who (taken together) are absolutely entitled to the property subject to the trust.

(4)   If a direction under subsection (2) of this section is given, the power to insure, so far as it is subject to the direction, ceases to be a delegable function for the purposes of section 11 of the Trustee Act 2000 (power to employ agents).

(5)   In this section "trust funds" means any income or capital funds of the trust.

(2)   In section 20(1) of the Trustee Act 1925 (application of insurance money) omit "whether by fire or otherwise".]'

(3)   The amendments made by this section apply in relation to trusts whether created before or after its commencement.

Purpose of the section

14.2   This section substitutes a new s 19 of the Trustee Act 1925, which contains the statutory power to insure.

The 'old' s 19

14.3   In its original form, until the amendments made by the Trusts of Land and Appointment of Trustees Act 1996 took effect, s 19 gave trustees power to insure any building and 'other insurable property', but only against loss or damage by fire and only up to three quarters of the full value and the premiums had to be paid out of income. The amendment to s 19 made by the Trusts of Land and Appointment of Trustees Act 1996 removed the reference to buildings and gave trustees power to insure 'any personal property' against any risks but still only up to three quarters of the full value of the property involved with premiums still having to be paid out of income. The position after the 1996 Act came into force on 1 January 1997 was therefore that trustees could insure 'personal property' against any risk but only up to three quarters of the value, while the position regarding buildings was uncertain. Presumably the removal of the reference to 'buildings' was because the wide powers given to trustees of a trust of land by s 6(1) of the 1996 Act were considered to extend to insurance[1]. However, the powers given by section 6(1) related to the trust land and it is not clear that they extend to income or other monies held by the trustees out of which they would be likely to be paying any premiums. The statutory power to insure has generally been considered unsatisfactory. It has been argued that the duty of trustees to protect the trust property gave them a wider power to insure than that contained in section 19 but this has never been established. In practice professionally drawn settlements and wills have frequently conferred wide powers of insurance on trustees.

1   The ambit of s 6 is considered at para 2.41 above.

The new section

14.4   The new substituted s 19, gives trustees power to insure any trust property against loss or damage by any risks and to any amount, and to pay the premiums out of either income or capital of the trust[1]. The only restriction is in the case of a 'bare trust' (defined as being a trust where there is one adult of full capacity absolutely entitled or where there is more than one beneficiary each of whom is adult and of full capacity and who taken together are absolutely entitled[2]). In this case the power is subject to any direction given by the absolutely entitled beneficiary (or by each of them where there are more than one), that any specified property is not to be insured or is to be insured only on stated conditions. If such a direction is given then the power to insure, so far as affected by the direction, ceases to be a power that the trustees concerned can delegate under section 11 of the Act[3].

1   For a consideration of this discretion given to trustees, see para 13.36 above.
2   The definition is considered to be defective in including the situation where property is held in trust for beneficiaries each of whom is of full age and who (taken together) are absolutely entitled to the property subject to the trust since this would include a trust for A for life reminder to B given that both are of full age – together they are absolutely entitled to the trust property but this is *not* a bare trust! Surely the provision should be limited to the situation where the beneficiaries are absolutely entitled 'to undivided shares'; for similar problems see Trusts of Land & Appointment of Trustees Act 1996, s 6(2) discussed at para 2.45 above.
3   See para 12.5 above.

Commencement

14.5   The substituted s 19 applies to trusts whether created before or after 1 February 2001. The amendments made by the Act to the Settled Land Act 1925 include an amendment to section 107 of that Act which has given the s 19 power to insure to the tenant for life as well as to the trustees[1]. The provisions of the Trustee Act 1925, s 20 as amended, concerning the application of insurance monies where the monies are received under an insurance policy effected under any power, are, save for a small textual alteration, unchanged.

1   As a result of an oversight neither the tenant for life nor anyone exercising his powers had a statutory power to insure after 1 January 1997. This amendment therefore restores the position.

Drafting

14.6   The power contained in the substituted s 19 is, of course, a power to insure trust property against risks. Trustees will continue to need an express power in the trust instrument to be able to effect life assurance policies on the lives of individuals, say the settlor or beneficiaries[1].

1   See **Precedent 46** below.

Duty of care

14.7   The duty of care under s 1 of the Act applies to the exercise of a power to insure whether it be the statutory power or one contained in the trust instrument. This duty will therefore be in point when trustees decide on the risks to be covered, the amount of the cover and choice of insurer. The explanatory notes to the Act point out that the substituted s 19 will not impose a *duty* to insure but expresses the view that trustees who fail to insure where a reasonable person would have insured are likely to be in breach of trust[1]. It is, however, the case that the express powers to insure contained in professionally drawn settlements often provide that the trustees are not to be liable for any failure to insure. Trustees with an express power to insure given by the settlement or will concerned, also have the widened statutory power given by the substituted s 19. It is, therefore, necessary, where settlors or testators do not wish the trustees to be liable for a failure to insure, that such an express provision extends to the statutory power as well as to any expressly conferred power. In the case of existing trusts it will be a matter of construction as to whether the exclusion of liability for failure to insure, applies to any power to insure or only to the express power contained in the trust instruction[2].

1   *Snell's Equity* (30th Ed) comments 'Trustees are not bound to insure the trust property against loss or damage by fire unless the trust instrument imposes such an obligation upon them' (at 12.12). The case law suggests, however, that the existence of a duty to insure (at least in some cases) may exist: compare *Re Betty* [1899] 1 Ch 821 and *Re McEacharn* (1911) 103 LT 900.
2   See **Precedent 51** below.

Conditionally exempt assets

14.8   When assets held in trust are conditionally exempt from Inheritance Tax[1], the loss of the item by fire or theft generally washes out of the deferred tax liability. Given that trustees will not replace such an asset the question arises as to the appropriate level of cover: is it the proceeds of sale less the tax that would have been paid if the asset had been sold? Incidentally a failure to insure is not a breach of the undertaking given in order to achieve conditional exemption[2].

1   See IHTA 1984, Pt II, Ch II. A similar exemption had been available from estate duty and capital transfer for tax.

2   In considering the appropriate level of cover the trustee should remember that a general averaging may apply if the property is under-insured.

Section 35 – Personal Representatives

14.9   Text of section 35

(1)   Subject to the following provisions of this section, this Act applies in relation to a personal representative administering an estate according to the law as it applies to a trustee carrying out a trust for beneficiaries.

(2)   For this purpose this Act is to be read with the appropriate modifications and in particular–

    (a)   references to the trust instrument are to be read as references to the will,

    (b)   references to a beneficiary or to beneficiaries, apart from the reference to a beneficiary in section 8(1)(b), are to be read as references to a person or the persons interested in the due administration of the estate, and

    (c)   the reference to a beneficiary in section 8(1)(b) is to be read as a reference to a person who under the will of the deceased or under the law relating to intestacy is beneficially interested in the estate.

(3)   Remuneration to which a personal representative is entitled under section 28 or 29 is to be treated as an administration expense for the purposes of–

    (a)   section 34(3) of the Administration of Estates Act 1925 (order in which estate to be paid out), and

    (b)   any provision giving reasonable administration expenses priority over the preferential debts listed in Schedule 6 to the Insolvency Act 1986.

(4)   Nothing in subsection (3) is to be treated as affecting the operation of the provisions mentioned in paragraphs (a) and (b) of that subsection in relation to any death occurring before the commencement of this section.

Purpose of the section

14.10   In relation to the matters contained in the Act, Personal Representatives ('PRs') have the same powers and duties when it comes to the administration of the estate of a deceased person as trustees have in relation to a trust fund. Previous Acts, such the Trustee Act 1925, had contained a similar provision[1].

1   See TA 1925, s 68(1)(17) and the Trusts of Land and Appointment of Trustees Act 1996, s 18.

Textual adjustments

14.11   The necessary adjustments are made by s 35(2): note especially that references to beneficiaries are generally to be construed as to 'persons interested in the due administration of the estate' which is sufficiently wide to include creditors of the deceased[1]. The one situation where 'beneficiary' is given a more restricted meaning is in relation to the possible exercise by PRs of the s 8(1)(b) power – to purchase a dwelling house for occupation by a beneficiary – where the word is limited to a person who is beneficially interested in the estate.

1   Note, therefore, that PRs cannot authorise a creditor to act as their agent (see s 12(3)). This would presumably mean that if the deceased owed fees to his portfolio manager then on his death the PRs cannot retain that person to act as their agent.

Remuneration

14.12   Changes in the treatment of remuneration paid to a trustee are made by ss 28-29 which have been considered at para 13.13 ff above. In the case of PRs two further significant changes have been effected:

(a)   any remuneration is treated as an administration expense for the purpose of the Administration of Estates Act 1925, s 34(3) (which lays down the order for the application of assets in the payment of funeral, testamentary and administration expenses);

(b)   in the case of insolvent estates the remuneration counts as an administration expense for the purpose of any provision which gives reasonable administration expenses priority over the preferential debts listed in the Insolvency Act 1986 Sch 6[1].

1   The preferential debts in that Schedule comprise debts due to the Inland Revenue, Customs and Excise, Social Security Contributions, contributions to Occupational Pension Schemes and the remuneration of employees. Because of the requirement that the administration expenses must be reasonable these may be allowed on a lower scale than would be permitted in the case of a solvent estate.

14.13   Under s 28(4)(a) remuneration of a PR is not treated as a gift for the purpose of the Wills Act 1837, s 15 (gifts to an attesting witness to be void).

14.14   These changes to the remuneration and to the treatment of remuneration of PRs do not affect the administration of estates in cases where the death has occurred before 1 February 2001.

Modifying the terms of TA 2000

14.15   In the same way that it is possible (and in a number of cases desirable) to provide expressly in a trust deed for matters otherwise dealt with in TA 2000, so wills should be drafted with such considerations in mind. The duty of care in Part 1 of the Act will apply to PRs and hence the will draftsman should consider whether that duty should be excluded or trustees protected by an exculpation clause[1]. In the case of an intestacy the Act must, of course, apply.

1   See generally para 10.20 above.

Section 36 – Pension Schemes

14.16   Text of section 36

(1)   In this section 'pension scheme' means an occupational pension scheme (within the meaning of the Pension Schemes Act 1993) established under a trust and subject to the law of England and Wales.

(2)   Part I does not apply in so far as it imposes a duty of care in relation to–

(a)   the functions described in paragraphs 1 and 2 of Schedule 1, or

(b)   the functions described in paragraph 3 of that Schedule to the extent that they relate to trustees–

(i)   authorising a person to exercise their functions with respect to investment, or

(ii)   appointing a person to act as their nominee or custodian.

(3)   Nothing in Part II or III applies to the trustees of any pension scheme.

(4)   Part IV applies to the trustees of a pension scheme subject to the restrictions in subsections (5) to (8).

(5)   The trustees of a pension scheme may not under Part IV authorise any person to exercise any functions relating to investment as their agent.

(6)   The trustees of a pension scheme may not under Part IV authorise a person who is–

(a)   an employer in relation to the scheme, or

(b)   connected with or an associate of such an employer,

to exercise any of their functions as their agent.

(7)   For the purposes of subsection (6)–

(a)   'employer', in relation to a scheme, has the same meaning as in the Pensions Act 1995;

(b)   sections 249 and 435 of the Insolvency Act 1986 apply for the purpose of determining whether a person is connected with or an associate of an employer.

(8)   Sections 16 to 20 (powers to appoint nominees and custodians) do not apply to the trustees of a pension scheme.

Purpose of the section

14.17   Trustees of an occupational pension scheme are subject to their own rules and hence various provisions of TA 2000 do not apply to them.

What is an occupational pension scheme?

14.18   This is a scheme within the meaning of the Pension Schemes Act 1993 established by means of a trust and subject to the laws of England and Wales[1].

1   Section 1 of that Act defines an occupational pension scheme as being a scheme which
     has, or is capable of having, effect in relation to a description or category of employment so
     as to provide benefits payable on termination of service, death or retirement or in respect
     of earners with qualifying service in an employment of any such description or category.

Investment and delegation of investment decisions

14.19   These matters are regulated by the Pensions Act 1995, s 34[1]. This section:

(a)   gives trustees the powers of an absolute owner in relation to the making of investments; and

(b)   by s 34(2) permits delegation to a fund manager who satisfies certain requirements.

1   See para 11.8 above.

14.20   Section 35 of the Act lays down a requirement that there must be a statement of investment principles[1] and by s 47 trustees are required, when the assets of the scheme include investments, to appoint a fund manager and can appoint nominees and custodians[2].

1   See paras 11.9 and 11.20 above.
2   Occupational Pension Schemes (Scheme Administration) Regs 1996, SI 1996/1715, rule
     2(c).

14.21   As a result the following parts of TA 2000 do not apply to occupational pension trustees when carrying out their investment functions:

(a)   Pt I;

(b)   Pt II;

(c)   Pt III;

(d)   Pt IV insofar as it confers powers to appoint nominees and custodians or, in relation to investments, an agent.

The parts of TA 2000 that do apply

14.22   The following parts of TA 2000 do apply to occupational pension trustees:

(a)   the duty of care in relation to matters *other than* investment, agency for investment purposes and the appointment of a nominee or custodian;

(b)   the delegation of non investment functions under Part IV but (to protect beneficiaries) delegation to a scheme employer or to a person who is connected with or is an associate of a scheme employer is prohibited[1].

1   TA 2000 s 36(6). Employer is defined in s 36(7)(a) by reference to the Pensions Act 1995
     ss 124(1) and 125(3). Section 124(1) provides that:

     ' "employer" in relation to an occupational pension scheme, means the employer of
     persons in the description or category or employment to which the scheme in question
     relates (but see section 125(3))'

and s 125(3) that:

> 'Regulations may, in relation to occupational pension schemes, extend for the purposes of this Part the meaning of "employer" to include persons who have been the employer in relation to the scheme.'

The question whether a person is connected with a company is governed by the Insolvency Act 1986 s 249 which provides as follows:

> ' . . . a person is connected with a company if:

(a) he is a director or shadow director of the company or an associate of such a director or shadow director, or

(b) he is an associate of the company;

(c) and "associate" has the meaning given by s 435.'

On the meaning of shadow director see *Secretary of State for Trade and Industry v Deverell* [2000] 2 All ER 365, CA. Section 435 defines an 'associate' as follows:

435(1) [Determination of whether associate] For the purposes of this Act any question whether a person is an associate of another person is to be determined in accordance with the following provisions of this section (any provision that a person is an associate of another person being taken to mean that they are associates of each other).

435(2) [Associate of individual] A person is an associate of an individual if that person is the individual's husband or wife, or is a relative, or the husband or wife of a relative, of the individual or of the individual's husband or wife.

435(3) [Associate of partner] A person is an associate of any person with whom he is in partnership, and of the husband or wife of a relative of any individual with whom he is in partnership; and a Scottish firm is an associate of any person who is a member of the firm.

435(4) [Associate of employee, employer] A person is an associate of any person whom he employs or by whom he is employed.

435(5) [Associate of trustee] A person in his capacity as trustee of a trust other than:

(a) a trust arising under any of the second Group of Parts or the Bankruptcy (Scotland) Act 1985, or

(b) a pension scheme or an employee's share scheme (within the meaning of the Companies Act),

is an associate of another person if the beneficiaries of the trust include, or the terms of the trust confer a power that may be exercised for the benefit of, that other person or an associate of that other person.

435(6) [Company associate of another company] A company is an associate of another company:

(a) if the same person has control of both, or a person has control of one and persons who are his associates, or he and persons who are his associates, have control of the other, or

(b) if a group of two or more persons has control of each company, and the groups either consist of the same persons by treating (in one or more cases) a member of either group as replaced by a person of whom he is an associate.

435(7) [Company associate of another person] A company is an associate of another person if that person has control of it or if that person and persons who are his associates together have control of it.

435(8) [Relatives] For the purposes of this section a person is a relative of an individual if he is that individual's brother, sister, uncle, aunt, nephew, niece, lineal ancestor or lineal descendant, treating:

(a) any relationship of the half blood as a relationship of the whole blood and the stepchild or adopted child of any person as his child, and

(b) an illegitimate child as the legitimate child of his mother and reputed father,

and references in this section to a husband and wife include a former husband or wife and a reputed husband or wife.

435(9) [Director employee] For the purposes of this section any director or other officer of a company is to be treated as employed by that company.

435(10) [Person with control] For the purposes of this section a person is to be taken as having control of a company if:

(a)   the directors of the company or of another company which has control of it (or any of them) are accustomed to act in accordance with his directions or instructions, or

(b)   he is entitled to exercise, or control the exercise of, one third or more of the voting power at any general meeting of the company or of another company which has control of it,

and where two or more persons together satisfy either of the above conditions, they are to be taken as having control of the company.

435(11) ['Company'] In this section 'company' includes any body corporate (whether incorporated in Great Britain or elsewhere); and references to directors and other officers of a company and to voting power at any general meeting of a company have effect with any necessary modifications.

This definition is widely framed and will, or course, catch spouses, close relatives, business partners (and their spouses) employers and employees.

Section 37 – Authorised Unit Trusts

14.23   Text of section 37

(1)   Parts II to IV do not apply to trustees of authorised unit trusts.

(2)   'Authorised unit trust' means a unit trust scheme in the case of which an order under section 78 of the Financial Services Act 1986 is in force.

Purpose of the section

14.24   This section provides that Pt II-IV of the Act do not apply to authorised unit trusts (as defined in s 37(2)).

Meaning of a unit trust scheme

14.25   A unit trust scheme is a collective investment scheme under which property is held in trust for the participants. Such a scheme will only be authorised if the Secretary of State is satisfied that the trust deed complies with regulations as to the powers and duties of the manager and trustees and hence there is no need for the powers conferred by Pts II-IV.

The duty of care

14.26   Part I of the Act applies to such trustees in the exercise of their express powers.

Section 38 – Common Investment Schemes for Charities etc

14.27   Text of section 38

Parts II to IV do not apply to—

(a)   trustees managing a fund under a common investment scheme made, or having effect as if made, under section 24 of the Charities Act 1993, other than such a fund the trusts of which provide that property is not to be transferred to the fund except by or on behalf of a charity the trustees of which are the trustees appointed to manage the fund; or

(b)   trustees managing a fund under a common deposit scheme made, or having effect as if made, under section 25 of that Act.

Purpose of the section

14.28   This section provides that Pts II-IV of the Act do not apply to trustees managing common investment and common deposit schemes under the Charities Act 1993.

What is a common investment and common deposit scheme?

14.29   Both schemes enable different charities to pool resources for investment purposes. These schemes can only be established by order of the Court or Charity Commissioners:

(a)   Charities Act 1993 s 24: this gives the Court or Charity Commissioners power to approve a common investment scheme involving any two or more charities[1]. The scheme will give trustees the powers provided for in Pts II-IV of the Trustee Act 2000 which powers, being unnecessary, are made inapplicable to such schemes;

(b)   Charities Act 1993, s 25: this enables schemes to be made to establish common deposit funds. There are obviously similar features to common investment schemes[2]: in this case the scheme will provide for repayment of the sum deposited and for interest thereon at a prescribed rate.

1   See generally Picarda, 'Law & Practice relating to Charities' (3rd Edn) at p 513 *et seq*.
2   Picarda, 'Law and Practice relating to Charities' (3rd Edn), at p 517.

'Or having effect as if made'

14.30   These words, added at Committee Stage in the House of Lords[1] make it clear that schemes made before the Charities Act 1993 came into effect (these are schemes made under the Charities Act 1960, s 22(1) and s 22A) are treated in the same way as schemes made under the 1993 Act.

1   Lords Hansard, 7 June 2000, Col CWH 11.

A pooling scheme

14.31   This enables a single body of trustees holding the investments of a number of charitable trusts to treat those investments, for investment purposes, as a single whole. Formerly, these schemes were made under the inherent jurisdiction of the court but they comprise common investment funds and hence they are now made under s 24. The final part of s 38(1) –

from 'other than' to 'the fund' – deals with such schemes and was added at Committee Stage in the House of Lords. The Lord Chancellor (Lord Irvine) explained this addition as follows:

> 'This amendment brings within the ambit of the Bill those schemes set up under Section 24 of the Charities Act 1993 known as pooling schemes, by which groups of small charities may consolidate their investments. These schemes often have no explicit powers of investment and thus the Charity Commission was of the view that there would be an advantage to bringing them within the new scheme[1].'

1   Lords Hansard, 7 June 2000, Col CWH 11.

The duty of care

14.32   Because Part I of the Act is not excluded, it is capable of applying to charitable trustees of schemes falling within s 38 when they exercise their express powers.

Section 39 – Interpretation

14.33   Text of section 39

(1)   In this Act–

'asset' includes any right or interest;

'charitable trust' means a trust under which property is held for charitable purposes and 'charitable purposes' has the same meaning as in the Charities Act 1993;

'custodian trustee' has the same meaning as in the Public Trustee Act 1906;

'enactment' includes any provision of a Measure of the Church Assembly or of the General Synod of the Church of England;

'exempt charity' has the same meaning as in the Charities Act 1993;

'functions' includes powers and duties;

'legal mortgage' has the same meaning as in the Law of Property Act 1925;

'personal representative' has the same meaning as in the Trustee Act 1925;

'settled land' has the same meaning as in the Settled Land Act 1925;

'trust corporation' has the same meaning as in the Trustee Act 1925;

'trust funds' means income or capital funds of the trust.

(2)   In this Act the expressions listed below are defined or otherwise explained by the provisions indicated–

asset management functions	section 15(5)
custodian	section 17(2)
the duty of care	section 1(2)
the general power of investment	section 3(2)

lay trustee	section 28(6)
power of intervention	section 22(4)
the standard investment criteria	section 4(3)
subordinate legislation	section 6(3)
trustee acting in a professional capacity	section 28(5)
trust instrument	sections 6(2) and 35(2)(a)

14.34   This is the definition section and the following matters may be noted:

(a)   certain terms are defined in the section of the Act in which they first appear and so are not found in this general definition section: see s 39(2);

(b)   although an 'asset' includes any right or interest the word is not otherwise defined. It is likely that the court will give it the widest meaning in line with the statutory definition for capital gains tax purposes: namely that 'all forms of property shall be assets for the purposes of this Act'[1];

(c)   'charitable purposes' are defined in the Charities Act 1993 as 'purposes which are exclusively charitable according to the law of England and Wales' (see CA 1993, s 97(1));

(d)   'exempt charities' are listed in the Second Schedule to the Charities Act 1993 and generally comprise charities which are outside the jurisdiction of the Charity Commissioners because they are sufficiently regulated by other statutory provisions;

(e)   'functions': the use of the expression 'functions as trustees' occurs in ss 6(1) and 9(1) of the Trusts of Land and Appointment of Trustees Act 1996 but in neither case is the word function defined (see also s 11(1) of that Act 'any function relating to the land'). Function is a singularly inelegant word and it is unfortunate that it has been employed instead of the more familiar (and accurate) 'powers and duties';

(f)   trust funds: this is defined as the income or capital funds of the trust (in common usage 'trust fund' is the corpus (capital) and the trust instrument will commonly refer to 'the income therefrom'). Some controversy has arisen from the provisions of TA 2000, s 31 (trustees' expenses) s 32 (remuneration and expenses of agents) and s 34 (payment of insurance premiums) since in each of these sections the trustees in their discretion are allowed to use trust funds to discharge the relevant expense. The now repealed TA 1925, s 30(2) had permitted trustee expenses to be discharged out of the 'trust premises' which presumably had much the same meaning as out of the trust funds. By contrast, the old power to insure had provided for premiums to be paid only out of income[2]: see the old TA 1925, s 19 which has now been replaced.

1   See TCGA 1992, s 21(1) and the case law thereon notably *O'Brien v Benson's Hosiery Ltd* [1979] 3 All ER 652, HL (rights under a service contract) and *Kirby v Thorn EMI plc* [1986] STC 200 (right to engage in commercial activity not an asset). See also *Swift v Dairywise Farms Ltd* [2000] 1 All ER 320.
2   Contrast the common law which had allowed the use of capital.

14.35 Two questions need to be considered:

(a) from what source do the trustees obtain reimbursement or extract funds to discharge their expenses? and

(b) as between income and capital beneficiaries who bears that expense?

14.36 A convenient statement of the law as it has always been understood is to be found in Pettit's *Equity and the Law of Trusts* (8th Edn) at p 458:

'As between the beneficiaries, the trustees' costs and expenses are normally payable out of capital but so far as the trustees are concerned their right to an 'indemnity against all costs and expenses properly incurred by them in their execution of the trust is a first charge on all the trust property both income and corpus[1].'

1   *Stott v Milne* (1884) 25 Ch D 710 per Selborne LC at 715.

14.37 Has TA 2000 effected any change in this position? To allow trustees a discretion to attribute any expenses to income or capital would have potentially startling consequences: they might, for instance, decide that a capital gains tax liability was to be set against income for the year and, presumably, an income tax liability against capital (of course in exercising any such discretion the trustees would presumably have to act fairly as between the beneficiaries!). There is certainly no suggestion in the Law Commission's Final Report that such a fundamental change was intended[1].

1   The contrary view is asserted by Kessler in *Drafting Trusts and Will Trusts* (5th Ed) at 18.29; the matter is also considered at para 13.36 above.

Section 40 – Minor and Consequential Amendments etc

14.38 Text of section 40

(1) Schedule 2 (minor and consequential amendments) shall have effect.

(2) Schedule 3 (transitional provisions and savings) shall have effect.

(3) Schedule 4 (repeals) shall have effect.

Section 41 – Power to Amend other Acts

14.39 Text of section 41

(1) A Minister of the Crown may by order make such amendments of any Act, including an Act extending to places outside England and Wales, as appear to him appropriate in consequence of or in connection with Part II or III.

(2) Before exercising the power under subsection (1) in relation to a local, personal or private Act, the Minister must consult any person who appears to him to be affected by any proposed amendment.

(3) An order under this section may–

(a)   contain such transitional provisions and savings as the Minister thinks fit;

(b)   make different provision for different purposes.

(4)   The power to make an order under this section is exercisable by statutory instrument which shall be subject to annulment in pursuance of a resolution of either House of Parliament.

(5)   'Minister of the Crown' has the same meaning as in the Ministers of the Crown Act 1975.

Section 42 – Commencement and Extent

14.40   Text of section 42

(1)   Section 41, this section and section 43 shall come into force on the day on which this Act is passed.

(2)   The remaining provisions of this Act shall come into force on such day as the Lord Chancellor may appoint by order made by statutory instrument; and different days may be so appointed for different purposes.

(3)   An order under subsection (2) may contain such transitional provisions and savings as the Lord Chancellor considers appropriate in connection with the order.

(4)   Subject to section 41(1) and subsection (5), this Act extends to England and Wales only.

(5)   An amendment or repeal in Part II or III of Schedule 2 or Part II of Schedule 4 has the same extent as the provision amended or repealed.

Section 43 – Short Title

14.41   Text of section 43

This Act may be cited as the Trustee Act 2000.

14.42   The following matters may be noted in connection with ss 40-43:

(a)   Power to amend other Acts (s 41): this is a 'Henry VIII clause'. In the House of Lords Debates, the Lord Chancellor commented as follows:

'Clause 41 is a Henry VIII power to amend other Acts. I am grateful to the Delegated Powers and Deregulation Committee of your Lordship's House who considered this matter . . . and accepted the reasoning for its inclusion in the Bill. The purpose of clause 41 is to allow those whose investment powers are governed by the 1961 Act but who would wish to take advantage of the new powers granted by Parts II and III of this Bill to apply to the Minister to be able to do so by the amendment of their governing statute. The Minister will be required to consult anyone who seems to him likely to be affected by the proposed amendment of a local personal or private Act. Sub-section (1) gives a minister of the Crown power to make such amendments to any act including an act extending to places outside England and Wales, as appear to him appropriate in consequence of or in connection with Part II or Part III. The reason for the extension of the power to Acts which operate beyond England and Wales is that, where a provision has UK wide application, it may be anomalous to amend it in relation to England and Wales but not otherwise. Over the years, the statutory investment powers of many organisations which are not trusts have nonetheless been defined in terms of the default powers contained in the 1961 Act. Many of those are thought to be governed by local personal or private Acts and so not all of them are amenable to identification by the usual methods such as LEXIS searches[1].'

A Minister of the Crown means the holder of an office in Her Majesty's Government in the UK and includes the Treasury, Board of Trade and Defence Council.

(b) Commencement: The Act was brought into force by SI 2001/49 with effect from 1 February 2001. No transitional provisions or savings were considered necessary. In general the Act extends to England and Wales only although the consequential amendments and repeals will depend upon the provision being amended.

1   House of Lords Debates, 14 April 2000, columns 379-380.

Schedule 1

14.43   This is considered in detail at para 10.7.

Schedule 2

14.44   This Schedule is printed in Appendix 4.

14.45   The Schedule is primarily concerned with the amendments brought about by the introduction of new general power of investment to the Trustee Investments Act 1961 and the Charities Act 1993.

14.46   Paragraph 1 repeals the provisions of the 1961 Act except in so far as those provisions continue to be applied by or under any other enactment. The repealed provisions in that Act are:

(a)   s 1 (power of investment of trustees);

(b)   s 2 (restrictions on wide range investments);

(c)   s 5 (valuations on a division of the fund);

(d)   s 6 (duty in choosing investments);

(e)   s 12 (power to add to the list of investments);

(f)   s 13 power to modify the rules as to the division of the trust fund);

(g)   s 15 (saving for court powers);

(h)   s 3 (relationship between the Act and other powers of investment);

(i)   Sch 2/3 (supplemental provisions);

(j)   s 8 (special cases);

(k)   s 9 (supplemental);

(l)   Sch 4, para 1(1); s 16(1) (construction of references to the replaced TA 1925, s 1).

14.47   So far as the Charities Act 1993 is concerned, ss 70 and 71 enabled the Secretary of State to expand the investment powers of charitable trustees. These provisions are no longer needed and the sections are accordingly repealed in Schedule 4.

14.48   Paras 7-17 make amendments to the Settled Land Act 1925. In brief:

(a)   paras 7-9 reflect the widening of the investment powers of trustees;

(b)   para 10 amends s 75 of the SLA 1925 in an important respect. The investment (or application) of capital money is now made a matter for the trustees rather than for the tenant for life. The tenant for life has to be consulted and, 'so far as consistent with the general interest of the settlement', the trustees should give effect to his wishes (compare the Trusts of Land and Appointment of Trustees Act 1996, s 11: see para 2.107 above). It would appear that in expressing his wishes the tenant for life will not have to act in a fiduciary manner. In exercising their function in this regard the trustees are subject to the statutory duty of care. Trustees can delegate under TA 2000, Pt IV but not so as to avoid consulting the tenant for life;

(c)   the new s 75A inserted by para 11 replaces TA 1925, s 10(2) which was repealed by TA 2000. It permits the tenant for life who sells settled land to leave up to two thirds of the purchase money outstanding on mortgage;

(d)   the repeal of s 96 mirrors the repeal of TA 1925, s 30(1). Because trustees are now responsible for the investment of capital monies s 98(1)-(2) have been repealed and s 100 (reimbursement of trustees) has been superseded by TA 2000, s 31. The replacement of s 102(E) reflects the widened insurance powers of trustees under TA 1925, s 19 (inserted by TA 2000);

(e)   para 16 is concerned with the situation where the life tenant has assigned his estate for value and identifies when the assignee is to be required to consent to the investment of capital money;

(f)   para 17 extends to the tenant for life the widened administrative powers given to trustees under TA 2000. Formerly the tenant for life did not have a statutory power to employ and pay agents: now he can employ an agent on a discretionary basis subject to the statutory duty of care (interestingly that duty does not apply to the tenant for life himself if he exercises management functions). Two issues may be noted: first, that although an agent may be remunerated out of the trust funds (ie both income and capital) the tenant for life will not have access to capital (other than to the settled land itself) which is of course vested in the trustees and, secondly, the new s 107(1A) power to appoint agents applies equally to the trustees although presumably only in relation to their statutory functions as trustees.

14.49 Paras 18-25 make a number of significant changes to the Trustee Act 1925 (the Act in amended form is printed in full in Appendix 1). Note the following:

(a) the provisions in TA 1925, ss 8-9 dealing with lending on mortgages of real property have been repealed although not so as to affect the operation of loans or investments made before 1 February 2001. A power to make such loans is now contained in the general power of investment (see TA 2000, s 3(3): its exercise is subject to the statutory duty of care);

(b) TA 1925, s 10(2) permitted trustees, on a sale of land, to leave part of the purchase price outstanding on mortgage. That section has been repealed and, except in the case of settled land[1] not replaced. Accordingly, such arrangements must now be dealt with under the general power of investment and hence the requirements of ss 4-5 will need to be met. A similar result follows from the repeal of TA 1925, s 10(1) (power to contract not to call in money): the trustees in exercising their s 3 powers will now need to decide whether it is appropriate to enter into the kind of long term mortgage investment that had been permitted by s 10(1);

(c) the express power conferred by TA 1925, s 2 to purchase redeemable stock at a premium (and to retain the same) has been repealed and not replaced. The question now for trustees is whether they should make such an investment: it falls within the general power of investment in s 3;

(d) similar comments may be made of the repeal – again with no replacement – of TA 1925, s 7 which gave trustees powers to invest in bearer securities (see also TA 2000, s 18 which generally requires trustees to vest such securities in a custodian);

(e) TA 1925, s 10(3) permitted trustees to concur in a scheme of arrangement in relation to securities held in the trust. The repeal of this provision (without any replacement) may present problems for trustees: obviously they have a power to sell their securities and to switch them on a reconstruction of a company for other securities (provided that acquisition is within the general power of investment) but they no longer have an express statutory power to consent to the sale by the company of any part of its property or undertaking (similarly it is not clear that trustees will be able to release rights attaching to their shares);

(f) the repeal (and non-replacement) of s 10(4) dealing with rights issues should not present difficulties for trustees. The investment of monies in a rights issue will be an investment decision within s 3 of the Act. (Of course, there may be strong reasons why trustees should take up the rights issue in view of the effect that it will have on the price of their existing shares);

(g)   S 11(2) of TA 1925 enabled trustees to apply capital money in paying calls on shares held in the trust and has been repealed without any replacement. Of course, there is nothing to stop trustees subscribing for partly paid shares: they are merely undertaking to pay the purchase price of their investment by instalments. What, however, if they purchase from a third party shares which are only partly paid? It is thought that the position is analogous: when the investment was made it was on the basis of the contingent liability;

(h)   the replacement of the good faith requirement with the statutory duty of care in ss 15 and 22(1) and (3) has been discussed at para 10.13 above.

1   See para 14.48 above.

14.50   The important changes made to the Trusts of Land and Appointment of Trustees Act 1996 by paras 45-48 have been considered earlier in a commentary on that Act.

Schedule 3

14.51   The Schedule is printed in Appendix 4.

14.52   The Schedule introduces various transitional provisions including:

(a)   a banker or banking company under TA 1925, s 7 holding bearer securities is to be treated as if it had been appointed a custodian under TA 2000, s 18;

(b)   the repeal of TA 1925, ss 8-9 does not affect loans made before 1 February 2001;

(c)   similar provisions to (a) in relation to the repeal of TA 1925, s 21;

(d)   an agent appointed under TA 1925, s 23(1) before 1 February 2001 is to be treated as if he had been appointed under s 11 and an agent already appointed under s 23(2) will retain his authority to act. Of course, the trustees having appointed an agent under s23(1) when they were only subject to the duty 'to act in good faith' in employing that agent will find that, as from 1 February 2001, they are subject to the statutory duty of care (for instance, in reviewing the activities of that agent); and

(e)   para 7 provides that a trustee shall not be liable for breach of trust merely by continuing to hold an investment that had been authorised by the Trustee Investments Act 1961, Sch 1, Pt II, para 14 (perpetual rent charges). A trustee should, of course, consider whether that investment remains appropriate under his general duty to review investments.

Excursus

Bare trusts

14.53 The only reference to bare trusts in TA 2000 is in s 34 which substitutes a new statutory power of insurance into TA 1925, s 19. That section as originally drafted also had such a reference in s 19(2): 'the section does not apply to any building or property which a trustee is bound forthwith to convey absolutely to any beneficiary upon being requested to do so.'

14.54 The Law Commission commented that:

'the fact that property is held on a bare trust should not alter or exclude the trustee's statutory powers of insurance. However . . . where there is either a bare trust or all the beneficiaries are of full age and capacity, and, taken together, are absolutely entitled to the trust property, the beneficiaries should be at liberty to direct the trustees not to insure the trust property . . . if that is their unanimous wish . . . the beneficiaries should be able to carry out the cost-benefit analysis involved in deciding whether or not to insure in the same way as an absolute owner[1].'

1   Law Commission, No 260, para 6.5.

14.55 The following matters may be noted:

What is a bare trust?

14.56 A bare (or 'simple' trust) arises when a trustee holds property for the sole benefit of one beneficiary who is of full age. Such trusts may be expressly created or may arise as a result from the termination of prior interests which leave a single beneficiary absolutely entitled to the trust property.

EXAMPLE 1

(1) Mr Taxconscious set up a trust for his granddaughter, Felicity (aged 2), under which she is absolutely entitled to the property. Such a trust may confer income and capital gains tax advantages in that it will enable use to be made of Felicity's income tax allowances and her CGT annual exemption.

(2) On the death of Mrs Lonelyheart her late husband's will trust is held for the benefit of his nephew absolutely.

14.57 It may be thought that the concept of a bare trust is also wide enough to encompass the following cases:

EXAMPLE 2

(3) Under the terms of the family's accumulation and maintenance trust the property vests in the twins, Jimmy and Jemima, absolutely when they become 25. Once that happens they are together absolutely entitled in undivided shares.

> (4) As in example (3) but the beneficiaries are not twins and Jimmy (only) has attained 25 (Jemima is 22). Under general rules Jimmy will be entitled to his share of the trust fund unless it comprises land or is otherwise subject to special rules[1]. Of course until such time as the assets are divided it will not be possible in either this example or in (3) to identify the property which is held for each absolutely entitled beneficiary.

1   See, for instance, *Snell's Equity*,30th Ed, 2000 at para 11.52 and note the important capital gains tax case of *Crowe v Appleby* [1976] 2 All ER 914, CA.

14.58   By contrast with the foregoing, the so-called rule in *Saunders v Vautier*[1] is capable of operating in a wider set of circumstances. It provides that, if the beneficiaries are *sui iuris* and together entitled to the whole beneficial interest, they can direct the trustees to hand over the trust property as they may direct.

> **EXAMPLE 3**
>
> (5) Property is held for Abel for life remainder to Cain. Together they could bring the trust to an end but there is no likely prospect of this happening[2].

1   (1841) 4 Beav 115; affd (1841) Cr & Ph 240.
2   Note also the possibility that they could replace the trustees under the Trusts of Land and Appointment of Trustees Act 1996, Pt II (see further para 3.8 above).

14.59   Whilst there is general agreement that examples (1) and (2) are bare trusts there is far from unanimity on the position of the trusts in examples (3), (4) and (5)[1].

1   Consider TA 2000, s 34 inserting TA 1925, s 19(3)(b) and compare Trusts of Land and Appointment of Trustees Act 1996, s 6(2) with s 7. The term 'a bare trust' has been described as 'ambiguous' (per Hall VC in *Christie v Ovington* (1875) 1 Ch D 279 at 281) and see also *Herdegen v Federal Comr of Taxation* (1988) 84 ALR 271 at 281 and the dissenting judgment of Millett LJ in *Ingram v IRC* [1997] 4 All ER 395, CA.

What duties do bare trustees have?

14.60   It is commonly said that bare trustees should act as directed by the absolutely entitled beneficiary. Whilst that is an accurate statement of their position in example (2) it cannot deal with the situation in example (1) until Felicity is of full age and able to exercise control over of the affairs of the trust. Likewise in examples (3) and (4) until the fund is appropriately divided and in (5) until the trust is brought to an end.

What powers do bare trustees have?

14.61   Bare trusts are, since 1 January 1997, capable of being trusts of land and hence the trustees possess all the powers of trustees of land and can, for instance, sell the property[1]. It seems clear that the powers given by the

Trustee Act 1925, the Trustee Investments Act 1961 and the Trustee Act 2000 all applied, or apply (as the case may be) to bare trustees.

1   For a consideration of the previous law see Megarry and Wade, *Law of Real Property*, (6th Ed) 2000 at para 8.129.

Other matters

14.62   First, an express bare trust may confer administrative powers on the trustees (this will commonly be the case when the trust is for an infant). Second, the bare trustees may have a lien over trust property in the case where there are contingent liabilities for which the trustees may be account-able and in such cases their powers to manage the property continue[1]. Finally, a nominee is usually considered to be a species of bare trustee but does it follow that, for instance, the nominee company of a bank holding securities for a customer has a duty to review those investments under TA 2000, s 4 and is subject to the duty of care? Surely not, and it is therefore suggested that, at least for these purposes, a distinction has to be drawn between nominees and bare trustees: it is obviously unfortunate that TA 2000 did not expressly deal with this matter.

1   See *X v A* [2000] 1 All ER 490.

Part IV:
Precedents

1 The Trusts of Land and Appointment of Trustees Act 1996

1

Express trust of land (discretionary)[1]

THIS SETTLEMENT is made the [   ] day of [   ]BETWEEN (1) [settlor] of [address] ('the Settlor') and (2) [original trustees] of [addresses] ('the Original Trustees')

WHEREAS

[(1)   By a conveyance of even date (executed contemporaneously with) and made between the same parties as this settlement ('the Convey-ance') the Settlor has conveyed to the Original Trustees certain freehold properties situated in the County of *(specify)* in fee simple subject as mentioned in the Conveyance to hold the same upon the trusts and with and subject to the powers and provisions declared and contained concerning the same in a settlement referred to in the Conveyance (meaning this settlement)]. [By a transfer of even date with this Deed the Settlor has transferred to the original trustees the property situated at [   ] and known as [   ] as the same is registered at HM Land Registry with absolute freehold title under title number [   ] to hold the same upon the trusts and with and subject to the powers and provisions of this settlement].

[(2)   The land [conveyed or transferred] to the Original Trustees to be held on the trusts of this settlement has been in the ownership of my family for many years and it is my wish that so far as is consistent with the interests of the beneficiaries under such trusts the Trustees should retain such land or the greater part of it so that it may remain in the possession of my family][2].

(3)   Further assets may in the future be paid or transferred to the Trustees to be held on and with and subject to such trusts powers and provisions.

[(4)   It is intended that this settlement shall be irrevocable][3]

[(5)   The Original Trustees have agreed to act as the first trustees of the settlement][4]

NOW THIS DEED WITNESSES as follows:

1   Definitions and interpretation

1.1   In this settlement the following expressions have where the context permits the following meanings:

1.1.1   'the Trustees' means the Original Trustees or other the trustees or trustee for the time being of this settlement and 'Trustee' means each and any of the Trustees;

1.1.2   'the Trust Fund' means the freehold properties [property] conveyed to the Original Trustees as recited above all property at any time added by way of further settlement accumulation of income capital accretion or otherwise and all property from time to time representing the same;

1.1.3   'the Discretionary Beneficiaries'[5] means (subject to the provisions of clause 6) the following persons:

1.1.3.1   the Settlor's [widow],

1.1.3.2   the issue (whether present or future) of the Settlor's grandfather [name of settlor's grandfather] but other than and excluding the Settlor,

1.1.3.3   any spouse for the time being and any widow or widower (whether or not for the time being remarried) of the individuals referred to in clause 1.1.3.2 above (but other than any spouse of the Settlor),

and 'Discretionary Beneficiary' has a corresponding meaning

1.1.4   'the Accumulation Period' means the period of 21 years commencing with the date of this deed;

1.1.5   'the Specified Period' means the period beginning at the date of this deed and enduring for 80 years and the said number of years shall be the perpetuity period applicable to this settlement;

1.1.6   'Charitable' means charitable (and exclusively charitable) according to the law for the time being of England and Wales;

1.1.7   'Charity' means a trust or corporation association society or other institution established only for Charitable purposes and 'Charities' have a corresponding meaning

[1.2   The provisions of this settlement shall be construed as though the Children Act 1989 the Legitimacy Act 1976 the Adoption Act 1976 and the Family Law Reform Act 1987 Sections 1 and 19 or any re-enactment of them had not been enacted][6]

[1.3   References in this settlement to the income of the Trust Fund shall
        (without any allocation or apportionment in favour of the Settlor)
        extend to the rents and profits now accrued or accruing but not yet
        actually payable][7]

2   Principal trusts[8]

2.1   The Trustees shall stand possessed of the Trust Fund and the income
        from it on such trusts and with and subject to such charges powers and
        provisions whatever in favour or for the benefit of all or any one or
        more exclusively of the others or other of the Discretionary Beneficiar-
        ies as the Trustees (being at least two in number or a trust corporation)
        in their absolute discretion shall at any time or times during the
        Specified Period by any deed or deeds revocable or irrevocable appoint
        (regard being had to the law relating to remoteness).

2.2   Subject as stated above and subject also as is provided in clause 2.4
        below any trust appointed under the power contained in clause 2.1
        above may be mandatory or discretionary and may create any
        interest or interests whatever whether absolute or limited and
        whether vested or contingent and whether in possession or rever-
        sion and may divide the property subject to it or the income from it
        into any shares and may provide for the accumulation of the whole
        or any part of the income subject to it during the Accumulation
        Period (or during any other permissible period) and any discretion-
        ary trust or power may by such appointment be conferred on any
        person or persons (not necessarily being or including the Trustees)
        and any such trusts or powers so conferred may authorise the
        delegation to an unlimited extent of any discretion.

2.3   Without prejudice to the generality of the above any appointment
        contained under the power contained in clause 2.1 may (if the
        Trustees in their absolute discretion think fit) appoint on trust or
        trusts to pay or transfer immediately any income or capital of the
        Trust Fund or any part or parts of it to the trustees of any other trust
        or settlement (wherever established or existing) under which any
        one or more of the Discretionary Beneficiaries is or are beneficially
        interested (whether or not such one or more of the Discretionary
        Beneficiaries is or are the only persons interested or capable of
        benefiting under such trust or settlement) so long as neither the
        settlor nor any spouse of the settlor shall be interested or capable of
        benefiting under such other trust or settlement.

2.4   PROVIDED always that:

        2.4.1   no exercise of the power of appointment conferred by clause
                 2.1 above shall affect any capital or income of the Trust Fund
                 (or any share or part of it) previously paid transferred or
                 applied (except merely by accumulation) to or for the benefit
                 of any person under the other provisions of this settlement
                 or any income (except accumulated income) of the Trust
                 Fund (or any share or part of it) accruing prior to such
                 appointment;

2.4.2   the Trustees (being at least two in number or a trust corporation) may at any time or times before the expiration of the Specified Period by deed or deeds extinguish (or restrict the future exercise of) the power conferred by clause 2.1 above.

3   Powers of maintenance

3.1   In default[9] of and until and subject to any and every appointment made under the power or powers conferred by clause 2.1 above the income of the Trust Fund shall during the Specified Period be held by the Trustees upon trust to pay or apply or (in the case of a minor) allocate the same to or for the maintenance support or otherwise for the benefit in any manner of all or any one or more exclusively of the others or other of the Discretionary Beneficiaries for the time being in existence and if more than one in such shares and in such manner in all respects as the Trustees shall in their absolute discretion without being liable in any such case to account for the exercise of such discretion think fit.

3.2   PROVIDED always that the Trustees shall not be bound to apply or allocate the whole or any part of the income accruing to the Trust Fund during the Accumulation Period but may during the Accumulation Period pay apply or allocate only so much of the income as the Trustees shall in their absolute discretion think fit and shall accumulate the surplus (if any) of such income at compound interest by investing the same and the resulting income from it in any of the investments authorised by this settlement and shall hold such accumulations as an accretion to (and as one fund with) the capital of the Trust Fund.

4   Trust for Discretionary Beneficiaries

In default[10] of and subject to any and every appointment made under the power or powers conferred by clause 2.1 above the Trust Fund and the future income from it shall from and after the end of the Specified Period be held upon trust absolutely for such of the Discretionary Beneficiaries as are living at the end of the Specified Period in equal shares per capita[11].

5   Ultimate trust

Subject to all the trusts powers and provisions of this settlement and if and so far as (for any reason whatever) not wholly disposed of by it the Trust Fund and the income from it shall be held upon trust for (name)[12].

6   Alteration of class of beneficiaries[13]

6.1   Subject to clause 6.2 below:

6.1.1   the Trustees (being at least two in number or a trust corporation) shall have power by any deed or deeds revocable or irrevocable executed during the Specified Period to declare that any individual or individuals (not being the Settlor or any spouse of the Settlor) whether or not then born or ascertained or any Charity or Charities (other than any individual then a Trustee and other than any individual or Charity previously excluded under the power set out in clause 6.1.2 below) shall from such time and (subject to any future exercise of the power contained in clause 6.1.2 below) either permanently or for such period or periods as shall be specified in any such deed or deeds be included in the class of the Discretionary Beneficiaries defined in clause 1.1.3 above;

6.1.2   the Trustees (being not less than two in number or a trust corporation) shall also have power by any deed or deeds revocable or irrevocable executed during the Specified Period to declare that any individual or individuals whether or not born or ascertained or any Charity or Charities who or which is or are a member or members (or eligible to be added as a member or members) of the class of the Discretionary Beneficiaries immediately prior to the execution of such deed or deeds shall from such time and either permanently or for such period or periods as shall be specified in any such deed or deeds cease to be a member or members (or eligible to become a member or members) of such class.

6.2   PROVIDED always that:

6.2.1   no such deed made in exercise of the power conferred by clause 6.1 above shall affect the validity or effect of:

6.2.1.1   any distribution previously made to or for the benefit of any beneficiary under or pursuant to any power or discretion,

6.2.1.2   any transmissible interest (whether vested or contingent) previously conferred on any beneficiary either by clauses 4 and 5 above or under or pursuant to any irrevocable exercise of the power of appointment conferred by clause 2 above, or

6.2.1.3   any future distribution to any beneficiary consequent on the absolute vesting in possession of any such interest as is mentioned in clause 6.2.1.2 above,

6.2.2   the Trustees being not less than two in number or a trust corporation may at any time or times during the Specified Period by deed or deeds extinguish (or restrict the future exercise of) the power (but not any of the restrictions applicable to the same) conferred by clause 6.1 above.

7   Exclusion of apportionment

Where under the trusts for the time being affecting the same there is a change in the person or persons beneficially or prospectively beneficially entitled to the income of any part of the Trust Fund (whether due to the birth or death of any person or for any other reason whatever) the provisions of the Apportionment Act 1870 shall not apply and no apportionment shall be made of income accruing or accrued or of outgoings being expended on the occasion of such change in beneficial entitlement but rather the same shall be treated as having accrued due or become a proper liability on the day of actual receipt or expenditure (as the case may be)[14].

8 Administrative provisions[15]

8.1 Subject to clause 8.2 below the Trustees shall during the Specified Period and during such further period (if any) as the law may allow have the additional powers set out in the Schedule.

8.2 PROVIDED always that the Trustees (being not less than two in number or a trust corporation) may at any time or times during the Specified Period by deed or deeds extinguish (or restrict the future exercise of) all or any of the powers (but not any of the restrictions applicable to them) conferred by clause 8.1 above.

[8.3 If in the administration of the Trust Fund any transaction is in the opinion of the Trustees expedient but the same cannot be effected by reason of the absence of any sufficient power for that purpose conferred by this deed or by law (or by any earlier exercise of the present power) than the Trustees may by deed confer upon themselves either generally or for the purpose of any particular transaction or transactions the necessary power and from the execution of such a deed the Trustees shall have such power as if it had been conferred by this Deed.] [Provided that before executing any such deed the Trustees shall obtain the written opinion of a counsel of at least ten years' standing practising in trust law that the possession by the trustees of such power is desirable in the interests of the beneficiaries.]

9 Trustees' charges and remuneration[16]

9.1 Any of the Trustees who shall be an individual engaged in any profession or business which consists of or includes the administration of trusts, or the management of assets of a type comprised in the Trust Fund or the advising of trustees either generally or in respect of any particular aspect of their functions or obligations either alone or in partnership shall be entitled to charge and be paid and to retain all professional or other charges for any business carried out or time spent or services rendered by him or his firm in connection with the trusts powers and provisions of this settlement or of any assurance of immovable property upon the trusts of his settlement and any of the Trustees being an individual who is employed by any company partnership or individual engaged in any such profession or business shall be entitled to charge and be paid and to retain reasonable charges for time spent and services rendered by him in connection with the trusts powers and provisions of this Deed and any such individuals respectively shall also be entitled to retain a share of brokerage or commission paid to him or his firm by any broker agent or insurance office in connection with any acquisition of or dealing with any investment or property or the effecting or payment of any premium or any policy of insurance subject to the trusts of this settlement.

9.2   None of the Trustees holding any directorship or other office or employment or retainer in relation to any company all or any of whose shares stock or securities shall at any time be subject to any trusts of this settlement shall be accountable for any remuneration received in connection with such directorship office employment or retainer.

9.3   Notwithstanding anything contained in this clause neither the Settlor nor any spouse of the Settlor who may be for the time being one of the Trustees shall be entitled to charge or be paid or retain any or any share of any professional or other charges by reason of this clause or be relieved thereby from any liability to account as a trustee for any money or assets[17].

10   Corporate Trustees

10.1   A corporation (whether or not a trust corporation) may at any time be appointed to be one of the Trustees on such reasonable terms as to remuneration and charging and otherwise however as shall be agreed at the time when the appointment is made between the person or persons making the appointment on the one hand and the corporation on the other.

10.2   The provisions of the Trustee Act 1925, s 37 in their application to this settlement shall be varied so that for each reference to 'a trust corporation' there shall be substituted a reference to 'a corporation (whether or not a trust corporation)'[18].

11   Exclusion of Self Dealing

Any of the Trustees may exercise or concur in exercising any powers and discretions given by this settlement or by law notwithstanding that he has a direct or other personal interest in the mode or result of any such exercise but any such Trustee may abstain from acting except as a merely formal party in any matter in which he may be so personally interested and may allow his co-trustees or co-trustee to act alone in relation thereto[19].

12   Protection of Trustees

12.1   In the professed execution of the trusts and powers of this settlement or of any assurance of immovable property upon the trusts of this settlement none of the Trustees (being an individual) shall be liable for any loss arising by reason of any improper investment made in good faith or the retention of any improper investment or any failure to see to the [insurance of or] preservation of any chattels or the making or revising of any inventory of them or for the negligence or fraud of any agent employed by him or by any other of the Trustees (although the employment of such agent was not strictly necessary or expedient) or by reason of any other matter or thing whatever except wilful and individual fraud or wrongdoing on the part of that one of the Trustees who is sought to be made liable[20].

12.2   The Trustees shall not be bound or required to interfere in the management or conduct of the affairs or business of any company in respect of which the Trustees shall hold or control the whole or a majority or any part of the shares carrying the control of the company or other the voting rights of the company and so long as there shall be no notice of any act of dishonesty or misappropriation of money on the part of the directors having the management of such company the Trustees shall be at liberty to leave the conduct of its business (including the payment or non-payment of dividends) wholly to such directors.

[12.3   The Trustees shall not be obliged to insure any buildings situate on land for the time being subject to the trusts of this settlement or any chattels or other assets for the time being so subject and shall not be liable for any loss resulting from any failure or omission to effect or maintain any such insurance or for the insufficiency of the amount of the cover or the risks covered under any insurance that is effected by them][21].

13   Exclusion of the Settlor and spouse from benefit

Notwithstanding anything in this settlement expressed or implied no money or other assets subject to the trusts of this settlement shall in any circumstances whatever be paid or transferred beneficially (except for full consideration) to or lent to or applied (whether directly or indirectly) for the benefit of the Settlor or any spouse of the Settlor[22].

14   Appointment of new Trustees

14.1   The power of appointing a new Trustee or new Trustees shall (subject to clause 14.3 below) be vested in the Settlor during the life of the Settlor[23].

14.2   Any individual or corporation may be appointed as a Trustee notwithstanding that such individual or corporation is resident domiciled or incorporated outside the United Kingdom and notwithstanding that as a result of such appointment (or any retirement occurring in connection with it) all or a majority of the Trustees are persons resident domiciled or incorporated outside the United Kingdom.

14.3   It is declared (for the avoidance of any doubt) that the Settlor may at any time or times by deed release (or restrict the future exercise of) the power conferred on the Settlor by clause 14.1 above and it is further declared that the provisions of the Trustee Act 1925, s 36 in their application to this settlement shall be varied so that it shall not be a ground for the appointment of a new Trustee that an existing Trustee has remained out of the United Kingdom for more than 12 months.

15 Exclusion of s 11

The provisions of s 11(1) of the Trusts of Land and Appointment of Trustees Act 1996 shall not apply to any land situated in England and Wales which is at any time subject to the trusts of this Deed[24].

[16 Exclusion of s 1]

The provisions of Sub-s (1) of s 1 of the Trustee Delegation Act 1999 shall not apply to any Trustee or Trustees for the time being of this settlement][25].

[17 Exclusion of the Duty of Care]

The duty of care contained in s 1 of the Trustee Act 2000 shall not apply to the Trustees in the exercise of any of the powers conferred on them by this settlement nor to any duties relating to the exercise of such powers nor to the exercise by the Trustees of any powers contained in or duties imposed by the Trustee Act 2000, the Trustee Act 1925, the Trusts of Land and Appointment of Trustees Act 1996 or any other statute where the duty of care is expressed to be applicable][26].

18 Clause headings

The headings to the clauses and paragraphs of this settlement are for the purposes of information only and are not part of and shall not be used in the construction of this settlement or any part of it.

IN WITNESS etc

SCHEDULE

Administrative Powers

1 Application of money requiring investment[27]

Power as regards any money for the time being subject to the provisions of this settlement and requiring investment to invest or lay out the same in the purchase or otherwise in the acquisition of or at interest upon the security of any shares stocks funds securities policies of insurance or other investments or property (movable or immovable) of whatever nature and wherever situated and whether or not productive of income and whether involving liability or not or upon such personal credit with or without security in all respects as the Trustees shall in their discretion think fit to the intent that the Trustees shall have the same full and unrestricted powers of investing and transposing investments and dealing with trust money and buying or selling property in all respects as if they were absolutely entitled beneficially and so that the acquisition with trust money of property with a view to its enjoyment in kind by a Discretionary Beneficiary or Discretionary Beneficiaries in accordance with the provisions of paragraph 22 below shall for the purpose of this settlement be deemed to be an investment of trust money.

2 Retention of assets

Power to accept or acquire and retain any assets subject or to be subject to the trusts declared by this settlement (including any uninvested money) in their actual state and condition for any period even although the whole or a substantial part of the assets so subject may be producing no or little income or may consist of shares or securities of a single company.

3 Transposition of investments

Power at any time or times to sell or convert or call in any investments or other property for the time being comprised in the Trust Fund or to transpose or convert the same into any other investments or property the acquisition of which with money subject to this settlement is by this settlement authorised.

4 Improvements to land

Power at any time or times to apply any money subject to the trusts of this settlement in making improvements to or otherwise developing or using any land or buildings or in erecting enlarging repairing decorating making alterations to or improvements in or pulling down and rebuilding any buildings which shall be subject to the same trusts.

5 Leases and mortgaging

Power to lease let licence mortgage and charge and to grant tenancies and licences and to accept surrenders of leases tenancies and licences and to enter into and carry into effect any grants agreements or arrangements whatever of or relating to and generally to manage and deal with any land or buildings which shall for the time being be subject to any trusts of this settlement in all respects as if the Trustees were an absolute beneficial owner of such land or buildings and so that no mortgagee or chargee or intending mortgagee or chargee dealing with the Trustees in regard to any such land or buildings shall be concerned to see for what purpose any money is raised or as to the application of such money PROVIDED that nothing in this paragraph shall affect or restrict any power conferred on the Trustees in respect of land situated in England and Wales or elsewhere in the United Kingdom conferred by the Trusts of Land and Appointment of Trustees Act 1996, s 6(1) or the Trustee Act 2000, s 8(3).

6 Hiring of chattels

Power to hire out or lend or bail any movable chattels for any period or periods and for any consideration whatever.

7 Mortgaging of chattels etc

In relation to any property other than land and buildings the like powers of mortgaging charging and entering into and carrying into effect any agreements or arrangements whatever as are given by paragraph 5 above in regard to land and buildings.

8 Borrowing

Power to borrow or raise money for the purposes of mere investment or for acquiring any property either without security or on the security of the whole or part of the Trust Fund and any property so acquired.

9 Guarantees

Without prejudice to the generality of paragraphs 5 and 7 of this schedule power to effect any mortgage or charge under those paragraphs as collateral security for or to guarantee money payable in respect of any loan to a Discretionary Beneficiary or Discretionary Beneficiaries upon such terms in all respects as the Trustees shall in their absolute discretion think fit PROVIDED that this power shall not be exercised except in conformity with the beneficial trusts for the time being governing the Trust Fund (or the part of it affected by such mortgage charge or guarantee) and the income from it.

10 Arbitration

Power to refer to arbitration or to the determination of any expert:

10.1   the amount of the money to be received or paid on any sale or purchase or exchange;

10.2   the amount of the rent or other payment to be reserved by any lease tenancy agreement or licence in respect of the whole or any part of the term or currency of such lease and the covenants and provisions to be contained in any such lease tenancy agreement or licence;

10.3   the terms for the surrender or other termination of any lease tenancy or licence; and

10.4   all disputes between any tenant or licensee and the reversioner or licensor.

11 Appropriation

Power from time to time to set such a value upon any investments or other property forming part of the Trust Fund as the Trustees shall think fit and to appropriate if they shall think fit any such investments or property at such value in or towards satisfaction of any share or interest under the trusts affecting the same[28]

12 Valuation

Power at any time or times to have any assets valued for any purpose in such manner as the Trustees shall in their discretion think fit.

13 Promotion of companies

Power to promote or form or join in promoting or forming any company or corporation for the purpose of acquiring or taking on lease or hire for any estate or interest all or any of the assets which are held on the trusts of this settlement or for any other purpose whatever connected with any assets which are subject or are to become subject to any of those trusts.

14 Subscription for shares etc

Power to subscribe for all or any of the shares debentures or other securities of any such company or corporation as is mentioned in paragraph 13 above.

15 Sales etc for paper consideration

Power to sell transfer let or hire out for any estate or interest any assets which are subject to any of the trusts of this settlement in consideration of the issue or transfer to the Trustees or their nominees of any stock shares debentures or other securities.

16 Rights attached to investments

Power to exercise or refrain from exercising (either themselves or by proxy) the rights attached to any investments subject to any of the trusts of this settlement in any manner whatever and in particular (without prejudice to the generality of the above) to wind up or dissolve or join in winding up or dissolving any company or corporation and to alter or join in altering any of those rights or any rights attached to any other investments or property.

17 Farming and other business activity

Power upon or in any land and buildings which are held upon any of the trusts of this settlement to carry on the business (whether alone or in partnership with any other person) of farming forestry fruit growing or market gardening or any other business of an agricultural horticultural or aboricultural nature or of any other nature and to employ in it all or any part or parts of any assets subject to the same trusts and to finance such business out of those trust assets with full power to engage remunerate and dismiss any managers bailiffs servants and agents and to appoint regulate and change their respective duties[29].

18 Nominees

Power to put or leave any shares stocks securities insurance policies or other property whatever (including money) in the name or names of any nominee or nominees for the Trustees and to put or leave any movable chattels for safe keeping in the possession or custody of any person or persons without being responsible for any loss or damage and on such terms and subject to such conditions including remuneration of any such nominee or custodian (other than the Settlor or any spouse of the Settlor) as the Trustees shall think fit and so that any such nominees or custodians may be or include any one or more of the Trustees[30]. [Sections 16 and 17 of the Trustee Act 2000 shall not apply to this Deed]. [The provisions of s 22 of the Trustee Act 2000 shall not apply to any nominee or custodian appointed by the Trustees pursuant to this power].

19   Insurance[31]

19.1   Power to effect maintain and deal with any insurance or insurances upon the life of any person PROVIDED:

19.1.1   that the Trustees may pay all premiums and other costs relating to such insurance out of the income or the capital of the Trust Fund,

19.1.2   that nothing in this paragraph shall authorise any accumulations of income within the Law of Property Act 1925 s 164.

19.2   The Trustees shall have in respect of any policy or policies entered into under the above power all the powers of an absolute owner including the power to surrender convert or otherwise deal with any such policy or policies or any bonuses attaching to them or part of them in such manner as the Trustees shall consider most beneficial to the persons beneficially interested under these trusts.

20   Maintenance etc of chattels

Power to maintain repair improve and alter any movable chattels and to take such steps as they may consider proper for the preservation of any movable chattels or other assets subject to any trusts of this settlement.

[21   Delegation[32]

Power to delegate all or any of the powers of the Trustees contained in this schedule (including this power) and any administrative power conferred by law (and all or any of the duties and discretions of the Trustees relating to the exercise of such powers) to any person or persons (not being the Settlor or any spouse of the Settlor) subject to such conditions (if any) and upon such terms (including the remuneration of any such delegate and so that in the case of a delegation to two or more persons such delegates may be authorised to act jointly and severally) as the Trustees shall think fit (without being liable for the acts or defaults of any such delegate) and to revoke or modify any such delegation or conditions or terms. [Section 11 of the Trustee Act 2000 shall not apply to this Deed]. [The provisions of s 22 of the Trustee Act 2000 shall not apply to any delegate or agent appointed by the Trustees pursuant to the foregoing power]].

22   Use of property in kind

Power (subject as provided below) to permit a Discretionary Beneficiary or Discretionary Beneficiaries (either alone or concurrently or successively) to occupy use or enjoy personally any movable or immovable property which may for the time being be comprised in the Trust Fund upon any terms or conditions whatever which the Trustees may think fit PROVIDED that this power shall not be exercised except in conformity with the beneficial trusts powers and provisions for the time being governing the Trust Fund (or the part of it in which such movable or immovable property is so comprised) and the income from it[33].

23   Loans to Discretionary Beneficiaries

Power (subject as provided below) to lend any money with or without security to a Discretionary Beneficiary or Discretionary Beneficiaries with or without payment of interest and upon such terms as to repayment and otherwise in such manner in all respects as the Trustees shall in their absolute discretion think fit PROVIDED that this power shall not be exercised except in conformity with the beneficial trusts powers and provisions for the time being governing the Trust Fund (or the part of it from which such loan is to be made) and the income from it[34].

24   Transactions with other trustees

Power from time to time in their absolute discretion to enter into any agreement or transaction with the trustee or trustees of any other settlement or will (being an agreement or transaction which apart from this present provision the Trustees could properly have entered into if one or more of them had not also been a trustee of such other settlement or will) notwith-standing that the Trustees or one or more of them may also be trustees or a trustee or the sole trustee of such other settlement or will and in like manner in all respects as if none of the Trustees were a trustee of such other settlement or will.

25   Power to sign cheques

Power to permit any one or more of the Trustees to sign cheques on any bank account in the names of the Trustees and generally to sign orders and authorities to any bank on behalf of the Trustees.

26   Additions

Power (if the Trustees think fit) to accept any assets which may be transferred or otherwise given to the Trustees as an addition to the capital of the Trust Fund on terms that any inheritance tax that is payable in consequence of such transfer or gift shall be payable out of and borne by the Trust Fund and not by the transferor or donor personally and also power (if the Trustees think fit) to pay any capital transfer tax or inheritance tax that may from time to time be levied on the Trust Fund or any part of it notwithstanding that some other person or persons may also be liable to pay such tax.

27 Receipts

27.1 Where the Trustees are authorised or required to pay or apply any capital money or income to or for the benefit of any person who does not have the capacity to give a valid receipt for it the Trustees may pay the same to any parent or guardian of such person for the benefit of such person without seeing to the application of it or themselves apply the same for the benefit of such person as may be directed in writing by such parent or guardian and the receipt of such parent or guardian shall be a sufficient discharge to the Trustees.

27.2 The receipt of the person professing to be the treasurer or other proper officer of any charity to which any capital or income may be payable or transferable under this settlement shall be a sufficient discharge to the Trustees.

28 Incidental costs

Power to pay out of the Trust Fund the costs of and incidental to the preparation and completion of this settlement (including any stamp duty payable on it).

[signatures of the parties]

[signatures of witnesses]

1 Stamp duty of £5 is payable on this declaration of trust. This settlement contains a discretionary trust for a wide range of beneficiaries both named and by way of class and is capable of lasting for at least 80 years. The settlor should supplement the trust deed with a letter of wishes which he can review from time to time. It is assumed that no trust for sale has been imposed in respect of the properties conveyed which are therefore held on a trust of land under which there is no duty to sell.

2 This recital has been included in the light of TA 2000, ss 4–5 and especially s 4(3)(b) which imposes a requirement on trustees to diversify the investments in the trust 'insofar as is appropriate to the circumstances of the trust'. See further para 11.34 above.

3 This provision is declaratory: settlements are irrevocable unless the deed of settlement provides to the contrary.

4 This provision is declaratory: the trustees agree to act by executing the deed. Similarly clause 14 is declaratory.

5 Discretionary beneficiaries are commonly defined to include the settlor's issue and spouses of such issue but to expressly exclude both the settlor and his spouse where they would otherwise be included. If this exclusion is not made then not only may income tax and capital gains tax problems arise but, in addition, the Inland Revenue may argue that the settlor has reserved a benefit in his settlement for inheritance tax purposes. Including the widow (or widower) of the settlor does not give rise to any of these difficulties. For the power to change the beneficial class see clause 6.

6 This clause excludes (so far as their benefits depend on description through relationship) all persons who are legitimated, adopted, or illegitimate and any person who traces a relationship through them. Consequently, the inclusion of this clause should be made only after express instructions have been taken from the settlor.

7 The rent produced by the land may require apportionment (although not if it was payable in advance).

8 This clause gives the trustees wide discretionary powers over the capital (and income) of the fund.

9 The default clause operates with regard to the income of the trust fund pending exercise by the trustees of the dispositive powers in clause 2. The accumulation period is defined as a period of 21 years running from the date of creation of the settlement. If desired one of the

alternative periods set out in the Law of Property Act 1925, s 164 as modified by the Perpetuities and Accumulations Act 1964, s 13 may be employed.

10   The default provision will apply (subject to any exercise of the powers given to the trustees in clause 2) at the end of the specified period.

11   Default trusts sometimes include a stirpital addition along the following lines:

'PROVIDED that if any of them shall have died during the Specified Period leaving issue living at the end of the Specified Period such issue shall take by substitution and if more than one in equal shares per stirpes the share of such part of the Trust Fund as stated above which the person so dying would have taken if he or she had survived until the end of the Specified Period but so that no issue shall take whose parent is alive at the end of the Specified Period and capable of taking'.

This would produce a most confusing situation in cases like this where the discretionary beneficiaries are defined as being all the issue of the settlor's grandfather. If a discretionary beneficiary therefore dies leaving children and grandchildren those children and grand-children themselves will be discretionary beneficiaries and therefore there could be a multiple claim: an individual might claim as being both a discretionary beneficiary living at the end of the specified period and also by substitution of part of a parent's share and/or part of a grandparent's share.

12   This clause is a long stop.

13   This clause enables the trustees to include or exclude, either permanently or for a specified period, any person (or charity) in or from the beneficial class. The exercise of this power does not affect the validity of anything which has already occurred.

14   It is usual to exclude apportionment calculations (which can be complex) under the Apportionment Act 1870.

15   The powers set out in the schedule supplement those already possessed by the trustees: eg under the Trusts of Land and Appointment of Trustees Act 1996 and under the Trustee Act 2000. Given changing conditions it can be useful to have the power to confer extra powers contained in sub-clause 8.3.

16   This provision is intended to circumvent that part of the conflict of interest rules developed by the courts: see further *Snell's Equity* (30th edn, 2000) para 11.87. For a consideration of the drafting of remuneration clauses after TA 2000, see **Precedent 53**. See also, on conflicts of interest, clause 11 below.

17   Neither the settlor nor his spouse may obtain any remuneration from the trust; this provision is important to avoid any suggestion that the reservation of benefit rules could apply. See note 4 above.

18   The amendment made to the wording of the Trustee Act 1925, s 37 is designed to avoid the difficulties that may arise if it is decided to export the trust. On exports of trust see further clauses 14.2 and 14.3 and para 6.68 above.

19   For the self dealing rule, see footnote 16 above. Although it may be argued that a trustee selected by the settlor, who is also a beneficiary, should be free to make appointments in his own favour, this clause is intended to put the matter beyond doubt.

20   This clause offers wide protection to trustees who have not committed wilful and individual fraud or wrongdoing. Express instructions from the settlor should be taken before including this clause.

21   The words between square brackets in sub-clause 12.1 should be omitted if the optional sub-clause 12.3 is included. There is some uncertainty as to whether if the trustees have a power to insure they have a duty to do so. Sub-clause 12.3 is designed to remove any such possible liability.

22   The exclusion of the settlor and his spouse from benefiting is dictated by tax considera-tions. See note 5 above.

23   The settlor should consider giving the main beneficiary the power to appoint new trustees after his death.

24   Although the Trusts of Land and Appointment of Trustees Act 1996, Pt II will not apply to the trust in its present form, the settlor may wish to exclude it in case the beneficiaries in the future fall within the terms of the Trusts of Land and Appointment of Trustees Act 1996, s 19(1)(b).

25   The provisions of the Trustee Delegation Act 1999, s 1 are often considered unsatisfactory in their application to a continuing trust. Its provisions can be excluded: s 1(3).

26   The statutory duty of care imposed by the Trustee Act 2000, s 1 can be excluded: see para 7 of the Schedule to the Act.

27   An express power of investment has been retained. It enables the trustees to:

(a)   acquire assets (including land) which are not income producing; and

(b)   irrespective of where such assets are situated; and to

(c)   acquire assets (including but not limited to land) for use by a Discretionary Beneficiary.

The provisions of TA 2000, Pts II and III will apply to supplement this clause: eg to enable land to be acquired for a purpose other than as an investment or for beneficial occupation (see further para 11.68 above).

28   The power of appropriation given in the Administration of Estates Act 1925, s 41 as amended does not extend to trustees.

29   This makes explicit what might otherwise be implied from the Trusts of Land and Appointment of Trustees Act 1996, s 6(1). However, it cannot be certain that s 6 can be used to establish business activities on land which might involve the use of trust assets other than land. For a general power to carry on a business see **Precedent 47** and to form a limited liability partnership, **Precedent 48**.

30   The use of an express clause to appoint nominees and/or custodians may be preferred to the statutory power in the Trustee Act 2000, ss 16 and 17 as the choice of nominees and custodians is not limited to those fulfilling the conditions contained in s 19 of the Act. The duty to review contained in s 22 of the Act can be excluded: see s 21(3).

31   This paragraph only confers a power to effect life insurance. The power to insure assets contained in the Trustee Act 1925, s 15 (as inserted by the Trustee Act 2000, s 34) would appear adequate. See also **Precedent 46**.

32   The use of an express clause giving a power of collective delegation of administrative powers may be considered preferable to the statutory former power now contained in the Trustee Act 2000, s 11 as the latter does not prevent delegation to a beneficiary. The duty to review contained in the Trustee Act 2000, s 22 can be excluded: see s 21(3).

33   Considerable care must be exercised by the trustees to ensure that any such exercise will not result in the beneficiary obtaining an interest in possession in the relevant property: see *Sansom v Peay* [1976] 3 All ER 375, [1976] 1WLR 1073; Inland Revenue Statement of Practice SP 10/79 (15 August 1979). The right to occupy provisions in the Trusts of Land and Appointment of Trustees Act 1996, ss 12, 13 do not apply to a trust in discretionary form.

34   The Inland Revenue have been known in the past to contend that the making of a loan can create an interest in possession and thereby create an exit charge for the purposes of inheritance tax. It is not thought that this is current practice.

2A

Conveyance of land to trustees on trust of land or trust for sale[1]

THIS CONVEYANCE is made the [   ] day of [   ] BETWEEN (1) [settlor] of [address] and (2) [trustee] of [address] and [trustee] of [address] ('the Trustees' which expression where the context permits includes the trustees or trustee for the time being of this deed)

WHEREAS

(1)   The Settlor is the estate owner in respect of the fee simple absolute in possession of the pieces of land described in the schedule ('the Property') and desires to make the following disposition.

(2)   This deed is made in consideration of the love and affection of the Settlor for the several persons designated as [Discretionary Beneficiaries] in a deed of settlement of even date (executed contemporaneously with) and made between the same parties as this conveyance ('the Deed of Settlement').

NOW THIS DEED WITNESSES as follows:

1   Conveyance

The Settlor conveys the Property to the Trustees TO HOLD to the Trustees in fee simple subject to all subsisting tenancies tithe redemption annuities easements restrictions and covenants as may affect the same or part of it on the trusts and with and subject to the powers and provisions [declared and contained below] or [declared and contained concerning the same in the Deed of Settlement][2].

2   Easements

It is agreed and declared that all existing easements or quasi-easements as to way drains light air flow of water eavesdrop fall pipes spouts electricity and water mains and all other matters and things which have been used and enjoyed by the Property and the adjoining land and property shall continue to be used and enjoyed accordingly notwithstanding severance of the ownership of the same.

[3   Trust for sale

The Trustees shall hold the Property on trust that the Trustees shall in their discretion sell the Property at such time or times as they think proper with full power to postpone the sale of all or any part of it (and so that all the powers and provisions in this deed regarding the Property until sale of it shall so far as the nature of the case admits apply to any unsold part or parts of it)][3].

[4   Trusts

The Trustees shall hold the net money to arise from any sale and the net rents and profits of the Property until sale on the trusts and with and subject to the powers and provisions declared and contained concerning the same in the Deed of Settlement][4].

5   Appointment of new Trustees

5.1   The power of appointing a new trustee or new trustees of this deed shall (subject to clause 5.3) be vested in the Settlor during the Settlor's life.

5.2   Any individual or corporation may be appointed as a trustee of this deed notwithstanding that such individual or corporation is resident domiciled or incorporated outside the United Kingdom and notwithstanding that as a result of such appointment (or any retirement occurring in connection therewith) all or a majority of the Trustees are persons resident domiciled or incorporated outside the United Kingdom and the provisions of the Trustee Act 1925, s 36 in their application to this deed shall be varied so that it shall not be a ground for the appointment of a new trustee of this deed that an existing trustee has remained out of the United Kingdom for more than 12 months.

5.3   For the avoidance of doubt it is declared that the Settlor may at any time or times by deed release (or restrict the future exercise of) the power conferred on [him] by clause 5.1 above.

5.4   A corporation (whether or not a trust corporation) may at any time be appointed to be a trustee of this deed upon such terms as to remuneration and charging and otherwise as shall be agreed at the time when the appointment is made between the person or persons making the appointment on the one hand and the corporation on the other.

5.5   The provisions of the Trustee Act 1925, s 37 in their application to this deed shall be varied so that for each reference in it to 'a trust corporation' there shall be substituted a reference to 'a corporation (whether or not a trust corporation)'[5].

6   Stamp duty

It is certified that this instrument falls within category L in the Schedule to the Stamp Duty (Exempt Instruments) Regulations 1987[6].

IN WITNESS etc

SCHEDULE

The Property

[describe property conveyed]

[signatures of the parties]

[signatures of witnesses]

1   This Precedent is for a voluntary disposition of land and may be used in conjunction with the express trust of land at **Precedent 1**. Such a disposition may attract a capital gains tax charge and (if the land is to be held on discretionary trusts) an inheritance tax liability (although if this is the case any capital gains tax charge may be postponed by a hold-over election). A stamp duty declaration is included.

2   The first set of wording should be inserted where the trustees are directed to hold the land on a trust for sale. If it is not desired to impose a trust for sale (but to have the land held on a trust of land) then the second set of wording should be inserted.

3   Clauses 3 and 4 should be inserted where the trustees are directed to hold the land on a trust for sale with an express power to postpone. If it is not desired to impose a trust for sale (but to have the land held on a trust of land) these clauses should be omitted.

4   Consideration should be given to excluding the operation of the Trusts of Land and Appointment of Trustees Act 1996, Pt II: see para 3.31 above.

5   Although 'persons' has now replaced 'individuals' in the Trustee Act 1925 s 37 as amended by the Trusts of Land and Appointment of Trustees Act 1996, Sch 3, para 3(12), it is still necessary to appoint at least two persons or a trust corporation. This sub-clause permits a single corporation to be appointed.

6   Ie the Stamp Duty (Exempt Instruments) Regulations 1987/516. Instruments correctly certified in accordance with these regulations are exempted from the fixed duty of £5 to which they would otherwise be liable.

2B

Transfer of land to trustees on trust of land or trust for sale

**Transfer of whole
of registered title(s)**

HM Land Registry TR1

(if you need more room than is provided for in a panel, use continuation sheet CS and staple to this form)

1. Stamp Duty
Place 'X' in the box that applies and complete the box in the appropriate certificate. ☒ I/We hereby certify that this instrument falls within category ⬛ in the Schedule to the Stamp Duty (Exempt Instruments) Regulations 1987 ☐ It is certified that the transaction effected does not form part of a larger transaction or of a series of transactions in respect of which the amount or value or the aggregate amount or value of the consideration exceeds the sum of £
2. Title Number(s) of the Property *(leave blank if not yet registered)*
3. Property   *If this transfer is made under section 37 of the Land Registration Act 1925 following a not-yet-registered dealing with part only of the land in a title, or is made under rule 72 of the Land Registration Rules 1925, include a reference to the last preceding document of title containing a description of the property.*

---

4. Date

---

5. Transferor *(give full names and Company's Registered Number if any)*

---

6. Transferee **for entry on the register** *(Give full names and Company's Registered Number if any; for Scottish Co. Reg. Nos., use an SC prefix. For foreign companies give territory in which incorporated.)*

Unless otherwise arranged with Land Registry headquarters, a certified copy of the transferee's constitution (in English or Welsh) will be required if it is a body corporate but is not a company registered in England and Wales or Scotland under the Companies Acts.

---

7. Transferee's intended **address(es) for service in the UK** *(including postcode)* **for entry on the register**

---

8. The Transferor transfers the property to the Transferee.

---

9. Consideration *(Place 'X' in the box that applies. State clearly the currency unit if other than sterling. If none of the boxes applies, insert an appropriate memorandum in the additional provisions panel.)*
☐ The Transferor has received from the Transferee for the property the sum of *(in words and figures)*
   (insert other receipt as appropriate)
☒ The Transfer is not for money or anything which has a monetary value

---

10. The Transferor transfers with *(place 'X' in the box which applies and add any modifications)*
☐ full title guarantee ☒ limited title guarantee

---

11. Declaration of trust *Where there is more than one transferee, place 'X' in the appropriate box.*

☐ The transferees are to hold the property on trust for themselves as joint tenants.

☐ The transferees are to hold the property on trust for themselves as tenants in common in equal shares.

☒ The transferees are to hold the property *(complete as necessary)* [*on the trusts of a settlement dated the [   ] day of [   ] [   ] and made between [   ] of the one part and [   ] and [   ] of the other part*].

12. Additional Provision(s) *Insert here any required or permitted statement, certificate or application and any agreed covenants, declarations, etc.*

[The provisions of section 11(1) of the Trusts of Land and Appointment of Trustees Act 1996 shall not apply to the Property].

13. *The Transferors and all other necessary parties should execute this transfer as a deed using the space below.* Forms of execution are given in Schedule 3 to the Land Registration Rules 1925. If the transfer contains transferees' covenants or declarations or contains an application by them (eg for a restriction), it must also be executed by the Transferees.

3

Appointment by supplemental deed under the Trustee Act 1925 of new trustee of settlement of land conveyed on trust in place of deceased trustee – appointment of new trustee of conveyance[1]

THIS DEED OF APPOINTMENT is made the [   ] day of [   ] BETWEEN (1) [surviving trustee] of [address] ('the Appointor') and (2) [new trustee] of [address] ('the New Trustee')

WHEREAS

(1)   This deed is supplemental to a conveyance ('the Conveyance') dated [date] and made between (1) [settlor] and (2) the Appointor and [deceased trustee] ('the Deceased Trustee') by which the property described in the first schedule was conveyed to the Appointor and the Deceased Trustee upon trust to hold upon the trusts of a settlement of even date referred to in the Conveyance.

(2)   No person was nominated by the Conveyance for the purpose of appointing new trustees.

(3)   The Deceased Trustee died on [date].

(4)   The property described in Part I of the second schedule has been sold and the property now subject to the trusts is described in Part II of second schedule.

(5)   The Appointor wishes to appoint the New Trustee to be a trustee of the Conveyance in place of the Deceased Trustee.

NOW THIS DEED WITNESSES that the Appointor in exercise of the power conferred upon him by the Trustee Act 1925 and of every other power enabling him appoints the New Trustee to be a trustee of the Conveyance in place of the Deceased Trustee and to act jointly with the Appointor[2].

IN WITNESS etc

FIRST SCHEDULE

The Property

[describe property conveyed]

SECOND SCHEDULE

Part I

[describe property sold]

Part II

[describe property now subject to trust]

[signatures of the parties]

[signatures of witnesses]

1   No stamp duty is payable. As to the necessity for appointments of new trustees of conveyances of land held on trust to be effected by separate instruments see para 6.47 above. For the power of a surviving or continuing trustee to appoint new or additional trustees under the Trustee Act 1925, s 36(1) see para 3.10 above. In the case of registered land there are two alternatives. The deed of appointment can itself be produced to the registry on an application to give effect to the implied (or express) vesting declaration contained in such deed under the Land Registration Act 1925, s 47. Alternatively, a transfer by the outgoing trustees in favour of the new trustees can be executed and registered, in which case the registered land in question should be excluded from the operation of the implied vesting declaration contained in the deed of appointment or deed or retirement of trustees of the trust instrument or will. If a transfer is used it has to be executed by all the proprietors, that is by all the trustees prior to the appointment or retirement (see further *Private Trusts of Land* (PAL 13: 2nd Edn, April 2000) published by the Land Registry).

2   It is not usual to include an express vesting declaration, reliance being placed on the implied vesting declaration under the Trustee Act 1925, s 40(1). It should be noted, however, that certain mortgage securities, shares, stock, etc are excluded from the vesting declaration implied by statute: see s 40(4).

4

Appointment by supplemental deed under the Trustee Act 1925 of new trustee of settlement of land conveyed on trust in place of deceased trustee – appointment of new trustee of trust instrument[1]

THIS DEED OF APPOINTMENT is made the [   ] day of [   ] BETWEEN (1) [surviving trustee] of [address] ('the Appointor') and (2) [new trustee] of [address] ('the New Trustee')

WHEREAS

(1)   This deed is supplemental to a trust instrument ('the Trust Instrument') dated [date] and made between (1) [settlor] and (2) the Appointor and [deceased trustee] ('the Deceased Trustee') by which trusts were declared of land conveyed on trust by a conveyance of even date with and made between the same parties as the Trust Instrument but no person was nominated by the Trust Instrument for the purpose of appointing new trustees of the same.

(2)   The Deceased Trustee died on [date].

(3)   The property described in Part I of the schedule has been sold and the property now subject to the Trust Instrument is described in Part II of the schedule.

(4)   The Appointor wishes to appoint the New Trustee to be a trustee of the Trust Instrument in place of the Deceased Trustee.

(5)   It is intended that the New Trustee shall by deed of even date be appointed a trustee of the conveyance of even date with the Trust Instrument and that the investments specified in Part II of the schedule shall be immediately separately transferred into the joint names of the Appointor and the New Trustee[2].

NOW THIS DEED WITNESSES that the Appointor in exercise of the power conferred upon him by the Trustee Act 1925 and of every other power enabling him appoints the New Trustee to be a trustee of the Trust Instrument in place of the Deceased Trustee and to act jointly with the Appointor[3].

IN WITNESS etc

SCHEDULE

Part I

[describe property sold]

Part II

[describe land and investments now subject to the Trust Instrument]

[signatures of the parties][4]

[signatures of witnesses]

1   No stamp duty is payable. For the power of a surviving or continuing trustee to appoint new or additional trustees under the Trustee Act 1925, s 36(1) see para 3.10 above.

2   Certain mortgage securities, shares, stock, etc are excluded from the vesting declaration implied by statute: see the Trustee Act 1925, s 40(4).

3   It is not usual to include an express vesting declaration, reliance being placed on the implied vesting declaration under the Trustee Act 1925, s 40(1).

4   An appointment should be executed by all parties since execution by a new trustee will operate as an acceptance of the trust.

5

Conveyance pursuant to the Trusts of Land and Appointment of Trustees Act 1996, s 6(2)[1]

THIS CONVEYANCE is made the [   ] day of [   ] BETWEEN (1) [trustee] of [address] and [trustee] of [address] ('the Trustees') and (2) [beneficiary] of [address] and [beneficiary] of [address] ('the Beneficiaries')

WHEREAS

(1)   The Trustees are the present trustees of a conveyance dated [date] ('the Conveyance') and made between (1) [settlor] and (2) [original trustees] ('the Former Trustees') by which the property described in the [first] schedule ('the Property') was conveyed to the Former Trustees upon trust to sell the same and to hold the net proceeds of any such sale upon the trusts declared by a settlement referred to in the Conveyance.

(2)   In the events that have happened the Beneficiaries are now entitled to the Property in equal shares absolutely.

(3)   The Trustees have resolved to convey the Property to the Beneficiaries (although the Beneficiaries have not requested the Trustees to do so) pursuant to the power conferred on them by the Trusts of Land and Appointment of Trustees Act 1996, s 6(1) and 6(2).

NOW THIS DEED WITNESSES as follows:

1   Conveyance

In exercise of the power conferred on them by the Trusts of Land and Appointment of Trustees Act 1996, s 6(1) and 6(2) and of all other powers enabling them the Trustees [with limited title guarantee] convey to the Beneficiaries the Property TO HOLD to the Beneficiaries in fee simple as beneficial tenants in common in equal shares discharged from the above trust for sale.

[2   Declaration of discharge

The Trustees pursuant to the Trusts of Land and Appointment of Trustees Act 1996, s 16(4) declare that they are discharged from the trusts of the conveyance in relation to the Property].

[3   Acknowledgment for production

The Trustees acknowledge the right of the Beneficiaries to production of the documents mentioned in the second schedule (the possession of which is retained by the Trustees) and to delivery of copies of them].

4   Stamp duty

It is certified that this instrument falls within category F in the Schedule to the Stamp Duty (Exempt Instruments) Regulations 1987[2].

IN WITNESS etc

[FIRST] SCHEDULE

The Property

[describe the Property]

[SECOND SCHEDULE

[insert details]]

[signatures of the parties]

[signatures of witnesses]

1   For a discussion of the Trusts of Land and Appointment of Trustees Act 1996, s 6(2) see para 2.45 above. The Precedent assumes two beneficiaries who, in the events that have happened, have become absolutely entitled as tenants in common in equal shares to land which was held on an old style trust for sale. Hence at the end of clause 1 there is a discharge from the trust for sale. Following the conveyance, the beneficiaries hold the land as joint tenants on trusts for themselves as tenants in common without the trust for sale. There are no inheritance tax or capital gains tax consequences and this is not an occasion of first registration.

The trustees should execute a deed of discharge pursuant to s 16(4) which has been included in this form: alternatively a separate deed may be employed: see **Precedent 16**.

2   Ie the Stamp Duty (Exempt Instruments) Regulations 1987/516. Instruments correctly certified in accordance with these regulations are exempted from the fixed duty of £5 to which they would otherwise be liable.

6

Consent to partition pursuant to the Trusts of Land and Appointment of Trustees Act 1996, s 7(3)[1]

To [trustee] of [address] and [trustee] of [address] the trustees of a conveyance dated [date] and made between [parties]

We [name] of [address] ('AB') [name] of [address] ('BC') and [name] of [address] ('CD') being entitled in equal undivided shares to the fee simple in the land described in the first second and third schedules consent to the partition proposed by you of such land pursuant to the provisions of the Trusts of Land and Appointment of Trustees Act 1996, s 7 under which partition:

1   the land more particularly described in the first schedule is allocated and is immediately to be conveyed in fee simple to AB;

2   the land more particularly described in the second schedule is allocated and is immediately to be conveyed in fee simple to BC; and

3   the land more particularly described in the third schedule is allocated and is immediately to be conveyed in fee simple to CD.

Dated: [date]

FIRST SCHEDULE
AB's Share
[describe land]

SECOND SCHEDULE
BC's Share
[describe land]

THIRD SCHEDULE

CD's Share

[describe land]

[signatures of the beneficiaries]

1   This is a form of consent by which the beneficiaries amongst whom the land in question
is being partitioned pursuant to the Trusts of Land and Appointment of Trustees Act
1996, s 7. Consent to the partitioning is required in s 7(3). This section in effect revamps
the Law of Property Act 1925, s 28 (repealed) where similar powers were restricted to
trusts for sale of land. Not much use was made of s 28(3), most partitions proceeding
purely on the basis of agreement. For a conveyance by trustees giving effect to an agreed
partition see Precedent 7. For a discussion of the Trusts of Land and Appointment of
Trustees Act 1996, s 7 see para 2.56 above.

Conveyance giving effect to a partition pursuant to the Trusts of Land and Appointment of Trustees Act 1996, s 7[1]

THIS CONVEYANCE is made the [   ] day of [   ] BETWEEN (1) [trustee] of [address] and [trustee] of [address] ('the Trustees') and (2) [beneficiary] of [address] ('the Beneficiary')

WHEREAS

(1)   The Trustees are the present trustees of a conveyance dated [date] and made between (1) [settlor] and (2) [original trustees] ('the Former Trustees') by which the property described in the first schedule ('the Property') was conveyed to the Former Trustees for a legal estate in fee simple in possession free from incumbrances on trust to sell the same and to stand possessed of the proceeds of such sale and the net rents and profits until sale upon trusts under which the Beneficiary and other persons have become absolutely entitled to such proceeds of sale in undivided shares.

(2)   The Trustees in exercise of the power conferred by the Trusts of Land and Appointment of Trustees Act 1996, s 7 have agreed with the Beneficiary and such other persons entitled to undivided shares in the proceeds of sale to partition the Property to which partition the Beneficiary and such other persons have all consented.

(3)   To give effect to such partition as regards the share of the Property to be taken by the Beneficiary (being the property described in the second schedule) the Trustees have agreed to make the conveyance below.

NOW THIS DEED WITNESSES as follows:

1   Conveyance

In pursuance of the arrangement for partition the Trustees in exercise of the power conferred on them by the Trusts of Land and Appointment of Trustees Act 1996, s 7 and of all other powers enabling them [with limited title guarantee] convey to the Beneficiary the property described in the second schedule TO HOLD to the Beneficiary in fee simple discharged from the trust for sale[2].

[2   Acknowledgment for production

The Trustees acknowledge the right of the Beneficiary to production of the documents mentioned in the third schedule (the possession of which is retained by the Trustees) and to delivery of copies of them].

IN WITNESS etc

FIRST SCHEDULE

The Property

SECOND SCHEDULE

Property allotted to the Beneficiary

[describe property]

[THIRD SCHEDULE

[insert details]]

[signatures of the parties]

[signatures of witnesses]

1   For a discussion of the Trusts of Land and Appointment of Trustees Act 1996, s 7 see para 2.56 above. Following on from the beneficiaries' consent this Precedent conveys to one of the beneficiaries the land to which he is entitled. For an appropriate consent see **Precedent 6** above. No equality money is payable.

For partitions of any estate or land a fixed stamp duty of £5 is charged unless consideration in excess of £100 is given for equality: FA 1999, Sch 13, para 21.

Following the execution of this Precedent, the trustees should execute a deed of discharge pursuant to the Trusts of Land and Appointment of Trustees Act 1996, s 16(4): see **Precedent 16** below.

2   The original trust was a trust for sale hence this discharge.

8

Clause for insertion in a disposition pursuant to the Trusts of Land and Appointment of Trustees Act 1996, s 8[1]

The provisions of the Trusts of Land and Appointment of Trustees Act 1996, s 6(2) and 7 shall not apply to the land which is at any time subject to the trusts of this deed[2].

1   The wording in the Trusts of Land and Appointment of Trustees Act 1996, s 8(1) 'insofar as provision . . .' means that it is possible to exclude some of the provisions in ibid s 6, which covers a number of matters, but not necessarily the whole section.

    It would appear from the wording of s 8(1) that the excluding provision has to be contained in the 'disposition' which creates the trust for land. That disposition will be the conveyance or transfer to the trustees on trust and so it is this deed which must have the exclusion in. In the past, where trusts for sale of land were created there was a series of deeds; ie a conveyance on trust for sale to the trustees and a separate deed which declared the trusts of the proceeds of sale. In future, if there is a trust for land (without creating a trust for sale) there will again be a tendency to have two deeds so as to keep the trusts off the title; ie a conveyance or transfer to the trustees and a declaration as to the trusts that apply. It will be essential to have the exclusion in the conveyance rather than in the deed which declares the trusts.

    If there is a personalty settlement and at some future date the settlor transfers land to the trustees to hold on the trusts of his trust, or the trustees purchase land, then the disposition creating the trust of the land will be the conveyance and not the original settlement which created the personalty settlement. If the settlor is adding property there will be no problem over his including in the conveyance an exclusion clause, but when the trustees are purchasing land they would not have authority to include an exclusion unless they had power to do so under the original trust deed. Accordingly, the safe course is to ensure that the exclusion is contained not only in the conveyance or transfer to the trustees, but also in the trust deed which sets out the applicable trusts. Oddly, the wording in s 11(2) (exclusion of provisions regarding consultation with beneficiaries) is not identical.

2   The provisions excluded have been selected purely for illustrative purposes: excluding s 7, for example, will be uncommon. Excluding s 6(2) makes sense given the uncertainties that exist as to its ambit!

9

Power of attorney granted pursuant to the Trusts of Land and Appointment of Trustees Act 1996, s 9[1]

THIS POWER OF ATTORNEY is given on the [   ] day of [   ] by [trustee] of [address] and [trustee] of [address] ('the Trustees')

WHEREAS

(1)   The Trustees are the present trustees of a conveyance dated [date] ('the Conveyance') and made between [parties]

(2)   The Trustees wish to appoint [attorney] of [address] ('the Attorney') being a person entitled to an interest in possession in the land subject to the trusts of the Conveyance ('the Land') to be their attorney and to delegate to him the following powers and discretions in respect of the Land.

NOW THIS DEED WITNESSES as follows:

1   Appointment

1.1   The Trustees in pursuance of the power conferred by the Trusts of Land and Appointment of Trustees Act 1996, s 9 appoint the Attorney to be their attorney in their name and on their behalf to exercise in respect of the Land (or so much of it as has not for the time being been sold and conveyed away) or any part or parts of it the powers vested in them to:

1.1.1   grant leases tenancies and licences;

1.1.2   accept surrenders of leases tenancies and licences;

1.1.3   vary the terms of any leases tenancies and licences;

1.1.4   serve any notices and grant any consents or approvals of plans under the terms of any leases tenancies or licences; and

1.1.5   generally to manage the Land.

1.2   PROVIDED that no delegation is made of the receipt or right to receive capital money payable in consideration of or in connection with any transaction effected by the Attorney under the powers and discretions now delegated or otherwise and that the Attorney is not authorised to receive such capital money on behalf of the Trustees[2].

2   Powers and discretions

For the purposes of executing or exercising the powers and discretions delegated the Attorney is empowered to settle sign and execute any deeds documents or contracts and to engage any adviser or agent.

3   Revocation

This appointment and delegation is revocable at any time by written notice given by the Trustees or either of them to the Attorney and shall be automatically revoked if the Attorney at any time ceases to be entitled to an interest in possession in the Land or if any person is appointed a trustee of the Conveyance in place of the Trustees or either of them or is appointed as an additional trustee to act with the Trustees[3].

4   Termination

If not previously revoked under the provisions contained in clause 3 above this appointment and delegation shall terminate at the expiration of two years from the date of this deed[4].

[5   Ratification

The Trustees undertake to ratify whatever the Attorney does under the authority or purported authority of this power of attorney[5]].

IN WITNESS etc

[signatures of the trustees]

[signatures of witnesses]

1   No stamp duty is payable. This Precedent delegates the trustees' powers of leasing, surrendering and varying leases etc to the beneficiary entitled to an interest in possession in the land. The power is similar to powers that were granted under the Law of Property Act 1925, s 29 (repealed). For a discussion of the Trusts of Land and Appointment of Trustees Act 1996, s 9 see para 2.77 ff above.

2   It is not possible to delegate the right to receive capital monies: see s 9(7) and para 2.82 above.

3   See s 9(3), (4).

4   See s 9(5).

5   On ratification, see **Precedent 32, footnote 5**.

10

Statutory declaration pursuant to the Trusts of Land and Appointment of Trustees Act 1996, s 9(2)[1]

I [declarant] of [address] do solemnly and sincerely declare as follows:

1   By a power of attorney dated [date] ('the Power of Attorney') [trustee] of [address] and [trustee] of [address] ('the Trustees') being the present trustees of a conveyance dated [date] and made between [parties] in exercise of the power conferred by the Trusts of Land and Appointment of Trustees Act 1996, s 9 appointed [attorney] of [address] ('the Attorney') to be their attorney and delegated to him [their power to grant leases and tenancies of the land subject to the trusts of the conveyance] and including the execution on their behalf of any deeds or documents in exercise of such power.

2   By a lease dated the [   ] day of [   ] and made between (1) the Trustees and (2) myself the property described in the schedule (being part of the land then vested in the Trustees) was demised to me for the term of [   ] years from the date thereof in consideration of the rent thereby reserved and such lease was effected by the Attorney in the names and on behalf of the Trustees in exercise of the power delegated to him by the Power of Attorney and such lease was executed by him in the name and on behalf of each of the Trustees.

3   I dealt in good faith with the Attorney and had no knowledge to the effect that the Attorney was not a person in whose favour the Trustees could execute such a power of attorney and delegate such powers under the provisions of the Trusts of Land and Appointment of Trustees Act 1996, s 9[2].

SCHEDULE

The Property

[describe property]

AND I make this solemn declaration conscientiously believing the same to be true and by virtue of the Statutory Declarations Act 1835

[signature of the declarant]

DECLARED at [   ] this [   ] day of [   ]

Before me

[signature of person before whom declaration is made]

[A commissioner for oaths *or* A solicitor empowered to administer oaths *or* (as appropriate)]

1   No stamp duty is payable. This statutory declaration must be made before, or within three months of, the completion of the purchase if the purchaser from a third party who dealt with the attorney is to obtain the benefit of the Trusts of Land and Appointment of Trustees Act 1996, s 9(2). As to the protection of third parties generally see para 2.86 above.

2   It may be appropriate to add a further declaration to take advantage of the Powers of Attorney Act 1971, s 5 along the following lines: 'I did not know of any revocation of the power of attorney'. See further para 2.89 above.

11

Clause pursuant to the Trusts of Land and Appointment of Trustees Act 1996, s 11(2)[1]

The provisions of the Trusts of Land and Appointment of Trustees Act 1996, s 11(1) (relating to consultation of beneficiaries) shall not apply to any land situated in England and Wales which is at any time subject to the trusts of this deed.

1   For a discussion of the consultation requirements see para 2.107 ff above. This clause is intended to completely exclude these provisions. The wording in the Trusts of Land and Appointment of Trustees Act 1996, s 11(2)(a) is somewhat different to that in s 8(1) regarding the exclusion of the provisions of ss 6 and 7. In s 8(1) there is a reference to 'a trust of land created by a disposition', the excluding provision having to be in the disposition. s 11(2)(a), however, refers to 'a trust created by a disposition', the exclusion again having to be in the disposition. Does this difference in wording imply anything? The authors consider that the disposition which creates the trust of land is the conveyance or transfer which transfers the land in question to trustees subject to the trust where there is an inter vivos transaction, so that again it is that document which needs to contain the exclusion. However, when there are different documents conveying the land and setting out the trusts applicable, it will be prudent to make sure that there is an exclusion in both. Compare the wording of SLA 1925, s 75(4) inserted by TA 2000, Sch 2, para 10: see para 14.48 above.

12

Deed by settlor pursuant to the Trusts of Land and Appointment of Trustees Act 1996, s 11(3)[1]

THIS DEED is made the [   ] day of [   ]BETWEEN (1) [settlor] of [address] ('the Settlor') and (2) [trustee] of [address] and [trustee] of [address] ('the Trustees')

WHEREAS

This deed is supplemental to:

(1)   a conveyance ('the Conveyance') dated [date] and made between (1) the Settlor and (2) the Trustees by which the Settlor conveyed the freehold property described in the schedule to the Trustees upon trust to sell such property and to hold the net proceeds of such sale and the net rents and profits until sale upon the trusts declared in the settlement referred to in the Conveyance;

(2)   a settlement ('the Settlement') of even date with and made between the same parties in the same order as the Conveyance (and being the settlement referred to in the Conveyance).

NOW THIS DEED WITNESSES that in exercise of the power conferred on the Settlor by s 11(3) of the Trusts of Land and Appointment of Trustees Act 1996 ('the Act') the Settlor declares that as and from the date of this deed the provisions of s 11 of the Act (relating to consultation of beneficiaries) shall apply to any land which is subject to the trusts declared in the Conveyance and in the Settlement or such of the same as may for the time being be subsisting.

IN WITNESS etc

SCHEDULE

The Property

[describe property]

[signatures of the parties]

[signatures of witnesses]

1   No stamp duty is payable. This Precedent is based on land held subject to a trust for sale: there were two deeds, a conveyance and an accompanying settlement of the proceeds of sale. For a discussion of the Trusts of Land and Appointment of Trustees Act 1996, s 11 see para 2.107 above.

13

Recital for inclusion in a settlement as to the purposes of the settlement having regard to the Trusts of Land and Appointment of Trustees Act 1996, s 12(1)[1]

The Settlor does not intend and it is not the purpose of this settlement that any land or building subject to the trusts of this deed should be occupied by or should be available for occupation by any beneficiary or beneficiaries under the settlement either as a residence or for any business or other purposes.

1   For a discussion of the ambit of the Trusts of Land and Appointment of Trustees Act 1996, s 12 conferring a right of occupation see para 2.128 above. Whilst it is not thought that this section can be excluded as such, entitlement (in part) depends upon the 'purposes of the trust': see s 12(1)(a). This recital indicates that providing land etc for occupation is not a trust purpose.

14

Sub-clause for inclusion in an investment clause of a will, or a settlement, excluding the investment in land or buildings for use by a beneficiary[1]

The power of investment contained in the preceding sub-clause shall not extend to or include power to purchase land or buildings or any interest in the same for occupation by any Beneficiary or Beneficiaries (whether as a residence or for use by any business carried on either alone or in partnership by a Beneficiary or Beneficiaries or for any other purpose) and the powers to invest in land contained in the Trusts of Land and Appointment of Trustees Act 1996, s 6(3) and the Trustee Act 2000, s 8 shall be restricted so that such powers do not extend to the purchase of land for occupation by any beneficiary.

1   This sub-clause seeks to back up **Precedent 13** above by restricting the investment powers of the trustees under the Trusts of Land and Appointment of Trustees Act 1996, s 6(1), (3) (as amended by TA 2000) and under the Trustee Act 2000 to exclude land bought for beneficial occupation. As such it restores the decision in *Re Power, Public Trustee v Hastings* [1947] Ch 572, [1947] 2 All ER 282: see para 11.72 above.

15

Agreement with beneficiary for occupation of a trust property pursuant to the Trusts of Land and Appointment of Trustees Act 1996, s 13[1]

THIS AGREEMENT is made the [   ] day of [   ] BETWEEN A [   ] of [   ] B [   ] of [   ] (hereinafter called 'the Trustees' of one part and C [   ] of [   ] (hereinafter called 'the Beneficiary') of the other part

WHEREAS

(1)   The Trustees are the present trustees of (a) a conveyance dated the [   ] day of [   ] and made between [   ] of the one part and [   ] of the other part and (b) settlement of even date with and made between the same parties in the same order as the conveyance.

(2)   The freehold property known as [   ] (hereinafter called 'the Property') is vested in the Trustees and is held on trusts whereunder the Beneficiary is entitled to an interest in possession therein.

(3)   The Trustees have determined in accordance with the provisions of the Trusts of Land and Appointment of Trustees Act 1996, s 13 and it has been agreed with the Beneficiary that the Beneficiary will pursuant to the right conferred on him by s 12 of that Act occupy the Property on the terms and conditions hereinafter contained including the payment by the Beneficiary to D (who is also entitled to an interest in possession under the trusts affecting the Property) of such annual sums as are hereinafter provided.

NOW IT IS HEREBY AGREED as follows:

1   Pursuant to the Trusts of Land and Appointment of Trustees Act 1996, ss 12 and 13 the Beneficiary shall be entitled to occupy the Property until this Agreement is determined in accordance with the provisions hereinafter contained[2].

2   The Beneficiary hereby undertakes to pay to the said D [   ] the annual sum of £[   ] by equal half yearly instalments payable in arrears throughout the currency of this Agreement so long as the said D [   ] shall be entitled to an interest in possession under the trusts affecting the Property the first such instalment to be paid on the [   ] day of [   ] next and subsequent instalments to be paid on the [   ] day of [   ] and the [   ] day of [   ] in each year and the last payment to be made on the termination of this Agreement or on such earlier date as the said D [   ] shall cease to be entitled to an interest in possession under the trusts affecting the Property (whether due to the death of the said D [   ] or for any other reason) and to be a proportionate payment[3].

3   The Beneficiary agrees with the Trustees:

3.1   to pay all Council Tax water rates and all other taxes impositions and outgoings which are now or may at any time during the currency of this Agreement be assessed levied charged or imposed on the Property or on the owner or occupier in respect thereof;

3.2   not to use the Property except as a residence for the Beneficiary and his family;

3.3   to keep the interior of the dwellinghouse on the Property and all fixtures and fittings therein (other than electrical wiring or pipes and apparatus for the supply of hot and cold water) in proper repair and good decorative condition throughout the currency of this Agreement;

3.4   to pay direct to the various supply authorities for all gas water and electricity consumed on the Property and the rent of the meters to regulate such supplies and to pay for the rental of any telephone or telephones installed at the Property and the costs of all calls;

3.5   to maintain the garden at the Property in a neat and tidy condition;

3.6   to insure and keep insured the dwellinghouse on the Property against loss from fire and all other perils usually covered by a householders' comprehensive policy in the names of the Trustees in an insurance office nominated by the Trustees and to produce a receipt for any premium paid to the Trustees or their agent on demand;

3.7   to permit the Trustees and their surveyors and agents at all reasonable times during the currency of this Agreement with or without workmen and others and with or without appliances to enter on the Property to view the state of repair and condition of the same and to repair the same;

3.8   not to make or allow to be made during the currency of this Agreement any new building on the Property or make or allow to be made any alteration or addition to the dwellinghouse on the Property;

3.9   not to do or permit anything to be done on the Property which may be or become a nuisance or annoyance or cause damage or inconvenience to the owners or occupiers of any adjoining or neighbouring property; and

3.10   forthwith on receipt of any notice or order or any proposal for the same from a planning or other authority to give full particulars to the Trustees or their agents and if required to do so to produce the same to the Trustees or their agents.

4   Nothing contained in this agreement shall create the relationship of landlord and tenant between the Trustees and the Beneficiary.

5.1   This Agreement shall automatically determine on the death of the Beneficiary or on the termination for any other reason of the Beneficiary's interest in possession in the Property:

    5.1.1   if at any time during the continuance of this Agreement the Trustees wish to sell the Property they shall be entitled to give the Beneficiary three months' notice to cease occupation of the Property and the Beneficiary shall cease occupation at the end of such period[4],

    5.1.2   if at any time during the continuance of this Agreement the Beneficiary shall be in breach of any of the terms and conditions of this Agreement the trustees shall be entitled to give the Beneficiary three months' notice to cease occupation of the Property and the Beneficiary shall cease occupation at the end of such period and the right to terminate the Beneficiary's occupation in respect of any breach of any terms or conditions shall not be waived solely by reason of any earlier waiver by the Trustees of any previous or continuing breach of that or any other condition.

5.2   The Beneficiary may at any time give to the Trustees one month's notice of his intention to vacate the Property and on the expiry of such period of one month this Agreement shall determine.

6.1   The expression 'the Trustees' herein shall include the trustees or the trustee for the time being of the said conveyance and the said settlement.

6.2   The expression 'interest in possession' herein shall have the same meaning as that expression has for the purposes of the Trusts of Land and Appointment of Trustees Act 1996.

SIGNED by the Trustees and the Beneficiary

1   This Precedent gives a beneficiary occupation of a dwelling house on terms that he is subject to interior repairs and the payment of all outgoings, and also subject to his making annual payments to another beneficiary entitled to an interest in possession. It is thought that the arrangement would be construed as a licence and not a tenancy in view of the fact that it is in favour of a beneficiary within a trust, and gives effect to the right of occupation of a beneficiary and the attendant powers of the trustees under the Trusts of Land and Appointment of Trustees Act 1996, ss 12, 13. For a discussion of s 13 see para 2.131 ff above.

2   For the inheritance tax implications of permitting one beneficiary to reside in the property and at the same time excluding another see para 2.138 above.

3   For the tax treatment of this payment so far as both beneficiaries are concerned see para 2.138 above.

4   The trustees can give notice to terminate the agreement if they wish to sell the property but the beneficiary would still be in occupation if he did not leave willingly and would come within the terms of s 13(7). In such circumstances the trustees would have to go to court to secure his removal.

16

Deed of discharge pursuant to the Trusts of Land and Appointment of Trustees Act 1996, s 16(4)[1]

THIS DEED OF DISCHARGE is made the [   ] day of [   ] by [trustee] of [address] and [trustee] of [address] ('the Trustees')

WHEREAS

This deed is supplemental to:

(1)   a conveyance ('the First Conveyance') dated [date] and made between (1) [settlor] and (2) the Trustees and

(2)   a conveyance ('the Second Conveyance') dated [date] and made between (1) the Trustees and (2) [beneficiaries] ('the Beneficiaries') by which the Trustees conveyed the property described in the schedule ('the Property') to the Beneficiaries in fee simple to be held by the Beneficiaries as beneficial tenants in common in equal shares.

NOW THIS DEED WITNESSES that pursuant to the Trusts of Land and Appointment of Trustees Act 1996, s 16(4) the Trustees declare that they are as regards the Property discharged from the trusts applicable to it by virtue of the First Conveyance.

IN WITNESS etc

SCHEDULE

The Property

[describe the Property]

[signatures of the parties]

[signatures of witnesses]

---

1   No stamp duty is payable. This Precedent corresponds to Precedent 5 above dealing with conveyance to beneficiaries under the Trusts of Land and Appointment of Trustees Act 1996, 6(2). The wording of s 16(4)(a) appears to contemplate a separate deed of discharge being executed by the trustees, although the authors suspect that practitioners may choose to ignore this apparent requirement and for simplicity's sake include the discharge in the conveyance. For a discussion of s 16 see para 2.165 ff above.

Prior to the commencement of the Trusts of Land and Appointment of Trustees Act 1996, there was generally no satisfactory machinery for ending a trust for sale without the equitable interests being brought on to the title (the main exception was a conveyance by a surviving joint tenant as 'beneficial owner' under the Law of Property (Joint Tenants) Act 1964). One solution was for the trustees to retain legal title until sale so that the purchaser could then rely on the Law of Property Act 1925, s 23 (repealed) (trusts for sale deemed to continue) and the overreaching mechanism in the Law of Property Act 1925, s 27 (now amended by the Trusts of Land and Appointment of Trustees Act 1996, Sch 3, para 4(8)). For a similar reason, personal representatives might delay vesting land in themselves as trustees: for example, when land was being enjoyed by an elderly life tenant they might wait until his death and then assent the land directly to the remainderman using the protection of the Administration of Estates Act 1925, s 36. These problems are largely solved by the Trusts of Land and Appointment of Trustees Act 1996, s 16(4). However, it is not thought that the new procedure will apply to events occuring before the commencement date: ie a beneficiary who received land before 1997 has no right to call for a discharge which even if given would not protect a purchaser (note that the wording of the subsection is 'convey' which looks to the future rather than the past).

17

Written direction to a trustee to retire pursuant to the Trusts of Land and Appointment of Trustees Act 1996, s 19(2)(a)[1]

To [trustee] of [address] being a trustee of a deed of settlement dated [date] ('the Settlement') and made between (1) [settlor] and (2) [trustees]

We [beneficiary] of [address] and [beneficiary] of [address] being both of full age and being together absolutely entitled to the trust fund subject to the trusts of the Settlement now subsisting in accordance with the provisions of the Trusts of Land and Appointment of Trustees Act 1996, s 19(2)(a) direct you immediately to retire as a trustee of the Settlement so that your co-trustees [trustee] of [address] *and* [trustee] of [address] shall alone continue as the trustees

Dated [date]

[signatures of the beneficiaries]

---

1   For the operation of the Trusts of Land and Appointment of Trustees Act 1996, s 19 see para 3.8 ff above. For a deed of retirement see **Precedent 18** below.

18

Deed of retirement by trustee pursuant to the Trusts of Land and Appointment of Trustees Act 1996, s 19(3)[1]

THIS DEED OF RETIREMENT is made the [   ] day of [   ] by (1) [retiring trustee] of [address] ('the Retiring Trustee') and (2) [continuing trustee] of [address] and [continuing trustee] of [address] ('the Continuing Trustees')

WHEREAS

(1)   This deed is supplemental to the will[2] dated [date] ('the Will') of [testator] late of [address] who died on [date] which will was on [date] proved in the [Principal *or* [name] District Probate] Registry of the Family Division of the High Court by the named executors.

(2)   The Retiring Trustee and the Continuing Trustees are the present trustees of the Will.

(3)   No person was named in the Will as having the power of appointing new trustees of the Will[3].

(4)   [Beneficiary] of [address] and [beneficiary] of [address] ('the Beneficiaries) being both of full age and together absolutely entitled to the trust fund subject to the now subsisting trusts of the Will have pursuant to the provisions of the Trusts of Land and Appointment of Trustees Act 1996, s 19(2) given a written direction dated [date] to the Retiring Trustee to retire from the trusts of the Will and this deed is made in compliance with such direction.

(5)   The property now subject to the trusts of the Will is specified in the first and second schedules.

(6)   The property specified in the second schedule is to be immediately and separately transferred into the joint names of the Continuing Trustees[4].

NOW THIS DEED WITNESSES as follows:

1   Retirement

The Retiring Trustee declares his retirement as a trustee of the Will and the Continuing Trustees consent to his retirement as such trustee (as testified by their execution of this deed) to the intent that the Retiring Trustee shall be deemed to have retired as such trustee and be discharged from the trusts of the Will.

[2   Residence

It is declared by the parties to this deed that there is no intention at the date of this deed that the trustees of the Will should become neither resident nor ordinarily resident in the United Kingdom][5].

IN WITNESS etc

FIRST SCHEDULE

[list property which will not be separately transferred]

SECOND SCHEDULE

[list property to be separately transferred]

[signatures of the parties]

[signatures of witnesses]

1   No stamp duty is payable. This Precedent assumes that the beneficiaries have directed the retiring trustee to retire and that no replacement is being appointed. For a written direction see Precedent 17 above. For the operation of the Trusts of Land and Appointment of Trustees Act 1996, s 19 see para 3.8 above.

2   The trust in this Precedent arose under the will of the deceased.

3   The existence of such a person would preclude the beneficiaries from directing the retirement and replacement of the retiring trustee: see the Trusts of Land and Appointment of Trustees Act 1996, s 19(1)(a).

4   Note the limits on the automatic vesting of trust property in the Trustee Act 1925, s 40 as amended by the Trusts of Land and Appointment of Trustees Act 1996, Sch 3, para 3(14).

5   This clause is inserted with the intention of affording a trustee some defence against a claim under the Taxation of Chargeable Gains Act 1992, s 82 to capital gains tax if the trust concerned is subsequently exported giving rise to a deemed disposal under s 80.

19

Written direction to trustee to appoint a specified person to be a trustee pursuant to the Trusts of Land and Appointment of Trustees Act 1996, s 19(2)(b)[1]

To [trustee] of [address] being the sole trustee of a deed of settlement dated [date] ('the Settlement') and made between (1) [settlor] and (2) [trustees]

We [beneficiary] of [address] and [beneficiary] of [address] being both of full age and being together absolutely entitled to the trust fund subject to the trusts of the Settlement now subsisting in accordance with the provisions of the Trusts of Land and Appointment of Trustees Act 1996, s 19(2)(b) direct you immediately to appoint [new trustee] of [address] to be a trustee of the Settlement and to act jointly with you

Dated [date]

[signatures of the beneficiaries]

---

1   For the operation of the Trusts of Land and Appointment of Trustees Act 1996, s 19 see para 3.8 ff above. For a deed of appointment see **Precedent 20** below.

20

Deed of appointment of new trustee pursuant to a direction given under the Trusts of Land and Appointment of Trustees Act 1996, s 19(2)(b)[1]

THIS DEED OF APPOINTMENT is made the [   ] day of [   ] by (1) [continuing trustee] of [address] ('the Continuing Trustee') and (2) [new trustee] of [address] ('the New Trustee')

WHEREAS

(1)   This deed is supplemental to the will dated [date] ('the Will') of [testator] late of [address] who died on [date] which will was on [date] proved in the [Principal *or* [name] District Probate] Registry of the Family Division of the High Court by the named executors.

(2)   The Continuing Trustee is the present trustee of the Will.

(3)   No person was nominated in the Will as having the power of appointing new trustees of the Will[2].

(4)   By a written notice dated [date] [beneficiary] of [address] and [beneficiary] of [address] ('the Beneficiaries) being both of full age and together absolutely entitled to the trust fund subject to the trusts of the Will directed the Continuing Trustee in accordance with the provisions of the Trusts of Land and Appointment of Trustees Act 1996, s 19(2) to appoint the New Trustee to be a trustee of the Will and the Continuing Trustee makes this deed of appointment in compliance with such direction.

(5)   The property now subject to the trusts of the Will is specified in the Schedule.

NOW THIS DEED WITNESSES that to give effect to the direction of the Beneficiaries and in exercise of the statutory power[3] in that behalf and of all other powers enabling him the Continuing Trustee appoints the New Trustee to be a trustee of the Will to act jointly with the Continuing Trustee.

IN WITNESS etc

SCHEDULE

The Property

[list of property subject to trusts of the Will]

[signatures of the parties]

[signatures of witnesses]

1   No stamp duty is payable. This Precedent assumes a sole trustee of a will trust who has been directed by the beneficiaries to appoint another trustee. For a written direction see **Precedent 19** above. For the operation of the Trusts of Land and Appointment of Trustees Act 1996, s 19 see para 3.8 ff above.

2   The existence of such a person would prevent the beneficiaries directing the appointment of an additional trustee: s 19(1)(a).

3   For a discussion of the relevant statutory power see para 3.19 ff above.

21

Notice to trustees of withdrawal by a beneficiary of a direction given pursuant to the Trusts of Land and Appointment of Trustees Act 1996, s 19[1]

To [trustee] of [address] and [trustee] of [address] being the present trustees of a deed of settlement dated [date] ('the Settlement') and made between (1) [settlor] and (2) [original trustees]

I [beneficiary] of [address] having with [beneficiary] of [address] given to you as the present trustees of the Settlement a written direction dated [date] to appoint [name] of [address] as an additional trustee of the Settlement pursuant to the provisions of the Trusts of Land and Appointment of Trustees Act 1996, s 19 (the two of us being together absolutely entitled to the trust fund subject to the trusts of the Settlement and such direction not having yet been complied with) NOW WITHDRAW the direction given by me

Dated [date]

[signature of the beneficiary]

---

1   See the Trusts of Land and Appointment of Trustees Act 1996, s 21(1) providing for a beneficiary to withdraw his direction and see also para 3.28 above.

22

Indemnity clause to be included in a deed of appointment of new trustee, where a trustee is retiring, giving the retiring trustee an indemnity against income tax and capital gains tax for which he may continue to be accountable[1]

The Continuing Trustee and the New Trustee jointly covenant with the Retiring Trustee that they will indemnify and keep indemnified the Retiring Trustee and his estate from and against all income tax payable in respect of the income of the property comprised or formerly comprised in the trust fund subject to the trusts of the Settlement and all capital gains tax payable in respect of any disposals or deemed disposals of assets comprised in the trust fund and any interest on it for which the Retiring Trustee as a trustee of the Settlement may be liable or accountable and which has not been settled or discharged at the date of this deed and from and against all claims demands costs and expenses whatsoever in respect of any such income tax or capital gains tax.

1   A trustee who is given a direction to retire by the beneficiaries is only obliged to retire when reasonable arrangements have been made for his protection: Trusts of Land and Appointment of Trustees Act 1996, s 19(3)(b). Trustees are liable for income tax and capital gains tax if they were trustees at any time in the tax year when the income/gain arose. In cases where the trustees are paying an inheritance tax liability by instalments, the retiring trustees will need to be assured that future instalments will be paid or, alternatively, may insist that the outstanding instalments are discharged before they retire (see *Howarth's Executors v IRC* [1997] STC (SCD) 162).

23

Clause pursuant to the Trusts of Land and Appointment of Trustees Act 1996, s 21(5)[1]

The provisions of the Trusts of Land and Appointment of Trustees Act 1996, ss 19 and 20 shall not apply to this [settlement *or* will].

1   For the operation of the Trusts of Land and Appointment of Trustees Act 1996, ss 19, 20 see para 3.1 ff above. Both sections can be excluded expressly in any disposition creating the trust. It is, of course, possible to exclude one but not the other or to modify their operation.

24

Deed made pursuant to the Trusts of Land and Appointment of Trustees Act 1996, s 21(6)[1]

THIS DEED is made the [   ] day of [   ] BETWEEN (1) [settlor] of [address] and (2) [trustee] of [address] and [trustee] of [address] ('the Trustees')

WHEREAS

(1)   This deed is supplemental to a settlement ('the Settlement') dated [date] and made between (1) the Settlor and (2) [original trustees].

(2)   The Trustees are the present trustees of the Settlement.

(3)   The Settlor wishes to exercise the power conferred on him by s 21(6) of the Trusts of Land and Appointment of Trustees Act 1996 ('the Act').

NOW THIS DEED WITNESSES that in exercise of the power conferred on him as the settlor of the Settlement by s 21(6) of the Act and of any and every other power enabling him the Settlor declares that as from the date of this deed the provisions of ss 19 and 20 of the Act shall not apply to the Settlement.

IN WITNESS etc

[signatures of the parties]

[signatures of witnesses]

1   No stamp duty is payable. So far as trusts created before 1 January 1997 are concerned, the Trusts of Land and Appointment of Trustees Act 1996, ss 19, 20 will apply unless the settlor, being of full capacity, provides for their exclusion by deed. For the operation of the Trusts of Land and Appointment of Trustees Act 1996, ss 19, 20 see para 3.1 ff above.

25

Conveyance of land to joint tenants[1]

THIS CONVEYANCE is made the [   ] day of [   ] BETWEEN (1) [vendor] of [address] ('the Vendor') and (2) [purchaser] of [address] and [purchaser] of [address] ('the Purchasers')

WHEREAS

(1)   The Vendor is seised of the property described in the [first] schedule ('the Property') for an estate in fee simple in possession free from incumbrances.

(2)   The Vendor has agreed to sell the Property to the Purchasers for the same estate for the sum of £[   ] and the Purchasers have agreed to hold the Property as beneficial joint tenants.

NOW THIS DEED WITNESSES as follows:

1   Conveyance

In consideration of £[   ] paid by the Purchasers to the Vendor (the receipt of which the Vendor acknowledges) the Vendor with [full *or* limited] title guarantee conveys to the Purchasers the Property TO HOLD to the Purchasers in fee simple as beneficial joint tenants.

[2   Acknowledgment for production

The Vendor acknowledges the right of the Purchasers to production of the documents mentioned in the second schedule (the possession of which is retained by the Vendor) and to delivery of copies of them].

[3   Certificate of value

[certificate of value if appropriate]][2]

IN WITNESS etc

[FIRST] SCHEDULE

The Property

[describe the Property]

[SECOND SCHEDULE

[insert details]]

[signatures of the parties]

[signatures of witnesses]

1   As a result of the Law of Property Act 1925, s 36 (as amended by the Trusts of Land and Appointment of Trustees Act 1996, s 5, Sch 2, para 4) the purchasers hold the property on a trust of land for themselves as beneficial joint tenants. This implied trust of land confers a power to sell (and retain) on the trustees: all the provisions of the Trusts of Land and Appointment of Trustees Act 1996 will apply (including the consultation rules in s 11 and the right to occupy in ss 12-13). For a consideration of whether it would be desirable to create an express trust for sale in such circumstances see para 6.38 above.

2   This certificate should be included where appropriate as the conveyance is a conveyance on sale.

26

Transfer of the whole of the land in a title to purchasers purchasing as beneficial joint tenants

Transfer of whole of registered title(s)

HM Land Registry TR1

(if you need more room than is provided for in a panel, use continuation sheet CS and staple to this form)

<table>
<tr><td>

1. Stamp Duty

Place 'X' in the box that applies and complete the box in the appropriate certificate.
☐ We hereby certify that this instrument falls within category ☐ in the Schedule to the Stamp Duty (Exempt Instruments) Regulations 1987
☐ It is certified that the transaction effected does not form part of a larger transaction or of a series of transactions in respect of which the amount or value or the aggregate amount or value of the consideration exceeds the sum of
£ [   ]

</td></tr>
<tr><td>

2. Title Number(s) of the Property *(leave blank if not yet registered)*

</td></tr>
</table>

3. Property

If this transfer is made under section 37 of the Land Registration Act 1925 following a not-yet-registered dealing with part only of the land in a title, or is made under rule 72 of the Land Registration Rules 1925, include a reference to the last preceding document of title containing a description of the property.

4. Date

5. Transferor *(give full names and Company's Registered Number if any)*

6. Transferee **for entry on the register** *(Give full names and Company's Registered Number if any; for Scottish Co. Reg. Nos., use an SC prefix. For foreign companies give territory in which incorporated.)*

Unless otherwise arranged with Land Registry headquarters, a certified copy of the transferee's constitution (in English or Welsh) will be required if it is a body corporate but is not a company registered in England and Wales or Scotland under the Companies Acts.

7. Transferee's intended **address(es) for service in the UK** *(including postcode) for entry on the register*

8. The Transferor transfers the property to the Transferee.

9. Consideration *(Place 'X' in the box that applies. State clearly the currency unit if other than sterling. If none of the boxes applies, insert an appropriate memorandum in the additional provisions panel.)*
☐ The Transferor has received from the Transferee for the property the sum of *(in words and figures)*
  (insert other receipt as appropriate)
☐ The Transfer is not for money or anything which has a monetary value

10. The Transferor transfers with *(place 'X' in the box which applies and add any modifications)*
☐ full title guarantee ☐ limited title guarantee

11. Declaration of trust *Where there is more than one transferee, place 'X' in the appropriate box.*

☒ The transferees are to hold the property on trust for themselves as joint tenants.

☐ The transferees are to hold the property on trust for themselves as tenants in common in equal shares.

☐ The transferees are to hold the property (complete as necessary)

12. Additional Provision(s) *Insert here any required or permitted statement, certificate or application and any agreed covenants, declarations, etc.*

13. The Transferors and all other necessary parties should execute this transfer as a deed using the space below. Forms of execution are given in Schedule 3 to the Land Registration Rules 1925. If the transfer contains transferees' covenants or declarations or contains an application by them (eg for a restriction), it must also be executed by the Transferees.

27

Assent on the trusts of the will by personal representatives in favour of themselves as trustees of the will[1]

BY THIS ASSENT dated the [   ] day of [   ] we [executor] of [address] and [executor] of [address] the executors of [testator] late of [address] who died on [date] and whose will was on [date] proved by us in the [Principal *or* [name] District Probate] Registry of the Family Division of the High Court as such personal representatives:

1   Assent to the vesting in ourselves [names of executors] of the freehold property described in the schedule to this assent ('the Property') for an estate in fee simple upon the [trusts *or* trust for sale][2] contained in clause *[specify]* of the will.

2   Declare that we have not previously given or made any assent or conveyance in respect of any legal estate in the Property or any part of it.

AS WITNESS etc

SCHEDULE

The Property

[describe the Property]

[signatures of the executors][3]

[signatures of witnesses]

---

1   No stamp duty is payable. For the requirements of a written assent in such circumstances see the Administration of Estates Act 1925, s 36(4). The assent is a crucial link in title to the legal estate showing that the property is no longer subject to the personal representatives powers of administration, albeit that it is vested in the same persons: see *Re King's Will Trusts, Assheton v Boyne* [1964] Ch 542, [1964] 1 All ER 833; *Re Edwards' Will Trusts, Edwards v Edwards* [1982] Ch 30, [1981] 2 All ER 941, CA. Note the protection of purchasers under the Administration of Estates Act 1925, s 36(7): following an assent of the legal estate, a purchaser may assume that it was made to the correct person and so is not concerned to see the contents of the will to confirm this. An assent is now an occasion of first registration and may be effected by Land Registry Form AS1 (see **Precedent 28** below).

2   For a consideration of when it will still be desirable for property to be held on trust for sale see para 6.38. This assent brings the will onto the title as far as the trust for sale/trust of land is concerned. Prior to 1 January 1997, this could create problems if the will inadvertently created a strict settlement. It automatically incorporates any restrictions on the trustees' powers.

3   A witness is not strictly required where an assent is not by deed but is helpful for evidential purposes.

28

Assent of the whole of a registered or an unregistered title – Land Registry Form AS1[1]

HM Land Registry AS1

(if you need more room than is provided for in a panel, use continuation sheet CS and staple to this form)

1. Title Number(s) of the Property *(leave blank if not yet registered)*
2. Property   *If this assent is made under section 37 of the Land Registration Act 1925 following a not-yet-registered dealing with part only of the land in a title, or is made under rule 72 of the Land Registration Rules 1925, include a reference to the last preceding document of title containing a description of the property.*
3. Date
4. Name of deceased proprietor (give full names)

5. Personal Representative of deceased proprietor *(give full names and Company's Registered Number if any)*

6. Recipient for entry on the register *(Give full names and Company's Registered Number if any: for Scottish Co. Reg. Nos., use an SC prefix. For foreign companies give territory in which incorporated.)*

Unless otherwise arranged with Land Registry headquarters, a certified copy of the transferee's constitution (in English or Welsh) will be required if it is a body corporate but is not a company registered in England and Wales or Scotland under the Companies Acts.

7. Recipient's intended **address(es) for service in the UK** *(including postcode)* **for entry on the register**

8. The Personal Representative assents to the vesting of the property in the Recipient.

9. The Personal Representative assents with *(place X in the box which applies and add any modifications)*
☐ full title guarantee ☐ limited title guarantee

10. Declaration of trust *Where there is more than one recipient, place 'X' in the appropriate box.*
☐ The recipients are to hold the property on trust for themselves as joint tenants.
☐ The recipients are to hold the property on trust for themselves as tenants in common in equal shares.
☐ The recipients are to hold the property *(complete as necessary)*

11. Additional Provision(s) *Insert here any required or permitted statement, certificate or application and any agreed covenants, declarations, etc.*

12. *The Personal Representatives and all other necessary parties should sign this assent in the presence of witnesses or execute it as a deed using the space below.* Forms of execution are given in Schedule 3 to the Land Registration Rules 1925. If the assent contains recipients' covenants or declarations or contains an application by them (eg for a restriction), it must also be executed by the Recipients.

Notes referring to specific panels of the Form appear below.

General

This assent is Form AS1 as prescribed under the Land Registration Rules 1925/1093 r 98(1)(b) as amended by the Land Registration Rules 1997/3037 r 2(1), Sch 1 para 23.

The Form is Crown copyright and must be prepared in accordance with the requirements of the Rules.

No stamp duty is payable.

This form of assent should be used for an assent of the whole of the land in one or more registered titles; or an assent of the whole of the land in a transfer or lease of part which has not yet been registered. It may also be used for an assent of unregistered land which is the whole of the land in the conveyance of the deceased.

If an assent is to included part only of the land in a registered title (whether or not it also includes as assent of the whole of the land in other registered titles) then Land Registry Form 56 should be used.

Registration. For registration the Form should be accompanied by:

(a) Land Registry Form AP1 – application for first registration of title must be made on Land Registry Form FR1;

(b) the land certificate (if outstanding) or all the documents evidencing the unregistered title under cover of Land Registry Form DL (a copy or sufficient abstract of the latest document of title, not being a document of record is required to be lodged: Land Registration Rules 1925, r 20(ii);

(c) appropriate evidence of the appointment of the personal representatives as indicated on the Form unless they have already been registered as proprietors of the land; and

(d) the requisite fee (if one is payable).

Method of reproduction. As to the method of reproduction of Land Registry forms see the Land Registration Rules 1925, rr 308-308B (as substituted by the Land Registration Rules 1997/3037, r 47):

'**308.**—(1)Subject to rule 308A, any application or instrument in one of the Schedule 1 forms must:

(a)be printed in black on durable white A4 size paper;

(b)be reproduced as set out in the Schedule, that is to say as to its wording, layout, ruling, font and point size, and

(c)contain all the information required in an easily legible form.

(2)Where on a Schedule 1 form (other than Form DL) any panel is insufficient in size to contain the required insertions, and the method of production of the form does not allow the depth of the panel to be increased, the information to be inserted in the panel shall be continued on a continuation sheet in form CS.

(3)When completing a Schedule 1 form containing an additional provisions panel, any statement, certificate or application required or permitted by these rules to be included in the form for which the form does not otherwise provide and any additional provisions desired by the parties shall be inserted in that panel or on a continuation thereof.

(4)Where the form consists of more than one sheet of paper, or refers to an attached plan or a continuation sheet, all the sheets including any plan shall be securely fastened together.

Electronically produced forms

308A. Where the method of production of a Schedule 1 form permits:

(a)the depth of a panel may be increased or reduced to fit the material to be comprised in it, and a panel may be divided at a page break;

(b)instructions in italics may be omitted;

(c)inapplicable certificates and statements may be omitted;

(d)the plural may be used instead of the singular and the singular instead of the plural;

(e) panels which would contain only the panel number and the panel heading, if any, may be omitted, but such omission shall not affect the numbering of subsequent panels.

(f)'x' boxes may be omitted where all inapplicable statements and certificates have been omitted;

(g)the sub-headings in an additional provisions panel may be added to, amended, repositioned or omitted;

(h)'Seller' may be substituted for 'Transferor' and 'Buyer' for 'Transferee' in a transfer on sale.

Paragraphs (f),(g) and (h) added by the Land Registration Rules 1999/128 r2(1) Sch 1, para 22.

Form of documents to be filed

308B. All documents (other than Schedule 1 forms, maps or plans) to be filed in the Registry shall be printed, typewritten, lithographed or written on durable paper, A4 size, and shall allow a sufficient margin, in order that they may be conveniently bound.'

Panel 2

Enter the full address, including postcode, or other description of the property. If the property is subject to a mortgage and the recipient is not entering into an indemnity covenant with the personal representatives the words 'subject to the mortgage dated (date) and made between (1) the Deceased and (2)(name of mortgagee)' should be added.

Panel 3

The date should be the date of the assent.

Panel 4

The deceased's full name should be reproduced as shown on the relevant grant of probate or letters of administration. If there is a discrepancy between that name and the name of the deceased as shown on the relevant register(s) of the title(s), it is helpful if the discrepancy is covered by suitable wording (eg 'FREDERICK ALAN SMITH also known as FREDERICK ALLAN SMITH'). There is no need to state the date of death nor to give particulars of the grant of representation: see the Administration of Estates Act 1925, s 36(4).

Panel 5

When the assent is made following a grant of probate, only proving executors should assent. There is no need to insert details of any executor who has died before the grant issued, or who has renounced probate, or to whom power has been reserved.

Panel 6

An assent not in favour of a named person shall not be effectual to pass a legal estate: Administration of Estates Act 1925, s 36(4).

Panel 7

This is the address which the Land Registry will use if they need to contact the recipient for any reason; eg for service of notices and correspondence.

Panel 9

If the personal representatives assent with full title guarantee they will give a covenant that they are disposing of the property free from all rights exercisable by third parties, other than any rights which they do not and could not reasonably be expected to know about: see the Law of Property (Miscellaneous Provisions) Act 1994, s 3(1)(b). Unless the personal representatives have personal knowledge of the property, it will be more usual for them to assent with limited title guarantee.

Panel 10

A reference to the recipients holding on trust for themselves as joint tenants informs the Registrar that the usual joint proprietor restriction need not be entered on the register (and the right of survivorship will apply). Conversely, if the recipients are to hold as tenants in common or as trustees for others (eg where personal representatives assent to themselves for the purpose of acting as continuing trustees of a will trust) a restriction will be entered. If the recipients are to hold as tenants in common in unequal shares, the third (bottom) box should be marked 'X' and the respective shares of each co-tenant expressly set out in the space below the box. The Registrar is bound to enter a restriction unless it is shown to his satisfaction that the joint proprietors are entitled for their own benefit, or can give a valid receipt for capital money or that one of them is a trust corporation: Land Registration Act 1925, s 58(3).

Panel 11

Additional clauses should be added here if required. It may, for example, be necessary to add:

(a)   an indemnity covenant given by the recipient(s) where the land is subject to restrictive covenants; or

(b)   in the case of unregistered land, confirmation that personal representatives have not given or made any previous assent or conveyance; or

(c)   prescribed statements where the assent is in favour of a charity; or

(d)   (if the assent is made by deed) a certificate that the document falls within the Stamp Duty (Exempt Instruments) Regulations 1987.

No acknowledgement for production of probate or letters of administration is required under the authority of which the transferor transfers, whether the land is registered or unregistered. The original or an office copy of the grant must accompany the application for registration; the Land Registry is not concerned with memoranda endorsed on the original grant and no copies are required by the Registry; however, it remains prudent conveyancing practice to endorse a memorandum of the assent on the original grant. Once the registration is completed there will be no future occasion upon which production of the original grant will be required by the Land Registry in relation to the land comprised in the assent.

Panel 12

The assent should be signed (or, if it contains covenants, executed as a deed) by the personal representatives in the presence of witnesses who should add their names and addresses. The recipient(s) will need to execute the document as a deed if they enter into covenants. For the prescribed forms of execution of transfers see the Land Registration Rules 1925/1093, Sch 3 as added by the Land Registration Rules 1997/3037 r 2(4), Sch 4.

To elaborate, the Land Registration Rules 1925/1093, Sch 3 as added by the Land Registration Rules 1997/3037, r 2(4), Sch 4 sets out forms of execution of deeds and, in a note which prefaces the Schedule, states that:

'All dispositions other than assents must be executed as a deed. In the case of an assent the words "as a deed" may be omitted.'

The net effect of this is that assents of registered land, where they are not executed as deeds, need to be signed under hand using the same wording, but modified as indicated so that such signatures require to be witnessed.

This panel should be completed with the inclusion of suitable words of execution in accordance with the requirements of the Land Registration Rules 1925. If a printed form is used and there is insufficient space to contain the execution clauses for all the executing parties, insert at the end of such clauses as are included in the panel 'Execution continued on Form CS' and set out the remaining clauses under the heading 'Execution of Form AS1 continued' on a continuation sheet in Form CS' attached to the main Form. If the method of production of the Form so allows, the depth of the panel may be varied to the extent necessary to allow all the necessary execution clauses to be included on the main form.

29

Assent on an independent trust for sale by personal representatives in favour of themselves as trustees of the will[1]

BY THIS ASSENT dated the [ ] day of [ ] we [executor] of [address] and [executor] of [address] the executors of [testator] late of [address] ('the Testator') who died on [date] and whose will was on [date] proved by us in the [Principal *or* [name] District Probate] Registry of the Family Division of the High Court as such personal representatives:

1   Assent to the vesting in ourselves [names of executors] of the freehold property described in the schedule to this assent ('the Property') for an estate in fee simple upon trust to sell the same or any part of it with full power to postpone the sale and to stand possessed of the net proceeds of sale and any other money applicable as capital and the net rents and profits until sale upon the trusts declared by the Testator in the will concerning his residuary estate[2].

2   Declare that we have not previously given or made any assent or conveyance in respect of any legal estate in the Property or any part of it.

[3   Declare that the power of appointing new trustees of this assent is vested in [name] during [her] life].

[4   *set out any limitation of the powers conferred by the Trusts of Land and Appointment of Trustees Act 1996, s 6 mirroring any such restriction contained in the Testator's will*[3]].

AS WITNESS etc

SCHEDULE

The Property

[describe the Property]

[signatures of the executors][4]

[signatures of witnesses]

1   No stamp duty is payable. For the requirements of a written assent in such circumstances see the Administration of Estates Act 1925, s 36(4). The assent is a crucial link in title to the legal estate showing that the property is no longer subject to the personal representatives powers of administration, albeit that it is vested in the same persons: see *Re King's Will Trusts, Assheton v Boyne* [1964] Ch 542, [1964] 1 All ER 833; *Re Edwards' Will Trusts, Edwards v Edwards* [1982] Ch 30, [1981] 2 All ER 941, CA. Note the protection of purchasers under the Administration of Estates Act 1925, s 36(7): following an assent of the legal estate, a purchaser may assume that it was made to the correct person and so is not concerned to see the contents of the will to confirm this. An assent is an occasion of first registration and may be effected by Form AS 1 (see **Precedent 28** above).

2   This assent, in contrast to **Precedent 27** above, creates an independent trust for sale (from the commencement date of the Trusts of Land and Appointment of Trustees Act 1996 it is a trust of land) ensuring that the will is kept off the title. Any conveyance will be pursuant to the trust created by the assent, not by the will. This remains the preferable course since otherwise the purchaser must look at the will which may continue to present problems despite the abolition of the involuntary strict settlement: compare *Dodsworth v Dodsworth* (1973) 228 Estates Gazette 1115, CA.

3   See para 2.68 above.

4   A witness is not strictly required where an assent is not by deed but is helpful for evidential purposes.

30

Assent by personal representatives in favour of tenants in common[1]

BY THIS ASSENT dated the [   ] day of [   ] we [executor] of [address] and [executor] of [address] the executors of [testator] late of [address] ('the Testator') who died on [date] and whose will was on [date] proved by us in the [Principal *or* [name] District Probate] Registry of the Family Division of the High Court as such personal representatives:

1   Assent to the vesting in [name] of [address] and [name] of [address] ('the Beneficiaries') of the freehold property described in the schedule to this assent ('the Property') TO HOLD to the Beneficiaries for an estate in fee simple as beneficial tenants in common in equal shares.

2   Declare that we have not previously given or made any assent or conveyance in respect of any legal estate in the Property or any part of it.

3   Acknowledge the right of the Beneficiaries to production of the probate of the will of the Testator (possession of which is retained by us) and to the delivery of copies of it.

AS WITNESS etc

SCHEDULE

The Property

[describe the Property]

[signatures of the executors][2]

[signatures of witnesses]

---

1   No stamp duty is payable. The beneficiaries will hold the property on a trust of land for themselves as beneficial tenants in common: see the Law of Property Act 1925, s 34 as amended by the Trusts of Land and Appointment of Trustees Act 1996 s 5, Sch 2, para 3, Sch 4. As a result there is no overriding duty to sell: instead there is both a power to sell and retain. An assent is an occasion of first registration and may be effected by Form AS1 (see **Precedent 28** above).

2   A witness is not strictly required where an assent is not by deed but is helpful for evidential purposes.

2 The Trustee Delegation Act 1999

31

Standard EPA Form

Part A: About using this form

1. You may choose one attorney or more than one. If you choose one attorney then you must delete everything between the square brackets on the first page of the form. If you choose more than one, you must decide whether they are able to act:

- jointly (that is, they must all act together and cannot act separately); or

- jointly and severally (that is, they can all act together but they can also act separately if they wish).

On the first page of the form, show what you have decided by crossing out one of the alternatives.

2. If you give your attorney(s) general power in relation to all your property and affairs, it means that they will be able to deal with your money or property and may be able to sell your house.

3. If you don't want your attorney(s) to have such wide powers, you can include any restrictions you like. For example, you can include a restriction that your attorney(s) must not act on your behalf until they have reason to believe that you are becoming mentally incapable; or a restriction as to what your attorney(s) may do. Any restrictions you choose must be written or typed where indicated on the second page of the form.

4. If you are a trustee (and please remember that co-ownership of a home involves trusteeship), you should seek legal advice if you want your attorney(s) to act as a trustee on your behalf.

5. Unless you put in a restriction preventing it your attorney(s) will be able to use any of your money or property to make any provision which you yourself might be expected to make for their own needs or the needs of other people. Your attorney(s) will also be able to use your money to make gifts, but only for reasonable amounts in relation to the value of your money and property.

6. Your attorney(s) can recover the out-of-pocket expenses of acting as your attorney(s). If your attorney(s) are professional people, for example solicitors or accountants, they may be able to charge for their professional services as well. You may wish to provide expressly for remuneration of your attorney(s) (although if they are trustees they may not be allowed to accept it).

7. If your attorney(s) have reason to believe that you have become or are becoming mentally incapable of managing your affairs, your attorney(s) will have to apply to the Court of Protection for registration of this power.

8. Before applying to the Court of Protection for registration of this power, your attorney(s) must give written notice that that is what they are going to do, to you and your nearest relatives as defined in the Enduring Powers of Attorney Act 1985. You or your relatives will be able to object if you or they disagree with registration.

9. This is a simplified explanation of what the Enduring Powers of Attorney Act 1985 and the Rules and Regulations say. If you need more guidance, you or your advisers will need to look at the Act itself and the rules and Regulations. The rules are the Court of Protection (Enduring Powers of Attorney) Rules 1986 (Statutory Instrument 1986/127). The Regulations are the Enduring Powers of Attorney (Prescribed Form) Regulations 1990 (SI 1990/1376).

10. Note to Attorney(s)

After the power has been registered you should notify the Court of Protection if the donor dies or recovers.

11. Note to Donor

Some of these explanatory notes may not apply to the form you are using if it has already been adapted to suit your particular requirements.

YOU CAN CANCEL THIS POWER AT ANY TIME BEFORE IT HAS TO BE REGISTERED

Part B: To be completed by the 'donor' (the person appointing the attorney(s))

Don't sign this form unless you understand what it means

Please read the notes
in the margin which
follow and which are
part of the form
itself.

Donor's name and
address.

[   ]

of

Donor's date of birth.

born on

See note 1 on the
front of this form. If
you are appointing
only one attorney,
you should cross out
everything between
the square brackets.
If appointing more
than two attorneys,
please give additional
name(s) on an
attached sheet.

appoint

of

- [and

    of

Cross out the one
which does not apply
(see note 1 on the
front of this form).

- jointly
- jointly and severally]

Cross out the one
which does not apply
(see note 2 on the
front of this form).
Add any additional
powers.

to be my attorney(s) for the purpose of the Enduring Powers of Attorney Act 1985
- with general authority to act on my behalf
- with authority to do the following on my behalf

If you don't want the
attorney(s) to have
general power, you
must give details here
of what authority you
are giving to the
attorney(s).

Cross out the one
which does not
apply.

in relation to
- all my property and affairs
- the following property and affairs

Part B: continued

Please read the notes in the margin which follow and which are part of the form itself.

If there are restrictions or conditions, insert them here; if not cross out these words if you wish (see note 3 on the front of this form).

If this form is being signed at your direction:
-the person signing must not be an attorney or any witness (to Parts B or C)
-you must add a statement that this form has been signed at your direction
-a second witness is necessary (please see below).

Your signature (or mark).

Date.

Someone must witness your signature.

Signature of witness

Your attorney(s) cannot be your witness. It is not advisable for your husband or wife to be your witness.

Signature of second witness.

A second witness is only necessary if this form is not being signed by you personally but at your direction (for example, if a physical disability prevents you from signing).

- subject to the following restrictions and conditions:

I intend that this power shall continue even if I become mentally incapable

I have read or have had read to me the notes in Part A which are part of, and explain this form

Signed by me as a deed...
and delivered

on

in the presence of

Full name of witness

Address of witness

in the presence of

Full name of witness

Address of witness

Part C: To be completed by the attorney(s)

Note: 1. This form may be adapted to provide for execution by a corporation.

2. If there is more than one attorney additional sheets in the form as shown below must

be added to this Part C.

Please read the notes in the margin which follow and which are part of the form itself.

I understand that I have a duty to apply for the Court for registration of this form under the Enduring Powers of Attorney Act 1985 when the donor is becoming or has become mentally incapable.

Don't sign this form before the donor has signed Part B or if, in your opinion, the donor was already mentally incapable at the time of signing Part B.

I also understand my limited power to use the donor's property to benefit persons other than the donor.

If this form is being signed at your direction:
-the person signing must not be an attorney or any witness (to Parts B or C)
-you must add a statement that this form has been signed at your direction
-a second witness is necessary (please see below).

I am not a minor.

Signature (or mark) of attorney.

Signed by me as a deed...
and delivered

Date.

on

Signature of witness.

in the presence of

The attorney must sign the form and his signature must be witnessed. The donor may not be the witness and one attorney may not witness the signature of the other.

Full name of witness

Address of witness

Signature of second witness.

in the presence of

A second witness is only necessary if this form is not being signed by you personally but at your direction (for example, if a physical disability prevents you from signing).

Full name of witness

Address of witness

32

Power of attorney pursuant to TDA 1999, s 1[1]

THIS POWER OF ATTORNEY is made the [   ] day of [   ] by [   ] of [   ] (hereinafter called 'the Donor')

WHEREAS:

1   The property known as [   ] at [   ] in the County of [   ] (hereinafter called 'the Property') is registered in the names of the Donor and X as proprietors at HM Land Registry with title absolute under Title No [   ][2].

2   The Property is vested in the Donor and X as trustees upon trust for themselves as tenants in common in equal shares[3].

3   The Donor wishes to appoint [   ] of [   ] (hereinafter called 'the Attorney') to be his attorney for the purposes hereafter mentioned.

4   The provisions of section 1 of the Trustee Delegation Act 1999 apply to this Power.

5   In this Power the expression 'the other trustee' means where the context permits the said X or other the trustees or trustee in whom the Property shall for the time be vested with the Donor as trustees.

NOW THIS DEED WITNESSES as follows:

1   The Donor HEREBY APPOINTS the Attorney to be his attorney to sell together with the other trustee the Property and for that purpose to employ agents and agree the terms and conditions of sale and together with the other trustee to receive the purchase money from the purchaser or purchasers and to deal with all matters ancillary to such sale and the Donor hereby delegates to the Attorney all trusts powers and discretions relating to such sale and matters ancillary to such sale vested in the Donor and the other trustee jointly and appoints the Attorney in his name and on his behalf to execute and do all deeds documents and acts required to be executed or done in the execution and exercise of such trusts powers and discretions[4]

2   [The Donor agrees to ratify and confirm whatever the Attorney shall in good faith do in the premises][5]

IN WITNESS etc

(to be executed as a deed by the Donor)[6]

1   The power is a general power satisfying the requirements of PAA 1971, s 10. It is not a trustee power under TA 1925, s 25 and accordingly may last for longer than 12 months. The fixed stamp duty of 50p on powers of attorney was abolished by FA 1984, s 85 and Sch 24.

2   Crucially the power falls within TDA 1999, s 1: see in particular the second recital indicating that the Donor has a beneficial interest in possession in land of which he is a trustee.

3   Had the Donor so wished he could have appointed X as his attorney. In such a case X could not, acting alone, give a good receipt for capital monies arising on a sale of the land and, because the conditions of TDA 1999, s 8 (see para 8.63 above) are not met, the Donor and X would together have had to act in that regard.

4   The power is limited to the sale of a particular property and matters ancillary thereto. It could, of course, have been granted in terms wide enough to allow the attorney to exercise all the Donor's trustee functions.

5   Clause 2 is not included in the statutory form set out in the Schedule to PAA 1971 and ratification will rarely be appropriate. In respect of acts of the Donee pursuant to the power it will not be necessary: in so far as the power is exceeded the Donor is not bound by his Donee's acts. Accordingly, only if the power is defective for a reason not apparent on its face is it thought that ratification may be appropriate.

6   Powers of attorney (other than enduring powers under the 1985 Act) are normally executed by the Donor alone.

33

Statement pursuant to TDA 1999, s 2(2)[1]

To: [purchaser]

The transfer dated the [   ] made between AB and CD of the one part and you of the other part, by which the freehold property known as [   ] at [   ] was transferred to you by AB and CD in consideration of the sum of £[   ], was executed on behalf of AB by me as his attorney under a general power of attorney made by AB on the [   ] appointing me to be his attorney in accordance with section 10 of the Powers of Attorney Act 1971. I now state and confirm that at the date of this transfer AB was, subject to the contract for the sale of this property made between him and CD and you, beneficially entitled to this freehold property as joint tenant with CD.

Dated the [   ]

[signature of attorney]

1   This precedent deals with the common situation where a land registry sale by joint tenants has been completed by a transfer executed on behalf of one of the owners by an attorney. It will not normally be satisfactory to incorporate the statement into the transfer since that would involve making the attorney a party to the document in his own right.

34

Clause excluding the operation of TDA 1999, s 1[1]

The provisions of sub-section (1) of section 1 of the Trustee Delegation Act 1999 shall not apply to any trustee or trustees for the time being of this settlement.

1   In the case of a settlement (as opposed to a statutory trust arising in cases of co-ownership) the operation of s 1 may give rise to anomalies and delegation under that section lacks the safeguards provided for in TA 1925, s 25 (as amended). Hence it will be desirable to include a provision in the settlement deed along the lines of this precedent especially when the trust fund includes, or may include, land.

35

Enduring power as a trust power under TA 1925, s 25 (as amended)[1]

Part A: About using this form

1. You may choose one attorney or more than one. If you choose one attorney then you must delete everything between the square brackets on the first page of the form. If you choose more than one, you must decide whether they are able to act:

- jointly (that is, they must all act together and cannot act separately); or

- jointly and severally (that is, they can all act together but they can also act separately if they wish).

On the first page of the form, show what you have decided by crossing out one of the alternatives.

2. If you give your attorney(s) general power in relation to all your property and affairs, it means that they will be able to deal with your money or property and may be able to sell your house.

3. If you don't want your attorney(s) to have such wide powers, you can include any restrictions you like. For example, you can include a restriction that your attorney(s) must not act on your behalf until they have reason to believe that you are becoming mentally incapable; or a restriction as to what your attorney(s) may do. Any restrictions you choose must be written or typed where indicated on the second page of the form.

4. If you are a trustee (and please remember that co-ownership of a home involves trusteeship), you should seek legal advice if you want your attorney(s) to act as a trustee on your behalf.

5. Unless you put in a restriction preventing it your attorney(s) will be able to use any of your money or property to make any provision which you yourself might be expected to make for their own needs or the needs of other people. Your attorney(s) will also be able to use your money to make gifts, but only for reasonable amounts in relation to the value of your money and property.

6. Your attorney(s) can recover the out-of-pocket expenses of acting as your attorney(s). If your attorney(s) are professional people, for example solicitors or accountants, they may be able to charge for their professional services as well. You may wish to provide expressly for remuneration of your attorney(s) (although if they are trustees they may not be allowed to accept it).

7. If your attorney(s) have reason to believe that you have become or are becoming mentally incapable of managing your affairs, your attorney(s) will have to apply to the Court of Protection for registration of this power.

8. Before applying to the Court of Protection for registration of this power, your attorney(s) must give written notice that that is what they are going to do, to you and your nearest relatives as defined in the Enduring Powers of Attorney Act 1985. You or your relatives will be able to object if you or they disagree with registration.

9. This is a simplified explanation of what the Enduring Powers of Attorney Act 1985 and the Rules and Regulations say. If you need more guidance, you or your advisers will need to look at the Act itself and the rules and Regulations. The rules are the Court of Protection (Enduring Powers of Attorney) Rules 1986 (Statutory Instrument 1986/127). The Regulations are the Enduring Powers of Attorney (Prescribed Form) Regulations 1990 (SI 1990/1376).

10. Note to Attorney(s)

After the power has been registered you should notify the Court of Protection if the donor dies or recovers.

11. Note to Donor

Some of these explanatory notes may not apply to the form you are using if it has already been adapted to suit your particular requirements.

YOU CAN CANCEL THIS POWER AT ANY TIME BEFORE IT HAS TO BE REGISTERED

Part B: To be completed by the 'donor' (the person appointing the attorney(s))

Don't sign this form unless you understand what it means

Please read the notes
in the margin which
follow and which are
part of the form
itself.

Donor's name and
address.

[   ]

of

Donor's date of birth.

See note 1 on the
front of this form. If
you are appointing
only one attorney,
you should cross out
everything between
the square brackets.
If appointing more
than two attorneys,
please give additional
name(s) on an
attached sheet.

born on

appoint

of

• [~~and~~

_____ ~~of~~

Cross out the one
which does not apply
(see note 1 on the
front of this form).

• ~~jointly~~
• ~~jointly and severally]~~

Cross out the one
which does not apply
(see note 2 on the
front of this form).
Add any additional
powers.

to be my attorney for the purpose of the Enduring Powers of Attorney Act 1985
• with general authority to act on my behalf
• ~~with authority to do the following on my behalf~~

If you don't want the
attorney(s) to have
general power, you
must give details here
of what authority you
are giving to the
attorney(s).

Cross out the one
which does not
apply.

in relation to
• ~~all my property and affairs~~
• the following property and affairs

the trust fund vested in me and X as trustees of a settlement dated the [ ] day of
[ ] [ ] and made between A of the one part and B and C of the other part and the
execution and exercise of all or any of the trust powers and discretions vested in me
and X jointly as the trustees of that settlement[2].

Part B: continued

Please read the notes in the margin which follow and which are part of the form itself.

- subject to the following restrictions and conditions:

The delegation under this power (made pursuant to section 25 of the Trustees Act 1925) is to commence on the [   ] day of [   ] [   ] and to continue only for nine months.

If there are restrictions or conditions, insert them here; if not cross out these words if you wish (see note 3 on the front of this form).

If this form is being signed at your direction:
-the person signing must not be an attorney or any witness (to Parts B or C)
-you must add a statement that this form has been signed at your direction
-a second witness is necessary (please see below).

I intend that this power shall continue even if I become mentally incapable

I have read or have had read to me the notes in Part A which are part of, and explain this form

Your signature (or mark).

Signed by me as a deed..
and delivered

Date.

Someone must witness your signature.

on

Signature of witness

Your attorney(s) cannot be your witness. It is not advisable for your husband or wife to be your witness.

in the presence of

Full name of witness

Address of witness

Signature of second witness.

A second witness is only necessary if this form is not being signed by you personally but at your direction (for example, if a physical disability prevents you from signing).

in the presence of

Full name of witness

Address of witness

Part C: To be completed by the attorney(s)[3]

Note: 1. This form may be adapted to provide for execution by a corporation.

2. If there is more than one attorney additional sheets in the form as shown below must be added to this Part C.

Please read the notes in the margin which follow and which are part of the form itself.

Don't sign this form before the donor has signed Part B or if, in your opinion, the donor was already mentally incapable at the time of signing Part B.

I understand that I have a duty to apply for the Court for registration of this form under the Enduring Powers of Attorney Act 1985 when the donor is becoming or has become mentally incapable.

I also understand my limited power to use the donor's property to benefit persons other than the donor.

If this form is being signed at your direction:
-the person signing must not be an attorney or any witness (to Parts B or C)
-you must add a statement that this form has been signed at your direction
-a second witness is necessary (please see below).

I am not a minor.

Signature (or mark) of attorney.

Signed by me as a deed...
and delivered

Date.

on

Signature of witness.

in the presence of

The attorney must sign the form and his signature must be witnessed. The donor may not be the witness and one attorney may not witness the signature of the other.

Full name of witness

Address of witness

Signature of second witness.

in the presence of

A second witness is only necessary if this form is not being signed by you personally but at your direction (for example, if a physical disability prevents you from signing).

Full name of witness

Address of witness

1   The enduring power falls within TA 1925, s 25 (as amended). Note that this precedent:

    (a)   delegates the trustee functions of the donor from a date that is set out in the instrument. As an alternative it could have specified from the date when the power was registered;

    (b)   is limited to a period of nine months: the maximum permitted period under TA 1925, s 25 is 12 months;

    (c)   delegates all the trustee's functions.

2   The power is not expressed to take effect under TDA 1999, s 1: it delegates X's trustee functions and does not indicate that these are limited to land etc in which X enjoys a beneficial interest as required by s 1.

3   The enduring power must be executed by the Donee (as well as the Donor).

36

Express trustee power of attorney[1]

THIS POWER OF ATTORNEY is made the [   ] day of [   ]

BY [   ] of [   ] ('the Principal')

WHEREAS the Principal and X are the present trustees of a Settlement ('the Settlement') dated the [   ] day of [   ] and made between A of the one part and B and C of the other part

NOW THIS DEED WITNESSES as follows:

1   The Principal HEREBY APPOINTS [   ] of [   ] ('the Attorney') to be his attorney in respect of the trusts powers and provisions of the Settlement in accordance with the provisions of section 25 of the Trustee Act 1925 (as substituted by the Trustee Delegation Act 1999).

2   The Principal hereby delegates to the Attorney for the period of [   ][2] months from the date hereof the execution and exercise on his behalf and in his name of all or any the trusts powers and discretions vested in the Principal and the said X jointly as trustees of the Settlement including all trusts powers and discretions implied or conferred by statute[3].

[3   The Principal agrees to ratify and confirm whatever the Attorney shall in good faith do in the premises][4].

IN WITNESS

(Executed as a Deed by the Principal)

1   This precedent effects the delegation by one trustee of all the trusts and powers vested in him and his co-trustee jointly as an alternative to the use of the statutory form contained in the Trustee Act 1925, s 25(6) (as substituted). It can readily be adapted for use when the statutory form cannot be used, for instance if joint attorneys are to be appointed or if only some of the trusts are to be delegated.

2   The period inserted must not exceed 12 months.

3   The statutory notices required by the Trustee Act 1925, s 25(4) (as substituted) must be given before or within seven days of the date of the power.

4   On ratification, see **Precedent 32, note 5** and on stamp duty see Precedent 32, note 1.

37

Notice given pursuant to the Trustee Act 1925, s 25(4) (as substituted by the TDA 1999)[1]

TO: A and B trustees of the Will dated the day of [   ] of the late C

I HEREBY GIVE YOU NOTICE that by a power of attorney dated the [   ] day of [   ] I delegated to [   ] of [   ] for the period of [   ] months from the date of such power all the trusts powers and discretions vested in me and you jointly as the trustees of the above Will. I have given this power of attorney as I expect to be abroad during much of this period.

1   For the requirement of notice, see TA 1925, s 25(4) as inserted by TDA 1999, s 5. Failure to give notice does not affect a third party dealing with the donee. As an internal trust matter, failure to give notice would appear to render the delegation invalid with the result that trustee decisions having been taken in the absence of the donor may be subject to attack and the attorney will have inter-meddled in the trust.

38

Power of attorney pursuant to the TA 1925, s 25 in favour of one attorney covering several trusts[1]

THIS POWER OF ATTORNEY is made the [   ] day of [   ] BY [   ] of

[   ] ('the Principal')

WHEREAS the Principal and AB are the present trustees of both the settlements short particulars of which are contained in the First Part of the Schedule hereto and the Principal and CD are the present trustees of the Will short particulars of which are contained in the Second Part of the said Schedule

NOW THIS DEED WITNESSES as follows:

1   The Principal HEREBY APPOINTS [   ] of [   ] ('the Attorney') to be his attorney in respect of the trusts powers and provisions of each of the said two settlements short particulars of which are contained in the First Part of the said Schedule ('the two settlements') and also in respect of the trusts powers and provisions of the Will short particulars of which are contained in the Second Part of the said Schedule ('the Will') in accordance with the provisions of Section 25 of the Trustee Act 1925 (as inserted by Section 5 of the Trustee Delegation Act 1999).

2.   The Principal hereby delegates to the Attorney for the period of [   ] months from the date of this Power First the execution and exercise on his behalf and in his name of all or any the trusts powers and discretions vested in the Principal and the said AB jointly as the trustees of each of the two settlements respectively including all trusts and powers implied or conferred by statute and Second the execution and exercise on his behalf and in his name of all or any the trusts powers and discretions vested in the Principal and the said CD jointly as the trustees of the Will including all trusts and powers implied or conferred by statute.

[3   The Principal agrees to ratify and confirm whatever the Attorney shall in good faith do in the premises][2].

IN WITNESS etc

THE SCHEDULE

First Part

[particular of the two settlements]

Second Part

[particulars of the Will]

[to be executed by the Principal]

1   Although the statutory form of power of attorney in s 25(6) does not deal with more than one trust it is not thought that the wording of the new s 25(5) is intended to prevent the administration of several trusts. This matter is explored in detail at para 8.44 above.

2   On ratification, see **Precedent 32, note 5** and for a form of notice to co-trustees see **Precedent 37** above.

39

Deed of appointment of additional trustee under TA 1925, s 36(6A)[1]

THIS DEED OF APPOINTMENT is made the [   ] day of [   ] BETWEEN [   ] of [   ] ('the Attorney') of the one part and [   ] of [   ] ('the New Trustee') of the other part AND IS SUPPLEMENTAL to a conveyance ('the Conveyance') dated the [   ] date of [   ] and made between A of the one part and B and C of the other part whereby the freehold property known as [   ] ('the Property') was conveyed to the said B and C upon trust for themselves as tenants in common in equal shares

WHEREAS:

1   By a Power of Attorney dated the [   ] day of [   ] the said B appointed the Attorney to be his attorney for the purposes of the Enduring Powers of Attorney Act 1985 with general authority to act on his behalf in relation to all his property and affairs and this enduring power of attorney was registered by the Court of Protection under section 6 of the said Act on the [   ] day of [   ].

2   The said C died on the [   ] day of [   ].

3   The said B is still beneficially entitled to a one half share of the property as tenant in common.

4   The Attorney wishes to sell part of the Property and accordingly to make the appointment hereafter contained.

NOW THIS DEED WITNESSES that in exercise of the power contained in section 36 (6A) of the Trustee Act 1925 (as inserted by the Trustee Delegation Act 1999) and of all other relevant powers the Attorney HEREBY APPOINTS the New Trustee to be an additional trustee of the Conveyance and to act jointly with the said B[2]

IN WITNESS etc

[To be executed as a deed by both the Attorney and the New Trustee]

1   TA 1925, s 36(6B) (inserted by TDA 1999) provides that the power of appointment arises if the attorney intends, *inter alia*, to exercise a function within TDA 1999, s 1. A trustee function is only within s 1 if the donor of the power has (at the time the act is done) a beneficial interest in the land etc.

2   Note carefully when the s 36(6A) power can be exercised: the attorney must be acting under a registered EPA.

40

Power for trustees to delegate both collectively and individually – exclusion of s 25[1]

Power for the Trustees collectively or for any of them individually (with the consent of the others or other of them) to delegate to any person or persons (not being the Settlor or any spouse of the Settlor but including in the case of delegation by an individual Trustee any other Trustee and including also any beneficiary or beneficiaries under the trusts of this Deed) at any time and for any period and in any manner and on any terms and conditions all or any of the trusts powers and discretions herein declared or conferred by this Deed or by law and section 25 of the Trustee Act 1925 (as substituted by the Trustee Delegation Act 1999) shall not apply to this Deed.

1 This express power ousts the statutory restrictions on trustee delegation in TDA 1999, s 1 and s 5 (recasting TA 1925, s 25). The delegation does not need to be by deed. It can be made 'in any manner' (hence permitting the use of both EPAs and general powers under PAA 1971, s 10). It removes the restrictions of TA 1925, s 25: eg as to a maximum duration of 12 months. Notice however that the two-trustee rule under TDA 1999, s 7 is mandatory and may create problems if a sole co-trustee has been appointed as attorney. For collective delegation, see **Precedent 56** below.

3 The Trustee Act 2000

41

Exclusion of the duty of care under
TA 2000, s 1[1]

The duty of care contained in section 1 of the Trustee Act 2000 shall not apply to the Trustees in the exercise of any of the powers conferred on them by this settlement nor to any duties relating to the exercise of such powers nor to the exercise by the Trustees of any powers contained in or duties imposed by the Trustee Act 2000 the Trustee Act 1925 the Trusts of Land and Appointment of Trustees Act 1996 or any other statute where that duty of care is expressed to be applicable[2].

1   The duty of care can be excluded in the trust instrument: see TA 2000, Sch 1, para 7. As an alternative to excluding the duty, draftsmen (obviously after agreeing the matter with the settlor) may prefer to deal with the matter in an exculpation clause: see further **Precedent 42** below. Of course this will mean that there may still be a breach of duty (albeit not actionable because of the exculpation clause) and if such breach was serious and repeated a court might remove the trustees.
2   Consider, as an alternative, replacing the statutory duty with a lesser obligation, 'to act in good faith' (see the now repealed TA 1925, s 23(1)).

42

Trustee exoneration clauses

(A)   'No trustee shall be liable for any loss or damage which may happen
        to [the Trust Fund] or any part thereof or the income thereof at any
        time or from any cause whatsoever unless such loss or damage shall
        be caused by his own actual fraud . . .'

Notes

1.   A longer exculpation clause is set out as clause 11 of **Precedent 1** and an alternative
        clause is at (B) below. The above clause was considered by the Court of Appeal in *Armitage
        v Nurse* [1998] Ch 241, [1997] 2 All ER 705.

2.   A clause will be effective to protect trustees against the consequences of mistake or
        negligence. A clause will not, however, be valid if it seeks to cover any dishonest intention
        eg if it purported to afford protection to trustees who had been fraudulent or recklessly
        indifferent to their fiduciary duties. Such a clause would offend 'the irreducible trust core'
        which was explained as follows by Millett LJ in the Court of Appeal:

        'there is an irreducible core of obligations owned by the trustees to the beneficiaries
        and enforceable by them which is fundamental to the concept of a trust. If the
        beneficiaries have no rights enforceable against the trustees there are no trusts. But I
        do not accept the further submission that these core obligations include the duties of
        skill and care, prudence and diligence. The duty of the trustees to perform the trusts
        honestly and in good faith for the benefit of the beneficiaries is the minimum necessary
        to give substance to the trusts, but in my opinion it is sufficient.'

        As a result this clause will be effective to protect trustees against a negligent breach of the
        statutory duty of care: it will also protect trustees who commit a 'judicious' breach of trust.
        However, it is not sufficient for the trustee to believe that he is acting in the interests of the
        beneficiaries by committing a breach of trust if that belief was so unreasonable that no
        reasonable solicitor-trustee could have held it (see the preliminary decision of the Court of
        Appeal in *Walker v Stones* [2000] 4 All ER 412, [2001] 2 WLR 623.

3.   The clause can be relied upon by the person who drafted it provided (and this is a general
        requirement for the validity of such clauses) that it had been agreed by the settlor or
        testator. Normally this will be presumed from his execution of the trust or will: see *Bogg v
        Raper* (1998) Times, 22 April, CA.

(B)   Alternative clause

        'No Trustee being an individual [who gives his services gratuitously]
        shall be liable for any loss to the capital or income of the Trust Fund
        caused by any improper investment or purchase made by him in
        good faith or for the negligence or fraud of any agent employed by
        him or by any other Trustee although the employment of such agent
        may not have been strictly necessary or resulting from any other
        cause whatever other than wilful and individual fraud or wrongdo-
        ing on the part of the Trustee who is sought to be made liable.'

(C)   Vicarious liability

At para 10.21 above it was stated that despite the repeal of TA 1925, s 30(2) a trustee will not become vicariously liable for the acts of his co-trustee. To put the matter beyond doubt a cautious draftsman might include the following clause (even in cases where the trustees were not otherwise being protected by an exoneration clause):

'A Trustee shall be liable and accountable only for money and property actually received by him and (subject to the provisions of clause [   ]¹ of this Deed) only for his own acts receipts omissions and defaults and not for those of any other Trustee.'

1   The number of the exoneration clause (if any) should be inserted here.

43

Power to invest only in ethical investments[1, 2]

(a)   Money for the time being subject to the trusts of this settlement and requiring investment shall be invested or laid out in the purchase or otherwise in the acquisition of shares stock debentures loan stock or other securities of companies which or the subsidiaries of which are engaged in one or some or other of the following activities:

[insert details]

(b)   The general power of investment contained in section 3 of the Trustee Act 2000 shall not apply to this settlement.

Notes

1.   For a consideration of ethical investment, see para 11.18 above.
2.   A clause on these lines will result in a somewhat narrow power of investment. It would be more usual to have a wide power of investment or adopt the general power of investment under the Trustee Act 2000, s 3 but exclude certain categories of investment considered by the Settlor to be unethical: see **Precedent 44** below.

44

Clause prohibiting certain investments[1]

Notwithstanding the provisions of the preceding sub-clause the Trustees shall not (whether in exercise of the power of investment conferred by that sub-clause or of the general power of investment contained in section 3 of the Trustee Act 2000) invest in the shares stock debentures loan stock or other securities of any company which is or any of the subsidiaries of which are engaged in any of the following activities:

[insert details]

1   This is a precedent for a sub-clause following another which conferred a wide power of investment excluding from its ambit and from the general power of investment under the Trustee Act 2000 certain investments which the settlor considers 'unethical'. The general power of investment may be excluded, see the Trustee Act 2000, s 6(1).

45

Power to retain assets (with particular reference to private company shares[1-4])

Power to retain any assets subject to the trusts of this settlement (including any uninvested money) in their actual state and condition for any period even though the whole or a substantial part of the assets so subject may be producing no or little income or may consist of shares or securities of a single company and in particular (but without prejudice to the generality of the foregoing) to retain any shares debentures loan stock or other securities of any private company (whether now transferred to them or acquired hereafter) and so that the Trustees shall not be liable for any loss occasioned to the Trust Fund by reason of the retention of any such shares debentures loan stock or other securities.

1 Many trusts are set up expressly to hold private company shares and the application of TA 2000, ss 4 and 5 can present problems in such cases.

2 This clause confers a power to retain with particular reference to private company shares. The duty to review the trust investments imposed by s 4(2) and to obtain proper advice when doing so under the Trustee Act 2000, s 5(2) will still apply to the retained investments since it would appear that the duties under ss 4 and 5 cannot be excluded.

3 For an illustration of the problems that may face trustees who hold shares in the 'family' company, see *Walker v Stones* [2000] 4 All ER 412, [2001] 2 WLR 623, CA.

4 Consider also including clauses:

 (a) which allow trustees to retain director's fees;

 (b) which exonerate trustees from liability for failure to interfere in the affairs of the company (and to obtain a distribution of profit by way of dividend).

46

Power to effect life assurance and appoint the policies on trust[1]

1 The Trustees shall have power to effect maintain and deal with any insurance or insurances upon the life of any person or persons and so that:

    (i)   the Trustees may pay all premiums and other costs relating to such insurance and any amounts necessary for keeping on foot or reinstating such policy or policies out of [the income or] the capital of the Trust Fund[2];

    [(ii)   nothing in this clause shall authorise any accumulations of income within section 164 of the Law of Property Act 1925[3].]

2 The Trustees shall in respect of any policy or policies effected under the power conferred by the preceding sub-clause have all the powers of an absolute owner including power to surrender convert or otherwise deal with any such policy or policies or any bonuses attaching thereto or part of them in such manner as the Trustees shall consider most beneficial to the persons beneficially interested therein.

3 The Trustees (being at least two in number or a trust corporation) shall have power at any time during the Trust Period to appoint that any policy effected on the life of any person or persons under the power contained in the preceding sub-clause (a) shall be held on such trusts and with and subject to such powers and provisions (including if thought fit protective and discretionary trusts and powers exercisable at the discretion of the Trustees or of any other person or persons and authorising the delegation of any discretion) in favour or otherwise for the benefit of all or any one or more of the Discretionary Beneficiaries as the Trustees in their absolute discretion (due regard being had to the law concerning remoteness) think fit. Provided that the Trustees (being at least two in number) may at any time or times during the Trust Period by deed or deeds extinguish (or restrict the future exercise of) the power conferred by this sub-clause.

---

1   This clause is intended for use in an interest in possession trust where the trustees might wish, in particular, to insure the life of the life tenant but ensure that the resulting policy is held on different trusts in which he/she does not have a life interest. It is assumed that the terms 'Trust Fund', 'Trust Period' and 'Discretionary Beneficiaries' have been defined.

2   It might be considered preferable to exclude the ability to pay premiums etc out of income lest this is prevents the settlement qualifying as an interest in possession trust for the purposes of inheritance tax: see *Pearson v IRC* [1981] AC 753, [1980] 2 All ER 479, HL. If the words in brackets are excluded, para (ii) of this sub-clause should be omitted.

3   There is some uncertainty as to whether payment of premiums out of income amounts to an accumulation of income. The better view is that being an administrative power it does not.

47

Power for trustees to carry on a business[1,2]

The Trustees shall have power from time to time to carry on whether by themselves or in partnership with any other individual or corporation (whether or not such individual shall be beneficially entitled under the trusts of this settlement) any trade or business which they consider to be for the benefit of the beneficiaries under this settlement and in connection with any such trade or business the Trustees may:

(a)   employ all or any part or parts of the capital of the Trust Fund;

(b)   be indemnified out of the Trust Fund against any liability which they may incur in connection with the setting up carrying on or dissolution of such trade or business;

(c)   use for the purposes of the trade or business any land or buildings which are subject to the trusts of this settlement;

(d)   exercise in relation to any such trade or business and the assets thereof any of the administrative powers conferred on the Trustees by this Deed or by law including (but without prejudice to the generality of the foregoing) powers of borrowing and charging and of delegation;

(e)   employ or join in employing on such terms as to remuneration and otherwise as they shall think fit any manager and other employees.

1   Trustees cannot carry on a trade or business without express authorisation: see *Re Berry* [1962] Ch 97, [1961], 1 All ER 529. A wide investment power does not allow trustees to 'invest' in a business.
2   'Business' is a wider word than 'trade'.

48

Sub-clause allowing trustees to form limited liability partnerships[1]

Any partnership formed by the Trustees to carry on any business pursuant to the preceding sub-clause may be a limited liability partnership under the Limited Liability Partnership Act 2000 and the Trustees may agree with the other partners therein (who may include any beneficiary or beneficiaries under the trusts of this settlement) such terms and conditions of the partnership as they shall think fit.

1   The Limited Liability Partnership Act 2000 came into force on 6 April 2001 and is expected to prove useful to trustees mindful of their personal liability for business debts which would apply if it was carried on as a 'sole trade' or through the medium of a simple partnership.

49

Power to borrow and charge property[1]

The Trustees shall have power to borrow money on such terms as to interest repayment and otherwise as they may think fit and whether upon the security of a mortgage or charge on any assets or property comprised in the Trust Fund or upon personal security only and to use the monies so borrowed in purchasing or subscribing for investments or property (including land) to be held as part of the Trust Fund or for any purpose for which capital money forming part of the Trust Fund may be used.

1   Trustees do not have power to borrow for investment purposes in the absence of express authorisation: see *Re Suenson's Settlement, Taylor* [1974] 3 All ER 397, *Moores v Moores* [1974] 1 WLR 1280.

50

Clause imposing an obligation to insure[1]

The Trustees shall insure and keep insured at the expense of the income or the capital of the Trust Fund to their full reinstatement value [all buildings situate on land in England and Wales for the time being subject to the trusts of this settlement] against loss or damage by fire aircraft explosion and the other risks usually covered by a comprehensive buildings' policy with an insurance office of repute[2].

1   For a consideration of the revised TA 1925, s 19, see para 14.1 above. A consideration of to what extent there may be a *duty* on the trustees to insure is at para 14.7.

2   The clause imposes an obligation to insure the property concerned as distinct from giving a power to insure. This clause applies to buildings but can be adapted so that it applies alternatively or in addition to other insurable property such as chattels or a particular class of chattels.

51

Clause negating any liability for failure to insure[1,2]

The Trustees shall not be obliged to insure any buildings situate on land for the time subject to the trusts of this settlement or any chattels or other assets for the time being so subject and shall not be liable for any loss resulting from any failure or omission to effect or maintain any such insurance or for the insufficiency of the amount of the cover or the risks covered under any insurance that is effected by them.

1   There is a default *power* to insure given by TA 1925, s 19 (as substituted by TA 2000, s 34);
2   *Snell's Equity* (30th edn) at para 12.12 states that trustees are not bound to insure the trust property against loss or damage by fire unless the trust instrument imposes such an obligation upon them (*Bailey v Gould* (1840) 4 Y & C 221). See further para 14.7 above and, in particular, footnote 1.

52

Power to appoint a custodian trustee[1]

1   Any incorporated body (whether or not a trust corporation) may at any time be appointed as a custodian trustee of this Deed by the person or persons having the power of appointing new trustees hereof [but so that such appointment shall be upon the condition that such custodian trustee may at any time be removed by the general trustees or trustee for the time being executing a deed of removal].

2   The person or persons appointing a custodian trustee may agree the terms and provisions for the remuneration of the incorporated body appointed out of the income or capital of the Trust Fund.

---

1   A custodian trustee is quite different from a custodian who may be appointed to hold trust documents or property. A custodian trustee is the creature of the Public Trustee Act 1906 in whom the ownership of all the trust property is vested while the active powers remain in the 'managing trustees'.

53

Trustee remuneration clause[1-3]

1   Any of the Trustees who shall be an individual engaged in any profession or business [which consists of or includes the administration of trusts or the management of assets of a type comprised in the Trust Fund or the advising of trustees either generally or in respect of any particular aspects of their functions or obligations] either alone or in partnership shall be entitled to charge and be paid and to retain all professional or other charges for any business done or time spent or services rendered by him or his firm in connection with the trusts powers and provisions of this settlement and shall also be entitled to retain any share of brokerage or commission paid to him or his firm by any broker agent or insurance office in connection with any acquisition of or dealing with any investments or property or the effecting or payment of any premium on any policy of insurance subject or intended to become subject to the trusts of this settlement.

2   None of the Trustees holding any directorship or other office or employment or retainer in relation to any company all or any of whose shares stock or securities shall at any time be subject to any trusts of this settlement shall be accountable for any remuneration received in connection with such directorship office employment or retainer[4].

3   Notwithstanding anything contained in this clause neither the Settlor nor any spouse of the Settlor who may for the time being be one of the Trustees shall be entitled to charge or be paid or retain all or any share of any professional or other charges by reason of this clause or be relieved thereby from any liability to account as a trustee for any money or assets[5].

1   Clause 1 is a standard precedent concerned with the question of which trustees should be remunerated. Should it only be a professional whose business involves acting as and advising trustees? TA 2000 defines when a trustee 'acts in a professional capacity' in s 28(5) and limits statutory remuneration accordingly. In this precedent, include the words in brackets if this restriction is required. If, on the other hand, it is desired to enable trustees who exercise *any* profession or vocation to charge then delete these words.

2   There may be some uncertainty as to what is included in the term 'profession or business'. Is it limited to a self employed person (compare the income tax distinction between trades professions and vocations falling under Sch D, Case I and offices and employments under Sch E)? If so, it excludes employees including (say) the senior investment manager of a merchant bank who may be *the* ideal trustee for the particular trust. It is arguable (although rather weakly) that such a person carries on a business (see Kessler *Drafting Trusts and Will Trusts* (5th edn, 2000) at para 18.56). Given these doubts it may be safer to employ a wider clause along the lines of the following:

> 'Any trustee, whether he is engaged in a profession or business or merely acts in a personal capacity, shall be entitled to charge and be paid all normal professional or other reasonable charges for business done, services rendered or time spent by such

trustee personally, or by such trustee's firm or company, in the administration of these trusts including acts which a trustee not engaged in any profession or business could have done personally.'

3   The wider formulation of **Precedent 53** prohibits a lay trustee from receiving remuneration but would, allow (say) a self-employed plumber or carpenter to be paid. This may not be thought entirely logical! Taking account of the remarks set out in this note and in the previous notes the authors incline to the view that although widely used in practice this clause may be unsatisfactory in trusts where trustees other than solicitors and accountants are involved.

4   Clause 2 is required to exclude the self dealing rule illustrated in cases such as *Re Dover Coalfield Extension Ltd* [1908] 1 Ch 65, CA: see further *Snell's Equity* (30th edn) para 11.76.

5   Clause 3 is designed to ensure the neither the settlor nor his spouse can benefit in any way from the trust and is primarily dictated by tax considerations.

54

Delegation of investment decisions by letter[1]

To: [   ] Ltd

We [   ] and [   ] being the present trustees of a settlement dated the
[   ] day of [   ] and made between [   ] (1) and [   ] and
[   ] (2) in exercise of the power contained in [clause [   ] of the
settlement or section 11 of the Trustee Act 2000] hereby delegate to you
[the power of investment and the power to sell convert and transpose
investments contained in clauses [   ] and [   ] of the settlement
respectively] [the general power of investment contained in section 3 of the
Trustee Act 2000] in respect of the investments and moneys from time to
time comprised in the Trust Fund (as defined in the settlement) such powers
to be exercised upon the terms and conditions set out in a letter of even date
herewith and addressed by us to you a copy of which is annexed hereto.

You are empowered to exercise any of the powers and discretions relating to
investment or ancillary to it conferred on us as the trustees of the settlement
by the settlement or by law including the power contained in [clause [   ]
of the settlement *or* section 16 of the Trustee Act 2000] to place investments
in the names of nominees and to give instructions to such nominees.

The delegation made hereby shall be revocable at any time by written notice
given by us (or the survivor of us) to you or by you to us (or the survivor of
us) but so that any person dealing with you in good faith shall be entitled to
assume that no notice has been given by either of us to the other revoking
this delegation.

DATED this [   ] day of [   ]]²

(To be signed by the Trustees)

1   This precedent is intended for use in conjunction with a letter on the lines of that
     contained in **Precedent 55** containing the terms of the delegation and the policy
     statement.
2   The delegation of the investment power is not by power of attorney, as this is not a
     requirement of the power contained in TA 2000, s 11 or usually of express powers to
     collectively delegate administrative powers. If any number of productions of the instru-
     ment of delegation are required, however, there is a practical advantage in using a power
     of attorney as copies, duly certified, can be used to prove its contents under the Powers of
     Attorney Act 1971, s 3. Any number of registrations or productions can then be dealt with
     at the same time and no harm ensues if a copy is lost or an institution fails to return one.

Letter to fund manager setting out the terms of his appointment and incorporating the policy statement

Dear Sirs

This letter is written in connection with the appointment by us today of you as our delegates in the exercise of our powers of investment under the settlement ('the Settlement') dated [date] and made between [parties] of which we are the present trustees.

The terms of the client agreement which is annexed to this letter will apply to your appointment except insofar as they are inconsistent with the terms set out in this letter.

We confirm that your appointment authorises you to make purchases and sales of investments on our behalf without previous reference to us in connection with the funds of this Settlement.

There are stated in the third schedule our powers of investment as trustees of the Settlement. We confirm that, within the scope of the those powers, and subject to the duties placed on trustees in selecting investments by the general law and to what is stated in the next paragraph, you are authorised to purchase stocks and shares throughout the world and units in all unit trusts and offshore funds, including unit trusts under your own management[1].

You will find listed in the first schedule:

(a)   any investments which are not to be sold without our specific authority; and

(b)   any investments in which we do not wish you to invest.

We will give you notice of any change in either of these categories of investment.

Subject to the duty imposed upon trustees by the general law to have regard to the interests of all beneficiaries, both present and future, and whether in capital or income, we have indicated in the second schedule the balance between income and capital growth which we consider appropriate to the circumstances of the Settlement. We will give you notice of any shift in emphasis that we may from time to time consider desirable. Valuations of the investments in the Settlement and reports on the portfolio should be sent to us at least [every [   ] months].

Any cash forming part of the portfolio which is not immediately required for the purpose of any transactions may, at your discretion, be placed on deposit in any currency at normal commercial rates of interest, but small balances of less than £[   ] may temporarily be held on current account.

We will pay your service charges (plus VAT where appropriate) in accordance with your current scale of stated charges as amended from time to time by prior written notice, which may be deducted from any cash balances held by you.

Please sign and return to us the attached copy of this letter to indicate your acceptance of its terms.

Yours faithfully

[signatures of the trustees]

FIRST SCHEDULE

1   We do not wish the following holdings to be sold without our prior consent:
       No investments in this category at present.

2   We do not wish any holdings to be bought in the following companies or sectors:
       No investments in this category at present.

SECOND SCHEDULE

We wish your investment policy for this account to be based on an even balance between income and capital growth.

THIRD SCHEDULE

[The general power of investment under section 3 of the Trustee Act 2000]

[Powers set out in the [name] settlement:

'Trust money may be invested or laid out in the purchase or otherwise in the acquisition of or at interest upon the security of any shares stocks funds securities policies of insurance or other investments or property (movable or immovable) of whatsoever nature and wheresoever situated and whether or not productive of income and whether involving liability or not or upon such personal credit with or without security in all respects as the Trustees shall in their discretion think fit to the intent that the Trustees shall have the same full and unrestricted powers of investing transposing investments and dealing with trust money and buying or selling property in all respects as if they were absolutely entitled beneficially.']

ANNEXURE

[client agreement]

1   See TA 2000, s 14(3)(4) under which an agent should not be permitted to act 'in circumstances capable of giving rise to a conflict of interest'. In practice fund managers are commonly allowed to invest in funds which they manage and such delegation is felt to be 'reasonably necessary' (see s 14(2)).

56

Clause providing for collective delegation by trustees of their administrative powers including delegation to beneficiaries[1]

1. Power to delegate all or any of the powers of the Trustees contained in the schedule and any administrative powers conferred by law (and all or any of the duties and discretions of the Trustees relating to the exercise of such powers) to any person or persons (not being the Settlor or any spouse of the Settlor) subject to such conditions (if any) and upon such terms (including the remuneration of any such delegate) as the Trustees shall think fit (without being liable for the acts or defaults of any such delegate) and to revoke or modify any such delegation or conditions or terms.

2. The persons in whose favour the Trustees may delegate all or any of such powers include any one or more of the Trustees and any one of more of the beneficiaries under the trusts of this settlement (but other than and excluding the Settlor or any spouse of the Settlor).

3. A delegation by the trustees under the foregoing power to two or more persons may authorise such delegates to exercise the powers duties and discretions delegated either jointly or jointly and severally.

4. Section 11 of the Trustee Act 2000 shall not apply to this Deed[2,3].

1   The power to delegate under the Trustee Act 2000, s 11 cannot be exercised in favour of a beneficiary. This precedent permits trustees to delegate administrative powers to any person (other than the settlor or his spouse) *including a beneficiary*. It also permits joint and several delegation (contrast TA 2000, s 12(2)) and see para 12.20 above.
2   The power to delegate contained in the Trustee Act 2000, s 11 may be excluded: see s 26(b) of that Act.
3   The duty to keep the arrangements with an agent under review and to intervene contained in the Trustee Act 2000, s 22 may also, if desired, be excluded in connection with this express power: see s 21(3) of the Act.

Part V:
Appendices

Appendix 1

Trustee Act 1925

Part I

[. . .]

Part II

General Powers of Trustees and Personal Representatives

Part V

General Provisions

Part I

2   [...]

[...]

Amendment

Repealed by the Trustee Act 2000, s 40(1), (3), Sch 2, Pt II, para 18, Sch 4, Pt II.
Date in force: 1 February 2001: see SI 2001/49, art 2.

3   [...]

[...]

Amendment

Repealed by the Trustee Act 2000, s 40(1), (3), Sch 2, Pt II, para 18, Sch 4, Pt II.
Date in force: 1 February 2001: see SI 2001/49, art 2.

4   [...]

[...]

Amendment

Repealed by the Trustee Act 2000, s 40(1), (3), Sch 2, Pt II, para 18, Sch 4, Pt II.
Date in force: 1 February 2001: see SI 2001/49, art 2.

5   [...]

[...]

Amendment

Repealed by the Trustee Act 2000, s 40(1), (3), Sch 2, Pt II, para 18, Sch 4, Pt II.
Date in force: 1 February 2001: see SI 2001/49, art 2.

6   [...]

[...]

Amendment

Repealed by the Trustee Act 2000, s 40(1), (3), Sch 2, Pt II, para 18, Sch 4, Pt II.
Date in force: 1 February 2001: see SI 2001/49, art 2.

7   [...]

[...]

Amendment

Repealed by the Trustee Act 2000, s 40(1), (3), Sch 2, Pt II, para 18, Sch 4, Pt II.
Date in force: 1 February 2001: see SI 2001/49, art 2.

8   [. . .]

[. . .]

Amendment

Repealed by the Trustee Act 2000, s 40(1), (3), Sch 2, Pt II, para 18, Sch 4, Pt II.

Date in force: 1 February 2001 (except in relation to loans or investments made before that date): see the Trustee Act 2000, s 40(2), Sch 3, para 2 and SI 2001/49, art 2.

9   [. . .]

[. . .]

Amendment

Repealed by the Trustee Act 2000, s 40(1), (3), Sch 2, Pt II, para 18, Sch 4, Pt II.

Date in force: 1 February 2001 (except in relation to loans or investments made before that date): see the Trustee Act 2000, s 40(2), Sch 3, para 3 and SI 2001/49, art 2.

10   [. . .]

[. . .]

Amendment

Repealed by the Trustee Act 2000, s 40(1), (3), Sch 2, Pt II, para 18, Sch 4, Pt II.

Date in force: 1 February 2001: see SI 2001/49, art 2.

11   [. . .]

[. . .]

Amendment

Repealed by the Trustee Act 2000, s 40(1), (3), Sch 2, Pt II, para 18, Sch 4, Pt II.

Date in force: 1 February 2001: see SI 2001/49, art 2.

Part II

General Powers of Trustees and Personal Representatives

12 Power of trustees for sale to sell by auction, etc

(1) Where [a trustee has a duty or power to sell property], he may sell or concur with any other person in selling all or any part of the property, either subject to prior charges or not, and either together or in lots, by public auction or by private contract, subject to any such conditions respecting title or evidence of title or other matter as the trustee thinks fit, with power to vary any contract for sale, and to buy in at any auction, or to rescind any contract for sale and to re-sell, without being answerable for any loss.

(2) A [duty] or power to sell or dispose of land includes a *trust* [duty] or power to sell or dispose of part thereof, whether the division is horizontal, vertical, or made in any other way.

(3) This section does not enable an express power to sell settled land to be exercised where the power is not vested in the tenant for life or statutory owner.

Amendment

Sub-ss (1), (2): words in square brackets substituted by the Trusts of Land and Appointment of Trustees Act 1996, s 25(1), Sch 3, para 3(2); for savings in relation to entailed interests created before the commencement of that Act, and savings consequential upon the abolition of the doctrine of conversion, see s 25(4), (5) thereof.

13 Power to sell subject to depreciatory conditions

(1) No sale made by a trustee shall be impeached by any beneficiary upon the ground that any of the conditions subject to which the sale was made may have been unnecessarily depreciatory, unless it also appears that the consideration for the sale was thereby rendered inadequate.

(2) No sale made by a trustee shall, after the execution of the conveyance, be impeached as against the purchaser upon the ground that any of the conditions subject to which the sale was made may have been unnecessarily depreciatory, unless it appears that the purchaser was acting in collusion with the trustee at the time when the contract for sale was made.

(3) No purchaser, upon any sale made by a trustee, shall be at liberty to make any objection against the title upon any of the grounds aforesaid.

(4) This section applies to sales made before or after the commencement of this Act.

14 Power of trustees to give receipts

(1) The receipt in writing of a trustee for any money, securities, [investments] or other personal property or effects payable, transferable, or deliverable to him under any trust or power shall be a sufficient discharge to the person paying, transferring, or delivering the same and shall effectually exonerate him from seeing to the application or being answerable for any loss or misapplication thereof.

(2) this section does not, except where the trustee is a trust corporation, enable a sole trustee to give a valid receipt for–

[(a)   proceeds of sale or other capital money arising under a trust of land;]

(b)   capital money arising under the Settled Land Act 1925.

(3)   This section applies notwithstanding anything to the contrary in the instrument, if any, creating the trust.

Amendment

Sub-s (1): word 'investments' in square brackets inserted by the Trustee Act 2000, s 40(1), Sch 2, Pt II, para 19.

15   Power to compound liabilities

A personal representative, or two or more trustees acting together, or, subject to the restrictions imposed in regard to receipts by a sole trustee not being a trust corporation, a sole acting trustee where by the instrument, if any, creating the trust, or by statute, a sole trustee is authorised to execute the trusts and powers reposed in him, may, if and as he or they think fit–

(a)   accept any property, real or personal, before the time at which it is made transferable or payable; or

(b)   sever and apportion any blended trust funds or property; or

(c)   pay or allow any debt or claim on any evidence that he or they think sufficient; or

(d)   accept any composition or any security, real or personal, for any debt or for any property, real or personal, claimed; or

(e)   allow any time of payment of any debt; or

(f)   compromise, compound, abandon, submit to arbitration, or otherwise settle any debt, account, claim, or thing whatever relating to the testator's or intestate's estate or to the trust;

and for any of these purposes may enter into, give, execute, and do such agreements, instruments of composition or arrangement, releases, and other things as to him or them seem expedient, without being responsible for any loss occasioned by any act or thing so done by him or them [if he has or they have discharged the duty of care set out in section 1(1) of the Trustee Act 2000].

Amendment

Words 'if he has or they have discharged the duty of care set out in section 1(1) of the Trustee Act 2000' in square brackets substituted by the Trustee Act 2000, s 40(1), Sch 2, Pt II, para 20.

Date in force: 1 February 2001: see SI 2001/49, art 2.

16   Power to raise money by sale, mortgage, etc

(1)   Where trustees are authorised by the instrument, if any, creating the trust or by law to pay or apply capital money subject to the trust for any purpose or in any manner, they shall have and shall be deemed always to have had power to raise the money required by sale, conversion, calling in, or mortgage of all or any part of the trust property for the time being in possession.

(2)   This section applies notwithstanding anything to the contrary contained in the instrument, if any, creating the trust, but does not apply to trustees of property

held for charitable purposes, or to trustees of a settlement for the purposes of the Settled Land Act 1925, not being also the statutory owners.

17 Protection to purchasers and mortgagees dealing with trustees

No purchaser or mortgagee paying or advancing money on a sale or mortgage purporting to be made under any trust or power vested in trustees, shall be concerned to see that such money is wanted; or that no more than is wanted is raised, or otherwise as to the application thereof.

18 Devolution of powers or trusts

(1) Where a power or trust is given to or imposed on two or more trustees jointly, the same may be exercised or performed by the survivors or survivor of them for the time being.

(2) Until the appointment of new trustees, the personal representatives or representative for the time being of a sole trustee, or, where there were two or more trustees of the last surviving or continuing trustee, shall be capable of exercising or performing any power or trust which was given to, or capable of being exercised by, the sole or last surviving or continuing trustee, or other the trustees or trustee for the time being of the trust.

(3) This section takes effect subject to the restrictions imposed in regard to receipts by a sole trustee, not being a trust corporation.

(4) In this section 'personal representative' does not include an executor who has renounced or has not proved.

[19 Power to insure]

[(1) A trustee may–

  (a) insure any property which is subject to the trust against risks of loss or damage due to any event, and

  (b) pay the premiums out of the trust funds.

(2) In the case of property held on a bare trust, the power to insure is subject to any direction given by the beneficiary or each of the beneficiaries–

  (a) that any property specified in the direction is not to be insured;

  (b) that any property specified in the direction is not to be insured except on such conditions as may be so specified.

(3) Property is held on a bare trust if it is held on trust for–

  (a) a beneficiary who is of full age and capacity and absolutely entitled to the property subject to the trust, or

  (b) beneficiaries each of whom is of full age and capacity and who (taken together) are absolutely entitled to the property subject to the trust.

(4) If a direction under subsection (2) of this section is given, the power to insure, so far as it is subject to the direction, ceases to be a delegable function for the purposes of section 11 of the Trustee Act 2000 (power to employ agents).

(5) In this section 'trust funds' means any income or capital funds of the trust.]

Amendment

Substituted by the Trustee Act 2000, s 34(1).

Date in force: 1 February 2001 (in relation to trusts created before or after that date): see the Trustee Act 2000, s 34(3) and SI 2001/49, art 2.

20   Application of insurance money where policy kept up under any trust, power or obligation

(1)   Money receivable by trustees or any beneficiary under a policy of insurance against the loss or damage of any property subject to a trust or to a settlement within the meaning of the Settled Land Act 1925 [. . .] shall, where the policy has been kept up under any trust in that behalf or under any power statutory or otherwise, or in performance of any covenant or of any obligation statutory or otherwise, or by a tenant for life impeachable for waste, be capital money for the purposes of the trust or settlement, as the case may be.

(2)   If any such money is receivable by any person, other than the trustees of the trust or settlement, that person shall use his best endeavours to recover and receive the money, and shall pay the net residue thereof, after discharging any costs of recovering and receiving it, to the trustees of the trust or settlement, or, if there are no trustees capable of giving a discharge therefor, into court.

(3)   Any such money—

    (a)   if it was receivable in respect of settled land within the meaning of the Settled Land Act 1925, or any building or works thereon, shall be deemed to be capital money arising under that Act from the settled land, and shall be invested or applied by the trustees, or, if in court, under the direction of the court, accordingly;

    (b)   if it was receivable in respect of personal chattels settled as heirlooms within the meaning of the Settled Land Act, 1925, shall be deemed to be capital money arising under that Act; and shall be applicable by the trustees, or, if in court, under the direction of the court, in like manner as provided by that Act with respect to money arising by sale of chattels as heirlooms as aforesaid;

    (c)   if it was receivable in respect of [land subject to a trust of land or personal property held on trust for sale], shall be held upon the trusts and subject to the powers and provisions applicable to money arising by a sale under such trust;

    (d)   in any other case, shall be held upon trusts corresponding as nearly as may be with the trusts affecting the property in respect of which it was payable.

(4)   Such money, or any part thereof, may also be applied by the trustees, or, if in court, under the direction of the court, in rebuilding, reinstating, replacing, or replacing the property loss or damaged, but any such application by the trustees shall be subject to the consent of any person whose consent is required by the instrument, if any, creating the trust to the investment of money subject to the trust, and, in the case of money which is deemed to be capital money arising under the Settled Land Act 1925, be subject to the provisions of that Act with respect to the application of capital money by the trustees of the settlement.

(5)   Nothing contained in this section prejudices or affects the right of any person to require any such money or any part thereof to be applied in rebuilding

reinstating, or repairing the property lost or damaged, or the rights of any mortgagee, lessor, or lessee, whether under any statute or otherwise.

(6)   This section applies to policies effected either before or after the commencement of this Act, but only to money received after such commencement.

Amendment

Sub-s (1): words omitted repealed by the Trustee Act 2000, ss 34(2), 40(3), Sch 4, Pt II.

Date in force: 1 February 2001 (in relation to trusts created before or after that date): see the Trustee Act 2000, s 34(3) and SI 2001/49, art 2.

Sub-s (3): in para (c) words 'land subject to a trust of land or personal property held on trust for sale' in square brackets substituted by the Trusts of Land and Appointment of Trustees Act 1996, s 25(1), Sch 3, para 3(5); for savings in relation to entailed interests created before the commencement of that Act, and savings consequential upon the abolition of the doctrine of conversion, see s 25(4), (5) thereof.

21   [...]

[...]

Amendment

Repealed by the Trustee Act 2000, s 40(1), (3), Sch 2, Pt II, para 21, Sch 4, Pt II.

Date in force: 1 February 2001: see SI 2001/49, art 2.

22   Reversionary interests, valuations and audit

(1)   Where trust property includes any share or interest in property not vested in the trustees, or the proceeds of the sale of any such property, or any other thing in action, the trustees on the same falling into possession, or becoming payable or transferable may—

(a)   agree or ascertain the amount or value thereof or any part thereof in such manner as they may think fit;

(b)   accept in or towards satisfaction thereof, at the market or current value, or upon any valuation or estimate of value which they may think fit, any authorised investments;

(c)   allow any deductions for duties, costs, charges and expenses which they may think proper or reasonable;

(d)   execute any release in respect of the premises so as effectually to discharge all accountable parties from all liability in respect of any matters coming within the scope of such release;

without being responsible in any such case for any loss occasioned by any act or thing so done by them [if they have discharged the duty of care set out in section 1(1) of the Trustee Act 2000].

(2)   The trustees shall not be under any obligation and shall not be chargeable with any breach of trust by reason of any omission—

(a)   to place any distringas notice or apply for any stop or other like order upon any securities or other property out of or on which such share or interest or other thing in action as aforesaid is derived, payable or charged; or

(b)   to take any proceedings on account of any act, default, or neglect on the part of the persons in whom such securities or other property or any of them or any part thereof are for the time being, or had at any time been, vested;

unless and until required in writing so to do by some person, or the guardian of some person, beneficially interested under the trust, and unless also due provision is made to their satisfaction for payment of the costs of any proceedings required to be taken:

Provided that nothing in this subsection shall relieve the trustees of the obligation to get in and obtain payment or transfer of such share or interest or other thing in action on the same falling into possession.

(3)   Trustees may, for the purpose of giving effect to the trust, or any of the provisions of the instrument, if any, creating the trust or of any statute, from time to time (by duly qualified agents) ascertain and fix the value of any trust property in such manner as they think proper, and any valuation so made [. . .] shall be binding upon all persons interested under the trust [if the trustees have discharged the duty of care set out in section 1(1) of the Trustee Act 2000].

(4)   Trustees may, in their absolute discretion, from time to time, but not more than once in every three years unless the nature of the trust or any special dealings with the trust property make a more frequent exercise of the right reasonable, cause the accounts of the trust property to be examined or audited by an independent accountant, and shall, for that purpose, produce such vouchers and give such information to him as he may require; and the costs of such examination or audit, including the fee of the auditor, shall be paid out of the capital or income of the trust property, or partly in one way and partly in the other as the trustees, in their absolute discretion, think fit, but, in default of any direction by the trustees to the contrary in any special case, costs attributable to capital shall be borne by capital and those attributable to income by income.

Amendment

Sub-s (1): words 'if they have discharged the duty of care set out in section 1(1) of the Trustee Act 2000' in square brackets substituted by the Trustee Act 2000, s 40(1), Sch 2, Pt II, para 22(a).

Date in force: 1 February 2001: see SI 2001/49, art 2.

Sub-s (3): words omitted repealed by the Trustee Act 2000, s 40(1), Sch 2, Pt II, para 22(b).

Date in force: 1 February 2001: see SI 2001/49, art 2.

Sub-s (3): words 'if the trustees have discharged the duty of care set out in section 1(1) of the Trustee Act 2000' in square brackets inserted by the Trustee Act 2000, s 40(1), Sch 2, Pt II, para 22(b).

Date in force: 1 February 2001: see SI 2001/49, art 2.

23 [. . .]

[. . .]

Amendment

Repealed by the Trustee Act 2000, s 40(1), (3), Sch 2, Pt II, para 23, Sch 4, Pt II.

Date in force: 1 February 2001 (except in so far as it does not affect the operation of an appointment made under this section before that date): see the Trustee Act 2000, s 40(2), Sch 3, para 6 and SI 2001/49, art 2.

24 Power to concur with others

Where an undivided share in [any] property, is subject to a trust, or forms part of the estate of a testator or intestate, the trustees or personal representatives may (without prejudice to the [trust] affecting the entirety of the land and the powers of the [trustees] in reference thereto), execute or exercise any [duty or] power vested in them in relation to such share in conjunction with the persons entitled to or having power in that behalf over the other share or shares, and notwithstanding that any one or more of the trustees or personal representatives may be entitled to or interested in any such other share, either in his or their own right or in a fiduciary capacity.

Amendment

Words in square brackets substituted by the Trusts of Land and Appointment of Trustees Act 1996, s 25(1), Sch 3, para 3(6); for savings in relation to entailed interests created before the commencement of that Act, and savings consequential upon the abolition of the doctrine of conversion, see s 25(4), (5) thereof.

[25 Delegation of trustees' functions by power of attorney]

[(1) Notwithstanding any rule of law or equity to the contrary, a trustee may, by power of attorney, delegate the execution or exercise of all or any of the trusts, powers and discretions vested in him as trustee either alone or jointly with any other person or persons.

(2) A delegation under this section—

    (a) commences as provided by the instrument creating the power or, if the instrument makes no provision as to the commencement of the delegation, with the date of the execution of the instrument by the donor; and

    (b) continues for a period of twelve months or any shorter period provided by the instrument creating the power.

(3) The persons who may be donees of a power of attorney under this section include a trust corporation.

(4) Before or within seven days after giving a power of attorney under this section the donor shall give written notice of it (specifying the date on which the power comes into operation and its duration, the donee of the power, the reason why the power is given and, where some only are delegated, the trusts, powers and discretions delegated) to—

    (a) each person (other than himself), if any, who under any instrument creating the trust has power (whether alone or jointly) to appoint a new trustee; and

    (b) each of the other trustees, if any;

but failure to comply with this subsection shall not, in favour of a person dealing with the donee of the power, invalidate any act done or instrument executed by the donee.

(5)   A power of attorney given under this section by a single donor–

    (a)   in the form set out in subsection (6) of this section; or

    (b)   in a form to the like effect but expressed to be made under this subsection,

shall operate to delegate to the person identified in the form as the single donee of the power the execution and exercise of all the trusts, powers and discretions vested in the donor as trustee (either alone or jointly with any other person or persons) under the single trust so identified.

(6)   The form referred to in subsection (5) of this section is as follows–

'THIS GENERAL TRUSTEE POWER OF ATTORNEY is made on [date] by [name of one donor] of [address of donor] as trustee of [name or details of one trust].

I appoint [name of one donee] of [address of donee] to be my attorney [if desired, the date on which the delegation commences or the period for which it continues (or both)] in accordance with section 25(5) of the Trustee Act 1925.

[To be executed as a deed]'.

(7)   The donor of a power of attorney given under this section shall be liable for the acts or defaults of the donee in the same manner as if they were the acts or defaults of the donor.

(8)   For the purpose of executing or exercising the trusts or powers delegated to him, the donee may exercise any of the powers conferred on the donor as trustee by statute or by the instrument creating the trust, including power, for the purpose of the transfer of any inscribed stock, himself to delegate to an attorney power to transfer, but not including the power of delegation conferred by this section.

(9)   The fact that it appears from any power of attorney given under this section, or from any evidence required for the purposes of any such power of attorney or otherwise, that in dealing with any stock the donee of the power is acting in the execution of a trust shall not be deemed for any purpose to affect any person in whose books the stock is inscribed or registered with any notice of the trust.

(10)   This section applies to a personal representative, tenant for life and statutory owner as it applies to a trustee except that subsection (4) shall apply as if it required the notice there mentioned to be given–

    (a)   in the case of a personal representative, to each of the other personal representatives, if any, except any executor who has renounced probate;

    (b)   in the case of a tenant for life, to the trustees of the settlement and to each person, if any, who together with the person giving the notice constitutes the tenant for life; and

    (c)   in the case of a statutory owner, to each of the persons, if any, who together with the person giving the notice constitute the statutory owner and, in the case of a statutory owner by virtue of section 23(1)(a) of the Settled Land Act 1925, to the trustees of the settlement.]

Amendment

Substituted by the Trustee Delegation Act 1999, s 5(1), (2).

Date in force: 1 March 2000 (in relation to enduring powers created after that date): see SI 2000/216, art 2.

Indemnities

26 Protection against liability in respect of rents and covenants

(1) Where a personal representative or trustee liable as such for—

    (a) any rent, covenant, or agreement reserved by or contained in any lease; or

    (b) any rent, covenant or agreement payable under or contained in any grant made in consideration of a rentcharge; or

    (c) any indemnity given in respect of any rent, covenant or agreement referred to in either of the foregoing paragraphs;

satisfies all liabilities under the lease or grant [which may have accrued and been claimed] up to the date of the conveyance hereinafter mentioned, and, where necessary, sets apart a sufficient fund to answer any future claim that may be made in respect of any fixed and ascertained sum which the lessee or grantee agreed to lay out on the property demised or granted, although the period for laying out the same may not have arrived, then and in any such case the personal representative or trustee may convey the property demised or granted to a purchaser, legatee, devisee, or other person entitled to call for a conveyance thereof and thereafter—

    (i) he may distribute the residuary real and personal estate of the deceased testator or intestate, or, as the case may be, the trust estate (other than the fund, if any, set apart as aforesaid) to or amongst the persons entitled thereto, without appropriating any part, or any further part, as the case may be, of the estate of the deceased or of the trust estate to meet any future liability under the said lease or grant;

    (ii) notwithstanding such distribution, he shall not be personally liable in respect of any subsequent claim under the said lease or grant.

[(1A) Where a personal representative or trustee has as such entered into, or may as such be required to enter into, an authorised guarantee agreement with respect to any lease comprised in the estate of a deceased testator or intestate or a trust estate (and, in a case where he has entered into such an agreement, he has satisfied all liabilities under it which may have accrued and been claimed up to the date of distribution)—

    (a) he may distribute the residuary real and personal estate of the deceased testator or intestate, or the trust estate, to or amongst the persons entitled thereto—

        (i) without appropriating any part of the estate of the deceased, or the trust estate, to meet any future liability (or, as the case may be, any liability) under any such agreement, and

        (ii) notwithstanding any potential liability of his to enter into any such agreement; and

(b)   notwithstanding such distribution, he shall not be personally liable in respect of any subsequent claim (or, as the case may be, any claim) under any such agreement.

In this subsection 'authorised guarantee agreement' has the same meaning as in the Landlord and Tenant (Covenants) Act 1995.]

(2)   This section operates without prejudice to the right of the lessor or grantor, or the persons deriving title under the lessor or grantor, to follow the assets of the deceased or the trust property into the hands of the persons amongst whom the same may have been respectively distributed, and applies notwithstanding anything to the contrary in the will or other instrument, if any, creating the trust.

(3)   In this section 'lease' includes an underlease and an agreement for a lease or underlease and any instrument giving any such indemnity as aforesaid or varying the liabilities under the lease; 'grant' applies to a grant whether the rent is created by limitation, grant, reservation, or otherwise, and includes an agreement for a grant and any instrument giving any such indemnity as aforesaid or varying the liabilities under the grant; 'lessee' and 'grantee' include persons respectively deriving title under them.

Amendment

Sub-s (1): words in square brackets substituted by the Law of Property (Amendment) Act 1926, ss 7, 8(2), Schedule.

Sub-s (1A): inserted by the Landlord and Tenant (Covenants) Act 1995, s 30(1), Sch 1, para 1.

This Act does not extend to Scotland.

27   Protection by means of advertisements

(1)   With a view to the conveyance to or distribution among the persons entitled to any real or personal property, the trustees of a settlement [, trustees of land, trustees for sale of personal property] or personal representatives, may give notice by advertisement in the Gazette, and [in a newspaper circulating in the district in which the land is situated] and such other like notices, including notices elsewhere than in England and Wales, as would, in any special case, have been directed by a court of competent jurisdiction in an action for administration, of their intention to make such conveyance or distribution as aforesaid, and requiring any person interested to send to the trustees or personal representatives within the time, not being less than two months, fixed in the notice or, where more than one notice is given, in the last of the notices, particulars of his claim in respect of the property or any part thereof to which the notice relates.

(2)   At the expiration of the time fixed by the notice the trustees or personal representatives may convey or distribute the property or any part thereof to which the notice relates, to or among the persons entitled thereto, having regard only to the claims, whether formal or not, of which the trustees or personal representatives then had notice and shall not, as respects the property so conveyed or distributed, be liable to any person of whose claim the trustees or personal representatives have not had notice at the time of conveyance or distribution; but nothing in this section—

(a)   prejudices the right of any person to follow the property, or any property representing the same, into the hands of any person, other than a purchaser, who may have received it; or

(b) frees the trustees or personal representatives from any obligation to make searches or obtain official certificates of search similar to those which an intending purchaser would be advised to make or obtain.

(3) This section applies notwithstanding anything to the contrary in the will or other instrument, if any, creating the trust.

Amendment

Sub-s (1): first words in square brackets substituted by the Trusts of Land and Appointment of Trustees Act 1996, s 25(1), Sch 3, para 3(7), for savings in relation to entailed interests created before the commencement of that Act, and savings consequential upon the abolition of the doctrine of conversion, see s 25(4), (5) thereof; final words in square brackets substituted by the Law of Property (Amendment) Act 1926, ss 7, 8(2), Schedule.

28 Protection in regard to notice

A trustee or personal representative acting for the purposes of more than one trust or estate shall not, in the absence of fraud, be affected by notice of any instrument, matter, fact or thing in relation to any particular trust or estate if he has obtained notice thereof merely by reason of his acting or having acted for the purposes of another trust or estate.

30 [. . .]

[. . .]

Amendment

Repealed by the Trustee Act 2000, s 40(1), (3), Sch 2, Pt II, para 24, Sch 4, Pt II.

Date in force: 1 February 2001: see SI 2001/49, art 2.

Maintenance Advancement and Protective Trusts

31 Power to apply income for maintenance and to accumulate surplus income during a minority

(1) Where any property is held by trustees in trust for any person for any interest whatsoever, whether vested or contingent, then, subject to any prior interests or charges affecting that property—

 (i) during the infancy of any such person, if his interest so long continues, the trustees may, at their sole discretion, pay to his parent or guardian, if any, or otherwise apply for or towards his maintenance, education, or benefit, the whole or such part, if any, of the income of that property as may, in all the circumstances, be reasonable, whether or not there is—

  (a) any other fund applicable to the same purpose; or

  (b) any person bound by law to provide for his maintenance or education; and

 (ii) if such person on attaining the age of [eighteen years] has not a vested interest in such income, the trustees shall thenceforth pay the income of that property and of any accretion thereto under subsection (2) of this section to him, until he either attains a vested interest therein or dies, or until failure of his interest:

Provided that, in deciding whether the whole or any part of the income of the property is during a minority to be paid or applied for the purposes aforesaid, the trustees shall have regard to the age of the infant and his requirements and generally to the circumstances of the case, and in particular to what other income, if any, is applicable for the same purposes; and where trustees have notice that the income of more than one fund is applicable for those purposes, then, so far as practicable, unless the entire income of the funds is paid or applied as aforesaid or the court otherwise directs, a proportionate part only of the income of each fund shall be so paid or applied.

(2) During the infancy of any such person, if his interest so long continues, the trustees shall accumulate all the residue of that income [by investing it, and any profits from so investing it] from time to time in authorised investments, and shall hold those accumulations as follows:–

(i) If any such person–

(a) attains the age of [eighteen years], or marries under that age, and his interest in such income during his infancy or until his marriage is a vested interest; or

(b) on attaining the age of [eighteen years] or on marriage under that age becomes entitled to the property from which such income arose in fee simple, absolute or determinable, or absolutely, or for an entailed interest;

the trustees shall hold the accumulations in trust for such person absolutely, but without prejudice to any provision with respect thereto contained in any settlement by him made under any statutory powers during his infancy, and so that the receipt of such person after marriage, and though still an infant, shall be a good discharge; and

(ii) In any other case the trustees shall, notwithstanding that such person had a vested interest in such income, hold the accumulations as an accretion to the capital of the property from which such accumulations arose, and as one fund with such capital for all purposes, and so that, if such property is settled land, such accumulations shall be held upon the same trusts as if the same were capital money arising therefrom;

but the trustees may, at any time during the infancy of such person if his interest so long continues, apply those accumulations, or any part thereof, as if they were income arising in the then current year.

(3) This section applies in the case of a contingent interest only if the limitation or trust carries the intermediate income of the property, but it applies to a future or contingent legacy by the parent of, or a person standing in loco parentis to, the legatee, if and for such period as, under the general law, the legacy carries interest for the maintenance of the legatee, and in any such case as last aforesaid the rate of interest shall (if the income available is sufficient, and subject to any rules of court to the contrary) be five pounds per centum per annum.

(4) This section applies to a vested annuity in like manner as if the annuity were the income of property held by trustees in trust to pay the income thereof to the annuitant for the same period for which the annuity is payable, save that in any case accumulations made during the infancy of the annuitant shall be held in trust for the annuitant or his personal representatives absolutely.

(5)   This section does not apply where the instrument, if any, under which the interest arises came into operation before the commencement of this Act.

Amendment

Sub-s (1): words in square brackets substituted by the Family Law Reform Act 1969, s 1(3), Sch 1, Part I.

Sub-s (2): words 'by investing it, and any profits from so investing it' in square brackets substituted by the Trustee Act 2000, s 40(1), Sch 2, Pt II, para 25.

Date in force: 1 February 2001: see SI 2001/49, art 2.

Sub-s (2): in para (i)(a) words 'eighteen years' in square brackets substituted by the Family Law Reform Act 1969, s 1(3), Sch 1, Part I.

Sub-s (2): in para (i)(b) words 'eighteen years' in square brackets substituted by the Family Law Reform Act 1969, s 1(3), Sch 1, Part I.

32   Power of advancement

(1)   Trustees may at any time or times pay or apply any capital money subject to a trust, for the advancement or benefit, in such manner as they may, in their absolute discretion, think fit, of any person entitled to the capital of the trust property or of any share thereof, whether absolutely or contingently on his attaining any specified age or on the occurrence of any other event, or subject to a gift over on his death under any specified age or on the occurrence of any other event, and whether in possession or in remainder or reversion, and such payment or application may be made notwithstanding that the interest of such person is liable to be defeated by the exercise of a power of appointment or revocation, or to be diminished by the increase of the class to which he belongs:

Provided that—

(a)   the money so paid or applied for the advancement or benefit of any person shall not exceed altogether in amount one-half of the presumptive or vested share or interest of that person in the trust property; and

(b)   if that person is or becomes absolutely and indefeasibly entitled to a share in the trust property the money so paid or applied shall be brought into account as part of such share; and

(c)   no such payment or application shall be made so as to prejudice any person entitled to any prior life or other interest, whether vested or contingent, in the money paid or applied unless such person is in existence and of full age and consents in writing to such payment or application.

[(2)   This section does not apply to capital money arising under the Settled Land Act 1925.]

(3)   This section does not apply to trusts constituted or created before the commencement of this Act.

Amendment

Sub-s (2): substituted by the Trusts of Land and Appointment of Trustees Act 1996, s 25(1), Sch 3, para 3(8); for savings in relation to entailed interests created before the commencement of that Act, and savings consequential upon the abolition of the doctrine of conversion, see s 25(4), (5) thereof.

33   Protective trusts

(1)   Where any income, including an annuity or other periodical income payment, is directed to be held on protective trusts for the benefit of any person (in this section called 'the principal beneficiary') for the period of his life or for any less period, then, during that period (in this section called the 'trust period') the said income shall, without prejudice to any prior interest, be held on the following trusts, namely:–

(i)   Upon trust for the principal beneficiary during the trust period or until he, whether before or after the termination of any prior interest, does or attempts to do or suffers any act or thing, or until any event happens, other than an advance under any statutory or express power, whereby, if the said income were payable during the trust period to the principal beneficiary absolutely during that period, he would be deprived of the right to receive the same or any part thereof, in any of which cases, as well as on the termination of the trust period, whichever first happens, this trust of the said income shall fail or determine;

(ii)   If the trust aforesaid fails or determines during the subsistence of the trust period, then, during the residue of that period, the said income shall be held upon trust for the application thereof for the maintenance or support, or otherwise for the benefit, of all or any one or more exclusively of the other or others of the following persons (that is to say)–

(a)   the principal beneficiary and his or her wife or husband, if any, and his or her children or more remote issue, if any; or

(b)   if there is no wife or husband or issue of the principal beneficiary in existence, the principal beneficiary and the persons who would, if he were actually dead, be entitled to the trust property or the income thereof or to the annuity fund, if any, or arrears of the annuity, as the case may be;

as the trustees in their absolute discretion, without being liable to account for the exercise of such discretion, think fit.

(2)   This section does not apply to trusts coming into operation before the commencement of this Act, and has effect subject to any variation of the implied trusts aforesaid contained in the instrument creating the trust.

(3)   Nothing in this section operates to validate any trust which would, if contained in the instrument creating the trust, be liable to be set aside.

[(4)   In relation to the dispositions mentioned in section 19(1) of the Family Law Reform Act 1987, this section shall have effect as if any reference (however expressed) to any relationship between two persons were construed in accordance with section 1 of that Act.]

Amendment

Sub-s (4): inserted by the Family Law Reform Act 1987, s 33(1), Sch 2, para 2, Sch 3, para 1.

Part III

Appointment and Discharge of Trustees

34   Limitation of the number of trustees

(1)   Where, at the commencement of this Act, there are more than four trustees of a settlement of land, or more than four trustees holding land on trust for sale, no new trustees shall (except where as a result of the appointment the number is reduced to four or less) be capable of being appointed until the number is reduced to less than four, and thereafter the number shall not be increased beyond four.

(2)   In the case of settlements and dispositions [creating trusts of land] made or coming into operation after the commencement of this Act—

(a)   the number of trustees thereof shall not in any case exceed four, and where more than four persons are named as such trustees, the four first named (who are able and willing to act) shall alone be the trustees, and the other persons named shall not be trustees unless appointed on the occurrence of a vacancy;

(b)   the number of the trustees shall not be increased beyond four.

(3)   This section only applies to settlements and dispositions of land, and the restrictions imposed on the number of trustees do not apply—

(a)   in the case of land vested in trustees for charitable, ecclesiastical, or public purposes; or

(b)   where the net proceeds of the sale of the land are held for like purposes; or

(c)   to the trustees of a term of years absolute limited by a settlement on trusts for raising money, or of a like term created under the statutory remedies relating to annual sums charged on land.

Amendment

Sub-s (2): words in square brackets substituted by the Trusts of Land and Appointment of Trustees Act 1996, s 25(1), Sch 3, para 3(9); for savings in relation to entailed interests created before the commencement of that Act, and savings consequential upon the abolition of the doctrine of conversion, see s 25(4), (5) thereof.

35   Appointments of trustees of settlements and [and trustees of land]

[(1)   Appointments of new trustees of land and of new trustees of any trust of the proceeds of sale of the land shall, subject to any order of the court, be effected by separate instruments, but in such manner as to secure that the same persons become trustees of land and trustees of the trust of the proceeds of sale.]

(2)   Where new trustees of a settlement are appointed, a memorandum of the names and addresses of the persons who are for the time being the trustees thereof for the purposes of the Settled Land Act 1925, shall be endorsed on or annexed to the last or only principal vesting instrument by or on behalf of the

trustees of the settlement, and such vesting instrument shall, for that purpose, be produced by the person having the possession thereof of the trustees of the settlement when so required.

[(3) Where new trustees of land are appointed, a memorandum of the persons who are for the time being the trustees of the land shall be endorsed on or annexed to the conveyance by which the land was vested in trustees of land; and that conveyance shall be produced to the persons who are for the time being the trustees of the land by the person in possession of it in order for that to be done when the trustees require its production.]

(4) This section applies only to settlements and dispositions of land.

Amendment

Section heading: words in square brackets substituted by the Trusts of Land and Appointment of Trustees Act 1996, s 25(1), Sch 3, para 3(10)(c); for savings in relation to entailed interests created before the commencement of that Act, and savings consequential upon the abolition of the doctrine of conversion, see s 25(4), (5) thereof.

Sub-ss (1), (3): substituted by the Trusts of Land and Appointment of Trustees Act 1996, s 25(1), Sch 3, para 3(10)(a), (b); for savings in relation to entailed interests created before the commencement of that Act, and savings consequential upon the abolition of the doctrine of conversion, see s 25(4), (5) thereof.

36   Power of appointing new or additional trustees

(1) Where a trustee, either original or substituted, and whether appointed by a court or otherwise, is dead, or remains out of the United Kingdom for more than twelve months, or desires to be discharged from all or any of the trusts or powers reposed in or conferred on him, or refuses or is unfit to act therein, or is incapable of acting therein, or is an infant, then, subject to the restrictions imposed by this Act on the number of trustees,–

(a) the person or persons nominated for the purpose of appointing new trustees by the instrument, if any, creating the trust; or

(b) if there is no such person, or no such person able and willing to act, then the surviving or continuing trustees or trustee for the time being, or the personal representatives of the last surviving or continuing trustee;

may, by writing, appoint one or more other persons (whether or not being the persons exercising the power) to be a trustee or trustees in the place of the trustee so deceased remaining out of the United Kingdom, desiring to be discharged, refusing, or being unfit or being incapable, or being an infant, as aforesaid.

(2) Where a trustee has been removed under a power contained in the instrument creating the trust, a new trustee or new trustees may be appointed in the place of the trustee who is removed, as if he were dead, or, in the case of a corporation, as if the corporation desired to be discharged from the trust, and the provisions of this section shall apply accordingly, but subject to the restrictions imposed by this Act on the number of trustees.

(3) Where a corporation being a trustee is or has been dissolved, either before or after the commencement of this Act, then, for the purposes of this section and of any enactment replaced thereby, the corporation shall be deemed to be and

to have been from the date of the dissolution incapable of acting in the trusts or powers reposed in or conferred on the corporation.

(4)   The power of appointment given by subsection (1) of this section or any similar previous enactment to the personal representatives of a last surviving or continuing trustee shall be and shall be deemed always to have been exercisable by the executors for the time being (whether original or by representation) of such surviving or continuing trustee who have proved the will of their testator or by the administrators for the time being of such trustee without the concurrence of any executor who has renounced or has not proved.

(5)   But a sole or last surviving executor intending to renounce, or all the executors where they all intend to renounce, shall have and shall be deemed always to have had power, at any time before renouncing probate, to exercise the power of appointment given by this section, or by any similar previous enactment, if willing to act for that purpose and without thereby accepting the office of executor.

[(6)   Where, in the case of any trust, there are not more than three trustees–]

    (a)   the person or persons nominated for the purpose of appointing new trustees by the instrument, if any, creating the trust; or

    (b)   if there is no such person, or no such person able and willing to act, then the trustee or trustees for the time being;

may, by writing appoint another person or other persons to be an additional trustee or additional trustees, but it shall not be obligatory to appoint any additional trustee, unless the instrument, if any, creating the trust, or any statutory enactment provides to the contrary, nor shall the number of trustees be increased beyond four by virtue of any such appointment.

[(6A) A person who is either–

    (a)   both a trustee and attorney for the other trustee (if one other), or for both of the other trustees (if two others), under a registered power; or

    (b)   attorney under a registered power for the trustee (if one) or for both or each of the trustees (if two or three),

may, if subsection (6B) of this section is satisfied in relation to him, make an appointment under subsection (6)(b) of this section on behalf of the trustee or trustees.

(6B)   This subsection is satisfied in relation to an attorney under a registered power for one or more trustees if (as attorney under the power)–

    (a)   he intends to exercise any function of the trustee or trustees by virtue of section 1(1) of the Trustee Delegation Act 1999; or

    (b)   he intends to exercise any function of the trustee or trustees in relation to any land, capital proceeds of a conveyance of land or income from land by virtue of its delegation to him under section 25 of this Act or the instrument (if any) creating the trust.

(6C)   In subsections (6A) and (6B) of this section 'registered power' means a power of attorney created by an instrument which is for the time being registered under section 6 of the Enduring Powers of Attorney Act 1985.

(6D) Subsection (6A) of this section—

(a) applies only if and so far as a contrary intention is not expressed in the instrument creating the power of attorney (or, where more than one, any of them) or the instrument (if any) creating the trust; and

(b) has effect subject to the terms of those instruments.]

(7) Every new trustee appointed under this section as well before as after all the trust property becomes by law, or by assurance, or otherwise, vested in him, shall have the same powers, authorities, and discretions, and may in all respects act as if he had been originally appointed a trustee by the instrument, if any, creating the trust.

(8) The provisions of this section relating to a trustee who is dead include the case of a person nominated trustee in a will but dying before the testator, and those relative to a continuing trustee include a refusing or retiring trustee, if willing to act in the execution of the provisions of this section.

[(9) Where a trustee is incapable, by reason of mental disorder within the meaning of [the Mental Health Act 1983], of exercising his functions as trustee and is also entitled in possession to some beneficial interest in the trust property, no appointment of a new trustee in his place shall be made by virtue of paragraph (b) of subsection (1) of this section unless leave to make the appointment has been given by the authority having jurisdiction under [Part VII of the Mental Health Act 1983].]

Amendment

Sub-s (6): words in square brackets substituted by the Trusts of Land and Appointment of Trustees Act 1996, s 25(1), Sch 3, para 3(11); for savings in relation to entailed interests created before the commencement of that Act, and savings consequential upon the abolition of the doctrine of conversion, see s 25(4), (5) thereof.

Sub-ss (6A)-(6D): inserted by the Trustee Delegation Act 1999, s 8.

Date in force: 1 March 2000 (in relation to powers created after that date): see SI 2000/216, art 2.

Sub-s (9): substituted by the Mental Health Act 1959, s 149(1), Sch 7, Part I; words in square brackets therein substituted by the Mental Health Act 1983, s 148, Sch 4, para 4.

37 Supplemental provisions as to appointment of trustees

(1) On the appointment of a trustee for the whole or any part of trust property—

(a) the number of trustees may, subject to the restrictions imposed by this Act on the number of trustees, be increased; and

(b) a separate set of trustees, not exceeding four, may be appointed for any part of the trust property held on trusts distinct from those relating to any other part or parts of the trust property, notwithstanding that no new trustees or trustee are or is to be appointed for other parts of the trust property, and any existing trustee may be appointed or remain one of such separate set of trustees, or, if only one trustee was originally appointed, then, save as hereinafter provided, one separate trustee may be so appointed; and

(c)   it shall not be obligatory, save as hereinafter provided, to appoint more than one new trustee where only one trustee was originally appointed, or to fill up the original number of trustees where more than two trustees were originally appointed, but, except where only one trustee was originally appointed, and a sole trustee when appointed will be able to give valid receipts for all capital money, a trustee shall not be discharged from his trust unless there will be either a trust corporation or at least two [persons] to act as trustees to perform the trust; and

(d)   any assurance or thing requisite for vesting the trust property, or any part thereof, in a sole trustee, or jointly in the persons who are the trustees, shall be executed or done.

(2)   Nothing in this Act shall authorise the appointment of a sole trustee, not being a trust corporation, where the trustee, when appointed, would not be able to give valid receipts for all capital money arising under the trust.

Amendment

Sub-s (1): in para (c) word in square brackets substituted by the Trusts of Land and Appointment of Trustees Act 1996, s 25(1), Sch 3, para 3(12); for savings in relation to entailed interests created before the commencement of that Act, and savings consequential upon the abolition of the doctrine of conversion, see s 25(4), (5) thereof.

38   Evidence as to a vacancy in a trust

(1)   A statement, contained in any instrument coming into operation after the commencement of this Act by which a new trustee is appointed for any purpose connected with land, to the effect that a trustee has remained out of the United Kingdom for more than twelve months or refuses or is unfit to act, or is incapable of acting, or that he is not entitled to a beneficial interest in the trust property in possession, shall, in favour of a purchaser of a legal estate, be conclusive evidence of the matter stated.

(2)   In favour of such purchaser any appointment of a new trustee depending on that statement, and any vesting declaration, express or implied, consequent on the appointment, shall be valid.

39   Retirement of trustee without a new appointment

(1)   Where a trustee is desirous of being discharged from the trust, and after his discharge there will be either a trust corporation or at least two [persons] to act as trustees to perform the trust, then, if such trustee as aforesaid by deed declares that he is desirous of being discharged from the trust, and if his co-trustees and such other person, if any, as is empowered to appoint trustees, by deed consent to the discharge of the trustee, and to the vesting in the co-trustees alone of the trust property, the trustee desirous of being discharged shall be deemed to have retired from the trust, and shall, by the deed, be discharged therefrom under this Act, without any new trustee being appointed in his place.

(2)   Any assurance or thing requisite for vesting the trust property in the continuing trustees alone shall be executed or done.

Amendment

Sub-s (1): word in square brackets substituted by the Trusts of Land and Appointment of Trustees Act 1996, s 25(1), Sch 3, para 3(13); for savings in relation to entailed interests created before the commencement of that Act, and savings consequential upon the abolition of the doctrine of conversion, see s 25(4), (5) thereof.

40   Vesting of trust property in new or continuing trustees

(1)   Where by a deed a new trustee is appointed to perform any trust, then—

(a)   if the deed contains a declaration by the appointor to the effect that any estate or interest in any land subject to the trust, or in any chattel so subject, or right to recover or receive any debt or other thing in action so subject, shall vest in the persons who by virtue of the deed become or are the trustees for performing the trust, the deed shall operate, without any conveyance or assignment, to vest in those persons as joint tenants and for the purposes of the trust the estate interest or right to which the declaration relates; and

(b)   if the deed is made after the commencement of this Act and does not contain such a declaration, the deed shall, subject to any express provision to the contrary therein contained, operate as if it had contained such a declaration by the appointor extending to all the estates interests and rights with respect to which a declaration could have been made.

(2)   Where by a deed a retiring trustee is discharged under [section 39 of this Act or section 19 of the Trusts of Land and Appointment of Trustees Act 1996] without a new trustee being appointed, then—

(a)   if the deed contains such a declaration as aforesaid by the retiring and continuing trustees, and by the other person, if any, empowered to appoint trustees, the deed shall, without any conveyance or assignment, operate to vest in the continuing trustees alone, as joint tenants, and for the purposes of the trust, the estate, interest, or right to which the declaration relates; and

(b)   if the deed is made after the commencement of this Act and does not contain such a declaration, the deed shall, subject to any express provision to the contrary therein contained, operate as if it had contained such a declaration by such persons as aforesaid extending to all the estates, interests and rights with respect to which a declaration could have been made.

(3)   An express vesting declaration, whether made before or after the commencement of this Act, shall, notwithstanding that the estate, interest or right to be vested is not expressly referred to, and provided that the other statutory requirements were or are complied with, operate and be deemed always to have operated (but without prejudice to any express provision to the contrary contained in the deed of appointment or discharge) to vest in the persons respectively referred to in subsections (1) and (2) of this section, as the case may require, such estates, interests and rights as are capable of being and ought to be vested in those persons.

(4)   This section does not extend—

(a)   to land conveyed by way of mortgage for securing money subject to the trust, except land conveyed on trust for securing debentures or debenture stock;

(b)   to land held under a lease which contains any covenant, condition or agreement against assignment or disposing of the land without licence or consent, unless, prior to the execution of the deed containing expressly or impliedly the vesting declaration, the requisite licence or consent has been obtained, or unless, by virtue of any statute or rule of law, the vesting declaration, express or implied, would not operate as a breach of covenant or give rise to a forfeiture;

(c)   to any share, stock, annuity or property which is only transferable in books kept by a company or other body, or in manner directed by or under an Act of Parliament.

In this subsection 'lease' includes an underlease and an agreement for a lease or underlease.

(5)   For purposes of registration of the deed in any registry, the person or persons making the declaration expressly or impliedly, shall be deemed the conveying party or parties, and the conveyance shall be deemed to be made by him or them under a power conferred by this Act.

(6)   This section applies to deeds of appointment or discharge executed on or after the first day of January, eighteen hundred and eighty-two.

Amendment

Sub-s (2): words in square brackets substituted by the Trusts of Land and Appointment of Trustees Act 1996, s 25(1), Sch 3, para 3(14); for savings in relation to entailed interests created before the commencement of that Act, and savings consequential upon the abolition of the doctrine of conversion, see s 25(4), (5) thereof.

Part IV

Powers of the Court

Appointment of new Trustees

41 Power of court to appoint new trustees

(1) The court may, whenever it is expedient to appoint a new trustee or new trustees, and it is found inexpedient difficult or impracticable so to do without the assistance of the court, make an order appointing a new trustee or new trustees either in substitution for or in addition to any existing trustee or trustees, or although there is no existing trustee.

In particular and without prejudice to the generality of the foregoing provision, the court may make an order appointing a new trustee in substitution for a trustee who [. . .] is [incapable, by reason of mental disorder within the meaning of [the Mental Health Act 1983], of exercising his functions as trustee], or is a bankrupt, or is a corporation which is in liquidation or has been dissolved.

(2) The power conferred by this section may, in the case of a deed of arrangement within the meaning of the Deeds of Arrangement Act 1914, be exercised either by the High Court or by the court having jurisdiction in bankruptcy in the district in which the debtor resided or carried on business at the date of the execution of the deed.

(3) An order under this section, and any consequential vesting order or conveyance, shall not operate further or otherwise as a discharge to any former or continuing trustee than an appointment of new trustees under any power for that purpose contained in any instrument would have operated.

(4) Nothing in this section gives power to appoint an executor or administrator.

Amendment

Sub-s (1): words omitted repealed by the Criminal Law Act 1967, s 10, Sch 3, Part III; first words in square brackets substituted by the Mental Health Act 1959, s 149(1), Sch 7, Part I, words in square brackets therein substituted by the Mental Health Act 1983, s 148, Sch 4, para 4.

42 Power to authorise remuneration

Where the court appoints a corporation, other than the Public Trustee, to be a trustee either solely or jointly with another person, the court may authorise the corporation to charge such remuneration for its services as trustee as the court may think fit.

43 Powers of new trustee appointed by the Court

Every trustee appointed by a court of competent jurisdiction shall, as well before as after the trust property becomes by law, or by assurance, or otherwise, vested in him, have the same powers, authorities, and discretions, and may in all respects act as if he had been originally appointed a trustee by the instrument, if any, creating the trust.

Vesting Orders

44 Vesting orders of land

In any of the following cases, namely:

(i)   Where the court appoints or has appointed a trustee, or where a trustee has been appointed out of court under any statutory or express power;

(ii)   Where a trustee entitled to or possessed of any land or interest therein, whether by way of mortgage or otherwise, or entitled to a contingent right therein, either solely or jointly with any other person—

    (a)   is under disability; or

    (b)   is out of the jurisdiction of the High Court; or

    (c)   cannot be found, or, being a corporation, has been dissolved;

(iii)   Where it is uncertain who was the survivor of two or more trustees jointly entitled to or possessed of any interest in land;

(iv)   Where it is uncertain whether the last trustee known to have been entitled to or possessed of any interest in land is living or dead;

(v)   Where there is no personal representative of a deceased trustee who was entitled to or possessed of any interest in land, or where it is uncertain who is the personal representative of a deceased trustee who was entitled to or possessed of any interest in land;

(vi)   Where a trustee jointly or solely entitled to or possessed of any interest in land, or entitled to a contingent right therein, has been required, by or on behalf of a person entitled to require a conveyance of the land or interest or a release of the right, to convey the land or interest or to release the right, and has wilfully refused or neglected to convey the land or interest or release the right for twenty-eight days after the date of the requirement;

(vii)   Where land or any interest therein is vested in a trustee whether by way of mortgage or otherwise, and it appears to the court to be expedient;

the court may make an order (in this Act called a vesting order) vesting the land or interest therein in any such person in any such manner and for any such estate or interest as the court may direct, or releasing or disposing of the contingent right to such person as the court may direct:

Provided that—

    (a)   Where the order is consequential on the appointment of a trustee the land or interest therein shall be vested for such estate as the court may direct in the persons who on the appointment are the trustees; and

    (b)   Where the order relates to a trustee entitled or formerly entitled jointly with another person, and such trustee is under disability or out of the jurisdiction of the High Court or cannot be found, or being a corporation has been dissolved, the land interest or right shall be vested in such other person who remains entitled, either alone or with any other person the court may appoint.

45   Orders as to contingent rights of unborn persons

Where any interest in land is subject to a contingent right in an unborn person or class of unborn persons who, on coming into existence would, in respect, thereof, become entitled to or possessed of that interest on any trust, the court may make an order releasing the land or interest therein from the contingent right, or may make an order vesting in any person the estate or interest to or of which the unborn person or class of unborn persons would, on coming into existence, be entitled or possessed in the land.

46 Vesting order in place of conveyance by infant mortgagee

Where any person entitled to or possessed of any interest in land, or entitled to a contingent right in land, by way of security for money, is an infant, the court may make an order vesting or releasing or disposing of the interest in the land or the right in like manner as in the case of a trustee under disability.

47 Vesting order consequential on order for sale or mortgage of land

Where any court gives a judgment or makes an order directing the sale or mortgage of any land, every person who is entitled to or possessed of any interest in the land, or entitled to a contingent right therein, and is a party to the action or proceeding in which the judgment or order is given or made or is otherwise bound by the judgment or order, shall be deemed to be so entitled or possessed, as the case may be, as a trustee for the purpose of this Act, and the court may, if it thinks expedient, make an order vesting the land or any part thereof for such estate or interest as that court thinks fit in the purchaser or mortgagee or in any other person:

> Provided that, in the case of a legal mortgage, the estate to be vested in the mortgagee shall be a term of years absolute.

48 Vesting order consequential on judgement for specific performance, etc

Where a judgment is given for the specific performance of a contract concerning any interest in land, or for sale or exchange of any interest in land, or generally where any judgment is given for the conveyance of any interest in land either in cases arising out of the doctrine of election or otherwise, the court may declare–

(a) that any of the parties to the action are trustees of any interest in the land or any part thereof within the meaning of this Act; or

(b) that the interests of unborn persons who might claim under any party to the action, or under the will or voluntary settlement of any deceased person who was during his lifetime a party to the contract or transaction concerning which the judgment is given, are the interests of persons who, on coming into existence, would be trustees within the meaning of this Act;

and thereupon the court may make a vesting order relating to the rights of those persons, born and unborn, as if they had been trustees.

49 Effect of vesting order

A vesting order under any of the foregoing provisions shall in the case of a vesting order consequential on the appointment of a trustee, have the same effect–

(a) as if the persons who before the appointment were the trustees, if any, had duly executed all proper conveyances of the land for such estate or interest as the court directs; or

(b) if there is no such person, or no such person of full capacity, as if such person had existed and been of full capacity and had duly executed all proper conveyances of the land for such estate or interest as the court directs;

> and shall in every other case have the same effect as if the trustee or other person or description or class of persons to whose rights or supposed rights the said provisions respectively relate had been an ascertained and existing person of full capacity, and had executed a conveyance or release to the effect intended by the order.

50 Power to appoint person to convey

In all cases where a vesting order can be made under any of the foregoing provisions, the court may, if it is more convenient, appoint a person to convey the land or any interest therein or release the contingent right, and a conveyance or release by that person in conformity with the order shall have the same effect as an order under the appropriate provision.

51 Vesting orders as to stock and things in action

(1) In any of the following cases, namely:–

   (i) Where the court appoints or has appointed a trustee, or where a trustee has been appointed out of court under any statutory or express power;

   (ii) Where a trustee entitled, whether by way of mortgage or otherwise, alone or jointly with another person to stock or to a thing in action–

     (a) is under disability; or

     (b) is out of the jurisdiction of the High Court; or

     (c) cannot be found, or, being a corporation, has been dissolved; or

     (d) neglects or refuses to transfer stock or receive the dividends or income thereof, or to sue for or recover a thing in action, according to the direction of the person absolutely entitled thereto for twenty-eight days next after a request in writing has been made to him by the person so entitled; or

     (e) neglects or refuses to transfer stock or receive the dividends or income thereof, or to sue for or recover a thing in action for twenty-eight days next after an order of the court for that purpose has been served on him;

   (iii) Where it is uncertain whether a trustee entitled alone or jointly with another person to stock or to a thing in action is alive or dead;

   (iv) Where stock is standing in the name of a deceased person whose personal representative is under disability;

   (v) Where stock or a thing in action is vested in a trustee whether by way of mortgage or otherwise and it appears to the court to be expedient;

the court may make an order vesting the right to transfer or call for a transfer of stock, or to receive the dividends or income thereof, or to sue for or recover the thing in action, in any such person as the court may appoint:

Provided that–

   (a) Where the order is consequential on the appointment of a trustee, the right shall be vested in the persons who, on the appointment, are the trustees; and

   (b) Where the person whose right is dealt with by the order was entitled jointly with another person, the right shall be vested in that last-mentioned person either alone or jointly with any other person whom the court may appoint.

(2) In all cases where a vesting order can be made under this section, the court may, if it is more convenient, appoint some proper person to make or join in making the transfer:

Provided that the person appointed to make or join in making a transfer of stock shall be some proper officer of the bank, or the company or society whose stock is to be transferred.

(3) The person in whom the right to transfer or call for the transfer of any stock is vested by an order of the court under this Act, may transfer the stock to himself or any other person, according to the order, and the Bank of England and all other companies shall obey every order under this section according to its tenor.

(4) After notice in writing of an order under this section it shall not be lawful for the Bank of England or any other company to transfer any stock to which the order relates or to pay any dividends thereon except in accordance with the order.

(5) The court may make declarations and give directions concerning the manner in which the right to transfer any stock or thing in action vested under the provisions of this Act is to be exercised.

(6) The provisions of this Act as to vesting orders shall apply to shares in ships registered under the [Merchant Shipping Act 1995] as if they were stock.

Amendment

Sub-s (6): words in square brackets substituted by the Merchant Shipping Act 1995, s 314(2), Sch 13, para 13.

52   Vesting orders of charity property

The powers conferred by this Act as to vesting orders may be exercised for vesting any interest in land, stock, or thing in action in any trustee of a charity or society over which the court would have jurisdiction upon action duly instituted, whether the appointment of the trustee was made by instrument under a power or by the court under its general or statutory jurisdiction.

53   Vesting orders in relation to infants' beneficial interests

Where an infant is beneficially entitled to any property the court may, with a view to the application of the capital or income thereof for the maintenance, education, or benefit of the infant, make an order—

(a) appointing a person to convey such property; or

(b) in the case of stock, or a thing in action, vesting in any person the right to transfer or call for a transfer of such stock, or to receive the dividends or income thereof, or to sue for and recover such thing in action, upon such terms as the court may think fit.

[54   Jurisdiction in regard to mental patients]

[(1) Subject to the provisions of this section, the authority having jurisdiction under [Part VII of the Mental Health Act 1983], shall not have power to make any order, or give any direction or authority, in relation to a patient who is a trustee if the High Court has power under this Act to make an order to the like effect.

(2) Where a patient is a trustee and a receiver appointed by the said authority is acting for him or an application for the appointment of a receiver has been made but not determined, then, except as respects a trust which is subject to an order for administration made by the High Court, the said authority shall have concurrent jurisdiction with the High Court in relation to—

(a)   mortgaged property of which the patient has become a trustee merely by reason of the mortgage having been paid off;

(b)   matters consequent on the making of provision by the said authority for the exercise of a power of appointing trustees or retiring from a trust;

(c)   matters consequent on the making of provision by the said authority for the carrying out of any contract entered into by the patient;

(d)   property to some interest in which the patient is beneficially entitled but which, or some interest in which, is held by the patient under an express, implied or constructive trust.

The Lord Chancellor may make rules with respect to the exercise of the jurisdiction referred to in this subsection.

(3)   In this section 'patient' means a patient as defined by [section 94 of the Mental Health Act 1983], or a person as to whom powers are [exercisable under section 98 of that Act and have been exercised under that section or section 104 of the Mental Health Act 1959].]

Amendment

Substituted by the Mental Health Act 1959, s 149(1), Sch 7, Part I.

Sub-ss (1), (3): words in square brackets substituted by the Mental Health Act 1983, s 148, Sch 4, para 4.

55   Orders made upon certain allegations to be conclusive evidence

Where a vesting order is made as to any land under this Act or under [Part VII of the Mental Health Act 1983], as amended by any subsequent enactment, or under any Act relating to lunacy in Northern Ireland, founded on an allegation of any of the following matters namely—

(a)   the personal incapacity of a trustee or mortgagee; or

(b)   that a trustee or mortgagee or the personal representative of or other person deriving title under a trustee or mortgagee is out of the jurisdiction of the High Court or cannot be found, or being a corporation has been dissolved; or

(c)   that it is uncertain which of two or more trustees, or which of two or more persons interested in a mortgage, was the survivor; or

(d)   that it is uncertain whether the last trustee or the personal representative of or other person deriving title under a trustee or mortgagee, or the last surviving person interested in a mortgage is living or dead: or

(e)   that any trustee or mortgagee has died intestate without leaving a person beneficially interested under the intestacy or has died and it is not known who is his personal representative or the person interested;

the fact that the order has been so made shall be conclusive evidence of the matter so alleged in any court upon any question as to the validity of the order; but this section does not prevent the court from directing a reconveyance or surrender or the payment of costs occasioned by any such order if improperly obtained.

Amendment

Words in square brackets substituted by the Mental Health Act 1983, s 148, Sch 4, para 4.

56 Application of vesting order to property out of England

The powers of the court to make vesting orders under this Act shall extend to all property in any part of His Majesty's dominions except Scotland.

Jurisdiction to make other Orders

57 Power of court to authorise dealings with trust property

(1) Where in the management or administration of any property vested in trustees, any sale, lease, mortgage, surrender, release, or other disposition, or any purchase, investment, acquisition, expenditure, or other transaction, is in the opinion of the court expedient, but the same cannot be effected by reason of the absence of any power for that purpose vested in the trustees by the trust instrument, if any, or by law, the court may by order confer upon the trustees, either generally or in any particular instance, the necessary power for the purpose, on such terms, and subject to such provisions and conditions, if any, as the court may think fit and may direct in what manner any money authorised to be expended, and the costs of any transaction, are to be paid or borne as between capital and income.

(2) The court may, from time to time, rescind or vary any order made under this section, or may make any new or further order.

(3) An application to the court under this section may be made by the trustees, or by any of them, or by any person beneficially interested under the trust.

(4) This section does not apply to trustees of a settlement for the purposes of the Settled Land Act 1925.

58 Persons entitled to apply for orders

(1) An order under this Act for the appointment of a new trustee or concerning any interest in land, stock, or thing in action subject to a trust, may be made on the application of any person beneficially interested in the land, stock, or thing in action, whether under disability or not, or on the application of any person duly appointed trustee thereof.

(2) An order under this Act concerning any interest in land, stock, or thing in action subject to a mortgage may be made on the application of any person beneficially interested in the equity of redemption, whether under disability or not, or of any person interested in the money secured by the mortgage.

59 Power to give judgment in absence of a trustee

Where in any action the court is satisfied that diligent search has been made for any person who, in the character of trustee, is made a defendant in any action, to serve him with a process of the court, and that he cannot be found, the court may hear and determine the action and give judgment therein against that person in his character of a trustee as if he had been duly served, or had entered an appearance in the action, and had also appeared by his counsel and solicitor at the hearing, but without prejudice to any interest he may have in the matters in question in the action in any other character.

60 Power to charge costs on trust estate

The court may order the costs and expenses of and incident to any application for an order appointing a new trustee, or for a vesting order, or of and incident to any such order, or any conveyance or transfer in pursuance thereof, to be raised and paid out of the property in respect whereof the same is made, or out of the income thereof, or to be borne and paid in such manner and by such persons as to the court may seem just.

61 Power to relieve trustee from personal liability

If it appears to the court that a trustee, whether appointed by the court or otherwise, is or may be personally liable for any breach of trust, whether the transaction alleged to be a breach of trust occurred before or after the commencement of this Act, but has acted honestly and reasonably, and ought fairly to be excused for the breach of trust and for omitting to obtain the directions of the court in the matter in which he committed such breach, then the court may relieve him either wholly or partly from personal liability for the same.

62 Power to make beneficiary indemnify for breach of trust

(1)   Where a trustee commits a breach of trust at the instigation or request or with the consent in writing of a beneficiary, the court may, if it thinks fit, [. . .] make such order as to the court seems just, for impounding all or any part of the interest of the beneficiary in the trust estate by way of indemnity to the trustee or persons claiming through him.

(2)   This section applies to breaches of trust committed as well before as after the commencement of this Act.

Amendment

Sub-s (1): words omitted repealed by the Married Women (Restraint upon Anticipation) Act 1949, s 1(4), Sch 2.

Payment into Court

63 Payment into court by trustees

(1)   Trustees, or the majority of trustees, having in their hands or under their control money or securities belonging to a trust, may pay the same into court; [. . .]

(2)   The receipt or certificate of the proper officer shall be a sufficient discharge to trustees for the money or securities so paid into court.

(3)   Where money or securities are vested in any persons as trustees, and the majority are desirous of paying the same into court, but the concurrence of the other or others cannot be obtained, the court may order the payment into court to be made by the majority without the concurrence of the other or others.

(4)   Where any such money or securities are deposited with any banker, broker, or other depository, the court may order payment or delivery of the money or securities to the majority of the trustees for the purpose of payment into court.

(5)   Every transfer payment and delivery made in pursuance of any such order shall be valid and take effect as if the same had been made on the authority or by the act of all the persons entitled to the money and securities so transferred, paid, or delivered.

Amendment

Sub-s (1): words omitted repealed by the Administration of Justice Act 1965, s 36(4), Sch 3.

[63A Jurisdiction of County Court]

[(1) The county court has jurisdiction under the following provisions where the amount or value of the trust estate or fund to be dealt with in the court does not exceed the county court limit–

section 41;

section 42;

section 51;

section 57;

section 60;

section 61;

section 62.

(2) The county court has jurisdiction under the following provisions where the land or the interest or contingent right in land which is to be dealt with in the court forms part of a trust estate which does not exceed in amount or value the county court limit–

section 44;

section 45;

section 46.

(3) The county court has jurisdiction–

(a) under sections 47 and 48 of this Act, where the judgment is given or order is made by the court;

(b) under sections 50 and 56, where a vesting order can be made by the court;

(c) under section 53, where the amount or value of the property to be dealt with in the court does not exceed the county court limit; and

(d) under section 63 (including power to receive payment of money or securities into court) where the money or securities to be paid into court do not exceed in amount or value the county court limit.

(4) Any reference to the court in section 59 of this Act includes a reference to the county court.

(5) In this section, in its application to any enactment, 'the county court limit' means the amount for the time being specified by an Order in Council under section 145 of the County Courts Act 1984 as the county court limit for the purposes of that enactment (or, where no such Order in Council has been made, the corresponding limit specified by Order in Council under section 192 of the County Courts Act 1959).]

Amendment

Inserted by the County Courts Act 1984, s 148(1), Sch 2, para 1.

Part V

General Provisions

64 Application of Act to Settled Land Act trustees

(1) All the powers and provisions contained in this Act with reference to the appointment of new trustees, and the discharge and retirement of trustees, apply to and include trustees for the purposes of the Settled Land Act 1925, and trustees for the purpose of the management of land during a minority, whether such trustees are appointed by he court or by the settlement, or under provisions contained in any instrument.

(2) Where, either before or after the commencement of this Act, trustees of a settlement have been appointed by the court for the purposes of the Settled Land Acts 1882 to 1890, or of the Settled Land Act 1925, then, after the commencement of this Act—

(a) the person or persons nominated for the purpose of appointing new trustees by the instrument, if any, creating the settlement, though no trustees for the purposes of the said Acts were thereby appointed; or

(b) if there is no such person, or no such person able and willing to act, the surviving or continuing trustees or trustee for the time being for the purposes of the said Acts or the personal representatives of the last surviving or continuing trustee for those purposes,

shall have the powers conferred by this Act to appoint new or additional trustees of the settlement for the purposes of the said Acts.

(3) Appointments of new trustees for the purposes of the said Acts made or expressed to be made before the commencement of this Act by the trustees or trustee or personal representatives referred to in paragraph (b) of the last preceding subsection or by the persons referred to in paragraph (a) of that subsection are, without prejudice to any order of the court made before such commencement, hereby confirmed.

66 Indemnity to banks, etc

This Act, and every order purporting to be made under this Act, shall be a complete indemnity to the Bank of England, and to all persons for any acts done pursuant thereto, and it shall not be necessary for the Bank or for any person to inquire concerning the propriety of the order, or whether the court by which the order was made had jurisdiction to make it.

67 Jurisdiction of the 'court'

(1) In this Act 'the court' means the High Court [...] or the county court, where those courts respectively have jurisdiction.

(2) The procedure under this Act in [...] county courts shall be in accordance with the Acts and rules regulating the procedure of those courts.

Amendment

Words omitted repealed by the Courts Act 1971, s 56, Sch 11, Part II.

68 Definitions

[(1)] In this Act, unless the context otherwise requires, the following expressions have the meanings hereby assigned to them respectively, that is to say:–

(1) 'Authorised investments' mean investments authorised by the instrument, if any, creating the trust for the investment of money subject to the trust, or by law;

(2) 'Contingent right' as applied to land includes a contingent or executory interest, a possibility coupled with an interest, whether the object of the gift or limitation of the interest, or possibility is or is not ascertained, also a right of entry, whether immediate or future, and whether vested or contingent;

(3) 'Convey' and 'conveyance' as applied to any person include the execution by that person of every necessary or suitable assurance (including an assent) for conveying, assigning, appointing, surrendering, or otherwise transferring or disposing of land whereof he is seised or possessed, or wherein he is entitled to a contingent right, either for his whole estate or for any less estate, together with the performance of all formalities required by law for the validity of the conveyance; 'sale' includes an exchange;

(4) 'Gazette' means the London Gazette;

(5) 'Instrument' includes Act of Parliament;

(6) 'Land' includes land of any tenure, and mines and minerals, whether or not severed from the surface, buildings or parts of buildings, whether the division is horizontal, vertical or made in any other way, and other corporeal hereditaments; also a manor, an advowson, and a rent and other incorporeal hereditaments, and an easement, right, privilege, or benefit in, over, or derived from [. . .]; and in this definition 'mines and minerals' include any strata or seam of minerals or substances in or under any land, and powers of working and getting the same [...]; and 'hereditaments' mean real property which under an intestacy occurring before the commencement of this Act might have devolved on an heir;

(7) 'Mortgage' and 'mortgagee' include a charge or chargee by way of legal mortgage, and relate to every estate and interest regarded in equity as merely a security for money, and every person deriving title under the original mortgagee;

(8) [. . .]

(9) 'Personal representative' means the executor, original or by representation, or administrator for the time being of a deceased person;

(10) 'Possession' includes receipt of rents and profits or the right to receive the same, if any; 'income' includes rents and profits; and 'possessed' applies to receipt of income of and to any vested estate less than a life interest in possession or in expectancy in any land;

(11) 'Property' includes real and personal property, and any estate share and interest in any property, real or personal, and any debt, and any thing in action, and any other right or interest, whether in possession or not;

(12) 'Rights' include estates and interests;

(13) 'Securities' include stocks, funds, and shares; [...] and 'securities payable to bearer' include securities transferable by delivery or by delivery and endorsement;

(14) 'Stock' includes fully paid up shares, and so far as relates to vesting orders made by the court under this Act, includes any fund, annuity, or security transferable in books kept by any company or society, or by instrument of transfer either alone or accompanied by other formalities, and any share or interest therein;

(15) 'Tenant for life', 'statutory owner', 'settled land', 'settlement', 'trust instrument', 'trustees of the settlement' [...] 'term of years absolute' and 'vesting instrument' have the same meanings as in the Settled Land Act 1925, and 'entailed interest' has the same meaning as in the Law of Property Act 1925;

(16) 'Transfer' in relation to stock or securities, includes the performance and execution of every deed, power of attorney, act, and thing on the part of the transferor to effect and complete the title in the transferee;

(17) 'Trust' does not include the duties incident to an estate conveyed by way of mortgage, but with this exception the expressions 'trust' and 'trustee' extend to implied and constructive trusts, and to cases where the trustee has a beneficial interest in the trust property, and to the duties incident to the office of a personal representative, and 'trustee' where the context admits, includes a personal representative, and 'new trustee' includes an additional trustee;

(18) 'Trust corporation' means the Public Trustee or a corporation either appointed by the court in any particular case to be a trustee, or entitled by rules made under subsection (3) of section four of the Public Trustee Act 1906, to act as custodian trustee;

(19) 'Trust for sale' in relation to land means an immediate [...] trust for sale, whether or not exercisable at the request or with the consent of any person [...];

(20) 'United Kingdom' means Great Britain and Northern Ireland.

[(2) Any reference in this Act to paying money or securities into court shall be construed as referring to paying the money or transferring or depositing the securities into or in the Supreme Court or into or in any other court that has jurisdiction, and any reference in this Act to payment of money or securities into court shall be construed–

(a) with reference to an order of the High Court, as referring to payment of the money or transfer or deposit of the securities into or in the Supreme Court; and

(b) with reference to an order of any other court, as referring to payment of the money or transfer or deposit of the securities into or in that court.]

Amendment

Sub-s (1): words omitted from paras (6), (19) repealed by the Trusts of Land and Appointment of Trustees Act 1996, s 25(2), Sch 4, for savings in relation to entailed interests created before the commencement of that Act, and savings consequential upon the abolition of the doctrine of conversion, see s 25(4), (5) thereof; para (8) repealed, and words omitted from para (13) repealed, by the Administration of Justice Act 1965, s 17(1), Sch 1; words omitted from para (15) repealed by the Mental Health Act 1959 s 149(2), Sch 8, Part I.

Sub-s (2): inserted by the Administration of Justice Act 1965, s 17(1), Sch 1.

69 Application of Act

(1) This Act, except where otherwise expressly provided, applies to trusts including, so far as this Act applies thereto, executorships and administratorships constituted or created either before or after the commencement of this Act.

(2) The powers conferred by this Act on trustees are in addition to the powers conferred by the instrument, if any, creating the trust, but those powers, unless otherwise stated, apply if and so far only as a contrary intention is not expressed in the instrument, if any, creating the trust, and have effect subject to the terms of that instrument.

(3) [. . .]

Amendment

Sub-s (3): repealed by the Statute Law (Repeals) Act 1978, s 1, Sch 1, Part XVII.

70 Enactments repealed

[. . .] without prejudice to the provisions of section thirty-eight of the Interpretation Act 1889:

(a) Nothing in this repeal shall affect any vesting order or appointment made or other thing done under any enactment so repealed, and any order or appointment so made may be revoked or varied in like manner as if it has been made under this Act;

(b) References in any document to any enactment repealed by this Act shall be construed as references to this Act or to the corresponding enactment in this Act.

Amendment

Words omitted repealed by the Statute Law Revision Act 1950.

71 Short title, commencement, extent

(1) This Act may be cited as the Trustee Act, 1925.

(2) [. . .]

(3) This Act, except where otherwise expressly provided, extends to England and Wales only.

(4) The provisions of this Act bind the Crown.

Amendment

Sub-s (2): repealed by the Statute Law Revision Act 1950.

Appendix 2

Trusts of Land and Appointment of Trustees Act 1996

Part I

Trusts of Land

Introductory

1   Meaning of 'trust of land'

(1)   In this Act—

(a)   'trust of land' means (subject to subsection (3)) any trust of property which consists of or includes land, and

(b)   'trustees of land' means trustees of a trust of land.

(2)   The reference in subsection (1)(a) to a trust—

(a)   is to any description of trust (whether express, implied, resulting or constructive), including a trust for sale and a bare trust, and

(b)   includes a trust created, or arising, before the commencement of this Act.

(3)   The reference to land in subsection (1)(a) does not include land which (despite section 2) is settled land or which is land to which the Universities and College Estates Act 1925 applies.

Settlements and trusts for sale as trusts of land

2   Trusts in place of settlements

(1)   No settlement created after the commencement of this Act is a settlement for the purposes of the Settled Land Act 1925; and no settlement shall be deemed to be made under that Act after that commencement.

(2)   Subsection (1) does not apply to a settlement created on the occasion of an alteration in any interest in, or of a person becoming entitled under, a settlement which—

(a)   is in existence at the commencement of this Act, or

(b)   derives from a settlement within paragraph (a) or this paragraph.

(3)   But a settlement created as mentioned in subsection (2) is not a settlement for the purposes of the Settled Land Act 1925 if provision to the effect that it is not is made in the instrument, or any of the instruments, by which it is created.

(4)   Where at any time after the commencement of this Act there is in the case of any settlement which is a settlement for the purposes of the Settled Land Act 1925 no relevant property which is, or is deemed to be, subject to the settlement, the settlement permanently ceases at that time to be a settlement for the purposes of that Act.

In this subsection 'relevant property' means land and personal chattels to which section 67(1) of the Settled Land Act 1925 (heirlooms) applies.

(5)   No land held on charitable, ecclesiastical or public trusts shall be or be deemed to be settled land after the commencement of this Act, even if it was or was deemed to be settled land before that commencement.

(6)   Schedule 1 has effect to make provision consequential on this section (including provision to impose a trust in circumstances in which, apart from this

section, there would be a settlement for the purposes of the Settled Land Act 1925 (and there would not otherwise be a trust)).

3   Abolition of doctrine of conversion

(1)   Where land is held by trustees subject to a trust for sale, the land is not to be regarded as personal property; and where personal property is subject to a trust for sale in order that the trustees may acquire land, the personal property is not to be regarded as land.

(2)   Subsection (1) does not apply to a trust created by a will if the testator died before the commencement of this Act.

(3)   Subject to that, subsection (1) applies to a trust whether it is created, or arises, before or after that commencement.

4   Express trusts for sale as trusts of land

(1)   In the case of every trust for sale of land created by a disposition there is to be implied, despite any provision to the contrary made by the disposition, a power for the trustees to postpone sale of the land; and the trustees are not liable in any way for postponing sale of the land, in the exercise of their discretion, for an indefinite period.

(2)   Subsection (1) applies to a trust whether it is created, or arises, before or after the commencement of this Act.

(3)   Subsection (1) does not affect any liability incurred by trustees before that commencement.

5   Implied trusts for sale as trusts for land

(1)   Schedule 2 has effect in relation to statutory provisions which impose a trust for sale of land in certain circumstances so that in those circumstances there is instead a trust of the land (without a duty to sell).

(2)   Section 1 of the Settled Land Act 1925 does not apply to land held on any trust arising by virtue of that Schedule (so that any such land is subject to a trust of land).

Functions of trustees of land

6   General powers of trustees

(1)   For the purpose of exercising their functions as trustees, the trustees of land have in relation to the land subject to the trust all the powers of an absolute owner.

(2)   Where in the case of any land subject to a trust of land each of the beneficiaries interested in the land is a person of full age and capacity who is absolutely entitled to the land, the powers conferred on the trustees by subsection (1) include the power to convey the land to the beneficiaries even though they have not required the trustees to do so; and where land is conveyed by virtue of this subsection–

(a)   the beneficiaries shall do whatever is necessary to secure that it vests in them, and

(b)   if they fail to do so, the court may make an order requiring them to do so.

(3)   The trustees of land have power to [acquire land under the power conferred by section 8 of the Trustee Act 2000].

(4)   [. . .]

(5)   In exercising the powers conferred by this section trustees shall have regard to the rights of the beneficiaries.

(6)   The powers conferred by this section shall not be exercised in contravention of, or of any order made in pursuance of, any other enactment or any rule of law or equity.

(7)   The reference in subsection (6) to an order includes an order of any court or of the Charity Commissioners.

(8)   Where any enactment other than this section confers on trustees authority to act subject to any restriction, limitation or condition, trustees of land may not exercise the powers conferred by this section to do any act which they are prevented from doing under the other enactment by reason of the restriction, limitation or condition.

[(9)   The duty of care under section 1 of the Trustee Act 2000 applies to trustees of land when exercising the powers conferred by this section.]

Amendment

Sub-s (3): words 'acquire land under the power conferred by section 8 of the Trustee Act 2000' in square brackets substituted by the Trustee Act 2000, s 40(1), Sch 2, Pt II, para 45(1).

Date in force: 1 February 2001: see SI 2001/49, art 2.

Sub-s (4): repealed by the Trustee Act 2000, s 40(1), (3), Sch 2, Pt II, para 45(2), Sch 4, Pt II.

Date in force: 1 February 2001: see SI 2001/49, art 2.

Sub-s (9): inserted by the Trustee Act 2000, s 40(1), Sch 2, Pt II, para 45(3).

Date in force: 1 February 2001: see SI 2001/49, art 2.

7   Partition by trustees

(1)   The trustees of land may, where beneficiaries of full age are absolutely entitled in undivided shares to land subject to the trust, partition the land, or any part of it, and provide (by way of mortgage or otherwise) for the payment of any equality money.

(2)   The trustees shall give effect to any such partition by conveying the partitioned land in severalty (whether or not subject to any legal mortgage created for raising equality money), either absolutely or in trust, in accordance with the rights of those beneficiaries.

(3)   Before exercising their powers under subsection (2) the trustees shall obtain the consent of each of those beneficiaries.

(4)   Where a share in the land is affected by an incumbrance, the trustees may either give effect to it or provide for its discharge from the property allotted to that share as they think fit.

(5)   If a share in the land is absolutely vested in a minor, subsections (1) to (4) apply as if he were of full age, except that the trustees may act on his behalf and retain land or other property representing his share in trust for him.

8   Exclusion and restriction of powers

(1)   Sections 6 and 7 do not apply in the case of a trust of land created by a disposition in so far as provision to the effect that they do not apply is made by the disposition.

(2)   If the disposition creating such a trust makes provision requiring any consent to be obtained to the exercise of any power conferred by section 6 or 7, the power may not be exercised without that consent.

(3)   Subsection (1) does not apply in the case of charitable, ecclesiastical or public trusts.

(4)   Subsections (1) and (2) have effect subject to any enactment which prohibits or restricts the effect of provision of the description mentioned in them.

9   Delegation by trustees

(1)   The trustees of land may, by power of attorney, delegate to any beneficiary or beneficiaries of full age and beneficially entitled to an interest in possession in land subject to the trust any of their functions as trustees which relate to the land.

(2)   Where trustees purport to delegate to a person by a power of attorney under subsection (1) functions relating to any land and another person in good faith deals with him in relation to the land, he shall be presumed in favour of that other person to have been a person to whom the functions could be delegated unless that other person has knowledge at the time of the transaction that he was not such a person.

And it shall be conclusively presumed in favour of any purchaser whose interest depends on the validity of that transaction that that other person dealt in good faith and did not have such knowledge if that other person makes a statutory declaration to that effect before or within three months after the completion of the purchase.

(3)   A power of attorney under subsection (1) shall be given by all the trustees jointly and (unless expressed to be irrevocable and to be given by way of security) may be revoked by any one or more of them; and such a power is revoked by the appointment as a trustee of a person other than those by whom it is given (though not by any of those persons dying or otherwise ceasing to be a trustee).

(4)   Where a beneficiary to whom functions are delegated by a power of attorney under subsection (1) ceases to be a person beneficially entitled to an interest in possession in land subject to the trust–

(a)   if the functions are delegated to him alone, the power is revoked,

(b)   if the functions are delegated to him and to other beneficiaries to be exercised by them jointly (but not separately), the power is revoked if each of the other beneficiaries ceases to be so entitled (but otherwise functions exercisable in accordance with the power are so exercisable by the remaining beneficiary or beneficiaries), and

(c)   if the functions are delegated to him and to other beneficiaries to be exercised by them separately (or either separately or jointly), the power is revoked in so far as it relates to him.

(5)   A delegation under subsection (1) may be for any period or indefinite.

(6)   A power of attorney under subsection (1) cannot be an enduring power within the meaning of the Enduring Powers of Attorney Act 1985.

(7)   Beneficiaries to whom functions have been delegated under subsection (1) are, in relation to the exercise of the functions, in the same position as trustees (with the same duties and liabilities); but such beneficiaries shall not be regarded as trustees for any other purposes (including, in particular, the purposes of any enactment permitting the delegation of functions by trustees or imposing requirements relating to the payment of capital money).

(8)   [. . .]

(9)   Neither this section nor the repeal by this Act of section 29 of the Law of Property Act 1925 (which is superseded by this section) affects the operation after the commencement of this Act of any delegation effected before that commencement.

Amendment

Sub-s (8): repealed by the Trustee Act 2000, s 40(1), (3), Sch 2, Pt II, para 46, Sch 4, Pt II.

Date in force: 1 February 2001: see SI 2001/49, art 2.

[9A   Duties of trustees in connection with delegation etc]

[(1)   The duty of care under section 1 of the Trustee Act 2000 applies to trustees of land in deciding whether to delegate any of their functions under section 9.

(2)   Subsection (3) applies if the trustees of land–

(a)   delegate any of their functions under section 9, and

(b)   the delegation is not irrevocable.

(3)   While the delegation continues, the trustees–

(a)   must keep the delegation under review,

(b)   if circumstances make it appropriate to do so, must consider whether there is a need to exercise any power of intervention that they have, and

(c)   if they consider that there is a need to exercise such a power, must do so.

(4)   'Power of intervention' includes–

(a)   a power to give directions to the beneficiary;

(b)   a power to revoke the delegation.

(5)   The duty of care under section 1 of the 2000 Act applies to trustees in carrying out any duty under subsection (3).

(6)   A trustee of land is not liable for any act or default of the beneficiary, or beneficiaries, unless the trustee fails to comply with the duty of care in deciding to delegate any of the trustees' functions under section 9 or in carrying out any duty under subsection (3).

(7)   Neither this section nor the repeal of section 9(8) by the Trustee Act 2000 affects the operation after the commencement of this section of any delegation effected before that commencement.]

Amendment

Inserted by the Trustee Act 2000, s 40(1), Sch 2, Pt II, para 47.

Date in force: 1 February 2001: see SI 2001/49, art 2.

Consents and consultation

10   Consents

(1)   If a disposition creating a trust of land requires the consent of more than two persons to the exercise by the trustees of any function relating to the land, the consent of any two of them to the exercise of the function is sufficient in favour of a purchaser.

(2)   Subsection (1) does not apply to the exercise of a function by trustees of land held on charitable, ecclesiastical or public trusts.

(3)   Where at any time a person whose consent is expressed by a disposition creating a trust of land to be required to the exercise by the trustees of any function relating to the land is not of full age—

    (a)   his consent is not, in favour of a purchaser, required to the exercise of the function, but

    (b)   the trustees shall obtain the consent of a parent who has parental responsibility for him (within the meaning of the Children Act 1989) or of a guardian of his.

11   Consultation with beneficiaries

(1)   The trustees of land shall in the exercise of any function relating to land subject to the trust—

    (a)   so far as practicable, consult the beneficiaries of full age and beneficially entitled to an interest in possession in the land, and

    (b)   so far as consistent with the general interest of the trust, give effect to the wishes of those beneficiaries, or (in case of dispute) of the majority (according to the value of their combined interests).

(2)   Subsection (1) does not apply—

    (a)   in relation to a trust created by a disposition in so far as provision that it does not apply is made by the disposition,

    (b)   in relation to a trust created or arising under a will made before the commencement of this Act, or

    (c)   in relation to the exercise of the power mentioned in section 6(2).

(3)   Subsection (1) does not apply to a trust created before the commencement of this Act by a disposition, or a trust created after that commencement by reference to such a trust, unless provision to the effect that it is to apply is made by a deed executed—

    (a)   in a case in which the trust was created by one person and he is of full capacity, by that person, or

    (b)   in a case in which the trust was created by more than one person, by such of the persons who created the trust as are alive and of full capacity.

(4)   A deed executed for the purposes of subsection (3) is irrevocable.

Right of beneficiaries to occupy trust land

12 The right to occupy

(1) A beneficiary who is beneficially entitled to an interest in possession in land subject to a trust of land is entitled by reason of his interest to occupy the land at any time if at that time—

  (a) the purposes of the trust include making the land available for his occupation (or for the occupation of beneficiaries of a class of which he is a member or of beneficiaries in general), or

  (b) the land is held by the trustees so as to be so available.

(2) Subsection (1) does not confer on a beneficiary a right to occupy land if it is either unavailable or unsuitable for occupation by him.

(3) This section is subject to section 13.

13 Exclusion and restriction of right to occupy

(1) Where two or more beneficiaries are (or apart from this subsection would be) entitled under section 12 to occupy land, the trustees of land may exclude or restrict the entitlement of any one or more (but not all) of them.

(2) Trustees may not under subsection (1)—

  (a) unreasonably exclude any beneficiary's entitlement to occupy land, or

  (b) restrict any such entitlement to an unreasonable extent.

(3) The trustees of land may from time to time impose reasonable conditions on any beneficiary in relation to his occupation of land by reason of his entitlement under section 12.

(4) The matters to which trustees are to have regard in exercising the powers conferred by this section include—

  (a) the intentions of the person or persons (if any) who created the trust,

  (b) the purposes for which the land is held, and

  (c) the circumstances and wishes of each of the beneficiaries who is (or apart from any previous exercise by the trustees of those powers would be) entitled to occupy the land under section 12.

(5) The conditions which may be imposed on a beneficiary under subsection (3) include, in particular, conditions requiring him—

  (a) to pay any outgoings or expenses in respect of the land, or

  (b) to assume any other obligation in relation to the land or to any activity which is or is proposed to be conducted there.

(6) Where the entitlement of any beneficiary to occupy land under section 12 has been excluded or restricted, the conditions which may be imposed on any other beneficiary under subsection (3) include, in particular, conditions requiring him to—

  (a) make payments by way of compensation to the beneficiary whose entitlement has been excluded or restricted, or

  (b) forgo any payment or other benefit to which he would otherwise be entitled under the trust so as to benefit that beneficiary.

(7) The powers conferred on trustees by this section may not be exercised—

    (a) so as prevent any person who is in occupation of land (whether or not by reason of an entitlement under section 12) from continuing to occupy the land, or

    (b) in a manner likely to result in any such person ceasing to occupy the land,

unless he consents or the court has given approval.

(8) The matters to which the court is to have regard in determining whether to give approval under subsection (7) include the matters mentioned in subsection (4)(a) to (c).

Powers of court

14 Applications for order

(1) Any person who is a trustee of land or has an interest in a property subject to a trust of land may make an application to the court for an order under this section.

(2) On an application for an order under this section the court may make any such order—

    (a) relating to the exercise by the trustees of any of their functions (including an order relieving them of any obligation to obtain the consent of, or to consult, any person in connection with the exercise of any of their functions), or

    (b) declaring the nature or extent of a person's interest in property subject to the trust,

as the court thinks fit.

(3) The court may not under this section make any order as to the appointment or removal of trustees.

(4) The powers conferred on the court by this section are exercisable on an application whether it is made before or after the commencement of this Act.

15 Matters relevant in determining applications

(1) The matters to which the court is to have regard in determining an application for an order under section 14 include—

    (a) the intentions of the person or persons (if any) who created the trust,

    (b) the purposes for which the property subject to the trust is held,

    (c) the welfare of any minor who occupies or might reasonably be expected to occupy any land subject to the trust as his home, and

    (d) the interests of any secured creditor of any beneficiary.

(2) In the case of an application relating to the exercise in relation to any land of the powers conferred on the trustees by section 13, the matters to which the court is to have regard also include the circumstances and wishes of each of the beneficiaries who is (or apart from any previous exercise by the trustees of those powers would be) entitled to occupy the land under section 12.

(3) In the case of any other application, other than one relating to the exercise of the power mentioned in section 6(2), the matters to which the court is to have regard also include the circumstances and wishes of any beneficiaries of full age and entitled to an interest in possession in property subject to the trust or (in case of dispute) of the majority (according to the value of their combined interests).

(4) This section does not apply to an application if section 335A of the Insolvency Act 1986 (which is inserted by Schedule 3 and relates to applications by a trustee of a bankrupt) applies to it.

Purchaser protection

16 Protection of purchasers

(1) A purchaser of land which is or has been subject to a trust need not be concerned to see that any requirement imposed on the trustees by section 6(5), 7(3) or 11(1) has been complied with.

(2) Where—

(a) trustees of land who convey land which (immediately before it is conveyed) is subject to the trust contravene section 6(6) or (8), but

(b) the purchaser of the land from the trustees has no actual notice of the contravention,

the contravention does not invalidate the conveyance.

(3) Where the powers of trustees of land are limited by virtue of section 8—

(a) the trustees shall take all reasonable steps to bring the limitation to the notice of any purchaser of the land from them, but

(b) the limitation does not invalidate any conveyance by the trustees to a purchaser who has no actual notice of the limitation.

(4) Where trustees of land convey land which (immediately before it is conveyed) is subject to the trust to persons believed by them to be beneficiaries absolutely entitled to the land under the trust and of full age and capacity—

(a) the trustees shall execute a deed declaring that they are discharged from the trust in relation to that land, and

(b) if they fail to do so, the court may make an order requiring them to do so.

(5) A purchaser of land to which a deed under subsection (4) relates is entitled to assume that, as from the date of the deed, the land is not subject to the trust unless he has actual notice that the trustees were mistaken in their belief that the land was conveyed to beneficiaries absolutely entitled to the land under the trust and of full age and capacity.

(6) Subsections (2) and (3) do not apply to land held on charitable, ecclesiastical or public trusts.

(7) This section does not apply to registered land.

Supplementary

17   Application of provisions to trusts of proceeds of sale

(1)   [. . .]

(2)   Section 14 applies in relation to a trust of proceeds of sale of land and trustees of such a trust as in relation to a trust of land and trustees of land.

(3)   In this section 'trust of proceeds of sale of land' means (subject to subsection (5)) any trust of property (other than a trust of land) which consists of or includes—

  (a)   any proceeds of a disposition of land held in trust (including settled land), or

  (b)   any property representing any such proceeds.

(4)   The references in subsection (3) to a trust—

  (a)   are to any description of trust (whether express, implied, resulting or constructive), including a trust for sale and a bare trust, and

  (b)   include a trust created, or arising, before the commencement of this Act.

(5)   A trust which (despite section 2) is a settlement for the purposes of the Settled Land Act 1925 cannot be a trust of proceeds of sale of land.

(6)   In subsection (3)—

  (a)   'disposition' includes any disposition made, or coming into operation, before the commencement of this Act, and

  (b)   the reference to settled land includes personal chattels to which section 67(1) of the Settled Land Act 1925 (heirlooms) applies.

Amendment

Sub-s (1): repealed by the Trustee Act 2000, s 40(1), (3), Sch 2, Pt II, para 48, Sch 4, Pt II.

Date in force: 1 February 2001: see SI 2001/49, art 2.

18   Application of Part to personal representatives

(1)   The provisions of this Part relating to trustees, other than sections 10, 11 and 14, apply to personal representatives, but with appropriate modifications and without prejudice to the functions of personal representatives for the purposes of administration.

(2)   The appropriate modifications include—

  (a)   the substitution of references to persons interested in the due administration of the estate for references to beneficiaries, and

  (b)   the substitution of references to the will for references to the disposition creating the trust.

(3)   Section 3(1) does not apply to personal representatives if the death occurs before the commencement of this Act.

Part II

Appointment and Retirement of Trustees

19 Appointment and retirement of trustee at instance of beneficiaries

(1) This section applies in the case of a trust where—

(a) there is no person nominated for the purpose of appointing new trustees by the instrument, if any, creating the trust, and

(b) the beneficiaries under the trust are of full age and capacity and (taken together) are absolutely entitled to the property subject to the trust.

(2) The beneficiaries may give a direction or directions of either or both of the following descriptions—

(a) a written direction to a trustee or trustees to retire from the trust, and

(b) a written direction to the trustees or trustee for the time being (or, if there are none, to the personal representative of the last person who was a trustee) to appoint by writing to be a trustee or trustees the person or persons specified in the direction.

(3) Where—

(a) a trustee has been given a direction under subsection (2)(a),

(b) reasonable arrangements have been made for the protection of any rights of his in connection with the trust,

(c) after he has retired there will be either a trust corporation or at least two persons to act as trustees to perform the trust, and

(d) either another person is to be appointed to be a new trustee on his retirement (whether in compliance with a direction under subsection (2)(b) or otherwise) or the continuing trustees by deed consent to his retirement,

he shall make a deed declaring his retirement and shall be deemed to have retired and be discharged from the trust.

(4) Where a trustee retires under subsection (3) he and the continuing trustees (together with any new trustee) shall (subject to any arrangements for the protection of his rights) do anything necessary to vest the trust property in the continuing trustees (or the continuing and new trustees).

(5) This section has effect subject to the restrictions imposed by the Trustee Act 1925 on the number of trustees.

20 Appointment of substitute for incapable trustee

(1) This section applies where—

(a) a trustee is incapable by reason of mental disorder of exercising his functions as trustee,

(b) there is no person who is both entitled and willing and able to appoint a trustee in place of him under section 36(1) of the Trustee Act 1925, and

(c) the beneficiaries under the trust are of full age and capacity and (taken together) are absolutely entitled to the property subject to the trust.

(2)   The beneficiaries may give to—

    (a)   a receiver of the trustee,

    (b)   an attorney acting for him under the authority of a power of attorney created by an instrument which is registered under section 6 of the Enduring Powers of Attorney Act 1985, or

    (c)   a person authorised for the purpose by the authority having jurisdiction under Part VII of the Mental Health Act 1983,

a written direction to appoint by writing the person or persons specified in the direction to be a trustee or trustees in place of the incapable trustee.

21   Supplementary

(1)   For the purposes of section 19 or 20 a direction is given by beneficiaries if—

    (a)   a single direction is jointly given by all of them, or

    (b)   (subject to subsection (2)) a direction is given by each of them (whether solely or jointly with one or more, but not all, of the others),

and none of them by writing withdraws the direction given by him before it has been complied with.

(2)   Where more than one direction is given each must specify for appointment or retirement the same person or persons.

(3)   Subsection (7) of section 36 of the Trustee Act 1925 (powers of trustees appointed under that section) applies to a trustee appointed under section 19 or 20 as if he were appointed under that section.

(4)   A direction under section 19 or 20 must not specify a person or persons for appointment if the appointment of that person or those persons would be in contravention of section 35(1) of the Trustee Act 1925 or section 24(1) of the Law of Property Act 1925 (requirements as to identity of trustees).

(5)   Sections 19 and 20 do not apply in relation to a trust created by a disposition in so far as provision that they do not apply is made by the disposition.

(6)   Sections 19 and 20 do not apply in relation to a trust created before the commencement of this Act by a disposition in so far as provision to the effect that they do not apply is made by a deed executed—

    (a)   in a case in which the trust was created by one person and he is of full capacity, by that person, or

    (b)   in a case in which the trust was created by more than one person, by such of the persons who created the trust as are alive and of full capacity.

(7)   A deed executed for the purposes of subsection (6) is irrevocable.

(8)   Where a deed is executed for the purposes of subsection (6)—

    (a)   it does not affect anything done before its execution to comply with a direction under section 19 or 20, but

    (b)   a direction under section 19 or 20 which has been given but not complied with before its execution shall cease to have effect.

Part III

Supplementary

22 Meaning of 'beneficiary'

(1) In this Act 'beneficiary', in relation to a trust, means any person who under the trust has an interest in property subject to the trust (including a person who has such an interest as a trustee or a personal representative).

(2) In this Act references to a beneficiary who is beneficially entitled do not include a beneficiary who has an interest in property subject to the trust only by reason of being a trustee or personal representative.

(3) For the purposes of this Act a person who is a beneficiary only by reason of being an annuitant is not to be regarded as entitled to an interest in possession in land subject to the trust.

23 Other interpretation provisions

(1) In this Act 'purchaser' has the same meaning as in Part I of the Law of Property Act 1925.

(2) Subject to that, where an expression used in this Act is given a meaning by the Law of Property Act 1925 it has the same meaning as in that Act unless the context otherwise requires.

(3) In this Act 'the court' means–

(a)   the High Court, or

(b)   a county court.

24 Application to Crown

(1) Subject to subsection (2), this Act binds the Crown.

(2) This Act (except so far as it relates to undivided shares and joint ownership) does not affect or alter the descent, devolution or nature of the estates and interests of or in–

(a)   land for the time being vested in Her Majesty in right of the Crown or of the Duchy of Lancaster, or

(b)   land for the time being belonging to the Duchy of Cornwall and held in right or respect of the Duchy.

25 Amendments, repeals etc

(1) The enactments mentioned in Schedule 3 have effect subject to the amendments specified in that Schedule (which are minor or consequential on other provisions of this Act).

(2) The enactments mentioned in Schedule 4 are repealed to the extent specified in the third column of that Schedule.

(3) Neither section 2(5) nor the repeal by this Act of section 29 of the Settled Land Act 1925 applies in relation to the deed of settlement set out in the Schedule to the Chequers Estate Act 1917 or the trust instrument set out in the Schedule to the Chevening Estate Act 1959.

(4)   The amendments and repeals made by this Act do not affect any entailed interest created before the commencement of this Act.

(5)   The amendments and repeals made by this Act in consequence of section 3–

(a)   do not affect a trust created by a will if the testator died before the commencement of this Act, and

(b)   do not affect personal representatives of a person who died before that commencement;

and the repeal of section 22 of the Partnership Act 1890 does not apply in any circumstances involving the personal representatives of a partner who died before that commencement.

26   Power to make consequential provision

(1)   The Lord Chancellor may by order made by statutory instrument make any such supplementary, transitional or incidental provision as appears to him to be appropriate for any of the purposes of this Act or in consequence of any of the provisions of this Act.

(2)   An order under subsection (1) may, in particular, include provision modifying any enactment contained in a public general or local Act which is passed before, or in the same Session as, this Act.

(3)   A statutory instrument made in the exercise of the power conferred by this section is subject to annulment in pursuance of a resolution of either House of Parliament.

27   Short title, commencement and extent

(1)   This Act may be cited as the Trusts of Land and Appointment of Trustees Act 1996.

(2)   This Act comes into force on such day as the Lord Chancellor appoints by order made by statutory instrument.

(3)   Subject to subsection (4), the provisions of this Act extend only to England and Wales.

(4)   The repeal in section 30(2) of the Agriculture Act 1970 extends only to Northern Ireland.

Schedules

Minors

1

(1)   Where after the commencement of this Act a person purports to convey a legal estate in land to a minor, or two or more minors, alone, the conveyance—

    (a)   is not effective to pass the legal estate, but

    (b)   operates as a declaration that the land is held in trust for the minor or minors (or if he purports to convey it to the minor or minors in trust for any persons, for those persons).

(2)   Where after the commencement of this Act a person purports to convey a legal estate in land to—

    (a)   a minor or two or more minors, and

    (b)   another person who is, or other persons who are, of full age,

the conveyance operates to vest the land in the other person or persons in trust for the minor or minors and the other person or persons (or if he purports to convey it to them in trust for any persons, for those persons).

(3)   Where immediately before the commencement of this Act a conveyance is operating (by virtue of section 27 of the Settled Land Act 1925) as an agreement to execute a settlement in favour of a minor or minors—

    (a)   the agreement ceases to have effect on the commencement of this Act, and

    (b)   the conveyance subsequently operates instead as a declaration that the land is held in trust for the minor or minors.

2

Where after the commencement of this Act a legal estate in land would, by reason of intestacy or in any other circumstances not dealt with in paragraph 1, vest in a person who is a minor if he were a person of full age, the land is held in trust for the minor.

Family charges

3

Where, by virtue of an instrument coming into operation after the commencement of this Act, land becomes charged voluntarily (or in consideration of marriage) or by way of family arrangement, whether immediately or after an interval, with the payment of—

    (a)   a rentcharge for the life of a person or a shorter period, or

    (b)   capital, annual or periodical sums for the benefit of a person,

the instrument operates as a declaration that the land is held in trust for giving effect to the charge.

Charitable, ecclesiastical and public trusts

4

(1)   This paragraph applies in the case of land held on charitable, ecclesiastical or public trusts (other than land to which the Universities and College Estates Act 1925 applies).

(2)   Where there is a conveyance of such land–

(a)   if neither section 37(1) nor section 39(1) of the Charities Act 1993 applies to the conveyance, it shall state that the land is held on such trusts, and

(b)   if neither section 37(2) nor section 39(2) of that Act has been complied with in relation to the conveyance and a purchaser has notice that the land is held on such trusts, he must see that any consents or orders necessary to authorise the transaction have been obtained.

(3)   Where any trustees or the majority of any set of trustees have power to transfer or create any legal estate in the land, the estate shall be transferred or created by them in the names and on behalf of the persons in whom it is vested.

Entailed interests

5

(1)   Where a person purports by an instrument coming into operation after the commencement of this Act to grant to another person an entailed interest in real or personal property, the instrument–

(a)   is not effective to grant an entailed interest, but

(b)   operates instead as a declaration that the property is held in trust absolutely for the person to whom an entailed interest in the property was purportedly granted.

(2)   Where a person purports by an instrument coming into operation after the commencement of this Act to declare himself a tenant in entail of real or personal property, the instrument is not effective to create an entailed interest.

Property held on settlement ceasing to exist

6

Where a settlement ceases to be a settlement for the purposes of the Settled Land Act 1925 because no relevant property (within the meaning of section 2(4)) is, or is deemed to be, subject to the settlement, any property which is or later becomes subject to the settlement is held in trust for the persons interested under the settlement.

SCHEDULE 2
AMENDMENTS OF STATUTORY PROVISIONS IMPOSING TRUST FOR SALE

Section 5

Mortgaged property held by trustees after redemption barred

1

(1)–(6)   [. . .]

(7)   The amendments made by this paragraph–

    (a)   apply whether the right of redemption is discharged before or after the commencement of this Act, but

    (b)   are without prejudice to any dealings or arrangements made before the commencement of this Act.

Land purchased by trustees of personal property etc

2

(1)   [. . .]

(2)   The repeal made by this paragraph applies in relation to land purchased after the commencement of this Act whether the trust or will in pursuance of which it is purchased comes into operation before or after the commencement of this Act.

Dispositions to tenants in common

3

(1)-(5)   [. . .]

(6)   The amendments made by this paragraph apply whether the disposition is made, or comes into operation, before or after the commencement of this Act.

Joint tenancies

4

(1)-(3)   [. . .]

(4)   The amendments made by this paragraph apply whether the legal estate is limited, or becomes held in trust, before or after the commencement of this Act.

Intestacy

5

(1)-(4)   [. . .]

(5)   The amendments made by this paragraph apply whether the death occurs before or after the commencement of this Act.

Reverter of sites

6

(1)-(5)   [. . .]

(6)   The amendments made by this paragraph apply whether the trust arises before or after the commencement of this Act.

Trusts deemed to arise in 1926

7

Where at the commencement of this Act any land is held on trust for sale, or on the statutory trusts, by virtue of Schedule 1 to the Law of Property Act 1925 (transitional provisions), it shall after that commencement be held in trust for the persons interested in the land; and references in that Schedule to trusts for sale or trustees for sale or to the statutory trusts shall be construed accordingly.

Amendment

Para 1: sub-paras (1)-(6) amend the Law of Property Act 1925, s 31.

Para 2: sub-para (1) repeals the Law of Property Act 1925, s 32.

Para 3: sub-paras (1)-(5) amend the Law of Property Act 1925, s 34.

Para 4: sub-paras (1)-(3) amend the Law of Property Act 1925, s 36(1), (2).

Para 5: sub-paras (1)-(4) amend the Administration of Estates Act 1925, s 33.

Para 6: sub-paras (1)-(5) amend the Reverter of Sites Act 1987, s 1.

SCHEDULE 3
MINOR AND CONSEQUENTIAL AMENDMENTS

Section 25(1)

[. . .]

Amendment

This Schedule contains amendments only.

Repealed in part by the Trustee Act 2000, s 40(1), (3), Sch 2, Pt II, para 49, Sch 4, Pt II.

Date in force: 1 February 2001: see SI 2001/49, art 2.

Repealed in part by the Countryside and Rights of Way Act 2000, s 102, Sch 16, Pt III.

Date in force: 30 January 2001: see the Countryside and Rights of Way Act 2000, s 103(2).

SCHEDULE 4
REPEALS

Section 25(2)

Chapter	Short title	Extent of repeal
3 & 4 Will 4 c 74	The Fines and Recoveries Act 1833	In section 1, the words ', and any undivided share thereof', in both places.
7 Will 4 & 1 Vict c 26	The Wills Act 1837	In section 1, the words 'and to any undivided share thereof',. Section 32.

Chapter	Short title	Extent of repeal
53 & 54 Vict c 39	The Partnership Act 1890	Section 22.
12 & 13 Geo 5 c 16	The Law of Property Act 1922	In section 188– in subsection (1), the words 'but not an undivided share in land;' and the words 'but not an undivided share thereof', and subsection (30).
15 & 16 Geo 5 c 18	The Settled Land Act 1925	Section 27. Section 29.
15 & 16 Geo 5 c 19	The Trustee Act 1925	In section 10(2)– in the first paragraph, the words 'by trustees or' and the words 'the trustees, or', and in the second paragraph, the words from the beginning to 'mortgage; and'. In section 19(1), the words 'building or', in the second place. In section 68– in subsection (6), the words ', but not an undivided share in land' and the words ', but not an undivided share thereof', and in subsection (19), the word 'binding', the words ', and with or without power at discretion to postpone the sale' and the definition of 'trustees for sale'.
15 & 16 Geo 5 c 20	The Law of Property Act 1925	In section 3– subsections (1)(b) and (2), and in subsection (5), the words 'trustees for sale or other'. In section 7(3), the second paragraph. In section 18–

Chapter	Short title	Extent of repeal
		in subsection (1), the words from ', and personal estate' to 'payable', in the second place, and the words "or is capable of being", and
		in subsection (2), the words "of the settlement or the trustees for sale", in both places.
		Section 19.
		Section 23 (and the heading immediately preceding it).
		Sections 25 and 26.
		Sections 28 to 30.
		Section 31(3).
		Section 32.
		In section 34–
		in subsection (3), the words from 'the trustees (if any)' to 'then to' and the words 'in each case', and
		subsection (4).
		Section 35.
		Section 42(6).
		In section 60, paragraphs (b) and (c) of the proviso to subsection (4).
		In section 130, subsections (1) to (3) and (6) (and the words "Creation of" in the sidenote).
		Section 201(3).
		In section 205(1)–
		in paragraph (ix), the words 'but not an undivided share in land;' and the words 'but not an undivided share thereof',
		in paragraph (x), the words 'or in the proceeds of sale thereof', and
		in paragraph (xxix), the

Chapter	Short title	Extent of repeal
		word 'binding', the words ', and with or without a power at discretion to postpone the sale' and the words 'and 'power" onwards.
15 & 16 Geo 5 c 21	The Land Registration Act 1925	In section 3– _ in paragraph (viii), the words 'but not an undivided share in land;', in paragraph (xi), the words 'or in the proceeds of sale thereof', in paragraph (xiv), the words ', but not an undivided share thereof', and paragraphs (xxviii) and (xxix).
15 & 16 Geo 5 c 23	The Administration of Estates Act 1925	In section 3(1)(ii), the words 'money to arise under a trust for sale of land, nor'. In section 39(1)(i), the words from ', and such power' to 'legal mortgage'. In section 51– in subsection (3), the word 'settled', and subsection (4). In section 55(1)– in paragraph (vii), the words 'or in the proceeds of sale thereof', in paragraph (xxiv), the word " "land" ", and paragraph (xxvii).
15 & 16 Geo 5 c 24	The Universities and College Estates Act 1925	In section 43(iv), the words ', but not an undivided share in land'.
16 & 17 Geo 5 c 11	The Law of Property (Amendment) Act 1926	In the Schedule, the entries relating to section 3 of the Settled Land Act 1925 and sections 26, 28 and 35 of the Law of Property Act 1925.

Chapter	Short title	Extent of repeal
17 & 18 Geo 5 c 36	The Landlord and Tenant Act 1927	In section 13– in subsection (1), the words from '(either" to "Property Act, 1925)', in subsection (2), the words', trustee for sale, or personal representative', and in subsection (3), the words ', and "settled land"' onwards.
22 & 23 Geo 5 c 27	The Law of Property (Entailed Interests) Act 1932	Section 1.
2 & 3 Geo 6 c 72	The Landlord and Tenant (War Damage) Act 1939	Section 3(c).
9 & 10 Geo 6 c 73	The Hill Farming Act 1946	Section 11(2).
12 & 13 Geo 6 c 74	The Coast Protection Act 1949	In section 11(2)(a)– the words ', by that section as applied by section twenty-eight of the Law of Property Act, 1925, in relation to trusts for sale', and the words ', by that section as applied as aforesaid'.
2 & 3 Eliz 2 c 56	The Landlord and Tenant Act 1954	In the Second Schedule, in paragraph 6– the words ', by that section as applied by section twenty-eight of the Law of Property Act, 1925, in relation to trusts for sale', and the words ', by that section as applied as aforesaid'.
7 & 8 Eliz 2 c 72	The Mental Health Act 1959	In Schedule 7, in Part I, the entries relating to sections 26 and 28 of the Law of Property Act 1925.
1964 No 2	The Incumbents and Churchwardens (Trusts) Measure 1964	In section 1, in the definition of 'land', the words 'nor an undivided share in land'.
1967 c 10	The Forestry Act 1967	In Schedule 2, paragraph 1(4).

Chapter	Short title	Extent of repeal
1967 c 88	The Leasehold Reform Act 1967	In section 6(5)– the words ', or by that section as applied by section 28 of the Law of Property Act 1925 in relation to trusts for sale,' the words 'or by that section as applied as aforesaid', and the words 'or by trustees for sale'. In Schedule 2, in paragraph 9(1)– the words ', or by that section as applied by section 28 of the Law of Property Act 1925 in relation to trusts for sale', and the words 'or by that section as applied as aforesaid'.
1969 c 10	The Mines and Quarries (Tips) Act 1969	In section 32(2)(a) and (b), the words ', by that section as applied by section 28 of the Law of Property Act 1925 in relation to trusts for sale'.
1970 c 40	The Agriculture Act 1970	In section 30 in subsection (1), the words '(including those provisions as extended to trusts for sale by section 28 of the Law of Property Act 1925)', and in subsection (2), the words 'the words from "(including those provisions" to "Law of Property Act 1925)" and'.
1972 c 61	The Land Charges Act 1972	In section 17(1), the definition of 'trust for sale'.
1976 c 31	The Legitimacy Act 1976	Section 10(4).
1976 c 36	The Adoption Act 1976	Section 46(5).
1977 c 42	The Rent Act 1977	In Schedule 2, in Part I, in paragraph 2(b), the words 'or, if it is held on trust for sale, the proceeds of its sale are'.

Chapter	Short title	Extent of repeal
1980 c 58	The Limitation Act 1980	In section 18– in subsection (1), the words ', including interests in the proceeds of the sale of land held upon trust for sale', and in subsections (3) and (4), the words '(including a trust for sale)'' and the words ''or in the proceeds of sale'. In section 38(1)– in the definition of 'land', the words ', including an interest in the proceeds of the sale of land held upon trust for sale', and the definition of 'trust for sale'. In Schedule 1, in Part I, in paragraph 9– the words 'or in the proceeds of sale', the words 'or the proceeds', and the words 'or the proceeds of sale'.
1981 c 54	The Supreme Court Act 1981	In section 128, in the definition of 'real estate', in paragraph (b), the words 'money to arise under a trust for sale of land, nor'.
1983 c 41	The Health and Social Services and Social Security Adjudications Act 1983	Section 22(3).
1984 c 28	The County Courts Act 1984	In Schedule 2, in Part II, in paragraph 2– in sub-paragraph (1), the entry relating to section 30 of the Law of Property Act 1925, sub-paragraph (2), and in sub-paragraph (3), '30(2)'.

Chapter	Short title	Extent of repeal
1984 c 51	The Inheritance Tax Act 1984	In section 237(3), the words 'and undivided shares in land held on trust for sale, whether statutory or not',.
1986 c 5	The Agricultural Holdings Act 1986	In section 89(1), the words 'or the Law of Property Act 1925'.
1986 c 45	The Insolvency Act 1986	In section 336– subsection (3), and in subsection (4), the words 'or (3)' and the words 'or section 30 of the Act of 1925'.
1988 c 50	The Housing Act 1988	In Schedule 1, in Part III, in paragraph 18(1)(b), the words 'or, if it is held on trust for sale, the proceeds of its sale are'.
1989 c 34	The Law of Property (Miscellaneous Provisions) Act 1989	In sections 1(6) and 2(6), the words 'or in or over the proceeds of sale of land'.
1990 c 8	The Town and Country Planning Act 1990	In section 328–
1991 c 31		in subsection (1)(a), the words 'and by that section as applied by section 28 of the Law of Property Act 1925 in relation to trusts for sale', and in subsection (2)(a), the words 'and by that section as so applied'.
1991 c 31	The Finance Act 1991	Section 110(5)(b).
1993 c 10	The Charities Act 1993	Section 37(6). Section 39(5).
1993 c 28	The Leasehold Reform, Housing and Urban Development Act 1993	In section 93A(4)– the words ', or by that section as applied by section 28 of the Law of Property Act 1925 in relation to trusts for sale', the words ', or by that section as so applied', and the words 'or by trustees for sale'.

Chapter	Short title	Extent of repeal
		In Schedule 2, paragraph 5(2)(b) and the word 'and' immediately preceding it.
1994 c 36	The Law of Property (Miscellaneous Provisions) Act 1994	In section 16– subsection (2), and in subsection (3), the words '; and subsection (2)' onwards.
1995 c 8	The Agricultural Tenancies Act 1995	In section 33– in subsections (1) and (2), the words from '(either " to "Property Act 1925)' and in subsection (4), the definition of 'settled land' and the word 'and' immediately preceding it.
1996 c 53	The Housing Grants, Construction and Regeneration Act 1996	Section 55(4)(b). Section 73(3)(b). In section 98(2)(a), the words 'or to the proceeds of sale of the dwelling'.

Appendix 3

Trustee Delegation Act 1999

SCHEDULE
REPEALS

Attorney of trustee with beneficial interest in land

1   Exercise of trustee functions by attorney

(1)   The donee of a power of attorney is not prevented from doing an act in relation to—

    (a)   land,

    (b)   capital proceeds of a conveyance of land, or

    (c)   income from land,

by reason only that the act involves the exercise of a trustee function of the donor if, at the time when the act is done, the donor has a beneficial interest in the land, proceeds or income.

(2) In this section—

    (a) 'conveyance' has the same meaning as in the Law of Property Act 1925, and

    (b) references to a trustee function of the donor are to a function which the donor has as trustee (either alone or jointly with any other person or persons).

(3) Subsection (1) above—

    (a) applies only if and so far as a contrary intention is not expressed in the instrument creating the power of attorney, and

    (b) has effect subject to the terms of that instrument.

(4) The donor of the power of attorney—

    (a) is liable for the acts or defaults of the donee in exercising any function by virtue of subsection (1) above in the same manner as if they were acts or defaults of the donor, but

    (b) is not liable by reason only that a function is exercised by the donee by virtue of that subsection.

(5) Subsections (1) and (4) above—

    (a) apply only if and so far as a contrary intention is not expressed in the instrument (if any) creating the trust, and

    (b) have effect subject to the terms of such an instrument.

(6) The fact that it appears that, in dealing with any shares or stock, the donee of the power of attorney is exercising a function by virtue of subsection (1) above does not affect with any notice of any trust a person in whose books the shares are, or stock is, registered or inscribed.

(7) In any case where (by way of exception to section 3(1) of the Trusts of Land and Appointment of Trustees Act 1996) the doctrine of conversion continues to operate, any person who, by reason of the continuing operation of that doctrine, has a beneficial interest in the proceeds of sale of land shall be treated for the purposes of this section and section 2 below as having a beneficial interest in the land.

(8) The donee of a power of attorney is not to be regarded as exercising a trustee function by virtue of subsection (1) above if he is acting under a trustee delegation power; and for this purpose a trustee delegation power is a power of attorney given under—

    (a) a statutory provision, or

    (b) a provision of the instrument (if any) creating a trust,

under which the donor of the power is expressly authorised to delegate the exercise of all or any of his trustee functions by power of attorney.

(9) Subject to section 4(6) below, this section applies only to powers of attorney created after the commencement of this Act.

2   Evidence of beneficial interest

(1)   This section applies where the interest of a purchaser depends on the donee of a power of attorney having power to do an act in relation to any property by virtue of section 1(1) above.

In this subsection 'purchaser' has the same meaning as in Part I of the Law of Property Act 1925.

(2)   Where this section applies an appropriate statement is, in favour of the purchaser, conclusive evidence of the donor of the power having a beneficial interest in the property at the time of the doing of the act.

(3)   In this section 'an appropriate statement' means a signed statement made by the donee—

(a)   when doing the act in question, or

(b)   at any other time within the period of three months beginning with the day on which the act is done,

that the donor has a beneficial interest in the property at the time of the donee doing the act.

(4)   If an appropriate statement is false, the donee is liable in the same way as he would be if the statement were contained in a statutory declaration.

3   General powers in specified form

In section 10(2) of the Powers of Attorney Act 1971 (which provides that a general power of attorney in the form set out in Schedule 1 to that Act, or a similar form, does not confer on the donee of the power any authority to exercise functions of the donor as trustee etc), for the words 'This section' substitute 'Subject to section 1 of the Trustee Delegation Act 1999, this section'.

4   Enduring powers

(1)   Section 3(3) of the Enduring Powers of Attorney Act 1985 (which entitles the donee of an enduring power to exercise any of the donor's functions as trustee and to give receipt for capital money etc) does not apply to enduring powers created after the commencement of this Act.

(2)   Section 3(3) of the Enduring Powers of Attorney Act 1985 ceases to apply to enduring powers created before the commencement of this Act—

(a)   where subsection (3) below applies, in accordance with that subsection, and

(b)   otherwise, at the end of the period of one year from that commencement.

(3)   Where an application for the registration of the instrument creating such an enduring power is made before the commencement of this Act, or during the period of one year from that commencement, section 3(3) of the Enduring Powers of Attorney Act 1985 ceases to apply to the power—

(a)   if the instrument is registered pursuant to the application (whether before commencement or during or after that period), when the registration of the instrument is cancelled, and

(b)   if the application is finally refused during or after that period, when the application is finally refused.

(4)   In subsection (3) above–

(a)   'registration' and 'registered' mean registration and registered under section 6 of the Enduring Powers of Attorney Act 1985, and

(b)   'cancelled' means cancelled under section 8(4) of that Act.

(5)   For the purposes of subsection (3)(b) above an application is finally refused–

(a)   if the application is withdrawn or any appeal is abandoned, when the application is withdrawn or the appeal is abandoned, and

(b)   otherwise, when proceedings on the application (including any proceedings on, or in consequence of, an appeal) have been determined and any time for appealing or further appealing has expired.

(6)   Section 1 above applies to an enduring power created before the commencement of this Act from the time when (in accordance with subsections (2) to (5) above) section 3(3) of the Enduring Powers of Attorney Act 1985 ceases to apply to it.

Trustee Delegation under section 25 of the Trustee Act 1925

5   Delegation under section 25 of the Trustee Act 1925

(1)   For section 25 of the Trustee Act 1925 substitute–

'25   Delegation of trustee's functions by power of attorney

(1)   Notwithstanding any rule of law or equity to the contrary, a trustee may, by power of attorney, delegate the execution or exercise of all or any of the trusts, powers and discretions vested in him as trustee either alone or jointly with any other person or persons.

(2)   A delegation under this section–

(a)   commences as provided by the instrument creating the power or, if the instrument makes no provision as to the commencement of the delegation, with the date of the execution of the instrument by the donor; and

(b)   continues for a period of twelve months or any shorter period provided by the instrument creating the power.

(3)   The persons who may be donees of a power of attorney under this section include a trust corporation.

(4)   Before or within seven days after giving a power of attorney under this section the donor shall give written notice of it (specifying the date on which the power comes into operation and its duration, the donee of the power, the reason why the power is given and, where some only are delegated, the trusts, powers and discretions delegated) to–

(a)   each person (other than himself), if any, who under any instrument creating the trust has power (whether alone or jointly) to appoint a new trustee; and

(b)   each of the other trustees, if any;

but failure to comply with this subsection shall not, in favour of a person dealing with the donee of the power, invalidate any act done or instrument executed by the donee.

(5)   A power of attorney given under this section by a single donor—

    (a)   in the form set out in subsection (6) of this section; or

    (b)   in a form to the like effect but expressed to be made under this subsection,

    shall operate to delegate to the person identified in the form as the single donee of the power the execution and exercise of all the trusts, powers and discretions vested in the donor as trustee (either alone or jointly with any other person or persons) under the single trust so identified.

(6)   The form referred to in subsection (5) of this section is as follows—

"THIS GENERAL TRUSTEE POWER OF ATTORNEY is made on [*date*] by [*name of one donor*] of [*address of donor*] as trustee of [*name or details of one trust*].

I appoint [*name of one donee*] of [*address of donee*] to be my attorney [*if desired, the date on which the delegation commences or the period for which it continues (or both)*] in accordance with section 25(5) of the Trustee Act 1925.

[*To be executed as a deed*]".

(7)   The donor of a power of attorney given under this section shall be liable for the acts or defaults of the donee in the same manner as if they were the acts or defaults of the donor.

(8)   For the purpose of executing or exercising the trusts or powers delegated to him, the donee may exercise any of the powers conferred on the donor as trustee by statute or by the instrument creating the trust, including power, for the purpose of the transfer of any inscribed stock, himself to delegate to an attorney power to transfer, but not including the power of delegation conferred by this section.

(9)   The fact that it appears from any power of attorney given under this section, or from any evidence required for the purposes of any such power of attorney or otherwise, that in dealing with any stock the donee of the power is acting in the execution of a trust shall not be deemed for any purpose to affect any person in whose books the stock is inscribed or registered with any notice of the trust.

(10)   This section applies to a personal representative, tenant for life and statutory owner as it applies to a trustee except that subsection (4) shall apply as if it required the notice there mentioned to be given—

    (a)   in the case of a personal representative, to each of the other personal representatives, if any, except any executor who has renounced probate;

    (b)   in the case of a tenant for life, to the trustees of the settlement and to each person, if any, who together with the person giving the notice constitutes the tenant for life; and

    (c)   in the case of a statutory owner, to each of the persons, if any, who together with the person giving the notice constitute the statutory owner and, in the case of a statutory owner by virtue of section 23(1)(a) of the Settled Land Act 1925, to the trustees of the settlement.'

(2)   Subsection (1) above has effect in relation to powers of attorney created after the commencement of this Act.

(3)   In section 34(2)(b) of the Pensions Act 1995 (delegation by trustees of trustee scheme under section 25 of the Trustee Act 1925), for 'during absence abroad' substitute 'for period not exceeding twelve months'.

6 Section 25 powers as enduring powers

Section 2(8) of the Enduring Powers of Attorney Act 1985 (which prevents a power of attorney under section 25 of the Trustee Act 1925 from being an enduring power) does not apply to powers of attorney created after the commencement of this Act.

Miscellaneous provisions about attorney acting for trustee

7 Two-trustee rules

(1) A requirement imposed by an enactment–

 (a) that capital money be paid to, or dealt with as directed by, at least two trustees or that a valid receipt for capital money be given otherwise than by a sole trustee, or

 (b) that, in order for an interest or power to be overreached, a conveyance or deed be executed by at least two trustees,

 is not satisfied by money being paid to or dealt with as directed by, or a receipt for money being given by, a relevant attorney or by a conveyance or deed being executed by such an attorney.

(2) In this section 'relevant attorney' means a person (other than a trust corporation within the meaning of the Trustee Act 1925) who is acting either–

 (a) both as a trustee and as attorney for one or more other trustees, or

 (b) as attorney for two or more trustees,

 and who is not acting together with any other person or persons.

(3) This section applies whether a relevant attorney is acting under a power created before or after the commencement of this Act (but in the case of such an attorney acting under an enduring power created before that commencement is without prejudice to any continuing application of section 3(3) of the Enduring Powers of Attorney Act 1985 to the enduring power after that commencement in accordance with section 4 above).

8 Appointment of additional trustee by attorney

(1) In section 36 of the Trustee Act 1925 (appointment of trustees), after subsection (6) (additional trustees) insert–

'(6A) A person who is either–

 (a) both a trustee and attorney for the other trustee (if one other), or for both of the other trustees (if two others), under a registered power; or

 (b) attorney under a registered power for the trustee (if one) or for both or each of the trustees (if two or three),

 may, if subsection (6B) of this section is satisfied in relation to him, make an appointment under subsection (6)(b) of this section on behalf of the trustee or trustees.

(6B) This subsection is satisfied in relation to an attorney under a registered power for one or more trustees if (as attorney under the power)–

 (a) he intends to exercise any function of the trustee or trustees by virtue of section 1(1) of the Trustee Delegation Act 1999; or

(b)   he intends to exercise any function of the trustee or trustees in relation to any land, capital proceeds of a conveyance of land or income from land by virtue of its delegation to him under section 25 of this Act or the instrument (if any) creating the trust.

(6C)   In subsections (6A) and (6B) of this section "registered power" means a power of attorney created by an instrument which is for the time being registered under section 6 of the Enduring Powers of Attorney Act 1985.

(6D)   Subsection (6A) of this section—

(a)   applies only if and so far as a contrary intention is not expressed in the instrument creating the power of attorney (or, where more than one, any of them) or the instrument (if any) creating the trust; and

(b)   has effect subject to the terms of those instruments.'

(2)   The amendment made by subsection (1) above has effect only where the power, or (where more than one) each of them, is created after the commencement of this Act.

9   Attorney acting for incapable trustee

(1)   In section 22 of the Law of Property Act 1925 (requirement, before dealing with legal estate vested in trustee who is incapable by reason of mental disorder, to appoint new trustee or discharge incapable trustee), after subsection (2) insert—

'(3)   Subsection (2) of this section does not prevent a legal estate being dealt with without the appointment of a new trustee, or the discharge of the incapable trustee, at a time when the donee of an enduring power (within the meaning of the Enduring Powers of Attorney Act 1985) is entitled to act for the incapable trustee in the dealing.'

(2)   The amendment made by subsection (1) above has effect whether the enduring power was created before or after the commencement of this Act.

Authority of attorney to act in relation to land

10   Extent of attorney's authority to act in relation to land

(1)   Where the donee of a power of attorney is authorised by the power to do an act of any description in relation to any land, his authority to do an act of that description at any time includes authority to do it with respect to any estate or interest in the land which is held at that time by the donor (whether alone or jointly with any other person or persons).

(2)   Subsection (1) above—

(a)   applies only if and so far as a contrary intention is not expressed in the instrument creating the power of attorney, and

(b)   has effect subject to the terms of that instrument.

(3)   This section applies only to powers of attorney created after the commencement of this Act.

Supplementary

11 Interpretation

(1) In this Act–

'land' has the same meaning as in the Trustee Act 1925, and

'enduring power' has the same meaning as in the Enduring Powers of Attorney Act 1985.

(2) References in this Act to the creation of a power of attorney are to the execution by the donor of the instrument creating it.

12 Repeals

The enactments specified in the Schedule to this Act are repealed to the extent specified in the third column, but subject to the note at the end.

13 Commencement, extent and short title

(1) The preceding provisions of this Act shall come into force on such day as the Lord Chancellor may by order made by statutory instrument appoint.

(2) This Act extends to England and Wales only.

(3) This Act may be cited as the Trustee Delegation Act 1999.

SCHEDULE
REPEALS

Section 12

1985 c 29 The Enduring Powers of Attorney Act 1985 Section 2(8)

The repeal of section 3(3) of the Enduring Powers of Attorney Act 1985 has effect in accordance with section 4 of this Act and the remaining repeals have effect in relation to powers of attorney created after the commencement of this Act.

Appendix 4

Trustee Act 2000

Part I

The Duty of Care

Part I

The Duty of Care

1   The duty of care

(1)   Whenever the duty under this subsection applies to a trustee, he must exercise such care and skill as is reasonable in the circumstances, having regard in particular—

(a)   to any special knowledge or experience that he has or holds himself out as having, and

(b)   if he acts as trustee in the course of a business or profession, to any special knowledge or experience that it is reasonable to expect of a person acting in the course of that kind of business or profession.

(2)   In this Act the duty under subsection (1) is called 'the duty of care'.

2   Application of duty of care

Schedule 1 makes provision about when the duty of care applies to a trustee.

Part II

Investment

3 General power of investment

(1) Subject to the provisions of this Part, a trustee may make any kind of investment that he could make if he were absolutely entitled to the assets of the trust.

(2) In this Act the power under subsection (1) is called 'the general power of investment'.

(3) The general power of investment does not permit a trustee to make investments in land other than in loans secured on land (but see also section 8).

(4) A person invests in a loan secured on land if he has rights under any contract under which—

(a) one person provides another with credit, and

(b) the obligation of the borrower to repay is secured on land.

(5) 'Credit' includes any cash loan or other financial accommodation.

(6) 'Cash' includes money in any form.

4 Standard investment criteria

(1) In exercising any power of investment, whether arising under this Part or otherwise, a trustee must have regard to the standard investment criteria.

(2) A trustee must from time to time review the investments of the trust and consider whether, having regard to the standard investment criteria, they should be varied.

(3) The standard investment criteria, in relation to a trust, are—

(a) the suitability to the trust of investments of the same kind as any particular investment proposed to be made or retained and of that particular investment as an investment of that kind, and

(b) the need for diversification of investments of the trust, in so far as is appropriate to the circumstances of the trust.

5 Advice

(1) Before exercising any power of investment, whether arising under this Part or otherwise, a trustee must (unless the exception applies) obtain and consider proper advice about the way in which, having regard to the standard investment criteria, the power should be exercised.

(2) When reviewing the investments of the trust, a trustee must (unless the exception applies) obtain and consider proper advice about whether, having regard to the standard investment criteria, the investments should be varied.

(3) The exception is that a trustee need not obtain such advice if he reasonably concludes that in all the circumstances it is unnecessary or inappropriate to do so.

(4) Proper advice is the advice of a person who is reasonably believed by the trustee to be qualified to give it by his ability in and practical experience of financial and other matters relating to the proposed investment.

6 Restriction or exclusion of this Part etc

(1) The general power of investment is–

(a) in addition to powers conferred on trustees otherwise than by this Act, but

(b) subject to any restriction or exclusion imposed by the trust instrument or by any enactment or any provision of subordinate legislation.

(2) For the purposes of this Act, an enactment or a provision of subordinate legislation is not to be regarded as being, or as being part of, a trust instrument.

(3) In this Act 'subordinate legislation' has the same meaning as in the Interpretation Act 1978.

7 Existing trusts

(1) This Part applies in relation to trusts whether created before or after its commencement.

(2) No provision relating to the powers of a trustee contained in a trust instrument made before 3rd August 1961 is to be treated (for the purposes of section 6(1)(b)) as restricting or excluding the general power of investment.

(3) A provision contained in a trust instrument made before the commencement of this Part which–

(a) has effect under section 3(2) of the Trustee Investments Act 1961 as a power to invest under that Act, or

(b) confers power to invest under that Act,

is to be treated as conferring the general power of investment on a trustee.

Part III

Acquisition of Land

8 Power to acquire freehold and leasehold land

(1) A trustee may acquire freehold or leasehold land in the United Kingdom—

 (a) as an investment,

 (b) for occupation by a beneficiary, or

 (c) for any other reason.

(2) 'Freehold or leasehold land' means—

 (a) in relation to England and Wales, a legal estate in land,

 (b) in relation to Scotland—

  (i) the estate or interest of the proprietor of the dominium utile or, in the case of land not held on feudal tenure, the estate or interest of the owner, or

  (ii) a tenancy, and

 (c) in relation to Northern Ireland, a legal estate in land, including land held under a fee farm grant.

(3) For the purpose of exercising his functions as a trustee, a trustee who acquires land under this section has all the powers of an absolute owner in relation to the land.

9 Restriction or exclusion of this Part etc

The powers conferred by this Part are—

(a) in addition to powers conferred on trustees otherwise than by this Part, but

(b) subject to any restriction or exclusion imposed by the trust instrument or by any enactment or any provision of subordinate legislation.

10 Existing trusts

(1) This Part does not apply in relation to—

 (a) a trust of property which consists of or includes land which (despite section 2 of the Trusts of Land and Appointment of Trustees Act 1996) is settled land, or

 (b) a trust to which the Universities and College Estates Act 1925 applies.

(2) Subject to subsection (1), this Part applies in relation to trusts whether created before or after its commencement.

Part IV

Agents, nominees and custodians

Agents

11 Power to employ agents

(1) Subject to the provisions of this Part, the trustees of a trust may authorise any person to exercise any or all of their delegable functions as their agent.

(2) In the case of a trust other than a charitable trust, the trustees' delegable functions consist of any function other than—

    (a) any function relating to whether or in what way any assets of the trust should be distributed,

    (b) any power to decide whether any fees or other payment due to be made out of the trust funds should be made out of income or capital,

    (c) any power to appoint a person to be a trustee of the trust, or

    (d) any power conferred by any other enactment or the trust instrument which permits the trustees to delegate any of their functions or to appoint a person to act as a nominee or custodian.

(3) In the case of a charitable trust, the trustees' delegable functions are—

    (a) any function consisting of carrying out a decision that the trustees have taken;

    (b) any function relating to the investment of assets subject to the trust (including, in the case of land held as an investment, managing the land and creating or disposing of an interest in the land);

    (c) any function relating to the raising of funds for the trust otherwise than by means of profits of a trade which is an integral part of carrying out the trust's charitable purpose;

    (d) any other function prescribed by an order made by the Secretary of State.

(4) For the purposes of subsection (3)(c) a trade is an integral part of carrying out a trust's charitable purpose if, whether carried on in the United Kingdom or elsewhere, the profits are applied solely to the purposes of the trust and either—

    (a) the trade is exercised in the course of the actual carrying out of a primary purpose of the trust, or

    (b) the work in connection with the trade is mainly carried out by beneficiaries of the trust.

(5) The power to make an order under subsection (3)(d) is exercisable by statutory instrument which shall be subject to annulment in pursuance of a resolution of either House of Parliament.

12 Persons who may act as agents

(1) Subject to subsection (2), the persons whom the trustees may under section 11 authorise to exercise functions as their agent include one or more of their number.

(2)   The trustees may not authorise two (or more) persons to exercise the same function unless they are to exercise the function jointly.

(3)   The trustees may not under section 11 authorise a beneficiary to exercise any function as their agent (even if the beneficiary is also a trustee).

(4)   The trustees may under section 11 authorise a person to exercise functions as their agent even though he is also appointed to act as their nominee or custodian (whether under section 16, 17 or 18 or any other power).

13   Linked functions etc

(1)   Subject to subsections (2) and (5), a person who is authorised under section 11 to exercise a function is (whatever the terms of the agency) subject to any specific duties or restrictions attached to the function.

For example, a person who is authorised under section 11 to exercise the general power of investment is subject to the duties under section 4 in relation to that power.

(2)   A person who is authorised under section 11 to exercise a power which is subject to a requirement to obtain advice is not subject to the requirement if he is the kind of person from whom it would have been proper for the trustees, in compliance with the requirement, to obtain advice.

(3)   Subsections (4) and (5) apply to a trust to which section 11(1) of the Trusts of Land and Appointment of Trustees Act 1996 (duties to consult beneficiaries and give effect to their wishes) applies.

(4)   The trustees may not under section 11 authorise a person to exercise any of their functions on terms that prevent them from complying with section 11(1) of the 1996 Act.

(5)   A person who is authorised under section 11 to exercise any function relating to land subject to the trust is not subject to section 11(1) of the 1996 Act.

14   Terms of agency

(1)   Subject to subsection (2) and sections 15(2) and 29 to 32, the trustees may authorise a person to exercise functions as their agent on such terms as to remuneration and other matters as they may determine.

(2)   The trustees may not authorise a person to exercise functions as their agent on any of the terms mentioned in subsection (3) unless it is reasonably necessary for them to do so.

(3)   The terms are—

(a)   a term permitting the agent to appoint a substitute;

(b)   a term restricting the liability of the agent or his substitute to the trustees or any beneficiary;

(c)   a term permitting the agent to act in circumstances capable of giving rise to a conflict of interest.

15   Asset management: special restrictions

(1)   The trustees may not authorise a person to exercise any of their asset management functions as their agent except by an agreement which is in or evidenced in writing.

(2) The trustees may not authorise a person to exercise any of their asset management functions as their agent unless—

    (a) they have prepared a statement that gives guidance as to how the functions should be exercised ('a policy statement'), and

    (b) the agreement under which the agent is to act includes a term to the effect that he will secure compliance with—

        (i) the policy statement, or

        (ii) if the policy statement is revised or replaced under section 22, the revised or replacement policy statement.

(3) The trustees must formulate any guidance given in the policy statement with a view to ensuring that the functions will be exercised in the best interests of the trust.

(4) The policy statement must be in or evidenced in writing.

(5) The asset management functions of trustees are their functions relating to—

    (a) the investment of assets subject to the trust,

    (b) the acquisition of property which is to be subject to the trust, and

    (c) managing property which is subject to the trust and disposing of, or creating or disposing of an interest in, such property.

Nominees and custodians

16 Power to appoint nominees

(1) Subject to the provisions of this Part, the trustees of a trust may—

    (a) appoint a person to act as their nominee in relation to such of the assets of the trust as they determine (other than settled land), and

    (b) take such steps as are necessary to secure that those assets are vested in a person so appointed.

(2) An appointment under this section must be in or evidenced in writing.

(3) This section does not apply to any trust having a custodian trustee or in relation to any assets vested in the official custodian for charities.

17 Power to appoint custodians

(1) Subject to the provisions of this Part, the trustees of a trust may appoint a person to act as a custodian in relation to such of the assets of the trust as they may determine.

(2) For the purposes of this Act a person is a custodian in relation to assets if he undertakes the safe custody of the assets or of any documents or records concerning the assets.

(3) An appointment under this section must be in or evidenced in writing.

(4) This section does not apply to any trust having a custodian trustee or in relation to any assets vested in the official custodian for charities.

18   Investment in bearer securities

(1)   If trustees retain or invest in securities payable to bearer, they must appoint a person to act as a custodian of the securities.

(2)   Subsection (1) does not apply if the trust instrument or any enactment or provision of subordinate legislation contains provision which (however expressed) permits the trustees to retain or invest in securities payable to bearer without appointing a person to act as a custodian.

(3)   An appointment under this section must be in or evidenced in writing.

(4)   This section does not apply to any trust having a custodian trustee or in relation to any securities vested in the official custodian for charities.

19   Persons who may be appointed as nominees or custodians

(1)   A person may not be appointed under section 16, 17 or 18 as a nominee or custodian unless one of the relevant conditions is satisfied.

(2)   The relevant conditions are that—

(a)   the person carries on a business which consists of or includes acting as a nominee or custodian;

(b)   the person is a body corporate which is controlled by the trustees;

(c)   the person is a body corporate recognised under section 9 of the Administration of Justice Act 1985.

(3)   The question whether a body corporate is controlled by trustees is to be determined in accordance with section 840 of the Income and Corporation Taxes Act 1988.

(4)   The trustees of a charitable trust which is not an exempt charity must act in accordance with any guidance given by the Charity Commissioners concerning the selection of a person for appointment as a nominee or custodian under section 16, 17 or 18.

(5)   Subject to subsections (1) and (4), the persons whom the trustees may under section 16, 17 or 18 appoint as a nominee or custodian include—

(a)   one of their number, if that one is a trust corporation, or

(b)   two (or more) of their number, if they are to act as joint nominees or joint custodians.

(6)   The trustees may under section 16 appoint a person to act as their nominee even though he is also—

(a)   appointed to act as their custodian (whether under section 17 or 18 or any other power), or

(b)   authorised to exercise functions as their agent (whether under section 11 or any other power).

(7)   Likewise, the trustees may under section 17 or 18 appoint a person to act as their custodian even though he is also—

(a)   appointed to act as their nominee (whether under section 16 or any other power), or

(b)   authorised to exercise functions as their agent (whether under section 11 or any other power).

20   Terms of appointment of nominees and custodians

(1)   Subject to subsection (2) and sections 29 to 32, the trustees may under section 16, 17 or 18 appoint a person to act as a nominee or custodian on such terms as to remuneration and other matters as they may determine.

(2)   The trustees may not under section 16, 17 or 18 appoint a person to act as a nominee or custodian on any of the terms mentioned in subsection (3) unless it is reasonably necessary for them to do so.

(3)   The terms are—

(a)   a term permitting the nominee or custodian to appoint a substitute;

(b)   a term restricting the liability of the nominee or custodian or his substitute to the trustees or to any beneficiary;

(c)   a term permitting the nominee or custodian to act in circumstances capable of giving rise to a conflict of interest.

Review of and liability for agents, nominees and custodians etc

21   Application of sections 22 and 23

(1)   Sections 22 and 23 apply in a case where trustees have, under section 11, 16, 17 or 18—

(a)   authorised a person to exercise functions as their agent, or

(b)   appointed a person to act as a nominee or custodian.

(2)   Subject to subsection (3), sections 22 and 23 also apply in a case where trustees have, under any power conferred on them by the trust instrument or by any enactment or any provision of subordinate legislation—

(a)   authorised a person to exercise functions as their agent, or

(b)   appointed a person to act as a nominee or custodian.

(3)   If the application of section 22 or 23 is inconsistent with the terms of the trust instrument or the enactment or provision of subordinate legislation, the section in question does not apply.

22   Review of agents, nominees and custodians etc

(1)   While the agent, nominee or custodian continues to act for the trust, the trustees—

(a)   must keep under review the arrangements under which the agent, nominee or custodian acts and how those arrangements are being put into effect,

(b)   if circumstances make it appropriate to do so, must consider whether there is a need to exercise any power of intervention that they have, and

(c)   if they consider that there is a need to exercise such a power, must do so.

(2)   If the agent has been authorised to exercise asset management functions, the duty under subsection (1) includes, in particular—

(a)   a duty to consider whether there is any need to revise or replace the policy statement made for the purposes of section 15,

(b)   if they consider that there is a need to revise or replace the policy statement, a duty to do so, and

(c)   a duty to assess whether the policy statement (as it has effect for the time being) is being complied with.

(3)   Subsections (3) and (4) of section 15 apply to the revision or replacement of a policy statement under this section as they apply to the making of a policy statement under that section.

(4)   'Power of intervention' includes–

(a)   a power to give directions to the agent, nominee or custodian;

(b)   a power to revoke the authorisation or appointment.

23   Liability for agents, nominees and custodians etc

(1)   A trustee is not liable for any act or default of the agent, nominee or custodian unless he has failed to comply with the duty of care applicable to him, under paragraph 3 of Schedule 1–

(a)   when entering into the arrangements under which the person acts as agent, nominee or custodian, or

(b)   when carrying out his duties under section 22.

(2)   If a trustee has agreed a term under which the agent, nominee or custodian is permitted to appoint a substitute, the trustee is not liable for any act or default of the substitute unless he has failed to comply with the duty of care applicable to him, under paragraph 3 of Schedule 1–

(a)   when agreeing that term, or

(b)   when carrying out his duties under section 22 in so far as they relate to the use of the substitute.

Supplementary

24   Effect of trustees exceeding their powers

A failure by the trustees to act within the limits of the powers conferred by this Part–

(a)   in authorising a person to exercise a function of theirs as an agent, or

(b)   in appointing a person to act as a nominee or custodian,

does not invalidate the authorisation or appointment.

25   Sole trustees

(1)   Subject to subsection (2), this Part applies in relation to a trust having a sole trustee as it applies in relation to other trusts (and references in this Part to trustees – except in sections 12(1) and (3) and 19(5) – are to be read accordingly).

(2)   Section 18 does not impose a duty on a sole trustee if that trustee is a trust corporation.

26 Restriction or exclusion of this Part etc

The powers conferred by this Part are—

(a)   in addition to powers conferred on trustees otherwise than by this Act, but

(b)   subject to any restriction or exclusion imposed by the trust instrument or by any enactment or any provision of subordinate legislation.

27 Existing trusts

This Part applies in relation to trusts whether created before or after its commencement.

Part V

Remuneration

28 Trustee's entitlement to payment under trust instrument

(1) Except to the extent (if any) to which the trust instrument makes inconsistent provision, subsections (2) to (4) apply to a trustee if–

    (a) there is a provision in the trust instrument entitling him to receive payment out of trust funds in respect of services provided by him to or on behalf of the trust, and

    (b) the trustee is a trust corporation or is acting in a professional capacity.

(2) The trustee is to be treated as entitled under the trust instrument to receive payment in respect of services even if they are services which are capable of being provided by a lay trustee.

(3) Subsection (2) applies to a trustee of a charitable trust who is not a trust corporation only–

    (a) if he is not a sole trustee, and

    (b) to the extent that a majority of the other trustees have agreed that it should apply to him.

(4) Any payments to which the trustee is entitled in respect of services are to be treated as remuneration for services (and not as a gift) for the purposes of–

    (a) section 15 of the Wills Act 1837 (gifts to an attesting witness to be void), and

    (b) section 34(3) of the Administration of Estates Act 1925 (order in which estate to be paid out).

(5) For the purposes of this Part, a trustee acts in a professional capacity if he acts in the course of a profession or business which consists of or includes the provision of services in connection with–

    (a) the management or administration of trusts generally or a particular kind of trust, or

    (b) any particular aspect of the management or administration of trusts generally or a particular kind of trust,

and the services he provides to or on behalf of the trust fall within that description.

(6) For the purposes of this Part, a person acts as a lay trustee if he–

    (a) is not a trust corporation, and

    (b) does not act in a professional capacity.

29 Remuneration of certain trustees

(1) Subject to subsection (5), a trustee who–

    (a) is a trust corporation, but

    (b) is not a trustee of a charitable trust,

is entitled to receive reasonable remuneration out of the trust funds for any services that the trust corporation provides to or on behalf of the trust.

(2) Subject to subsection (5), a trustee who—

(a) acts in a professional capacity, but

(b) is not a trust corporation, a trustee of a charitable trust or a sole trustee,

is entitled to receive reasonable remuneration out of the trust funds for any services that he provides to or on behalf of the trust if each other trustee has agreed in writing that he may be remunerated for the services.

(3) 'Reasonable remuneration' means, in relation to the provision of services by a trustee, such remuneration as is reasonable in the circumstances for the provision of those services to or on behalf of that trust by that trustee and for the purposes of subsection (1) includes, in relation to the provision of services by a trustee who is an authorised institution under the Banking Act 1987 and provides the services in that capacity, the institution's reasonable charges for the provision of such services.

(4) A trustee is entitled to remuneration under this section even if the services in question are capable of being provided by a lay trustee.

(5) A trustee is not entitled to remuneration under this section if any provision about his entitlement to remuneration has been made—

(a) by the trust instrument, or

(b) by any enactment or any provision of subordinate legislation.

(6) This section applies to a trustee who has been authorised under a power conferred by Part IV or the trust instrument—

(a) to exercise functions as an agent of the trustees, or

(b) to act as a nominee or custodian,

as it applies to any other trustee.

30 Remuneration of trustees of charitable trusts

(1) The Secretary of State may by regulations make provision for the remuneration of trustees of charitable trusts who are trust corporations or act in a professional capacity.

(2) The power under subsection (1) includes power to make provision for the remuneration of a trustee who has been authorised under a power conferred by Part IV or any other enactment or any provision of subordinate legislation, or by the trust instrument—

(a) to exercise functions as an agent of the trustees, or

(b) to act as a nominee or custodian.

(3) Regulations under this section may—

(a) make different provision for different cases;

(b) contain such supplemental, incidental, consequential and transitional provision as the Secretary of State considers appropriate.

(4)   The power to make regulations under this section is exercisable by statutory instrument, but no such instrument shall be made unless a draft of it has been laid before Parliament and approved by a resolution of each House of Parliament.

31   Trustees' expenses

(1)   A trustee—

(a)   is entitled to be reimbursed from the trust funds, or

(b)   may pay out of the trust funds,

expenses properly incurred by him when acting on behalf of the trust.

(2)   This section applies to a trustee who has been authorised under a power conferred by Part IV or any other enactment or any provision of subordinate legislation, or by the trust instrument—

(a)   to exercise functions as an agent of the trustees, or

(b)   to act as a nominee or custodian,

as it applies to any other trustee.

32   Remuneration and expenses of agents, nominees and custodians

(1)   This section applies if, under a power conferred by Part IV or any other enactment or any provision of subordinate legislation, or by the trust instrument, a person other than a trustee has been—

(a)   authorised to exercise functions as an agent of the trustees, or

(b)   appointed to act as a nominee or custodian.

(2)   The trustees may remunerate the agent, nominee or custodian out of the trust funds for services if—

(a)   he is engaged on terms entitling him to be remunerated for those services, and

(b)   the amount does not exceed such remuneration as is reasonable in the circumstances for the provision of those services by him to or on behalf of that trust.

(3)   The trustees may reimburse the agent, nominee or custodian out of the trust funds for any expenses properly incurred by him in exercising functions as an agent, nominee or custodian.

33   Application

(1)   Subject to subsection (2), sections 28, 29, 31 and 32 apply in relation to services provided to or on behalf of, or (as the case may be) expenses incurred on or after their commencement on behalf of, trusts whenever created.

(2)   Nothing in section 28 or 29 is to be treated as affecting the operation of—

(a)   section 15 of the Wills Act 1837, or

(b)   section 34(3) of the Administration of Estates Act 1925,

in relation to any death occurring before the commencement of section 28 or (as the case may be) section 29.

Part VI

Miscellaneous and Supplementary

34 Power to insure

(1) For section 19 of the Trustee Act 1925 (power to insure) substitute—

19 'Power to insure

(1) A trustee may—

(a) insure any property which is subject to the trust against risks of loss or damage due to any event, and

(b) pay the premiums out of the trust funds.

(2) In the case of property held on a bare trust, the power to insure is subject to any direction given by the beneficiary or each of the beneficiaries—

(a) that any property specified in the direction is not to be insured;

(b) that any property specified in the direction is not to be insured except on such conditions as may be so specified.

(3) Property is held on a bare trust if it is held on trust for—

(a) a beneficiary who is of full age and capacity and absolutely entitled to the property subject to the trust, or

(b) beneficiaries each of whom is of full age and capacity and who (taken together) are absolutely entitled to the property subject to the trust.

(4) If a direction under subsection (2) of this section is given, the power to insure, so far as it is subject to the direction, ceases to be a delegable function for the purposes of section 11 of the Trustee Act 2000 (power to employ agents).

(5) In this section "trust funds" means any income or capital funds of the trust.'

(2) In section 20(1) of the Trustee Act 1925 (application of insurance money) omit 'whether by fire or otherwise'.

(3) The amendments made by this section apply in relation to trusts whether created before or after its commencement.

35 Personal representatives

(1) Subject to the following provisions of this section, this Act applies in relation to a personal representative administering an estate according to the law as it applies to a trustee carrying out a trust for beneficiaries.

(2) For this purpose this Act is to be read with the appropriate modifications and in particular—

(a) references to the trust instrument are to be read as references to the will,

(b) references to a beneficiary or to beneficiaries, apart from the reference to a beneficiary in section 8(1)(b), are to be read as references to a person or the persons interested in the due administration of the estate, and

(c) the reference to a beneficiary in section 8(1)(b) is to be read as a reference to a person who under the will of the deceased or under the law relating to intestacy is beneficially interested in the estate.

(3)   Remuneration to which a personal representative is entitled under section 28 or 29 is to be treated as an administration expense for the purposes of—

    (a)   section 34(3) of the Administration of Estates Act 1925 (order in which estate to be paid out), and

    (b)   any provision giving reasonable administration expenses priority over the preferential debts listed in Schedule 6 to the Insolvency Act 1986.

(4)   Nothing in subsection (3) is to be treated as affecting the operation of the provisions mentioned in paragraphs (a) and (b) of that subsection in relation to any death occurring before the commencement of this section.

36 Pension schemes

(1)   In this section 'pension scheme' means an occupational pension scheme (within the meaning of the Pension Schemes Act 1993) established under a trust and subject to the law of England and Wales.

(2)   Part I does not apply in so far as it imposes a duty of care in relation to—

    (a)   the functions described in paragraphs 1 and 2 of Schedule 1, or

    (b)   the functions described in paragraph 3 of that Schedule to the extent that they relate to trustees—

        (i)   authorising a person to exercise their functions with respect to investment, or

        (ii)   appointing a person to act as their nominee or custodian.

(3)   Nothing in Part II or III applies to the trustees of any pension scheme.

(4)   Part IV applies to the trustees of a pension scheme subject to the restrictions in subsections (5) to (8).

(5)   The trustees of a pension scheme may not under Part IV authorise any person to exercise any functions relating to investment as their agent.

(6)   The trustees of a pension scheme may not under Part IV authorise a person who is—

    (a)   an employer in relation to the scheme, or

    (b)   connected with or an associate of such an employer,

to exercise any of their functions as their agent.

(7)   For the purposes of subsection (6)—

    (a)   'employer', in relation to a scheme, has the same meaning as in the Pensions Act 1995;

    (b)   sections 249 and 435 of the Insolvency Act 1986 apply for the purpose of determining whether a person is connected with or an associate of an employer.

(8)   Sections 16 to 20 (powers to appoint nominees and custodians) do not apply to the trustees of a pension scheme.

37 Authorised unit trusts

(1)   Parts II to IV do not apply to trustees of authorised unit trusts.

(2)   'Authorised unit trust' means a unit trust scheme in the case of which an order under section 78 of the Financial Services Act 1986 is in force.

38   Common investment schemes for charities etc

Parts II to IV do not apply to—

(a)   trustees managing a fund under a common investment scheme made, or having effect as if made, under section 24 of the Charities Act 1993, other than such a fund the trusts of which provide that property is not to be transferred to the fund except by or on behalf of a charity the trustees of which are the trustees appointed to manage the fund, or

(b)   trustees managing a fund under a common deposit scheme made, or having effect as if made, under section 25 of that Act.

39   Interpretation

(1)   In this Act—

'asset' includes any right or interest;

'charitable trust' means a trust under which property is held for charitable purposes and 'charitable purposes' has the same meaning as in the Charities Act 1993;

'custodian trustee' has the same meaning as in the Public Trustee Act 1906;

'enactment' includes any provision of a Measure of the Church Assembly or of the General Synod of the Church of England;

'exempt charity' has the same meaning as in the Charities Act 1993;

'functions' includes powers and duties;

'legal mortgage' has the same meaning as in the Law of Property Act 1925;

'personal representative' has the same meaning as in the Trustee Act 1925;

'settled land' has the same meaning as in the Settled Land Act 1925;

'trust corporation' has the same meaning as in the Trustee Act 1925;

'trust funds' means income or capital funds of the trust.

(2)   In this Act the expressions listed below are defined or otherwise explained by the provisions indicated—

asset management functions	section 15(5)
Custodian	section 17(2)
the duty of care	section 1(2)
the general power of investment	section 3(2)
lay trustee	section 28(6)
power of intervention	section 22(4)
the standard investment criteria	section 4(3)
subordinate legislation	section 6(3)
trustee acting in a professional capacity	section 28(5)
trust instrument	sections 6(2) and 35(2)(a)

40 Minor and consequential amendments etc

(1) Schedule 2 (minor and consequential amendments) shall have effect.

(2) Schedule 3 (transitional provisions and savings) shall have effect.

(3) Schedule 4 (repeals) shall have effect.

41 Power to amend other Acts

(1) A Minister of the Crown may by order make such amendments of any Act, including an Act extending to places outside England and Wales, as appear to him appropriate in consequence of or in connection with Part II or III.

(2) Before exercising the power under subsection (1) in relation to a local, personal or private Act, the Minister must consult any person who appears to him to be affected by any proposed amendment.

(3) An order under this section may–

(a) contain such transitional provisions and savings as the Minister thinks fit;

(b) make different provision for different purposes.

(4) The power to make an order under this section is exercisable by statutory instrument which shall be subject to annulment in pursuance of a resolution of either House of Parliament.

(5) 'Minister of the Crown' has the same meaning as in the Ministers of the Crown Act 1975.

42 Commencement and extent

(1) Section 41, this section and section 43 shall come into force on the day on which this Act is passed.

(2) The remaining provisions of this Act shall come into force on such day as the Lord Chancellor may appoint by order made by statutory instrument; and different days may be so appointed for different purposes.

(3) An order under subsection (2) may contain such transitional provisions and savings as the Lord Chancellor considers appropriate in connection with the order.

(4) Subject to section 41(1) and subsection (5), this Act extends to England and Wales only.

(5) An amendment or repeal in Part II or III of Schedule 2 or Part II of Schedule 4 has the same extent as the provision amended or repealed.

43 Short title

This Act may be cited as the Trustee Act 2000.

SCHEDULE 1
APPLICATION OF DUTY OF CARE

Section 2

1

The duty of care applies to a trustee—

(a) when exercising the general power of investment or any other power of investment, however conferred;

(b) when carrying out a duty to which he is subject under section 4 or 5 (duties relating to the exercise of a power of investment or to the review of investments).

Acquisition of land

2

The duty of care applies to a trustee—

(a) when exercising the power under section 8 to acquire land;

(b) when exercising any other power to acquire land, however conferred;

(c) when exercising any power in relation to land acquired under a power mentioned in sub-paragraph (a) or (b).

Agents, nominees and custodians

3

(1) The duty of care applies to a trustee—

(a) when entering into arrangements under which a person is authorised under section 11 to exercise functions as an agent;

(b) when entering into arrangements under which a person is appointed under section 16 to act as a nominee;

(c) when entering into arrangements under which a person is appointed under section 17 or 18 to act as a custodian;

(d) when entering into arrangements under which, under any other power, however conferred, a person is authorised to exercise functions as an agent or is appointed to act as a nominee or custodian;

(e) when carrying out his duties under section 22 (review of agent, nominee or custodian, etc).

(2) For the purposes of sub-paragraph (1), entering into arrangements under which a person is authorised to exercise functions or is appointed to act as a nominee or custodian includes, in particular—

(a) selecting the person who is to act,

(b) determining any terms on which he is to act, and

(c) if the person is being authorised to exercise asset management functions, the preparation of a policy statement under section 15.

Compounding of liabilities

4

The duty of care applies to a trustee—

(a)   when exercising the power under section 15 of the Trustee Act 1925 to do any of the things referred to in that section;

(b)   when exercising any corresponding power, however conferred.

Insurance

5

The duty of care applies to a trustee—

(a)   when exercising the power under section 19 of the Trustee Act 1925 to insure property;

(b)   when exercising any corresponding power, however conferred.

Reversionary interests, valuations and audit

6

The duty of care applies to a trustee—

(a)   when exercising the power under section 22(1) or (3) of the Trustee Act 1925 to do any of the things referred to there;

(b)   when exercising any corresponding power, however conferred.

Exclusion of duty of care

7

The duty of care does not apply if or in so far as it appears from the trust instrument that the duty is not meant to apply.

SCHEDULE 2
MINOR AND CONSEQUENTIAL AMENDMENTS

Section 40

Part I
The Trustee Investments Act 1961 and the Charities Act 1993

The Trustee Investments Act 1961 (c 62)

1

(1) Sections 1, 2, 5, 6, 12, 13 and 15 shall cease to have effect, except in so far as they are applied by or under any other enactment.

(2) Section 3 and Schedules 2 and 3 shall cease to have effect, except in so far as they relate to a trustee having a power of investment conferred on him under an enactment—

    (a) which was passed before the passing of the 1961 Act, and

    (b) which is not amended by this Schedule.

(3) Omit—

    (a) sections 8 and 9,

    (b) paragraph 1(1) of Schedule 4, and

    (c) section 16(1), in so far as it relates to paragraph 1(1) of Schedule 4.

The Charities Act 1993 (c 10)

2

(1) Omit sections 70 and 71.

(2) In section 86(2) in paragraph (a)—

    (a) omit '70', and

    (b) at the end insert 'or'.

(3) Omit section 86(2)(b).

Part II

Other Public General Acts

The Places of Worship Sites Act 1873 (c 50)

3

In section 2 (payment of purchase money, etc) for "shall be invested upon such securities or investments as would for the time being be authorised by statute or the Court of Chancery" substitute "shall be invested under the general power of investment in section 3 of the Trustee Act 2000".

The Technical and Industrial Institutions Act 1892 (c 29)

4

In section 9 (investment powers relating to proceeds of sale of land acquired under the Act) for subsection (5) substitute–

'(5)   Money arising by sale may, until reinvested in the purchase of land, be invested–

    (a)   in the names of the governing body, in any investments in which trustees may invest under the general power of investment in section 3 of the Trustee Act 2000 (as restricted by sections 4 and 5 of that Act), or

    (b)   under the general power of investment in section 3 of that Act, by trustees for the governing body or by a person authorised by the trustees under that Act to invest as an agent of the trustees.

(6)   Any profits from investments under subsection (5) shall be invested in the same way and added to capital until the capital is reinvested in the purchase of land.'

The Duchy of Cornwall Management Act 1893 (c 20)

5

The 1893 Act is hereby repealed.

The Duchy of Lancaster Act 1920 (c 51)

6

In section 1 (extension of powers of investment of funds of Duchy of Lancaster) for 'in any of the investments specified in paragraph (a) of section one of the Trustees Act 1893 and any enactment amending or extending that paragraph' substitute 'under the general power of investment in section 3 of the Trustee Act 2000 (as restricted by sections 4 and 5 of that Act)'.

The Settled Land Act 1925 (c 18)

7

In section 21 (absolute owners subject to certain interests to have the powers of tenant for life), in subsection (1)(d) for 'income thereof' substitute 'resultant profits'.

8

In section 39 (regulations respecting sales), in subsection (2), in the proviso, for the words from 'accumulate' to the end of the subsection substitute 'accumulate the profits from the capital money by investing them and any resulting profits under the general power of investment in section 3 of the Trustee Act 2000 and shall add the accumulations to capital.'

9

In section 73 (modes of investment or application), in subsection (1) for paragraph (i) substitute—

> '(i) In investment in securities either under the general power of investment in section 3 of the Trustee Act 2000 or under a power to invest conferred on the trustees of the settlement by the settlement;'.

10

(1) In section 75 (regulations respecting investment, devolution, and income of securities etc), for subsection (2) substitute—

'(2) Subject to Part IV of the Trustee Act 2000, to section 75A of this Act and to the following provisions of this section—

> (a) the investment or other application by the trustees shall be made according to the discretion of the trustees, but subject to any consent required or direction given by the settlement with respect to the investment or other application by the trustees of trust money of the settlement, and

> (b) any investment shall be in the names or under the control of the trustees.'

(2) For subsection (4) of that section substitute—

'(4) The trustees, in exercising their power to invest or apply capital money, shall—

> (a) so far as practicable, consult the tenant for life; and

> (b) so far as consistent with the general interest of the settlement, give effect to his wishes.

(4A) Any investment or other application of capital money under the direction of the court shall not during the subsistence of the beneficial interest of the tenant for life be altered without his consent.

(4B) The trustees may not under section 11 of the Trustee Act 2000 authorise a person to exercise their functions with respect to the investment or application of capital money on terms that prevent them from complying with subsection (4) of this section.

(4C) A person who is authorised under section 11 of the Trustee Act 2000 to exercise any of their functions with respect to the investment or application of capital money is not subject to subsection (4) of this section.'

(3) Nothing in this paragraph affects the operation of section 75 in relation to directions of the tenant for life given, but not acted upon by the trustees, before the commencement of this paragraph.

11

After section 75 insert—

'75A Power to accept charge as security for part payment for land sold

(1)   Where—

    (a)   land subject to the settlement is sold by the tenant for life or statutory owner, for an estate in fee simple or a term having at least five hundred years to run, and

    (b)   the proceeds of sale are liable to be invested,

    the tenant for life or statutory owner may, with the consent of the trustees of the settlement, contract that the payment of any part, not exceeding two-thirds, of the purchase money shall be secured by a charge by way of legal mortgage of the land sold, with or without the security of any other property.

(2)   If any buildings are comprised in the property secured by the charge, the charge must contain a covenant by the mortgagor to keep them insured for their full value against loss or damage due to any event.

(3)   A person exercising the power under subsection (1) of this section, or giving consent for the purposes of that subsection—

    (a)   is not required to comply with section 5 of the Trustee Act 2000 before giving his consent, and

    (b)   is not liable for any loss incurred merely because the security is insufficient at the date of the charge.

(4)   The power under subsection (1) of this section is exercisable subject to the consent of any person whose consent to a change of investment is required by the instrument, if any, creating the trust.

(5)   Where the sale referred to in subsection (1) of this section is made under the order of the court, the power under that subsection applies only if and as far as the court may by order direct.'

12

Omit section 96 (protection of each trustee individually).

13

In section 98 (protection of trustees in particular cases), omit subsections (1) and (2).

14

Omit section 100 (trustees' reimbursements).

15

In section 102 (management of land during minority or pending contingency), in subsection (2) for paragraph (e) substitute—

    '(e)   to insure against risks of loss or damage due to any event under section 19 of the Trustee Act 1925;'.

16

(1)   In section 104 (powers of tenant for life not assignable etc)–

    (a)   in subsection (3)(b) omit 'authorised by statute for the investment of trust money', and

    (b)   in subsection (4)(b) for the words from 'no investment' to 'trust money;' substitute 'the consent of the assignee shall be required to an investment of capital money for the time being affected by the assignment in investments other than securities, and to any application of such capital money;'.

(2)   Sub-paragraph (1) applies to the determination on or after the commencement of that sub-paragraph of whether an assignee's consent is required to the investment or application of capital money.

17

In section 107 (tenant for life deemed to be in the position and to have the duties and liabilities of a trustee, etc) after subsection (1) insert–

'(1A) The following provisions apply to the tenant for life as they apply to the trustees of the settlement–

    (a)   sections 11, 13 to 15 and 21 to 23 of the Trustee Act 2000 (power to employ agents subject to certain restrictions),

    (b)   section 32 of that Act (remuneration and expenses of agents etc),

    (c)   section 19 of the Trustee Act 1925 (power to insure), and

    (d)   in so far as they relate to the provisions mentioned in paragraphs (a) and (c), Part I of, and Schedule 1 to, the Trustee Act 2000 (the duty of care).'

The Trustee Act 1925 (c 19)

18

Omit Part I (investments).

19

In section 14 (power of trustees to give receipts) in subsection (1) after 'securities,' insert 'investments'.

20

In section 15 (power to compound liabilities), for 'in good faith' substitute 'if he has or they have discharged the duty of care set out in section 1(1) of the Trustee Act 2000'.

21

Omit section 21 (deposit of documents for safe custody).

22

In section 22 (reversionary interests, valuations, and audit)–

    (a)   in subsection (1), for 'in good faith' substitute 'if they have discharged the duty of care set out in section 1(1) of the Trustee Act 2000', and

    (b)   in subsection (3), omit 'in good faith' and at the end insert 'if the trustees have discharged the duty of care set out in section 1(1) of the Trustee Act 2000'.

23

Omit section 23 (power to employ agents).

24

Omit section 30 (implied indemnity of trustees).

25

In section 31(2) (power to invest income during minority) for 'in the way of compound interest by investing the same and the resulting income thereof' substitute 'by investing it, and any profits from so investing it'.

The Land Registration Act 1925 (c 21)

26

In section 94(1) (registered land subject to a trust to be registered in the names of the trustees), at the end insert 'or in the name of a nominee appointed under section 16 of the Trustee Act 2000'.

The Administration of Estates Act 1925 (c 23)

27

In section 33, in subsection (3) (investment during minority of beneficiary or the subsistence of a life interest) for the words from 'in any investments for the time being authorised by statute' to the end of the subsection substitute 'under the Trustee Act 2000'.

28

In section 39 (powers of management) after subsection (1) insert—

'(1A) Subsection (1) of this section is without prejudice to the powers conferred on personal representatives by the Trustee Act 2000'.

The Universities and College Estates Act 1925 (c 24)

29

In section 26 (modes of application of capital money) in subsection (1) for paragraph (i) substitute—

'(i)   In investments in which trustees may invest under the general power of investment in section 3 of the Trustee Act 2000 (as restricted by sections 4 and 5 of that Act);'.

The Regimental Charitable Funds Act 1935 (c 11)

30

In section 2(1) (application of funds held on account of regimental charitable funds)—

(a)   in paragraph (a) for 'in some manner' to 'trusts' substitute 'under the general power of investment in section 3 of the Trustee Act 2000';

(b)   in paragraph (b) after 'the income' insert 'or the other profits'.

The Agricultural Marketing Act 1958 (c 47)

31

(1) In section 16 (investment of surplus funds of boards) for paragraph (a) substitute—

'(a) the moneys of the board not for the time being required by them for the purposes of their functions are not, except with the approval of the Minister, invested otherwise than in investments in which trustees may invest under the general power of investment in section 3 of the Trustee Act 2000 (as restricted by sections 4 and 5 of that Act); and'.

(2) Any scheme made under the 1958 Act and in effect before the day on which sub-paragraph (1) comes into force shall be treated, in relation to the making of investments on and after that day, as including provision permitting investment by the board in accordance with section 16(a) of the 1958 Act as amended by sub-paragraph (1).

The Horticulture Act 1960 (c 22)

32

In section 13 (miscellaneous financial powers of organisations promoting home-grown produce) for subsection (3) substitute—

'(3) A relevant organisation may invest any of its surplus money which is not for the time being required for any other purpose in any investments in which trustees may invest under the general power of investment in section 3 of the Trustee Act 2000 (as restricted by sections 4 and 5 of that Act)'.

The House of Commons Members' Fund Act 1962 (c 53)

33

(1) In section 1 (powers of investment of trustees of House of Commons Members' Fund)—

(a) in subsection (2) omit 'Subject to the following provisions of this section';

(b) omit subsections (3) to (5).

(2) In section 2 (interpretation etc) omit subsection (1).

The Betting, Gaming and Lotteries Act 1963 (c 2)

34

In section 25(1) (general powers and duties of the Horserace Betting Levy Board) for paragraph (e) substitute—

'(e) to make such other investments as—

(i) they judge desirable for the proper conduct of their affairs, and

(ii) a trustee would be able to make under the general power of investment in section 3 of the Trustee Act 2000 (as restricted by sections 4 and 5 of that Act);'.

The Cereals Marketing Act 1965 (c 14)

35

(1) In section 18, in subsection (2) (Home-Grown Cereals Authority's power to invest reserve funds) for 'in accordance with the next following subsection' substitute 'in any investments in which trustees may invest under the general power of investment in section 3 of the Trustee Act 2000 (as restricted by sections 4 and 5 of that Act)!

(2) Omit section 18(3).

The Agriculture Act 1967 (c 22)

36

(1) In section 18, in subsection (2) (Meat and Livestock Commission's power to invest reserve fund) for 'in accordance with the next following subsection' substitute 'in any investments in which trustees may invest under the general power of investment in section 3 of the Trustee Act 2000 (as restricted by sections 4 and 5 of that Act)!

(2) Omit section 18(3).

The Solicitors Act 1974 (c 47)

37

In Schedule 2, for paragraph 3 (power of Law Society to invest) substitute—

'3

The Society may invest any money which forms part of the fund in any investments in which trustees may invest under the general power of investment in section 3 of the Trustee Act 2000 (as restricted by sections 4 and 5 of that Act)!

The Policyholders Protection Act 1975 (c 75)

38

In Schedule 1, in paragraph 7, for sub-paragraph (1) (power of Policyholders Protection Board to invest) substitute—

'(1) The Board may invest any funds held by them which appear to them to be surplus to their requirements for the time being—

(a) in any investments in which trustees may invest under the general power of investment in section 3 of the Trustee Act 2000 (as restricted by sections 4 and 5 of that Act); or

(b) in any investment approved for the purpose by the Treasury!

The National Heritage Act 1980 (c 17)

39

In section 6 for subsection (3) (powers of investment of Trustees of National Heritage Memorial Fund) substitute—

'(3) The Trustees may invest any sums to which subsection (2) does not apply in any investments in which trustees may invest under the general power of investment in section 3 of the Trustee Act 2000 (as restricted by sections 4 and 5 of that Act).

The Licensing (Alcohol Education and Research) Act 1981 (c 28)

40

In section 7 (powers of investment of Alcohol Education and Research Council) for subsection (5) substitute—

'(5)   Any sums in the Fund which are not immediately required for any other purpose may be invested by the Council in any investments in which trustees may invest under the general power of investment in section 3 of the Trustee Act 2000 (as restricted by sections 4 and 5 of that Act).'

The Fisheries Act 1981 (c 29)

41

For section 10 (powers of investment of Sea Fish Industry Authority) substitute—

10   'Investment of reserve funds

Any money of the Authority which is not immediately required for any other purpose may be invested by the Authority in any investments in which trustees may invest under the general power of investment in section 3 of the Trustee Act 2000 (as restricted by sections 4 and 5 of that Act)'.

The Duchy of Cornwall Management Act 1982 (c 47)

42

For section 1 (powers of investment of Duchy property) substitute—

1   'Powers of investment of Duchy property

The power of investment conferred by the Duchy of Cornwall Management Act 1863 includes power to invest in any investments in which trustees may invest under the general power of investment in section 3 of the Trustee Act 2000 (as restricted by sections 4 and 5 of that Act).'

43

In—

(a)   section 6(3) (Duchy of Cornwall Management Acts extended in relation to banking), and

(b)   section 11(2) (collective citation of Duchy of Cornwall Management Acts),

for 'Duchy of Cornwall Management Acts 1868 to 1893" substitute "Duchy of Cornwall Management Acts 1863 to 1868'.

The Administration of Justice Act 1982 (c 53)

44

In section 42 (common investment schemes) in subsection (6) for paragraph (a) substitute—

'(a)   he may invest trust money in shares in the fund without obtaining and considering advice on whether to make such an investment; and'.

The Trusts of Land and Appointment of Trustees Act 1996 (c 47)

45

(1)   In section 6 (general powers of trustees), in subsection (3) for 'purchase a legal estate in any land in England and Wales' substitute 'acquire land under the power conferred by section 8 of the Trustee Act 2000.'

(2)   Omit subsection (4) of that section.

(3)   After subsection (8) of that section insert–

'(9)   The duty of care under section 1 of the Trustee Act 2000 applies to trustees of land when exercising the powers conferred by this section.'

46

In section 9 (delegation by trustees) omit subsection (8).

47

After section 9 insert–

'9A   Duties of trustees in connection with delegation etc

(1)   The duty of care under section 1 of the Trustee Act 2000 applies to trustees of land in deciding whether to delegate any of their functions under section 9.

(2)   Subsection (3) applies if the trustees of land–

(a)   delegate any of their functions under section 9, and

(b)   the delegation is not irrevocable.

(3)   While the delegation continues, the trustees–

(a)   must keep the delegation under review,

(b)   if circumstances make it appropriate to do so, must consider whether there is a need to exercise any power of intervention that they have, and

(c)   if they consider that there is a need to exercise such a power, must do so.

(4)   'Power of intervention' includes–

(a)   a power to give directions to the beneficiary;

(b)   a power to revoke the delegation.

(5)   The duty of care under section 1 of the 2000 Act applies to trustees in carrying out any duty under subsection (3).

(6)   A trustee of land is not liable for any act or default of the beneficiary, or beneficiaries, unless the trustee fails to comply with the duty of care in deciding to delegate any of the trustees' functions under section 9 or in carrying out any duty under subsection (3).

(7)   Neither this section nor the repeal of section 9(8) by the Trustee Act 2000 affects the operation after the commencement of this section of any delegation effected before that commencement.'

48

Omit section 17(1) (application of section 6(3) in relation to trustees of proceeds of sale of land).

49

In Schedule 3 (consequential amendments) omit paragraph 3(4) (amendment of section 19(1) and (2) of Trustee Act 1925).

Part III

Measures

The Ecclesiastical Dilapidations Measure 1923 (No 3)

50

In section 52, in subsection (5) (investment of sums held in relation to repair of chancels)–

(a) for 'in any investment permitted by law for the investment of trust funds, and the yearly income resulting therefrom shall be applied', substitute 'in any investments in which trustees may invest under the general power of investment in section 3 of the Trustee Act 2000, and the annual profits from the investments shall be applied'; and

(b) in paragraph (iii) for 'any residue of the said income not applied as aforesaid in any year' substitute 'any residue of the profits from the investments not applied in any year.'

The Diocesan Stipends Funds Measure 1953 (No 2)

51

In section 4 (application of moneys credited to capital accounts) in subsection (1) for paragraph (bc) substitute–

'(bc) investment in any investments in which trustees may invest under the general power of investment in section 3 of the Trustee Act 2000 (as restricted by sections 4 and 5 of that Act);'.

The Church Funds Investment Measure 1958 (No 1)

52

In the Schedule, in paragraph 21 (range of investments of deposit fund) for paragraphs (a) to (d) of sub-paragraph (1) substitute–

'(aa) In any investments in which trustees may invest under the general power of investment in section 3 of the Trustee Act 2000 (as restricted by sections 4 and 5 of that Act);'.

The Clergy Pensions Measure 1961 (No 3)

53

(1) In section 32 (investment powers of Board), in subsection (1), for paragraph (a) substitute–

'(a) in any investments in which trustees may invest under the general power of investment in section 3 of the Trustee Act 2000 (as restricted by sections 4 and 5 of that Act);'.

(2) Omit subsection (3) of that section.

The Repair of Benefice Buildings Measure 1972 (No 2)

54

In section 17, in subsection (2) (diocesan parsonages fund's power of investment), for 'who shall have the same powers of investment as trustees of trust funds:' substitute 'who shall have the same power as trustees to invest in any investments in which trustees may invest under the general power of investment in section 3 of the Trustee Act 2000 (as restricted by sections 4 and 5 of that Act):

The Pastoral Measure 1983 (No 1)

55

In section 44, for subsection (6) (Redundant Churches Fund's power of investment) substitute—

'(6)   The powers to invest any such sums are—

(a)   power to invest in investments in which trustees may invest under the general power of investment in section 3 of the Trustee Act 2000 (as restricted by sections 4 and 5 of that Act); and

(b)   power to invest in the investments referred to in paragraph 21(1)(e) and (f) of the Schedule to the Church Funds Investment Measure 1958:

The Church of England (Pensions) Measure 1988 (No 4)

56

Omit section 14(b) (amendment of section 32(3) of the Clergy Pensions Measure 1961).

The Cathedrals Measure 1999 (No 1)

57

In section 16 (cathedral moneys: investment powers, etc), in subsection (1)—

(a)   for paragraph (c) substitute—

'(c)   power to invest in any investments in which trustees may invest under the general power of investment in section 3 of the Trustee Act 2000 (as restricted by sections 4 and 5 of that Act)', and

(b)   omit the words from 'and the powers' to the end of the subsection.

SCHEDULE 3
TRANSITIONAL PROVISIONS AND SAVINGS

Section 40

The Trustee Act 1925 (c 19)

1

(1) Sub-paragraph (2) applies if, immediately before the day on which Part IV of this Act comes into force, a banker or banking company holds any bearer securities deposited with him under section 7(1) of the 1925 Act (investment in bearer securities).

(2) On and after the day on which Part IV comes into force, the banker or banking company shall be treated as if he had been appointed as custodian of the securities under section 18.

2

The repeal of section 8 of the 1925 Act (loans and investments by trustees not chargeable as breaches of trust) does not affect the operation of that section in relation to loans or investments made before the coming into force of that repeal.

3

The repeal of section 9 of the 1925 Act (liability for loss by reason of improper investment) does not affect the operation of that section in relation to any advance of trust money made before the coming into force of that repeal.

4

(1) Sub-paragraph (2) applies if, immediately before the day on which Part IV of this Act comes into force, a banker or banking company holds any documents deposited with him under section 21 of the 1925 Act (deposit of documents for safe custody).

(2) On and after the day on which Part IV comes into force, the banker or banking company shall be treated as if he had been appointed as custodian of the documents under section 17.

5

(1) Sub-paragraph (2) applies if, immediately before the day on which Part IV of this Act comes into force, a person has been appointed to act as or be an agent or attorney under section 23(1) or (3) of the 1925 Act (general power to employ agents etc).

(2) On and after the day on which Part IV comes into force, the agent shall be treated as if he had been authorised to exercise functions as an agent under section 11 (and, if appropriate, as if he had also been appointed under that Part to act as a custodian or nominee).

6

The repeal of section 23(2) of the 1925 Act (power to employ agents in respect of property outside the United Kingdom) does not affect the operation after the commencement of the repeal of an appointment made before that commencement.

The Trustee Investments Act 1961 (c 62)

7

(1)   A trustee shall not be liable for breach of trust merely because he continues to hold an investment acquired by virtue of paragraph 14 of Part II of Schedule 1 to the 1961 Act (perpetual rent-charges etc).

(2)   A person who—

    (a)   is not a trustee,

    (b)   before the commencement of Part II of this Act had powers to invest in the investments described in paragraph 14 of Part II of Schedule 1 to the 1961 Act, and

    (c)   on that commencement acquired the general power of investment,

shall not be treated as exceeding his powers of investment merely because he continues to hold an investment acquired by virtue of that paragraph.

The Cathedrals Measure 1963 (No 2)

8

While section 21 of the Cathedrals Measure 1963 (investment powers, etc of capitular bodies) continues to apply in relation to any cathedral, that section shall have effect as if—

(a)   in subsection (1), for paragraph (c) and the words from 'and the powers' to the end of the subsection there were substituted—

    '(c)   power to invest in any investments in which trustees may invest under the general power of investment in section 3 of the Trustee Act 2000 (as restricted by sections 4 and 5 of that Act)', and

(b)   in subsection (5), for 'subsections (2) and (3) of section six of the Trustee Investments Act 1961' there were substituted 'section 5 of the Trustee Act 2000'.

SCHEDULE 4
REPEALS

Section 40

Part I

The Trustee Investments Act 1961 and the Charities Act 1993

Chapter	Short title	Extent of repeal
1961 c 62	The Trustee Investments Act 1961	Sections 1 to 3, 5, 6, 8, 9, 12, 13, 15 and 16(1). Schedules 2 and 3. In Schedule 4, paragraph 1(1).
1993 c 10	The Charities Act 1993	Sections 70 and 71. In section 86(2) in paragraph (a), "70" and paragraph (b).

Note: the repeals in this Part of this Schedule have effect in accordance with Part I of Schedule 2.

Part II

Other Repeals

Chapter	Short title	Extent of repeal
1893 c 20.	The Duchy of Cornwall Management Act 1893	The whole Act.
1925 c 18	The Settled Land Act 1925	Section 96. Section 98(1) and (2). Section 100. In section 104(3)(b) the words 'authorised by statute for the investment of trust money'.
1925 c 19	The Trustee Act 1925	Part I. In section 20(1) the words 'whether by fire or otherwise'. Sections 21, 23 and 30.
1961 No 3	The Clergy Pensions Measure 1961	Section 32(3).

1962 c 53	The House of Commons Members' Fund Act 1962	In section 1, in subsection (2) the words 'Subject to the following provisions of this section' and subsections (3) to (5). Section 2(1).
1965 c 14	The Cereals Marketing Act 1965	Section 18(3).
1967 c 22	The Agriculture Act 1967	Section 18(3).
1988 No 4	The Church of England (Pensions) Measure 1988	Section 14(b).
1996 c 47	The Trusts of Land and Appointment of Trustees Act 1996	Section 6(4). Section 9(8). Section 17(1). In Schedule 3, paragraph 3(4).
1999 No 1	The Cathedrals Measure 1999	In section 16(1), the words from 'and the powers' to the end of the subsection.

Appendix 5

Extracts from an exchange of correspondence published in the *Tax Journal* on 30 January 1997 and 6 February 1997

The following extract is a slightly amended version of the correspondence between Chris Jarman of Payne Hicks Beech (Solicitors) and Brian Mace of the Inland Revenue relating to the Trusts of Land and Appointment of Trustees Act 1996:

Power to exclude beneficiaries and impose conditions

Section 12 of the Act gives a right of occupation to any beneficiary of a trust of land who is beneficially entitled to an interest in possession in land subject to a trust of land. (This article is not concerned with the identification of property to which the right applies.) Section 13 deals with several matters in connection with that basic right of occupation.

Section 13(3) allows the trustees to impose reasonable conditions on a beneficiary's occupation.

Where two or more beneficiaries are given a right of occupation under s 12 – in other words, where two or more of them are beneficially entitled to an interest in possession in the land – s 13(1) gives the trustees power to exclude or restrict the entitlement of any one or more (but not all) of them to occupy the land.

This power of exclusion may not be exercised unreasonably (s 13(2)), nor, without the beneficiary's consent or an order of the court, so as to exclude a beneficiary who is already in occupation (s 13(7)).

In exercising their powers under s 13 the trustees must have regard inter alia to the intentions of the settlor, the purposes for which the land is held, and the circumstances and wishes of the beneficiaries who have a prima facie right of occupation. (Similar principles apply to any exercise of the court's jurisdiction in the event of a dispute on such matters.)

Where a beneficiary has been excluded or restricted under the power in s 13(1), s 13(6) allows the trustees to imposed further requirements on the beneficiary who remains entitled to occupy the land. He may be required to make payments by way of compensation to the excluded beneficiary; alternatively, so as to benefit the excluded beneficiary, to forgo any payment or other benefit to which he (the occupying beneficiary) would otherwise be entitled under the trust. It is this provision which throws up the most queries in the taxation context.

Conditions to be satisfied by beneficiary

Some of the questions which arise depend on an analysis of the concept of a 'beneficiary of a trust of land who is beneficially entitled to an interest in possession in land subject to a trust of land'. Whilst agreeing that this is property legislation, not tax legislation, the Inland Revenue has confirmed its agreement generally that:

- The person concerned must be a beneficiary (within the definition in s 22(1)) under the trust [of land] and that a beneficiary under a sub-settlement is not a 'beneficiary' (of the trust of land itself) for the purpose of the Act.

- The beneficiary must be entitled to an interest in the land – as opposed to merely having an interest, eg as a discretionary beneficiary.

- His interest must be in possession in the sense explained in *Pearson v IRC*. Annuitants are excluded, for the specific purposes of the Act, by s 22(3).

- His entitlement must be for his own benefit, not just as a trustee or personal representative.

I had put it to the Inland Revenue that it seemed fundamental to the operation of s 13 that no exercise of the trustees' powers under that section would alter the nature of the beneficiaries' interests in the land concerned. A condition requiring compensation to be paid to a non-occupying beneficiary can only be imposed if he has been excluded under the section; he can only be excluded if he is one of two or more beneficiaries with a prima facie right of occupation; and to have such a prima facie right he must have an interest in possession. Therefore, my argument ran, an exclusion under s 13(1), whether or not accompanied by a requirement to pay compensation or forgo benefits under s 13(6), must still leave the excluded beneficiary with a beneficial interest in possession in the land.

The Inland Revenue says in reply to this that it accepts that an exclusion under s 13 powers, by itself, would not necessarily affect the nature of the excluded beneficiary's interest. It does not, however, agree with the general proposition that the exclusion could in no circumstances have that effect. The Inland Revenue's view, therefore, is that the precise implications of any exercise of the particular powers would need to be considered in the light of all the relevant facts including the various matters to which the trustees are required to have regard under s 13(4).

Questions arising in particular situations

I then posed various questions by reference to a series of example situations. Examples 1-4 are set out and illustrated on the following page, and the income tax questions and answers are reproduced in the box. The others will appear in Part 2 of the article.

Question 1

Where compensation is paid by A, the occupying beneficiary in Examples 1, 2 and 3, will this be regarded as taxable income in the hands of B, the recipient, and if so under which schedule?

Answer 1

The compensation would be regarded as taxable income under Schedule A if B were party to the decision to exclude him from occupation of the land.

Question 2

Will A, the occupying beneficiary in Examples 1, 2 and 3, be entitled to a deduction for income tax purposes in respect of the compensation which he has to pay B? Does this depend on whether he occupies the land for the purposes of a business as in Example 2, and if so is the position affected in any way if A is not the sole proprietor of the business (the partnership variant in Example 2)? Is the position affected by whether the land is settled property as in Example 3?

Answer 2

If A occupies the land for the purposes of a trade and can demonstrate that the payments are made for bona fide commercial reasons in connection with that trade, they would fall within s 347A(c) ICTA and be treated as annual payments. A would get relief as a charge on income and B would be chargeable under Schedule D Case III.

If the payments do not fall to be treated as a charge, but A still occupies the land for the purposes of a trade, the question whether the compensation is an allowable deduction in computing A's trading profits will depend upon the precise terms of the conditions imposed by the trustees under s 13(3). If the exclusive rights to occupy the land that A obtains are of an enduring nature, the compensation will be capital in nature and not an allowable deduction. If the rights are not of an enduring nature, the compensation is likely to be an allowable deduction.

The same principles apply whether A carries on the trade on his own account or in partnership. Nor will the position be directly affected by whether the land is settled property.

If A does not occupy the land for the purposes of a trade, it seems that no deduction will be available.

Question 3

Where the requirement imposed by the trustees on A, the occupying beneficiary (in Example 4), is to forgo payments to which he would otherwise be entitled under the settlement, in favour of B, the excluded beneficiary, which of the two beneficiaries is treated as entitled, for income tax purposes, to any income which A has to forgo in this way? If the underlying income must still be regarded as arising to A, what are the income tax implications, for both beneficiaries, of the transfer of income pursuant to the condition imposed by the trustees?

Answer 3

Our view is that the income forgone is likely to be the income of the beneficiary who becomes entitled to receive it, but this will depend on the precise facts of particular cases.

In reading the Inland Revenue's replies, it must be borne in mind that it prefaced its comments by emphasising that they are necessarily provisional; the Inland Revenue stressed that it is not possible or, indeed, appropriate to express any final view on hypothetical situations, especially as so much would depend on the precise facts of particular cases.

Question 4

Will the Inland Revenue accept the analysis set out in the first part of this article to the effect that an exercise of the trustees' powers under s 13(1) to exclude beneficiaries from occupation cannot alter the status (or proportions) of the two beneficiaries' continuing interests in possession in the land – whether or not any condition as to compensation or forgoing payments is imposed under s 13(6). This is obviously a fundamental issue for inheritance tax purposes, and also for the purposes of TCGA 19992, s 72. The result in Example 3 would be that each of A and B continues to have a 50 per cent interest in possession in the house. Would the Inland Revenue take a different view if:

- the terms of the exclusion did not require any compensation to be paid; or

- (as in Example 5) B is not excluded but simply chooses not to exercise his right of occupation?

Answer 4

As I have explained, the tax implications (if any) would depend on the precise facts. The amount of any compensation payable to the excluded beneficiary could be an important, but not the sole, relevant factor; and in Example 5, depending on the full facts, B's decision to forgo his right of occupation might amount to a disposal of his interest in possession.

Question 5

Correspondingly, where trustees impose a condition on an occupying beneficiary under s 13(6)(b), will the Inland Revenue accept that this does not affect the continuance of any interest in possession of the occupying

beneficiary, A, in the investments from which the forgone income arises –
nor give rise to any interest in possession in those investments in favour of B,
the excluded beneficiary? In other words, in Example 4, will both A and B be
regarded as entitled, throughout, to a 50 per cent interest in possession in the
house and in the investment fund?

Answer 5

Again, we would need to look at the relevant facts. However, on the basis
that the diversion of income from A to B at the full market rate can properly
be construed as a purely administrative adjustment to the distribution of trust
income, the nature of A and B's respective interests seems unlikely to be
affected if the value of those interests remains unchanged. These comments
do not apply to any appropriation of trust assets, which would apparently be
outside the provisions under consideration.

Question 6

If the Inland Revenue regards the answer to this last question as being in the
negative, will it at least accept, in circumstances such as Example 5 where
one beneficiary is out of occupation without having been excluded by the
trustees that any alteration in the beneficiaries' interests in possession only
occurs on exercise of the trustees' powers – in other words that the very
existence of the powers (or the voluntary non-occupation of the land by B)
does not prevent the existence of interests in possession, for example as a
power to divert the investment income of A in Example 4?

Answer 6

Yes.

Question 7

What effect, if any, do the provisions of ss 12-13 have on the Inland
Revenue's practice as set out in SP10/79? For example, the final sentence of
the statement suggests that where a beneficiary (X) is allowed to occupy, as a
permanent home, a property in which another beneficiary (Y) had an
interest in possession, X will be regarded, as far as the Inland Revenue is
concerned, as obtaining an interest in possession (and it appears to be
implied that Y's interests in possession will be regarded as terminating
accordingly).

You are probably aware that many property lawyers are at a loss to
understand the basis of that view generally – as at noted earlier the meaning
of interest in possession is a matter for property and law not tax law.
However, without this correspondence opening the debate on the position
prior to the Act coming into force, that practice, if continued in the
circumstances of Example 7, would appear to be at variance with the concept
behind ss 12-13.

Answer 7

SP 10/97 envisages the exercise of a wide fiduciary power to permit occupation of trust property. Where the exercise had the effect of terminating a person's existing interest in possession in the particular property, it would also extinguish his entitlement under s 12 which is restricted to person(s) beneficially entitled to an interest in possession in the subject land. So we do not see any substantive conflict between our approach under SP 10/79 and the concept behind ss 12-13.

Orders of the Court

Question 8

Would it make any difference to your replies to questions 1 to 6 if the exclusion, and/or conditions applicable to it, were ordered by the court under s 14 rather than imposed by the trustees under s 13?

Answer 8

No.

Conferring of benefits

Question 9

In cases where:

(a) one of several beneficiaries with interests in possession is not in fact occupying the land, without having been excluded from it by the trustees; or

(b) if he has been excluded, the terms of the exclusion do not include a s 13(6) condition;

will the Inland Revenue seek to argue that there is some benefit flowing from the trustees, or from the non-occupying beneficiary, to the occupying beneficiary, with any tax consequences? It is clear from Example 7 that there could be good reasons for matters being left as they are. In particular, would these circumstances have implications in the context of:

• TCGA 1992, s 87 or ICTA 1988, s 740 (capital gains tax and income tax charges on beneficiaries of non-resident trusts); or

• FA 1986, s 102 (inheritance tax: gifts with reservation)?

If so, will the same point be taken even where a s 13(6) condition is imposed, if the Inland Revenue considers that the trustees could, within the overriding requirement of reasonableness under s 13(3), have imposed more conditions, or more stringent conditions, on the occupying beneficiary?

Answer 9

Under TCGA 1992, s 87 the question is whether a particular person has received a capital payment within the meaning of s 97. Where benefits have been conferred, the only question is how to value them under s 97(4). Section 87 works on the actual benefit and subject to the facts of any particular case, we should not expect to be concerned with what the trustees could have done. [**Note:** The receipt of a capital payment, to be relevant, must be from the trustees (within the expansive definition of that concept in s 97(5)).]

A similar approach would be adopted for the purposes of ICTA 1988, s 740.

Depending on the full facts, there could be implications for FA 1986, s 102.

Question 10

Will any similar point be taken in circumstances such as Example 6, notwithstanding that S is not a beneficiary of the trust of the legal estate, and the will trustees are not beneficially entitled to an interest in possession under the trust of the legal estate, so that W is the only beneficiary with a right of occupation and there is no ground on which the trustees could seek to impose any conditions on her occupation under s 13?

Answer 10

For s 102 the answer is no.

The question of applying s 87 or s 740 in the circumstances of Example 6 could be relevant only if the will trustees were non-resident. But if S is not receiving any benefit, that is an end of the matter. [**Note:** The Inland Revenue has subsequently clarified this by confirming that, as it sees the position, W is entitled to occupy the property pursuant to her statutory right as tenant in common and beneficiary of the trust of land; and that in its view she is not, therefore, in receipt of a benefit from either the will trustees or S.]

Example 1

Trustees hold a house on behalf of A and B as beneficial tenants in common absolutely. They exercise their discretion to exclude B, and require A, who is in occupation, to pay compensation of £500 per month to B in consequence.

Example 2

Facts as Example 1 but the land comprises 100 acres of farm land which A farms (as sole trader or in partnership with another). A pays the compensation from the farm account (ie in the partnership case, from the partnership account).

Example 3

Trustees own a house as settled property in respect of which A and B have a joint life interest, with remainders over. The trustees exercise their discretion to exclude B, and require A, who is in occupation, to pay B compensation of £500 per month.

Example 4

Facts as Example 3, but the settled property also includes an investment fund yielding £20,000 per year net of income tax at the 'savings' rate. The trustees exercise their discretion to exclude B, and require A to forgo £6,000 per annum in favour of B out of the net investment income to which A would otherwise be entitled under the trust.

Example 5

Trustees own a house as settled property in respect of which A and B have a joint life interest, with remainders over. The trustees do not use their powers to exclude either beneficiary. In practice, B chooses not to live at the property.

Example 6

Trustees (call them the land trustees) hold a house in trust in equal shares absolutely for W and for the trustees of H's will (call them the will trustees; they, or some of them, might or might not be included among the land trustees). S has a life interest under the will; but for the purposes of the Act he would not be regarded as a beneficiary under the trust of land itself (see discussion in the text of the article). Accordingly, unless perhaps S also happened to be one of the will trustees, the only person with a right of occupation under s 12 is W, so that no question can arise of S (or any other trustee or beneficiary of the will) being excluded from occupation under s 13 – nor, therefore, of W being required by the land trustees under that section to pay compensation to anyone even if in practice W is the only person actually in occupation. The position in this respect would be all the more obvious if no interest in possession subsisted under the will).

Example 7

Trustees hold two houses, of significantly different size and value, as settled property (not under the SLA 1925). A and B have a joint life interest in both houses, with remainders over. In practice, A occupies one property and B occupies the other, each bearing the outgoings of their respective properties (a much heavier burden for the larger and more valuable property). The trustees do not exercise their discretion to exclude B from A's property and vice versa, but consider that if they were to do so they would not require the payment of compensation, or the forgoing of other benefits, under s 13(6), because the burden of outgoings assumed by the beneficiaries (and which would be made a condition of occupation if the trustees were going to exercise their discretions under s 13 in any event) might otherwise fall on the trust as a whole and therefore work, by one means or another, by the detriment of both beneficiaries equally in any event.

Appendix 6

Land Registry Practice Leaflet 32: Powers of Attorney and Registered Land

A What the Land Registry needs to know

B Types of power of attorney

    1. General powers under section 10 of the Powers of Attorney Act 1971

    2. Other general and special powers

    3. Security powers

    4. Enduring powers

    5. Trustee Act powers

    6. Power given by all the trustees to a beneficiary under section 9 of the Trusts of Land and Appointment of Trustees Act 1996

C Joint Proprietors – receipts for capital money

D Joint Proprietors – evidence that the donor of a power had a beneficial interest

E Powers more than 12 months old – evidence of non-revocation

F Evidence of the power

G Checklists

    1. Power given by a sole proprietor (not a trustee)

    2. Power given by one of joint proprietors dated before 1 March 2000

    3. Power given by one of joint proprietors dated after 29 February 2000

    4. Power given to beneficiaries by all the joint proprietors of the land

Annex – Statutory declaration/certificate as to non-revocation

A What the Land Registry needs to know

When we are registering a document signed by an attorney, we need to be sure that the document binds the individual or company on whose behalf it was signed. We do this by checking that the power of attorney:

- was validly executed as a deed;
- was still in force at the date of the document;
- authorised the attorney to take the action in question; and
- was, where necessary, made under the correct statutory provision.

There are cases where, even though the power does not meet these requirements, the person who relied on the document can assume that the power was correctly made or that it was still in force at the time it was used. In those cases we may need confirmatory evidence from that person.

When an individual executes a deed, it must be clear that the document is signed as a deed and the signature must be made in the presence of a witness who attests the signature. Practice Advice Leaflet No.6 deals in detail with execution of deeds by different types of legal person. Copies are available from any district land registry.

This leaflet takes account of the changes in the law made by the Trustee Delegation Act 1999, in force from 1 March 2000.

This leaflet does not cover the more complex issues involved when a power of attorney is granted under the law of another jurisdiction. In such a case we may require an opinion as to the matters specified above from a lawyer qualified in that jurisdiction.

B   Types of power of attorney

1. General powers under section 10 of the Powers of Attorney Act 1971

The 1971 Act provides a short form of general power of attorney that can be used by a sole beneficial owner of land. It operates to give the attorney authority to do anything that the donor can lawfully do by an attorney. However, powers in that form dated before 1 March 2000 are never suitable for dealing with land of which the donor is a joint proprietor. And those dated after 29 February 2000 may only be used by a joint proprietor if the donor has a beneficial interest in the land. The death, bankruptcy or mental incapacity of the donor will automatically revoke the power. The donor may also revoke it at any time.

2. Other general and special powers

A person wishing to appoint an attorney does not have to use the form set out in the 1971 Act. The only strict requirement is that the donor must execute the power as a deed. The donor may use any form of wording, giving the attorney either general authority to act or limited powers, for example in connection with a particular transaction or dealings with specified property. A power that does not follow any of the statutory forms may be used on behalf of a donor who is a joint proprietor only if:

- it is dated after 29 February 2000; and

- the donor has a beneficial interest in the land; and
- there is no indication in the power that the donor did not intend the attorney to exercise trustee functions.

Unless it is a security power the donor may revoke such a power and the death, bankruptcy or mental incapacity of the donor will automatically revoke it.

3. Security powers

A security power is a power of attorney that is expressed to be irrevocable and is given to secure:

- a proprietary interest of the attorney; or
- the performance of an obligation owed to the attorney.

While the donee has the interest or until the obligation is discharged the donor can only revoke the power with the attorney's consent and the death, bankruptcy or mental incapacity of the donor does not revoke it.

4. Enduring powers

An enduring power of attorney is one made by an individual under the Enduring Powers of Attorney Act 1985. It must be in the form prescribed under that Act at the date that the power was granted. An enduring power is not revoked by the donor's mental incapacity. But the attorney must apply to register the power with the Court of Protection if there is reason to believe that the donor is becoming mentally incapable. After the power is registered the donor can only revoke it if the Court confirms that he or she is mentally capable of doing so. The bankruptcy or death of the donor will automatically revoke the power whether or not it is so registered. The bankruptcy of the attorney will also revoke the power.

Enduring powers dated after 29 February 2000 may only be used on behalf of a donor who is a joint proprietor if:

- the donor has a beneficial interest in the land; and
- there is no indication in the power that the donor did not intend the attorney to exercise trustee functions.

There are transitional provisions in the 1999 Act for enduring powers dated before 1 March 2000. Until 1 March 2001 such a power may be used on behalf of any donor who is a joint proprietor. From 1 March 2001 an enduring power dated before 1 March 2000 may only be so used if:

- the donor has a beneficial interest in the land; and
- there is no indication in the power that the donor did not intend the attorney to exercise trustee functions;

or

- the power is registered with the court following an application made to the Court before 1 March 2001;

or

- an application made to the Court for registration of the power before 1 March 2001 has not been finally refused.

An attorney under an enduring power can make gifts and confer benefits on behalf of the donor only in very limited circumstances – see section 3 (4) and (5) of the 1985 Act. We will usually refuse to register a transfer involving a gift or benefit that is executed under an enduring power unless the Court has authorised the transfer under section 8 (2) (e) of the Act.

5. Trustee Act powers

Section 25 of the Trustee Act 1925 allows a trustee to grant a power of attorney delegating his or her functions as a trustee to the attorney. The original section 25 was substantially amended by the Powers of Attorney Act 1971 and, with effect from 1 March 2000, the Trustee Delegation Act 1999 has substituted a new section 25.

The new section 25 provides a short form of power by which a single donor can delegate trustee functions under a single trust to a single donee. Trustees can use other forms. The short form would not, for example, be appropriate where the donor wishes to delegate functions under several trusts to one attorney or wishes to limit the range of functions to be delegated.

A Trustee Act power can be granted only for a period of up to twelve months. For powers granted before 1 March 2000 that period commenced on the date of the power. For those granted after 29 February 2000 the twelve months period may start at a later date specified in the power.

A Trustee Act power can always be used, while in force, to execute dispositions of land on behalf of a donor who is a joint proprietor, whether or not the donor has a beneficial interest in the land. Before 1 March 2000 a trustee could not grant such a power to an attorney who was also the only other trustee under the trust. The 1999 Act has removed that limitation. However, where there are only two trustees, it will always be sensible to appoint a third party. This is because, as explained in part D below, a trustee who is also acting as attorney for the only other co-trustee will not be able to give valid receipts for capital money.

6. Power given by all the trustees to a beneficiary under section 9 of the Trusts of Land and Appointment of Trustees Act 1996

All the trustees of a trust of land can together appoint a beneficiary or the beneficiaries to exercise their functions in relation to the land. But the attorney cannot give a receipt for capital money, so the trustees would, in any event, need to join in any disposition of the land where such a receipt was required. This type of power is, therefore, likely to be encountered rarely in the context of dispositions of registered land. It could only be used effectively when no capital money is passing, e.g. on the grant of a rack rent lease.

Where this form of power is used for a registered disposition we need a statutory declaration from the person(s) who dealt with the attorney that they:

- acted in good faith; and

- had no knowledge at the time of completion of the transaction that the attorney was not a person to whom the functions of the trustees in relation to the land to which the application relates could be delegated under section 9 of the 1996 Act. – see rule 82B of the Land Registration Rules 1925.

Alternatively, we will accept a certificate to the same effect from a solicitor or licensed conveyancer. The combined form of the statutory declaration and certificate, set out in the Annex to this leaflet, covers the above points as well as the evidence we need if this form of power is over twelve months old at the date of the disposition.

C   Joint Proprietors – receipts for capital money

For dispositions dated after 29 February 2000, section 7 of the Trustee Delegation Act 1999 provides that a receipt for capital money will overreach beneficial interests only if an attorney acts with at least one other person. This means that a receipt clause in a disposition by joint proprietors is not acceptable if it is signed only by one person both as proprietor and as attorney for the other proprietor(s). Nor is it acceptable for one person to sign as attorney for all the proprietors.

If such a document is lodged we will return it for execution by the donor of the power. If the document is not re-executed we will enter a joint proprietor restriction on the register to protect any beneficial interests that may still subsist.

There is an exception to this rule under the transitional provisions of the Trustee Delegation Act 1999, described in paragraph B4 above. This applies where an enduring power of attorney dated before 1 March 2000 still covers all trustee functions, even though the donor of the power may have no beneficial interest in the land.

D   Joint Proprietors – evidence that the donor of a power had a beneficial interest

All joint proprietors hold the registered legal estate as trustees. Until 1 March 2000 this meant that a joint proprietor always had to appoint an attorney by a power under the Trustee Act 1925 or the Enduring Powers of Attorney Act 1985 if the attorney was to be able to execute dispositions of registered land. The Trustee Delegation Act 1999, in force on that date, has relaxed this rule where the joint proprietor has a beneficial interest in the land.

The 1999 Act allows a general or an enduring power of attorney dated after 29 February 2000 to be used in relation to trust property if, at the time it is used, the donor of the power owns a beneficial interest in that property. The same rule will apply to enduring powers of attorney dated before 1 March 2000 once the transitional provisions mentioned in paragraph B4 above have expired.

A written statement by the attorney given within three months of the date of the document confirming that the donor had a beneficial interest in the property is, in favour of a purchaser, conclusive evidence that the power could be used (section 2 (2) Trustee Delegation Act 1999).

The most convenient place for the attorney to make this written statement will be in the disposition itself. The attorney may:

- include a statement on the following lines in the additional provisions panel of a TR1 or other prescribed form, or in the body of a lease or charge:

'(Name of attorney) confirms that (donor of the power) has a beneficial interest in the property at the date of this (transfer, charge etc.)'

or

- adapt the attestation clause as follows:

'Signed as a deed by (name of donor of the power), who has a beneficial interest in the property at the date of this (transfer, charge etc.), acting by (his/her) attorney (name of attorney) in the presence of'

or

- expand the words of signature as follows:

'John Smith by his attorney Jane Brown who confirms that the donor has a beneficial interest in the Property at the date hereof'

The written statement can also be made separately as long as it is dated within three months of the date of the document.

If an applicant for registration cannot produce such a statement we will consider other evidence that the donor had a beneficial interest at the relevant time. A statutory declaration to that effect by a responsible person with full knowledge of the facts may be acceptable in some cases. But if the applicant does not produce sufficient evidence of the donor's beneficial entitlement the document will need to be executed by the donor of the power.

E Powers more than 12 months old – evidence of non-revocation

A purchaser from a person who has dealt with an attorney is entitled to assume that the power of attorney has not been revoked if the transaction in question took place within twelve months of the date when the power came into operation.

This general presumption about non-revocation does not apply to powers of attorney that are more than twelve months old. Under rule 82A of the Land Registration Rules 1925, if your application to the Registry relies on such a power you must produce evidence of non-revocation. This evidence will be either:

- a statutory declaration as to non-revocation in the appropriate form made **by the person dealing with the attorney**; or

- a certificate to the same effect given by that person's solicitor or licensed conveyancer.

The form of statutory declaration and certificate set out in the Annex to this leaflet covers all the information that we might require. You may photocopy it or reproduce it on your own word processor.

Trustee Act powers of attorney can only operate for twelve months. We will not, therefore, need evidence of non-revocation for these powers.

F   Evidence of the power

The Registry will need to see either the original or a sufficient copy of any power of attorney that you are relying on to establish that a document lodged with your application is validly executed. We will retain the evidence lodged in our files. If, therefore, you need to keep the original you should lodge a copy with your application.

Section 3 of the Powers of Attorney Act 1971 prescribes a strict method of proving the contents of a power of attorney. To follow this procedure a solicitor, notary public or stockbroker must certify:

- at the end of a photocopy of the power that it is a true and complete copy of the original; and

- on each page of the photocopy, if the power includes more than one page, that the page is a true and complete copy of the corresponding page of the original.

In practice, we will usually accept a photocopy that is certified, by a solicitor or licensed conveyancer, to be a true copy of the original power. However, in any case of doubt, we would need to ask you to produce either the original or the more formal certified copy mentioned above.

G   Checklists

The following checklists are set out below:

1.   Power given by a sole proprietor (not a trustee)

2.   Power given by one of joint proprietors date before 1 March 2000

3.   Power given by one of joint proprietors dated after 29 February 2000

4.   Power given to beneficiaries by all the joint proprietors of the land.

We hope that the checklists will help you, in the cases that they cover, to lodge the correct documents and evidence with your applications. Unless you can answer 'yes' to all the questions that apply, the donor of the power will need to execute the document personally before we can register it.

1. Power given by a sole proprietor (not a trustee)

- Are you able to lodge the original or a certified copy of the power?
- Is the power validly executed as a deed?
- Is the power wide enough to cover what the attorney has done?
- If the power was more than 12 months old when the attorney signed the document are you able to lodge the additional evidence that we need? – see part E.

2. Power given by one of joint proprietors dated before 1 March 2000

- Are you able to lodge the original or a certified copy of the power?
- Is the power validly executed as a deed?
- Is the power a Trustee Act power? – see paragraph B5.

or

- Is the power an enduring power and was the transfer or other document dated before 1 March 2001 (or within the transitional period if registered with the court)? – see paragraph B4.

or

- Is the power an enduring power and did the donor have a beneficial interest in the property, there being no intention, expressed in the power, of excluding functions that the donor held as a trustee? – see paragraph B4 and part D.
- Is the power wide enough to cover what the attorney has done?

For documents signed by the attorney after 29 February 2000

- Has at least one other proprietor of the land (or a third party as attorney on that proprietor's behalf) also given any necessary receipt for capital money?

or

- Is the power an enduring power dated before 1 March 2000 and was the document dated before 1 March 2001 (or within the transitional period if registered with the court)? – see paragraph B4.

- If the power was more than 12 months old when the attorney signed the document are you able to lodge the additional evidence that we need? – see part E.

3. Power given by one of joint proprietors dated after 29 February 2000

- Are you able to lodge the original or a certified copy of the power?
- Is the power validly executed as a deed?
- Is the power made under the Trustee Act 1925? – see paragraph B5.

or

- Did the donor of the power have a beneficial interest in the property, there being no intention, expressed in the power, of excluding functions that the donor held as a trustee? – see paragraphs B1, B2 and B4 and part D.
- Is the power wide enough to cover what the attorney has done?
- Has at least one other proprietor of the land (or a third party as attorney on that proprietor's behalf) also given any necessary receipt for capital money? – see part C.
- If the power was more than 12 months old when the attorney signed the document are you able to lodge the additional evidence that we need? – see part E.

4. Power given to beneficiaries by all the joint proprietors of the land

- Are you able to lodge the original or a certified copy of the power?
- Is the power validly executed as a deed?
- Is the power made under the Trusts of Land and Appointment of Trustees Act 1996? – see paragraph B6.
- Is the power wide enough to cover what the attorney has done?
- If the transaction involved the payment of capital money did the trustees join in to give a receipt?
- If the power was more than 12 months old when the attorney signed the document are you able to lodge the additional evidence that we need? – see part E.

Peter Collis, Chief Land Registrar
HM Land Registry
February 2000
© Crown Copyright

Annex

Statutory declaration/certificate as to non-revocation for powers more than 12 months old at the date of the disposition for which they are used

Date of power of attorney...

Donor of power of attorney..

I/We ....

of ....

do solemnly and sincerely declare, or certify, that at the time of completion of the .... to me/us/my client, I/we/my client had no knowledge

either

- of a revocation of the power

- of the death or bankruptcy of the donor or, if the donor is a corporate body, its winding up or dissolution

- of any incapacity of the donor where the power is not a valid enduring power

- if the power is in the form prescribed for an enduring power

  - of the bankruptcy of the attorney

  - of an order or direction of the Court of Protection which revoked the power

  - that the power was not in fact a valid enduring power

- if the power was given under section 9 of the Trusts of Land and Appointment of Trustees Act 1996

  - of an appointment of another trustee of the land in question

  - of any other event which would have had the effect of revoking the power

  - of any lack of good faith on the part of the person(s) who dealt with the attorney

  - that the attorney was not a person to whom the functions of the trustees could be delegated under section 9

or

- if the power is expressed to be given by way of security

  - that the power was not in fact given by way of security

  - of any revocation of the power with the consent of the attorney

  - of any other event which would have had the effect of revoking the power.

Where a Certificate is given

Signature of Solicitor/Licensed Conveyancer .... Date ....

Where a Statutory Declaration is made

And I/We make this solemn declaration conscientiously believing the same to be true and by virtue of the provisions of the Statutory Declarations Act 1835.

Signature of Declarant(s) .... Date ....

DECLARED at .... before me, a person entitled to administer oaths,

Name ....

Address ....

Qualification .... Signature ....

Please note a certificate can only be given by a solicitor or licensed conveyancer who has knowledge of the relevant facts. If such a certificate cannot be given, the person(s) who dealt with the attorney (e.g. the transferee(s) in the case of a transfer signed by an attorney on behalf of the transferor) must make the statutory declaration.

Index